Negotiating Crime

Negotiating Crime

Plea Bargaining, Problem Solving, and Dispute Resolution in the Criminal Context

SECOND EDITION

Cynthia Alkon
Professor of Law & Director of the
Criminal Law, Justice & Policy Program
Texas A&M University School of Law

Andrea Kupfer Schneider
Professor of Law & Director of the
Kukin Program for Conflict Resolution
Benjamin N. Cardozo School of Law

CAROLINA ACADEMIC PRESS

Library of Congress Cataloging-in-Publication Data

Names: Alkon, Cynthia author | Schneider, Andrea Kupfer author
Title: Negotiating crime : plea bargaining, problem solving, and dispute resolution in the criminal context / Cynthia Alkon, Andrea Kupfer Schneider.
Description: Second edition. | Durham, North Carolina : Carolina Academic Press, LLC, 2025. | Includes bibliographical references and index.
Identifiers: LCCN 2025039278 | ISBN 9781531032180 paperback | ISBN 9781531032197 ebook
Subjects: LCSH: Criminal procedure—United States | Plea bargaining—United States | Restorative justice—United States | Therapeutic jurisprudence—United States | LCGFT: Casebooks (Law)
Classification: LCC KF9619 .A72195 2025 | DDC 345.73/05—dc23/eng/20250822
LC record available at https://lccn.loc.gov/2025039278

Carolina Academic Press
700 Kent Street
Durham, North Carolina 27701
Telephone (919) 489-7486
www.cap-press.com

Printed in the United States of America

Contents

Table of Principal Cases

Preface to the Second Edition

When the first edition of *Negotiating Crime* appeared six years ago, we wanted it to reflect the criminal legal system in all of its concerns and potential. We hoped that both teachers and practitioners in the criminal legal space would find it useful to focus on criminal law from the dispute resolution perspective. Shifting away from a focus on trial and the typical "bail to jail" class, the book was designed to cover plea bargaining and problem solving in the resolution of criminal cases. And, of course, the book reflected the political and social context of its time.

In 2019, there seemed to be wide agreement across the political aisle that we, as a nation, needed to move beyond mass incarceration. Progressive prosecutors were still on the increase. Incarceration rates were declining, albeit slowly. It was widely recognized that crime rates were low and decreasing every year. Then 2020 hit. The pandemic reshaped aspects of the criminal legal system, exposing both vulnerabilities and possibilities for reform. Some violent crime rates increased, while arrest rates plummeted, and incarceration rates dipped and then climbed back higher than before. The murder of George Floyd sparked nation-wide protests with calls to defund the police and for prosecutors to hold police accountable.

Moreover, since 2019, our political climate has become even more polarized. Progressive prosecutors have been voted out of office and governors have started to question (or exert pressure on) prosecutorial decision-making in new ways. Crime rates, calls for law and order, and stronger punishments are again at the forefront of both national and local politics.

Between the pandemic and the murder of George Floyd, the pressure to reform the criminal legal system inspired a surge of creative writing and critical thinking about the future of the criminal legal system and we are delighted to include many of these articles. The ABA Task Force on Plea Bargaining report from 2023 is also included.

You will see updates throughout the book discussing these issues, what they might mean in practice, and suggestions for possible reforms. In addition, after teaching with the book for six years, and receiving helpful feedback from professors and students, we have made other changes. We no longer have the text of US Supreme Court cases on plea bargaining in the book. Instead, we have synopsis of the cases and have consolidated the discussion about plea bargaining case law into one chapter instead of two. This gave us leeway to add an important new final chapter to the book, pushed by student feedback.

While students gave us lots of helpful feedback on everything from typos to news items to other discussion questions, the most significant feedback was to reflect on the emotional seesaw of the first edition. As one student said,

> First, I read about plea bargaining, and I thought, "This is great!" Then, I read about the concerns and I thought "This is awful! We need to abolish it!" Then, I read about problem solving courts, and I thought, "This is it! This is the answer." Then I read about the concerns and thought, "No, we have to stop this!" And so it went. As each new process was introduced, I loved it. Then I was devastated. And when I got to the end of the book, it just ended. I didn't know where to go from here. How should I think about these processes?

Our final chapter responds to this concern by considering how the insights of dispute resolution theory can inform the next generation of criminal justice reform. Chapter 15 looks to dispute system design as a framework for creating more integrated and sustainable changes. It reminds readers that the criminal legal system's complexity defies simple solutions—piecemeal efforts, like the introduction of drug courts, cannot on their own deliver meaningful transformation.

As the criminal legal system continues to change and reform, this last chapter can provide the tools to do so in a more thoughtful and effective manner, and we look forward to hearing from students who can use these tools to make a difference.

Preface to the First Edition

This book is about how we resolve criminal cases in processes other than trials. Until now there has not been a single book that brings together reading about the concerns, critiques, proposals for reform, as well as focusing on the skills needed for the variety of processes beyond trial through which criminal cases are resolved.

To our readers who are law professors and law students, we understand that this book may look and feel different from a standard law school casebook. We do not focus on cases but instead have brought together reading from criminal law scholars, dispute resolution scholars, social scientists, and the media. Our focus is not on doctrine, in large part because there is very little doctrine in this area. Instead we focus on giving the reader a basic introduction, with a large dose of critical readings, to how criminal cases are actually resolved in the United States.

This book covers four topics: Plea bargaining, restorative justice, therapeutic justice, and juvenile justice. In covering each of these four topics we will first discuss what is happening on a practical level (for example, what are the stages of a plea negotiation? Who has more power in the plea negotiation process? How can you build your negotiation skills?) We will also discuss the evolution of these policies (for example, how did drug courts develop? How are these different than restorative justice processes?) Embedded into these discussions will be the policy reasons for these processes. Finally, for each topic, we will discuss concerns and recommendations for reform.

Each of the four topics that we are covering in this book is a rich area for scholarship and writings, although the four topics have not yet been brought together in one book. In fact, this likely means that some material is very familiar for our readers and some is not. For those of us steeped in criminal law and process, readings on negotiation skills and perhaps some of the alternative processes of problem solving courts or restorative justice will be relatively novel. For those of us coming from the dispute resolution field, we expect that the early chapters on plea bargaining might be particularly necessary to remind us of the current state of criminal practice or that much of the materials from criminal procedure cases to state regulations to ethical guidelines is completely unfamiliar. And for those of us from a clinical perspective, there will yet again be certain readings or theories that seem familiar while others are quite foreign. Although this may at times be frustrating, we also hope that this cross-disciplinary approach reflects the richness of this area of the law... as well as the need to bring all of these streams together in order to capture a fuller picture of what 21st Century lawyers need to know.

Each chapter in this book includes original text and excerpts from published material. Each chapter also includes discussion points, and questions to give additional information and to focus classroom discussion. Due to the wonderful wealth of material it is impossible for us to include everything in each chapter. Instead, we have pulled together some reading that helps to start the conversation in each topic and hope that classroom time will give rise to even more discussion. We have also included a list, at the end of each chapter, of additional resources. These lists include books, scholarly articles, and other materials that further illuminate the topics covered in each chapter.

Given the cross-disciplinary nature of the book, this book can easily be used in a variety of ways. This book could be used as the text in a standard 3-credit course or seminar or as the text for clinical classes in prosecution or defense. Parts of this book could be pulled out for stand-alone classes, such as a course on plea bargaining. Parts of this book could supplement reading in more standard doctrinal classes such as in criminal procedure. This book is intended to give students a basic introduction in these areas, to challenge our thinking about these topics, and to be a jumping off point for skill building, simulations and other exercises.

Finally, we want to note that this book is premised on the fact that criminal practice is constantly evolving. It is because of that evolution, and the likely continuation of change, that we think it is so important for new lawyers to understand all of the different processes that occur under the rubric of the criminal legal system. For example, mass incarceration was not always a defining feature of the US criminal legal system. Drug courts are also fairly new. We want to equip our readers with a critical understanding of how we resolve criminal cases now so that they can be part of the continuing process of change and contribute to improving our criminal legal system. We hope that this book will support more thoughtful and meaningful approaches to criminal justice reform.

Acknowledgments

This book has been a wonderful collaboration and we are grateful to many supporters for all of their help along the way. When we first hatched this idea, we decided to spend a week together at Marquette to block out what we thought the book should look like and to write a book proposal. This one-week visit became a regular staple of our summers and we are thankful to both Texas A&M School of Law and Marquette Law School for supporting this time together as well as Susan Campbell and Tom Content for hosting Cynthia every summer in their subterranean suite! Now working on our second edition, we are also grateful to Cardozo School of Law, where Andrea has moved, for its support.

As we started to write the first edition, we knew that this book would build on both shared expertise in dispute resolution and separate expertise in criminal law, criminal procedure and restorative justice. Our colleagues in all of these linked fields have been so helpful in reviewing everything from the book proposal to the table of contents to reading particular chapters. Much appreciation to Cara Drinan, Michael O'Hear, Peter Reilly, Jenny Roberts, and Ron Wright. Thank you also to Richard Birke, Amy Cohen, Aliza Cover, Eve Hanan, Art Hinshaw, Carrie Menkel-Meadow, and Melanie Reid. We are particularly grateful to Jen Reynolds who took our page proofs and taught with this book during her visit at Harvard Law School to really give this a test run. Thank you as well to Amber Baylor who introduced plea bargaining to her students in the Texas A&M Criminal Defense Clinic also using page proofs. And we thank all of the students in our respective classes at Texas A&M and Marquette who commented on the materials as they were being developed. For the second edition, we circled back to previous readers Michael O'Hear, Jenny Roberts, and Ron Wright for more fabulous advice and also are thankful for such helpful comments from Bennet Capers, Erin Collins, Hadar Dancig-Rosenberg, Tali Gal, Kay Levine, Justin Murray, and Andrea's new Cardozo colleagues Alma Magana and Katy Miller.

Andrea's assistant at Marquette, Carrie Kratochvil, managed the permission process to permit us the wonderful excerpts in the book. And, for round two, Scott Goodman, Andrea's research assistant at Cardozo, was a master of organization and persistence! Thanks to Andrea's research assistants at Marquette, Dom Rosso and Will Ruffing, for their work on first edition of book, and to her research assistants at Cardozo for the second edition, Madison Gagne, Matt Kee, Dighan Kelly, and Alexa Miller. Additional thanks on the second edition to Cynthia's research assistants Kyle Christman, Dalia El-Giar, and Brandon Yim. We also want to thank all the students who have taken the course, used the book, and provided such great feedback for this second edition.

Special thanks to Armand Avila for suggesting that we needed a better conclusion and final chapter, and to Ilhyung Lee at the University of Missouri School of Law, who hosted the conference where we were able to bring our thoughts together for that new final chapter. We agreed that being more hopeful about what dispute resolution can do is a great way to end!

Finally, thanks to Carolina Academic Press—to Carol McGeehan for pushing us to write the book and the second edition, and to Susan Trimble and Ryland Bowman for their great work in production.

We look forward to adding more thanks to each of you as you use these innovative materials and let us know how to continue to improve the book!

Part I

Chapter 1

Introduction

The trial of Derek Chauvin for the murder of George Floyd, the New York trial of Donald Trump for falsifying business records, and the trials of Adnan Masud Syed (from the podcast *Serial*), George Zimmerman, Casey Anthony, Jodi Arias, and O.J. Simpson all captured public attention. In their times, millions were glued to the podcasts, their TV sets, or watching the court proceedings on the internet. However, the reality in the criminal legal system is far removed from these high profile cases. Most cases never go to trial. Between 94–97% of all criminal convictions nationwide are due to plea bargains. And many of these cases are not simple plea bargains for time in prison or a fine, but instead involve an agreement to go to an alternative process such as drug court or mental health court. To understand the U.S. criminal legal system in the 21st Century, it is crucial to understand the variety of ways in which criminal cases are resolved. This book will introduce you to the variety of processes that are part of the U.S. criminal legal system including plea bargaining, problem-solving courts (or therapeutic justice), restorative justice and juvenile justice. Each one of these processes has a unique history that has developed in response to how the criminal legal system operates in the United States. Therefore, it is useful to first understand how the criminal legal system in the United States operates, including the major players, the theories of punishment, and issues surrounding the high incarceration rate in this country.

I. The U.S. Criminal Legal System: A Basic Introduction

This book will use the term "criminal legal system." However, in fact, there is no one criminal legal system in the United States. Crime is prosecuted locally and federally. Police forces, prosecutors, judges, juries, and the system of providing indigent defense are different depending on the location and the jurisdiction. There are often vast differences in both the procedural and substantive criminal law. There can also be differences in the institutional cultures. For example, the District Attorney (DA)'s Office in Los Angeles could have different policies than another DA's office in another part of the state, such as San Francisco. Policing agencies may also have very different approaches regarding who they will arrest or, for example, how they deal with the local homeless population (who disproportionately suffer from mental illness and substance abuse problems). As John Pfaff observed, "there is no single 'criminal justice system,' but instead a vast patchwork of systems that vary in almost every conceivable way."[1] As will be discussed later in this book, it is this very diversity that can make reform challenging.

However, there are also many points in common in terms of how crime is handled, and this is why we have decided to continue to use the term "criminal legal system" in this book. When the United States declared its independence in the late 18th Century, it was a small, mostly rural country. Crime was handled locally, and trials tended to be quick. Plea bargaining existed, but it was not commonly used. As the population grew, so did the number of criminal cases. The use of plea bargaining also grew to the point that, throughout the United States, plea bargaining became the dominant form of criminal case resolution. There are different theories about why plea bargaining grew to such prominence. One theory is that it was due to the caseload pressure. As the criminal legal system in this country grew, it became harder and harder for the courts to have the resources to conduct a trial for every case. A related theory is that pressure increased as protections for defendants became more formalized in the latter half of the 20th Century, and trials took longer. As William Stuntz commented, "[b]efore the last half-century, the law of trial procedure made jury trials cheap and reasonably effective, and therefore common. Today's elaborate body of procedural rules has made trials expensive, rare and error prone."[2] Another related theory is that, as the criminal legal system professionalized, it brought justice out of the town square and into courthouses as the "insiders" (professionals) took over the process.[3]

Already, by the late 1800s, the United States had a formal, largely professional criminal legal system with professional prosecutors (victims no longer had to handle their own cases) and judges. This was also a period of prison reform. The reformers sought to change U.S. prisons from the dangerous, filthy, scary places they were into institutions that would reform inmates and allow them to reenter society as productive citizens. The reform movements made progress in cleaning up the physical environment, but included putting prisoners in solitary confinement and requiring silence under the theory that doing so would help in the rehabilitation process.

Despite these often harsh conditions, incarceration rates in the United States held fairly steady into the late-20th Century when incarceration rates rose dramatically:

---

1. John Pfaff, Locked In: The True Causes of Mass Incarceration and How to Achieve Real Reform, 13 (2017).

2. William Stuntz, The Collapse of American Criminal Justice, 39 (2011).

3. Stephanos Bibas, The Machinery of Criminal Justice (2012).

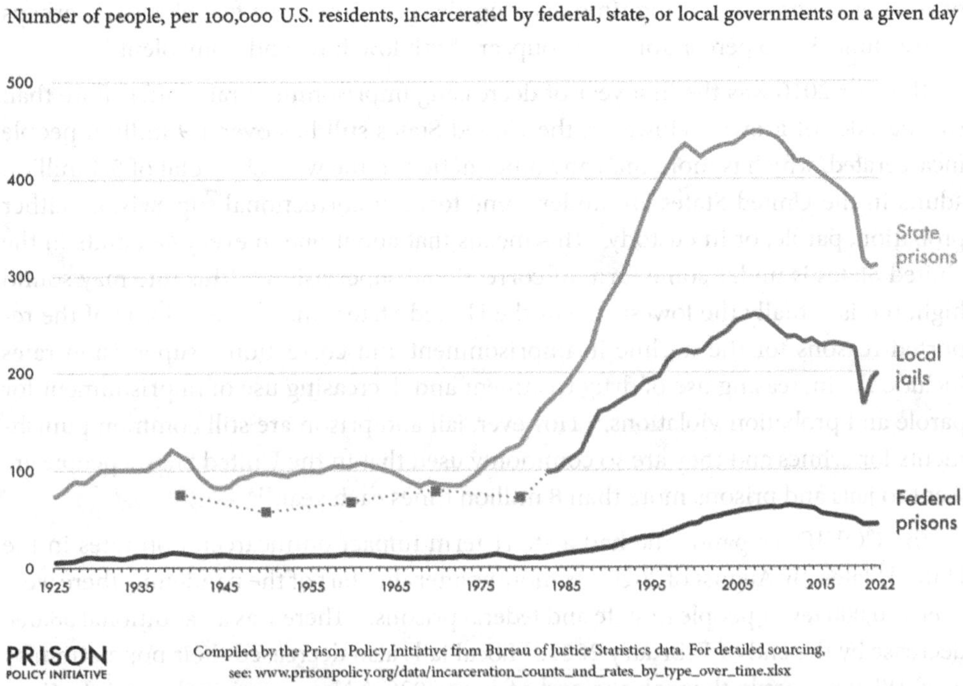

Source: Prison Policy Initiative

Just as there is no one criminal legal system in the United States, there is also no single reason for the increase in incarceration rates. The reasons for the increase in incarceration rates include the War on Drugs, the War on Crime, longer terms of incarceration, and how probation and parole violations were handled. In the U.S., defendants are sentenced to incarceration for violations of probation and parole more than in other countries. For example, up to 40% of all people are incarcerated due to a parole violation, not due to a sentence for the underlying crime.[4] One scholar, John Pfaff, argues that it is not higher arrest rates that led to higher incarceration rates. Pfaff concludes that while arrest rates held steady in the 1990s, imprisonment rates increased because prosecutors increased their felony filing rates. This meant that a much higher percentage of those arrested were ultimately charged with a criminal case.[5] As Pfaff stated, "[s]topping prosecutors from sending people to prison to start with would be far more effective in cutting incarceration rates than reducing the amount of time that prisoners spend in prison once they get there."[6] Pfaff also challenges the argument that the War on Drugs was a major driver of mass incarceration, as "only about 16 percent

4. The Growth of Incarceration in the United States: Exploring Causes and Consequences 41 (Jeremy Travis, et al. eds., National Academy of Sciences 2014).

5. John. F. Pfaff, *The Micro and Macro Causes of Prison Growth*, 28 Ga. St. U. L. Rev. 1239, 1242 (2012).

6. John Pfaff, Locked In: The True Causes of Mass Incarceration and How to Achieve Real Reform 6 (2017).

of state prisoners are serving time on drug charges—and very few of them, perhaps only around 5 or 6 percent of that group, are both low-level and nonviolent."[7]

The year 2010 was the first year of decreasing imprisonment rates after more than two decades of growth. However, the United States still has over 1.9 million people incarcerated, which is more than any other nation in the world.[8] A total of 5.4 million adults in the United States are under some form of correctional supervision, either probation, parole, or in custody.[9] This means that about one in every 48 adults in the United States is under some form of correctional supervision.[10] This rate may sound high, but is actually the lowest rate in the United States since 1996.[11] Some of the reported reasons for the decline in imprisonment and correctional supervision rates include the increasing use of drug treatment and decreasing use of imprisonment for parole and probation violations.[12] However, jail and prison are still common punishments for crimes and they are so commonly used that in the United States, people are "sent to jails and prisons more than 8 million times each year."[13]

The COVID-19 pandemic had a short-term impact on incarceration rates in the United States. By August of 2020, six months after the start of the pandemic, there were over 150,000 fewer people in state and federal prisons.[14] There was an additional 58,000 decrease by the end of February 2021.[15] Local jails also decreased their population, by over 185,000 people through the end of June 2020.[16] Not surprisingly, an infectious disease like COVID-19 spread quickly in crowded jail and prison environments. Incarcerated people were infected at a rate five times higher than the general population.[17] The death rate was also higher at 39 deaths per 100,000 people compared to the national average of 29 deaths per 100,000.[18] Some states and the federal government started early release programs that allowed eligible defendants to be released from custody

---

7. *Id.* at 6. *See also* Michael O'Hear, Wisconsin Sentencing in the Tough-on-Crime Era: How Judges Retained Power and Why Mass Incarceration Happened Anyway (University of Wisconsin Press 2017) (confirming that drug incarcerations were not the primary contributor to mass incarceration).

8. The United States also has the highest incarceration rate in the world, imprisoning 830 people per 100,000 in population in 2016.

9. Emily D. Buehler & Rich Kluckow, *Correctional Populations in the United States, 2022*, Statistical Tables, U.S. Department of Justice, Bureau of Justice Statistics, May 2024.

10. *Id.*

11. *Id.*

12. Erica Goode, *U.S. Prison Populations Decline, Reflecting New Approach to Crime*, N.Y. Times, July 25, 2013.

13. *Vera Incarceration Trends*, October 31, 2024.

14. E. Ann Carson, et al., *Impact of COVID-19 on State and Federal Prisons*, March 2020–February 2021, August 2022, Bureau of Justice Statistics.

15. *Id.*

16. Todd D. Minton, et al., *Impact of COVID-19 on the Local Jail Population, January–June 2020*, March 2021, Bureau of Justice Statistics.

17. Brendan Saloner, et al., *COVID-19 Cases and Deaths in Federal and State Prisons*, JAMA Network, July 8, 2020.

18. *Id.*

if they were more vulnerable to death due to COVID-19 (older prisoners, those with pre-existing conditions ... etc.). There were also increased efforts to decrease the number of people in pre-trial incarceration in local jails. However, local jail populations and prisons, not only returned to pre-COVID levels within a few years, but they have also increased beyond those levels. One reason for the increase may be the rise in incarceration rates from smaller and mid-sized cities and rural areas.[19]

Later in this chapter, you will read more about the incarceration rate in the United States. First, however, it is important to understand the major players in the criminal legal system.

II. The Players

The popular television series, *Law and Order*, opens with the now iconic saying: "In the criminal justice system, the people are represented by two separate, yet equally important groups: the police who investigate crime, and the district attorneys who prosecute the offenders. These are their stories." While this might be a useful dramatic device, it leaves out some important players in the criminal legal system. It also fails to capture the variety of motivations and policies at play, as the criminal legal system doesn't exist simply to prosecute offenders, but to try to protect the rights of all accused which includes, at least ideally, preventing innocent people from being convicted of crimes. The three main professional players, once a criminal case is filed, are judges, prosecutors, and defense lawyers, all with different roles, different powers, and different constraints on that power.

A. Judges

In our adversarial system of justice, judges are considered to be neutral umpires who do not play an active role in the case. This means that they are not involved with collecting evidence or investigating, as judges are in some civil law systems with a tradition of an investigating magistrate. Judges have the authority to decide motions, such as a motion to release a defendant on their own recognizance or a motion to reduce bail, or a motion to suppress evidence due to an illegal search. Judges also decide any legal questions that might arise during a jury trial, including what evidence can be admitted and what instructions to give the jury. In cases that do not go to trial, the judge can decide whether to accept the guilty or no contest plea. Judges can also put tremendous pressure on the prosecutors and defense lawyers to resolve more cases or handle them faster. Depending on the jurisdiction, the judge may have the authority to decide whether a defense lawyer will get funds to prepare the case, including hiring an expert in a particular case. Judges may even be the ones deciding which lawyers will get court appointments, authorizing the lawyer's pay directly, and they may need to sign and agree to each payment request.

---

19. Jacob Kang-Brown, et al., *People in Jail and Prison in 2022*, June 2023, Vera Institute.

Judges are either appointed or elected depending on the jurisdiction. Some judges are appointed for a limited period of time and then must stand for election. Other judges, such as federal judges, are appointed for life and never stand for election. How a judge gets their job, and how they keep it, can have a profound impact on how they exercise their power. Although it is unusual for a sitting judge to lose his seat due to a contested election, it does happen. The fact that it could happen can be something that is a part of how judges view the cases that come before them. Other factors that can influence how judges make decisions include their prior professional experience (were they a prosecutor or defense lawyer?), gender, age, ethnic group, where they went to law school, and other personal-identity characteristics.[20]

Budgets for the courts are determined by state legislatures or by the U.S. Congress. Judges may control aspects of how money is spent in the court, but they do not control the overall budget, or make decisions about their own salaries. Judges also do not make the final decision on how many judges to hire for a particular jurisdiction or if appointments are needed, as they do not control the appointment process. This means that while judges can control the workload to a degree in their particular courtrooms, they cannot control these larger factors which can result in heavier caseloads and put additional pressures on judges to manage these caseloads.

B. Prosecutors

Prosecutors are often referred to as "ministers of justice," as it is their ethical duty to "seek justice." This means that a prosecutor's job is broader than the single-minded view that *Law and Order* offers as their jobs and a prosecutor's ethical duties go beyond simply "prosecuting offenders." Prosecutors are bound by the same ethical duties as all lawyers, which means, they cannot lie or fabricate evidence. Prosecutors have an additional duty to turn over all exculpatory evidence to the defense.[21] Prosecutors have broad powers and broad discretion in the exercise of those powers. Prosecutors have the power to decide who to charge with a crime or what cases to bring to a grand jury for indictment. They have the power to dismiss some or all of the charges in a particular case. They also have the power to decide if they are going to make a plea offer in the case and what that offer will be. Although, as will be discussed, a defendant can often "plead open" to a judge, prosecutors regularly wield the ultimate power in deciding how cases will be resolved in terms of making plea offers or dismissing the charges altogether.

There are a variety of prosecuting agencies. Federal prosecutions are handled by the Department of Justice. The Attorney General of the United States is appointed by the President and serves as a member of the Cabinet. The Attorney General's appointment, like all cabinet level appointments, is subject to Congressional confirmation. The

---

20. *See e.g.*, Lee Epstein, et al., The Behavior of Federal Judges: A Theoretical and Empirical Study of Rational Choice (2012); Anna Spain Bradley, *The Disruptive Neuroscience of Judicial Choice*, 9 U.C. Irvine L. Rev. 1 (2018).

21. Brady v. Maryland, 373 U.S. 83 (1963).

The Mindset of Judges

Judge Young of the Western District of Massachusetts, began a written opinion admitting his own error with:

> There is a derisive ditty going around the courthouse as this opinion is being written. Set to the music of "Happy Together" by The Turtles, in relevant part it goes:
>
> > Imagine me as God. I do.
> > I think about it day and night. It feels so right
> > To be a federal district judge and know that I'm Appointed forever.
> >
> > I was anointed by the President,
> > And revelation told him I was heaven-sent.
> > And Congress in their wisdom granted their consent. Appointed forev-er.
> >
> > I'm a federal judge
> > And I'm smarter than you For all my life.
> > I can do whatever I want to do For all my life.
> >
> > Even at the very worst,
> > If you take me up to get reversed,
> > You'll have to get the circuit court to hear you first, And that takes for-ever.

Suboh v. Borgioli, 298 F. Supp. 2d 192, 194 (D. Mass. 2004) (quoting Bar & Grill Singers, *Appointed Forever,* on Licensed To Grill (1997), http://volokh.blogspot.com/2003_04_13_volokh_ archive.html#2001549 16).

As a prosecutor or defense lawyer, how might the attitudes reflected in these lyrics influence how you might approach motions that you argue in front of a judge? For example, if you are a prosecutor with a very weak case, and are making a good offer to the client where you are dismissing a number of charges, and giving the defendant time served in an otherwise serious tax fraud case, what might you want to do, before the case is called, to make sure the judge will accept the guilty plea without incident?

Department of Justice handles prosecution of federal crimes. Each state also has an Attorney General, which are elected positions in forty-three states. Usually, however, the most active local prosecutors are the district attorney (DA) in each county. The DA is almost always an elected position. The Deputy DAs, the lawyers who work in the DA's office, tend to be civil servants, which means there is less turnover at the lower levels if or when the District Attorney is voted out of office and replaced. However, this may be less true in smaller communities with smaller offices. Generally, the DA stands for re-election every four years. As with judges, the DA does not control their budget.

It is usually set by each county, but the state or federal government may contribute to portions of the budget through grants for various purposes.

> The ABA Guidelines on the Prosecution Function Standard 3-1.2(b):
>
> The primary duty of the prosecutor is to seek justice within the bounds of the law, not merely to convict. The prosecutor serves the public interest and should act with integrity and balanced judgment to increase public safety both by pursuing appropriate criminal charges of appropriate severity, and by exercising discretion to not pursue criminal charges in appropriate circumstances. The prosecutor should seek to protect the innocent and convict the guilty, consider the interests of victims and witnesses, and respect the constitutional and legal rights of all persons, including suspects and defendants.

DA decision-making tends to be very hierarchical. The courtroom level prosecutor generally has a number of office-wide policies that constrain what he or she can do on each individual case. These policies may be specific to the type of offense, for example, "never strike a gun allegation on a sexual assault." They may also constrain more general behavior, such as requiring higher level approval to dismiss any charges as part of a plea deal. Critics complain that these office-wide policies are instituted for political reasons to protect the re-election of the incumbent. And the typical response is that the policies are instituted to try to bring some consistency to how cases are handled.

In 2017, Larry Krasner was elected as the District Attorney for Philadelphia. He was the first prosecutor to run as a "progressive prosecutor." He has since been re-elected twice. Of the over 2300 elected prosecutor offices in the United States, it is estimated that less than 100 are led by "progressive prosecutors." There is no single definition of a progressive prosecutor, and those who do not define themselves as progressive may still agree with and promote policies that progressive prosecutors support. Often progressive prosecutors emphasize rehabilitation over punishment and are more skeptical about prosecuting cases brought by police officers with a history of dishonesty or misconduct. Progressive prosecutors may also focus on decreasing disparate treatment of different racial and ethnic groups. In recent years a number of progressive prosecutors have been voted out of office, including Chesa Boudin (recalled as San Francisco DA in 2022), George Gascón (voted out of office as the Los Angeles DA in November 2024), and Pamela Price (voted out of office as Alameda County DA in November 2024). Some progressive prosecutors have been attacked when they have exercised their discretion to not prosecute certain kinds of cases. For example, Governor Ron DeSantis, in Florida, suspended Andrew Warren, the 13th Judicial Circuit State Attorney, in August of 2022 when he refused to prosecute certain cases including those related to abortion. It is still to be determined what the long term impact of progressive prosecutors, and prosecutors who support similar policies, will be on the criminal legal system and mass incarceration.

C. Defense Attorneys

Defense attorneys are probably the most diverse group of players in the criminal legal system. Some are privately retained, some are appointed by the state to handle individual indigent defendants, and a large number work for public defender offices. The basic ethical duty of every defense lawyer is to "zealously represent" their client. This means it is not the defense attorney's job to find evidence for the prosecutor or otherwise help them to build their case against the defendant. Defense lawyers are bound by the same ethical duties as every other lawyer, which means they cannot lie or fabricate evidence. However, defense lawyers also owe a duty of confidentiality to their clients, which means they cannot divulge the content of their conversations with their clients without permission. Furthermore, defense attorneys are not obligated to turn over evidence in the same way as the prosecution due to their different role in our adversarial legal system, as they do not share the same ethical duties as prosecutors, who are required to turn over exculpatory evidence.

> ABA Guidelines on the Defense Function, Standard 4-1.2(b):
>
> Defense counsel have the difficult task of serving both as officers of the court and as loyal and zealous advocates for their clients. The primary duties that defense counsel owe to their clients, to the administration of justice, and as officers of the court, are to serve as their clients' counselor and advocate with courage and devotion; to ensure that constitutional and other legal rights of their clients are protected; and to render effective, high-quality legal representation with integrity.

It has been over fifty years since the U.S. Supreme Court held that indigent defendants have a right to a lawyer in the landmark case of *Gideon v. Wainwright*.[22] Most people arrested and charged with a crime cannot afford a lawyer. Despite *Gideon*, defendants on low-level misdemeanors still go unrepresented. Over 80% of those charged with felonies rely on the services of a public defender.[23] There are a few different types of appointed lawyers. The most common are public defenders. Los Angeles County opened the first Public Defender Office in 1913. It remains the largest in the country and currently employs over 700 lawyers. The office began due to the efforts of the District Attorney at the time, Clara Foltz, who was also the first woman lawyer in California. Foltz recognized the need for competent defense for indigent defendants

22. Gideon v. Wainwright, 372 U.S. 335 (1963).

23. United States Department of Justice, Office of Justice Programs, Bureau of Justice Statistics, *Defense Counsel in Criminal Cases* 1 (2000).

and championed the effort to establish a county-funded office to provide legal services. Under a public defender system, lawyers are paid a salary to handle criminal cases. Generally, a public defender's salary is decided by their civil service rank, which is tied to their experience level. They are not paid on a case-by-case basis. The federal system also uses a public defender system through the Federal Defender Service. Approximately twenty-seven states have state-wide public defender offices.[24] The rest of the states leave each county to decide how to handle indigent defense. This means that states like California and Texas have a variety of approaches, depending on the county. Most larger counties use public defender offices, although they may also have private appointed counsel to handle conflicts of interest (for example, when there is a two-defendant case, the public defender won't handle both defendants). Lawyers working in a public defender office are county or state employees. Some enjoy "parity" with the DA, meaning they get the same pay and benefits. The head of the public defender's office is appointed and is not an elected official, except in a handful of places around the country including Florida, some cities in Nebraska, San Francisco, and some parts of Tennessee.

Another type of appointed counsel is private counsel who are paid either as individuals or as a firm to handle a contract for the entire county (usually for a flat fee) or private lawyers who are retained and paid on a case-by-case basis. Some counties have a system in place where lawyers can qualify to get on lists to handle various types of cases, for example, misdemeanors or lower level felonies or capital cases. Once a lawyer is on the list, he or she will get appointments either directly from the judge, or through a random appointment system. Some counties mandate the maximum that they will pay per case, others will pay an hourly rate or set rate, depending on the actual work done. Even in counties with a public defender, there is still a need for an alternate appointment system, so there are lawyers available to handle conflicts of interest. For example, on behalf of one client, the public defender cannot cross-examine another. In that case, a lawyer from outside the public defender's office would have to be appointed.

Finances are a serious issue for indigent defense services. The way in which a lawyer is paid may determine the kind of job they are able to do for individual clients. For example, if a lawyer is paid a small fee per case, they may not have the ability to do more than meet once with the client, which is often the same day that they enter a guilty plea. And, while public defenders are not paid by the case, if the office as a whole is not adequately funded, they may be short-staffed. The result can be that individual public defenders have high caseloads and are unable to spend enough time on each case or with each client. Public defenders can be hard hit when budget cuts happen. For example, the Federal Defender Service suffered debilitating reductions after the 2013 budget sequester. The budget was cut by 23%, and lawyers, investigators, and other

24. Alissa Pollitz Worden & Andrew Lucas Blaize Davies, *A Patchwork of Policies: Justice, Due Process, and Public Defense Across American States*, 74 ALB. L. REV. 1423 (2010–2011).

staff suffered furloughs or were laid off.[25] In a 2023 study of public defender workloads revised the workload standards for defense lawyers concluding that earlier standards underestimated the time needed to competently represent clients for different kinds of criminal proceedings from probation or parole violations up to high level felonies.[26] Based on these standards, a study found that public defenders across the United States "work triple the cases they can effectively handle, and some work upwards of 10 times too many cases."[27]

Public defenders are often unable to decline cases due to heavy caseloads. Competent assistance of counsel is also affected by whether lawyers can hire experts or investigators to help prepare their cases. For many lawyers, such appointments depend on a judge signing an order to pay for the extra services. In some states, or some counties (often those with public defender offices), there is a specific budget for defense services. But often the money for defense services comes from the general judicial budget. And, in tougher economic times, judges may hesitate to spend limited funds on investigators or expert appointments.

Now that you have a basic introduction to the various players in the system, it is important to understand some of the basic theories that explain why the criminal legal system operates the way it does.

III. Theories of Punishment

Why do you think people follow the law? Your answer to this question will probably explain why you think certain approaches in the criminal legal system make sense and others make less sense. For example, if you think that people follow the law because they are scared of the consequences of not following the law, you probably think stiff penalties and punishments make sense, as they would encourage people to be more law-abiding. If you think people follow the law because they believe it is the right thing to do, then you might think that it makes sense to educate people who are not following the law so they understand why what they are doing is wrong. As you probably remember from your first year criminal law course, there are four basic theories of punishment on which the U.S. criminal legal system is based: incapacitation/public protection; deterrence; retribution; and treatment/rehabilitation. Another, more recent theory is to abolish prisons.

25. Based on data from 530 public defender offices in twenty-seven states and the District of Columbia. *Census of Public Defender Offices, County Based and Local Public Defender Office*, 2007, at 1, 3, and 8–10, U.S. Department of Justice, Bureau of Justice Statistics, available at http://www.bjs.gov/index.cfm?ty=pbdetail&iid=2211.

26. Nicholas M Pace et al., *National Public Defense Workload Study*, July 27, 2023, Rand Research Report.

27. Emily Hammer, *Public Defenders Work 3 Times Too Many Cases, Milestone Study and New Data Show*, Longview Daily News, September 12, 2023.

A. Incapacitation/Public Protection

The goal under this theory of punishment is to take the offender off the streets and thereby prevent him from committing more crimes. U.S. legislators have favored this approach and written it into our laws at the state and federal level. "Three strikes and you are out" laws and other "career criminal" sentencing enhancements are due to this approach. Throughout the United States, we have increased punishments for certain offenses and added enhancements for things like "using a gun." These approaches do indeed take convicted criminals off the street and, as is discussed below, have contributed to the high incarceration rates in the United States.

It is an open question whether these increased punishments provide a better level of protection as it is difficult to draw a direct connection between these laws and reduced crime rates. Worldwide, crime rates have fallen in developed countries, even in countries that have taken a far less punitive approach to punishment.[28] The United States saw increases in some crime rates during COVID-19—notably murder rates. However, the overall rates continue to decline, and violent crime rates have returned to pre-COVID levels.[29] U.S. policy favoring the incapacitation approach to punishment is starting to change after decades of steadily increasing penalties written into penal codes around the United States. For example, in 2012, California changed its three-strikes law to include only offenders with three serious and violent offenses. Previously, the law required anyone who had been convicted of two prior serious or violent felonies (which included residential burglary as well as crimes of violence) to be sentenced to 25-years-to-life on any new felony. This law led to thousands of people serving life terms when the new offense was neither serious or violent and was often a petty theft, or possession of a single rock of cocaine. Under the new law, only those convicted of a third serious or violent felony face life in prison.

B. Deterrence

Another theory of punishment is that the criminal legal system should work to deter future crime. This theory is also used to justify stiff sentences and sentencing enhancements. The idea is different from incapacitation, as the point is to have a penalty that will discourage people from committing the act in the first place. Deterrence can also be directed at particular types of offenders to try to get them to stop committing particular offenses, such as increasing penalties for each future criminal act, or making the punishment worse on each subsequent drunk driving conviction.

It is an open question whether deterrence works. It is unclear if the people who might commit crimes are actually deterred (or is this only people who are generally law abiding anyway). A separate concern is that a deterrence approach is meaningless

---

28. *Where have all the burglars gone*? ECONOMIST, July 20, 2013, available at: http://www.economist.com/news/briefing/21582041-rich-world-seeing-less-and-less-crime-even-face-high-unemployment-and-economic?frsc=dg%7ca.

29. Lori Robertson, *Crime Stats Still Show a Decline Since 2020*, FactCheck.Org, October 23, 2024.

for many people most likely to commit offenses such as drug addicts or the mentally ill. Their illnesses may prevent them from thinking rationally about actions and consequences, which means that the possibility of stiff penalties is unlikely to change their behavior.

C. Retribution

A third theory of criminal punishment which underlies our criminal legal system is retribution. This is the idea that people who commit crime deserves punishment and should be held accountable for their crimes. Retribution includes the idea that the punishment should be proportional. This means a minor offense, such as a petty theft, should not be punished too strongly while more serious crimes should be more severely punished. Those who hold a theory of retribution often have a hard time accepting alternative approaches that include treatment and not punishment. However, there are increasing calls for the criminal legal system to move away from a retributive approach. One reason is because of the costs involved in incarcerating large numbers of people. Others disagree with the underlying philosophy, as retribution does not address problems that may have led to the criminal behavior, and "[t]he vast majority of criminal offenders have multiple disorders, deficits, impairments, and conditions that are fundamentally related to their criminal behavior, which punishment does nothing to change."[30]

D. Treatment/Rehabilitation

Early criminal justice reform movements advocated moving beyond the retributive model of criminal justice, which they viewed as punishment for punishment's sake, and argued that the criminal legal system should strive to rehabilitate offenders to prevent future crimes and to "save" the individual offender. This idea of rehabilitation as a goal of criminal legal systems is a continuing theme. Traditionally, prison was referred to as a possible place for rehabilitation. As incarceration rates grew, many states stopped looking to prison as a rehabilitation location and instead focused on the punishment or retributive function of prisons. However, as will be discussed later in this book, starting in 1989, with the development of the first drug court in Dade County, Florida, the United States is in a new era of increasingly using problem-solving courts. These are premised on the theory that these courts can help rehabilitate defendants and, thereby, help to not only improve the lives of the individual defendants, but also decrease recidivism rates. Critics argue that the failure to provide treatment and address underlying causes is why over 65% of people who go to prison or jail will return to prison or jail. Critics also argue that these high recidivism rates indicate the failure of the criminal legal system and the need to focus on rehabilitation and treatment.

30. William R. Kelly, et al., From Retribution to Public Safety: Disruptive Innovation of American Criminal Justice 2 (2017).

E. Abolition

> "Mass incarceration is not a solution to unemployment, nor is it a solution to the vast array of social problems that are hidden away in a rapidly growing network of prisons and jails. However, the great majority of people have been tricked into believing in the efficacy of imprisonment, even though the historical record clearly demonstrates that prisons do not work."
>
> Angela Y. Davis, *Masked Racism: Reflections on the Prison Industrial Complex*, 1 Colorlines, 11 (Oct. 31, 1998).

In recent years, some have argued that prisons should be abolished. Many proponents of abolition view the carceral punishment system in the United States as being built on the legacy of slavery and are concerned that modern day prisons are used to continue a system of oppression, particularly against African Americans. The scholar and activist Angela Y. Davis focuses on the history of racism and the prison industrialist complex in advocating for prison abolition.[31] The abolitionist movement often includes calls to decriminalize specific types of offenses and all offenses. Within the abolition movement, there are different suggestions of what to do instead of prison. Some suggest a restorative justice approach. Others focus on rehabilitation. As one proponent of abolition said:

> Abolitionists don't stop at the prison walls, however: They aim to reshape our society as a whole. We are not doing nearly enough to address the root causes of poverty, addiction, homelessness, and mental-health crises, abolitionists contend, and criminalizing poverty through harsh fines and debt regulation; criminalizing addiction through drug laws; criminalizing homelessness by conducting sweeps of people sleeping in parks; and criminalizing mental illness by turning prisons into de facto psychiatric hospitals is all treating the symptom instead of the disease. This is one of the key differences between reform and abolitionism: The former deals with pain management and the latter with the actual source of the pain.[32]

Abolitionists challenge our traditional views of whether punishment is appropriate and how to manage people who commit crimes (and whether to even consider their acts criminal).[33]

---

31. Angela Y. Davis, Are Prisons Obsolete? (2003).

32. John Washington, *What Is Prison Abolition? The Movement that Is Trying to Think Beyond Prisons as a Tool to Solve Society's Problems*, The Nation, July 21, 2018.

33. Adam Gopnik, *Should We Abolish Prisons? Our Carceral System Is Characterized by Frequent Brutality and Ingrained Indifference. Finding a Better Way Requires that We Freely Imagine Alternatives*, The New Yorker, July 22, 2024.

IV. Incarceration in the United States

As was discussed briefly above, the United States continues to incarcerate more people than any other country in the world. In 2010, the incarceration rate went down for the first time in decades. However, the reduction has not been large enough to dramatically reduce the incarceration rates or the disparate impact of these rates on some communities in the United States. The high incarceration rate, also referred to as mass incarceration, is an inescapable fact that regularly features in any discussion about the U.S. criminal legal system, policy debates, and decisions about reform to the criminal legal system. Throughout this book, there will be readings that touch on the high incarceration rate or recommend changes in policy to address the high incarceration rate. The following readings help to give context and background regarding the impact of the high incarceration rates and some historical perspective on how we got to this point.

- In addition to the total number of people incarcerated in the United States, there are an additional estimated 4.5 million under community supervision, including probation and parole.
- These numbers are equivalent to the entire population of Tennessee or Massachusetts and would be the 16th largest state in the nation.

Prison Policy Initiative, *Correctional Control 2018: Incarceration and Supervision by the State*. https://www.prison policy.org/reports/correctionalcontrol 2018.html.

Let's start with some basic statistics before moving to a historical perspective:

- Despite making up close to 5% of the global population, the U.S. has nearly 20% of the world's prison population. Since 1970, our incarcerated population has increased by 700%—although there have been some decreases and we currently have 1.9 million people in jail and prison, far outpacing population growth and crime.
- Under current policies, one out of every three Black boys born today can expect to go to prison in his lifetime, as can one of every six Latino boys—compared to one of every 17 white boys. At the same time, women are the fastest growing incarcerated population in the United States.
- There are twice as many people sitting in local jails awaiting trial and presumed innocent than in the entire federal prison system. And each year, 650,000 men and women nationwide return from prison to their communities. They face nearly 50,000 federal, state, and local legal restrictions that make it difficult to reintegrate back into society.
- Our prison system costs taxpayers $80 billion per year.[34]

34. ACLU, *Mass Incarceration*, https://www.aclu.org/issues/smart-justice/mass-incarceration.

Jacob Kang-Brown, Oliver Hinds, Jasmine Heiss & Olive Lu, *A Brief History of Mass Incarceration: From Unified Growth to an Era of Reform*

THE NEW DYNAMICS OF MASS INCARCERATION 8
(Vera Institute June 2018)

After decades of stability, the U.S. incarceration rate increased markedly between 1970 and 2000, growing by an average of 12 percent each year to reach a total increase of about 400 percent—and the highest rate of incarceration in the world. The rise of mass incarceration was not perfectly even: the incarceration rate in states like California and Georgia began growing earlier, while in states like Minnesota and Massachusetts the increase came later. Wisconsin and Pennsylvania had notably high growth rates, but ultimately no state resisted the trend. Increased reliance on incarceration became mainstream public policy. For example, policy researchers at the National Institute of Justice argued that incarceration was a cost-effective way to reduce crime. Most elected officials fully supported policies reflecting that approach—as well as the appropriations necessary to expand and build new prisons and jails. Investment in prison and jail construction and expansion was so widespread and intensive that this era is now known as the "prison boom." As the boom progressed, courts and legislatures became less responsive to incarcerated people's claims to constitutional rights of speech, association, and freedom from cruel punishments. Close review of ill-treatment or harm arising from overcrowding and use-of-force incidents were largely replaced with deference to wardens' justifications of policies and practices in the service of institutional safety and security, and the 1996 Prison Litigation Reform Act further closed the door of the courthouse as an avenue for improving conditions. This created a unified trend wherein every state increased the use of prisons and jails and legislatures and courts felt little pressure to address the mounting human toll of incarceration.

The new millennium marked a turning point and ushered in a high plateau in the national incarceration rate: the nationwide growth of incarceration rates slowed, even falling slightly since the peak in 2007. In part, this change was due to increasing fiscal pressures states felt as a result of the recession crisis of the early 2000s, but it solidified with the subsequent financial crisis of 2008. As leaders responded to the financial crisis with calls for austerity, the budgetary implications began to make continued incarceration growth seem untenable in many states. This was complemented by a growing awareness that locking up huge numbers of people had, at best, a marginal benefit to and, at worst, a corrosive effect on, public safety. Courts began to be more responsive to mistreatment claims from prisoners. But incarceration's decline has been far less pronounced and much more uneven than its rise, with wide variation across states and counties.

* * *

The Vera Institute Report, quoted above, took a hard look at the data regarding incarceration and cautions that recent reductions in incarceration rates are not uniform,

How many years until incarceration in the United States falls to 1970 rates?

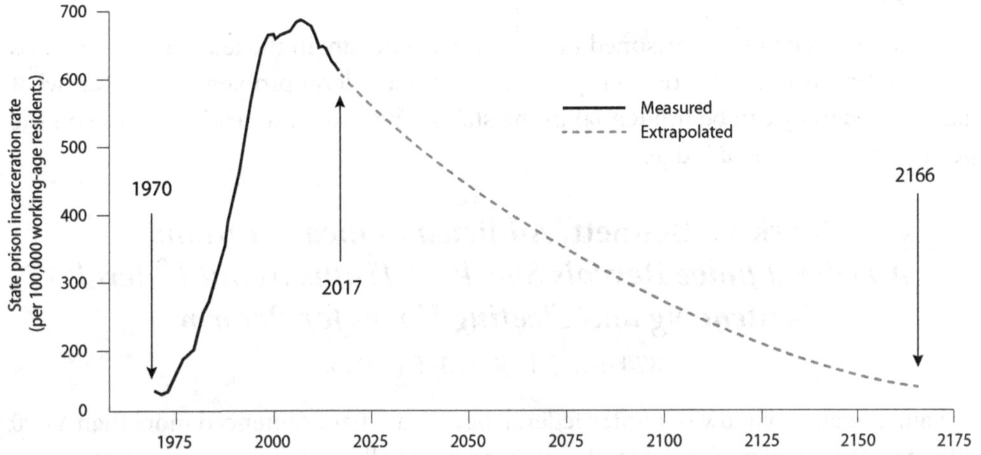

Note: This projection is based on the average annual rate of decline in the state prison incarceration rate since its peak in 2007.

in contrast to the single uniform trend upwards that lead to mass incarceration. For example, the Vera Institute found that cities tend to be "leading the way" in terms of decarceration. The challenge is that rural areas, in the same states, are continuing to incarcerate at the same or higher rates. As the report stated, "in the 35 states for which there is reliable county-level data, there is an almost universal urban-to-rural shift in prison admissions, regardless of whether admissions are declining in the state as a whole."[35] This data means that practicing lawyers need to understand the dynamics at play within their communities. Are they in a community that is committed to decreasing incarceration rates? If yes, that community may be more open to alternative processes, like problem solving courts. It also means that policy-makers can't ignore rural areas if they want to have a more lasting impact in terms of decarceration.

Incarceration rates are declining, but the decline is slow, and inconsistent. In 2018, The Vera Institute estimated that, at the current rates of decline, the United States would 150 years to return to the incarceration rates of 1975. It should be noted that that estimate does not include more recent data that has shown an increase, not a continuing decrease, in incarcerations rates. By another estimate that uses data up to 2020, the U.S. prison population will decrease by half by 2078, under the current rates of decline.[36] Lawyers and policymakers in the criminal legal system will have to make more serious and far-reaching reforms than they have so far if they want to end mass

---

35. Jacob Kang-Brown, et al., The New Dynamics of Mass Incarceration 22 (Vera Institute June 2018), available at: https://storage.googleapis.com/vera-web-assets/downloads/Publications/the-new-dynamics-of-mass-incarceration/legacy_downloads/the-new-dynamics-of-mass-incarceration-report.pdf.

36. Nazgol Ghandnoosh, *Can We Wait 60 Years to Cut the Prison Population in Half?* Policy Brief, The Sentencing Project, January 22, 2021.

incarceration and return to lower incarceration rates that were the norm for most of U.S. history.[37]

Only 13% of people imprisoned in the United States are in the federal system. Mass incarceration is not only (or even predominately) a federal problem. However, what happens federally can be influential in the states. The following reading gives you the perspective of a federal judge.

Mark W. Bennett, *Addicted to Incarceration: A Federal Judge Reveals Shocking Truths About Federal Sentencing and Fleeting Hopes for Reform*

87 UMKC L. Rev. 3–5 (2018)

I am a small-town Iowa-country federal judge, but I have sentenced more than 4,000 offenders to federal prison. Federal sentences, especially in drug cases, are all too often bone-crushingly severe. That is especially true for most of the endless drug offenders I see: non-violent, low-level, long-term and severe drug addicts. These folks stand before me for sentencing in sharp contrast to the super violent drug cartel kingpins we read about and see on television, Netflix, and in the movies. I can count on one hand the number of kingpins I have sentenced, and each received a very severe sentence, including affirming a sentence of death imposed by a jury after a three-month trial. In contrast, ninety-five percent or more of those I sentence in drug cases cannot afford to hire counsel, pay their rent or mortgage, or adequately provide for their children because of their severe addiction. Their sole focus in life becomes snorting, smoking, or injecting drugs. Their prior station in life is irrelevant to them. Their prior productive lives are a distant, hazy, and foggy memory. They are the grist of the federal sentencing mill and federal mass incarceration. Of those who come before me for an addiction to crack cocaine, they are almost always Black. If it is methamphetamine, they are usually White or Hispanic, and are often employed in blue collar industrial jobs like meat packing....

There are two other issues that have also led to the mass incarceration of federal drug offenders: 1) Congressionally-mandatory minimum sentences; and 2) Congressionally-mandated sentencing enhancements that often result in low level, non-violent, addict drug offenders having their already harsh mandatory minimum sentence doubled or even enhanced to a life sentence with no release except with a Presidential pardon or commutation. My favorite target for criticism of these unfair, arbitrarily and capriciously applied sentencing enhancements is known as a § 851 enhancement [increasing prison sentences for defendants with prior drug convictions].

The nation's federal prisons are bursting at the seams with the offenders that I just described. The simple truth is that Congress, the United States Sentencing Commission, and federal trial and appellate judges are addicted to incarceration.

---

37. The preceding chart is also from the Vera Institute. *Id.*

Erik Eckholm, *In Prisoners' Wake, a Tide of Troubled Kids*, N.Y. Times A13, July 5, 2009

The chances of seeing a parent go to prison have never been greater, especially for poor black Americans, and new research is documenting the long-term harm to the children they leave behind. Recent studies indicate that having an incarcerated parent doubles the chance that a child will be at least temporarily homeless and measurably increases the likelihood of physically aggressive behavior, social isolation, depression and problems in school—all portending dimmer prospects in adulthood.

"Parental imprisonment has emerged as a novel, and distinctly American, childhood risk that is concentrated among black children and children of low-education parents," said Christopher Wildeman, a sociologist at the University of Michigan who is studying what some now call the "incarceration generation."

Among those born in 1990, one in four black children, compared with one in 25 white children, had a father in prison by age 14. Risk is concentrated among black children whose parents are high-school dropouts; half of those children had a father in prison, compared with one in 14 white children with dropout parents, according to a report by Dr. Wildeman recently published in the journal Demography.

For both blacks and whites, the chances of parental incarceration were far higher than they were for children born just 12 years earlier, in 1978....

While poor urban children had a 3 percent chance of experiencing a period of homelessness over the previous year, those with an incarcerated parent had a 6 percent chance, one study found.

The United States of America leads the world in mass incarceration. We incarcerate more people per capita than China, Saudi Arabia, Russia, and even North Korea. In fact, we incarcerate a higher percentage of our population than any nation on Earth. The majority of those incarcerated are poor and people of color. Sections of most major metropolitan cities have been ravaged by the many effects of mass incarceration: families being ripped apart, a generational cycle of incarceration, inadequate housing, and diminished employment opportunities for felons. The list goes on and on. This mantra has become well known. Less has been written, however, about why federal judges seem to be addicted to incarceration. As the above dictionary definition provides, do federal judges incarcerate such a high percentage of defendants because they are in "the state of being enslaved to habit or practice" or because of a strong and harmful need to regularly do something?

In a prior article on mass incarceration and the role of discretion, my co-author (a former federal prosecutor and one of the nation's leading critics of federal sentencing and mass incarceration) and I started the piece with this:

> Speaking to the camera in Eugene Jarecki's film, *The House I Live In*, David Simon said, "The drug war is a holocaust in slow motion." Simon, who created the seminal television series about narcotics, *The Wire*, did not use the word "holocaust" casually.
>
> Like most provocative allusions, applying the word "holocaust" to the drug war is part truth and part gross exaggeration. The drug war clearly differs from a holocaust in terms of outcome, certainly: It primarily seeks the imprisonment of millions rather than death. The drug war and a holocaust, though, do share one crucial commonality. Both occur when thousands who work within the system are complicit in something they should know is wrong. Both represent a failure of the moral compass, not only of society as a whole, but of those who exercise their discretion to build and maintain the mechanism of injustice. We write this not only as a societal critique, but also as a confession. As a former federal prosecutor and a sitting federal judge, respectively, we have been among those pulling the levers that operate this cruel machine of mass incarceration.

* * *

Mass incarceration impacts not only those who are sentenced to jail and prison, but also their family, including children.

Notes/Questions

1. Should the incarceration rate in the United States matter to individual prosecutors, defense lawyers, and judges when considering plea bargaining individual cases?

2. As a prosecutor, should it matter that different communities are impacted differently? The National Academies of Science wrote:

> As a result of the lengthening of sentences and greatly expanded drug law enforcement and imprisonment for drug offenses, criminal defendants became more likely to be sentenced to prison and remained there significantly longer than in the past. The policy shifts that propelled the growth in incarceration had disproportionately large effects on African Americans and Latinos. Indeed, serving time in prison has become a normal life event among recent birth cohorts of African American men who have not completed high school.[38]

As you continue reading this book, think about how these inequalities could, or should, impact how you would do your job as a prosecutor, defense lawyer, and/or judge.

---

38. National Research Council of the National Academies of Science, The Growth of Incarceration in the United States Exploring Causes and Consequences 34 (Jeremy Travis, Bruce Western & Steve Redburn, eds., The National Academies Press 2014).

3. If you were a prosecutor, would your answer be different if the county you worked in would be responsible for all of the incarceration costs for each non-violent, non-serious offender that you sentenced to incarceration? Consider the following:

> In 2011 [California] Governor Jerry Brown signed Assembly Bill 109, commonly referred to as "prison realignment," which shifted to counties the responsibility for monitoring, tracking, and incarcerating lower-level offenders previously bound for state prison. In brief, AB 109 (and AB 117, a companion bill) altered both sentencing and post-prison supervision for the newly statutorily classified "non-serious, non-violent, non-sex" offenders. While the legislation is comprehensive and complex, three major groups are affected by Realignment. First, felony offenders who have never been convicted of a "serious" or "violent" crime or an aggravated white collar crime and are not required to register as sex offenders (colloquially referred to as the "triple-nons") will now serve their sentences in local custody. Second, released prisoners whose current commitment offense qualifies them as "triple-non" offenders are diverted to the supervision of county probation departments under "Post Release Community Supervision (PRCS)." Third, if persons on PRCS violate the technical conditions of their supervision (rather than committing a new crime), they can no longer be returned to State prison but must be sanctioned in local (county) jail or community alternatives, including house arrest, drug treatment, or flash incarceration."[39]

The state of California does not cover county jail imprisonment costs; instead, that comes out of local county budgets. This means that Realignment shifts the costs for imprisonment back to the counties for the categories of defendants described above.

4. Should the consequence for children of defendants be considered during plea negotiations? As many as 1 of every 28 children in the United States has a parent who is incarcerated. This is compared to 1 in every 125 children twenty-five years ago. As with other incarceration rate statistics, the impact is different in different communities. Approximately 13% of African American children, 20% of native children, and 6% of Latinx children have an incarcerated parent.[40] Currently 2.7 million children have a parent in custody in the United States, and over 5. 2 million children will have a parent incarcerated during their lives.[41]

Most families with an incarcerated parent also suffer economically. There are also studies that indicate increased problems in school, including expulsions and suspensions for children with one or more parent incarcerated. For more information, see The Pew Charitable Trusts, *Collateral Costs: Incarceration's Effect on Economic Mobility*, 17–20 (Washington, DC, 2010).

---

39. Stanford Criminal Justice Center, California Realignment, available at: http://www.law.stanford. edu/organizations/programs-and-centers/stanford-criminal-justice-center-scjc/california-realignment.

40. Nazgol Ghandnoosh, et al., *Parents in Prison*, The Sentencing Project, Feb. 2021.

41. *Id.*

Should prosecutors consider the impact on children as a factor in deciding whether to offer a non-prison sentence? As a defense lawyer, would you consider using the fact that your client has young children to try to encourage a non-custodial sentence during plea bargaining negotiations? Would your answer be different if your client was a man or a woman?

5. Incarceration of parents is so common that in 2013, Sesame Street introduced a new series to help children whose parents are in prison. The website introduction reads:

> Little Children, Big Challenges: Incarceration
>
> The incarceration of a loved one can be very overwhelming for both children and caregivers. It can bring about big changes and transitions. In simple everyday ways, you can comfort your child and guide her through these tough moments. With your love and support she can get through anything that comes her way. Here are some tools to help you with the changes your child is going through.[42]

6. How should a prosecutor weigh the impact of future employment prospects in deciding what plea bargain to offer individual defendants and whether to dismiss the case or allow it to go to some form of diversion? In the book, MARKED: RACE, CRIME, AND FINDING WORK IN AN ERA OF MASS INCARCERATION, author Devah Pager concluded that a criminal record, including for drug offenses, made it "nearly impossible" for African Americans in Milwaukee to get a job. Other authors have explored how mass incarceration has impacted African American communities. For example, Bruce Western in HOMEWARD: LIFE IN THE YEAR AFTER PRISON wrote:

> In the United States, pervasive incarceration remains a daily reality in poor and minority neighborhoods.[43] ... If we are going to reduce our prison populations, we must acknowledge that human frailty under conditions of poverty puts people at risk of simultaneously becoming both the perpetrator and the victim of violence.[44]
>
> People who go to prison have slipped through the holes of the American safety net. Many struggle with a human frailty where adversities of mental illness, untreated addiction, and physical disability all come together under conditions of poverty.[45]

Bruce Western in PUNISHMENT AND INEQUALITY IN AMERICA wrote about high incarceration rates for African American men who did not have a college education—30% have been to prison. The rates jump to 59% for African American men who are high-school dropouts. Western was quoted as saying:

---

42. http://www.sesamestreet.org/parents/topicsandactivities/toolkits/incarceration.

43. BRUCE WESTERN, HOMEWARD: LIFE IN THE YEAR AFTER PRISON 187 (Russel Sage Foundation, 2018).

44. *Id.* at 186.

45. *Id.* at 6.

"I don't think the really deep penetration of the criminal justice system into poor and minority communities has been fully understood by people outside these communities," says Western.

Mass incarceration, Western argues, also renders invisible a substantial portion of American poverty. At the height of the tech boom in 2000, he points out, 65 percent of black male high school dropouts weren't working. Government statistics, however, said the unemployment level of this group was 33 percent, because government surveys exclude prisoners....

A handful of cities ... no longer ask applicants for city jobs whether they have a criminal record, although their backgrounds can still be checked later. A growing "Ban the Box" movement—referring to the check-off box on an application, signaling a conviction—is designed to reduce the kind of upfront discrimination....

[We could] add a policy modeled on how we treat debtors: After a certain amount of time, records of most convictions, especially for nonviolent offenses, would be expunged. Stigma would have a deadline.[46]

7. Would you agree, as a prosecutor, that criminal records should be regularly expunged if the defendant is not re-arrested? Should this only apply to non-violent offenses? As a defense lawyer, should you negotiate for terms such as later expungements, or is it your duty only to handle the case and not other collateral matters?

8. Most people sentenced to prison are not sentenced to life without parole. This means that they will ultimately be released. In the United States, roughly 600,000 people are released from jail or prison every year. Every year Texas releases approximately 40,000 people from state prison to return to their communities. Approximately 30,000 return to Los Angeles, 20,000 return to New York, and 15,000 return to Chicago. Forty percent of those released will be back behind bars within three years, although this varies greatly by state and the national data has not been updated since 2012 by the Bureau of Justice Statistics. As a future prosecutor or defense lawyer, do these statistics matter in thinking about what to do with individual cases? If they do matter, how do they matter? Does it make you more or less hesitant to negotiate a plea agreement involving time in prison?

9. Increasing incarceration rates, and the increased costs, have motivated some states to make changes in their overall criminal justice policies and have stopped the otherwise steady increase in prison population rates. Texas used to have the highest incarceration rate in the United States, but in 2007, the nonpartisan Legislative Budget Board estimated that if incarceration rates kept rising at the rates they had been, Texas would need to build 17,000 more prison beds at a cost of $2 billion, plus the costs to

46. Christopher Shea, *Life Sentence: It's a government program whose impact rivals the New Deal*, Boston Globe, 1E, March, 2007.

Should Sentences Be Reduced for Violent Crime?

Between 2007 and 2018, the United States reduced the number of people imprisoned for a drug offense by 31%. During that same period, the number of people imprisoned for property offenses declined by 24%. But, between 2009–2018, the number of people imprisoned for a violent offense decreased by 5%. Reducing sentences for violent offenses would significantly reduce incarceration rates in the United States. Nazgol Ghandnoosh, *Can we wait 60 years to cut the prison population in half? Policy Brief*, the Sentencing Project, January 22, 2021.

The United States tends to give longer prison terms than many other countries: "The U.S. holds a substantial portion (40%) of the world's population of people serving life sentences, as well as the vast majority (83%) of those sentenced to life without the possibility of parole. While most jurisdictions with life sentencing laws have a provision for release, the amount of time people must serve before becoming eligible varies widely. In Belgium, Denmark, and Finland, it's 12 years or less. In Georgia, it's 30 years and in Texas it's 40 years." Lila Kazemian, Long Sentences: An International Perspective, Council on Criminal Justice, December 2022.

How might a state legislature think about reforming their sentencing laws to decrease sentences for violent offenses? What are the different goals? As you will read later in the book, the older a person gets, the more likely they are to "age out of" criminal behavior. Should laws be amended to allow an offender to be considered for parole after they reach a certain age? What age? At 30, 40, 50? Should their health be a part of the criteria making those in worse health eligible for parole considerations sooner? Or should the laws be rewritten to decrease the possible sentences or to not allow consecutive sentences? As you will read, even without a legislature changing the law, prosecutors could exercise their discretion and file different charges or seek different sentences in plea bargaining. Should prosecutors act on their own to decrease the possible sentences for violent offenses, even if the legislature has not?

run the new prisons.[47] According to an ACLU report, this "shocked legislators into enacting large reforms to move away from the state's overreliance on prisons."[48]

> Imprisonment fell in Texas, but critics point out that some of the decrease was due to non-prison alternatives, such as beds in locked-down substance abuse treatment centers and intermediate sanction facilities that are, for all practical purposes, places of confinement, although not technically prisons or jails.

---

47. American Civil Liberties Union, *Smart Reform Is Possible: States Reducing Incarceration Rates and Costs While Protecting Communities*, 18, August 2011.

48. *Id.*

The ACLU applauded the reforms in Texas, but also recommended a focus on "front-end" reforms "like decriminalizing low-level drug and property offenses, reducing sentences for some crimes, and mandating alternatives to incarceration for low-level crimes" instead of focusing on parole and probation.[49]

10. During COVID-19 prisons in some states and in the federal system allowed people to request or petition for early release. One requirement to be eligible to apply was whether the incarcerated person was more vulnerable to serious illness or death due to COVID-19, such as the elderly or those with other serious illnesses. At the same time, there was an effort to decrease pre-trial incarceration and allowing some people who were arrested to be cited and released pending their future court date. In the federal system more than 11,000 people were sent home and many of those were released on home confinement, which means they were not really released. Starting in 2022, some of those people were returned to prison. There is only limited data on criminal case processing during the pandemic and it is unclear if prosecutors agreed to lesser sentences during the pandemic to help keep people out of jails and prisons to help prevent the spread of COVID. As you read this book, you may want to think about whether or how risk of illness or injury in prison or jail should impact what plea bargain a prosecutor might offer. Should people who are more vulnerable, such as the elderly, the disabled, or juveniles, be treated differently?

11. George Floyd's murder by police officers in Minneapolis in 2020 sparked calls for reform including defunding the police. The Black Lives Matter (BLM) movement galvanized protests for police and criminal legal system reform across the United States. The protests sparked changes. Some communities reallocated funds away from the police (such as Los Angeles County), others restricted the use of chokeholds, and some enacted or strengthened "duty-to-intervene" policies so police officers would step in if a colleague used excessive force.

12. Over four years later, there are concerns that the reforms from the BLM movement were limited and there is backtracking on broader criminal reform. There has also been concern that we are moving out of an era when there was wide bipartisan support for criminal legal system reform. For example, in 2024, San Franciscans not only voted to remove their DA (see discussion above about progressive prosecutors) but also voted to give the police expanded surveillance powers (including the use of drones and more cameras) under Proposition E. Some states have voted to return to earlier practices. For example, Louisiana repealed a 2017 law that changed the age of adult criminal responsibility from 17 to 18 and returned it to 17 years old. Louisiana also reduced opportunities for parole and early release. It is not clear whether we are entering a longer period of backtracking and an end to more bipartisan criminal system reform efforts. What is clear is that crime and how prosecutors, police, judges, and lawyers handle criminal cases continue to be at the forefront of both news and politics.

---

49. *Id.*

V. Structure of This Book

This book is divided into four broad topics: plea bargaining, therapeutic justice, restorative justice and juvenile legal system. Plea bargaining is by far the predominant process through which criminal cases are resolved. This book will begin with plea bargaining due to its importance within the criminal legal system in the United States and also due to the fact that it is because of plea bargaining's flexibility that other alternative processes, such as therapeutic justice and restorative justice, have developed. Juvenile courts are often called the first problem-solving courts, and this book will close with a discussion of why that is and how juvenile courts work in ways that are similar and different from adult criminal courts. This book concludes by bringing together the discussion about these various alternative processes, through a dispute resolution lens, to consider what might bring lasting and meaningful reform.

Unlike a traditional criminal procedure text, this book will not focus only on the caselaw or even the statutory law surrounding these various processes. You will read about the major U.S. Supreme Court cases that touch on these subjects, but, as you will discover, the formal caselaw only discusses a small part of the practical and policy-level issues. Therefore, this book will move beyond the law and discuss policy, proposals for reform, and basic negotiation skills for criminal practitioners (prosecutors and defense lawyers). What follows is a brief introduction to each of these four topics.

A. Plea Bargaining

The overwhelming majority of criminal cases are resolved through plea bargaining in the United States. There are some types of cases (such as drug cases) that are almost never tried, and some jurisdictions see almost no jury trials. The U.S. criminal legal system relies on plea bargaining to process criminal cases. As Chief Justice Burger stated, "If every criminal charge were subjected to a full-scale trial, the States and the Federal Government would need to multiply by many times the number of judges and court facilities."[50] As Justice Kennedy observed, in reality, the "criminal justice system is for the most part a system of pleas, not a system of trials."[51]

Plea bargaining is defined as "... a form of negotiation by which the prosecutor and defense counsel enter into an agreement resolving one or more criminal charge against the defendant without a trial."[52] In the U.S., the two most common types of plea bargaining are charge bargaining and sentence bargaining. Under charge bargaining, the prosecutor may agree to dismiss one or more of the charges or to not charge particular offenses. Sentence bargaining occurs when the prosecution and defense negotiate the sentence, or punishment, while agreeing to the charges as filed. A third form of plea bargaining is sentencing recommendation agreements where the prosecutor agrees to recommend a particular sentence to the judge and is more common in the federal sys-

50. Santobello v. New York, 404 U.S. 2567, 260 (1971).

51. Lafler v. Cooper, 132 S. Ct. 1376, 1387 (2012).

52. G. Nicholas Herman, Plea Bargaining, 1 (2004).

tem. Plea negotiations often include both sentence and charge bargaining. Depending on the seriousness and complexity of the case, plea negotiations can be simple and fast, or extended and drawn out.

As you will read later in this book, critics have serious concerns about how plea bargaining works in practice, and there are repeated calls for reform. Yet the general response to calls to abolish plea bargaining is that there are just too many criminal cases to be able to do a jury trial for each one. Often, the best that is said about plea bargaining is that it is a necessary evil. Without it, our criminal legal system could not function.

However, as you will read, there is an underappreciated advantage of plea bargaining, which is that it is a process that allows for flexibility in the system. Thanks to plea bargaining, the criminal legal system can experiment, innovate, and take alternative approaches to punishment. The best example of this, which is covered later in this book, is the development of problem-solving courts such as drug courts, veterans courts, and mental health courts. Without a flexible and informal system of case resolution, it would be difficult, if not impossible, to agree to a resolution of the case that was outside the existing laws.

As you have seen from the discussion of incarceration rates, the United States has taken a punitive approach to crime. The penalties are high for a wide range of offenses. Plea bargaining allows the parties to agree to other outcomes for cases. Sometimes this means using newer approaches such as a drug court or mental health court. Sometimes it means agreeing to take the case outside the formal criminal legal system and resolve it through a restorative justice process. So, while there are serious criticisms of plea bargaining, it is important to keep in mind that the informality in the way we resolve criminal cases through plea bargaining allows for alternative options that otherwise might not be possible without first passing new laws.

Our six chapters on plea bargaining will introduce you to the background of plea bargaining, the concerns of critics, proposals for reform and discuss plea bargaining as a form of dispute resolution and the skills that lawyers (both prosecutors and defense lawyers) need to effectively plea bargain.

B. Problem-Solving Courts/Therapeutic Justice

A significant percentage of defendants suffer from mental illness, substance abuse, cognitive disabilities, and/or traumatic brain injuries. Problem-solving courts developed to move towards a more therapeutic/rehabilitative approach with the goal of addressing these underlying factors that lead to criminal offenses and thereby helping to reduce recidivism rates. The most common problem-solving courts in the United States are Drug Courts. However, problem-solving courts are not limited to drug offenses. Mental Health Courts, Domestic Violence Courts, Veterans Courts, and Community Courts are other common problem-solving courts. When a defendant's case is transferred to a problem-solving court, it is usually within the context of a plea agreement and is in lieu of a jury trial. Defendants may go to problem-solving courts to avoid a criminal conviction (as a form of diversion) or as a post-conviction probationary sentence.

All problem-solving courts have "five common features:

1. Close and ongoing judicial monitoring.
2. A multidisciplinary or team-oriented approach.
3. A therapeutic or treatment orientation.
4. The altering of traditional roles in the adjudication process.
5. An emphasis on solving the problems of individual offenders."[53]

Problem-solving courts are a combination of counseling and punishment. If a defendant fails to comply with the requirements, he/she may be sentenced to time in jail. And, if the failure is serious enough (or frequent enough), the court may decide to end the defendant's participation in the program entirely.

Drug courts are probably the fastest growing and most common alternative form of dispute resolution within the criminal legal system. Some states have legislated the creation and use of drug courts. For example, in 2001, Texas required drug courts for all jurisdictions with a population over 550,000.[54] That requirement was expanded in 2007, and currently, Texas requires any county with a population over 200,000 to have a drug court.[55] Proponents support the problem-solving approach due to the belief that by helping the offender with their underlying problems, it may prevent recidivism. Critics are concerned about whether problem-solving courts adequately protect defendants' rights. Some raise concerns about the impact on legal professionals, as problem-solving courts are not adversarial courts and require both lawyers and judges to behave differently and take on new roles. As with plea bargaining, the victim has no role in deciding whether a particular defendant should go to a problem-solving court instead of a traditional adversarial process. There are also criticisms about which defendants are sent to drug courts, with the concern that those with the most serious addiction problems may not be targeted.[56] We cover the problem-solving courts, and concerns, in Chapters 9 and 10.

C. Restorative Justice

Scholars and practitioners use the term "restorative justice" to describe a range of processes. Restorative justice processes include victim-offender mediation, family group conferencing, peacemaking circles, community reparative boards, and victim impact panels. As with problem-solving courts, restorative justice processes often

53. James L. Nolan Jr., Legal Accents, Legal Borrowing: The International Problem-Solving Court Movement 11 (2009).

54. Texas H.B. 1287 (77th legislature 2001).

55. Texas H.B. 530 (80th legislature 2007). This requirement is contingent on state or federal funding being available.

56. *See generally*, National Association of Criminal Defense Lawyers, *America's Problem-Solving Courts: The Criminal Costs of Treatment and the Case for Reform*, September 2009.

occur within the context of a plea agreement and may be in lieu of conviction or post-conviction. Some restorative justice processes occur after the conviction and are unrelated to the criminal process. For the purposes of this book, we will not focus on restorative justice processes that take place after or outside the criminal process.

Restorative justice and therapeutic justice/problem-solving courts share an emphasis on "emotions, empathy, healing, and the psychological well-being of individuals encountering the legal system."[57] On a practical level, one difference between restorative justice and therapeutic justice is that the victim is often directly involved in restorative justice proceedings.

Regardless of when the restorative justice process happens as an alternative process for the criminal legal system or outside it, all restorative processes share a basic definition. Howard Zehr, a leading scholar in the restorative justice field, defines restorative justice as "a process [that] involve[s], to the extent possible, those who have a stake in a specific offense and ... collectively identif[ies] and address[es] harms, needs, and obligations, in order to heal and put things as right as possible."[58] Other authors define "restorative justice [as] seek[ing] to balance the concerns of the victim and the community with the need to re-integrate the offender into society. It seeks to assist the recovery of the victim and enable all parties with a stake in the justice process to participate fruitfully in it."[59]

Restorative justice may be referred to as "mediation of criminal cases," but there are some key differences between restorative justice processes and civil mediation. One key difference is that the offender must accept responsibility for the "harm" or offense as a pre-condition to participating in a restorative justice process. This means that unlike in the civil mediation context, all parties are not equal. One party, the offender, must acknowledge responsibility for the crime, and the other is the acknowledged victim. The question in a restorative justice proceeding is not who did the crime, but rather what the offender should do to "repair the harm" of the crime he/she committed. These processes and concerns are the subjects of Chapters 11 and 12.

D. Juvenile Legal System

Juvenile courts were established in the United States to rehabilitate the juvenile offender and to provide a clear alternative to the adversarial process for adults. Due to this early emphasis on rehabilitation, juvenile courts have been referred to as the "original problem-solving courts." Currently, many states have no minimum age and allow juveniles to be prosecuted if they meet certain minimum competency requirements. Some states specifically state that only children ages 10–13 are old enough to be prosecuted. An increasing number of juveniles have been prosecuted as adults. Yet,

57. James L. Nolan Jr., Legal Accents, Legal Borrowing: The International Problem-Solving Court Movement, 32 (2009).

58. Howard Zehr, Changing Lenses: A New Focus for Crime and Justice 130 (1990).

59. Ivo Avertsen, et al. Rebuilding Community Connection: Mediation and Restorative Justice in Europe 14 (Council of Europe 2004).

in recent years, the U.S. Supreme Court has decided cases that have forced a change in how some juveniles are treated in the adult system. In 2005, in *Roper v. Simmons,* the Supreme Court held that juveniles cannot be executed.[60] In 2010, the Supreme Court held that it was unconstitutional to sentence a juvenile to life in prison without the possibility of parole for a non-homicide offense.[61] In 2012, the Court held that the Constitution prohibits a sentencing system that requires a juvenile to be sentenced to life in prison without the possibility of parole in a homicide offense without considering other possible sentences.[62]

In addition to looking at the current state of the juvenile court system, this book will also examine various alternatives within the juvenile legal system such as Teen Courts, Youth Courts, and other therapeutic and problem-solving courts directed at juvenile offenders. These alternatives often happen in lieu of sending a juvenile to the traditional juvenile legal system. Our final three chapters in the book delve into the juvenile system.

Basic Criminal Process

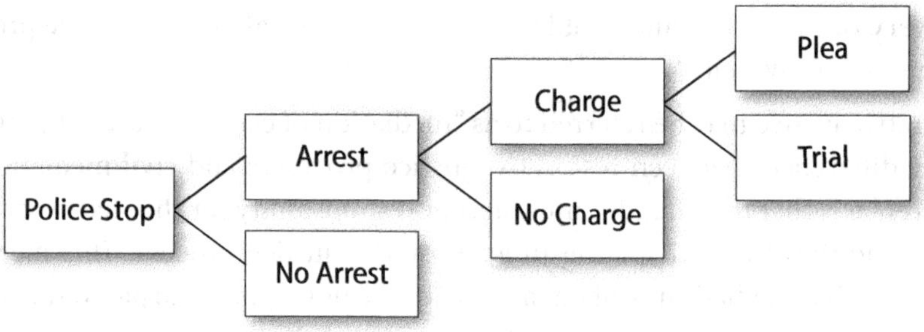

Standard Plea Outcomes

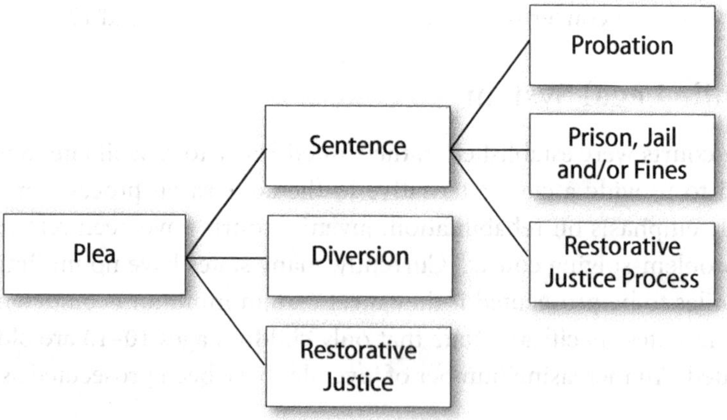

60. 543 U.S. 551 (2005).
61. Graham v. Florida, 560 U.S. 48 (2010).
62. Miller v. Alabama, 567 U.S. 460 (2012).

Standard Trial Outcomes

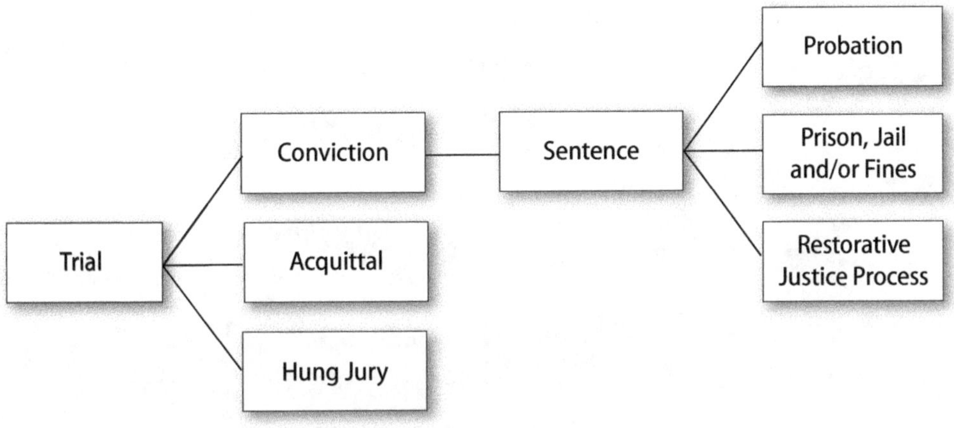

Additional Resources

Michelle Alexander, The New Jim Crow: Mass Incarceration in the Age of Colorblindness (The New Press 2012).

Amy Bach, Ordinary Injustice: How America Holds Court (Holt 2009).

Rachel Elise Barkow, Prisoners of Politics: Breaking the Cycle of Mass Incarceration (Harvard University Press, 2019).

Stephanos Bibas, The Machinery of Criminal Justice (Oxford University Press 2012).

Decarcerating America: From Mass Punishment to Public Health, Ernest Druker ed. (The New Press 2018).

James Forman Jr., Locking up Our Own (Farrar, Straus and Giroux 2017).

National Research Council of the National Academies of Science, The Growth of Incarceration in the United States: Exploring Causes and Consequences (National Academies Press 2014).

John. F. Pfaff, Locked In: The True Causes of Mass Incarceration and How to Achieve Real Reform (Basic Books 2017).

William J. Stuntz, The Collapse of American Criminal Justice (Harvard 2011).

Transforming Criminal Justice: An Evidence Based Agenda for Reform, Jon B. Gould & Pamela R. Metzger eds. (NYU Press 2022)

Chapter 2

Charging, Discretion, and Diversion

Before discussing plea bargaining and other processes that resolve criminal cases, it is important to understand the role and power of prosecutors at the beginning of the criminal process, when formal charges are filed. The prosecutor's initial decision of whether to file a case, which charges to file, and whether to file a case as a misdemeanor or a felony, can be the most important decision that is made in a criminal case in terms of determining the eventual outcome for the defendant. Prosecutors are part of the executive branch of government and have wide discretion to decide what cases to bring into the formal criminal legal system. They also have wide discretion to decide how to proceed once a case is filed, including whether to make a plea offer. As you will read in later chapters, there are few constraints on these prosecutorial powers.

Prosecutors are not alone in having discretionary powers. The U.S. criminal legal system is a system of discretion that gives the various players power to decide how to proceed with a case, including whether to proceed. This discretionary power starts with police officers who can decide, with some exceptions, who to stop and who to arrest. Once an arrest is made, prosecutors have discretion to decide whether to bring the case formally into the criminal legal system. Once a case goes into the criminal legal system, prosecutors retain discretion to decide whether to dismiss charges, add charges, or dismiss the case entirely. Judges have more limited discretion to dismiss charges or the entire case. Judges do not have the power to add charges to existing cases, or to file charges to start a criminal prosecution.

This chapter begins with readings on the prosecutor's wide-ranging, and largely unchecked, discretionary power in the decision to bring formal charges (or not). This chapter will then cover the role of prosecutors in grand jury indictments. You will also read how this discretion has come under attack for its seemingly unfettered power as well as the potential for abuse. We will then discuss diversion, as that was a process that started at the discretion of the prosecutor, although it is now often statutory. Finally, this chapter will end by comparing other models of prosecutorial power and discretion. All of the processes that this book will discuss in later chapters exist because there is discretion within the criminal legal system. The readings in this chapter focus on the impact of one player, the prosecutor, having such wide ranging and largely unchecked discretionary power. You will want to keep this in mind in future chapters as you learn how plea bargaining and other dispositive processes work, and particularly as you consider various proposals for reform.

I. Prosecutorial Power in Filing Charges

Criminal charges are brought either by grand jury indictment or by the prosecutor filing an information (directly filing charges with the court). Every state has grand juries, but less than half use them regularly; a smaller number require grand jury indictments in criminal cases; and some require grand jury indictments only in particular types of cases. Prosecutorial charging power is different depending on how charges are brought.

This section will focus on direct filing of charges, and later in the chapter, you will read more about the role of prosecutors in grand jury indictments. The readings in this section discuss the extent of prosecutorial discretion when deciding what charges to file, or not to file. In his study of discretionary justice in the United States, Kenneth Culp Davis commented, "[v]iewed in broad perspective, the American legal system seems to be shot through with many excessive and uncontrolled discretionary powers but the one that stands out above all others is the power to prosecute or not to prosecute."[1] It is this stand out power that you will now read more about.

Peter Krug, *Prosecutorial Discretion and Its Limits*

50 Am. J. Comp. L. 643, 644–649 (Fall 2002)

II. The Charging Function: Institutional Setting and the Nature of Prosecutorial Discretion

A. Institutional Setting

Prosecutorial functions are widely dispersed among different offices in the United States. Fifty-two jurisdictions—the federal government, each of the fifty states, and the District of Columbia—are competent to enact their own criminal laws and laws of criminal procedure, and to establish their own criminal justice systems. The only source of legal regulation that is applicable to all of these jurisdictions is the U.S. Constitution, which provides a common core of basic principles in the structure of criminal procedure. As to statutory law, there is a "fair degree of uniformity" among the different jurisdictions. Although the scope and volume of federal criminal statutes have expanded dramatically over the past several decades, most criminal laws are those of the states, and the vast majority of criminal cases are prosecuted by state and local authorities.

All fifty-two jurisdictions have their own, separate, prosecutorial organizations. Within the state systems, the prosecution function is de-centralized, so that in most states local prosecutorial offices function autonomously and the state attorneys general exercise very little effective control over them. Federal government prosecutorial agencies, meanwhile, are found in the United States Department of Justice and in offices within federal regulatory agencies. The Department of Justice includes the headquar-

1. Kenneth Culp Davis, Discretionary Justice: A Preliminary Inquiry (1971).

ters in Washington, D.C. and the ninety-three United States Attorneys who are located in the federal judicial districts throughout the United States.

The great majority of prosecutorial offices are led by chief prosecutors who are elected officials. Most are elected local officials who in turn appoint their assistant prosecutors. In four states (Connecticut, Delaware, New Jersey, and Rhode Island), local chief prosecutors are appointed by elected officials. In the federal system, the Department of Justice is led by the U.S. Attorney General, who is nominated by the President of the United States and approved by the U.S. Senate. United States Attorneys are appointed by the President, and Assistant U.S. Attorneys are appointed by the Attorney General.

B. The Nature of Prosecutorial Charging Discretion

The charging function has two decision-making components: the initial screening determination as to whether or not to charge (the "screening function"); and, if the answer is yes, the subsequent decisions as to choice and number of charges (the "selection function"). The extent of the prosecutor's discretion in making these decisions is measured by examining two separate indicia: the degree of freedom to act unilaterally in making the charging decisions themselves ("charging autonomy"); and the degree of insulation from subsequent judicial review of those decisions ("review autonomy").

In general, legislatures and courts rarely have taken steps to interfere with the prosecutorial exercise of discretion in the charging function; as a result, particularly in regard to review autonomy, prosecutors act with nearly unfettered independence. Many justifications have been articulated for this maximization of the prosecutor's decision-making. Those advanced or identified by courts, other public officials, and commentators can be grouped in four categories: constitutional separation of powers theories, grounded in the commonly-held view that the prosecutorial function lies in the executive branch of government; deference to prosecutorial expertise; administrative necessity; and individualized justice. According to the proponents of broad discretion, the positive public benefits derived from it dictate that the most appropriate mechanism for monitoring and curbing abuse of the charging function is the electoral process, not legal regulation.

1. Charging Autonomy

In theory, mechanisms for limiting charging autonomy could include legislative or judicial measures injecting external agencies or individuals into the decision-making process, as well as legislative or judicial rules circumscribing the scope of the prosecutor's discretionary charging authority. In practice, these are not widely employed.

Prosecutors enjoy something close to a monopoly on the use of prosecutorial authority. For one thing, the opportunities afforded by the criminal justice systems for private prosecutions are sparse and rarely utilized. For another, prosecutors generally discharge their charging responsibilities without any legal mandate to include other agencies in that process, although legislatures have required such intrusion in certain specific areas However, it is also important at the same time to note one example of shared decision-making in all U.S. criminal justice systems that often is overlooked.

As one commentator has noted, the systems provide "reasonably effective controls" in the form of judicial checks against abusive prosecutions not grounded in sufficient evidence. Thus, it can be said in this regard that prosecutors must in theory share decision-making authority with the judiciary on the question of whether a case will advance to the trial phase, and that it will not in that small number of cases when evidence for so proceeding is insufficient. It is in those cases where there is sufficient evidence to go forward that judicial intervention gives way and the prosecutor in practice exercises exclusive authority as to whether to press and maintain formal charges....

In general, prosecutors also exercise the charging function with statutory limitations, although again legislatures have acted to impose some constraints as to certain classes of offenses or persons. An example of legislative limitation on discretion in the screening function is in a State of Minnesota Statute that requires local (county) prosecutors to file charges for failure to report physical or sexual child abuse or neglect, certain acts of criminal sexual conduct, and environmental law violations.

2. Review Autonomy

The courts very infrequently will uphold challenges to prosecutorial charging decisions. Put another way, they rarely compel prosecutors either to charge or to withdraw charges.

a. Decisions Not to Charge

Although judicial mechanisms exist in the U.S. legal systems for individuals to compel a prosecutor to bring charges, it is generally accepted that they are used in-frequently and are rarely successful. In many states, the attorneys general of the various states have the power under judicially-created remedies to initiate local prosecution, but again this rarely occurs. The situation is slightly different in cases where the prosecutor has filed charges and then seeks to withdraw them without any negative consequences for the accused, the act known as *nolle prosequi* in the common law. In such cases, statutes in some jurisdictions require judicial approval of such an action. However, the courts have ruled that they will not interfere with a prosecutor's withdrawal of charges unless it can be shown that dismissal of the charges is clearly contrary to a manifest public interest—a finding that rarely is made.

b. Decisions to Prosecute

The criminal justice systems afford some opportunity for individuals or government actors to challenge decisions to file charges. However, in reality, the chances for successful pursuit of such opportunities are extremely limited. One reason is that the remedies are limited. In this regard, one potential vehicle for subsequent judicial review—a civil damages remedy—is not generally available to defendants who claim that prosecutors acted unconstitutionally in bringing charges against them. In a 1976 decision, the U.S. Supreme Court extended absolute immunity to prosecutors in regard to such civil lawsuits.

Thus, the only judicial remedy available against a decision to charge is dismissal of the prosecution. However, the grounds upon which courts will uphold a challenge are strictly limited to certain specific constitutional claims of denial of equal protection or due process, and courts have taken this interventionist step in only a very few cases.

An equal protection challenge must allege discriminatory or selective prosecution, and must overcome a "presumption of regularity" that supports prosecutorial decisions. In this regard, the U.S. Supreme Court has ruled that "[t]he conscious exercise of some selectivity in enforcement is not in itself a federal constitutional violation."[2] In order to overcome the presumption of regularity, a defendant must satisfy what the U.S. Supreme Court has recognized as a "demanding" standard: a showing, based on "clear evidence to the contrary", that (1) other persons similarly situated to the defendant have not been prosecuted; and (2) the prosecution's selection of this particular defendant for prosecution was invidious (based on constitutionally impermissible grounds such as race or religion) or in bad faith.

As to invidiousness, a claimant must demonstrate that the prosecutor's decision had a discriminatory effect and was motivated by a discriminatory purpose. The latter element calls upon a defendant to ascertain the prosecutor's motives by obtaining factual information that usually will be found only in the possession of the prosecutor. In *United States v. Armstrong*, the U.S. Supreme Court imposed a "rigorous standard" for such discovery, requiring the defendant to produce as a threshold requirement "some evidence tending to show the existence of the essential elements of the defense."[3] In justifying such a significant barrier to discovery, the Court cited the costs that discovery requirements would impose on the prosecutor, diverting resources and perhaps disclosing the prosecutor's litigation strategy.

Another potential basis for challenging the decision to prosecute is that of prosecutorial "vindictiveness"—i.e., punishment, in violation of due process rights, of a defendant in retaliation for his or her decision to exercise a constitutional right. Thus, a successful claim of vindictive prosecution might be one that shows that the prosecutor added more severe charges against a defendant who rejected a plea bargain in favor of exercising the constitutional right to a trial with a jury of one's peers. Commentators point out that the judicial standards governing the resolution of vindictiveness claims are not uniform; however, the U.S. Supreme Court has signaled that some measure of vindictiveness on the prosecutor's part is acceptable. Therefore, each case will rest on its particular facts to permit determination of the sufficient level of vindictiveness for a claimant to succeed.

* * *

2. [36] Oyler v. Boles, 368 U.S. 448, 456 (1962).
3. [39] United States v. Armstrong, 517 U.S. 456, 468 (1996).

The ABA Criminal Justice Section Standards on the Prosecution Function set out minimum standards for how prosecutors should handle their power to charge criminal cases. As a prosecutor, do these standards help to guide you in terms of when to file charges?

Standard 3-3.4 Decision to Charge

(a) The decision to institute criminal proceedings should be initially and primarily the responsibility of the prosecutor.

(b) Prosecutors should take reasonable care to ensure that investigators working at their direction or under their authority are adequately trained in the standards governing the issuance of arrest and search warrants and should inform investigators that they should seek the approval of a prosecutor in close or difficult cases.

(c) The prosecutor should establish standards and procedures for evaluating complaints to determine whether criminal proceedings should be instituted.

(d) Where the law permits a citizen to complain directly to a judicial officer or the grand jury, the citizen complainant should be required to present the complaint for prior approval to the prosecutor, and the prosecutor's action or recommendation thereon should be communicated to the judicial officer or grand jury....

Standard 3-3.8 Discretion as to Noncriminal Disposition

(a) The prosecutor should consider in appropriate cases the availability of noncriminal disposition, formal or informal, in deciding whether to press criminal charges which would otherwise be supported by probable cause; especially in the case of a first offender, the nature of the offense may warrant noncriminal disposition.

(b) Prosecutors should be familiar with the resources of social agencies which can assist in the evaluation of cases for diversion from the criminal process.

Standard 3-3.9 Discretion in the Charging Decision

(a) A prosecutor should not institute, or cause to be instituted, or permit the continued pendency of criminal charges when the prosecutor knows that the charges are not supported by probable cause. A prosecutor should not institute, cause to be instituted, or permit the continued pendency of criminal charges in the absence of sufficient admissible evidence to support a conviction.

(b) The prosecutor is not obliged to present all charges which the evidence might support. The prosecutor may in some circumstances and for good cause consistent with the public interest decline to prosecute, notwithstanding that sufficient evidence may exist which would support a conviction. Illustrative or the factors which the prosecutor may properly consider in exercising his or her discretion are:

(i) the prosecutor's reasonable doubt that the accused is in fact guilty;

(ii) the extent of the harm caused by the offense;

(iii) the disproportion of the authorized punishment in relation to the particular offense or the offender;

(iv) possible improper motives of a complainant;

(v) reluctance of the victim to testify;

(vi) cooperation of the accused in the apprehension or conviction of others; and

(vii) availability and likelihood of prosecution by another jurisdiction.

(c) A prosecutor should not be compelled by his or her supervisor to prosecute a case in which he or she has a reasonable doubt about the guilt of the accused.

(d) In making the decision to prosecute, the prosecutor should give no weight to the personal or political advantages or disadvantages which might be involved or to a desire to enhance his or her record of convictions.

(e) In cases which involve a serious threat to the community, the prosecutor should not be deterred from prosecution by the fact that in the jurisdiction juries have tended to acquit persons accused of the particular kind of criminal act in question.

(f) The prosecutor should not bring or seek charges greater in number of degree than can reasonably be supported with evidence at trial or than are necessary to fairly reflect the gravity of the offense.

(g) The prosecutor should not condition a dismissal of charges, nolle prosequi, or similar action on the accused's relinquishment of the right to seek civil redress unless the accused has agreed to the action knowingly and intelligently, freely and voluntarily, and where such waiver is approved by the court.

In recent years, as victim's rights movements have become more politically active, legislatures have placed some minimal limits on prosecutorial discretion in charging or declining to charge. We return to Peter Krug's article for a focus on the victim.

Peter Krug, *Prosecutorial Discretion and Its Limits*

50 Am. J. Comp. L. 643, 660–662 (Fall 2002)

....

D. Victims' Interests

Traditionally, prosecutors have not been compelled to represent the interests of the victim. Indeed, prosecutors as a general matter continue to exercise broad, unreviewable discretion in determining the extent to which the wishes of the victim should govern considerations in the charging function. Although in theory several remedies potentially are available to victims, commentators note that these are almost never invoked. Meanwhile, as stated above, legal systems in the United States place stringent limits on private prosecutions. Several policy considerations underlie the reluctance to place emphasis on victims' interests, including: the belief that crime in general is a matter of erga omnes concern; concern that prosecutors not be influenced to the detriment of protection of the rights of suspects and defendants; and concern that suspects might threaten or otherwise unduly influence victims to request that prosecution not proceed.

However, in a comparatively recent development, steps have been taken in response to an active victims' rights movement to address the concerns of victims in the overall criminal justice process. Some of these changes have had an impact on prosecutorial discretion in the charging function. More specifically, some jurisdictions have acted via legislation either to limit the breadth of prosecutorial discretion in the exercise of the charging decision, or to mandate subsequent judicial review in regard to certain specific classes of offenses. For example, in the past two decades some jurisdictions via controversial "no-drop" legislation have imposed mandatory prosecution of domestic violence cases, regardless of the desires of the victim. Commentators have distinguished between "soft" no-drop approaches, where victims are encouraged to cooperate with prosecutors but may also exercise some discretion as to the extent of their participation in the proceeding, and "hard" no-drop approaches under which they may not drop charges under any circumstances and may be subject to subpoenas and contempt of court charges. Other jurisdictions require prosecutors to consult with the victim before making a charging decision, at least in serious cases.

The area of victims' rights also includes one of the few examples of legislatively mandated subsequent judicial review of prosecutorial charging decisions. In certain circumstances, federal legislation provides a remedy by which victims can bring federal civil rights actions alleging racially selective exercise of prosecutorial discretion.

Written criteria also address these questions to some degree, and in doing so they reflect the tension between competing interests raised by long-held concerns about victim influence and the goals of the victims' rights movement. Of the seventeen "factors to consider" in deciding whether to file charges listed in the NDAA [National District Attorneys Association] Standards, one factor is the "interests of the victim" and another is "possible improper motives of a victim or witness." The DOJ Principles do not include the interests of the victim in the text setting forth the standards; however, in discussing the question of whether there might be a "substantial federal interest" in pursuing or declining prosecution, the U.S. Department of Justice commentary states that one factor that is "obviously of primary importance is the actual or potential impact of the offense on the community and on the victim."

The ABA Standards also reflect the countervailing issues at work in this aspect of the prosecution function. Among the factors "which the prosecutor may properly consider" in exercising his or her charging discretion, the Standards include "the extent of the harm caused by the offense" and the "reluctance of the victim to testify." Another factor, however, is "the possible improper motives of a complainant."

The State of Washington statutory guidelines for prosecutors also direct prosecutors to take victims' interests into account to a certain degree in the charging function. Among the satisfactory reasons for declining prosecution, the statute includes cases in which a victim so requests; however, the statute narrowly confines such cases to several enumerated "crimes or situations," and warns that "care should be taken to insure that the victim's request is freely made and is not the product of threats or pressure by the accused." Meanwhile, in cases where the prosecutor is considering pre-trial diversion or has decided in the screening function to proceed with prosecution, the statute permits discussion with victims as to the appropriateness of pretrial diversion or the selection of charges in the selection function. As to pre-trial diversion, the statute states that prosecutors should take such discussions into account before reaching any agreement with the defendant.

Notes/Questions

1. As a prosecutor, would you want to work in a state that adopted a law like the State of Washington, as outlined at the end of the Krug article? What are the advantages and disadvantages in terms of how you would do your job?

2. As a defense lawyer, would you support increased victims' rights, including the right of the victim to be consulted before a case goes out for diversion? You may want to keep this question in mind later in the chapter when you read more about diversion. We will return to the victim's perspective in later chapters on restorative justice.

The View of a Defense Lawyer

I was a public defender at the Public Defender Service for the District of Columbia (PDS) for 12 years. It was then that I learned of the formidable power and vast discretion of prosecutors. During my years at PDS, I noticed that prosecutors held almost all of the cards, and that they seemed to deal them as they saw fit. Although some saw themselves as ministers of justice and measured their decision carefully, very few were humbled by the power they held. Most wanted to win every case, and winning meant getting a conviction.

Angela J. Davis, *The American Prosecutor: Power, Discretion, and Misconduct* 23-SPG Crim. Just. 24 (2008).

Should prosecutors be humbled by the power they hold? What is the impact of not being humble on how prosecutors will behave in charging decisions and plea bargaining?

II. Prosecutorial Power/ Role in Grand Jury Indictments

In jurisdictions that have them, grand juries are charged with investigating and deciding whether there is probable cause to indict the defendant. The prosecutor decides which cases to bring to the grand jury. Grand jury proceedings are not public. Lay people are called to serve on a grand jury in a way that is similar to other forms of jury service (for trials). However, unlike a trial jury, grand juries generally serve for an extended period of time (such as four or six months). The length of grand jury service can affect how representative the grand jury is of the larger community. A judge will charge the grand jury but does not preside over the grand jury after giving them their charge. The prosecutor leads the grand jury investigation, including deciding what cases to bring to the grand jury. If a grand jury decides there is sufficient evidence to establish probable cause, they can return a "true bill" of indictment in the case. Grand juries could also decide that there is not sufficient evidence to establish probable cause and decide to "no bill" or "no true bill" a case. Indictments were referred to as "bills of indictment," so a grand jury is charged with finding whether there was sufficient evidence, or not, to support the finding of a true bill of indictment.

The U.S. Constitution guarantees the right to grand jury indictment in the Fifth Amendment:

> No person shall be held to answer for a capital, or otherwise infamous crime, unless on a presentment or indictment of a Grand Jury, except in cases arising in the land or naval forces, or in the Militia, when in actual service in time of War or public danger....

However, this right has not been incorporated as applicable to the states, and a majority of states do not use grand juries for all indictments. The frequency and circumstances in which grand juries are used varies widely from state to state within the twenty-two states that use some form of a grand jury more regularly.[4] As with other rights, the defendant can agree to waive grand jury indictment as part of a plea deal. The defense rights during the grand jury process are limited. Defendants do not have a right to present a defense during grand jury proceedings. Defendants do not even have a right to be notified about the grand jury process. Grand juries have the power to investigate and to subpoena witnesses. Grand jury hearings are not public. Defendants, defense lawyers, and the general public often view grand juries as willing tools of the prosecutor who will do whatever the prosecutor asks including "indicting a ham sandwich."[5]

---

4. *See e.g.*, Sara Sun Beale, et al., Grand Jury Law and Practice § 8:2 (2d ed.); John. F. Decker, *Legislating New Federalism: The Call for Grand Jury Reform in the States*, 58 Okla. L. Rev. 341, 354–55 (Fall 2005).

5. Glenn Harlan Reynolds, *Ham Sandwich Nation: Due Process When Everything Is a Crime*, 113 Colum. L. Rev. Sidebar 102 (2013) footnote 15: "The phrase, made famous in Tom Wolfe's novel, *The Bonfire of the Vanities*, apparently originates with New York City federal judge Sol Wachtler in a lunchtime interview with a reporter from the *New York Daily News*. Barry Popik, 'Indict a ham sand-

Some states give prosecutors the option of either filing charges directly or bringing the charges to a grand jury. In these jurisdictions, prosecutors may bring the tougher, or more politically volatile cases to the grand jury so they don't have to decide whether to file charges or not.

In more politically charged cases, such as police shootings, a prosecutor may not want to file charges but may also not want to face political fall-out for failing to file charges. Sending the case to a grand jury, in states where that is optional, can provide political cover to a prosecutor and allow them to avoid responsibility for failing to bring charges forward. In 2015, the local DA in Cleveland brought the police killing of twelve-year-old Tamir Rice to a grand jury for consideration. The grand jury declined to indict, as did the US. Department of Justice.[6] A prosecutor in Texas brought the jail death of Sandra Bland to a grand jury who also declined to prosecute. One of the criticisms leveled at the DA in the Bland case was that the office had maintained that there was sufficient evidence that the death was a suicide. But, bringing a case to a grand jury to make the final decision can take pressure off the local prosecutor, although this does not always avoid political fallout. The Cleveland DA lost his next election, a year after not filing charges in the Rice case and, reportedly, lost the vote in all of the majority African American precincts.[7] Depending on local practices, one way that prosecutors can flag to the grand jury that they don't want charges filed is send the case to a grand jury but not recommend filing of charges. It is not unusual for the grand jury to decide to "no bill" the case if the prosecutor doesn't recommend filing charges.

Defense lawyers often try to intervene early in a case, before it goes to a grand jury or to try to get additional information in the grand jury process to encourage a "no bill" for the case. This stage can be the single most important point in the negotiation of a criminal case, especially if the defense is successful in persuading the prosecutor to not bring the case to the grand jury. In those circumstances the case is over before it begins, and that may be the only negotiation that needs to be done in the case. In jurisdictions that widely use grand juries for indictment, defense lawyers may persuade the prosecutor to delay bringing the case to the grand jury as they investigate and gather evidence to present to the prosecutor to persuade them not to proceed.

Jeopardy does not attach at the grand jury stage. This means that if a grand jury decides to "no bill" a case, the prosecutor could bring the case back again to the grand jury and try again to get an indictment, unless it is after the statute of limitations has expired for the particular offense.

---

wich' Big Apple (July 15, 2004) http://www.barrypopik.com/index.php/new_york_city/entry/indict_a_ham_sandwich (on file with the *Columbia Law Review*)."

6. Ari Melber, *The Tamir Rice case shows how prosecutors twist grand juries to protect police*, The Washington Post, December 29, 2015.

7. Rich Exner, Vote in black communities seeps Michael O'Mallery to victory over Cuyahoga County Prosecutor Timothy McGinty, March 17, 2016, *Cleveland.com*.

The grand jury was intended to act as a check on governmental (particularly federal) power. However, as you will read in the next article, this is not the current view of how grand juries do their jobs.

The ABA Criminal Justice Section Standards on the Prosecution Function set out minimum standards for how prosecutors should handle relations with and presenting evidence to a grand jury. As a prosecutor, do these standards give you enough guidance?

Standard 3-3.5 Relations with Grand Jury

(a) Where the prosecutor is authorized to act as legal advisor to the grand jury, the prosecutor may appropriately explain the law and express an opinion on the legal significance of the evidence but should give due deference to its status as an independent legal body.

(b) The prosecutor should not make statements or arguments in an effort to influence grand jury action in a manner which would be impermissible at trial before a petit jury.

(c) The prosecutor's communications and presentations to the grand jury should be on the record.

Standard 3-3.6 Quality and Scope of Evidence Before Grand Jury

(a) A prosecutor should only make statements or arguments to the grand jury and only present evidence to the grand jury which the prosecutor believes is appropriate or authorized under law for presentation to the grand jury. In appropriate cases, the prosecutor may present witnesses to summarize admissible evidence available to the prosecutor which the prosecutor believes he or she will be able to present at trial. The prosecutor should also inform the grand jurors that they have the right to hear any available witnesses, including eyewitnesses.

(b) No prosecutor should knowingly fail to disclose to the grand jury evidence which tends to negate guilt or mitigate the offense.

(c) A prosecutor should recommend that the grand jury not indict if he or she believes the evidence presented does not warrant an indictment under governing law.

(d) If the prosecutor believes that a witness is a potential defendant, the prosecutor should not seek to compel the witness's testimony before the grand jury without informing the witness that he or she may be charged and that the witness should seek independent legal advice concerning his or her rights.

(e) The prosecutor should not compel the appearance of a witness before the grand jury whose activities are the subject of the inquiry if the witness states in advance that if called he or she will exercise the constitutional privilege not to testify, unless the prosecutor intends to judicially challenge the exercise of the privilege or to seek a grant of immunity according to the law.

(f) A prosecutor in presenting a case to a grand jury should not intentionally interfere with the independence of the grand jury, preempt a function of the grand jury, or abuse the processes of the grand jury.

(g) Unless the law of the jurisdiction so permits, a prosecutor should not use the grand jury in order to obtain tangible, documentary or testimonial evidence to assist the prosecutor in preparation for trial of a defendant who has already been charged by indictment or information.

(h) Unless the law of the jurisdiction so permits, a prosecutor should not use the grand jury for the purpose of aiding or assisting in any administrative inquiry.

Ric Simmons, *The Role of the Prosecutor and the Grand Jury in Police Use of Deadly Force Cases: Restoring the Grand Jury to Its Original Purpose*

65 Clev. St. L. Rev. 519, 520–523 (2017)

I. The Role of the Prosecutor and the Grand Jury

A. *The Prosecutor*

The prosecutor is the most powerful figure in the criminal justice system. No criminal case can begin without her, and any criminal case can end at any time based solely on her decision. Moreover, in the 95% of criminal cases that end in a plea bargain, it is the prosecutor who dominates the negotiation, with her hand strengthened by the proliferation of crimes in our penal codes and the high potential sentences authorized by legislatures.

Along with this power comes the ability to exercise discretion in each individual case. The prosecutor is supposed to use her training and experience to exercise this discretion and determine the just outcome for each case. However, that ideal model is not always borne out in practice. Exercising this discretion—deciding whether to charge and what to charge—is the most important role of the prosecutor, and it is a fundamental aspect of our criminal justice system.

In deciding whether and what to charge, the prosecutor looks to three different factors:

(1) Legal—Is there probable cause that the defendant committed this crime?

(2) Practical—If the case goes to trial, will there be sufficient evidence to convict the defendant beyond a reasonable doubt of this crime?

(3) Equitable—Should the defendant be charged with this crime?

The prosecutor is uniquely qualified to answer the first and second question. She is the legal actor who is most familiar with the facts and available evidence in the case, and she has been trained to know what constitutes probable cause and proof beyond a reasonable doubt. But the third question is a bit trickier. The prosecutor has some expertise in deciding what a fair and equitable charge would be based on her own past cases and those of others in her office. She is also (hopefully) responsive to the local community, whose members may care far more about enforcing some crimes than others. For example, in some jurisdictions, the community may want the prosecutor to focus on firearms possession but is not as concerned about marijuana possession or shoplifting. The prosecutor, or her supervisor, also may have her own political or personal agenda and decide to crack down on drug crimes, domestic violence, or white-collar crimes while saving resources by undercharging other types of cases. And, as this author has argued elsewhere, the grand jury conceivably could provide input on this equitable question, serving as the voice of the community with regard to certain types of crimes or to specific defendants. If a prosecutor has a particularly sympathetic defendant, or if the case involves significant but legally irrelevant mitigating factors, the prosecutor could present these facts to the grand jury to determine whether the grand jury still wants to go forward with the case. But for the most part, this role for the grand jury is only theoretical; in practice, the grand jury usually adds very little of substance to the charging decision.

B. *The Grand Jury*

The widespread impotence and irrelevance of the grand jury has been well documented elsewhere; this Article only reviews the highlights here. On the federal level, grand juries indict over 99% of the cases brought before them, while currently over half of the states do not even require a grand jury in order to initiate a felony case. In states where prosecutors do utilize a grand jury, the presentation is typically quick and perfunctory, involving a law enforcement officer reading a case file, and then the prosecutor initiates a legal charge.

A more interesting question is *how* the grand jury evolved into a mere rubber stamp for the prosecutor—after all, this was an institution so revered that it was included in the Bill of Rights and used in some administrative and quasi-legislative roles in the early days of the Republic. But two major changes have occurred over the centuries to siphon power away from the grand jury. The first is the rise of the professional prosecutor, who now essentially fulfills the grand jury's traditional role, both in terms of gathering evidence and reviewing cases. The second is a series of legal changes: as professional prosecutors became more widespread, a series of Supreme Court cases shifted power from the grand jury to the prosecutor. These decisions gave prosecutors the right to present hearsay testimony in the grand jury, held that the exclusionary rule does not apply to grand jury proceedings, applied a harmless error analysis to any procedural errors that occur during the proceedings, and ruled that a prosecutor had no duty to present exculpatory evidence to a grand jury. Through this series of decisions, the Supreme Court made it clear that the courts should exercise virtually no supervision of the grand jury. This notion was based on the legal fiction that the grand jury was an independent body, separate from both the prosecutor's office and the court system. As a result, in almost all jurisdictions, if the prosecutor wants an indictment from the grand jury, she can easily obtain one. The grand jury was originally meant to be a "shield" of independent citizens protecting the general public from the government's charging power; today, it is simply unable to perform that function....

Notes/Questions

1. The United States is one of only two countries (the other being Liberia) that still uses grand juries—and not in every state (as stated above, less than half of U.S. states use grand juries regularly). A key concern about grand juries is that they are not used as a check against government power but instead used to enable the government to proceed unchecked. Consider the following:

> Legal scholarship is disjointed and in disagreement over many points of law, but the assessment that the federal grand jury system has collapsed is held universally. Scholars and professionals quibble only over what to call this procedural step. A "rubber stamp," a "handmaiden" of prosecutors, a "kangaroo" proceeding, a "mockery," a "charade," a "lap dog," "a tool" of prosecutors, or simply "puppetry" have all been suggested. The American Bar Association, the National Association of Criminal Defense Lawyers, the American Jury Institute and even the U.S. Justice Department have all acknowledged that modern federal prosecutors have much more power over grand jury outcomes than the Constitution's Framers intended. A number of congressional investigations have also scrutinized the institution, each featuring testimony by numerous witnesses decrying the pathetic state of modern federal grand jury practice.[8]

2. An example of a grand jury working as intended?

> Following Hurricane Katrina, the attorney general of Louisiana demanded prosecution of medical workers who had remained at a New Orleans hospital with critically ill patients. When numerous patients died at the hospital while awaiting rescue, the attorney general focused blame on a surgeon and accused her of murdering some of the patients. When the local district attorney moved slowly to press charges, the state attorney general began an investigation and ordered a local grand jury from Orleans Parish to be empanelled to hear the charges. As the grand jury investigation proceeded, the local community support shifted toward the surgeon. In New Orleans, she became "something of a folk hero" for staying behind to help critically ill patients. While other doctors had fled the oncoming storm, the surgeon had provided care for four days in a "sweltering" hospital that had lost electricity and sometimes reached 110 degrees until all the surviving patients were evacuated. Thirty-four patients died during the ordeal. Though prosecutors accused the surgeon of administering lethal doses of painkillers and sedatives, the Orleans Parish grand jury refused to issue indictments and instead returned a "no true bill" decision.

---

8. Roger Roots, *Grand Juries Gone Wrong*, 14 RICH. J.L. & PUB. INT. 331 (2010)

Viewed from the outside, this New Orleans grand jury appeared to have done exactly what the founders intended. It prevented an official exercising central statewide authority (the state attorney general) from using his power to charge a local citizen with a serious crime. Who better to make the decision to prosecute actions under such circumstances than other citizens from the same community who faced the same unusual hardships? It is this ability, rarely seen in modern grand juries, that ought to be restored....

To restore the grand jury to its original role, reformers must make a subtle but important shift in focus. Reform proposals ought to be focused not so much on making the grand jury more independent of the prosecutor, but on making the grand jury less independent of the people in the local community. Such a shift would not only align the grand jury more closely with its original constitutional purpose, and better serve all communities, but it might also have a particularly good effect in minority communities. It might help to restore the legitimacy of the criminal justice system in such communities by improving their democratic involvement in these important issues.[9]

How might that work in practice? How would you make a grand jury reflect the local community? Should grand juries serve for less time (days instead of weeks)? Should defense lawyers have a right to participate and/or should the grand jury process not be secret?

III. Concerns about Prosecutorial Discretionary Power

The following articles take a critical look at prosecutorial discretionary power. As you will read, courts rarely intervene to limit prosecutorial power. As you are reading these articles, pay attention to descriptions of how this power is used in the plea bargaining process.

Angela J. Davis, *The American Prosecutor: Independence, Power, and the Threat of Tyranny*

86 Iowa L. Rev. 393, 408–415 (2001)

The Supreme Court has consistently upheld the broad exercise of prosecutorial discretion—a power that affords prosecutors far-reaching control over the outcome of criminal cases. Prosecutorial discretion and power expanded early in the development of the current system of public prosecution. As early as the 1920s, crime commissions and scholars criticized this power and proposed reforms to promote accountability This part focuses on the current scope of prosecutorial discretion and how it is abused.

9. Kevin K. Washburn, *Restoring the Grand Jury*, 76 Fordham L. Rev. 2333 (2008).

1. The Power to Charge

The charging decision is arguably the most important prosecutorial power and the strongest example of the influence and reach of prosecutorial discretion. Prosecutors decide whether and how to charge an individual. They decide whether to offer a plea to a lesser charge, set the terms of the plea, and assess whether the conditions have been met. In federal and state jurisdictions governed by sentencing guidelines, these decisions often predetermine the outcome of a case since the sentencing judge has little, if any, discretion in determining the length, nature, or severity of the sentence. The defendant certainly has the option of exercising her right to trial and leaving her fate in the hands of the jury or judge, but often she is not willing to run the risk of additional and more serious convictions and more prison time. Consequently, in most jurisdictions, plea bargaining resolves more than ninety percent of all criminal cases. Prosecutors on both the state and federal levels control this process. In some smaller offices, typically state and county prosecutor offices, the decisions concerning whether to charge and what to charge become routine. Police officers arrest a suspect, recommend a charge, and, if there is probable cause and supporting evidence, the prosecutor formalizes the charges by filing an information or seeking an indictment through the grand jury process. In other offices, prosecutors exercise discretion in a variety of ways. They may decline to bring charges, bring only charges that they believe they can prove, or "inflate" the charges—convincing a grand jury to indict a defendant for more and greater charges than they can establish.

The decision to forego charges may be based on practical considerations such as the triviality of the offense and/or the victim's lack of interest in prosecution. The decision may also be based on considerations of fairness and justice in a particular case. For example, some jurisdictions offer alternative dispositions such as diversion programs for certain less serious offenses. On the other hand, the decision either to forego or bring charges may be the result of a prosecutor's bias toward or against a particular defendant or victim. At any rate, the decision to forego charges is entirely within the discretion of the prosecutor.

2. Prosecutorial Misconduct: Abuse of Discretion

The many forms of prosecutorial misconduct that occur at numerous stages of the criminal process belie the courts' presumption of regularity for prosecutors. At the pretrial stage, prosecutors have been accused of intimidating witnesses, engaging in selective and vindictive prosecution, and abusing the grand jury process. During trial, prosecutorial misconduct may consist of inappropriate opening statements, cross-examination, or closing arguments. Prosecutors frequently violate their obligation to reveal exculpatory information to criminal defendants at various stages of the process.

Like so many other prosecutorial acts, misconduct often occurs in private and never becomes public. The victim of misconduct may be wholly unaware of its occurrence, especially if it takes place during the pretrial stage. Even when misconduct is discovered and litigated by criminal defendants, it is rarely exposed to the public. Judicial review of such misconduct is extremely limited. Under the harmless error rule, appellate courts affirm convictions if the evidence supports the defendant's guilt, even if she did not receive a fair trial. This rule permits, perhaps even encourages, prosecutors to engage in misconduct during trial with the assurance that so long as the evidence of the defendant's guilt is clear, the conviction will be affirmed.

The American Bar Association (ABA) Standards on the Prosecution Function state that a prosecutor should only bring charges that she believes she can prove beyond a reasonable doubt. This rule seems to state the obvious. A prosecutor's decision to bring charges she cannot prove would be unethical and harmful to the defendant. Even if a jury ultimately found the defendant not guilty of these false charges, she would bear the emotional—and perhaps financial—burden of defending against them. Furthermore, the defendant might labor under the shadow of suspicion that often lingers even after charges are dismissed or unproven.

Despite the ABA standards, prosecutors frequently charge more and greater offenses than they can prove beyond a reasonable doubt. This tactic offers the prosecutor more leverage during plea negotiations, causing the defendant to plead guilty to "reduced charges" offered by the prosecutor for fear of being convicted of all of the charges brought in the indictment. Often these "reduced charges" are the most the prosecutor believes she might be able to prove at trial. Sometimes, they are more than she knows she can prove. Indigent defendants with overworked counsel and limited resources often lack the ability to investigate the strength of the government's charges and may plead guilty out of fear of the unknown.

Many of the most damaging forms of misconduct occur behind closed doors. Inappropriate or unethical charging decisions, intimidating conversations with witnesses, selective and vindictive prosecutions, and grand jury abuse all occur in the privacy of prosecution offices—away from the public and the parties whose cases are affected by the harmful behavior. The courts have shielded many of these behaviors from scrutiny by establishing nearly impossible standards for obtaining the necessary discovery to seek judicial review.

On the rare occasion when prosecutorial misconduct is discovered, courts seldom use their supervisory power to curtail it. In addition to its constitutional power to reverse lower court convictions, the Supreme Court's supervisory authority to oversee the implementation of criminal justice grants the Court powers to regulate lower court procedures. For example, in *McNabb v. United States*, the Court concluded that when determining the admissibility of evidence, it obeys the Constitution, and, under its power of judicial supervision, formulates "additional civilized standards of procedure and evidence." These standards are to be applied in federal criminal prosecutions, in an effort to deter governmental misconduct and preserve judicial integrity. The Court's standards are satisfied by more than simple adherence to due process laws and are derived from considerations of "evidentiary relevance" and justice. In *United States v. Russell*, however, the Supreme Court drastically curtailed the supervisory power doctrine by reversing a lower court's use of the power in a case involving questionable law enforcement tactics. The Court invoked the separation of powers doctrine as it warned lower courts not to meddle in the business of law enforcement. In a further effort to limit the reach of a federal court's supervisory power, in *United States v. Hasting*, the Court held that judges may not reverse convictions because of prosecutorial misconduct in cases involving harmless error. Civil lawsuits have proven equally ineffective as remedies for prosecutorial misconduct. The Supreme Court established a broad rule of absolute immunity from civil liability for prosecutors in *Imbler v. Pachtman*. This rule immunizes prosecutors from liability for acts "intimately associated with the judicial phase of the criminal process." The Court expressed concern that prosecutors might be deterred from zealously pursuing their law enforcement responsibilities if they faced the possibility of civil liability and suggested that attorney disciplinary authorities address prosecutorial misconduct.

Shelby A. Dickerson Moore, *Questioning the Autonomy of Prosecutorial Charging Decisions: Recognizing the Need to Exercise Discretion—Knowing There Will Be Consequences for Crossing the Line*

60 LA. L. REV. 371, 377–378 (2000)

....

II. The Continuum of Prosecutorial Charging Decisions

Although the unbridled discretion granted to prosecutors in the charging process can lead to abuses, prosecutors nonetheless need to be entrusted with some degree of discretion for the criminal justice system to function efficiently. This section examines critically the reasons typically advanced for allowing prosecutors discretion in deciding when, what, and whom to charge.

A. The Need for Limited Discretion in Charging

The decision to charge an individual with a particular crime is a critical step in the criminal justice process. In determining whether to charge and what to charge, the prosecutor must assess whether a particular set of facts fits within the criminal code, weighing the strengths of the case and determining whether the alleged perpetrator is guilty or innocent. Even when the circumstances point to guilt, prosecutors must consider the sufficiency of the evidence to sustain a conviction. And even if the evidence proves sufficient, the determination must be made whether criminal sanctions are appropriate or criminal prosecution is in the community's best interest. All of these decisions are currently left to the prosecutor's discretion.

Among the principal reasons advanced for allowing the prosecutor such discretion is that it serves to mitigate the ill effects of the trend toward legislative overcriminalization. According to this view, prosecutorial discretion functions as a kind of safety valve that alleviates the pressures of a criminal code that tends to make a crime of everything that people find objectionable, but which fails to take into account issues of enforceability or changing social mores. Thus, while many states criminalize most forms of gambling, the enforcement of these gambling laws depends very much on the circumstances of the particular case, there being, for example, a general feeling that the legislature never intended to proscribe private gambling among friends. Other laws, such as adultery statutes, are passed as "state-declared ideals." These statutes are "unenforced because we want to continue our conduct and [are] unrepealed because we want to preserve our morals." Still other criminalized activities were enacted into law in the heat of a certain moment in time, when a particular mood dominated a tribunal or legislature or as a response to public reaction to a particular event. These archaic laws whose "time has passed" go unenforced, yet remain on the books for a variety of reasons, not least of which is the general public's ignorance of their very existence and consequential indifference to their repeal.

Clearly, some degree of prosecutorial discretion is desirable to avoid clogging the justice system with criminal prosecutions that are incompatible with current social views or goals. Prosecutors' offices are already heavily overworked. To require the mandatory charging of all offenses within the criminal code would drive them to the breaking point and make effective law enforcement virtually impossible.

An equally defensible reason for allowing a limited degree of prosecutorial discretion is essentially economic in nature. The government simply does not have sufficient resources to investigate, charge, and prosecute all offenses which come to its attention. Were society willing to pay for more police officers, prosecutors, public defenders, judges, courtrooms, and prisons, the exercise of prosecutorial discretion would be less justifiable. Since society has been unwilling to pay for full enforcement, the government must have some discretion in determining what cases to charge.

Notes/Questions

1. These articles have noted that legislatures and courts rarely take steps to interfere with the prosecutor's discretion. What would be the arguments for and against more legislative oversight? For the courts to be more involved? And, if we determined that the legislature should "interfere," what would this look like?

2. In recent years, there have been examples of governors acting to limit the discretion of local prosecutors. As discussed in Chapter One, Governor Rick DeSantis in Florida suspended a local State Attorney for failing to prosecute certain cases including those related to abortion. In 2023, Governor Abbot of Texas advocated for and signed into law House Bill 17 which expanded of the definition of "official misconduct" to allow a resident in the county to call for the removal of a local district attorney who refuses to prosecute certain kinds of offenses. This bill was in response to progressive prosecutors in the state refusing to prosecute low-level offenses such as marijuana possession or investigating families for child abuse in cases where their child was receiving transgender medical care. On the other side of the political aisle, Governor Tim Walz of Minnesota appointed Minnesota Attorney General Keith Ellison to "take the lead" in the prosecution of Derek Chauvin and the three other police officers who were tried for the murder of George Floyd in 2020. Walz did this after

the local Hennepin County DA delayed filing charges for many days against the other police officers. Should governors be directing what local, county level prosecutors do? Does it matter that these prosecutors are elected by their communities and charged with representing community values and standards? Should a governor with different views from an elected prosecutor step in like these governors have? Would it change your view if instead of stepping in to assure prosecution, the governor was stepping in to stop prosecutions of crimes or certain kinds of crimes?

3. Note that in all of these instances above, the governors were stepping in to make sure that prosecutions occurred. Would it change your view if a state wanted to decrease prosecutions, for example to not prosecute non-violent misdemeanors, and was stepping in to dictate change to local prosecutorial charging practices?

4. In 2021, a judge rejected a plea deal in Loudoun County, Virginia. In rejecting the deal, the judge removed and disqualified the entire prosecutors' office from the case. The defendant had multiple charges over four counties in Northern Virginia relating to what was described as a "smash and grab rampage." It was in one of those cases that the judge, who had seen the defendant in another courthouse where he also presides, refused to accept the plea deal and questioned why the prosecutor's office had not informed him about the other plea deals. The Commonwealth Attorney (the DA), Buta Biberaj, was considered a progressive prosecutor and was under attack for being "too lenient" in a number of cases and in this particular case the judge was the former Commonwealth Attorney. Biberaj appealed the removal of her office to the Virginia Supreme Court who reinstated her office on the case on the grounds that the Commonwealth Attorney had been denied due process to fight the removal. Biberaj was elected to office in 2019 and lost her re-election bid by 300 votes in 2023. Should judges have the power to remove an entire prosecutor's office from a case because they disagree with how they exercise their discretion?

5. Do you agree with Shelby A. Dickerson Moore, that prosecutors need to have some discretion? What are the advantages and disadvantages of prosecutors having discretion in charging decisions? You may want to keep this question in mind when you get to the end of this chapter and learn about other approaches, in other countries, to prosecutorial power.

6. Prosecutors' offices tend to have policies that guide or direct what an individual prosecutor within that office can do, both in charging cases and when making plea offers. Attorney General Sessions issued a Department of Justice Department Charging and Sentencing Policy Memo in May of 2017 that stated, in part:

> First, it is a core principle that prosecutors should charge and pursue the most serious, readily provable offense. This policy affirms our responsibility to enforce the law, is moral and just, and produces consistency. This policy fully utilizes the tools Congress has given us. By definition, the most serious offenses are those that carry the most substantial guidelines sentence, including mandatory minimum sentences.

> There will be circumstances in which good judgment would lead a prosecutor to conclude that a strict application of the above charging policy is not warranted. In that case, prosecutors should carefully consider whether an exception may be justified. Consistent with longstanding Department of Justice policy, any decision to vary from the policy must be approved by a United States Attorney or Assistant Attorney General, or a supervisor designated by the United States Attorney or Assistant Attorney General, and the reasons must be documented in the file.
>
> If you were a federal prosecutor working in the DOJ while this memo was in force, would you have the independent authority to charge a lesser offense? If not, what would you expect you would need to do if you wanted to charge a lesser offense? What does this policy encourage you to do?

7. On December 16, 2022, Attorney General Garland issued a memo on "Additional Department Policies Regarding Charging, Pleas, and Sentencing in Drug Cases." Under Garland's leadership, the DOJ's General Policies Memorandum called for "charges that subject a defendant to a mandatory minimum sentence should ordinarily be reserved for instances in which the remaining charges ... would not sufficiently reflect the seriousness of the defendant's criminal conduct, danger to the community, harm to victims" and "such purposes of the criminal law as punishment, protection of the public, specific and general deterrence, and rehabilitation." According to this Memo:

> ... in cases in which Title 21 mandatory minimum sentences are applicable based on drug type and quantity, prosecutors should decline to charge the quantity necessary to trigger a mandatory minimum sentence if the defendant satisfies all of the following criteria:
>
> - The defendant's relevant conduct does not involve: the use of violence, the direction to another to use violence, the credible threat of violence, the possession of a weapon, the trafficking of drugs to or with minors, or the death or serious bodily injury of any person;
> - The defendant does not have a significant managerial role in the trafficking of significant quantities of drugs;
> - The defendant does not have significant ties to a large-scale criminal organization or cartel, or to a violent gang; and
> - The defendant does not have a significant history of criminal activity that involved the use or threat of violence, personal involvement on multiple occasions in the distribution of significant quantities of illegal drugs, or possession of illegal firearms

Under the General Memorandum and this one, "any decision to include a mandatory minimum charge in a charging document or plea agreement must be approved by a supervisory attorney as designated by the United States Attorney."

As these two memos illustrate, what is charged and how a case is charged in the federal system can be different depending on the Administration in charge. As a federal prosecutor, under Attorney General Sessions, would you have the authority, on your own, to determine whether to seek a mandatory minimum sentence in a drug case? Are you concerned about these different policies from one administration to another? Remember, the underlying federal laws have not changed, just how prosecutors decide to charge cases and what sentences they seek.

8. Progressive prosecutors have been vocal about changing how their offices would exercise their discretionary power to charge crimes. For example, Philadelphia District Attorney Larry Krasner, was voted into office in November of 2017 with a platform promising change. In February of 2018 a memo was released which said, in part:

> These policies are an effort to end mass incarceration and bring balance back to sentencing. All policies are presumptive, not mandatory requirements. Where extraordinary circumstances suggest that an exception is appropriate, specific supervisory approval must be obtained. Wherever the term "supervisory approval" is used, it means that:
>
> (1) An Assistant District Attorney must obtain approval of the unit's supervisor, and
>
> (2) The supervisor must then obtain approval from the District Attorney, or in his absence, the approval of First Assistant Carolyn Temin or Robert Listenbee
>
> (3) Bona fide verbal approvals and disapprovals are sufficient and must be noted in the case file, including the date of approval and identity of the requesting Assistant District Attorney and the supervisor who obtained approval or disapproval from the District Attorney.
>
> DECLINE CERTAIN CHARGES
>
> 1. Do not charge possession of marijuana (cannabis) regardless of weight.
> 2. Do not charge any of the offenses relating to paraphernalia or buying from a person (BFP) where the drug involved is marijuana.
> 3. Do not charge prostitution cases against sex workers where a person who has been arrested has two, one or no prostitution convictions. Withdraw all pending cases in these categories that would be declined for charging under this policy.
> 4. Individuals who have three or more prostitution convictions will be charged with prostitution and immediately referred to DAWN Court.
>
> CHARGE LOWER GRADATIONS FOR CERTAIN OFFENSES
>
> **Rationale: summary gradation greatly reduces pre-trial incarceration rates as no bail is required and the shorter time required for hearings expedites Municipal Court and Common Pleas dockets.**
>
> 1. Charge and dispose of Retail Theft cases as summary offenses unless the value of the item(s) stolen in a particular case exceeds $500.00 or where the defendant has a very long history of theft and retail theft convictions.

2. You must seek supervisory approval to charge and dispose of retail theft cases at misdemeanor or felony levels.
3. Remember, that a summary conviction permits a sentence of 90 days incarceration, fines of up to $250, and full restitution. These penalties are sufficient to hold a retail thief accountable.
4. In all cases, seek full restitution.

What are the main differences between the Philadelphia DA's policies and the Department of Justice policies, under Attorney General Sessions and under Attorney General Garland? If you were a prosecutor, which office would you rather work in? Does one approach or the other seem a better fit with your values? If you were a defense lawyer, which jurisdiction would you rather work in?

9. Note that these policies are promulgated by individual DAs (or the US Attorney General) in separate jurisdictions. Is there a risk of different types of prosecutions depending on where you commit the crime? Is this an instance where it would be appropriate for state-wide or circuit-wide oversight? What role should the legislature or any individual judge play in determining appropriate charging? Should the law be changed to allow for this oversight?

10. What happens when the prosecutor uses her discretion in the opposite direction? When she chooses not to prosecute based on the police involved?

> In the racially divided city of St. Louis the chief prosecutor has embraced a controversial tool to hold police accountable: blacklisting cops who she says are too untrustworthy to testify in court. So far, Kim Gardner has dropped more than 100 cases that relied on statements from the 29 officers who got on the list for alleged lying, abuse or corruption. And she won't accept new cases or search-warrant requests from them, either. From Philadelphia to Houston to Seattle, district attorneys recently elected on platforms of criminal justice reform are building similar databases of their own. Often known as "do not call" lists, they are also called "exclusion lists" or "Brady lists" after a famous Supreme Court decision requiring prosecutors to disclose to defense lawyers information about unreliable police officers or other holes in their cases. The goal is to help prosecutors avoid bringing cases built on evidence from officers who are likely to be challenged in court, these new DAs say. Having a centralized list at a district attorney's office, they say, allows for the gathering of institutional knowledge, so that if one prosecutor on staff knows about a bad cop, all the prosecutors do. But the strategy has infuriated police unions and some law-enforcement officials, who say they should get a say in who's named on the lists—or else crime victims will pay the price."[10]

What do you think about this strategy? What might be your concerns as a prosecutor? As a defense attorney?

---

10. Justin George & Eli Hager, *One Way to Deal with Cops Who Lie? Blacklist Them, Some Das Say*, The Marshal Project, January 17, 2019.

11. Other decisions not to prosecute could be even more politically fraught. Consider this from Peter Krug:

> According to critics, who often cite statements of local prosecutors themselves, local prosecutors infrequently pursue prosecution of police officers. For one thing, it is difficult to obtain a conviction from a jury or judge. For another, prosecutors work closely with police on an on-going basis, and their ability to succeed in their general responsibilities of prosecuting routine crimes depend to a considerable extent on the work and cooperation of police officers. Thus, when faced with the question of prosecuting a police officer, prosecutors often face "an impossible conflict of interest". In addition, prosecutors also often confront intense political pressures from the police and government officials. The severity of these apparent obstacles to local prosecution has led to proposals for other institutional or legal means of increasing the accountability of police officers. One such effort has been to direct investigation and prosecution of alleged police misconduct away from prosecutors of general jurisdiction, to creation of civilian review boards as a means of alternate disposition of charges of police misconduct.
>
> Another approach has been to look to the federal government, raising the complex issues of dual, state/federal, prosecution. A federal civil rights statute, 18 U.S.C. 242 ("Deprivation of rights under color of law"), has long been available for federal prosecution of public officials who willfully subject persons to the deprivation of any rights secured by the U.S. Constitution or laws.[11]

What do you think about these proposals?

12. On the other end of the spectrum, consider the following excerpt: Prosecutors themselves understand just how much discretion they enjoy. As Tim Wu recounted in 2007, a popular game in the U.S. Attorney's Office for the Southern District of New York was to name a famous person—Mother Teresa, or John Lennon—and decide how he or she could be prosecuted:

> It would then be up to the junior prosecutors to figure out a plausible crime for which to indict him or her. The crimes were not usually rape, murder, or other crimes you'd see on *Law & Order* but rather the incredibly broad yet obscure crimes that populate the U.S. Code like a kind of jurisprudential minefield: Crimes like "false statements" (a felony, up to five years), "obstructing the mails" (five years), or "false pretenses on the high seas" (also five years). The trick and the skill lay in finding the more obscure offenses that fit the character of the celebrity and carried the toughest sentences. The, result, however, was inevitable: "prison time."[12]

---

11. Peter Krug, *Prosecutorial Discretion and Its Limits*, 50 Am. J. Comp. L. 643 (Fall 2002).

12. [7] Tim Wu, *American Lawbreaking*, Slate (Oct. 14, 2007, 8:03 AM), http://www.slate.com/articles/news_and_politics/jurisprudence/features/2007/american_lawbreaking/introduction.html (on file with the Columbia Law Review).

With so many federal laws and regulations, a prosecutor's task of first choosing a possible target and then pinning a crime on him or her is easier. If prosecutors were not motivated by politics, revenge, or other improper motives, the risk of improper prosecution would not be particularly severe.[13]

Do you think the game recounted above is appropriate for prosecutors to play? What would be a game that you would want prosecutors to play instead of the one recounted above? What is the underlying message in playing the game recounted above to newer prosecutors in an office? If you were a newer prosecutor, would you want to work in an office with this approach to filing charges? Why or why not? Would you want to know that prosecutors in your courthouse play this game if you were a defense lawyer? Why?

IV. Diversion

More recently, the discretion of the prosecutor *not* to charge has been standardized into systems of diversion—the idea that prosecution is either delayed or eliminated pending good behavior or treatment. Diversion can happen at several stages of a criminal case. It is possible for law enforcement to immediately divert a person into treatment and not place them under arrest. Diversion at this stage,

> often occurs through various models of partnership between law enforcement and the mental health community, wherein police work together in some manner with mental health professionals to manage incidents involving individuals who have mental illness. Such programs are often based on robust collaborative efforts between local law enforcement, mental health and substance use providers and advocates, individuals with mental health and/or substance use issues, and their families.[14]

Diversion also happens after charges have been filed and before conviction. Diversion that happens once criminal charges have been filed is our focus. While previous sections focused on the prosecutor's discretion as perhaps ratcheting lesser crimes into more serious charges, note how the prosecutor's discretion can also result in lower or no charges under diversion. As you read the following excerpts, consider how prosecutors can control (or not) the decision of whether a particular case goes into some form of diversion. How does diversion play a role in plea bargaining? The next article will give you a historical perspective on pre-trial diversion and a basic explanation of how diversion is administered.

---

13. Glenn Harlan Reynolds, *Ham Sandwich Nation: Due Process When Everything is a Crime*, 113 COLUM. L. REV. SIDEBAR 102, 103–104 (2013).

14. Center for Health and Justice at TASC, *A National Survey of Criminal Justice Diversion Program and Initiatives*, 12 (2013), available at http://www2.centerforhealthandjustice.org/sites/www2.center forhealthandjustice.org/files/publications/CHJ%20Diversion%20Report_web.pdf.

Thomas E. Ulrich, *Pretrial Diversion in the Federal Court System*

66-DEC Fed. Probation 30–31 (December 2002)

Pretrial Diversion is a voluntary program that provides an alternative to prosecution for an individual selected for placement in a program of supervision administered by a pretrial services or probation office. The offender who is selected for pretrial diversion enters into a contract with the U.S. attorney's office, pledging to meet certain conditions and to refrain from criminal activity for a specified period of time. Because participation is voluntary, persons may decline to enter the program and instead exercise their right to proceed with a trial on the charges against them.

History

The roots of pretrial diversion in the federal system lie in the treatment of juveniles facing judicial action in the federal courts. In 1947, the Judicial Conference recommended that courts be encouraged to use what was termed "deferred prosecution" in the cases of "worthy" juveniles, by placing them under the informal supervision of probation officers for a definite period. In the 1960s, growth in pretrial release programs spurred interest in going beyond assuring appearance in court and led to efforts to focus on addressing the reasons for arrest. In the 1970s, diversion programs expanded following the recommendations of the 1967 President's Commission on Law Enforcement and the Administration of Justice. Diversion thus emerged as a national crime control strategy.

By addressing the reasons for arrest, pretrial diversion is intended to reduce the likelihood of recidivism. Under diversion, the possibility that prosecution in the defendant's case might be suspended is meant to serve as an incentive to defendants to change their behavior and habits, particularly because it is clear that prosecution will occur if diversion is not completed successfully. Changed behavior through successful completion of diversion is also of value to the community and the courts.

Anticipated benefits arising from pretrial diversion also include conservation of court time and resources for more serious crimes, as well as the opportunity for rehabilitation, which can reduce the likelihood of future criminal activity. For the individual, who is often a first-time offender charged with a less-serious offense, satisfactory completion of the period of diversion offers the possibility of avoiding a charge on the record and a possible conviction. Positive outcomes for society occur when an individual receives treatment as a condition of diversion and when a pattern of illegal behavior is broken, which reduces that person's risk of becoming a repeat offender. Society also benefits when diversion results in restitution in the form of financial repayment to victims or service to the community.

Diversion Procedures

In the federal system, the Department of Justice (DOJ) has responsibility for pretrial diversion and creates policies and procedures for persons diverted from prosecution under this program. *The U.S. Attorney's Manual* includes eligibility criteria for divertees and describes procedures to be followed. When pretrial diversion is used, a written agreement between the U.S. attorney and the chief pretrial services or probation officer defines aspects of its implementation. The agreement describes the responsibilities of the U.S. attorney for referring potential candidates for pretrial diversion to the pretrial services or probation office, outlines the procedures to be followed if the individual breaches the conditions of the agreement, and describes actions that are taken upon successful completion of the requirements.

A pretrial services or probation officer typically prepares a diversion report that describes the offense, the candidate's personal history, including any criminal record, and an assessment of the person's risk factors; it also contains a recommendation regarding the person's participation in a pretrial diversion program. When the officer recommends an individual as a candidate for placement in pretrial diversion, the report typically suggests possible conditions, as well as a recommended length of diversion supervision.

The National Association of Pretrial Services Agencies (NAPSA) has developed a set of standards for diversion entitled *The Performance Standards and Goals for Pretrial Release and Diversion*. The original standards were developed in 1978, then revised in 1995. NAPSA defines a pretrial diversion program that includes the following standards:

- persons charged with criminal offenses are provided with alternatives to traditional criminal justice or juvenile justice proceedings;
- the accused participates in the program only on a voluntary basis;
- the accused has access to defense counsel prior to a decision to participate;
- service plans developed with the candidate are designed to address the needs of that candidate, and are structured to assist that person in avoiding behavior likely to lead to future arrests; and
- the program results in the dismissal of charges or the equivalent if the divertee successfully completes the diversion process.

In the federal court system, the use of diversion varies across districts, reflecting the discretion of the U.S. Attorney's Offices and district characteristics. How supervision is conducted also differs depending upon the types of offenses, needs of the divertees, and supporting programs available.

Participation in pretrial diversion is voluntary and may require a waiver of the individual's Sixth Amendment right to a speedy trial, because participation in the program causes prosecution to be deferred pending satisfactory completion of the diversion period. Prosecutors have the discretion to determine whether a defendant is suited for pretrial diversion, but are not authorized to selectively prosecute defendants based on impermissible considerations such as race or religion.

* * *

The Hallmarks of Pretrial Diversion Programs

1) the deferment of traditional justice processing pending completion of the program;
2) specific guidelines for eligibility, either in law or practice;
3) interagency decision-making about participation (e.g., the agreement of the prosecuting attorney and the judge) with one entity serving as final arbiter;
4) managed supervision and reporting, typically by a pretrial service agency or local non-for-profit entity; and
5) articulated criteria for determining success or failure and implications of both.

Center for Health and Justice at TASC, *A National Survey of Criminal Justice Diversion Programs and Initiatives*, 16 (2013).

Angela J. Davis, *The Prosecutor's Ethical Duty to End Mass Incarceration*

44 Hofstra L. Rev. 1063, 1081–1083 (2016)

A. Expanded Use of Diversion

State prosecutors should expand existing diversion programs to include all misdemeanors and all nonviolent felonies. Currently, most prosecutor offices have diversion programs for first-time offenders charged with minor misdemeanors. These diversion programs offer defendants the opportunity to have their charges dismissed if they meet certain conditions within a certain time period. For example, they might be required to complete a drug or alcohol program, do community service, pay restitution, or enroll in an education or employment program. Upon successful completion of the program or other conditions, the prosecutor dismisses the charges. These diversion programs are very beneficial in that the defendant avoids a criminal conviction and all its collateral consequences. Most prosecutor offices, however, only offer diversion for very minor offenses (possession of marijuana, petty theft, littering, etc.). These programs have been in existence for decades. Their continued use serves an important purpose, but they do not address the crisis of mass incarceration.

Since about half of all prisoners are serving time for nonviolent offenses, expanding diversion programs to include this category of offenses would significantly reduce the number of people going to prison. The devastating effects and financial and human costs of mass incarceration demand a comprehensive, impactful solution. Prosecutors should implement policies that result in a term of imprisonment for those who threaten the safety of others, while seeking alternatives to incarceration for others who break the law.

Every defendant charged with a misdemeanor or nonviolent felony would not receive diversion. Prosecutors would set eligibility criteria and conditions that would have to be fulfilled before the case is dismissed. For example, it would be reasonable to exclude defendants with a violent criminal record or extensive criminal history. However, restricting the programs to first offenders only may not be reasonable, especially when one considers the effects of previous arrest and charging policies, racial profiling, and other practices. Once criteria are set, participants would be required to fulfill conditions based on individualized assessments. For example, defendants with substance abuse problems would be required to complete rehabilitative programs. Those with education or mental health needs would complete appropriate programs. Defendants charged with theft or other property crimes might be required to make restitution to their victims or do some form of community service. Defendants who fail to meet the required conditions would be discharged from the program and prosecuted in accordance with normal office policies.

Some prosecutor offices offer diversion to individuals charged with felonies, but the requirements are usually very restrictive. One prosecutor, who has successfully used diversion in a wide range of felony cases, is John Chisholm, the District Attorney for Milwaukee County, Wisconsin. Chisholm implemented an early intervention program that results in either dismissal or reduction of charges for those who successfully comply with prescribed conditions. Chisholm does not offer the program to defendants charged with very violent offenses, but it is not restricted to misdemeanor offenders. Eligibility is determined by a detailed assessment of each defendant that includes an examination of his criminal record, background, lifestyle, and other relevant factors. Individuals admitted to the program are closely supervised and required to participate in programs that address their individual needs. Chisholm's efforts have resulted in a significant reduction in misdemeanor prosecutions.

Notes/Questions

1. What do you think about the idea that prosecutors have an *ethical* duty to use diversion? How would you structure who does or does not go into these programs?

2. You read part of the February 2018 memo for Philadelphia District Attorneys above. The memo also specifically discusses the policy regarding diversion:

> DIVERT MORE
>
> All attorneys are directed to approach diversion and re-entry with greater flexibility and an eye toward achieving accountability and justice while avoiding convictions where appropriate. For example:
>
> 1. An otherwise law-abiding, responsible gun owner who is arrested because he does not have a permit to carry a firearm may apply for individualized consideration for diversion.
>
> 2. An otherwise law-abiding, first DUI (driving under the influence) defendant who has no driver's license (regardless of whether or not that defen-

dant's immigration status interferes with obtaining a license under Pa. law) may apply for individualized consideration for diversion with a requirement of efforts to overcome license impediments where possible as an aspect of any diversionary program.

3. A defendant charged with marijuana (cannabis) delivery or PWID (Possession with the Intent to Deliver) may apply for diversion.

This is not a comprehensive list.

As a prosecutor, why might you support this policy? As a defense lawyer, would this kind of policy make a difference to your clients? Are there other offenses you would add to this list?

3. In June of 2018, the ACLU filed a lawsuit against the Montgomery County [Kansas] Attorney, Larry Markle, for his alleged failure to use diversion as required by Kansas Law.

In the brief, the ACLU sought the following relief:

a. An order compelling Respondent to create diversion policies and guidelines that fully and accurately describe the entire diversion program, including what charges are eligible and what factors are disqualifying.
b. An order compelling Respondent to provide written notice of diversion to all defendants in accordance with Respondent's clearly defined legal duty under K.S.A. § 22-2907(3).
c. An order compelling Respondent to provide diversion conferences to all eligible defendants in accordance with Respondent's clearly defined legal duty under K.S.A. § 22-2907(2) and (3).

One of the ACLU attorneys who filed the law suit said that, "we're taking action in Kansas to send a message to prosecutors that it's their obligation to uphold the law and serve their community, not just rack up as many convictions as they can." According to an ACLU report in 2017, Kansas prosecutors used diversion in felony cases half as often as the national average. That same report found that if Kansas used diversion at the same level as the national average, the state would save $8.9 million annually in incarceration costs. Should prosecutors change their policies to save money? What if there is a state law requiring different policies which a local DA does not agree with (such as in Kansas regarding diversion)? Should the DA disregard the law?

In 2022, after five years of litigation in Kansas, under a new Montgomery County Attorney, the lawsuit settled with the County Attorney agreeing to adopt a new diversion policy. The new policy included changes in the application process and to remove financial barriers to participating in the diversion program.

4. In his article above, Peter Krug noted how, under regulatory prosecution, it is up to each agency to determine whether or not to prosecute (and that there is no judicial review for this decision). One might worry about capture—where corporations are so closely linked to their regulators, that diversion sentencing simply forgives and excuses prior bad acts (if you promise not to pollute anymore, we will not prosecute you indi-

vidually for previous violations or if you promise to end predatory lending, we will not prosecute for violations leading to the housing crash in 2008). How might this type of discretion be regulated?

V. Comparative Prosecutorial Powers

Before leaving the topic of prosecutorial power and discretion in charging, consider that the model in the United States is not universal. As you read the following excerpt, keep in mind that plea bargaining is not the dominant case resolution process in the other countries discussed. As you continue reading the next chapters on plea bargaining, you might want to consider if, or how, the prosecutor's powers in the United States have shaped plea bargaining compared to how it might be if prosecutorial discretion were more restrained as it is in other countries.

Ronald F. Wright, *Reinventing American Prosecution Systems*

46 Crime & Just. 395, 401–405 (2017)

Legal systems in much of the world aspire to a prosecutorial service that is insulated from political pressures and is able to draw on professional expertise. Several features of these legal systems combine to keep the criminal prosecutor within the bounds of law without resorting to elections or other methods of popular control.

First, some criminal justice systems ask their apolitical prosecutors to follow the "principle of legality"—that is, the tradition of mandatory prosecution. Under this conception of the role, a prosecutor does not exercise legitimate discretion over the criminal charges. If the evidence supports a criminal charge, the prosecutor in theory is obliged to file those charges and does not ask if the prosecution is a wise use of limited resources or if it serves appropriate social objectives. The prosecutor's limited role resembles that of a judge. While the principle no longer carries the weight it once did, largely because of increased case volume in many systems, it is still foundational to the prosecutor's role in much of the world.

Prosecution systems in other countries operate under a "principle of expediency," which does authorize discretionary case-by-case decisions. But even those countries recognize the German doctrine of the *Rechtsstaat,* the state governed by law, which treats all citizens equally. This principle creates both institutional and personal psychological reasons for prosecutors (and judges) to treat similar cases similarly.

Fidelity to a criminal code is a meaningful guide for prosecutors' choices within this tradition because criminal codes in civil law countries present a relatively narrow and coherent set of choices. Codes in other nations also provide for less severe penalties for comparable crimes than one finds in criminal codes in the United States. Less severe codes mean that prosecutors in those systems remain within narrower bounds.

Within the outer boundaries set by law, prosecutors elsewhere in the world also produce consistent and proportional results because of tight bureaucratic controls on their work. New prosecutors join the prosecutorial service immediately after completion of legal education and successful completion of an entrance examination targeted specifically to the work of prosecutors. The typical new arrival in the public prosecutor service intends to work for an entire career as a criminal prosecutor.

Once the new prosecutors in civil systems join the service, they receive training that is more systematic than prosecutors usually receive in the United States. They also operate under written guidelines that address a wide range of the routine decisions that individual prosecutors face. Finally, the daily decisions of the line prosecutor in most prosecution services go through an internal review process, leaving relatively few prosecutorial decisions that are truly the work of an individual.

Consider, for example, the bureaucratic reviews at work for Japanese prosecutors. All levels of the bureaucracy are tied together by "the principle of prosecutor unity," which declares that subordinate prosecutors must obey superiors. On the basis of oral summaries of more serious cases and a review of documents in minor cases, managers must approve several key decisions in the case: whether to arrest a suspect, whether to file charges, and how to dispose of a case. Random audits of cases also expose prosecutor choices to more intensive review further up the bureaucratic chain. In Sweden, for another example, both defendants and victims can file administrative appeals of individual prosecutors' decisions in their cases within the prosecution service. Dutch prosecutors' decisions about diversion from prosecution, and about sentence recommendations to judges, are governed by a system of numerical guidelines.

These internal bureaucratic tools—training, articulated standards, and internal review of recorded individual decisions—all strengthen the concept of the prosecutor's job as a neutral quasi-judicial officer. The end result, in theory, produces prosecutorial decisions that are more consistent with one another and more consistent with the values embodied in the criminal code.

In the United States, the archetypal role of a prosecutor rejects the apolitical, bureaucratic concept of the role found elsewhere in the world. State legal systems treat chief prosecutors as political figures. Prosecutors must answer directly to the local voters through elections, and every line attorney who works in the office serves at the pleasure of the elected chief prosecutor. Only a few states (Alaska, Connecticut, Delaware, New Jersey, and Rhode Island) depart from this model: they empower a statewide elected official (typically the attorney general) to appoint the chief prosecutors in each local office.

In this essay, I embrace this vision of the prosecutor as a responsive government official. Rather than asking American prosecutors to become more like their colleagues in the rest of the world, I explore various ways to refine the methods of holding them accountable to the wishes of the community—the entire community. Elections are highly imperfect mechanisms, but the objective of asking prosecutors to respond to local priorities and values is worthwhile. In the American context, prosecutors should seek a balance between apolitical professionalism on the one hand and responsiveness to the community and to other official criminal justice actors on the other hand.

In part, this strategy is a concession to an immovable reality. The tradition of prosecutorial discretion is too strong to ignore in the American legal culture; judges and prosecutors who talk about their respective roles speak in terms of a constitutional concept, the separation of powers. Set against this background that celebrates and protects prosecutorial discretion, purely legal or bureaucratic methods do not effectively constrain that discretion. In this sort of legal culture, the best strategy is to supplement legal and bureaucratic controls by asking what the local community wants to fund or to tolerate.

The strategy also fits best with the two-step process that characterizes the prosecutor's role in the United States. American criminal codes are expansive, built around the assumption that prosecutors will go through two different stages of evaluation in every case. First the prosecutor asks if the evidence is present to prove each element of the crime. Second, prosecutors add a second level of judgment to their application of the broad criminal code: they must ask not only whether the evidence can support charges under the criminal statute but also whether the limited resources of the office justify this particular use of the criminal sanction. And even further, the prosecutor should ask, apart from limited resources, whether provable criminal charges would "do justice" and serve the overall social good; if the answer is no, then the prosecutor should decline charges from the outset or dismiss them as soon as possible.

This second layer of prosecutorial judgment, focused on the fit between the criminal law and the larger social good, is not just a theoretical possibility. It also describes the mental process that prosecutors actually follow in the United States as they evaluate potential charges and the best disposition of those charges. The legal sufficiency of the case dominates the prosecutor's thinking early in the case, at the charging stage; the proportionality of the outcome becomes more important later, at the disposition and sentencing stages.

The bureaucratic devices that work quite well in other parts of the world are well suited to create prosecutors who follow the criminal law on a consistent basis, producing restrained and proportional choices. Those same devices, however, would fail in the American context because they constrain the first level of prosecutor reasoning but leave the second level unguided. The legal culture in the United States relies more heavily on local public values to direct prosecutors' choices on that second level as they interpret the proper reach—in a particular time and place—of the over-broad criminal code language. The ideal prosecutor in the United States responds to the demands of the criminal law on one level while listening to the priorities of the local public on a second level when deciding how to do justice.

Notes/Questions

1. What do you think are the advantages and disadvantages of Professor Wright's proposal to balance professionalism and responsiveness?

2. What might a non-US prosecutor think about our system? How would they perceive the advantages and disadvantages of how we use a prosecutor versus how other countries do?

Additional Resources

Can a Good Person Be a Good Prosecutor in 2018?, Fordham L. Rev. Online 2018 (contributions from Bruce A. Green, Abbe Smith, Angela J. Davis, Vida B. Johnson, David E. Patton, Rebecca Roiphe, Jessica A. Roth, Ellen Yaroshefsky), available at: https://fordhamlawreview.org/online/.

Angela J. Davis, Arbitrary Justice: The Power of the American Prosecutor (2007, Oxford Press).

Bruce Green & Ellen Yaroshefsky, *Prosecutorial Accountability 2.0*, 92 Notre Dame L. Rev 51 (2016).

David Alan Sklansky, *The Nature and Function of Prosecutorial Power*, 106 J. Crim. L. & Criminology 473 (2016).

David Alan Sklansky, *The Progressive Prosecutor's Handbook*, 50 U.C. Davis L. Rev. Online 25 (2017).

Michael Tonry, Prosecutors and Politics: A Comparative Perspective (2012).

Russ Weaver, et al., Criminal Procedure: Adjudicative, 963–1044 (2d ed. 2018, West Publishing).

Chapter 3

Plea Bargaining: A Short History

Television and popular media give the impression that plea bargains are the exception and trials are the norm. The Sixth Amendment to the U.S. Constitution guarantees that "the accused shall enjoy the right to a speedy and public trial, by an impartial jury" But few understand that, in reality, if they are charged with a crime, they are most likely going to accept a plea deal and not go to trial. Why is it that so few defendants exercise this Constitutional right? As you will read in Chapter 4, defendants face tremendous pressure to accept plea deals to avoid higher sentences. But, what about the innocent? In TV and movies, the innocent always go to trial and win their cases. In reality, as you will read in Chapter 4, tremendous pressure is also put on innocent defendants to plead guilty.

The professionals within the system, the lawyers and the judges, also feel pressure to settle cases before trial. Trials take time and therefore require resources (courtrooms, judges, lawyers) and money (to pay for the courtrooms, judges and lawyers). A typical jury trial takes at least a few days of court time. The jury has to be selected, there may be pre-trial motions that the judge has to decide, there are opening arguments, witnesses who testify in both direct and cross examination, closing arguments, and jury instructions. Each of these parts of the trial takes time. The more complex the case, the longer it will take. A case with two defendants will usually have two defense lawyers, which means an additional opening argument, an additional closing argument, and additional questioning of witnesses. A case with more witnesses or more physical evidence will take longer, as each witness needs to testify and each piece of evidence will need to be formally entered into evidence. The professional players in the system understand the time it will take to do a jury trial. As you will read, time can be one important factor encouraging the use of plea bargaining.

Plea bargaining, like other types of negotiation, largely happens outside the formal legal system. This means that most plea bargains are negotiated off the record and often outside the courtroom. In many jurisdictions, the prosecutor makes the first offer on the case electronically when they include the offer as part of the initial electronic discovery given to the defense. Negotiations between the defense and prosecution may be through email, text message, phone calls, and/or face-to-face meetings. Negotiations may take minutes or extend over days or weeks. Negotiations may happen directly between the prosecutor and defense lawyer. Depending on the court and practices, the judge may get involved in the negotiation process. Defense attorneys may also involve more senior prosecutors, particularly if approval is needed to make an offer beyond standard policies. Prosecutors may make an offer and keep it "open" for weeks or put a tight time limit on it. Defense lawyers may have all the discovery on a case, or very little, before negotiating. Defense lawyers may have met with their clients before or during the negotiation process, or they may have never met their clients and have their first conversations after the plea negotiation process is over. In other words, there is no one standard approach, or a mandated approach, to where, when, how, or if plea bargaining occurs.

This chapter will introduce you to the history of plea bargaining, the underlying interests that plea bargaining meets and the basic caselaw from the US Supreme Court. The chapter begins with the history of guilty pleas and plea bargaining. Then you will read about why plea bargaining continues to be the dominant form of criminal case resolution. Next you will consider what underlying interests of the various players are met through plea bargaining instead of going to trial.

This chapter will introduce you to the rules and caselaw, such as it is, for plea bargaining. This chapter will discuss the cases that established that plea bargaining is constitutional, the rules surrounding prosecutorial behavior, the basic requirements for the defendant's competency in plea bargaining, and the standards for competent assistance of counsel in plea bargaining.

This chapter will also review the rules for the formal taking of a guilty plea in court, including what rights the defendant must waive to establish that the plea was "freely and voluntarily" given. Finally, you will read about the requirements, or lack of requirements, for discovery in plea bargaining. As you read this chapter, consider whether the rules, including the caselaw, would help you to understand both your responsibilities and your limitations while negotiating plea bargains as either a prosecutor or a defense lawyer.

I. A Short History of Plea Bargaining

Defendants could plead guilty in colonial America. However, plea bargaining became more common in the 19th Century. By the early 20th Century, plea bargaining had become the dominant form of case resolution. The following readings will give you some background on guilty pleas and early plea bargaining. You will want to keep this history in mind in future chapters as you read concerns about plea bargaining and proposals for reform. Knowing and understanding this history may help you to think about what is possible to make meaningful changes in plea bargaining in the future.

Albert A. Alschuler, *Plea Bargaining and Its History*

79 COLUM. L. REV. 1, 7–13 (1979)

....

III. An Early History of the Guilty Plea

A. The Judicial Discouragement of Confessions

From the earliest days of the common law, it has been possible for an accused criminal to convict himself by acknowledging his crime. "Confession" was in fact a possible means of conviction even prior to the Norman conquest of England. Nevertheless, the first common-law treatises ... fail to mention any procedure resembling the guilty plea, and confessions of guilt were apparently extremely uncommon during the medieval period. In hundreds of reported cases, medieval defendants denied "word for word, the felony, the king's peace, and all of it," but historians have found only a handful of recorded instances of confession.

When common-law treatises first adverted to the guilty plea, they indicated that the courts were extremely hesitant to receive it. By 1680, Sir Mathew Hale had written, "[W]here the defendant upon hearing of his indictment ... confesses it, this is a conviction; but it is usual for the court ... to advise the party to plead and put himself upon his trial, and not presently to record his confession, but to admit him to plead." Earlier, Ferdinando Pulton had written that the plea of not guilty was "the most common and usual plea" and that "it receiveth great favour in the law."

Statements like Hale's persisted in criminal law treatises until the end of the nineteenth century. For example, Blackstone's *Commentaries on the Laws of England* observed in the mid-eighteenth century that the courts were "very backward in receiving and recording [a guilty plea] ... and generally advise the prisoner to retract it." ...

In the early nineteenth century, Jeremy Bentham declared:

> In practice, it is grown into a sort of fashion, when a prisoner has [entered a plea of guilty], for the judge to endeavour to persuade him to withdraw it, and substitute the opposite plea, the plea of not guilty, in its place. The wicked man, repenting of his wickedness, offers what atonement is in his power: the judge, the chosen minister of righteousness, bids him repent of his repentance, and in place of the truth substitute a barefaced lie.

....

The earliest reported American decision on the guilty plea reveals that the practice in America was no different. In Massachusetts in 1804, a twenty-year-old black man was accused of raping a thirteen-year-old white girl, breaking her head with a stone, and throwing her body into the water, thereby causing her death. When the defendant pleaded guilty to indictments for rape and murder,

> The court informed him of the consequences of his plea, and that he was under no legal or moral obligation to plead guilty—but that he had a right to deny the several charges and put the government to the proof of them.—He would

> not retract his pleas—whereupon the court told him that they would allow him a reasonable time to consider of what had been said to him—and remanded him to prison. They directed the clerk not to record his pleas, at present.

When the defendant was returned to the courtroom, he again pleaded guilty.

> Upon which the court examined, under oath, the sheriff, the gaoler, and the justice [who had conducted the preliminary examination of the defendant] as to the sanity of the prisoner; and whether there had not been tampering with him, either by promises, persuasions, or hopes of pardon, if he would plead guilty. On a very full enquiry, nothing of that kind appearing, the prisoner was again remanded, and the clerk directed to record the plea on both indictments.

The report concluded that the defendant "has since been executed." In the only other American decision prior to the Civil War to discuss the guilty plea extensively, the persuasion of the court was successful, and the defendant withdrew his plea.

Even at the end of the nineteenth century, courts sometimes followed a procedure reminiscent of the one that Hale had described more than two hundred years earlier. The United States Supreme Court first upheld a guilty-plea conviction in *Hallinger v. Davis*, [146 U.S. 314 (1892),] decided in 1892. The Court observed, "The [trial] court refrained from at once accepting [the defendant's] plea of guilty, assigned him counsel, and twice adjourned, for a period of several days, in order that he might be fully advised of the truth, force and effect of his plea of guilty." ...

There were several reasons for the reluctance of the courts to receive pleas of guilty during the formative period of the common law and for centuries thereafter. First, these pleas were apparently distrusted. William Auckland, a contemporary of Blackstone, observed:

> [W]e have known instances of murder avowed, which never were committed; of things confessed to have been stolen, which never had quitted the possession of the owner. It is both ungenerous therefore, and unjust, to suffer the distractions of fear, or the misdirected hopes of mercy to preclude that negative evidence of disproof, which may possibly, on recollection, be in the power of the party; *we should never admit, when it may be avoided, even the possibility of driving the innocent to destruction.*

Probably more important than the judicial distrust of guilty pleas was the fact that English felony defendants were not represented by counsel. It was a basic duty of trial judges to see that these defendants should "suffer nothing for [their] want of knowledge in [the] matter of law." The common advice to stand trial was probably presented not in what we would today regard as a judicial capacity but in the court's capacity as counselor.

Still another reason for the courts' discouragement of guilty pleas was that death was the prescribed penalty for every felony. When a guilty plea is an act of suicide, it is understandable that the acceptance of it should evoke squeamish feelings. One should not suppose, however, that the English penalty structure was simply too rigid to permit any development of plea negotiation. When capital punishment reached its high-water mark in England in 1819, death was the authorized punishment for 220 offenses. Of the 1254 defendants convicted of capital crimes during the preceding year, however, only ninety-seven were executed. Alongside England's system of capital punishment had grown an extensive system of executive reprieves. A recommendation by the trial judge ensured the King's pardon, and other techniques for nullifying the death penalty were also available. In practice, therefore, judges did exercise substantial discretion in their recommendations concerning executive clemency, but their exercise of this discretion apparently did not lead to the exchange of leniency for pleas of guilty.

B. The Requirement of Voluntariness

Common-law courts apparently took a negative view, not of plea bargaining specifically, but of guilty pleas of any description. The courts therefore discouraged the entry even of guilty pleas that would qualify as voluntary under virtually any definition. Nevertheless, the formal requirement that a guilty plea be voluntary is at least as old as the first English treatise devoted exclusively to criminal law, Staundforde's Pleas of the Crown. This work, published in 1560, declared that a guilty plea arising from "fear, menace, or duress" should not be recorded. A half century later, Ferdinando Pulton wrote that the plea must "proceed freely, and of [the defendant's] own good will."

Perhaps because guilty pleas were infrequent and even voluntary guilty pleas discouraged, the courts articulated the meaning of the concept of voluntariness exclusively in cases involving out-of-court confessions. The principles developed in these cases, however, suggest a basic incompatibility between plea bargaining and traditional common-law assumptions. The most famous of the confession cases was probably *Rex v. Warickshall,* [1 Leach 263, 168 Eng. Rep. 234 (1783),] which in 1783 held any confession obtained "by promises of favor" to be inadmissible. The court declared, "[A] confession forced from the mind by the flattery of hope, or by the torture of fear, comes in so questionable a shape ... that no credit ought to be given to it." It soon became clear that any confession "obtained by [a] direct or implied promise[], however slight" could not be received in evidence. Even the offer of a glass of gin was a "promise of leniency" capable of coercing a confession.

The basic rule was, and is still, that a promise of leniency by a person in authority invalidates an out-of-court confession. Were this rule applied to pleas of guilty, every bargained plea would of course be invalid. Although some modern courts and scholars have attempted to escape this conclusion by suggesting distinctions between guilty pleas and out-of-court confessions, there was apparently no such distinction in history. Indeed, while the legal phenomenon that we call a guilty plea has existed for more than eight centuries, the term "guilty plea" came into common use only about one century ago. During the previous 700 years, what we call a guilty plea was simply called a "confession."

* * *

Jennifer L. Mnookin, *Uncertain Bargains: The Rise of Plea Bargaining in America*

57 Stan. L. Rev. 1721–1724, 1725–1726, 1728–1729 (2005)

....

In *Plea Bargaining's Triumph: A History of Plea Bargaining in America*, George Fisher offers an impressively researched and fascinating account of how plea bargaining was transformed over the course of the nineteenth century from a "tiny beachhead" of little general importance to "the dominant force in criminal procedure." Over the course of the century, plea bargaining came to be in the interest of prosecutors and judges alike, and once the principal institutional players shared an interest in facilitating deals, plea bargains quickly became both prevalent and entrenched. At the most basic level, Fisher's argument is that when parties have both the incentive and power to bargain, they will, almost inevitably, bargain.

At some risk of oversimplification, four central claims can be drawn from Fisher's rich and careful narrative. First, Fisher's historical investigations show that prosecutors will tend to bargain whenever they have the power to do so. Plea bargains, Fisher maintains, are "an almost primordial instinct of the prosecutorial soul." They provide a guaranteed conviction for the prosecutor, thereby enhancing his "win" rate, and they are far less time-consuming and resource-intensive than a trial. In the early nineteenth century, prosecutors often combined their responsibilities with other forms of lawyering, and for such part-time prosecutors, quick guilty pleas provided more time for the rest of their (paying) clientele. Even for full-time prosecutors, caseload pressures—or even just a taste for leisure or a preference for anything apart from work—made guilty pleas a satisfying alternative to trial, so long as the defendant could be persuaded to accept terms that still provided adequate punishment from the prosecutorial perspective.

Second, Fisher emphasizes that to create incentives for defendants to plead guilty, prosecutors must have the power to offer a carrot, a stick, or both. They need to be able credibly to establish that a plea will result in a better outcome for the defendant than he could realistically expect from going to trial. The prosecutor must therefore have a relatively high degree of control over, or at least clear knowledge of, the likely sentence that would result from trial. Until judges became willing partners in plea bargaining in the last quarter of the nineteenth century, indeterminate sentencing schemes or substantial judicial discretion severely limited a prosecutor's plea bargaining power. The greater a judge's sentencing discretion, the more uncertainty about what punishment would actually result from conviction; this greater uncertainty made it difficult to "price" a conviction with any confidence. Thus bargains flourished only in limited nooks and crannies of the system, until judges' civil caseload pressures shifted their attitudes about the merits of negotiated pleas.

The third central argument is that once bargains took hold within our criminal justice system, only those institutions and devices that proved compatible with plea bargaining have survived and flourished; Fisher provides examples such as probation and the public defender. Even those procedural devices that might have conceivably limited or slowed the advance of plea bargaining—the bench trial or the rule of evidence restricting the use of prior convictions to impeach a testifying criminal defendant—developed in ways that in fact stanched its advance only slightly, if at all.

Finally, though plea bargaining is sufficiently well entrenched at this point as to be practically unstoppable, this does not mean that all approaches to plea bargaining are created equal. In the final chapter of the book, Fisher's generally descriptive history takes a more normative turn, and he suggests that plea bargaining will be fairest to defendants when there is an appropriate "balance of power" between judge and prosecutor, so that each may operate as a check on unreasonably severe sentences even for those defendants who plead. The Federal Sentencing Guidelines, in Fisher's view, have shifted this balance of power too decisively to prosecutors as opposed to judges, and this new equilibrium may have contributed to pushing the rate of plea bargains still higher in recent years.

As this thumbnail sketch of the book's central arguments suggests, Fisher's explanations focus on the institutional dynamics that made plea bargaining an increasingly attractive alternative for all of the principal players in the criminal justice system—primarily prosecutors and judges, but also defense counsel and even defendants themselves. He looks to explain the rise of plea bargaining through mechanisms internal to the criminal justice system, emphasizing conditions such as caseload pressures, evidence rules, and the structure of sentencing rather than any broader social forces or cultural dynamics....

I. Plea Bargaining's Triumph

Fisher's story begins in the early nineteenth century, in Massachusetts; his prodigious research focuses on Middlesex County. In 1809, Samuel Dana, the first Middlesex County attorney, brought a four-count indictment against Nathan Corey, charging him with being a "common seller of alcohol" and with three counts of making unlicensed alcohol sales. In exchange for a plea of no contest, Dana dropped three of the four charges, and Corey paid a fine and court costs on the remaining charge. This was one of the earliest examples Fisher found of a "clear plea bargain," an overt agreement between prosecutor and defendant to reduce the penalty in exchange for a plea. In Fisher's close examination of the middle-tier courts of Middlesex County, he found that between 1787 and 1849, clear bargains of this sort were rare, but when they did occur, nearly two-thirds of them took place in liquor cases. Why? Liquor cases in this period were unusual in that the penalty structure was carefully prescribed: anyone convicted of being a "common seller of alcohol" had to pay a twenty-pound fine, and individual sales called for a payment between two and six pounds, as well as whatever costs were assessed by the prosecutor.

Unlike most other criminal matters, in which the judge had enormous sentencing discretion regarding both the amount of fine and length of imprisonment, these liquor statutes left judges with little choice about what sentence to impose upon either a conviction or a guilty plea. It was precisely this lack of judicial sentencing discretion that created for prosecutors the opportunity to deal. Because the charges themselves determined the punishment, prosecutors could manipulate the charges to produce their desired result. Specifically, a prosecutor could overcharge and then drop some of the most serious charges in exchange for a guilty plea. Since the sentences were determinate, a defendant could know with precision what punishment he risked if he were convicted at trial of the charges in their entirety and could also know with confidence what punishment would be exacted if he agreed to the prosecutor's terms.

At first, such bargains were rare, even in liquor cases. But as caseloads increased, Middlesex prosecutors began to make greater use of the technique.... By 1849, the county attorney used multicount indictments in 89% of liquor cases and, even using a conservative definition of what counts as a plea bargain that quite possibly understates the actual proportion, Fisher finds that at least 35% of liquor cases that year were resolved through clear plea bargains.

....

Gradually, however, judges became full-fledged partners in plea bargaining. Fisher's innovation is to recast one of the traditional explanations for why judges increasingly supported pleas. Some of the earliest analysts of the rise of plea bargaining, such as Justin Miller in 1927, emphasized that plea bargaining had dramatically increased because of the increasing caseload pressure on courts and prosecutors alike. Fisher largely buys the caseload-pressure explanation, but he emphasizes that it was the dramatically increasing civil caseloads that prompted courts to embrace deals. Between 1880 and 1900, the quantity of civil suits filed in Boston increased dramatically, from 120 to about 3300. But courts had more power to coerce criminal plea bargains than they did civil settlements, so "overworked judges of the last quarter of the century turned to plea bargaining for relief from their out-of-control civil caseloads." The increasing need for some mechanism to reduce workload was abetted by the rise of the probation officer, who could offer the judge a relatively impartial assessment of the defendant to help him assess the facts of the case and the character of the defendant even without the benefit of a trial. Practically speaking, the dominant way that judges assisted with plea bargaining was simply to acquiesce to the sentencing recommendation of the parties. Once such acquiescence became routine and predictable, it had the benefit of encouraging the defendant to strike a deal while avoiding the need to put the judge in the unseemly position of overtly haggling over terms....

Fisher's account also reveals how certain evidentiary changes had the probably unintended consequence of further entrenching plea bargains. In 1866, Massachusetts began to allow criminal defendants to testify under oath in their own trials, making it the third state to permit such testimony. While this change was linked to much broader eliminations of competency restrictions, it ended up creating quite literal prisoners' dilemmas for defendants, especially for those who had a rap sheet. If the defendant chose not to testify, it was highly probable that the jury would draw a negative inference from this refusal, notwithstanding jury instructions declaring that no such inference should be drawn. But if the defendant did testify, then because he was a witness, he was subject to the full panoply of cross-examination techniques, including impeachment for lack of credibility because of a prior criminal record. So if the defendant testified, his prior crimes would be introduced against him; if he stayed silent, his failure to testify would likely be taken as evidence of guilt. Either way, defendants were worse off than they were before they had the so-called right to testify, and they were now worse off at trial, which probably increased the chances that they would accept a plea. The plea-encouraging dynamic of these testimonial changes was further enhanced when judges began to give especially stiff sentences to those defendants who had testified but were nonetheless convicted, as on top of whatever crime they had presumably committed, they were taken to be perjurers to boot. This meant that all defendants, recidivists or not, now faced a genuine bind: "All defendants risked being convicted for their silence, and when tried before judges intent on penalizing them for their perjury, all defendants risked being punished for their speech."

* * *

Historical Factors Leading Plea Bargaining to Become the Dominant Process for Resolving Criminal Cases

a. **Caseload Pressure**: as caseloads increased, there was increasing pressure to manage the volume of cases.

b. **Length of Trials**: As more procedures and protections were built into trials, they were no longer as short as they had been, and guilty pleas did save more significant amounts of time.

c. **Professionalism of Police and Prosecutors' Offices**: This resulted in more information about a case earlier in the process putting greater pressure on defendants to accept plea deals.

d. **Key Structural Shifts**: Judges and prosecutors began to be elected, which focused more attention on "measures of success such as conviction rates."

Brian D. Johnson et al., *Sociolegal Approaches to the Study of Guilty Pleas and Prosecution*, 12 Annu. Rev. Law. Soc. Sci, 479, 482–83 (2016).

II. Why We Have Plea Bargaining

Moving beyond the history of how plea bargaining developed and took root, what are the reasons that plea bargaining continues to be the dominant form of criminal case resolution? Consider the following reading, which explains some practical reasons plea bargaining continues to be used at significantly higher rates than trial. In Chapter 7, you will learn more about negotiating plea bargains. You may want to refer back to these reasons after you have done that reading to think about how they may, or may not, help you in a plea negotiation.

Cynthia Alkon, *The U.S. Supreme Court's Failure to Fix Plea Bargaining: The Impact of* Lafler *and* Frye

41 Hastings Const. L.Q. 561, 588–593 (2014)

IV. Reasons for Plea Bargaining

There are four basic reasons plea bargaining exists: (1) it resolves cases when there are no issues in dispute; (2) it is an efficient way to handle cases; (3) it gives an incentive for cooperating witnesses; and (4) it allows for more creativity in resolving criminal cases. The first reason—that there are no issues in dispute—means that the defendant did what he is accused of and there are no legal issues to litigate. These cases are often factually fairly simple, making scientific evidence and extensive investigation unnecessary. If there are no issues to litigate, the extended process of a trial is unnecessary. On a practical level, the question in most criminal cases is not whether the defendant committed the crime, but what is the fairest way to handle the particular offense. Because the parties within the criminal justice system recognize that this is the issue to be resolved in most cases, they tend to resist efforts to force more "unnecessary" trials, as attempts to ban plea bargaining have illustrated.

The second and most often cited reason for plea bargaining is the efficient handling of cases. Jury trials in the United States can take considerable time and resources. Increasing the number of jury trials by even twenty percent would carry significant costs, due to the need for more courts, judges, and lawyers. Although some jurisdictions have experimented with abolishing plea bargaining, the prevailing wisdom is that most busy jurisdictions do not have sufficient resources or staffing to ban plea bargaining or even significantly reduce its use. Judges, prosecutors, and defense attorneys all rely on plea bargaining to manage their caseloads. These "insiders" consider plea bargaining to be an indispensable part of how they do their jobs and manage work-life balance. As such, they would strongly resist plea bargaining reform if it were to slow down or reduce plea bargaining (and thereby interfere with caseload management). Prosecutors, in particular, would resist plea bargaining reform if such changes were thought to undermine their power in the system which, in part, enables them to exercise control over their caseloads. The Supreme Court also recognizes that our criminal justice system depends on plea bargaining to function. This may be one reason why the Court has, for the most part, allowed "business as usual" and has not yet required a major overhaul of plea bargaining.

The third reason for plea bargaining, usually offered by prosecutors and law enforcement, is that offering plea deals to cooperating witnesses is an important tool in complex prosecutions. For example, the Federal Sentencing Guidelines allow for a "sentence departure" for cooperating witnesses, and a significant number of defendants in the federal system take advantage of this. Organized crime prosecutions often depend on arresting and "flipping" lower-level players to prosecute the leaders. Prosecutors also regularly use cooperating witnesses to build corruption and drug trafficking cases. Federal prosecutors tend to see this kind of deal-making as a necessary crime-fighting tool. Critics dismiss the use of informants as "notoriously unreliable," especially when done in exchange for a better deal. However, for many prosecutors, not having this option would impact their ability (or at least their perceived ability) to put together the more difficult cases.

The fourth reason for plea bargaining is rarely stated, but is perhaps the most valuable: It allows for flexibility and creativity in a system that rarely fosters either. Thanks to plea bargaining, the criminal justice system can experiment, innovate, and take alternative approaches. This means that practices in the criminal justice system can change without having to draft and enact legislation. To try a new approach within the criminal justice system, all that is needed is for the professionals in the system to agree. The best example is the development of problem-solving courts, such as drug courts, veterans courts, and mental health courts. These courts started because professionals in the system, often judges, pushed to try new approaches due to their concern that the existing system was inadequate. [You will read more about these in Chapters 9 and 10.]

... Due to the flexibility in plea bargaining, all that is required to impose a punishment other than jail, imprisonment, or a fine is for a judge, prosecutor, and defendant to agree—through a plea bargain—to resolve the case through an alternative process. This may be more complicated in systems with sentencing guidelines or with charges that carry mandatory minimums; this may explain, in part, why there is relatively little creative sentencing in the federal system and more innovative plea bargains at the local level....

III. The Underlying Interests

The previous reading discussed why plea bargaining is useful to the criminal legal system, but beyond the larger systemic reasons, why do the various individual players in the system support such a widespread use of this process over trials? The simple answer is that plea bargaining works not just for the system, but for the individuals who make the system work. Below is a partial list of some of the reasons, or interests, that different players have to support plea bargaining. As you will see, the list includes idealistic reasons, such as justice and fairness. The list includes practical reasons such as managing a caseload. The list also includes personal reasons, such as having a home life, individual reputation, or career advancement. Many of these interests, if not most of these interests, are present in some form or another during every plea negotiation. Some of these interests may be the reason a prosecutor or defendant does not want to conclude a plea deal in a particular case and instead chooses to go to trial.

As you look at this list consider whether plea bargaining fits these interests better than jury trials or court trials. Or could some of these interests also explain why a trial might be preferred? What might be most important to each player? Will it vary depending on the individual prosecutor or defense lawyer, or will these interests be equally important and valued regardless of who is in the role? Are some of these interests in conflict with each other? For example, can a prosecutor have as an underlying interest both doing justice and managing their caseload? Can a defense lawyer have as an underlying interest both minimizing the sentence and maintaining a good relationship with prosecutors and judges? As you consider the following lists of interests, consider which players in the criminal legal system may have this interest? Does it matter to the prosecution, the defense, the defendant, the victim, and/or the judge? When might one interest or another matter more?

Interests in Plea Bargaining

Justice/Fairness	Prevention/Safety
Rehabilitation	Protection of Rights
Efficiency/Docket Management	Sentencing—Appropriate/Max/Min
Consistency/Uniformity/Rules	Home/Family Life
Career/Employment	Political/Reelection
Good Relationships	Day in Court
Reputation	Freedom
Revenge/Restitution/Punishment	Closure/Certainty
Financial Costs	Mental Health

Now that you have looked at the list, what is missing? What else might the players in the system care about? You might want to consider whether when the outward interests appear to be the same (for example, reputation or appropriate punishment), the various players will want the same outcome. For example, if a prosecutor wants to protect their reputation, might that mean more or less time in prison as part of a plea offer? And what about for a defense lawyer? And does it matter what defendants and victims want?

Do Prosecutors Up for Re-Election Behave Differently?

One study found that trial rates rose in the year before an incumbent prosecutor runs for re-election, and it rises even higher if the incumbent has a competitor either in the primary or general election. The study found a 24.3% increase in trials in jurisdictions when a challenger ran against the incumbent.

Siddhartha Bandyopadhyay & Bryan C. McCannon, *The Effect of the Election of Prosecutors on Criminal Trials*, 161 Public Choice 141, 143 (2014).

In Chapter 6 you will learn more about how to negotiate criminal cases. Understanding the underlying interests of the various parties is one key to successful negotiation. You may want to refer back to this list after you read Chapter 6 and think again about how understanding these various interests may help you to negotiate individual criminal cases. As a prosecutor, how might you negotiate with a defense lawyer if you understand that they value defending their client's rights? As a defense lawyer, how might you negotiate with a prosecutor if you understand that they want to do justice and do what is fair? What if you understand that your counterpart has an ill family member and needs to not be delayed at work? Or that they are very ambitious in their career goals?

In Chapter 5 you will consider various proposals to reform plea bargaining. When you read that Chapter, you may want to think about how these underlying interests may impact reform efforts. Should reform proposals consider the underlying interests of judges and lawyers to manage their dockets and caseloads? Should reform proposals focus on defendants' underlying interest in certainty of the process or limiting the time they spend waiting in court? Should reformers consider that judges and prosecutors are often elected and operate in a political environment?

Every negotiation includes underlying interests. But how much do individual interests of the players matter in determining trial rates? Would there be higher trial rates if individual prosecutors or defense attorneys saw an individual interest in doing more trials (i.e., building their own skills and making themselves more marketable)? One study concluded that "drug-trafficking cases are more likely to be tried in high-private-salary districts than in low-private-salary districts."[1] The study also concluded that if private salaries were higher, then there were higher rates of prosecutor turnover. Civil trial rates are lower than criminal trial rates.[2] Civil law firms often seek out lawyers with criminal law experience because it is one of the few practice areas where lawyers get significant trial experience. The fact that individual lawyers may have aspirations beyond their current jobs are often an unspoken part of the plea negotiation process.

Notes/Questions

1. Is it ethical for a prosecutor to take cases to trial simply to get more trial experience? What do the Model Rules (or any other ethical guideline) say about this?

2. Is it ethical for a prosecutor to increase trial rates during election years?

3. Imagine that you are a supervisor in a prosecutor's office that has a high attrition rate. The prosecutors who work under you regularly resign to take much more lucrative positions in the private sector. What kind of office policies might you introduce that could decrease the problem of prosecutors trying cases to get more experience?

---

1. Richard T. Boylan, et al., *Salaries, Plea Rates, and the Career Objectives of Federal Prosecutors*, 48 J. L. & Econ. 627 (2005).

2. Mark Galanter, *The Vanishing Trial: An Examination of Trials and Related Matters in Federal and State Courts*, 161 J. of Empirical L. Stud. 459 (Nov. 2004).

IV. The Caselaw

The U.S. Supreme Court has held that plea bargaining is constitutional, but that there is no right to a plea bargain. The Court has held that plea bargains are valid only if they are knowing and voluntary, and that the right to effective assistance of counsel extends to plea bargaining, not just to trial. However, as you will read, the Court has only recently begun to grapple with the question of what is effective representation by counsel in the plea bargaining process. Overall, the plea bargaining process is not well defined, and there are few clear instructions about how plea bargaining should work and few constraints on either defense lawyers or prosecutors to guide or restrict their behavior as they negotiate plea deals. Overall, as you will see, the Supreme Court decisions barely scratch the surface of the criticisms of plea bargaining and how it works. You may want to refer to this section after you read the next chapter discussing the concerns that surround plea bargaining and consider whether the existing caselaw addresses most (or any) of those concerns.

A. Plea Bargaining Is Constitutional

The U.S. Constitution does not mention plea bargaining. The Sixth Amendment guarantees the right to "fair and speedy public trial by jury." The Fifth Amendment guarantees the right against self-incrimination. Despite its not being mentioned in the Constitution, plea bargaining has been a part of criminal practice since Colonial times and dominant since the early 20th Century. The U.S. Supreme Court has looked at various issues involving guilty pleas. For example, in 1968, the Court, in *United States v. Jackson*,[3] considered the constitutionality of a federal kidnapping statute that limited the power to impose the death penalty to juries, thereby allowing defendants who plead guilty to avoid the death penalty without any agreement with the prosecution to not seek death. The Court invalidated this provision of the statute, stating, in part, that it "needlessly penalizes the assertion of a constitutional right" (the Sixth Amendment right to trial). In *Boykin v. Alabama*, the Court held that a defendant's guilty plea should be "voluntary" and "intelligent."[4] However, despite these earlier cases and the frequent use of plea bargaining, it was not until 1970 that the U.S. Supreme Court, in *Brady v. United States*, explicitly held that plea bargaining is constitutional. In *Brady*, the Court stated that *Jackson* did not hold that "all pleas of guilty encouraged by the fear of a possible death sentence are involuntary pleas nor that such encouraged pleas are invalid whether involuntary or not."[5]

---

3. 390 U.S. 570 (1968).
4. 395 U.S. 238 (1969).
5. Brady v. United States, 397 U.S. 742, 756 (1970).

Brady v. United States

397 U.S. 742 (1970)

The Basics: The Brady case was the first time that the US Supreme Court explicitly recognized the constitutionality of plea bargaining. In doing so, the Court discussed what it called the "mutuality of advantage" to both sides in plea bargaining. Under the facts, in 1959, the defendant was charged with kidnapping in which the victim was "not liberated unharmed" so the maximum penalty was death. The defendant plead guilty "upon learning that his co-defendant, who had confessed to the authorities, would plead guilty and be available to testify against him." The judge, before accepting his plea, asked questions to establish if the defendant was pleading voluntarily. The defendant was sentenced to 50 years based on the plea of guilty which was later reduced to 30 years. The defendant appealed, in part, on the grounds that his plea was not, in fact, voluntary due to the threat of facing the death penalty under 18 U.S.C. § 1201(a). The court recognized that "at present well over three fourths of the criminal convictions in this country rest on pleas of guilty, a great many of them no doubt motivated at least in part by the hope or assurance of a lesser penalty than might be imposed if there were a guilty verdict after a trial to judge or jury." The Court held that even if Brady were motivated by a "desire to avoid the death penalty, we are convinced that his plea was voluntarily and intelligently made...."

Takeaway: Brady established that plea bargaining is not unconstitutional and, further, that it is not coercion in the plea bargaining process if the prosecutor threatens to impose a penalty allowed under the law, even if that penalty is death.

Is the Supreme Court Right?

"It is this mutuality of advantage that perhaps explains the fact that at present well over three-fourths of the criminal convictions in this country rest on pleas of guilty, a great many of them no doubt motivated at least in part by the hope or assurance of a lesser penalty than might be imposed if there were a guilty verdict after a trial to judge or jury."

Is it a "mutuality of advantage" or fear of harsher penalties that motivates defendants? What do you think motivates defendants? You may want to refer back to this question after reading about the "trial penalty" in Chapter 4.

No Right to a Plea Bargain

In 1977, the U.S. Supreme Court held that there is no right to a plea bargain. In *Weatherford v. Bursey*, 429 U.S. 545 (1977), the Court held that "there is no constitutional right to plea bargain; the prosecutor need not do so if he prefers to go to trial."

Prosecutors are more likely to *not* make a plea offer in serious cases. As a result, trial rates are higher for more serious cases. As you continue reading, consider how the fact that prosecutors are not obligated to offer plea deals impacts plea bargaining.

Notes/Questions

1. Should plea bargains with defendants facing life sentences or the death penalty be held up to greater scrutiny to make sure the pleas are voluntary?

2. If the Prosecutor offers a plea bargain in a death penalty case, should they no longer be able to seek death if the defendant rejects the plea deal? You will want to remember this question when you read about the trial penalty and the death penalty in Chapter 4.

3. Do you agree that the ultimate sentence a defendant is facing is not coercive in the plea bargaining process? Would your answer be different if the plea offer were substantially different from the possible maximum sentence? For example, is it coercive if a defendant is offered a deal of one year in jail for a crime that could carry a maximum life sentence? Is it coercive if the offer is time-served when the defendant has been in jail overnight, or a maximum of one year in jail if they go to trial?

4. Do you agree with Justice White when he wrote in the *Brady v. United States* opinion "that courts will satisfy themselves that pleas of guilty are voluntarily and intelligently made by competent defendants with adequate advice of counsel and that there is nothing to question the accuracy and reliability of the defendants' admissions that they committed the crimes with which they are charged"? Or are you concerned that innocent defendants might plead guilty? You will read more about this issue in Chapter 4.

5. Does *Brady* seem to reflect any of the underlying interests given earlier in this Chapter for why judges, prosecutors, or defendants might want plea bargaining?

B. Limits on Prosecutorial Power?

The Supreme Court has decided few cases examining prosecutorial power in plea bargaining. In *Brady* the Court allowed prosecutors to threaten to seek the death penalty. As you will read there are only a few cases where the Supreme Court has placed any checks on prosecutorial power during plea bargaining.

Santobello v. New York

404 U.S. 257 (1971)

The Basics: The defendant was charged with two felonies, promoting gambling in the first degree and possession of gambling records in the first degree. During plea negotiations the prosecutor agreed that the defendant could plead guilty to a lesser included offense which carries a maximum of one year. The prosecutor agreed to not make any recommendations as to sentencing. Based on this understanding of the plea deal, the defendant withdrew his not-guilty plea and entered a plea of guilty. The court accepted the plea and set a date for sentencing. There were a series of delays for a number of reasons including that the defendant changed defense lawyers and various motions were filed on his behalf, including a motion to withdraw his guilty plea. All of the motions were denied and nearly six months after entering his guilty plea, the defendant was sentenced. The judge who had accepted the guilty plea had retired. So the case was in front of a new judge and a new prosecutor was handling the case. The prosecutor recommended the maximum sentence of one year. Defense counsel objected because the deal included a promise by the prosecution that they would not make a recommendation at the sentencing hearing. The prosecutor argued that there was nothing in the record to support that claim. The judge imposed the maximum sentence. The Court held that even though high workloads in the prosecutor's office may "explain" the reason for the "lapse" "it does not excuse them." The Court stated that plea bargaining is

> an essential component of the administration of justice. If every criminal charge were subjected to a full-scale trial, the States and the Federal Government would need to multiply by many times the number of judges and court facilities.

The Court held that when a plea "rests in any significant degree on a promise or agreement of the prosecutor ... such promise must be fulfilled."

Takeaway: Prosecutors will be held to their promises when the defendant accepts a plea deal, regardless of change in personnel within the prosecutor's office.

Notes/Questions

1. The Supreme Court did not remand this case with instructions to allow the defendant to withdraw his plea. Justices Marshall, Brennan, and Stewart concurred in part of the opinion but dissented in part because the "petitioner must be permitted to withdraw his guilty plea. This is the relief petitioner requested and, on the facts set out by the majority, it is a form of relief to which he is entitled." As Justice Marshall wrote, "I believe that where the defendant presents a reason for vacating his plea and the government has not relied on the plea to its disadvantage, the plea may be vacated and the right to trial regained at least where the motion to vacate is made prior to sentence and judgment. In other words, in such circumstances I would not deem the earlier plea to

have irrevocably waived the defendant's federal constitutional right to a trial." Do you agree? Is this the relief that the Court should have granted?

2. One problem with the power that prosecutors hold is that it creates power imbalances in the plea negotiation process. Can a defendant effectively negotiate with a prosecutor who has virtually unchecked power to add more charges or enhancements? You will want to keep this in mind when you read about negotiation skills in Chapter 6.

Bordenkircher v. Hayes

434 U.S. 357 (1978)

The Basics: The Defendant was indicted on a forgery charge and could receive two to ten years in prison. During plea negotiations, the prosecutor offered to recommend a sentence of five years, but if the defendant rejected the deal, the prosecutor would "return to the grand jury to seek an indictment under the Kentucky Habitual Criminal Act ... which would subject Hayes to a mandatory sentence of life" due to his prior convictions. The defendant rejected the plea deal, the grand jury indicted under the habitual offender statute, and the defendant went to trial. The defendant was convicted and sentenced to life in prison. The Court stated that,

> by tolerating and encouraging the negotiation of pleas, this Court has necessarily accepted as constitutionally legitimate the simple reality that the prosecutor's interest at the bargaining table is to persuade the defendant to forgo his right to plead not guilty.

The Court went on to state that the decision of whether to file charges and what charges to file are entirely within the discretion of the prosecutor as long as the prosecutor has probable cause to believe that those offenses were committed by the defendant. The Court held that there is no due process violation if the prosecutor simply tells defendant the "unpleasant alternatives of forgoing trial...."

Takeaway: Prosecutors can threaten to add more serious charges or enhancements if they have probable cause to do so. It is within their discretionary power.

Notes/Questions

1. In the dissent, Justice Powell expressed concern that the due process clause was violated because the prosecutor's "admitted purpose was to discourage and then to penalize with unique severity [the defendant's] exercise of constitutional rights. Implementation of a strategy calculated solely to deter the exercise of constitutional rights is not a constitutionally permissible exercise of discretion." Do you agree?

2. Justice Powell also said in his dissent that plea bargaining "normally affords genuine benefits to defendants as well as to society. And if the system is to work effectively, prosecutors must be accorded the widest discretion, within constitutional limits, in conducting bargaining.... This is especially true when a defendant is represented by counsel and presumably is fully advised of his rights. Only in the most exceptional case

should the court conclude that the scales of the bargaining are so unevenly balanced as to arouse suspicion." Do you agree? You may want to return to this question after reading about the concerns with plea bargaining in Chapter 4.

3. What do you think are the differences between *Santobello* and *Bordenkircher*? Why did the Court find for the defendant in one set of circumstances and not in another? You should think about these questions as you do the next reading.

C. Requirements of a Guilty Plea

A guilty plea can be accepted by a court if it is voluntarily and intelligent.[6] The U.S. Supreme Court has said this means that the defendant must understand what he is doing, act freely and knowingly, and accept (or decline) a plea bargain without physical coercion.[7] In addition, there must be some showing on the record that the defendant is, in fact, knowingly and voluntarily giving up his constitutional rights and pleading guilty.[8] Due to this requirement, as you will see later in this chapter, statutory plea bargaining rules tend to focus on the rights a defendant will waive and what must be put on the record as part of the plea colloquy.[9]

However, what is voluntary and intelligent in practice? One clear line that the Court has drawn is that the defendant cannot be threatened with physical violence if he fails to plead guilty. As you will read in the discussion of the next case, the defendant should be competent, but what does that mean in the context of plea bargaining?

Godinez v. Moran

509 U.S. 389 (1993)

The Basics: The defendant shot and killed a bartender and a patron of the bar. Nine days later he shot and killed his ex-wife. He also shot himself and slit his wrists. He confessed to the three killings from his hospital bed, while recovering from his self-inflicted injuries. Defendant plead not guilty to three counts of first degree murder. The court ordered a psychiatric examination and both of the psychiatrists concluded that the defendant was competent to stand trial. At a subsequent court appearance, the defendant informed the court that he wanted his lawyers removed so he could represent himself and he wanted to change his plea to guilty. The defendant wanted to do this to prevent mitigating evidence from being entered at a sentencing hearing. Based on the psychiatric reports the court found that the defendant was competent to represent himself and to enter a plea of guilty as "he knew the nature and quality of his acts ... knows the consequences of entering a plea of guilty ... and that he can intelligently and knowingly waive his constitutional right to assistance of an attorney." Just under three months later a three-judge panel sentenced the defendant to death for each of the murders. On appeal the Nevada Supreme Court reversed the murder sentence and remanded for the lower court to impose a sentence of life without the possibility of parole. The Supreme Court considered the question of whether the competency standard for pleading guilty and waiving counsel is higher than that for trial.

The Court concluded that it was not as the Due Process Clause "does not impose these additional requirements."

Takeaway: There is just one competency standard for defendants regardless of whether they go to trial or represent themselves and/or plead guilty. Pleading guilty does not require a different or higher level of competency.

Notes/Questions

1. When a defendant represents himself, depending on the jurisdiction, he may have plea negotiation conversations with the prosecutor that are off the record and not in open court. Does a defendant need a higher level of competence, beyond simple competence to stand trial, to be able to have these kinds of conversations? Should plea negotiation conversations with pro se defendants be required to be in open court or on the record? Some jurisdictions, including the federal system, prohibit judges from being involved in any plea discussions. Should those jurisdictions carve out an exception allowing for judicial involvement in plea bargain discussions when a defendant represents themselves? We will return to the question of increased judicial involvement in Chapter 5 when discussing possible reforms to the plea bargaining system.

2. Justice Thomas wrote the majority opinion in Godinez and stated,

> In sum, *all* criminal defendants—not merely those who plead guilty—may be required to make important decisions once criminal proceedings have been initiated. And while the decision to plead guilty is undeniably a profound one, it is no more complicated than the sum total of decisions that a defendant may be called upon to make during the course of a trial. (The decision to plead guilty is also made over a shorter period of time, without the distraction and burden of a trial.)

Does a shorter time frame for guilty pleas make the decision to plead guilty somehow less complicated? You may want to think about this again after reading more about hard bargaining in plea bargaining in Chapter 4.

3. Justices Blackmun and Stevens dissented, stating that the trial court judge who accepted the guilty plea should have inquired further into Moran's mental state, including the medications he was taking. Should asking about medication or other mood altering substances be a required part of every plea colloquy? You may want to reconsider this question after reading more about plea colloquies later in this chapter.

D. The Right to Effective Assistance of Counsel

The U.S. Supreme Court has looked at the issue of competent assistance of counsel during plea bargaining in three main cases, *Padilla*, *Lafler*, and *Frye*. In this section you may want to pay attention to how the Court speaks about plea bargaining and the role of lawyers in the process. These cases focus exclusively on the client counseling phase of plea bargaining. Is the Court missing anything in this approach? Do these cases give direction to prosecutors in terms of how to handle plea negotiations in their cases? Do these cases seem to consider the issues of limited access to defense lawyers or limited resources for defense lawyers?

Padilla v. Kentucky

559 U.S. 356 (2010)

The Basics: The defendant was a lawful permanent resident of the United States for over 40 years, including serving in the US Army during the Vietnam War. Padilla was a licensed commercial truck driver and plead guilty to transporting a "large amount" of marijuana in his "tractor-trailer" in Kentucky. The defendant on appeal alleged that his lawyer failed to advise him of the possible immigration consequences. After his guilty plea deportation proceedings began. The question the Supreme Court considered was whether Padilla's lawyer had an obligation to advise him of the collateral immigration consequences of his guilty plea. The Supreme Court held that Padilla's lawyer should have advised him of the immigration consequences as part of his constitutional right to "effective assistance of competent counsel." The Court specifically limited this holding to the question of whether competent lawyers should advise their clients about collateral immigration consequences due to the "unique nature of deportation."

Takeaway: It is incompetent assistance of counsel for a lawyer to fail to advice their client about the immigration consequences of a guilty plea. This decision does not apply to other collateral consequences.

The U.S. Supreme Court handed down their opinions on the following companion cases on the same day, in a move that raised considerable interest and hope that the Court was entering into a new era to better regulate plea bargaining.

Missouri v. Frye

566 U.S. 134 (2012)

The Basics: The defendant was charged with driving with a revoked license and because he had been convicted of the same offense three other times he was charged with a class D Felony that carried a maximum term of four years in prison in Missouri. On November 15, 2007, the prosecutor sent a letter offering two possible plea deals to the defendant. One involved a plea to a felony, with a recommendation that the defendant serve ten days in jail and no recommendation regarding probation. The alternative offer was that the defendant would plead to a misdemeanor and receive ninety days in jail. The letter said that the offers would expire on December 28. The preliminary hearing on the case was scheduled for January 4, 2008; however, on December 30, 2007, the defendant was arrested again for driving with a revoked license. At the January 4th hearing the defendant waived his right to a preliminary hearing and then later plead guilty without a plea agreement. At the sentencing hearing the prosecutor recommended a three year sentence, made no recommendation about probation, and requested 10 days of "shock time." The judge sentenced the defendant to three years in prison. The Court quoted their decision in *Padilla* when they said that "the negotiation of a plea bargain is a critical phase of litigation for purposes of the Sixth Amendment right to effective assistance of Counsel." The Court holds that, "as a general rule, defense counsel has the duty to communicate formal offers from the prosecution." The Court said that "when defense counsel allowed the offer to expire without advising the defendant or allowing him to consider it, defense counsel did not render the effective assistance the Constitution requires."

Takeaway: Lawyers have a duty to convey all plea offers made by the prosecution. A failure to convey an offer means that a lawyer has failed to give effective assistance of counsel.

"Bargaining is, by its nature, defined to a substantial degree by personal style. The alternative courses and tactics in negotiation are so individual that it may be neither prudent nor practicable to try to elaborate or define detailed standards for the proper discharge of defense counsel's participation in the process." *Missouri v. Frye*, 566 U.S. 134, 145 (2012).

Is Justice Kennedy right? Or can there be standards for plea bargaining? You will consider this question again when you read Chapters 7 and 8.

Notes/Questions

1. Justice Scalia, in his dissent, expressed concern about the remedy of requiring the prosecution to re-open the plea offer. Determining what kind of remedy is appropriate when a defendant doesn't take a plea deal is a difficult question. Professor Jenia Iontcheva Turner concludes that the Court's remedy was correct in *Lafler*, as a court's goal after finding a Sixth Amendment violation should be to "restore the defendant as fully as possible to the position he occupied before being victimized by his counsel's incompetence or neglect." Jenia Iontcheva Turner, *Effective Remedies for Ineffective Assistance*, 48 Wake Forest L. Rev. 949 (2013).

2. As part of a plea deal, defendants commonly agree to waive their appellate rights. Over two-thirds of all cases in the federal system include an appeal waiver. Nancy J. King & Michael E. O'Neill, *Appeal Waivers and the Future of Sentencing Policy*, 55 Duke L.J. 209, 212 (2005). As a defense lawyer, is it ethical for you to recommend that a defendant accept a plea deal that includes an appellate waiver? What if the appellate waiver specifically precludes appealing any claim of ineffective assistance of counsel? A Florida ethics opinion held that it was not ethical to waive a claim of ineffective assistance of counsel, as "a criminal defense lawyer has a personal conflict of interest when advising a client regarding waiving the right to later collateral proceedings regarding ineffective assistance of counsel." Prof. Ethics of the Fla. Bar Op. 12-1 (June 2011).

3. Should appeals based on plea bargaining be limited to defendants that actually plead guilty? What about defendants who reject plea deals and then have a fair jury trial? What are the reasons to allow an appeal in these cases? And what might be the reasons to limit appeals to those who take an offer versus rejecting it? You may want to consider this question again after you read about the following case.

Lafler v. Cooper

566 U.S. 156 (2012)

The Basics: The defendant was charged with assault with intent to murder and three other offenses and for being a habitual offender after he shot the victim four times, in her buttock, hip, and stomach. The prosecution offered to dismiss two of the charges and recommend a sentence of 51–85 months. The defendant's lawyer advised him that the prosecution would be "unable to establish his intent to murder [because the victim] had been shot below the waist." The defendant rejected the first offer and rejected another offer just before trial. The defendant was convicted at trial and sentenced to 185–360 months in prison. On appeal, all parties agreed that the lawyer had given bad advice. As in *Frye*, the Court found that "but for counsel's deficient performance there is a reasonable probability that he would have accepted the guilty plea." In addition, he was prejudiced by a sentence that was three and a half times longer after trial than the plea offer had been.

Takeaway: It is ineffective assistance of counsel to give bad advice on the defendant's possible criminal liability. In this case, the lawyer advised the defendant to reject the plea deal with advice that he could not be convicted of attempted murder if the victim was shot four times, but only below the waist. All sides agree that this could, without question, qualify as attempted murder.

Notes/Questions

1. In looking at *Lafler v. Cooper* and *Missouri v. Frye*, would it make a difference to you if you discovered that either or both of these defendants had lengthy criminal records? Why? Would it make a difference to you if you discovered that each of these defendants had never been arrested before? Does a defendant's prior experience with the criminal legal system equal informed consent?

2. Are you concerned about the impact that finding for the defendants in *Padilla*, *Frye*, and *Lafler* might have on how plea bargaining is conducted in future cases? Should this concern judges when deciding cases that might have far-reaching consequences?

3. Do these cases give you guidance on what constitutes effective assistance of counsel in the plea bargaining context?

4. Do you think Justice Scalia would have written about plea bargaining differently if he had been a prosecutor or a defense lawyer and thereby had actual experience in the criminal legal system? If yes, what might have been different? There are two Jus-

tices currently sitting on the Supreme Court with criminal practice experience: Justice Sotomayer, who was a state level prosecutor in New York City; and Justice Kentaji Brown Jackson, who was a Federal Public Defender in Washington DC. Would having more Justices on the Supreme Court with criminal practice experience change how the Court is deciding plea bargaining cases? (Note that even the *Strickland* test, discussed in the above cases, had a strong dissent from Justice Marshall arguing that the bar of competent representation for criminal counsel was set much too low. At the time he the only Justice on the Supreme Court with criminal law experience.)

5. A type of plea bargaining that the Court did not consider was appellate plea bargaining. Cases on appeal can be settled before a court considers the appeal. It is unclear how frequently this happens, as there is no clear data. But, as a prosecutor, if you had been given the *Lafler* case to handle on appeal, would you have wanted to try to plea bargain the case to prevent it from being heard, ultimately, by the Supreme Court? Why or why not? Would your answer be different if you were a defense lawyer?

6. After *Lafler* and *Frye* were decided, prosecutors were concerned about protecting the record for appeal. An Assistant U.S. Attorney in the Western District of Tennessee filed a motion for the plea offer to be clearly stated on the record and that the defense state the content of "any plea related discussions" including the "attorneys' advice to their clients." The motion recognized that these discussions could be privileged and therefore said that they should be sealed and not shown to the prosecution. Is the sealing of the record enough or do you see any ethical problems with this prosecutorial request?

7. Despite Justice Scalia's concern that *Lafler* and *Frye* would open the floodgates to many more plea bargaining cases going up on appeal, there have been very few. As is mentioned above, one issue is that an appeal waiver is part of many plea bargains. As you read about the concerns regarding plea bargaining in the next chapter, you may want to consider which of those concerns could be litigated through appeals in individual cases and which might be larger policy questions that are better addressed through legislation or other methods, such as policy changes in prosecutors' offices.

E. Competent Assistance beyond Counseling?

In *Padilla*, *Lafler*, and *Frye*, the Supreme Court focused on defense lawyer behavior during the counseling phase of plea bargaining. But, as you will learn in future chapters, negotiation has multiple phases, and lawyers have key roles beyond what they discuss with their clients when conveying offers or advising the clients about whether to accept the plea deal. The Court has not yet focused on what is competent assistance of counsel in the preparation phase of the plea bargain. For example, is it a violation of the Sixth Amendment right to counsel if the lawyer doesn't speak to their client before starting the negotiation? Is it a failure to competently prepare for negotiation if a lawyer doesn't calculate the maximum possible sentence correctly? The Court has also not defined what is required to be competent in the negotiation process itself. Is a defense lawyer incompetent if they do not try to plea bargain a case? What if the defendant tells his lawyer that he doesn't want to plead guilty? Does that change a lawyer's responsibilities? Thus far, the Court has not answered any of these questions.

V. Statutes Regulating Plea Bargaining

Many of the countries that have more recently adopted plea bargaining have first passed new laws formalizing the process.[6] These laws can include limitations on the types of cases that can be plea bargained (such as only less serious cases). The laws can also restrict whether charge bargaining is allowed, or if bargaining is limited to sentence bargaining. As you know from your reading earlier in this chapter, plea bargaining in the United States has a different history and did not start with the passage of new laws, nor was it a product of carefully considered policy. Instead, plea bargaining developed as an informal practice with little law, either statutory or caselaw, that defines or limits its practice.

Most states, and the federal system, have laws about plea bargaining. However, these statutes are limited to outlining the process for a court to accept a guilty plea and do not regulate the process of negotiating plea bargains. Rule 11 of the Federal Rules of Criminal Procedure is an example of the approach which has been adopted by most legislatures. As you read these rules, consider whether they would help you as a new prosecutor or defense lawyer to better understand the rules surrounding what you can or cannot do in the plea bargaining process with your counterpart (opposing counsel). As a defense lawyer, do these rules help you to understand your obligations towards your client? And does asking the defendant this series of questions guarantee that he is, in fact, fully advised and freely and voluntarily waiving his constitutional right to trial?

Federal Rules of Criminal Procedure, Rule 11

....

(b) **Considering and Accepting a Guilty or Nolo Contendere Plea.**

1. **Advising and Questioning the Defendant.** Before the court accepts a plea of guilty or nolo contendere, the defendant may be placed under oath, and the court must address the defendant personally in open court. During this address, the court must inform the defendant of, and determine that the defendant understands, the following:

    (A) the government's right, in a prosecution for perjury or false statement, to use against the defendant any statement that the defendant gives under oath;

    (B) the right to plead not guilty, or having already so pleaded, to persist in that plea;

    (C) the right to a jury trial;

    (D) the right to be represented by counsel—and if necessary have the court appoint counsel—at trial and at every other stage of the proceeding;

6. For more information, see Cynthia Alkon, *Plea Bargaining as a Legal Transplant: A Good Idea for Troubled Criminal Justice Systems?* 19 Transnat'l L. & Contemp. Probs. 355 (2010).

(E) the right at trial to confront and cross-examine adverse witnesses, to be protected from compelled self-incrimination, to testify and present evidence, and to compel the attendance of witnesses;

(F) the defendant's waiver of these trial rights if the court accepts a plea of guilty or nolo contendere;

(G) the nature of each charge to which the defendant is pleading;

(H) any maximum possible penalty, including imprisonment, fine, and term of supervised release;

(I) any mandatory minimum penalty;

(J) any applicable forfeiture;

(K) the court's authority to order restitution;

(L) the court's obligation to impose a special assessment;

(M) in determining a sentence, the court's obligation to calculate the applicable sentencing-guideline range and to consider that range, possible departures under the Sentencing Guidelines, and other sentencing factors under 18 U.S.C. § 3553(a);

(N) the terms of any plea-agreement provision waiving the right to appeal or to collaterally attack the sentence; and

(O) that, if convicted, a defendant who is not a United States citizen may be removed from the United States, denied citizenship, and denied admission to the United States in the future.

2. **Ensuring That a Plea Is Voluntary.** Before accepting a plea of guilty or nolo contendere, the court must address the defendant personally in open court and determine that the plea is voluntary and did not result from force, threats, or promises (other than promises in a plea agreement).

3. **Determining the Factual Basis for a Plea.** Before entering judgment on a guilty plea, the court must determine that there is a factual basis for the plea.

....

Notes/Questions

1. If you were a criminal defense lawyer, what would you want to be sure to advise your client based on Rule 11? What would you want to be sure to document in your file?

2. If you were a prosecutor, is anything in Rule 11 that is important to consider during your plea negotiations with the defense?

3. If you were a federal judge, what would you want to do to be sure any plea taken in your court fully complied with Rule 11?

How to Explain the Process to Defendants

From a Pennsylvania defense attorney blog:

> In Bucks County, most guilty plea colloquys are verbal. They are performed by the judge. In Montgomery County, they are written. You review a form and initial each page while signing the last page. In Philadelphia, the colloquy can be done by the District Attorney or the judge.
>
> The judge will typically line up several defendants and individually address them regarding their alleged crime(s). The judge will further discuss the elements of the crimes with individual defendants and will then address the group as a whole. This will include asking if the group/individuals know what they are doing, have had time to speak to their [lawyer], understand they have a right to a trial, understand the burden is on the Commonwealth to prove their case beyond a reasonable doubt, and understand that they are giving up those rights by pleading guilty. The judge will also make sure you aren't on any alcohol or drugs that would preclude your ability to enter into the plea. The judge will further stress, pursuant to *Padilla* [*v. Kentucky*, 559 U.S. 356 (2010)], that you have had time to speak to an immigration lawyer about your plea if you are not a U.S. citizen.
>
> Therefore, the colloquy does not have to be in writing. The judge will most likely go over the general elements of the crime(s) you are pleading to. The judge and/or the DA will provide a factual basis (what they are alleging) to establish a conviction....

The Colloquy of a Guilty Plea, Bucks County Criminal Defense Lawyers Blog, Sept. 19, 2014, available at: http://buckscountycriminaldefenselawyers.posthaven.com/the-colloquy-of-the-guilty-plea.

- Does this explain what rights a defendant gives up when pleading guilty?
- What else would you need to explain if you were a defense lawyer?

Consider the following example from Texas:

Texas Code of Criminal Procedure Article 26.13

(a) Prior to accepting a plea of guilty or a plea of nolo contendere, the court shall admonish the defendant of:

(1) the range of the punishment attached to the offense;

(2) the fact that the recommendation of the prosecuting attorney as to punishment is not binding on the court. Provided that the court shall inquire as to the existence of a plea bargain agreement between the state and the defendant and, if an agreement exists, the court shall inform the defendant whether it will follow or reject the agreement

in open court and before any finding on the plea. Should the court reject the agreement, the defendant shall be permitted to withdraw the defendant's plea of guilty or nolo contendere;

(3) the fact that if the punishment assessed does not exceed the punishment recommended by the prosecutor and agreed to by the defendant and the defendant's attorney, the trial court must give its permission to the defendant before the defendant may prosecute an appeal on any matter in the case except for those matters raised by written motions filed prior to trial;

(4) the fact that if the defendant is not a citizen of the United States of America, a plea of guilty or nolo contendere for the offense charged may result in deportation, the exclusion from admission to this country, or the denial of naturalization under federal law;

(5) the fact that the defendant will be required to meet the registration requirements of Chapter 62, if the defendant is convicted of or placed on deferred adjudication for an offense for which a person is subject to registration under that chapter; and

(6) the fact that if the defendant is placed on community supervision, after satisfactorily fulfilling the conditions of community supervision and on expiration of the period of community supervision, the court is authorized to release the defendant from the penalties and disabilities resulting from the offense as provided by Article 42A.701(f).

(b) No plea of guilty or plea of nolo contendere shall be accepted by the court unless it appears that the defendant is mentally competent and the plea is free and voluntary.

(c) In admonishing the defendant as herein provided, substantial compliance by the court is sufficient, unless the defendant affirmatively shows that he was not aware of the consequences of his plea and that he was misled or harmed by the admonishment of the court.

(d) The court may make the admonitions required by this article either orally or in writing. If the court makes the admonitions in writing, it must receive a statement signed by the defendant and the defendant's attorney that he understands the admonitions and is aware of the consequences of his plea. If the defendant is unable or refuses to sign the statement, the court shall make the admonitions orally.

(e) Before accepting a plea of guilty or a plea of nolo contendere, the court shall, as applicable in the case:

(1) inquire as to whether a victim impact statement has been returned to the attorney representing the state and ask for a copy of the statement if one has been returned; and

(2) inquire as to whether the attorney representing the state has given notice of the existence and terms of any plea bargain agreement to the victim, guardian of a victim, or close relative of a deceased victim, as those terms are defined by Article 56.01.

(f) The court must substantially comply with Subsection (e) of this article. The failure of the court to comply with Subsection (e) of this article is not grounds for the defendant to set aside the conviction, sentence, or plea.

(g) Before accepting a plea of guilty or a plea of nolo contendere and on the request of a victim of the offense, the court may assist the victim and the defendant in participating in a victim-offender mediation program.

....

Notes/Questions

1. How does the law in Texas give greater definition than Rule 11? To whom is this most helpful? Based on this, what edits might you suggest for the Federal Rule? Are there other elements you would add to both Texas law and Federal Rule 11?

2. As a criminal defense lawyer or a prosecutor in Texas, what would you want to consider during your plea negotiations to make sure you are complying with this law?

3. Do these laws help you to understand, as either a prosecutor or defense lawyer, *how* you can or should negotiate a plea deal?

VI. Right to Discovery

One key element of any negotiation is information. In the civil system, where a considerable number of cases settle out of court, much like plea bargaining, there are numerous rules concerning discovery, and lawyers regularly consider how much discovery is needed before opening settlement discussions. The typical source of information in criminal cases is the police investigation primarily conducted prior to charges being filed which could include information regarding witnesses, evidence, other potential suspects, and the like. This type of information would be considered a key element of negotiation. There are some state laws requiring prosecutors to turn over discovery to defendants. But these laws are not the norm. Nationwide, the U.S. Supreme Court, in *Brady v. Maryland*, required prosecutors to turn over all exculpatory evidence.[7] However, in *United States v. Ruiz*, the Court held that the defense has no right, pre-plea bargain, to impeachment information.[8] As you read the following excerpt, think about what this kind of a holding means in practice. Does this holding mean that the prosecutor should not surprise the defense with this kind of informa-

7. 373 U.S. 83 (1963).
8. 536 U.S. 622 (2002).

tion? Is there information that is useful in the plea negotiation context that is not exculpatory? What does this opinion reflect in terms of whether the Supreme Court recognizes the value of information in the plea negotiation process?

Cynthia Alkon, *The Right to Defense Discovery in Plea Bargaining Fifty Years after* Brady v. Maryland

38 NYU Rev. L. & Soc. Change 407, 409–415 (2014)

....

II. The Supreme Court's Failure to Understand How Discovery Matters in Plea Bargaining

The Supreme Court has left both plea bargaining and the defense right to discovery largely unregulated. The basic requirements for valid guilty pleas are that the defendant should knowingly, intelligently, and voluntarily accept the plea deal and that this acceptance should not be due to improper threats or coercion The Court has allowed what might be considered hard bargaining tactics, such as prosecutors threatening to seek the death penalty or adding an enhanced penalty if the defendant refuses the plea offer as long as such threats can be lawfully imposed "[F]undamental fairness remains the principle approach" that the Court uses in evaluating the constitutionality of plea bargaining practices, including whether the plea is voluntary. However, the Court has limited its definition of fairness to preventing "unfair surprise." Under this narrow concept of fundamental fairness in plea bargaining, defendants have prevailed by arguing that they were surprised by the prosecutor's breach of a previous agreement or by their defense lawyer failing to advise them of the immigration consequences of the guilty plea.

The discovery that prosecutors must give to the defense is similarly broad and, as stated above, not specific to plea bargaining. *Brady* simply requires the prosecution to disclose "evidence favorable to an accused ... where the evidence is material either to guilt or to punishment." The *Brady* Court expressed doubt about whether a trial could be fair if a prosecutor failed to disclose exculpatory evidence, stating that "our system of the administration of justice suffers when any accused is treated unfairly." Nevertheless, the Court has not specifically required prosecutors to disclose exculpatory evidence to a defendant before entering a guilty plea. Moreover, the Court has not yet clearly examined whether failure to turn over discovery to the defense during plea negotiations violates the plea bargain's fundamental fairness.

In the 2002 case *United States v. Ruiz*, the Supreme Court examined the question of a defense right to discovery in plea bargaining, but ultimately found this right had not been violated. Instead, the Court decided, in part, that a defendant did not have a constitutional right to impeachment information before pleading guilty. Pursuant to a "fast track" plea agreement, the defendant in *Ruiz* would have had the right to receive any information relating to her "factual innocence" but would have also been required to waive the right to impeachment information about any witnesses and any information that might support an affirmative defense at trial. The defendant turned down that deal, as she was unwilling to waive the right to impeachment information, but ultimately pled guilty without the benefit of any deal. The Court specifically rejected the lower court's finding that failure to disclose impeachment evidence violated the requirement that the plea be voluntary, holding instead that "impeachment information is special in relation to the *fairness of the trial*, not in respect to whether a plea is *voluntary*." The Court further stated that "the Constitution does not require the prosecutor to share all useful information with the defendant." The Court did not question whether the failure to turn over impeachment evidence was a violation of the fundamental fairness required for constitutional plea bargains. Indeed, the Court failed to understand that impeachment information is useful not only at trial and in evaluating the chances of success at trial, but also in plea bargaining because it gives the defense leverage in the negotiation process.

The *Ruiz* case illustrates the overall attitude the Court holds towards plea bargaining. The Court was concerned that requiring disclosure of impeachment information would "seriously interfere with the Government's interest in securing those guilty pleas that are factually justified, desired by defendants, and help to secure the efficient administration of justice." Through this statement, the Court made it clear that its main concern, in addition to efficiency, was the "accuracy" of the plea, which means that the Court was satisfied of the defendant's guilt and considered pleading guilty an acceptable outcome.

In *Ruiz*, the Court applied the *Brady* standard but failed to see that impeachment evidence, even under the limited standards of *Brady*, is exactly the kind of evidence to which the defense should be entitled. As stated above, *Brady* held that the prosecution must turn over evidence that is "material ... to punishment." In *Brady*, the defendant was convicted of first degree murder and sentenced to death. The prosecution turned over many statements but failed to turn over the one statement in which Brady's friend (and co-arrestee) Boblit stated that he, not Brady, did the actual killing. If this evidence had been disclosed at trial, the jury might have agreed to a lesser punishment and not returned a death sentence. In *Ruiz*, however, the Court was quick to dismiss the potential importance of impeachment information in the negotiation process despite its potential to similarly impact the defendant's punishment. This problem stems from the Court analyzing the relevance of discovery using a trial model instead of a plea bargaining model. As a result, the Court failed to ask what discovery might be needed during plea negotiations to reduce the risk of an innocent person pleading guilty and the risk of a defendant getting a worse deal. The Court stated that "[i]t is particularly difficult to characterize impeachment information as critical information of which the defendant must always be aware prior to pleading guilty given the random way in which such information may, or may not, help a particular defendant." The Court does not understand that impeachment evidence can impact punishment by giving the defendant leverage in the plea negotiation process to persuade the prosecutor to offer a better deal.

Ruiz illustrates how little the Court understands the plea negotiation process and the potential value of impeachment information to ensure a more just outcome. Plea bargaining is not simply a zero sum game in which the defendant either accepts or rejects the deal; instead, plea bargaining is more often about what the deal will be. Plea bargaining is often a fast and simple process, with both felony and misdemeanor cases frequently pleading out on the day of arraignment. In this fast-moving environment, as in every negotiation, information is crucial. The more a defense attorney knows about her client's case and the prosecutor's case, the more likely she is to be able to work out a deal that more accurately reflects the weight of the evidence. While a plea negotiation might involve the prosecutor simply making an offer and the defense accepting it without further negotiation, this is not the only way that plea negotiations happen. Instead, plea negotiations regularly involve offers and counter-offers that may be exchanged quickly at arraignment or extend over days, weeks, or, in some cases, months. Prosecutors will reduce charges, time in custody, or both if there are "bad facts" in their case. Impeachment information is exactly the kind of bad fact that can help a defense lawyer negotiate a better deal. The final offer may change as the defense lawyer points out to the prosecutor why such information could weaken their case, a conclusion the prosecutor may not have reached without discussions with the defense. Impeachment information is just one example of evidence to which defendants have no constitutional entitlement. Yet, such important evidence can be the difference between a defense lawyer's ability to negotiate a better deal and defendants being stuck with no option but to "take or leave" the original prosecution offer.

The Court in *Ruiz* also did not consider that plea negotiations are multi-party negotiations and are therefore a more complex type of negotiation. Plea bargains are commonly a "three-way" negotiation (between the prosecutor, defense attorney, and the defendant) and often a "four-way negotiation" (adding in the prosecutor's boss). In some situations, it may become a "five-way" negotiation if the judge who needs to accept the plea deal is, for whatever reason, reluctant to do so. As with a two-party negotiation, information is key to successful negotiations between multiple parties and the lack of information can impede settlement. This can be a concern that goes to the fundamental fairness of the process, particularly during the negotiation between the defendant and his lawyer. In *Ruiz*, the Court barely mentioned that the defendant turned down the "fast track" deal and later pled guilty without any deal (after unsuccessfully asking the court to honor the earlier plea offer from the prosecution). The Court failed to consider how the defendant's lack of information influenced her decision-making, leading her to reject an earlier and better offer only to realize later in the process that she wanted the original deal.

Ruiz is an example of the Court failing to see that information can be material to the decision-making process of the parties during plea bargaining. Defendants often do not trust their lawyers or believe that they are getting the best deal when it is the first offer they have heard, and they generally do not understand how the criminal justice system works. Some defendants are also in denial about the strength of the case against them The more information the defense lawyer has, the more they can work through those issues with their clients and assist them to make informed decisions that often may mean agreeing to take the "good deal" early in the case. For the negotiation with the prosecutor and his chain of command, the more information a defense lawyer has, the more she may be able to convince the prosecutor, or more importantly, his boss, that this particular case deserves a better deal. Information can also contribute to convincing a judge to accept a plea that she might otherwise reject.

Information helps at every level of every negotiation that is part of the plea bargaining process. Conversely, a lack of information can affect the fundamental fairness of the plea bargaining process by, in part, having a direct impact on the punishment the defendant ultimately receives or by preventing the defendant from understanding the reasons to accept or reject a particular plea offer. Defense lawyers need access to information, such as impeachment evidence, that could be used to negotiate a better deal. In addition, defense lawyers need more complete information to adequately advise their clients regarding whether to accept the plea offer and to protect defendants from accepting or rejecting deals without adequate information for informed decision-making.

* * *

What Evidence Matters to Lawyers in Decision-Making about Plea Bargaining?

A study found that defense attorneys look at more information as part of the process of evaluating their cases for plea bargaining. The study gave defense lawyers and prosecutors a variety of factors (information) for each case and asked them to look at whatever they wanted and evaluate the case for plea bargaining. Because it was done on-line, the researchers could track exactly what information the lawyers looked at. Defense lawyers viewed an average of 23 factors, compared to prosecutor and judges viewing fewer than 20. The researchers do not draw conclusions about why there is this difference. It could be because defense lawyers are looking for more information to help improve the deal, while prosecutors think they have enough to evaluate the case. But, understanding that there is this difference, does that raise questions about making more information available to the defense as prosecutors may not consider some information as relevant as defense lawyers do.

See Allison D. Redlich, et al., *Plea Decision-Making by Attorneys and Judges*, 12 J. Exp. Criminol. 537 (2016). Is this an argument for turning over more evidence and sooner to the defense?

Additional Resources

Cynthia Alkon, *Plea Bargaining as a Legal Transplant: A Good Idea for Troubled Criminal Justice Systems?* 19 Transnational Law & Contemporary Problems 355 (2010).

Albert W. Alschuler, *The Prosecutor's Role in Plea Bargaining*, 36 Chicago L. Rev. 50 (1968).

Albert W. Alschuler, *The Defense Attorney's Role in Plea Bargaining*, 84 Yale L.J. 1179 (1975).

Albert W. Alschuler, *The Trial Judges' Role in Plea Bargaining, Part I*, 76 Columbia L. Rev. 1059 (1976).

Malcolm M. Feeley, The Process Is the Punishment: Handling Cases in a Lower Criminal Court (1979).

George Fisher, Plea Bargaining's Triumph: A History of Plea Bargaining in America (2003).

Rebecca K. Helm & Valerie F. Reyna, *Logical but Incompetent Plea Decisions: A New Approach to Plea Bargaining Grounded in Cognitive Theory*, 23 Psychology, Public Policy, and Law 367–380 (2017).

G. Nicholas Herman, Plea Bargaining (5th ed. 2020).

Milton Heumann, Plea Bargaining: The Experiences of Prosecutors, Judges, and Defense Attorneys (1978).

Brian D. Johnson, Ryan D. King & Cassia Spohn, *Sociolegal Approaches to the Study of Guilty Pleas and Prosecution,* 12 Annual Rev. Law Soc. Sci. 479, 484 (2016).

Brian D. Johnson et al., *Sociolegal Approaches to the Study of Guilty Pleas and Prosecution*, 12 Annu. Rev. Law Soc. Sci 479–495 (2016).

Nancy J. King & Michael E. O'Neill, *Appeal Waivers and the Future of Sentencing Policy*, 55 Duke L.J. 209, 212 (2005).

Mike McConville & Chester L. Mirsky, Jury Trials and Plea Bargaining: A True History (2005).

Peter F. Nardulli et al., The Tenor of Justice: Criminal Courts and the Guilty Plea Process (1988).

Allison Redlich & Miko M. Wilford, *Understanding Guilty Pleas Through the Lens of Social Science*, 23 Psychology, Public Policy, and Law 458–471 (2017).

Allison D. Redlich et al., *The Influence of Confessions on Guilty Pleas and Plea Discounts*, 24 Psychology, Public Policy, and Law 147–157 (2018).

Robert E. Scott & William J. Stuntz, *Plea Bargaining as Contract*, 101 Yale L.J. 1909 (1992).

Jenia I. Turner, Plea Bargaining Across Borders (2009).

Pamela J. Utz, Settling the Facts: Discretion and Negotiation in Criminal Court (1978).

Chapter 4

Plea Bargaining Concerns

Policy-makers, practitioners, judges, and scholars routinely criticize plea bargaining. Some critics focus on the impact on the legal system as a whole and whether plea bargaining prevents justice or undermines the adversarial system. Other critics are concerned about the impact on individual defendants, including those who are innocent. Some critics focus on how plea bargaining impacts how prosecutors or defense lawyers do their jobs. As was discussed at the beginning of this book, a backdrop to all of the specific concerns about plea bargaining is the high incarceration rate in the United States, including concerns about higher incarceration rates for racial and ethnic minorities.

This chapter begins with the concern that plea bargaining is overly coercive for defendants. As you will read, critics who are concerned about coercion in plea bargaining often also discuss whether coercion influences innocent defendants to plead guilty. One of the early critics drawing the connection between coercion and plea bargaining was John Langbein, who compared the use of plea bargaining in the U.S. to the use of torture and argued that torture and plea bargaining are both coercive and have "condemnation without adjudication."[1]

Another concern focused on plea bargaining's impact on individual defendants is the "trial penalty" or the "trial tax." Defendants who go to trial and are found guilty can receive sentences in prison that are over four times as high those who plead guilty. Critics are concerned that fear of these harsher post-trial sentences puts pressure on defendants to take plea deals. And there is the particular concern that innocent defendants may be even more susceptible to the pressure and plead guilty due to fears about the risk of going to trial and the potentially harsh penalties.

Critics are also concerned about disparate treatment of defendants, noting that defendants with similar records and similar offenses can receive vastly different sentences under plea bargaining. The single biggest factor in case outcomes can be *where* the defendant was arrested and therefore what laws apply and what prosecutor and prosecutor's office is deciding how to handle the case. Similarly situated defendants are not treated the same. One recurring concern is the impact of race and socio-economic status on how defendants are treated in the criminal legal system, as incarceration rates are significantly higher for African Americans and Latinos.

---

1. John H. Langbein, *Torture and Plea Bargaining*, 46 U. Chi. L. Rev. 8, 14 (1978). Although Langbein concedes that "the tortured confession is ... markedly less reliable than the negotiated plea, because the degree of coercion is greater." *Id. at* 15.

Racial Inequality and Plea Bargaining

In 2023 the ABA Plea Bargain Task Force released their report. The Task Force reported that it "heard many ways in which plea bargaining promotes and exacerbates existing racial inequality in the criminal system.... [T]hroughout the plea process similarly situated defendants of color fare worse than white defendants. Black defendants in drug cases, for instance, are less likely to receive favorable plea offers that avoid mandatory minimum sentences and, as a result, receive higher sentences for the same charges as white defendants. The same is true for gun cases, in which Black defendants are more often subjected to charge stacking—a technique that allows prosecutors to pile on many charges, increasing the likely sentence after trial and the government's leverage during plea negotiations—than white defendants. In fact, across all charges the Task Force found evidence of significant racial disparities in prosecutorial decisions to drop or reduce charges. For example, white defendants who face initial felony charges are less likely than Black defendants to be convicted of a felony, and white defendants facing misdemeanor charges are more likely than Black defendants to have their cases dismissed or resolved without incarceration." ABA 2023 Plea Bargain Task Force Report.

Related to the concern of disparate treatment is the concern that plea bargaining creates a "game" atmosphere where more sophisticated defendants, or those with more skilled or knowledgeable defense lawyers, are able to get better deals. As Robert Kagan observed in his book, *Adversarial Legalism: The American Way of Law*, "[Plea bargaining] transforms the act of confession from a ritual of moral and social healing into a cynical game, reinforcing the criminal's alienated view of society."[2] This is one of the reasons proponents of restorative justice offer as to why restorative justice may reduce recidivism, as it requires a different level of participation from the defendant and is harder to "game." We will discuss this further in Chapters 11 and 12.

Plea bargaining critics also express concern that defendants do not get appropriate deals because their lawyers are not skilled negotiators. As you have read, the system of indigent representation in the United States is under-funded, and lawyers tend to carry heavy caseloads. Lawyers may not, therefore, spend the time they should on individual cases. As you will read in Chapter 7, lawyers may also not know how to negotiate as few prosecutors or defense lawyers are sufficiently trained in negotiation skills. Another reason that lawyers may not be skilled negotiators is because they do not get the infor-

---

2. Robert A. Kagan, Adversarial Legalism: The American Way of Law 85 (2001); *see also* Nancy J. King, *Regulating Settlement: What Is Left of the Rule of Law in the Criminal Process?* 56 DePaul L. Rev 389 (2007) (criticizing plea bargaining for allowing rights to be exchanged for guilty pleas and recommending structural changes in plea bargaining to better protect innocent defendants who might plead guilty). *See also*, John Kaplan, *American Merchandising and the Guilty Plea: Replacing the Bazaar with the Department Store*, 5 Am. J. Crim. L. 215, 218 (1977).

mation they need about the case. Lawyers may not get full discovery from prosecutors before the first plea deal is offered, and they may be pressured through hard bargaining tactics to have their clients take the deal before discovery has been turned over or before investigation is complete.

Critics regularly express concern about the extraordinary power that prosecutors have in plea bargaining. Prosecutors have the power to decide what charges to file and what charges to drop. They have the power to decide whether to offer a plea bargain or not. As you have read, there are few restrictions on prosecutorial power. Concern about coercion is often actually a concern about prosecutorial power. The concern about innocent defendants being pressured into pleading guilty is often, at its root, also a concern about unrestricted prosecutorial power. One aspect of these concerns is the way prosecutors negotiate plea deals and their use of hard bargaining tactics, which can increase the coercive atmosphere in plea bargaining.

Finally, as you will read, critics are concerned about the reliance on plea bargaining and negotiated case resolution instead of jury trials. Lawyers who do not try cases may not fully develop their lawyering skills, and it is hard to assess the quality of a witness or of certain pieces of evidence if a lawyer has never tried to introduce such evidence at trial. Judges who do not try cases may also be less skilled. As you know, the United States has an adversarial system, not an inquisitorial system. Yet critics wonder, if negotiation is the predominate form of case resolution, does this undermine our adversarial system of justice?

I. Coercion

John H. Langbein, *Torture and Plea Bargaining*

46 U. Chi. L. Rev. 8, 12–15, 17–18 (1978)

I am now going to cross the centuries and cross the Atlantic in order to speak of the rise of plea bargaining in twentieth-century America. The description of the European law of torture that I have just presented has been meant to stir among American readers an unpleasant sensation of the familiar. The parallels between the modern American plea bargaining system and the ancient system of judicial torture are many and chilling.... By way of preface, let me set forth briefly some of the rudiments of our plea bargaining system. Plea bargaining occurs when the prosecutor induces a criminal accused to confess guilt and to waive his right to trial in exchange for a more lenient criminal sanction than would be imposed if the accused were adjudicated guilty following trial. The prosecutor offers leniency either directly, in the form of a charge reduction, or indirectly, through the connivance of the judge, in the form of a recommendation for reduced sentence that the judge will follow. In exchange for procuring this leniency for the accused, the prosecutor is relieved of the need to prove the accused's guilt, and the court is spared having to adjudicate it. The court condemns the accused on the basis of his confession, without independent adjudication....

In twentieth-century America we have duplicated the central experience of medieval European criminal procedure: we have moved from an adjudicatory to a concessionary system. We coerce the accused against whom we find probable cause to confess his guilt. To be sure, our means are much politer; we use no rack, no thumbscrew, no Spanish boot to mash his legs. But like the Europeans of distant centuries who did employ those machines, we make it terribly costly for an accused to claim his right to the constitutional safeguard of trial. We threaten him with a materially increased sanction if he avails himself of his right and is thereafter convicted. This sentencing differential is what makes plea bargaining coercive. There is, of course, a difference between having your limbs crushed if you refuse to confess, or suffering some extra years of imprisonment if you refuse to confess, but the difference is of degree, not kind. Plea bargaining, like torture, is coercive. Like the medieval Europeans, the Americans are now operating a procedural system that engages in condemnation without adjudication....

I have said that European law attempted to devise safeguards for the use of torture that proved illusory; these measures bear an eerie resemblance to the supposed safeguards of the American law of plea bargaining. Foremost among the illusory safeguards of both systems is the doctrinal preoccupation with characterizing the induced waivers as voluntary. The Europeans made the torture victim repeat his confession "voluntarily," but under the threat of being tortured anew if he recanted. The American counterpart is Rule 11(d) of the Federal Rules of Criminal Procedure, which forbids the court from accepting a guilty plea without first "addressing the defendant personally in open court, determining that the plea is voluntary and not the result of force or threats or of promises apart from a plea agreement." Of course, the plea agreement is the source of the coercion and already embodies the involuntariness.

The architects of the European law of torture sought to enhance the reliability of a torture-induced confession with other safeguards designed to substantiate its factual basis. We have said that they required a probable cause determination for investigation under torture and that they directed the court to take steps to verify the accuracy of the confession by investigating some of its detail. We have explained why these measures were inadequate to protect many innocent suspects from torture, confession, and condemnation. Probable cause is not the same as guilt, and verification, even if undertaken in good faith, could easily fail as a safeguard, either because the matters confessed were not susceptible of physical or testimonial corroboration, or because the accused might know enough about the crime to lend verisimilitude to his confession even though he was not in fact the culprit. The American law of plea bargaining has pursued a similar chimera: the requirement of "adequate factual basis for the plea." Federal Rule 11(f) provides that "the court should not enter judgment upon [a guilty] plea without making such inquiry as shall satisfy it that there is a factual basis for the plea." As with the tortured confession, so with the negotiated plea: any case that has resisted dismissal for want of probable cause at the preliminary hearing will rest upon enough inculpating evidence to cast suspicion upon the accused. The function of trial, which plea bargaining eliminates, is to require the court to adjudicate whether the facts proven support an inference of guilt beyond a reasonable doubt. Consider, however, the case of *North Carolina v. Alford*, [400 U.S. 25 (1970),] decided in this decade, in which the U.S. Supreme Court found it permissible to condemn without trial a defendant who had told the sentencing court: "I pleaded guilty on second degree murder because they said there is too much evidence, but I ain't shot no man.... I just pleaded guilty because they said if I didn't they would gas me for it. I'm not guilty but I plead guilty." I invite you to compare Alford's statement with the explanation of one Johannes Juilius, seventeenth-century burgomaster of Bamberg, who wrote from his dungeon cell where he was awaiting execution, in order to tell his daughter why he had confessed to witchcraft "for which I must die. It is all falsehood and invention, so help me God.... They never cease to torture until one says something." The tortured confession is, of course, markedly less reliable than the negotiated plea, because the degree of coercion is greater. An accused is more likely to bear false witness against himself in order to escape further hours on the rack than to avoid risking a longer prison term. But the resulting moral quandary is the same....

Our law of plea bargaining has not only recapitulated much of the doctrinal folly of the law of torture, complete with the pathetic safeguards of voluntariness and factual basis that I have just discussed, but it has also repeated the main institutional blunder of the law of torture. Plea bargaining concentrates effective control of criminal procedure in the hands of a single officer. Our formal law of trial envisages a division of responsibility. We expect the prosecutor to make the charging decision, the judge and especially the jury to adjudicate, and the judge to set the sentence. Plea bargaining merges these accusatory, determinative, and sanctional phases of the procedure in the hands of the prosecutor. Students of the history of the law of torture are reminded that the great psychological fallacy of the European inquisitorial procedure of that time was that it concentrated in the investigating magistrate the powers of accusation, investigation, torture, and condemnation. The single inquisitor who wielded those powers needed to have what one recent historian has called "superhuman capabilities [in order to] keep himself in his decisional function free from the predisposing influences of his own instigating and investigating activity." The dominant version of American plea bargaining makes similar demands: it requires the prosecutor to usurp the determinative and sentencing functions, hence to make himself judge in his own cause. I cannot emphasize too strongly how dangerous this concentration of prosecutorial power can be. The modern public prosecutor commands the vast resources of the state for gathering and generating accusing evidence. We allowed him this power in large part because the criminal trial interposed the safeguard of adjudication against the danger that he might bring those resources to bear against an innocent citizen-whether on account of honest error, arbitrariness, or worse. But the plea bargaining system has largely dissolved that safeguard.

* * *

Notes/Questions

1. Professor Langbein's devastating critique was written in 1978. This was just at the beginning of the time when imprisonment rates started to increase dramatically. Do his observations stand the test of time? Are they still relevant to plea bargaining discussions in the 21st Century?

2. Defendants are commonly held in custody pending the posting of bail, even on misdemeanor charges. Prosecutors regularly argue against releasing defendants on their own recognizance. Yet, these will soon be the exact same defendants that they will offer a time-served deal. Many have noted the incongruity, and critics argue that keeping defendants in custody pending a guilty plea coerces them into pleading guilty. Human Rights Watch studied the bail system in California and found that 70–90% of all misdemeanor and non-serious felony defendants pled guilty and were released before trial, lending evidence to the concern that defendants plead guilty to get out of jail before trial. Human Rights Watch, *Not In It For Justice, How California's Pretrial Detention and Bail System Penalizes Poor People*, April 2017, https://www.hrw.org/ sites/default/files /report_pdf/usbail0417_web_0.pdf.

3. As a prosecutor, is it ethical to argue against pre-trial release for a defendant at the same time you are offering a time-served plea deal to? Does it matter, ethically, if the evidence against the defendant is strong or weak? Is it less ethical, to offer a time-served deal and then argue against release of the defendant pending trial when the evidence is weak?

II. The Trial Penalty

A second concern with plea bargaining is the impact of the trial penalty. As you have likely already concluded, a plea often makes sense to the defendant compared to trial because the sentence will be less than what will happen if they are convicted after trial. The trial penalty (or plea discount as it is called in some writings) can be significant, cutting potential jail time in half or even more. For our purposes in understanding the practicalities of plea bargaining, we need to consider how this incentive structure of bargaining operates. Imagine that a civil defendant facing a middling plaintiff was told that they could pay $100,000 now or, perhaps while sitting in jail (!), could wait one year, perhaps pay nothing but, if the jury agreed with the plaintiff, would pay $500,000 later. The trial penalty varies. It depends on the type of offense, the court, the judge, whether it was a jury trial or a bench trial, and whether the jury is charged with sentencing or the judge will do the sentencing.[3] Defendants routinely have to decide if they will take a deal or face a sentence, after trial, that could be five or more times higher than the plea offer. They often have very little time to make that decision. The

3. Nancy J. King et al., *When Process Affects Punishment: Differences in Sentences After Guilty Plea, Bench Trial, and Jury Trial in Five Guidelines States*, 105 Colum. L. Rev. 959 (2005); *The Trial Penalty: The Sixth Amendment Right to Trial on the Verge of Extinction and How to Save It*, The National Association of Criminal Defense Lawyers, July 2018.

trial penalty data generally doesn't include sentence bargaining, but instead compares sentences after trial to sentences due plea deals on the same charge before trial.[4] This means that the actual trial penalty could be far higher in jurisdictions or with offenses that routinely engage in charge bargaining as part of plea bargaining.

The Trial Penalty in the Federal System

If defendants "clearly demonstrate[] acceptance of responsibility," courts can then grant defendants two-level sentence reductions, even without prosecutors' consent. Defendants can receive three-level reductions if their cases are sufficiently serious, and the government files motions indicating the timeliness of such acceptance. Acceptance of responsibility can significantly reduce defendants' sentences, and qualifying for this exception can mean the difference between receiving a split sentence (partially served in home confinement without parole) instead of prison time, or receiving twenty years instead of life imprisonment on the high end of the Sentencing Table. There is, however, a limitation to receiving this reduction. If defendants opt to go to trial, they typically do not receive acceptance of responsibility credit. Moreover, the Guidelines permit the court to add two offense levels when defendants willfully commit or suborn perjury. Going to trial unsuccessfully sometimes results in defendants experiencing a "five-level swing" under the Guidelines.

Robert J. Conrad Jr. & Katy L. Clements, *The Vanishing Criminal Jury Trial: From Trial Judges to Sentencing Judges*, 86 GEO. WASH. L. REV. 99, 102 (January 2018).

Notes/Questions

1. Is it really a "trial penalty" if a defendant rejects a plea bargain and goes to trial and loses? Or is it the reduced sentence due to a plea bargain a fair trade in exchange for not having to spend resources and time of going to trial?

2. If defendants don't get sentenced to a higher amount of time after trial, what incentive do they have to accept a plea deal? Should we provide (other) incentives for pleas?

3. As a defense lawyer in the federal system, would you recommend that your client accept responsibility for the crime and plead guilty to get the sentencing reduction? What if he was innocent? You may want to think about this question as you read the next section.

4. Does the trial penalty increase the likelihood that innocent defendants will plead guilty? If yes, what reforms could address this concern? You will want to keep this question in mind as you continue reading this chapter and in the next chapter.

---

4. Russell Covey, *Reconsidering the Relationship Between Cognitive Psychology and Plea Bargaining*, 91 MARQ. L. REV. 213, at 224–30.

Do Plea Bargains Occur in the Shadow of the Law (Trial Outcomes)?

"Although there are few criminal trials, one continuing area of inquiry is whether plea bargaining occurs in the shadow of trial—whether plea deals are negotiated based on expected trial outcomes. The data surrounding the trial penalty, or trial tax, suggests that discounts are given based on the defendant pleading guilty. The Shadow of Trial Theory was originally developed to examine family (divorce) cases and settlements." Robert H. Mnookin & Lewis Kornhauser, *Bargaining in the Shadow of the Law: The Case of Divorce*, 88 Yale L.J. 950 (1979).

Yet, this theory may not apply as smoothly to plea bargaining, as "[p]rosecutors do not necessarily try to maximize total prison time in the same way that civil litigants try to maximize dollars; they lack the time to take every winnable case to trial, and sometimes the law mandates more punishment than the prosecutor desires." Brian D. Johnson, Ryan D. King & Cassia Spohn, *Sociolegal Approaches to the Study of Guilty Pleas and Prosecution,* 12 Annual Rev. Law Soc. Sci. 479, 484 (2016).

Empirical studies have ranged from looking at available data sets to survey data and have both found support for the shadow model and questioned it. One of the studies in favor confirmed that prosecutors and defense lawyers (although not judges) make decisions on cases based on the shadow of trial. Shawn D. Bushway, et al., *An Explicit Test of Plea Bargaining in the "Shadow of Trial,"* 52 Criminology 723 (2014).

A more recent survey of prosecutors concluded that prosecutors' plea bargaining decisions (what charges to file and what offer to make) are not influenced by the shadow of the trial. Instead, other factors, such as the criminal record of the defendant, the custody status of the defendant and their office norms for disposing of cases were the more dominant factors in their decision making. Casey N. Tisdale & Ashley M. Votruba, *Prosecutors' considerations when initiating plea bargaining*, Anal Soc Issues Public Policy, 1 (2023).

Is this just an academic question? If you were a defense lawyer or a prosecutor, would you consider possible trial outcomes as part of your evaluation of the plea deal? If this matters to you as a lawyer, it might be important to think about how the underlying criminal law (and the trial penalty) may influence your decision-making.

III. Innocent Defendants

A third concern with plea bargaining is the impact that the structure—limited information, perhaps already being held in jail, and a trial penalty—might have on the innocent. Is this a real concern? We might assume that innocent defendants are the ones who will insist on going to trial. Yet studies have shown that is not true. "A standard concern of plea bargaining critics is that innocent defendants plead guilty due to the overall coercive atmosphere of plea bargaining. Unfortunately, we now know that innocent people plead guilty in the United States. For example, 17 percent of those exonerated in 2013 first pled guilty to the charges. Overall, out of the 344 DNA exonerations nationwide, thirty-six (or just over 10 percent) pled guilty to the crime before being exonerated. One reason that innocent people may plead guilty is because 'the offer is too good to refuse,' which is tied to defendants evaluating the possible maximum compared to the plea offer. Innocent defendants may also be more risk averse than the guilty and, therefore, more likely to take deals."[5]

The following articles discuss this concern and consider reforming or changing plea bargaining practices to protect the innocent.

Jed S. Rakoff, *Why Innocent People Plead Guilty*

New York Review of Books, Nov. 20, 2014

In this typical situation, the prosecutor has all the advantages. He knows a lot about the case (and, as noted, probably feels more confident about it than he should, since he has only heard from one side), whereas the defense lawyer knows very little. Furthermore, the prosecutor controls the decision to charge the defendant with a crime. Indeed, the law of every US jurisdiction leaves this to the prosecutor's unfettered discretion; and both the prosecutor and the defense lawyer know that the grand jury, which typically will hear from one side only, is highly likely to approve any charge the prosecutor recommends.

But what really puts the prosecutor in the driver's seat is the fact that he—because of mandatory minimums, sentencing guidelines (which, though no longer mandatory in the federal system, are still widely followed by most judges), and simply his ability to shape whatever charges are brought—can effectively dictate the sentence by how he publicly describes the offense. For example, the prosecutor can agree with the defense counsel in a federal narcotics case that, if there is a plea bargain, the defendant will only have to plead guilty to the personal sale of a few ounces of heroin, which carries no mandatory minimum and a guidelines range of less than two years; but if the defendant does not plead guilty, he will be charged with the drug conspiracy of which his sale was a small part, a conspiracy involving many kilograms of heroin, which could mean a ten-year mandatory minimum and a guidelines range of twenty years or more. Put

5. Cynthia Alkon, *Hard Bargaining in Plea Bargaining: When do Prosecutors Cross the Line?* 17 Nev. L.J. 401, 414 (2017).

another way, it is the prosecutor, not the judge, who effectively exercises the sentencing power, albeit cloaked as a charging decision.

The defense lawyer understands this fully, and so she recognizes that the best outcome for her client is likely to be an early plea bargain, while the prosecutor is still willing to accept a plea to a relatively low-level offense. Indeed, in 2012, the average sentence for federal narcotics defendants who entered into any kind of plea bargain was five years and four months, while the average sentence for defendants who went to trial was sixteen years....

Though there are many variations on this theme, they all prove the same basic point: the prosecutor has all the power. The Supreme Court's suggestion that a plea bargain is a fair and voluntary contractual arrangement between two relatively equal parties is a total myth: it is much more like a "contract of adhesion" in which one party can effectively force its will on the other party.

As for the suggestion from some academics that this is the equivalent of a regulatory process, that too is a myth: for, quite aside from the imbalance of power, there are no written regulations controlling the prosecutor's exercise of his charging power and no established or meaningful process for appealing his exercise of that power. The result is that, of the 2.2 million Americans now in prison—an appalling number in its own right—well over two million are there as a result of plea bargains dictated by the government's prosecutors, who effectively dictate the sentences as well....

... [T]he prosecutor-dictated plea bargain system, by creating such inordinate pressures to enter into plea bargains, appears to have led a significant number of defendants to plead guilty to crimes they never actually committed. For example, of the approximately three hundred people that the Innocence Project and its affiliated lawyers have proven were wrongfully convicted of crimes of rape or murder that they did not in fact commit, at least thirty, or about 10 percent, pleaded guilty to those crimes. Presumably they did so because, even though they were innocent, they faced the likelihood of being convicted of capital offenses and sought to avoid the death penalty, even at the price of life imprisonment. But other publicized cases, arising with disturbing frequency, suggest that this self-protective psychology operates in noncapital cases as well, and recent studies suggest that this is a widespread problem. For example, the National Registry of Exonerations (a joint project of Michigan Law School and Northwestern Law School) records that of 1,428 legally acknowledged exonerations that have occurred since 1989 involving the full range of felony charges, 151 (or, again, about 10 percent) involved false guilty pleas.

It is not difficult to perceive why this should be so. After all, the typical person accused of a crime combines a troubled past with limited resources: he thus recognizes that, even if he is innocent, his chances of mounting an effective defense at trial may be modest at best. If his lawyer can obtain a plea bargain that will reduce his likely time in prison, he may find it "rational" to take the plea.

Every criminal defense lawyer (and I was both a federal prosecutor and a criminal defense lawyer before going on the bench) has had the experience of a client who first tells his lawyer he is innocent and then, when confronted with a preview of the government's proof, says he is guilty. Usually, he is in fact guilty and was previously lying to his lawyer (despite the protections of the attorney-client privilege, which many defendants, suspicious even of their court-appointed lawyers, do not appreciate). But sometimes the situation is reversed, and the client now lies to his lawyer by saying he is guilty when in fact he is not, because he has decided to "take the fall."

In theory, this charade should be exposed at the time the defendant enters his plea, since the judge is supposed to question the defendant about the facts underlying his confession of guilt. But in practice, most judges, happy for their own reasons to avoid a time-consuming trial, will barely question the defendant beyond the bare bones of his assertion of guilt, relying instead on the prosecutor's statement (untested by any cross-examination) of what the underlying facts are. Indeed, in situations in which the prosecutor and defense counsel themselves recognize that the guilty plea is somewhat artificial, they will have jointly arrived at a written statement of guilt for the defendant to read that cleverly covers all the bases without providing much detail. The Supreme Court, for its part, has gone so far (with the *Alford* plea of 1970) as to allow a defendant to enter a guilty plea while factually maintaining his innocence.

While, moreover, a defendant's decision to plead guilty to a crime he did not commit may represent a "rational," if cynical, cost-benefit analysis of his situation, in fact there is some evidence that the pressure of the situation may cause an innocent defendant to make a less-than-rational appraisal of his chances for acquittal and thus decide to plead guilty when he not only is actually innocent but also could be proven so. Research indicates that young, unintelligent, or risk-averse defendants will often provide false confessions just because they cannot "take the heat" of an interrogation. Although research into false guilty pleas is far less developed, it may be hypothesized that similar pressures, less immediate but more prolonged, may be in effect when a defendant is told, often by his own lawyer, that there is a strong case against him, that his likelihood of acquittal is low, and that he faces a mandatory minimum of five or ten years in prison if convicted and a guidelines range of considerably more—but that, if he acts swiftly, he can get a plea bargain to a lesser offense that will reduce his prison time by many years.

How prevalent is the phenomenon of innocent people pleading guilty? The few criminologists who have thus far investigated the phenomenon estimate that the overall rate for convicted felons as a whole is between 2 percent and 8 percent. The size of that range suggests the imperfection of the data; but let us suppose that it is even lower, say, no more than 1 percent. When you recall that, of the 2.2 million Americans in prison, over 2 million are there because of plea bargains, we are then talking about an estimated 20,000 persons, or more, who are in prison for crimes to which they pleaded guilty but did not in fact commit.

* * *

Notes/Questions

The next chapter will cover suggested reforms. Should plea bargaining reform efforts be aimed at reducing the problem of innocent defendants pleading guilty, particularly in light of what you have just read about how many innocent people may have pled guilty? You will want to keep this question in mind when you read about suggested reforms in the next chapter and think about whether these proposed reforms will help to reduce or prevent innocent defendants from pleading guilty.

Josh Bowers, *Punishing the Innocent*

156 U. Penn. L.R. 1117, 1119–1120, 1122–1128, 1130–1131, 1158–1160, 1178–1179 (2008)

Introduction

No doubt, punishment of the innocent is a tragedy and a failure. Yet, inaccurate guilty pleas are merely symptomatic of errors at the points of arrest, charge, or trial—not at the point of plea bargaining. The relevant plea-bargaining question is only how bad the failure will be—how great the tragedy. From that understanding, the inescapable, if seemingly unsavory, ultimate conclusion is that many innocent defendants are better off in a world with plea bargaining than one without it.

For the typical innocent defendant in the typical case—which I will demonstrate is a recidivist facing petty charges—the best resolution is generally a quick plea in exchange for a light, bargained-for sentence. And such a plea is frequently available because prosecutors do not try to maximize sentence length in low-stakes cases. Moreover, defendants possess certain underappreciated bargaining advantages in these cases. Finally, even for innocent defendants facing more serious charges, plea bargaining may be, at a minimum, the manifestly least-bad option....

Second, most plea bargains terminate petty cases in exchange for trivial sentences, notwithstanding academic and popular over attention to uncommon instances of high-stakes bartering over years in prison in high-profile cases.

Third, the pretrial process is painful. Punishment does not begin with sentence. Many defendants—even the innocent—do not welcome a process that frequently constitutes most, if not all, of the punishment they will face. For the typical innocent recidivist defendant facing the typical petty charge, the more abbreviated the process, the less the punishment....

Prosecutors make such lenient offers because they can. They enjoy little public or official scrutiny in low-stakes cases. In these cases, prosecutors are much more interested in reducing their own administrative costs while earning some type (any type) of undelayed conviction. The adversarial model breaks down, or at least becomes a secondary consideration to workgroup cooperative principles. For all involved, the best pleas are quick pleas. And quick pleas are most efficiently reached at low market prices, because—although prosecutors may abandon sentence maximization—defendants always remain sentence minimizers. The threat that defendants might demur leads even self-interested defense attorneys and prosecutors to set prices low ex ante as the most efficient way to ensure that the largest number of defendants plead guilty with the least amount of hesitation.

As stakes rise, however, plea bargaining comes to resemble more closely the orthodox ideal of adversarial gamesmanship: prosecutors more often yield only enough to purchase pleas and use overcharging to compel defendants' acceptance of high prices. In these serious cases, bargaining provides an escape only from the prohibitive risk of substantial trial penalties, not from trial processes that defendants might otherwise welcome. Bargaining may be rational here, but it creates no normative good. Yet, significantly, this overcharging criticism is an objection to bargaining and charging discretion generally. The problem affects all defendants; it is not exclusive to the innocent....

I. The Usual Suspects

There is no longer any serious question that innocent people are charged with and convicted of crimes. These instances of wrongful conviction may be uncommon, but even so, they likely affect thousands of people per year nationwide. Still, public perceptions of the characteristics of the innocent accused remain fuzzy, if not inaccurate. Commonly, the media portrays the innocent accused as the railroaded "good person"—the law-abiding citizen robbed of liberty and tossed in a dank cell by incompetent or even crooked prosecutors and police. Undoubtedly, such cases exist. But they are the rarest type of a rare category. In fact, recidivists are the most likely innocent defendants. First, recidivists comprise the majority of criminal defendants overall. Specifically, in 2002, in the nation's seventy-five largest counties, seventy-six percent of state-court felony defendants had at least one prior arrest, fifty percent had five arrests or more, fifty-nine percent had at least one prior conviction, and twenty-four percent had five or more convictions. Second, this recidivist majority is overrepresented among the population of wrongfully accused, because institutional biases select for erroneous arrest, prosecution, and trial conviction of recidivist defendants.

A. Arrest Biases

Recidivists are common first targets when crime happens, or even when they are simply on public sidewalks or in building lobbies in high-crime areas. They are stopped because they are known to police or just because they are more likely to look the criminal part. This on-the-beat selection bias for repeat players is most pronounced when police enforce minor crime—particularly the petty public-order offenses that have increasingly become the grist of criminal court mills. But even in more serious cases, police are prone to arrest recidivists on less concrete evidence, because police often start with the recidivists—for instance, by directing crime victims to mug-shot books composed exclusively of prior arrestees. In short, when police lack solid leads—or even when they just need higher arrest numbers—the time has come to "round up the usual suspects," as Captain Renault announced in Casablanca.

B. Charging Biases

At the screening phase, prosecutors err on the side of charging—a predisposition that affects all arrestees, not just recidivists. There are two principal reasons. First, in the interest of comity, prosecutors must level charges against a significant portion of the arrestees that police process. Second, prosecutors carry a general "presumption of guilt" that leads them to resolve inconsistencies in favor of guilt. This charging presumption is strongest when police arrest recidivists. Prosecutors assume—perhaps with good reason—that recidivists are guilty of some crime. As such, prosecutors are unlikely to exercise discretion to decline prosecution. Even in the weakest cases, prosecutors can go forward with charges and anticipate pleas because they know that recidivists cannot easily fight charges at trial under existing evidence rules.

C. Dismissal Aversion

Once charged, innocent defendants—particularly recidivists—are unlikely to convince prosecutors that the charges are erroneous. Prosecutors have every incentive to spin away stories of innocence. First, prosecutors retain the same presumption of guilt that led them to charge erroneously in the first instance. Second, even if prosecutors were receptive to protests of innocence, innocent defendants cannot effectively signal genuine innocence because prosecutors are aware that guilty defendants will attempt to copy any halfway persuasive signal. In any event, in many low-stakes cases there is no time for thorough signaling. Third, prosecutors can justify incuriosity as appropriately leaving proof questions to the judge or jury. Fourth, line prosecutors often must obtain supervisory approval before dismissing cases, even though they enjoy no similar official oversight over their bargaining, charging, and trial decisions generally. At bottom, prosecutors carry mindsets of "nondefeat"—aversions to dismissal that they keep in all cases, but that are most pronounced in cases against recidivists. In this sense, prosecutors consistently function as conviction maximizers even if they only rarely operate as sentence maximizers....

D. Trial Biases

Innocent recidivist defendants who choose to go to trial face a number of hurdles that raise the prospect of wrongful conviction. First, innocent defendants are less likely to rely solely on putting the prosecution to its burden. They have stories of innocence to tell—typically of alibi. But they cannot testify without potentially opening the door to past-crimes evidence that may be used against them for impeachment purposes. In any event, juries may not credit even true stories. Second, recidivist innocent defendants are more likely to be held pretrial, and this confinement impacts their ability to communicate with their attorneys, contact witnesses, and plan defenses. Third, "usual-suspects" policing creates early opportunities for false identification. False identification is the leading cause of wrongful arrest and conviction because police, prosecutors, and juries give undue credence to its probative strength. Fourth, juries and judges are more likely to be predisposed toward conviction of recidivist defendants all the more so if they can intuit, as is often manifest, that a particular defendant is currently confined. For these reasons, it is no surprise that the great majority of DNA exonerations involve recidivist defendants wrongfully convicted after trial, and that over three-quarters of these erroneous convictions were based at least partly on inaccurate eyewitness identification evidence....

VI. Objections

To sum up, plea bargaining works best for innocent defendants for whom the process is the punishment. However, because the system condones overcharging (and consequently substantial de facto trial penalties), bargaining may also prove to be the least-bad option for some innocent defendants for whom process would otherwise be welcome. After all, trials are imperfect, particularly for recidivist defendants who cannot so easily challenge wrongful charges. Accordingly, it seems wrongheaded and even unjust to allow a factually guilty defendant to make a rational choice in the face of plea bargaining's benefits and trial's potential penalties and travails, but to force an innocent defendant—who, by her nature as innocent and facing criminal charges, has already been systemically abused once—to risk, against her will, an uncertain trial with significant downside. Yet, that is precisely what some commentators and courts piously demand when they insist that the innocent should never plead guilty.

What are these critics' principal concerns? There seem to be four concrete reasons for potential pause: bargained-for convictions of the innocent may (1) engender disaffection with the criminal justice system; (2) permit real perpetrators to escape punishment; (3) incentivize prosecutors to charge marginal cases because they can anticipate pleas; and (4) enable police misconduct by insulating unlawful searches, seizures, and other police procedures from constitutional review. Further, these problems carry greater moral weight if—as one might expect—they disproportionately affect poor or minority communities....

Conclusion

... [I]nnocent defendants are plainly better off in a world with plea bargaining. Bargains provide these innocent defendants a means to escape their own process costs and receive light unmaximized sentences, rather than endure full process and risk considerable posttrial sanctions. It is wholly secondary whether the lenient offers are normatively and systematically good or bad. For the innocent accused, it is enough that they exist. Lenient offers create opportunities. A top-most normative demand should be to ensure that the innocent have the same access to those opportunities. Of course, even an abbreviated sentence and any brand of conviction of the innocent is a systemic failure. The plea bargain, however, does not create this failure; the false arrest and the prosecutorial decision to make and carry out charges do. And, although the offer may seem foolhardy to decline, the defendant—innocent or guilty—always retains the right to fight on for acquittal.

The question is pricklier in high-stakes cases. In these cases, all defendants—innocent and guilty—are better off in a world without plea bargaining, or, at least, in a world with fewer plea-bargaining pressures. If prosecutors were unable to exploit overinclusive criminal statutes to overcharge defendants, then there would be far less concern over de facto trial penalties. Nevertheless, it does not follow from this objection that innocent defendants should have no right to plead guilty in serious felony cases. The innocent would be at a great disadvantage if the culpable could plead guilty to avoid large sentence disparities and rampant overcharging but the innocent could not....

Notes/Questions

1. An interesting empirical study suggested that it might be common for innocent people to plead guilty, due to fear of the consequences. In the study, college students were put into different groups and accused of cheating. In this controlled experiment some had "cheated" and some were "innocent." The "innocent" students took the equivalent of the "deal" to avoid more serious disciplinary proceedings that could have had lasting consequences on their college careers. The clear implication from this study is that innocent people will fear the consequences and be as likely (if not more likely) to take deals. As has been discussed, there are serious consequences in terms of trial penalties for defendants who do not accept plea deals. This may make it more likely that innocent defendants will feel the pressure and decide to plead guilty. This may be more likely when they are charged with offenses that carry serious potential penalties, making the pressure to accept a deal even more attractive. Lucian E. Dervan & Vanessa A. Edkins, *The Innocent Defendant's Dilemma: An Innovative Empirical Study of Plea Bargaining's Innocence Problem*, 103 J. Crim. L. & Criminology 1, 3–4 (2013).

2. Another study looked at whether innocent people would be more likely to plead guilty if they were jailed pre-trial and had the added risk of COVID-19 exposure. Using a computer simulation the study concluded that the added concern about COVID-19 "weighed more heavily" on innocent defendants than the guilty, making it more likely that they would plead guilty. This article was published in June of 2021, when vaccines were still fairly new and the serious impact of the pandemic was fresher. But, the findings complement the study above in finding that the innocent might be more risk averse (whatever the particular risk they are concerned about) and more likely to take a deal. Miko M Wilford et al., *Innocence in the Shadow of COVID-19: Plea Decisions Making During a Pandemic*, 27 Journal of Experimental Psychology: Applied 739 (2021).

3. Do you agree with Josh Bowers that innocent defendants, at least for the less serious offenses and defendants with prior convictions, pleading guilty really isn't a problem?

4. In contrast to Bowers' view about the impact of misdemeanor convictions, Professor Jenny Roberts details the penalties and consequences including immigration consequences, of misdemeanor convictions. For more on this, see Jenny Roberts, *Why Misdemeanors Matter: Defining Effective Advocacy in the Lower Criminal Courts*, U.C. Davis L. Rev. 277 (2011).

5. As a defense lawyer or prosecutor, should you think that misdemeanors don't matter, or that it matters less if the defendant might be innocent if he or she has prior

convictions? Is it ethical to treat a defendant with prior convictions differently? What if you are a prosecutor; is it ethical? Is the answer different if you are a defense lawyer?

IV. Prosecutorial Conduct and Power in Plea Bargaining

Underlying the concerns addressed in this chapter are the power and discretion currently accorded to prosecutors in our system. As you read further, consider how each of the concerns above are impacted by prosecutors and their decisions in plea bargaining.

A. Power to Charge

As you read in Chapter Two, prosecutors enjoy extraordinary powers in making decisions about charging. Prosecutors can decide what charges and what enhancements to file. They can also decide whether to make a plea offer and what plea offer to make. Consider the following readings that focus on prosecutorial power in plea bargaining and whether there are any constraints on their powers both within the plea bargaining process and beyond. As a defense lawyer, what would this power mean in terms of how you do your job? What if you were a prosecutor?

Cynthia Alkon, *The U.S. Supreme Court's Failure to Fix Plea Bargaining: The Impact of* Lafler *and* Frye

41 Hastings Const. L.Q. 561, 582–583, 586–587 (2014)

...

Prosecutors have virtually unchecked discretion to charge more- or less-serious penalties for the same act. They can also penalize defendants who refuse plea offers by adding enhancements or charges—potentially adding significant amounts of time that a defendant will spend in custody if convicted. Furthermore, because prosecutors are rarely hesitant to wield this power, they contribute to the United States' high incarceration rates and to the reality that first-time offenders are regularly sentenced to time in custody even for nonviolent, nonserious offenses....

The increase in penalties and enhancements, zero-tolerance policies, and sentencing guidelines gave prosecutors tools, embedded within the structure of the criminal justice system, to pressure defendants to plead guilty during plea bargaining.... Structural changes in penal codes around the country gave prosecutors more choices when deciding how to charge an offense and what offers to make; these legislative changes have often been made precisely to give prosecutors more "bargaining chips." A prosecutor can now routinely decide whether to charge the same act as a misdemeanor or a felony; whether to add an enhancement (e.g., use of a firearm in the commission of the offense); whether to add a prior conviction; or whether to allege the offense happened "in a school zone" or another location that will increase the potential punishment.

Adding charges, enhancements, or prior convictions can substantially increase the severity of a sentence. In the course of plea negotiations, a prosecutor can agree to drop each time-adding allegation or threaten to add more serious charges if the defendant refuses to "take the deal." ...

Notes/Questions

1. Prosecutors have extraordinary power, but they aren't the only players in the system that can decide what charges to file. In fourteen states, police officers have the power to file charges, and act as the prosecutor, in misdemeanor courts. In these courts, the police officer is also the witness and can be the only player to negotiate a plea deal. For example, in South Carolina, there are no prosecutors in 400 magistrate and municipal courts. This means that defendants in those courts are negotiating deals with the police officer who arrested them. The judges in these courts are not required to be lawyers, and 90% of defendants go unrepresented. Another concern is that prosecutors are not exercising any oversight and instead routinely file all minor cases brought to them by police, even in courts where prosecutors do file the charges. The challenge is that once a case is filed, most defendants are convicted. Alexandra Natapoff, *When Police Become the Prosecutors: Officers Quietly Wield a Lot of Unchecked Prosecutorial Power*, N.Y. Times, Dec. 26, 2018.

2. As a prosecutor, do you think you are exercising your ethical duty by filing virtually every case brought to you by the police? The percentage of cases where prosecutors decline to file are widely variable. In Mecklenburg County, North Carolina, prosecutors declined 4% of drug offenses (and 0% of those where the defendant was an African American woman). In Texas, prosecutors declined to file 8% of non-traffic misdemeanors. By contrast, federal prosecutors decline approximately one-third of felony cases. Alexandra Natapoff, *When Police Become the Prosecutors: Officers Quietly Wield a Lot of Unchecked Prosecutorial Power*, N.Y. Times, Dec. 26, 2018.

3. Alexandra Natapoff refers to police officers as "accidental prosecutors" in jurisdictions where prosecutors file cases brought by the police without any serious screening or oversight. In New York, in over 98% of misdemeanor cases, prosecutors file exactly what the police recommend.[6] Does it matter that these cases are often "only" misdemeanors? Or should prosecutors subject these cases to more scrutiny in the filing decisions?

4. Should prosecutors not file as many misdemeanor cases as they do? One study found that when prosecutors decide not to file low-level non-violent misdemeanor cases, it reduces recidivism for those people. These researchers found that staying out of the criminal legal system is the best protection against future cases. If you understand that not prosecuting reduces future criminal behavior, should you, as a prosecutor, use this information in deciding whether to file cases? Amanda Agan, et al., *Misdemeanor*

---

6. Cynthia Alkon et al., *Disposing of Misdemeanors: An Empirical Perspective*, 99 St. John's Law Review 101 (2025).

Prosecution, 138 QUARTERLY JOURNAL OF ECONOMICS, 1453 (August 2023).You might want to keep these questions in mind as you read the next article discussing how existing laws give prosecutors power in charging decisions that impacts their power in plea negotiations. Note the different types of negotiation strategies that prosecutors have at their disposal to encourage (or coerce?) a plea agreement. You will also want to consider the impact this has had on incarceration rates in the United States.

Cynthia Alkon, *An Overlooked Key to Reversing Mass Incarceration: Reforming the Law to Reduce Prosecutorial Power in Plea Bargaining*

15 MD. L.J. OF RACE, RELIGION, GENDER & CLASS 191, 197–201 (Fall 2015)

...

Complicating the situation, prosecutors' offices regularly evaluate prosecutors based on their conviction rates—a practice that can encourage a range of problematic practices, such as discovery violations, which sometimes goes hand-in-hand with coercive plea bargaining practices. The decision to file charges has been described as "the most dangerous power of the prosecutor" and is one that is rarely subject to review. Criminal codes are structured to allow prosecutors wide latitude in deciding what to file. Prosecutors routinely use this power to pressure defendants to take deals or face harsher penalties. Prosecutors operate in a culture where they know that once they file charges, the charges will stand, and they will likely get convictions through guilty pleas. This gives prosecutors few incentives not to file charges. These factors contribute to a prosecutorial culture that supports, or at the very least, doesn't discourage increased filing of charges, and, as will be discussed below, this might be the single most important contributing factor to dramatically increased incarceration rates.

I. Prosecutors and Mass Incarceration

One scholar examining the data surrounding incarceration rates in the United States is John Pfaff. Pfaff's work focuses on the state-level data provided by just over thirty states. Examining state-level data is important, as that is where most incarceration happens. For example, federal incarceration accounts for only 12 percent of the total incarcerated population in the United States. Pfaff has drawn several key conclusions from his empirical work. The first is that drug offenses are not the main reason that incarceration rates have soared as they account for only 17 percent of those incarcerated. Pfaff acknowledges that drug offenses can drive up incarceration rates as they may, for example, be the first offense that is then used for heavier sentences in future offenses....

Pfaff concludes that the main driver for mass incarceration is prosecutors who are filing more felony charges. As Pfaff explains, the admission to prison rate per criminal filing has not changed, what has changed is that a higher percentage of people arrested are ultimately charged with crimes as prosecutors decide to file felony charges more frequently than they did in previous eras.

... As Pfaff observed, "prosecutors have become substantially more aggressive over the past 25 years, for reasons that are not yet understood."

Pfaff's work challenges the predominant narrative that mass incarceration is due to the war on drugs and longer prison sentences. Pfaff doesn't examine whether changes in the law and the embedded power imbalances may be contributing to this prosecutorial culture of increasing criminal filings. Pfaff also doesn't examine how plea bargaining may contribute to mass incarceration and how certain reforms may change bargaining behavior by reducing power imbalances and thereby contribute to reducing mass incarceration. Nor is Pfaff alone. Michelle Alexander also only briefly touches on the relationship between plea bargaining and mass incarceration. Although Pfaff disagrees with Alexander's conclusion about the impact of the war on drugs on mass incarceration, both agree that prosecutors are the key players. As Alexander states, "the prosecutor holds the cards" in plea-bargaining.[7] One reason that prosecutors may be filing a higher percentage of cases than in previous eras is that they can expect cases to be easily resolved in the plea bargaining process. This is due, in no small part, to how the laws are currently structured, allowing prosecutors to get away with being highly aggressive with few checks or limits on that power.

Notes/Questions

1. Should judges have the power to review charging decisions to reduce the impact on imprisonment rates?

2. Are there changes that you might suggest that would help to reduce the impact of prosecutorial power to file charges?

B. Prosecutor Conduct during Plea Bargaining

Cynthia Alkon, *Hard Bargaining in Plea Bargaining: When Do Prosecutors Cross the Line?*

17 Nev. L.J. 401, 406–413 (2017)

II. Hard Bargaining

....

In the negotiation literature, hard bargaining can refer to a vast array of negotiation tactics that fall broadly under the category of adversarial, competitive, distributive, positional, or zero-sum bargaining. These terms are often used inter-changeably to describe a type of negotiation behavior that is not problem-solving, cooperative, integrative, or interest based. However, this article is not using the term "hard bargaining" in this broad sense but rather is defining hard bargaining to be specific prosecutorial

---

7. Michelle Alexander, The New Jim Crow: Mass Incarceration in the Age of Color-Blindness 86 (2010).

Does Every Crime Have to Be Charged?

As you read in Chapter 2, long-time criminal defense lawyer Larry Krasner was elected DA in Philadelphia in November 2017. Krasner instructed his lawyers to:

> decline charges for marijuana possession, no matter the weight, effectively decriminalizing possession of the drug in the city for all nonfederal cases. Sex workers will not be charged with prostitution unless they have more than two priors, in which case they'll be diverted to a specialized court. Retail theft under $500 is no longer a misdemeanor in the eyes of Philly prosecutors, but a summary offense—the lowest possible criminal charge. And when ADAs give probation charges they are to opt for the lower end of the possible spectrum. "Criminological studies show that most violations of probation occur within the first 12 months," the memo reads. "Assuming that a defendant is violation free for 12 months, any remaining probation is simply excess baggage requiring unnecessary expenditure of funds for supervision."

Maura Ewing, *Philadelphia's New Top Prosecutor Is Rolling Out Wild, Unprecedented Criminal Justice Reforms,* Slate, March 14, 2018, available at: https://slate.com/news-and-politics/2018/03/phillys-new-top-prosecutor-is-rolling-out-wild-unprecedented-criminal-justice-reforms.html.

As a criminal defense lawyer working in Philadelphia, how would these policy changes impact your negotiation strategies in plea bargaining new cases? As a prosecutor, how would you react to this change in policy?

tactics in plea bargaining that make further negotiation nearly impossible and leave the defendant with an immediate, or near immediate decision of whether to take the deal or go to trial.

Even under this narrower definition, prosecutorial hard bargaining tactics are routine. But, this is not to suggest that every plea negotiation or even a majority of plea negotiations include hard bargaining tactics. Young and less experienced prosecutors may use hard bargaining tactics. Prosecutors who are difficult people or who think that all negotiations should be highly adversarial may use hard bargaining tactics. Prosecutors who have political motivations, such as wanting to show they are "tough on drunk driving" may use hard bargaining practices. Prosecutors who want to manage their caseloads may use hard bargaining tactics. Prosecutors may also use hard bargaining tactics on some cases when they are, for whatever reason, reacting more emotionally to the case and want to ensure a conviction. And, in cases that bring even greater concern, prosecutors may use hard bargaining tactics to cover up for a weak case where they are concerned they might not otherwise secure a conviction or when they are worried that they will lose in an expected search and seizure motion. It is hard to know how frequently hard bargaining tactics are used, as there are so few empirical studies of the plea bargaining process itself. However, the likely fact that prosecutors are not using hard bargaining tactics in the majority of their cases does not mean that there is not a need for restrictions and better rules to prevent hard bargaining tactics.

Examples of hard bargaining tactics include "exploding offers" when a prosecutor threatens that the deal is good "today only" or for some other restricted time period (such as until the case is called). Another standard hard bargaining tactic is for the prosecutor to threaten to add an enhancement, such as the use of a gun, which adds mandatory minimum jail time. A third hard bargaining tactic is to threaten to add additional charges that carry additional time, sometimes also as a mandatory minimum. A fourth hard bargaining tactic is to phrase the offer as a "take it or leave it" offer and refuse any further negotiation. Finally, a fifth concern is when prosecutors threaten to proceed with the case as a death penalty case unless the defendant takes the deal. As will be discussed below, prosecutors often use more than one hard bargaining tactic in the same case.

A. Exploding Offers

Plea offers are often made with time limits attached. Prosecutors can put time limits on a plea offer for legitimate reasons. For example, if a case involves child witnesses or sexual assault victims, making an offer that is good until the first proceeding when the child or sexual assault victim may have to take the witness stand and testify, is appropriate. The goal in these circumstances would be to protect the victims from having to testify. However, exploding offers are often made with no reason beyond pressuring the defendant to take the deal. This happens in both misdemeanor and felony cases. Defendants are routinely put in the position of having to decide on the day of the arraignment, which is often the first day they are meeting and talking with their lawyer, whether to accept a plea deal or not. Prosecutors routinely tell defendants and their lawyers that if they reject the deal that is good "today only" they will face a higher sentence as the prosecutor will never again make that "low" plea offer. In some cases prosecutors will make a specific threat, such as, "today I'm offering 6 months in the county-jail, if you don't accept this deal today, the next time out the best we will do is 3 years in state prison."

B. Threats to Add Enhancements

Over the last four decades, penal codes have been amended and revised to allow the same act to be charged in a variety of ways. One of the standard changes in penal codes has been the addition of a number of enhancements that can add time to the underlying criminal offense. Often these enhancements, once added to the offense, add mandatory time. This means that if the defendant is convicted of the offense, including the enhancement, the judge will not be able, under the law, to sentence the defendant to anything but the mandatory time. For example, the offense of sales of a controlled substance has one penalty, but if the sale was in a school zone, additional time is added. Gun use and prior criminal convictions are also standard enhancements that can add serious time. One example, from the federal system, is the case of Lulzim Kupa who was charged with distributing cocaine.[8] Mr. Kupa rejected the initial plea offer, however two weeks prior to his trial date, the prosecution gave notice of two prior marijuana convictions. The addition of these two prior convictions increased the possible penalty to life in prison. The federal system has no parole, so life in prison is life without parole. Mr. Kupa then agreed to accept a plea offer and was sentenced to eleven years in prison and the prosecution agreed to withdraw the notice of the prior convictions. While there might be reasons other than putting pressure on the defendant that the notice of prior convictions was added after Mr. Kupa rejected the plea deal, the timing is suspect and appears to have been done to exert pressure on Mr. Kupa to take the deal.

Criminal codes allow for extreme mandatory penalties if prosecutors add the right enhancement. Once the enhancement is added, and the defendant is convicted at trial, the law often allows for no discretion by a sentencing judge. However, the prosecution has the discretion to withdraw the enhancement as part of a plea deal, as ultimately happened with Mr. Kupa.

C. Threats to Add Additional Charges

Just as criminal codes now allow for a variety of possible enhancements, there are also a variety of ways in which the same act can be charged. For example, many acts can be charged as either felonies or misdemeanors. In addition, the same act can result in one criminal charge, or multiple criminal charges, depending on how the prosecutor chooses to look at it. One example of this is the case of Marissa Alexander.[9] Ms. Alexander was originally charged with one count of aggravated assault with a deadly weapon in Florida. The case started when Ms. Alexander shot her gun in the air "one time" during a fight with her estranged husband. Ms. Alexander's defense was that on the day in question her husband grabbed her neck and threatened to kill her. The trial judge, in error, shifted the burden of proof in the "stand your ground" defense to Ms. Alexander during jury instructions. The jury convicted Ms. Alexander and due to the mandatory "use a gun" law in Florida, Ms. Alexander was sentenced to twenty years in prison. Ms. Alexander's case was overturned on appeal due to an error in the jury instructions and sent back for a re-trial. Before her first trial the prosecution offered three years in prison in exchange for a guilty plea to aggravated assault (without the gun use allegation). Ms. Alexander rejected that deal and went to trial. After the appellate court ordered a re-trial, the prosecutor added additional charges of aggravated assault, one for each of her two children who were present, in addition to her estranged husband. Those additional charges made the possible maximum sentence sixty years in prison, as there was a mandatory twenty year "use a gun" allegation with each charge. Ms. Alexander ultimately chose to take the three year plea deal that the prosecutor eventually

---

8. United States v. Kupa, No. 11-CR-345 (E.D.N.Y. Oct. 9, 2013). See also Human Rights Watch, An Offer you Can't Refuse: How US Federal Prosecutors Force Drug Defendants to Plead Guilty 5 (2013), https://www.hrw.org/report/2013/12/05/offer-you-cant-refuse/how-us-federal-prosecutors-force-drug-defendants-plead [https://perma.cc/K9C2-KUTN].

9. Marissa Alexander v. State of Florida, 121 So. 3d 1185, 1186 (Fla 1st DCA 2013).

offered again. By that time, Ms. Alexander was just weeks away from completing the three year term.

D. Take It or Leave It Offers

Related to and often accompanying threats to add enhancements and charges are take-it-or-leave-it offers. The prosecution may decide early on in the case that only a certain penalty is appropriate and refuse to negotiate. This happens in the context of "standard deals" when certain kinds of cases are routinely plea bargained for the same punishment. Driving under the influence of alcohol and drug possession cases are examples of cases that often have standard offers. The Aaron Swartz case provides an example of prosecutors using stiff penalties in the existing law and refusing to negotiate beyond a take it or leave it deal. Aaron Swartz was an activist who thought there should be free access to information on the internet. He set up a computer at MIT to download articles from the database JSTOR. Mr. Swartz intended to make the information freely available and never intended to sell it or profit from it. Initially Mr. Swartz was charged with four counts of violating federal computer fraud and abuse statutes, which carried a maximum of thirty-five years in prison and a $1 million fine. Fourteen months later, the Department of Justice indicted Mr. Swartz on thirteen counts of violating federal computer fraud and abuse statutes, increasing the possible penalty to fifty years in prison. Mr. Swartz had no prior criminal record. JSTOR was not "interested in this becoming an on-going legal matter" as all of the information was returned.

The prosecutor offered six months in custody in exchange for pleading to several felony counts. Mr. Swartz rejected the offer. On January 13, 2013, a year and half after the prosecution began, Mr. Swartz committed suicide. Mr. Swartz's suicide led to a flurry of questions about the aggressive prosecution and the plea bargaining process in his case, as Swartz's family and friends argued that the aggressive prosecution was a contributing factor to his suicide. One commentator asked "If [the prosecutor] thought that Swartz only deserved to spend 6 months in jail, why did she charge him with crimes carrying a maximum penalty of 50 years?" Darrell Issa, the Chairman of the House Committee on Oversight and Government Reform asked "[a]re we using excess prosecution, excess claims, in order to force guilty pleas?" In a letter to then Attorney General Eric Holder, the House Committee asked questions about the plea offers and how the charges and offers compared to other cases prosecuted under the Computer Fraud and Abuse Act. During the hearing itself, Texas Senator John Cornyn said, "I'm concerned that average citizens, if you can call them that, like Aaron Swartz, people who don't have status and power, perhaps, in dealing with the federal government, could be bullied."

Mr. Kupa's drug case and Ms. Alexander's assault case were both also "take it or leave it" plea offers. And, both also carried potentially high sentences if the defendant refused the plea deal. The problem with take it or leave it offers, especially when combined with potentially heavy sentences after trial, is that defendants often consider cases with good defense (such as Ms. Alexander's case) to be too risky to take to trial. Prosecutors can ratchet up the possible penalties on weaker cases, such as Ms. Alexander's case, and

No More Overcharging in Philadelphia?

Philadelphia DA Larry Krasner said "We are not going to overcharge ... we are not going to try to coerce defendants. We are going to proceed on charges that are supported by the facts in the case, period. The era of trying to get away with the highest charge regardless of the facts is over." Krasner also requires that he personally agree to offer any plea deal over 15–30 years in prison. This has included a willingness to charge homicides as manslaughter and not murder, as would have happened under other DAs in Philadelphia.

Maura Ewing, *America's Leading Reform-Minded District Attorney Has Taken His Most Radical Step Yet*, Slate, December 4, 2018.

A New Era in San Francisco?

In contrast to Philadelphia, after San Francisco voted out progressive prosecutor Chesa Boudin in 2022 as District Attorney, long time Deputy District Attorney Brooke Jenkins was appointed and then elected to the position. After her first year in office, Jenkins said, "We have filed almost doubled the number of cases the prior administration filed in the same period of time. That's over 800 cases that were filed in my first year." In addition, Jenkins pledged that any drug dealer who is linked to a victim's fatal overdose will be charged with murder.

Amy Larson & Haaziq Madyun, "Jenkins talks about her first year as San Francisco DA", KRON 4, July 12, 2023.

refuse to negotiate a better deal (for example, insisting that first time offenders must go to prison), and leave defendants with the choice to either plead guilty to cases where they may not be guilty, or to accept higher sentences than the case may deserve.

E. Threats to Seek the Death Penalty

Although a threat to seek the death penalty can be considered a threat to add an enhancement, or new charge (depending on the jurisdiction), this prosecutorial threat is different in that the threat is to impose the ultimate penalty. In the context of this discussion, therefore, it is potentially even more coercive, although it involves a smaller sub-set of defendants.

It is not unusual for the defendant to offer to plead guilty in exchange for life in prison without parole in death penalty cases. However, this is when the prosecution has already filed the charges, or sought an indictment, for the case as a death penalty case. Although there is undoubtedly pressure to accept any offered plea deal in a death penalty case, the concern, for purposes of this discussion, is those cases where the prosecution is using the possibility of the death penalty as leverage to extract a guilty plea.

Notes/Questions

1. If you were a prosecutor, would you want to use any of these hard bargaining tactics? Why?

2. If you were a defense lawyer, would you want to use any of these hard bargaining tactics? Which ones do you think might be more realistic for a defense lawyer to use?

3. When you read Chapter Seven, you will want to think about what negotiation tactics and skills may help you if you confront hard bargaining tactics during plea negotiations.

4. Should hard bargaining tactics be limited? In other negotiation contexts, hard bargaining is restricted. For example, in labor negotiations, hard bargaining can be a form of bad faith negotiation, which is prohibited under the National Labor Relations Act. Should a similar restriction be adopted in the context of plea bargaining? See Cynthia Alkon, *Hard Bargaining in Plea Bargaining: When Do Prosecutors Cross the Line?*, 17 Nev. L.J. 401 (2017).

5. Should prosecutors get bonuses for how they do their jobs? A District Attorney in Colorado gave prosecutors bonuses if they had "at least five trials during the year, with 70 percent of them ending in a felony conviction. Plea bargains or mistrials don't count."[10] The DA, in explaining this policy said, "this is a trial office. I don't think that comes as a surprise to anyone If you are doing the job, you are going to necessarily go to trial. We plea bargain most of our cases so that we can try the others." A DA from another county in Colorado expressed concern about this policy stating, "If you're to seek justice and yet your pay is based on the number of cases you take to trial or your conviction rate, then it clouds your discretion. They have an incentive not to make a reasonable disposition if they need one more trial or another conviction in order to get a bonus." Will this incentive structure encourage fair plea bargains? Are there ethical issues? What might be the unintended consequences of this policy?

6. Prosecutors may offer a defendant a better deal if they will "cooperate" by giving information on others who could be prosecuted. This is done more often in the federal system and under federal law, where a defendant who agrees to cooperate could get a sentence reduction for the assistance (which should be substantial assistance) or a post-sentence reduction. One defense lawyer remarked: "Cooperation is a horrible thing for clients. Doing law enforcement's job and requiring someone to bargain for their freedom encourages an ugly, unfair, and unjust system to become even more so

---

10. Jessica Fender, *DA Chambers Offers Bonuses for Prosecutors Who Hit Conviction Targets*, Denver Post, March 23, 2011, available at http://www.denverpost.com/2011/03/23/da-chambers-offers-bonuses-for-prosecutors-who-hit-conviction-targets/.

that way."[11] A recent study found that defense lawyers view the process as unfair and would like more training on this topic. Law enforcement considers cooperation in some cases, such as organized crime cases, to be vital to secure convictions for higher level operators. Defendants can face retaliation and social stigma as snitches. From a plea bargaining point of view, a prosecutor's offer to cooperate could be a hard bargaining tactic. If a defendant has little leverage, and is facing serious time in prison, the offer of a sentence reduction may look attractive and a defendant may not think they have any other option. What if a prosecutor knows that the defendant has no prior criminal record? What if they file charges that virtually guarantee time in prison, unless the defendant cooperates? Or guarantee substantial time in prison? What about an innocent defendant who is faced with this choice? Should there be strict guidelines about cooperation? Should those be internal prosecutor office policies, or should the criminal codes limit what reductions can, or should, be given in sentences due to cooperation? For more information see Jessica A. Roth, et al., *Why Criminal Defendants Cooperate: The Defense Attorney's Perspective*, 117 Northwestern University Law Review, 1351 (2023).

C. Constraints on Prosecutorial Power?

Related to the concern about prosecutorial conduct during plea bargaining is the concern that the Supreme Court has failed to place any meaningful limits on prosecutor's power in the context of plea bargaining. This next reading will refer to cases discussed in Chapter Three.

Josh Bowers, *Fundamental Fairness and the Path from* Santobello *to* Padilla: *A Response to Professor Bibas*

2 Cal. L. Rev. Circuit 52, 56–61 (2011)

....

II. THE PATH TO *PADILLA*

Significantly, however, what is true of constitutional trial procedure is not true of constitutional guilty-plea procedure. In the plea-bargaining and guilty-plea contexts, the accuracy principle has played a smaller role as compared to fundamental fairness. For example, consider the Court's early plea-bargaining ruling in *Santobello v. New York* [404 U.S. 257 (1971)]. In that case, the Court held that prosecutors violated a defendant's constitutional rights by promising to make no sentencing recommendation, but by thereafter asking the sentencing judge to impose the maximum sentence on a reduced charge. The Court reasoned that "when a plea rests in any significant degree

11. Anonymous federal defense lawyer from a survey in Jessica A. Roth, et al., *Why Criminal Defendants Cooperate: The Defense Attorney's Perspective*, 117 Northwestern University Law Review, 1351 (2023).

on a promise or agreement of the prosecutor, so that it can be said to be part of the inducement or consideration, such promise must be fulfilled."

The significance of the decision is often misunderstood. Bibas cites the case only to underscore the point that the Court encourages disposition by plea. And, no doubt, *Santobello* stands for that proposition. However, the decision signifies much more. First, it is noteworthy that the Court vacated the sentence *even though* it found no prejudice. Specifically, the Court took the government at its word that the prosecutor's breach of the plea agreement was inadvertent, and accepted the trial judge's assertion that he would have imposed the maximum sentence in any event:

> We need not reach the question whether the sentencing judge would or would not have been influenced had he known all the details of the negotiations for the plea. He stated that the prosecutor's recommendation did not influence him *and we have no reason to doubt that.*

In short, the Court accepted that the sentence was *accurate*—that is, that the defendant would have received the same sentence even in the absence of a constitutional violation. Nevertheless, the Court provided a constitutional remedy, because the Court concluded that it would have been fundamentally unfair to do otherwise. Thus, accuracy played no part in the Court's calculation.

Second, the opinion is remarkably uninformative. Indeed, the Court never even signaled what constitutional right the prosecutor violated. Perhaps the opinion's obscurity was tactical. In any event, it is telling. A frank discussion of due-process jurisprudence would have forced the Court to acknowledge that it was applying a more expansive version of fundamental fairness to guilty-plea procedures than to trial procedures. Specifically, the prevailing fundamental-fairness test at the time was whether the procedure in question "shock[ed] the conscience"—whether it "more than offend[ed] some fastidious squeamishness or private sentimentalism." But, significantly, had the Court applied such a rigorous fundamental-fairness standard to the facts of *Santobello*, it would have had no choice but to reject the defendant's constitutional claim, because a prosecutor's inadvertent breach surely does not shock the conscience, especially where—as the *Santobello* Court assumed—the breach had no influence on the sentencing judge.

Essentially, the *Santobello* Court held unconstitutional a plea-bargaining breach that was more slip-up than "rack and screw." Thus, the import of *Santobello* is not just that the Court appealed to fundamental fairness as opposed to accuracy, but that it did so *generously*. The question is why the Court deemed it appropriate to adopt what might be called a kind of *fundamental fairness with bite* for pleas but not for trials. On this score, I think Bibas has hit upon the answer: when it comes to guilty pleas, the Court assumes that the pleading defendant is factually guilty. Thus, fundamental fairness is the focus because there is little else on which to concentrate once the Court has deemed the accuracy question beside the point. Put differently, if fundamental fairness lacks bite, then the Constitution has almost no bite at all in the guilty-plea context.

And, significantly, *Santobello* is no outlier. Rather, the case is consistent with the Court's conventional methodological approach to plea-bargaining and guilty-plea cases. For example, in *Brady v. United States*, [397 U.S. 742 (1970),] the Court held that a conviction by plea must be intelligent and voluntary—that is, that the conviction must be the product of fair procedures designed to promote fully informed and free choice. First, as to the voluntariness requirement, the *Brady* Court forbade "actual or threatened physical harm ... [,] mental coercion overbearing the will of the defendant," and "misrepresentation[s] ..., or ... promises that ... hav[e] no proper relationship to the prosecutor's business." In other words, it prohibited prosecutors from engaging in manifestly unfair conduct of the kind that might invalidate a civil contract. Second, as to the intelligence requirement, the *Brady* Court demanded that a defendant be made aware of the nature of the charges, the rights waived, and the consequences of pleading guilty. Taken together, then, these constitutional requirements protect against unfair threats or promises and the unfair surprise of unforeseen consequences, misrepresentations, or other shady dealings.

Even the Court's somewhat infamous decision in *Bordenkircher v. Hayes* [434 U.S. 357 (1978)] was not inattentive to principles of fundamental fairness. In that decision, the Court found no due-process violation where the defendant declined a plea to a five-year prison term, whereupon the prosecutor made good on a threat to file a habitual-offender charge that carried a mandatory life sentence. Unquestionably, the *Bordenkircher* Court authorized hard bargaining. However, hard bargaining and unconstrained bargaining are not one and the same. Significantly, the Court found dispositive the fact that the defendant saw the habitual-offender charge coming. It held, therefore, that the prosecutor's threat was merely part of the transparent "give-and-take" of plea-bargaining. In short, the defendant was not *surprised* by the added charge, and, thus, he could make no constitutional claim.

Notice, then, that this same notion of unfair surprise runs through all three cases—*Brady*, *Santobello*, and *Bordenkircher*. The only difference is that in *Santobello*, the Court found unfair surprise, whereas in *Brady* and *Bordenkircher*, it did not. This is not to say that the Court sufficiently regulated the guilty-plea regime pre-*Padilla* [*v. Kentucky*, 559 U.S. 356 (2010)], but only that its approach was consistent, coherent, and decidedly not *caveat emptor*. And this is the point that I think Bibas misses. He confuses an indifference toward accuracy with an indifference toward constitutional regulation altogether. He mistakes an under-regulated market for an unregulated market. Put simply, he sees too little in the path to *Padilla*. And, beyond that, he sees too much in the *Padilla* decision itself. Precisely, he considers *Padilla* to be an opinion principally about substance, not procedure—an effort by the Court to substantively "evaluate whether [a plea] punishment is fitting." But *Padilla* is no more a case about *substantive* fairness than *Brady* or *Santobello*, and it is therefore no obvious harbinger of substantive things to come. In all three cases, substantive results are regulated practically only to the extent that they are products of unfair *procedures*: *Brady* instituted minimum (and, as indicated, almost certainly insufficient) procedural safeguards; *Santobello* ensured that prosecutors act according to their promises; and *Padilla* obliged counsel to advise noncitizen clients about certain sufficiently serious noncriminal consequences of conviction. Thus, a clean line runs from *Brady* to *Padilla*, and it is a principally procedural line—to wit, *Brady* made certain that the defendant is "fully aware of the direct consequences" of pleading guilt, and *Padilla* extended that guarantee to immigration consequences (and possibly much more).

Moreover, the Court achieved this procedural extension without abandoning its former interpretive commitments. As before, unfair surprise remains the focus, and accuracy remains a practical irrelevancy. The difference is that now, for the first time, the Court has announced that it may constitute unfair surprise for a defendant to plead guilty when he is blind to certain meaningful consequences that were formerly considered collateral. On this reading, the Court did not "drag the law into the twenty-first century." It gave the old law new teeth.

The consistency of the Court's interpretive approach raises a more general point about fundamental fairness. Some have faulted the concept as too mutable to provide the basis for principled constitutional regulation. But it is this very same capacious quality that permits fundamental fairness to occasionally admit appropriate change over time. I concede that there are dangers to the enterprise of constitutional regulation premised on soft principle, but, sometimes, fundamental fairness may provide the Court with a useful and constructive foothold. And, to my thinking, this is just such a setting. More than ever, the severity and scope of so-called collateral consequences are genuine, expansive, and significant. In *Padilla*, the Court justifiably recognized and responded to this reality. It determined that counsel can, and constitutionally *must*, advise clients about all sufficiently meaningful consequences of conviction—that is, all consequences that are "intimately related to the criminal process" or that are "integral part[s] of the penalty."

Nevertheless, because *Padilla*—like *Santobello*, *Brady*, and *Bordenkircher* before it—principally regulates the fairness of constitutional criminal *procedure*, it can do only so much to promote what Bibas and I both believe ought to be a paramount objective: *substantively* fair guilty-plea sentencing. The decision fails to constrain constitutionally the breadth and depth of criminal codes, and, thus, it cannot address adequately what Bibas appropriately identifies as some of plea-bargaining's most significant dangers. Specifically, a prosecutor still may stack criminal charges "to hide [her] weak hand" or to "induce [the] defendant[] to surrender [his] Cadillac trial[] in exchange for [a] scooter plea bargain[]." And a legislature still may "multiply overlapping criminal statutes and inflate sentences to give prosecutors extra plea-bargaining chips." Bibas recognizes that an increasing proportion of convictions "trigger automatic collateral consequences, such as deportation or sex-offender residency restrictions," but he does not appreciate sufficiently that *Padilla* has left those triggers firmly in place. The decision has merely changed what a defense attorney must say *ex ante* to her client about the potential application of those triggers.

Thus, even after *Padilla*, the defendant has no constitutional claim as long as he pleads guilty with his eyes open. *Padilla* has merely made bargaining *processes* fairer. Any unduly harsh penalty that may follow such fair processes is taken to be, in *Bordenkircher*'s words, just part of the "give-and-take" of plea-bargaining. Put differently, the substantive law may be unfair, but the well-informed defendant is never *unfairly surprised*. Once again, the *Padilla* decision has kept true to its roots. In *Bordenkircher*, the Court affirmed the ability of a prosecutor to threaten a substantively draconian life sentence for a relatively nominal offense like forgery, and, in *Padilla*, the Court affirmed the ability of the prosecutor to threaten automatic deportation for even a marijuana conviction.

Notes/Questions

1. What kinds of rules or limitations on prosecutorial behavior might make sense to add into the plea bargaining process?

2. As a prosecutor, what might you want to do in the plea bargaining process to be sure that there would be no "unfair surprises" such as in *Santobello*?

V. Impact on Lawyering Skills Development and the Adversarial System

The United States has an adversarial system of justice. As we have noted (and criticized in the context of plea bargaining), procedural and evidentiary rules developed to work within an adversarial system. If most cases are negotiated, and not tried, does this undermine our adversarial system? One related issue is the impact that this has on overall lawyering skills. Can prosecutors who rarely try cases appropriately evaluate the strength of their evidence when plea bargaining? Is there a risk that they may not be able to recognize bad evidence or recognize when there might be a problem with the evidence at trial? Although there are fewer criminal trials, as you will read in the next chapter, training in prosecutor and public defender offices still focuses more on trial skills and less on negotiation skills. Many prosecutors and defense lawyers receive no training for negotiation. The next two articles were written by federal judges, in 2006 and 2018, both decrying the decrease in trial rates and the impact this is having both on society at large and on how law is practiced. As you read these two articles, consider the impact of low trial rates on lawyering skills.

Honorable William G. Young, *Vanishing Trials, Vanishing Juries, Vanishing Constitution*

40 Suffolk L. Rev. 67, 76, 79–81 (2006)

...

Consider the judicial role in the decline of the American jury. Part of the picture is substantive. In *Patton v. United States*, the Supreme Court held that the "framers of the Constitution simply were intent upon preserving the right of trial by jury primarily for the protection of the accused." In so holding, the Court essentially read Article III's jury mandate out of the Constitution. Today, our federal criminal justice system is all about plea bargaining. Trials—and, thus, juries—are largely extraneous. An accused individual who requests a trial may, as a functional matter (though we obstinately deny it), be punished severely for requesting what was once a constitutional right. Moreover, offenders today are routinely and severely punished for crimes with which they have never been charged, and, even more incredibly, for crimes for which a jury has acquitted them....

Of paramount importance, however, is a matter neither of substance nor procedure, but culture. We federal trial judges appear no longer to revere the jury trial as the central and paramount goal of our American system of justice. We have so "deconstructed the role of the trial judge" that today far too many judges do not understand the concept. Between 1980 and 2002, average on-bench time among active district judges declined from 790 hours to 490 hours. Indeed, some knowledgeable commentators observe that we "trial" judges appear no longer very interested in doing our jobs.

The results of our own indifference toward jury trials are already sadly apparent. Because we no longer seem very interested in using our courtrooms, we are losing them. Further, the institutional judiciary seems bent on dismantling the superb professional teams so essential to sustained trial operations. Somehow, we seem to be forgetting that the very reason for our judicial existence is to afford jury trials to our people pursuant to the United States Constitution. Ironically, our ability to control our dockets to avoid the quotidian details of daily jury trials and save ourselves instead for "really big" constitutional adjudication insures that such cases will come our way less frequently.

The shift from trials as the central icon of the federal courts to a "settlement culture" may be traced back to the tenure of Chief Justice Warren E. Burger. This "settlement culture" reached its apogee between 1990 and 1995, when the Hon. William W. Schwarzer served as Director of the Federal Judicial Center. A distinguished judge and author, Judge Schwarzer is an outspoken advocate of managing cases toward settlement.

Having set themselves adrift from their constitutional partner—the American Jury—federal trial judges now find themselves bereft of the central wellspring of their moral authority. Public disparagement and Congressional disdain follow in the wake of this trend.

* * *

Twelve years later, Judge Robert Conrad, and Katy Clements wrote about the continuing decrease in jury trials stating that federal "trial judges" are now "increasingly seen as 'sentencing judges'" while criminal defense attorneys are more "sentencing advocates" than "trial lawyers." Conrad and Clements conclude that the reasons for the decrease in trial rates include the increase in mandatory minimums and the impact of the *United States v. Booker*, which declared the federal sentencing guidelines were not mandatory and by doing so increased the importance of the sentencing hearing. Conrad and Clements discuss the reasons we should care about the decrease in jury trial rates in the excerpt below.

Robert J. Conrad Jr. & Katy L. Clements, *The Vanishing Criminal Jury Trial: From Trial Judges to Sentencing Judges*

86 Geo. Wash. L. Rev. 99, 157–163 (January 2018)

. . .

IV. THE CONSEQUENCES

Jury trials are on the verge of extinction, but so what? Does the jury trial diminution truly represent an American tragedy? Or, is it a sign of national progress and improved productivity? Part IV explores the ramifications of a system dominated by plea agreements.

A. *The System's Loss*

The absence of jury trials makes the judicial process more secretive and contravenes the "presumption of openness [that] inheres in the very nature of a criminal trial under [the American] system of justice." Trials provide a public forum for the airing of grievances, yet the death of trials marks the end of doing justice where disputes are played out under the attentive eye of judge and jury. In an adversarial trial system, judges and lawyers welcome the presence of outsiders, both as witnesses and as active participants. The courtroom becomes a theater, where all actors and observers are welcome. The courtroom record created in trials becomes a script, immortalizing the details of the case, the attorneys' arguments, and the jury's final decision. And trials attract media attention, expanding awareness to the general public.

These realities are not present in the plea process. Following the Rule 11 hearing, United States Probation Officers prepare and distribute presentence reports to the parties under seal. Each side has an opportunity to contest the factual and legal conclusions. Parties often file sentencing memoranda under seal as a result of citation to the sealed presentence reports. Much has already been agreed to on paper without adversarial testing. That which is to be litigated at the sentencing hearing frequently involves Babel-like intramural fights between attorneys, refereed by the judge, over cryptic terms. For example, the parties may litigate whether a defendant's mitigating role can be described as minimal (four-level reduction) or minor (two-level reduction), or if the court cannot choose between the two, then it can grant a three-level reduction. The determination of whether an enhancement should apply for possession of a firearm in connection with an offense—another recurring squabble at sentencing hearings—depends on whether it is "clearly improbable" that the weapon was connected to the offense. The ever-changing Guidelines contain over 600 pages of these relevant, yet non-self-defining, distinctions. Lawyers are directed to consult the Guidelines language and where there is ambiguity, glean from the commentary, to assist in the determination. Never-ending circuit court opinions construing both the Guidelines and commentary in question require a third level of scrutiny. The circuits often split and rarely does the Supreme Court enter the fray to resolve the issue.

Suppose you are a courtroom spectator, a mother whose son has just been sentenced, or a victim whose life's savings have been swindled. You cannot understand a word that is being said. The lawyers speak in strange ways about unseen things, in foreign phrases and terms that do not seem connected to ultimate or tangible matters. Usually the first question asked of the lawyer at the end of the sentencing hearing is, "What happened?" This everyday occurrence is the antithesis of the catharsis and clarity that emerge from a well-tried jury case. Trials send a clear message that wrongdoing has consequences and innocence has rewards. There is third-party (jury) validation of the government's use of power. Or not. The current dominance of plea resolution eliminates all this and adds to the perception of an impersonalized justice system. Obscurity and secrecy supplant the public-square openness of trials.

B. *The Guild's Loss*

In addition to sparking a trial decline, settling criminal cases by plea agreements stunts the development of case law. Precedential rulings undergird the American judicial system. A lawyer's ability to successfully analogize or distinguish his case to or from prior cases can determine the outcome of his client's case. Just as the mandatory Guidelines gave attorneys a barometer for predicting sentencing outcomes given similar offense conduct and criminal histories, jury verdicts inform lawyers' future advice on guilt and innocence questions.

New law develops when appellate judges review decisions reached by lower courts. In the criminal system, lower courts most frequently make those decisions through trials. In the civil system, new law can be formed through summary judgments and judgments on the pleadings. The criminal system does not contain analogs to these civil dispositions. In contrast, plea agreements often contain mandatory waiver provisions of the defendant's rights to trial and appeal. These provisions could also be termed "precedent waivers" as they essentially ensure that no new case law will develop from these defendants' cases. Plea agreements eliminate the need for judges to decide difficult evidentiary questions. The vanishing trial trend could curtail the development of legal doctrine and perpetuate the gradual staling of case law. Appellate courts are not given opportunities to develop or apply precedent to new facts. And lawyers are left on increasingly shaky ground when advising future clients in novel areas of law.

Lost opportunity to apply precedent to new facts is not the only negative consequence to the legal guild. Trial skills are both art and science and are lost if not practiced. Instructional programs in law schools and other trial advocacy settings have admirably attempted to fill the gap. But there is nothing like a jury trial with real-life consequences to equip lawyers to better handle real-life cases. The more time that passes between trials, the more time lost confidence has to set in. With fewer trials come fewer opportunities to hone trial skills. More attorneys fear going to trial because of lack of experience and diminished confidence. This presents a catch-22 dilemma: attorneys have more incentive to avoid trial because of their lack of experience, which in turn prevents them from ever gaining trial experience. Less trial experience also weakens attorneys' abilities to accurately evaluate case outcomes, which results in less-informed plea negotiations.

What has been said about the atrophy of attorney trial skills applies with equal force to trial judges. Judges need regular opportunities to sharpen their presiding skills. One of the remarkable things learned when the undersigned switched seats in the courtroom from advocate to presider (or as one coauthor's friend suggested, from player to benchwarmer) is the different skill set necessary to excel. As an advocate, outcomes turn on preparation—interviews, strategy, examination outlines, and anticipation of evidentiary issues. As a judge, success often depends on reflexive ruling relying on past experience to resolve present trial objections. It takes practice and repetition to do this well. And judges are not getting it. This lack of trial experience over the long term will result in fewer skilled trial advocates being nominated to the bench. And once confirmed, those on the bench will have less opportunity to warm it. In today's trial-less climate, judges have fewer occasions to improve their trial skills. This bodes poorly for our justice system.

C. *The Defendant's Loss*

The absence of the jury trial negatively impacts criminal defendants. By accepting a plea agreement, a defendant waives his constitutional right to present his story to a fresh set of eyes. Deciding the fate of a potential criminal is not a normal, everyday occurrence for the jury. Juries know that being selected to play this important role in the administration of justice is an honor and a duty, and the court instructs jurors not to take their job lightly. Juries understand that their decisions have great implications.

Most defendants recognize that the guilt determination will likely be the same regardless of whether they accept a plea agreement or proceed to trial. The high federal conviction rate solidifies this reality. However, the United States has always ascribed value to processes, not merely outcomes. Indeed, one of *Gideon*'s central tenets is that the Constitution entitles all defendants to have equal access to a right to fight. In a system where conviction is almost certain, the level of process received becomes a paramount concern of defense counsel and their clients. If the government is going to deprive defendants of their liberty, defendants at least want to be able to tell their side of the story. Brokering plea agreements, while faster and easier to process, necessarily involves less process than trials provide. Therefore, when defendants plead out, they forfeit their right to fight and minimize their opportunity to tell their stories.

In the overwhelming majority of cases resolved by plea, the presumption of innocence has been overcome by the defendant's admission of guilt. In many cases, this is just and fair to both sides. In close or weak cases, the absence of the potential for independent fact-finding by a neutral jury has weightier justice implications.

D. *The Jury's Loss*

The forgotten player of the criminal justice system—the jury—perhaps represents the gravest concern to those considering the disappearing criminal jury trial. The right to jury trial in criminal cases and concomitant presumption of innocence is a constitutional right that the jury and our society cannot "disregard[] ... at [their] pleasure." The jury, "the spinal column of American democracy" and only entity that the Framers designed to exist as a truly independent check on the criminal adjudication system, risks becoming obsolete. Jurors enjoy autonomy and take their oath of service seriously. They are told at the end of the case that they have been on the court's schedule throughout the trial, but now the court is on their schedule. They may stay late into the night or come back early the next week. On occasion, they choose to work over a weekend, and the court accommodates them. Rarely has the U.S. District Court for the WDNC interacted with a jury after a verdict without being left with a sense of wonder at the ability of a jury to get it right. Rarer still has been the occasion where the jurors do not leave with a sense of meaningful participation in the democratic process which jury service affords.

The paucity of trials deprives citizens of this meaningful opportunity to participate in democracy. Jury duty empowers the average citizen and elevates a citizen's role from member to decisionmaker. Besides voting, jury service is one of the only ways citizens can directly engage in and affect our government. The U.S. Court Handbook aptly states that "[t]here is no more valuable work that the average citizen can perform in support of our Government than the full and honest discharge of jury duty." In the WDNC, it is the court's practice to stand as the jury enters and leaves the courtroom. Jurors are the judges of the facts, and the judges of law acknowledge that in a small way by extending this courtesy.

Jurors often leave the jury-duty experience with a renewed sense of faith in the fairness and integrity of our government. However, as trials disappear, the risk of the public becoming increasingly disenchanted and distrustful of the American judicial system, and more importantly, of our democracy as a whole, becomes more real.

Notes/Questions

1. Do you share the judges' concern that not regularly exercising the constitutional right to trial is undermining that right?

2. And what about the concern of fewer jury trials? Although it is not the subject of this section, we can consider the larger impact of fewer jury trials and the community

connection (and support) that jury trials convey. Might jurisdictions that have very few jury trials lack support from the public? Or might the judges and prosecutors in that jurisdiction feel less connected and responsive to the community?

3. Do you share the concern that doing fewer trials is having a negative impact on lawyering skills? Conrad & Clements reported that sixteen out of thirty-three prosecutors in the Western District of North Carolina appeared "as counsel of record in a criminal trial" in 2016. During that same year, all thirty-three lawyers appeared in more than 900 sentencing hearings and supervised release revocation hearings.[12]

4. As a new prosecutor, would you want to go to a jurisdiction with higher or lower trial rates, particularly for misdemeanors (the type of case you would start your career prosecuting)?

5. As a new defense lawyer, would you want to be in a job where you would likely do more or less trials? Why?

6. If you support the idea that there should be more trials, how can you encourage more trials without the fear of poor incentives as is discussed above in the example from Colorado?

7. Beyond trial skills, does doing more trials help you to negotiate better deals? New public defenders are routinely advised to do as many trials as quickly as they can so "they will know you are not afraid of trial." Is that good advice? Why? Does it apply to prosecutors also? How does having a solid trial record help in negotiation?

Additional Resources

Albert W. Alschuler, *Plea Bargaining and Mass Incarceration*, 76 NYU Annual Survey of American Law, 205 (2021).

Lucian E. Dervan, *Bargained Justice: Plea-Bargaining's Innocence Problem and the Brady Safety-Valve*, 2012 UTLR 51 (2012).

Vanessa A. Edkins & Lucian Dervan, *Freedom Now or a Future Later: Pitting the Lasting Implications of Collateral Consequences Against Pretrial Detention in Decisions to Plead Guilty*, 24 Psychology, Public Policy, and Law 204–215 (2018).

A System of Pleas: Social Science's Contributions to the Real Legal System (Vanessa A. Edkins & Allison D. Redlich, eds) (2019).

Lisa Kern Griffin, *State Incentives, Plea Bargaining Regulation, and the Failed Market for Indigent Defense*, 80 Law & Contemp. Probs. 83 (2017).

Rebecca K. Helm, et al., *Too Young to Plead? Risk, Rationality and Plea Bargaining's Innocence Problem in Adolescents*, 24 Psychology, Public Policy, and Law 180–191 (2018).

12. Robert J. Conrad Jr. & Katy L. Clements, *The Vanishing Criminal Jury Trial: From Trial Judges to Sentencing Judges*, 86 Geo. Wash. L. Rev. 99, 102 (2018).

Rebecca K. Helm et al., *Limitations on the Ability to Negotiate Justice: Attorney Perspectives on Guilty, Innocence, and Legal Advice in the Current Plea System*, 24 PSYCHOLOGY, CRIME & LAW 915–934 (2018).

Kelsey S. Henderson & Lora M. Levett, *Investigation Predictors of True and False Guilty Pleas*, 42 LAW AND HUMAN BEHAVIOR 427–441 (2017).

Nancy J. King & Ronald F. Wright, *The Invisible Revolution in Plea Bargaining: Managerial Judging and Judicial Participation in Negotiations*, 95 TEX L. REV. 325 (2016).

Allison D. Redlick & Revka V. Shteynberg, *To Plead or Not to Plead: A Comparison of Juvenile and Adult True and False Plea Decisions*, 40, LAW AND HUMAN BEHAVIOR 611–625 (2016).

Allison D. Redlich et al., *The Psychology of Defendant Plea Decision Making*, 72 AM. PSYCHOLOGIST 339–352 (2017).

Miko M. Wilford & Gary Wells, *Bluffed by the Dealer: Distinguishing False Pleas from False Confessions*, 24 PSYCHOLOGY, PUBLIC POLICY, AND LAW 158–170 (2018).

Chapter 5

Plea Bargaining Reform

The concerns about plea bargaining have led to a variety of proposals for reform ranging from banning it outright to changes in law and practices. As you have read, plea bargaining is deeply embedded into the criminal legal system despite not being deeply woven into the laws. These long-standing practices are resistant to change. As you read about proposed reforms, and experiments with change, think about what types of policies might help to reduce the concerns of plea bargaining critics. For example, what policies or reforms might reduce the pressure on defendants to plead guilty when they are innocent? What kinds of changes in how plea bargaining works will be likely to have more support from the professionals in the system? And should that support matter? Understanding some of the basic concerns will help you to think about what reforms may help or what types of reform might be more of a priority, depending on the specific concern.

There are a variety of proposals to reform plea bargaining. This chapter will divide these proposals for change into four broad categories. The first category you will read about is changes in the underlying criminal law to lessen the pressure put on defendants to plead guilty. The second category for reform is to change the plea bargaining process itself through regulation and to encourage a focus on procedural justice through either banning plea bargaining or increasing trial rates. The third broad category of reform is to change how the defense lawyers, prosecutors and judges do their jobs. For example, giving defense lawyers better access to information may change how and if they plea bargain. Limiting hard bargaining behavior from prosecutors could limit the pressure put on defendants to plead guilty. Finally, judges could be more involved to help to lessen the power imbalances in plea bargaining. A recent study found that judges in many states are already involved in plea bargaining in ways that work both for prosecutors and defense lawyers. The fourth category, systemic change, would look at the larger criminal legal system and move beyond limited solutions and piecemeal approaches. Rather than only focusing on case resolution, system change would focus on how to make meaningful change as part of the larger and more complex criminal legal system. As you read these various reform proposals, think about what part of the criminal justice process is involved and who is required to act for the particular reform to happen. Some proposals focus on making change through the courts. Some proposals focus on legislative changes to the existing laws. Finally, some proposals seek to make change through changing policies and practices, not the law. Systemic change could focus on changes through all of these approaches working together.

Policy-makers and legislators often do not consider the impact that their changes in the law may have on plea bargaining practice. One example of this was the wave of legislative changes that increased possible criminal penalties and added a range of enhancements, such as the "use a gun go to jail" or "three strikes and you are out." These changes increased pressure on defendants to plead guilty to lessor offenses or face stiff penalties if they were convicted. Some of these defendants, as you have read, are innocent. An unintended consequence of these provisions, therefore, was to increase pressure on innocent defendants to plead guilty. Keep this example in mind as you read about these various reform proposals. What might be the unintended consequences? Would it help if policy-makers and legislators had a better understanding of how plea bargaining actually works so they could avoid these unintended consequences?

Since plea bargaining is deeply embedded into the criminal legal system, and, as was discussed in the beginning of the book, we in fact have many criminal legal systems in this country, changing how plea bargaining works is not something that can likely be achieved with one simple reform proposal. Even some of the simplest proposals, like banning plea bargaining, are difficult to implement and can create unintended consequences. As you read about possible reforms, you may want to refer back to Chapter 3's discussion about the reasons we have plea bargaining and the interests of the various players in the process and think about whether these various reform proposals support or are in conflict with these underlying interests and reasons for plea bargaining.

I. Change the Law

There are two basic proposals under this broad category: to change the underlying criminal law, or to put limits on the possible discount defendants can gain through plea bargaining.

A. Reform the Underlying Criminal Law

As you have read, one concern about plea bargaining is the trial penalty—that defendants who exercise their right to trial suffer harsher penalties than those who take a plea deal. One proposal, as you read about in Chapter One, for reforming the law is abolition of prison. More traditional proposals are related to the concern about the trial penalty and the extreme punishments are embedded into the criminal codes in every state in the United States and federally. As has been discussed, these potentially high sentences may be why some innocent people plead guilty. The potential high sentences also give prosecutors ammunition to use in hard bargaining. This is related to the concern that prosecutors have extraordinary powers in plea bargaining. Therefore, one reform proposal is to change the underlying criminal codes to reduce the amount of power that prosecutors have.

Cynthia Alkon, *An Overlooked Key to Reversing Mass Incarceration: Reforming the Law to Reduce Prosecutorial Power in Plea Bargaining*

15 Md. L.J. of Race, Religion, Gender & Class 191, 201–207 (Fall 2015)

...

III. Legislative Reform to Reduce Prosecutorial Power in Plea Bargaining

As long as prosecutors hold unfettered power, there is little incentive for them to not charge people with crimes when they have the evidence to support a conviction. Simply asking for prosecutors to exercise more discretion to return to earlier filing rates, and file fewer cases, is unlikely to have the necessary far-reaching impact. This means that legislative change, aimed at reducing some prosecutorial power, and aimed at making high filing rates less attractive, should be part of any meaningful discussion about how to reduce incarceration rates. This is not to suggest that legislative reform would be quick or easy, although some states have started to make some of the changes discussed in this section. This is also not to suggest that legislative reform alone will dramatically change how prosecutors approach their jobs. But, legislative reform in a few key areas could reduce the pressure put on defendants to accept plea deals and might, therefore, help to reduce the number of cases that prosecutors file, as extracting guilty pleas will not be as easy. The first suggested category for reform is to change how crimes are defined to reduce the number of crimes that can be charged as both misdemeanors and felonies and to reduce some felonies to misdemeanors. The second category is to reduce potential punishment ranges by eliminating mandatory minimums for most crimes and for enhancements. These reforms would reduce the pressure that prosecutors now routinely put on defendants to plead guilty.

A. Revise How Crimes Are Defined

If a crime is a felony, or potentially a felony, the consequences of conviction are more severe. This can mean more time in jail or prison, and the collateral consequences are significantly more serious for felony convictions. Prosecutorial discretion determines which charges will be filed, as so many acts can be punished as both felonies and misdemeanors. The threats of re-filing as a felony or reducing to a misdemeanor are both powerful threats. To avoid a felony conviction, a defendant may agree to plead guilty to a misdemeanor, even if they are innocent or otherwise have a strong defense. One way to help prevent this type of pressure from prosecutors is to redefine crimes both by reducing the number that can be charged as both felonies and misdemeanors and by reducing some felonies to misdemeanors.

1. Reducing the Number of Acts that Can Be Charged as Either Felonies or Misdemeanors

Theft offenses and assaults are two common types of crimes that can be charged as both misdemeanors and felonies, depending on the seriousness of the offense. For example, an assault that includes serious bodily injury is more likely to be a felony. Likewise, a theft that involves property that is worth over a certain amount of money (for example, $2,500.00) is often a felony. Prior offenses can also be a factor. For example, petty theft with a prior conviction can be charged as a felony or a misdemeanor in California, regardless of the value of the stolen property.

Some of these distinctions make sense and shouldn't be eliminated. For example, a spousal battery where there is serious bodily injury is clearly a more serious crime than a simple punch or single slap. But some of these distinctions simply allow prosecutors to exert pressure during the plea bargaining process to encourage defendants to take the plea deal. In addition, when given the option to file a felony, the prosecutor may decide that the case should at least be filed as a misdemeanor, even if it is not a serious offense. Legislatures should review the full list of criminal charges that can be filed as both misdemeanors or felonies and make sure the distinctions support a real public policy objective and are not simply there to add to the arsenal of charges that prosecutors can file. One simple proposal is to eliminate petty theft with a prior as a felony charge. If the amount stolen is a small amount and not enough to rise to the level of a felony, it should stay a misdemeanor, regardless of the record of the defendant.

2. Reducing Felonies to Misdemeanors

Related to reducing or eliminating crimes that can be both misdemeanors and felonies is reducing crimes from felonies to misdemeanors. For example, Proposition 47, which passed in California in November 2014, reduced some felonies to misdemeanors, including drug and property crimes. It is still too early to evaluate the long-term impact. Early reports indicate that arrests are down dramatically for narcotics offenses, which are no longer felonies. Overall, in Los Angeles County, narcotics arrests decreased by 30 percent and overall bookings into the Los Angeles County Jail were down by 23 percent in the initial months after the adoption of Proposition 47. It is unclear what impact Proposition 47 has on plea bargaining or prosecutorial behavior. If the long-term impact is a reduction in arrests, this would reduce the number of cases that prosecutors can ultimately file, although without prosecutorial involvement or impacting the relative power that prosecutors hold in the system. One unknown is the impact that having fewer arrests, and thereby fewer potential cases to file, may have on prosecutors' institutional culture. Will seeing fewer cases reduce the punitive approach by prosecutors? It is clear that if California's initial experience continues, and there are fewer arrests, this change in law will reduce incarceration rates, albeit for reasons not necessarily envisioned by the voters who likely thought Proposition 47 would just reduce felony convictions rates, not arrest rates.

B. Eliminate Most Mandatory Sentences

Both state and federal criminal codes include a large number of mandatory minimum sentences both for the underlying criminal charge and for added enhancements. If a defendant is convicted at trial of a crime or an enhancement that includes a mandatory minimum sentence, the judge usually has no choice but to impose the sentence. The practical effect of mandatory minimums is to give prosecutors more power as the threat of adding an enhancement with a mandatory minimum or proceeding on a charge with a mandatory minimum can mean that the defendant will get significantly more time if they are convicted and do not accept the plea deal. In all but the most serious of crimes, legislatures should remove mandatory minimums from criminal codes both for the underlying offense and for enhancements.

1. Eliminating Mandatory Minimum Sentences in Most Charges

Mandatory minimums should be reserved for only the most serious crimes. Currently, mandatory minimums exist for everything ranging from less serious misdemeanors to murder. For example, driving under the influence of alcohol, if the blood alcohol level is over a certain amount, often includes mandatory jail time. At the other extreme is California's three-strike law, which mandates a term of 25 years to life for conviction of a third strike offense. For the purposes of this discussion, to aid in reducing mass incarceration, the concern is about mandatory minimums that carry significant potential time in prison. For a variety of reasons, including practical political constraints, it may make sense to continue to have mandatory minimums for violent crimes such as murder in the first degree. The clear category of crimes to focus on first is to remove mandatory minimums for non-violent offenses. This would mean focusing on drug cases and theft cases. Pfaff's research supports focusing on property offenses as he identifies this category of offenses as being part of the reason for increased incarceration rates because of the overall increase in property crime rates. Each state should carefully examine how non-violent property crimes and drug crimes are punished and eliminate mandatory minimums in these categories.

2. Eliminating Mandatory Minimum Sentences in Enhancements

Prosecutors routinely threaten to add enhancements, such as the use of a gun, that include mandatory minimum sentences in order to put pressure on defendants to plead guilty. Although at first glance many enhancements support clear policy goals, such as discouraging the use of a gun during the commission of a felony, the mandatory sentences are often excessive of the stated reason for the enhancement. For example, the use of a gun regularly carries mandatory minimums of a decade or more in prison. There are questions about what is added, from a public policy point of view, by these enhancements. For example, if a gun is used and causes serious bodily injury, the underlying offense—assault with serious bodily injury—would include increased punishment for the injury. In that example, the gun use enhancement simply acts to put additional pressure on a defendant to take a deal, as the penalty can be so much more severe. Most codes allow for a great variety of enhancements based on where the crime was committed (i.e. was the defendant in a school zone?); what was used (a gun or other deadly weapon?); and whether the defendant has prior convictions. Legislative reform needs to include a full overhaul of what kinds of enhancements are allowed, eliminate mandatory sentences, and reduce the time for enhancements. Mandatory minimums in enhancements give prosecutors tremendous power to pressure defendants to plead guilty in exchange for an offer to strike the enhancement or not add it in the first place.

Notes/Questions

An empirical study found that the more possible crimes a prosecutor can charge, the more there is charge bargaining. However, if prosecutors have more options in terms of what felony charge they can file for the same offense, they are less likely to reduce felonies to misdemeanors. If prosecutors "have felony options, they generally choose them." Ronald F. Wright & Rodney L. Engen, *Charge Movement and Theories of Prosecutors*, 91 MARQUETTE L. REV. 9 (2007). If you were in the legislature in your state, what changes in the law might you suggest based on this information?

B. Limits on the Possible Plea Discount

This type of reform proposal is aimed at reducing the possible trial penalty by limiting how good the deal can be under a plea deal. One approach could be to do abbreviated trials. This process exists in a number of civil law countries outside the United States. Under an abbreviated trial system, the criminal code allows for a standardized reduction if defendants plead guilty to the case. The amount of the reduction in sentence is written into the Criminal Code so there is no question of disparate treatment.[1] Another possible approach was proposed by Russell D. Covey, the "plea-based ceiling," which:

> ... [W]ould establish mandatory caps or ceilings on trial sentences. Pursuant to the ceiling, no defendant could receive a punishment after trial that exceeded the sentence he could have had as a result of a plea offer by more than a modest, predetermined amount. Ceilings would thus limit the sentencing differential and enforce a fixed discount by capping the punishment that could be imposed on the defendant who pleads not guilty.[2]

Covey suggests that one advantage of this proposal, over a firm fixed discount system, like abbreviated trials, is that prosecutors would be free to offer the same full range of discounts that they currently offer in plea bargaining, including reducing charges.

---

1. *See Plea Bargaining as a Legal Transplant: A Good Idea for Troubled Criminal Justice Systems?*, 19 TRANSNATIONAL LAW & CONTEMPORARY PROBLEMS 355 (2010); Ena Dion, *Introducing Plea Bargaining into Post-Conflict Legal Systems*, Research Memorandum for the International Network to Promote the Rule of Law (March 2014).

2. Russell D. Covey, *Fixed Justice: Reforming Plea Bargaining with Plea-Based Ceilings*, 82 TUL. L. REV. 1237 (2008).

> **Does the U.S. Military Have a Better System?**
>
> Under the U.S. Code of Military Justice, service members facing court martial can make a "pre-trial agreement." The court, which includes the Military Judge and court members, are not informed about the sentence agreed to. Evidence is then presented, and the tribunal decides the sentence. If it is higher than what was agreed to in the pre-trial agreement, the lower sentence prevails. If it was lower, then that sentence prevails. The pre-trial agreement acts as a "ceiling" for the sentence. Do you think civilian criminal legal systems should adopt this system?
>
> *See* Rodger A. Drew, Jr., *An Introduction to the U.S. Military Justice System*, 43 No. 3 JUDGES J. 7, 10–11 (2006). *See generally* R. Peter Masterton, *Pretrial Agreement Negotiations: A Defense Perspective*, 1990-APR ARMY LAW 28; Maj. Mary M. Foreman, *Let's Make a Deal! The Development of Pretrial Agreements in Military Criminal Justice Practice*, 170 MIL. L. REV. 53 (2001).

Prosecutors would not be locked into standardized reductions. However, this system would likely change the type of offers that prosecutors would be willing to make:

> Obviously, plea-based ceilings would have a dramatic impact on the kinds of plea offers a prosecutor would be willing to make in the first instance. In a plea-based ceiling system, the prosecutor could not make extremely lenient plea offers in order to induce a guilty plea because this would simultaneously reduce the defendant's incentive to avoid trial without changing the likelihood of conviction. Because a lenient offer would not result in a plea agreement, the prosecutor will be far less likely to make such an offer, unless she believed it represented a substantively fair outcome.[3]

Covey suggests that plea-based ceilings would prevent some prosecutorial hard bargaining tactics, like exploding offers. Covey's proposed plea-based ceilings would also prevent prosecutors from threatening to seek the death penalty.

> Because plea-based ceilings would effectively bar prosecutors from making plea offers in any case where they wish to seek a death sentence or to keep that option open, the threat of capital punishment would lose its value as leverage in securing guilty pleas in serious cases, perhaps undermining one of its principal uses.[4]

Covey argues that adopting plea based ceilings would have a number of advantages including that innocent defendants would be "more likely to contest their cases."[5] He also argues that this proposal would help the goal of changing prosecutorial cultures

3. *Id.* at 1275.
4. *Id.* at 1284.
5. *Id.* at 1290.

by discouraging prosecutors from over charging and encouraging them to screen their cases better. Covey acknowledges that judges might not like this change as it would limit their sentencing options.

Notes/Questions

1. Do you agree with Professor Covey's suggestion to have plea based ceilings? If you were a prosecutor, would you think this is a good idea? Would your opinion change if you were a defense attorney?

2. As explained above, many civil law countries that do not have plea bargaining have, instead, a system of abbreviated trials. Under these systems, if a defendant agrees to the abbreviated trial, he pleads guilty and receives a standard sentence reduction. During the abbreviated trial, the judge reviews the documentary evidence, including the defendant's guilty plea, and if the judge finds the defendant guilty, s/he sentences him to the reduced sentence. What advantages do you think there are to this system for the prosecutor? What advantages do you think there are to this system for the defense?

3. Do you think that standard sentence reductions would limit creativity in plea bargaining and limit the possibility for non-custodial sentences?

4. Oren Gazal-Ayal and Avishalom Tor offer a different proposal aimed at reducing coercion to accept plea deals by requiring judges to reject any plea offers that "include a sentence that is significantly lower than the sentence expected following conviction by a jury trial."[6] The idea is that this would prevent innocent defendants from pleading guilty, as they would be more likely to get deep discounts in the plea offer. The challenge with this proposal, unlike with Covey's plea-based ceilings, is that it provides no protection for the defendant whose deal is refused by the judge and who then goes to trial and loses. A defendant in this situation is looking at the same potentially stiff penalty that they were looking at before trial. This proposal does not limit the post-trial sentence. It potentially just forces more defendants to go to trial and risk the outcome.

II. Change the Process

Another category of reform proposal involves changing the process of plea bargaining. One set of proposals under this category is to adopt clear regulations for the process of plea bargaining. Another proposal is to change how plea bargaining works for defendants by giving them a better voice in the process through procedural justice. Finally, the third suggestion is to increase the number of trials and decrease the rate of plea bargaining.

6. Oren Gazal-Ayal & Avishalom Tor, *The Innocence Effect*, 62 Duke L.J. 339, 395 (2012).

A. Better Regulation of Plea Bargaining

One of the leading critics of plea bargaining, Stafanos Bibas, has called for regulation of the plea bargaining process to help better protect defendants and to restrict some prosecutorial excesses.

Stephanos Bibas, *Regulating the Plea-Bargaining Market: From Caveat Emptor to Consumer Protection*

99 Cal. L. Rev. 1117, 1153–1158 (2011)

. . .

It is astonishing that a $100 credit-card purchase of a microwave oven is regulated more carefully than a guilty plea that results in years of imprisonment. It would not take much to extend the consumer protection analogy to plea bargains. Legislatures and rules commissions could forbid some terms outright. Mostly, however, they would regulate the contracting process procedurally to ensure a modicum of understanding and advice.

Many cognitive deficits plague plea bargaining and merit fixing. Probably the most basic is sheer incomprehension because defendants often are unsophisticated laymen facing repeat-player prosecutors. Many defendants also feel pressured to make hurried decisions based on advice by lawyers whom they may not yet have come to trust. Defense lawyers are often overburdened, of varying ability and experience, and may have incentives to plead cases out quickly. Framing, anchoring, and loss aversion are also factors. Overconfidence and impulsivity probably play lesser roles because impulsive, overconfident defendants are more likely to go to trial or hold out for better deals. Solutions should attack each of these problems, especially poor defense lawyering and incomprehension, followed by excessive pressure to plead quickly. The following list is not meant to be a comprehensive blueprint for legislation, but rather an effort to brainstorm about possible solutions.

Improving Comprehension. The most basic and important reforms focus on ensuring that defendants know what they are doing. Most critically, they need better defense lawyers, as I will discuss, and simpler, clearer plea bargains. But for starters, all plea agreements should be in writing. While many plea bargains are written down, not all are. Their terms may be set forth at the plea hearing in full, in part, or not at all. Simply memorializing all agreements in writing, ahead of time, would go a long way toward reducing confusion and later evidentiary disputes about what was promised or understood. A simple check-the-box form with blanks for the defendant's name, the charge(s), and the sentence might suffice for simple misdemeanors and the like.

Another comprehension problem is that innumeracy hinders defendants' grasp of the risks of various outcomes, such as the chance of various convictions or sentences after trial. Following standard best practices for translating numbers into commonsense terms can help. Psychological research shows that displaying numerical information visually, and phrasing risks in absolute rather than relative terms, help people to understand risks better. It is also important to use standard numerical formats and to reduce the number of calculations and inferences that readers must make. For example, lawyers and plea agreements could phrase sentencing ranges not as 126 to 144 months but as 10 to 12 years....

Clear numbers should be accompanied by clear language. To improve defendants' comprehension, drafting commissions could require summaries of agreements in plain English. Studies consistently show that laymen understand very little of the boilerplate legalese in jury instructions and the like. Rewriting legalese in simpler, shorter terms using the active voice increases readers' understanding markedly....

Prosecutors would remain free to bargain for nonstandard terms, but those could face closer scrutiny and regulation. For example, prosecutors sometimes ask one defendant to plead guilty in exchange for lenient treatment of a close relative, but these terms are often criticized as coercive. For such package deals, prosecutors might have to display the provisions in large, boldfaced type, specifically discuss them at plea colloquies, and have defendants initial those paragraphs individually. That would both improve defendants' understanding and perhaps offset one of the most coercive pressures to plead.

Moderating Pressures. Defendants often face great pressure to plead out quickly, which may lead them to make life-altering decisions before they come to appreciate the consequences. One way to reduce this pressure would be a cooling-off period for plea bargains authorizing five years' imprisonment or more. The law could forbid guilty pleas at the initial appearance for serious felonies, to avoid pressure to plead immediately after first meeting with one's defense lawyer. It could also require prosecutors to disclose the deal's terms and defense lawyers to offer advice at least three days before the plea hearing, unless the court finds compelling reasons to allow an immediate plea. (The final plea deal might need to be put on the table a week before trial, to allow time for advice and avoid pressure for last-minute deals.) Cooling-off periods help to make decisions more dispassionate and to reduce second-guessing of rash snap judgments. They are most valuable when (1) people make a decision infrequently and are therefore inexperienced, and (2) the decision is an emotional one. Felony guilty pleas satisfy both criteria....

Prosecutorial Disclosure. In addition to rules of construction, prosecutors might be subject to certain disclosure obligations, even when defendants decide to plead guilty without plea agreements. The Second Circuit, for example, encourages prosecutors to send defendants letters setting forth their understandings of how the U.S. Sentencing Guidelines should apply to each defendant's case. These Pimentel letters, as they are called, give defendants fair warnings of the sentences they are likely to receive in exchange for their pleas and any enhancements that arguably apply. Other mandatory disclosures could cover concurrent versus consecutive sentencing for all pending charges, as well as possible or mandatory parole, supervised release, civil commitment, and asset forfeiture. These disclosures would help to inform defendants' decisions about whether (and how) to plead guilty.

Prosecutors and courts could likewise have to clarify the consequences defendants face in other ways. For example, they ought to notify defendants of possible departures from presumptive sentences. They might also have to consolidate all outstanding cases for sentencing, so defendants have a comprehensive picture of the exposure they face. Indeed, the ABA's Standards for Criminal Justice: Sentencing already require both of these steps....

Improving Defense Lawyering. Most important of all would be the advice of counsel. Defendants must trust their lawyers because they cannot begin to learn enough and their lawyers are experts. Defense lawyers may need training, guidance, and reminders to ensure that they advise their clients competently. Bar associations could help to address this concern by developing best practices for advising defendants on guilty pleas. Checklists or computer programs could flag typical collateral consequences of which defense lawyers must warn, based on each defendant's charges, jurisdiction, immigration status, address, and job. They could do the same for defense lawyers' duties to investigate, prepare, meet with clients, and advise. Checklists sound too obvious to be much of a change, but they would offer much more concrete guidance than current law [see the plea bargaining preparation sheet in Chapter 7]. Strickland shied away from rules or even rules of thumb to guide defense lawyers and lower courts, making review difficult and prey to the inevitability bias. As Dr. Atul Gawande has argued, checklists remain an underused solution to the modern problem of extreme complexity. They remind professionals to avoid common errors by going by the book. These measures are incremental, practical starting points. One can at least hope for more radical reforms, such as alleviating the chronic underfunding, overwork, and agency costs that plague appointed defense counsel.

Notes/Questions

1. In an earlier article, Stephanos Bibas made this recommendation:

   Additionally, better sharing of sentencing information could help nonrepeat players to understand the going rates or prices for crimes. For example, just as commercial markets increase efficiency by posting the recent prices of particular commodities or stocks, so plea-bargaining markets could use a database of prices. A database of past trial and plea-bargain outcomes would give lawyers access to information that some repeat players already know (individually or collectively as an office). Plea bargains, however, are often complex, multidimensional agreements in which the parties need to know the defendant's criminal history and the strength of the evidence as well as the likely sentence. While a database could not capture these facts fully, it could at least provide a starting point or relevant anchor for researching, comparing prices, and bargaining.[7]

Is this practical? What concerns would you have as a prosecutor to having such a database? What concerns would you have as a defense lawyer? What about if you were a judge and a database were collected about all your sentences? Would you think this was a good idea? Would you be concerned about unintended consequences?

2. Is it appropriate to analogize plea bargaining to consumer law?

3. If you were a prosecutor, which of Stephanos Bibas' suggestions would you support? If you were a defense lawyer, which of Stephanos Bibas' suggestions would you support?

B. Give Defendants More of a Role in the Process

Critics of plea bargaining often focus on how plea bargaining works from the perspective of the defendant. Defendants rarely speak in court, except to enter their plea. They do not tell their story, unless they testify at trial. One of the reasons that plea bargaining can seem like a game is because defendants are often cut off from the process. Lawyers convey offers, but defendants do not see the negotiation that resulted in the offer. One scholar, Michael O'Hear, calls for the introduction of procedural justice to address concerns about how defendants perceive plea bargaining working in practice.

Michael O'Hear, *Plea Bargaining and Procedural Justice*

42 GA. L. REV. 407, 420–422, 426–431 (2008)

...

[A] person's perception of whether a decision making process was fair does not depend solely on the outcome, but also on various attributes of the process used to reach the outcome. Those attributes include: (1) whether the person had an opportunity to tell his or her side of the story ("voice"); (2) whether the authorities were seen as unbiased, honest, and principled ("neutrality"); (3) whether the authorities were seen as benevolent and caring ("trustworthiness"); and (4) whether the person was treated with dignity and respect. The perception of voice, neutrality, trustworthiness, and respect can promote the acceptance of decisions that are otherwise believed to be incorrect or substantively unfair. Indeed, in many settings, perceptions of process fairness exert greater influence over acceptance of the result than do the outcomes themselves. Second, the extent to which decision making processes are perceived as fair helps shape beliefs regarding the legitimacy of the legal authorities responsible for the decision. And third, the perception that legal authorities have legitimacy enhances the sense that the authorities are entitled to be obeyed. Fair procedures thus promote

---

7. Stephanos Bibas, *Plea Bargaining Outside the Shadow of Trial*, 117 HARV. L. REV. 2463, 2532 (2004).

cooperation with the authorities and compliance with their directives, as well as the development of a more general sense of obligation to obey the law.

These three claims are backed, to a greater or lesser extent, by three decades of social psychology research, encompassing both laboratory and field studies. The studies are too numerous to summarize (or even cite) here, but a brief description of two especially relevant studies will illustrate the nature of the available empirical support. In one, Jonathan Casper and his colleagues interviewed 628 felony defendants in three cities. They found that procedural justice in the processing of the defendants' cases made a significant contribution to outcome satisfaction. They further found a significant correlation between defendants' perceptions of procedural justice and the amount of time they spent speaking with their lawyers (which they associated with voice) and the respectfulness of the treatment they received from police officers at the time of arrest. In a second criminal justice study, Raymond Paternoster and his colleagues gathered information regarding 479 domestic violence arrestees. They determined that "[w]hen police acted in a procedurally fair manner when arresting assault suspects, the rate of subsequent domestic violence was significantly lower than when they did not." They measured procedural justice by reference to such variables as whether officers "took the time" to listen to the arrestee's side of the story and whether the arrestee was handcuffed in front of the victim (which they related to respectful treatment)....

How might these factors be translated into plea bargaining practice? Let us consider each in turn.

Defendants have voice to the extent they perceive an opportunity to tell their side of their story. Interestingly, some research suggests that voice matters even if the opportunity to be heard does not occur until after the relevant decision has been made. Voice effects are greater, however, if the opportunity to be heard is provided earlier in the process. Prosecutors should thus ensure such an opportunity is available before presenting an offer to a defendant.

One common method for prosecutors to learn the defendant's side of the story is through police reports. Police, however, are not always diligent about collecting the defendant's side of the story. Moreover, defendants may not think much of their opportunity to be heard by the police. Their "hearing," for instance, may have occurred in an emotionally charged arrest context, or may have been colored by coercive or deceptive police practices. Thus, a serious commitment to voice cannot be satisfied through an uncritical reliance on police reports.

Instead, before making a plea offer, the prosecutor should affirmatively ascertain whether the defendant had a meaningful opportunity to convey his or her side of the story, either through appropriately sensitive police processes or through an attorney. Thus, for instance, in cases in which police documentation does not indicate meaningful voice opportunities, the prosecutor should dig a little deeper, refraining from plea negotiations until after he or she has discussed the matter with the officers involved or has provided the defendant with a meaningful voice opportunity through counsel. And, to the extent that counsel is regarded as the guarantor of defendant voice, plea negotiations should wait until after the defendant and the lawyer have conferred for more than just a few moments in a crowded holding pen or the back of a noisy courtroom, as is the norm for indigent defendants in some jurisdictions. In support of this view, one might recall Casper's finding of a significant correlation between defendant perceptions of procedural justice and the amount of time simply spent talking with a lawyer.

Neutrality is associated with a decisionmaker who is unbiased, honest, and principled. Most prosecutors doubtlessly believe they are neutral, but the trick is to reassure defendants of this. [Tom] Tyler identifies the use of objective criteria as an important means by which a decisionmaker can establish his or her neutrality. Decisions, moreover, should be explained so as to demonstrate that a neutral process was followed. In the plea bargaining context, then, prosecutors might enhance procedural justice by adopting objective criteria to guide their decisions and explaining to defendants why they take the positions they do. Explanations ought to be conveyed through defense counsel, but, recognizing that busy counsel may not effectively convey the information, prosecutors also should explain their reasoning in open court when the defendant is physically present to offer his or her guilty plea.

People infer trustworthiness when they believe "that the authorities with whom they are dealing are concerned about their welfare and want to treat them fairly." Perceived trustworthiness is enhanced when the authorities demonstrate that they have actually considered the information offered during voice opportunities. Thus, in the plea bargaining context, when explaining his or her positions, the prosecutor should expressly address any claims asserted by the defendant in support of more lenient treatment, that is, provide what was termed "principled engagement" above.

Perceptions of respect are associated with simple politeness by the authorities, as well as the acknowledgement of citizens' legal rights. In the plea bargaining context, prosecutors might undertake a number of measures to enhance perceptions of respect. They might, for instance, take care to use the appropriate honorific when referring to the defendant (e.g., Mr. Smith, Ms. Jones) and discourage unnecessary handcuffing and other forms of rough treatment. They also should avoid exploding offers that expire before defendants have had a meaningful opportunity to confer with counsel or to litigate colorable suppression motions as such offers convey a disregard for the defendants' legal rights. Finally, after formal charges have been filed, prosecutors should avoid threats of enhanced charges in order to extract guilty pleas. A guilty plea represents the waiver of numerous constitutional rights, including the right to a jury trial and the privilege against self-incrimination. A prosecutor shows disrespect for these rights when she threatens a recalcitrant defendant with charges that she evidently did not think appropriate to pursue in the first instance.

In sum, it is not hard to imagine a number of conceptually simple protocols that could be implemented by prosecutors in order to enhance defendants' perceptions of procedural justice: (1) before starting plea negotiations, ensure that defendants have had a meaningful opportunity to tell their side of the story, either through police officers during pre-charge processing or through counsel after charging; (2) develop objective criteria to guide plea negotiations; (3) explain positions taken in negotiations; (4) expressly acknowledge arguments for more lenient treatment; and (5) refrain from pressure tactics like exploding offers and charging threats.

C. Ban Plea Bargaining or Increase the Number of Trials

Some critics of plea bargaining suggest either an outright ban on plea bargaining or a concerted effort to increase the number of trials. As you will read, the concerns motivating these suggestions are different. Michelle Alexander is primarily concerned about eliminating mass incarceration. Jenny Roberts is focused on increasing fairness and demanding a change from business as usual with misdemeanor cases. Finally, you will read about two examples of jurisdictions that tried to ban plea bargaining entirely. In El Paso, Texas, two judges started the ban after a political dispute with the District Attorney. By contrast, in the Bronx, the ban was started by the District Attorney who was concerned about judges being too lenient. As you read these suggestions, consider how realistic they are. What are the intended and unintended consequences of doing what these reformers suggest?

Michelle Alexander suggested that large numbers of defendants should stop pleading guilty, as it could "crash the system" if they exercised their rights to trial.

> The system of mass incarceration depends almost entirely on the cooperation of those it seeks to control. If everyone charged with crimes suddenly exercised his constitutional rights, there would not be enough judges, lawyers or prison cells to deal with the ensuring tsunami of litigation. Not everyone would have to join for the revolt to have an impact; as the legal scholar Angela J. Davis noted, "if the number of people exercising their trial rights suddenly doubled or tripled in some jurisdictions, it would create chaos."[8]

As a defense lawyer, is it ethical to suggest that your client go to trial instead of taking a plea deal that is a fraction of the possible maximum sentence? As a prosecutor, what would you do if, suddenly, in your court, defense lawyers stopped pleading out a large percentage of their cases?

Jenny Roberts built onto Michelle Alexander's suggestion focusing on misdemeanor cases. Roberts asked,

> What if indigent defense counsel triaged in favor of misdemeanor representation, and in particular focused on the "petty," quality-of-life misdemeanors that flood the system and result in disproportionately harsh, permanent criminal records? What if defenders put sufficient resources into such cases so that clients felt they actually had the true choice of refusing to plead guilty? ...

---

8. Michelle Alexander, *Go to Trial: Crash the Justice System*, N.Y. Times, March 10, 2012.

> Yet truly minor misdemeanors are precisely the types of cases in which a plea bargain is rarely much of a bargain for the defendant. For example, a defendant might be "offered" a sentence of time already served—which can mean the night spent in jail awaiting arraignment, or even a fictional time period if the person was never incarcerated—in exchange for pleading guilty to a misdemeanor of disorderly conduct. This may sound advantageous, or at least not harmful, until the actual consequences of this plea are added into the equation. This conviction can, and does, lead to proceedings to evict an individual from public housing. It can, and does, pose a bar to demonstrating "good moral conduct" for citizenship. Perhaps most significantly, in an era in which employers can, and do, easily access electronic criminal records, the person taking the "harmless" disorderly conduct plea will have difficulty finding work. Indeed, this employment issue alone starkly illustrates the way in which the most minor misdemeanor conviction has serious implications for so many people.
>
> The underlying goal of this Article's proposal to focus defender resources on minor misdemeanors is to have more defendants choose trial over a guilty plea, or at least reject a quick, early guilty plea—understanding that declining to plead guilty may lead to trial, but may also lead to deferral or dismissal. More misdemeanor trials, or fewer guilty pleas at an early court appearance, would impose serious strain on the criminal justice system. If these costs filter down, prosecutors would be forced to decline prosecution in more cases. This may, in turn, affect law enforcement, potentially leading the police to exercise discretion in deciding whom they actually put through the system. Finally, making the system bear more of the true costs of adjudicating misdemeanor arrests would, hopefully, give legislators a concrete reason (and perhaps some political coverage) to decriminalize and to refrain from creating more minor criminal offenses. In these ways, zealous attention to misdemeanor representation—in addition to being one way of dealing directly with the misdemeanor crisis—may advance other methods of dealing with the misdemeanor crisis.[9]

Roberts suggests that higher trial rates for less serious cases could change how those cases are handled in fundamental ways. What would it take to implement this proposal? Is it a different ethical question if the consequences of going to trial are potentially far less harmful than they could be in a felony case? Is taking more cases to trial a realistic proposal for reform? Who might resist higher trial rates?

The other option beyond increasing trial rates could be a formal ban of plea bargaining. However, as you will read with these next two excerpts, it is not easy to ban a deeply embedded practice. Both El Paso, Texas, and the Bronx, New York, banned plea bargaining in 1975. In both jurisdictions, banning plea bargaining increased trial rates, but a significant number of cases still pled out before trial.

---

9. Jenny Roberts, *Crashing the Misdemeanor System*, 70 WASH. & LEE L. REV. 1089, 1094–1100 (Spring 2013).

In El Paso, two criminal court judges banned plea bargaining after a political dispute with the District Attorney. The DA's office refused to recommend probation, "under any circumstances" for some specific offenses, including burglary. But the judges thought that refusing probation for first time offenders was out of step with what juries would do (in Texas, defendants can opt to have the jury do the sentencing after trial). The judges did not want to give tougher sentences than what they perceived a jury would give. They did not want to undercut the DA, as that made them look weak on crime in that they were giving lesser sentences than the plea offers. The judges also expressed concern that judges should be responsible for sentencing instead of a system of negotiated justice. As a result, the two judges issued a ban on sentence negotiation. They would, instead, sentence any defendant who wanted to plead guilty under guidelines that they developed. The DA responded by banning all sentence and charge bargaining in felony cases. The ban in El Paso held until the early 1980s. During that time, caseloads grew and case delay increased. In less than three years, the open criminal cases increased by 250%. The increased caseload meant more delays in case processing. When Texas passed a new law mandating speedy trials, more judges were shifted from the civil to the criminal docket to help manage the increased caseload due to fewer guilty pleas.

However, even during the ban, there were guilty pleas and prosecutors who acted contrary to the stated DA office policy. El Paso is an example of the challenge of maintaining a ban when professionals, including, ultimately, other judges, decide to exercise their discretionary power and not go along with the ban.[10]

Another example of banning plea bargaining is from the Bronx, New York, but this example was limited to banning post-indictment bargaining. The El Paso ban was instituted by judges who were concerned about how the DA was exercising power. The DA in El Paso, in response, also declared a ban on plea bargaining. In contrast, the Bronx District Attorney instituted the ban due to concern that judges were being too lenient and that the case management was resulting in case backlogs that caused case delays that made it harder for the prosecution to win convictions. The goal, therefore, was to change judicial behavior. The ban did decrease guilty pleas by 11%, but it also led to a 24% increase in the backlog of cases. This delay led to the unintended consequence of increasing the dismissal rate by 21%—or one in ten cases. For those defendants whose cases were not dismissed immediately, the backlog lead to more defendants being jailed for longer, with 47% being in jail for over a year. The Bronx ban cost taxpayers more money, as they were paying for longer, and therefore more expensive, pre-trial detention. The Bronx example raises a number of interesting questions, including whether the ban had the consequences it intended.

* * *

---

10. See generally, Robert A. Weninger, *The Abolition of Plea Bargaining: A Case Study of El Paso County, Texas*, 35 UCLA L. Rev. 265 (1987).

Roland Acevedo, *Is a Ban on Plea Bargaining an Ethical Abuse of Discretion? A Bronx County, New York Case Study*

64 FORDHAM L. REV. 987, 999–1000, 1005–1007, 1013 (1995)

...

More troubling than the rise in the dismissal rate and the concomitant threat posed to society by the release of potentially guilty defendants is the probability that innocent defendants are being convicted because of the Bronx ban. This probability results from a combination of three factors. First, under the new plea policy, defendants must usually decide within six days, before they are indicted, whether to accept a prosecutor's offer and plead guilty. This time limit places tremendous pressure on a defendant who, from a jail cell, must attempt to contact and consult with family and counsel before making a decision that could affect him for the rest of his life. Furthermore, not only must a defendant make this crucial decision within a few days, he must do so without the benefit of necessary information to assist him. Finally, because innocent defendants are highly risk averse, they will likely succumb to the pressure of making a rushed decision without adequate information. These defendants will often conclude that their interests are best served by pleading guilty, accepting the certainty of a lesser punishment, and avoiding the risk of a longer period of incarceration.

III. An Examination of the Effects of the Ban Under Ethics Rules

A. The Bronx District Attorney's Duty to "Seek Justice"

Foremost among the special ethics rules governing the Bronx District Attorney's conduct is N.Y. Code EC 7-13, which states that prosecutors have a "duty to seek justice [and] not merely to convict." In seeking justice, the prosecutor performs an "oversight function" and must be mindful of his responsibilities to the community, victim, defendant, and state. The prosecutor must protect the community, quench the victim's desire for vengeance, safeguard the defendant's rights, and ensure that the state has a fair and efficient criminal justice system. An examination of the effects of the Bronx plea bargaining ban suggests that the District Attorney may have neglected his obligation to certain constituencies.

While the community and victims are applauding the plea bargaining ban because felons are being increasingly convicted on the highest counts of indictments, defendants are lamenting its effects. The ban has not only resulted in a substantial increase in the average length of defendants' pre-trial detention, but has also heightened the possibility that innocent defendants are being unjustly convicted. Additionally, the increased reliance on SCIs as a means of prosecution deprives defendants of the constitutional protections afforded by the grand jury process.

The state also suffers as a result of the Bronx District Attorney's failure to maintain a fair and efficient criminal justice system. The large increase in the backlog of pending cases and the number of dismissals undermines the efficiency of the system. Further, a system that convicts innocent defendants and holds others in lengthy pre-trial detention leads the public to question its fairness. In sum, the effects of the Bronx ban strongly suggest that the District Attorney is failing to seek justice for segments of society that he is responsible for representing....

B. The Prosecutor's Duty to Identify and Correct Deficiencies in the Criminal Justice System

As a key player in the criminal justice system, the Bronx District Attorney also has an ethical duty to "recognize deficiencies in the legal system and to initiate corrective measures therein." This ethical obligation to innovate imposes a duty on the Bronx District Attorney to encourage and aid in making needed changes in the legal system. Arguably, the Bronx District Attorney was implementing needed changes when he banned plea bargaining. First, restrictive plea bargaining policies are associated with efforts to crack down on crime by refusing to offer lenient sentences. In a borough that has sixteen percent of New York City's population yet twenty-five percent of its homicides, twenty-two percent of its drug arrests, and twenty percent of its rapes, the public may perceive the plea bargaining ban as a welcome and needed change to combat the disproportionate amount of crime in the Bronx. The public may also perceive the Bronx ban as an innovative attempt to secure desperately needed additional courtrooms and judges from the state. While some may view the Bronx ban as an innovative corrective measure designed to improve the legal system, others perceive it as a death knell for criminal justice in the Bronx. The plea bargaining ban has not only increased the backlog of pending cases and the number of dismissals, but has also forced defendants to remain in pre-trial detention longer and has cost the state millions of extra dollars. In light of these results, there is support for the proposition that the Bronx District Attorney is impairing the quality of justice rather than fulfilling his ethical obligation to improve the legal system....

Conclusion

The ban on plea bargaining has severely impacted the Bronx criminal justice system. The overall adverse effects of the plea bargaining ban suggest that the Bronx District Attorney may be acting unethically. An examination of the relevant ethics rules, however, reveals that the standards governing the Bronx District Attorney's behavior are nebulous, provide no concrete standards upon which to judge his behavior, and afford him tremendous latitude in exercising his discretion. This discretion makes the Bronx District Attorney's behavior nearly irreproachable under ethical standards. Furthermore, not all of the effects of the Bronx plea bargaining ban have been adverse. The few positive effects of the plea bargaining ban could lead one to conclude that the Bronx District Attorney was being innovative in his attempt, through the ban, to pressure the state to provide much needed additional courtroom space and judges.

But while the Bronx District Attorney's behavior does not appear to violate any ethics rules, his behavior is nonetheless adversely impacting the Bronx criminal justice system. To avoid further deterioration and possible irreparable harm to the Bronx criminal justice system, the Bronx District Attorney needs to take prompt and definitive action. Two possible courses of action are available. First, the District Attorney could expand the time allotted for plea bargaining so that defendants would have sufficient time to secure the information necessary to assist them in deciding whether or not to plead guilty. Second, the District Attorney could implement written guidelines governing the plea bargaining process to prevent abuses of discretion and to ensure that appropriate sentences are imposed on defendants....

Notes/Questions

1. If you were a prosecutor would you try to ban plea bargaining? If yes, why? If no, why not? You might want to keep this question in mind as you continue reading this chapter.

2. If you were a defense attorney what advantages might there be for your clients if there were no plea bargaining? You might want to keep this question in mind as you continue reading this chapter.

3. The ban in both locations cost taxpayers more money. Should this matter? Should the DA consider the financial implications of changes in policies?

4. The article reported that, due to the change in policy, it is possible that innocent defendants are pleading guilty. Should that be a factor that is considered before any policy change? Is there something that could have been done to prevent this unintended consequence of the policy change?

In addition to the argument that banning plea bargaining would destroy efficient case processing, what about the impact on defendants who want to plead guilty? Is there a value in allowing guilty pleas beyond efficiency? Consider this:

> Abolishing guilty pleas is completely contrary to existing psychological research. Acceptance of responsibility and expression of remorse are critical psychological factors preventing people from committing more crimes. Simply put, greater remorse leads to less recidivism. A person who admits that they committed a robbery and sincerely apologizes to the victim is significantly less likely to rob again. It is not only psychologists who have recognized this fact; every parent knows that a child who admits to stealing cookies and cries after being caught is less likely to keep stealing cookies. The proposal to abolish guilty pleas is an invitation for defendants to establish a pattern of dishonest defiance that will lead to more crime.[11]

You may want to consider this again after reading the chapters on restorative justice. Are guilty pleas, and a system of plea bargaining, the only way that people can take responsibility and feel remorse about having committed a crime?

---

11. Tom Hogan, *The Movement to Abolish Guilty Pleas: A Critical Analysis*, 3 Practical Lawyer 69 (2023).

III. Change the Players

The third category is reform proposals that recommend changes in how the professionals in the system do their jobs. The section below is divided into three parts, one for each of the main professional players in plea bargaining: defense lawyers, prosecutors, and judges. As you are reading this section, you will want to consider what difference these proposals might make and what underlying concerns they address. For example, if defense lawyers had more resources, would it encourage them to spend the time to adequately investigate and research their cases? What if prosecutors could not easily engage in hard bargaining tactics during plea bargaining? Would that lead to fewer innocent defendants pleading guilty? And if judges were more involved in the plea bargaining process, could that help to even out the power imbalances?

A. Changes in How Defense Lawyers Do Their Job

A type of plea bargaining reform that has gotten the most attention so far is reforming or changing how defense lawyers do their jobs. Before discussing what reforms might make a difference, it is important to understand how indigent defense is structured in the United States and the constraints that impact how defense lawyers can do their jobs, including plea bargaining on behalf of their clients.

Cynthia Alkon, *The U.S. Supreme Court's Failure to Fix Plea Bargaining: The Impact of* Lafler *and* Frye

41 Hastings Const. L.Q. 561, 576, 580, 582 (Spring 2014)

....

The vast majority of criminal defendants in the United States rely on appointed counsel, which has a substantial impact on how the criminal justice system, including plea bargaining, works. For indigent defendants, access to legal counsel is still a serious challenge despite the Supreme Court's decision over fifty years ago in *Gideon v. Wainwright* [372 U.S. 335 (1963)] that indigent defendants have a right to state-appointed counsel. In reality, defendants may wait months before a lawyer is appointed.

In misdemeanor cases, defendants are more likely to go unrepresented and waive their right to a lawyer under questionable circumstances. Misdemeanor defendants overwhelmingly enter guilty pleas, often without knowing the serious collateral consequences of the conviction. Defendants facing both misdemeanor and felony charges often do not meet their lawyer until their first court date—which for many defendants may be their last court date because they plead guilty at arraignment to get out of jail.

Defendants suffering from mental illness, developmental disabilities, or substance abuse—a significant percentage of all criminal defendants—often have cognitive limitations that may make it difficult for them to quickly understand what is happening with their cases and what their options are. The fact that a client may need more time to talk with their lawyer and to understand what is being explained is rarely an acceptable reason to give these clients more time with their appointed lawyer because appointed lawyers work under a system that constrains the amount of time they can spend with each client. The end result is that appointed lawyers often do not have enough time for meaningful communications with their clients, particularly in less serious cases.

As will be discussed, money can have a significant impact on how well lawyers can do their jobs. Budget limitations can mean that lawyers have less time to talk to their clients, limited ability to investigate cases, and fewer experts to aid in case preparation. So far, the Court has not directly confronted these systemic problems in examining claims of effective assistance of counsel. However, to understand how plea bargaining works, it is important to first understand the variety of ways in which indigent defendants get a lawyer and what this may mean for the quality of their defense. This section will then discuss how budgetary problems can influence effective assistance of counsel.

1. Appointment of Lawyers

There is no uniform approach to appointing indigent defense lawyers as each jurisdiction uses different systems, including public defenders and publicly appointed private counsel. Most large counties rely on public defender offices. There are continuing questions about whether the way in which a lawyer is appointed to handle an indigent defendant's case impacts the quality of his representation. In comparing public defenders, publicly appointed private counsel, contract lawyers, and privately retained lawyers, studies vary on which type of counsel results in better outcomes for the client. Overall, however, researchers have found that publicly appointed private counsel tend to perform worse than professional public defenders in both federal and state courts. So far, the Supreme Court has not examined how the right to a lawyer may be affected by the way that a lawyer is hired and paid, which are factors that these studies indicate may have a significant impact on whether an indigent defendant receives adequate assistance of counsel.

Indigent defendants who rely on appointed counsel commonly face the problem of lacking access to a lawyer or having access only to an overextended lawyer. These problems are due to the indigent defendant's inability to pay for a private lawyer's time and attention. Due to caseload pressures and pay structures, most appointed lawyers cannot take most cases to trial. However, as discussed above, most cases likely do not need to go to trial. Thus, for defendants who rely on appointed counsel, the more pressing issue is their lawyer's limited time to conduct basic interviews and counseling, and to prepare the case for a better plea deal. [We will discuss the importance of preparation for plea bargaining in Chapter Seven.]

2. Limited Indigent Defense Budgets

Regardless of how lawyers are appointed, due to budgetary constraints they tend to carry high caseloads and have limited time for each individual client. In 1973, the National Advisory Commission on Criminal Justice Standards and Goals recommended that criminal defense lawyers carry no more than 150 felonies or 400 misdemeanor cases in any given year. However, most public defender offices are unable to enforce these caseload limits. For example, the Department of Justice reported in 2007 that seventy-three percent of "county-based public defender offices" nationwide exceeded this limit. Contributing to the higher caseloads is the lack of formal caseload limits, with the Department of Justice reporting that only fifteen percent of surveyed public defender offices had such formal limits and only thirty-six percent had the authority to refuse cases due to high caseloads.

....

Indigent defense lawyers may have limited, or no, resources to investigate a case or appoint an expert. In the context of plea bargaining, these limitations create a perfect storm that encourages high plea rates, discourages negotiation, and contributes to many defendants feeling that they are simply getting processed through the system, but are not receiving individualized attention or justice. These combined realities are serious structural problems facing the criminal defense bar that make it difficult to reform plea bargaining without providing more resources. Simply mandating that defense lawyers do better without increased resources is unlikely to have much impact.

* * *

What If Defendants Only Plead After They Had Full Discovery from the Prosecution?

Few states require the prosecution to turn over all discovery before plea bargaining or before a plea deal is concluded. Prosecutors are required to turn over exculpatory information, but this is subject to interpretation (what is exculpatory?), and this does not include a requirement to turn over all information supporting the charges. Without a clear right to discovery, prosecutors may not provide it. Consider this situation:

> Here's how it went. [A] client would hire me for a DWI or weed case. I'd go to court and ask for a copy of the police report. I'd be told that they could read it to me (no seriously, they would say this), or sometimes even let me read it. But if I wanted a copy then I would have to file a discovery motion and then they would withdraw all plea offers and force my client to trial. So basically they set up a closed file system to bully defendants into pleading guilty without looking at the evidence.

Cynthia Alkon, *The Right to Defense Discovery in Plea Bargaining: Fifty Years After Brady v. Maryland*, 38 N.Y.U. Rev. L. & Soc. Change 407 (2014). Quote above from Robert Guest, *Michael Morton Act Becomes Law—No More Closed Files in Texas*, Dallas Crim. Def. Lawyer Blog (May 16, 2013), https://www.dallascriminaldefenselawyerblog.com/michael-morton-act-beco-mes-law-no-more-closed-files-in-texas/.

One reform proposal, increasingly adopted by states, is to mandate that prosecutors turn over all information to the defense so defendants know the strength of the case against them, and so their lawyers know all the information that might be relevant for the plea negotiation.

Should Defense Lawyers Adopt an "Abolitionist Ethic"?

"What does an abolitionist ethic mean for a public defender? Fundamentally, it is a merger of retail-scale zealous criminal defense with wholesale structural change aimed at dismantling the criminal system. Beyond that, it means building a world in which police, jails, and prisons are obsolete. And it employs frameworks and advocacy tools that are accessible to public defense. A public defender's abolitionist ethic combines a racial justice lens informed by Critical Race Theory to understand the forces that animate the criminal system; zealous holistic defense of individuals infused with the spirit of resistance lawyering; movement lawyering to support social justice advocacy aimed at reducing the size, scope, and scale of the system on the way to dismantling it; and organized efforts to render the carceral state dispensable.

Shifting the paradigm of public defense and the work of public defenders is no easy task. Indeed, it is laden with challenges. Inadequate funding, the skepticism that travels with abolition, the sheer difficulty of criminal defense work, and the seemingly intractable nature of the criminal system can make the turn to an abolitionist ethic seem like a fruitless pursuit.... Defenders fight against long odds in an unforgiving system. They do so for a host of reasons, among them the hope that what they do will make a difference in the broader fight for the dignity and humanity of those they represent...." Vincent M. Southerland, *Public Defense and an Abolitionist Ethic*, 99 New York University Law Review, 635 (2024).

Is this something that defense lawyers should fight for? How realistic is this for a new public defender in a large and established public defenders office? Or for a more senior public defender in a smaller and newly established office?

As you have read, the most recent U.S. Supreme Court cases on plea bargaining focused on the client counseling phase of plea bargaining. In *Padilla v. Kentucky*, 559 U.S. 356 (2010), the Court held that lawyers should advise their clients of the collateral immigration consequences of a plea bargain. In *Lafler v. Cooper,*132 S. Ct. 1376 (2012), the Court held that it was incompetent assistance of counsel for a lawyer to wrongly advise their client about their case. In *Missouri v. Frye*, 566 U.S. 134 (2012), the Court held that it was incompetent assistance of counsel to not advise a client about an offer. *Lafler*, *Frye*, and *Padilla* do not represent changes in how defense lawyers do their jobs, as it has been clear for decades that good lawyers should do these things, and more. These cases are a step forward in that they are a formal recognition that defendants have a Constitutional right to competent representation in plea bargaining.

Another focus of reform has been to improve indigent defense. As you have read, the vast majority of criminal defendants cannot afford to hire a lawyer. In major urban areas, the predominate model of criminal defense is through public defender offices. Some of the finest defense lawyers in the United States work in these offices, such as the Federal Public Defender, the Los Angeles County Public Defender (with over 600 lawyers) and the Public Defender Service for the District of Columbia. Some states have statewide public defender offices, so the representation is not different in each county.

But, for most defendants, the quality of the defense lawyer depends entirely on where they are arrested and whether it is a county with few resources and a system of poorly paid appointed counsel, or a larger county with more resources. One basic reform proposal is to increase funding to defense services to guarantee that every defendant has a lawyer who can put the necessary time into client interviewing and counseling, investigating the case, and appointing any relevant experts, such as a psychologist to evaluate the client. The goal of this reform proposals is to move beyond the "meet and plead" system that exists in some counties.

B. Change Prosecutorial Behavior

As you have read, the extraordinary power that prosecutors enjoy in the plea bargaining process raises concerns, including that innocent defendants may feel pressured into pleading guilty. The following reform proposals focus on how to lessen that problem. First you will read about hard bargaining in plea bargaining and proposals to limit it. Next you will read the suggestion that if prosecutors took the time and put resources into changing how cases are screened before charges are filed, it could lessen the trial penalty problem, and it could also help to increase public confidence in the criminal legal system, as cases would not settle for a fraction of the original charges.

1. Reduce Prosecutorial Hard Bargaining

One reform proposal is to limit when prosecutors can engage in hard bargaining What tactics are appropriate and which tactics cross the line? Hard bargaining tactics remain legal and, with only a few narrow exceptions, prosecutors are free to engage in hard bargaining. One argument against hard bargaining is that it can work to undermine the defense lawyer's role, as it leaves defendants with no options and forces a plea deal. The challenge is figuring out when hard bargaining behavior should be restricted. In the previous chapter, Cynthia Alkon outlined several of the questionable hard bargaining tactics. In a continuation of that article, she now argues for how and why these tactics should be limited.

Cynthia Alkon, *Hard Bargaining in Plea Bargaining: When Do Prosecutors Cross the Line?*

17 Nev. L.J. 401, 425–427 (2017)

...

VII. Which Hard Bargaining Tactics Should Be Restricted?

A. Exploding Offers

This might be the easiest category to consider. In ordinary criminal cases, prosecutors should not rush defendants in their decision of whether to accept a deal or not. No defendant should be forced to decide on the day of arraignment whether to take a particular plea offer. As noted above, there can be good reasons to place time limits on offers—but those reasons should be clearly stated on the record and should involve goals beyond simply moving the docket. It should be acceptable to limit an offer until the day a child victim or victim of a violent crime, including sexual assault, would have to come to court and testify. It should not, however, be acceptable for prosecutors to keep offers open only until a police officer testifies. Testifying is part of a police officer's official duties. As such, there would ordinarily be no reason to pressure defendants to accept plea deals to spare police officers from testifying. Defendants should never face the choice between taking an offer and getting discovery on a case. The U.S. Supreme Court has not yet held that defendants have a right to all discovery, prior to plea bargaining. However, as a basic rule, prosecutors, even in jurisdictions without open file discovery rules, should not make a plea offer at arraignment that is good only for that day. This is due to the concern that, as a practical matter, forcing pleas at arraignment shuts off the defendant's ability to get full discovery in the case. If there is a good reason to resolve cases at arraignment, prosecutors and courts should allow the defense to continue the arraignment until a day when the defense will have full discovery and will have had an opportunity to speak to the defendant about the case and about options. If a defense lawyer does not have full discovery in the case, she cannot competently advise her client about what to do. This includes whether there should be further investigation or motions. Depriving a defense lawyer of discovery is a clear usurpation of the representation function. Doing so reduces the defense lawyer to merely a conduit for conveying the offer without the ability to provide any meaningful advice or to make meaningful counter-offers because the defense lawyer may not know enough about the case to do either. Prosecutors should also not be allowed to continue the practice of taking offers off the table if or when the defense files certain motions, such as search and seizure motions. Prosecutors often use the threat of withdrawing the offer to prevent defense lawyers from making motions, including, in some cases, to prevent them from requesting discovery. The fact that the defense may want to explore the strength of the prosecution's discovery and file motions should not result in offers being withdrawn. Prosecutors who engage in this practice are clearly usurping the defense attorney's role, and can be acting to prevent effective assistance of counsel. The fact that the defendant may not prevail in the motion should not be dispositive in determining whether the prosecutor engaged in hard bargaining tactics. Search and seizure motions can be difficult to win, but there are good tactical reasons to file such motions, including that it may give the defense lawyer a better sense of how an individual police officer will be as a witness. If the prosecutor makes a direct threat to withdraw an offer when the defense files a motion, or states an intention to file a motion, that should be considered inappropriate hard bargaining.

B. Threats to Add Charges or Enhancements

Once a prosecutor has made a plea offer and the defense has rejected it, they should not be allowed to add additional charges or enhancements. Prosecutors should also not be allowed to threaten to add charges if the defense rejects the offer. As discussed above, the threat to add additional charges also acts to undermine the defense lawyer's role. The challenge with establishing this as a clear rule is that it will likely lead to prosecutors adding enhancements and charges at the beginning of the case. This could have the effect of adding pressure on the defendant and being even more coercive because the first charges and potential maximum will be so much more serious. This challenge points out the reality that simply restricting prosecutorial hard bargaining tactics, in the absence of other substantive reforms to the criminal justice system, can be easily worked around by professionals in the system who choose to "game it." What makes these threats so powerful is that the existing laws allow for extreme penalties for acts that might not [otherwise] be so serious....

C. Take-It-or-Leave-It Offers

There can be times when it is appropriate for the prosecution to make a set plea offer and not negotiate further. The question would be why is the prosecutor refusing to negotiate? If it is to pressure the defendant to plead guilty, and the prosecutor is refusing to listen to new evidence or mitigating circumstances that call for a reconsideration of the plea offer, then it would be an unacceptable hard bargaining tactic. If the reason is simply that the case is standard, the offer is standard, and there is no reason to change it, this would not in and of itself constitute unacceptable prosecutorial hard bargaining. A district attorney's office may have decided to adopt a policy to handle particular crimes in a uniform way. There are good policy arguments against both mandatory minimums and adopting such sweeping policies. However, looking at the totality of the circumstances, if the prosecutor's office is making take-it-or-leave-it offers as part of a policy of making uniform offers, and not as part of an effort to pressure defendants to take the plea deals, this would not cross the line in terms of hard bargaining practices.

D. Threats to Seek the Death Penalty

... [C]oncern is raised when prosecutors threaten the death penalty to pressure defendants to accept plea deals when they have not already filed as a capital case. The challenge is the same as above in that a clear rule prohibiting prosecutors from filing later to seek death may just encourage more capital-case indictments earlier in the process and not reduce the actual number of times the threat of death is used to encourage defendants to take plea deals. A rule preventing later filing of capital charges could also work to undermine prosecutors' offices that have adopted policies to make sure their death prosecutions are well-considered and happen later in the process, not at the initial filing. However, it is time for the Court to move beyond a blanket acceptance of prosecutors threatening to seek the death penalty simply because the defendant is aware of the "relevant circumstances" and the result (death) would be a lawful penalty.

* * *

Change the Prosecutor?

Is yet another option to change the prosecutor? Since 2016, a number of reform-minded prosecutors have been elected around the country including in Philadelphia, Chicago, Cleveland, Denver, Orlando, Houston, and Corpus Christi. If the laws do not change, will these prosecutors change the practices in meaningful ways? Some prosecutors, such as Larry Krasner in Philadelphia whom we have already highlighted, are former defense lawyers.

These prosecutors have been making statements recognizing the inequities and bias in the criminal legal system and moving beyond standard "tough on crime" rhetoric. They are making changes in bail and changes in terms of which crimes they will or will not prosecute.

For example, the New York DA announced in August 2018 it would no longer prosecute marijuana possession and smoking cases. The Press Release reported:

> … the policy is expected to reduce Manhattan marijuana prosecutions from approximately 5,000 per year to approximately 200 per year, a 96% reduction.
>
> "The dual mission of the Manhattan DA's Office is a safer New York and a more equal justice system," said District Attorney Vance. "The ongoing arrest and criminal prosecution of predominantly black and brown New Yorkers for smoking marijuana serves neither of these goals. Effective August 1st, my Office will decline to prosecute marijuana possession and smoking cases…."

Others have questioned whether even the best progressive prosecutors will bring far-reaching change:

> [for] many prosecutors the essential purpose of the job is, after all, to prosecute—that is, to investigate, charge, convict, and punish. Further, an entrenched culture quickly culturizes even new prosecutors who purport to share progressive ideals. As two scholars have noted, "[o]ver time, the new hires became increasingly punitive, and no amount of training could counter this trend." And even when new policies are implemented, strong resistance can come from judges, many of whom were themselves prosecutors who, as institutional actors in the criminal legal system, can cling tightly to the status quo.

Brooks Holland & Steven Zeidman, *Progressive Prosecutors or Zealous Defenders, from Coast-to-Coast*, 60 Am. Crim. L. Rev. 1467 (2023).

As you have read earlier in this book, there has been pushback against progressive prosecutors. Some have been voted out of office. Some have had their powers limited by the governors of their state. And, judges have pushed back. How far reaching is changing the DA? Would it concern you to practice in a county, or live in a county, where the elected DA changes every four years (or less) due to controversies about how they are doing their job? You may want to consider these questions as you continue reading.

2. Improve Prosecutorial Screening of Cases

Professors Ron Wright and Marc Miller, in the article below, suggest that "a more structured and reasoned charge selection process" could be a third alternative between plea bargaining and trials. This would include four "interrelated features, all internal to the prosecutor's office: early assessment, reasoned selection, barriers to bargains, and enforcement." In more detail, these four features are:

1. "[T]he prosecutor's office must make an early and careful assessment of each case, and demand that police and investigators provide sufficient information before the initial charge is filed."
2. "[T]he prosecutor's office must file only appropriate charges. Which charges are 'appropriate' is determined by several factors. A prosecutor should only file charges that the office would generally want to result in a criminal conviction and sanction. In addition, appropriate charges must reflect reasonably accu-

One concern about prosecutorial conduct during plea bargaining is that prosecutors may have both implicit and explicit bias that could influence their decision-making about what is an appropriate offer to a particular defendant in their case. As you have read earlier, people of color are pulled into the criminal legal system at disproportionately high numbers. One proposal is that prosecutors should do a blind assessment when making their first offer. This means that when they review the file all identifying information, such as the defendant's name, race, address, age, and gender should be removed. Depending on the jurisdiction, this could also extend to deleting information about the arresting officer (if that will identify the neighborhood). Demographic information about the witnesses or victims may also need to be anonymized. This would leave a prosecutor focused on the facts of the case in determining what plea offer to make.

See Cynthia Alkon, *Bargaining Without Bias*, 73 Rutgers University Law Review 1337 (Summer 2021).

rately what actually occurred. They are charges that the prosecutor can very likely prove in court."

3. "Third, and critically, the office must severely restrict all plea bargaining, and most especially charge bargains. Prosecutors should also recognize explicitly that the screening process is the mechanism that makes such restrictions possible."
4. "Fourth, the kind of prosecutorial screening we advocate must include sufficient training, oversight, and other internal enforcement mechanisms to ensure reasonable uniformity in charging and relatively few changes to charges after they have been filed."

Wright and Miller studied the impact of a more robust screening process on how criminal cases were handled in New Orleans.

Ronald Wright & Marc Miller, *The Screening/Bargaining Tradeoff*

55 Stan. L. Rev. 29, 34, 58–68, 74, 84 (2002)

... We know this practice [improved screening] is viable because it is now operating in a few American jurisdictions, without much controversy and without attracting the attention it deserves. For instance, over the last three decades New Orleans District Attorney Harry Connick has emphasized early screening of cases and has actively discouraged any changes of criminal charges as a result of negotiations after the charges are filed. Furthermore, the office maintains an extraordinary database, containing detailed information on more than ten years' worth of felony cases. This data allows us to test whether the District Attorney's policies have any real impact.

The heart of this paper ... is our study of the New Orleans data. It confirms that a prosecutor can invest serious resources in early evaluation of cases and maintain this practice over the long run. This screening leads to relatively high rates of declination (that is, refusals to prosecute a case after the police recommend charges). When combined with policies discouraging reductions in charges once they are filed, the results are lower levels of negotiated pleas, slightly higher rates of trial, and notably higher rates of open guilty pleas than in typical American jurisdictions. This combination of policies can survive political and administrative challenges of many types....

What should we expect to happen when a prosecutor decides to shift the screening/bargaining tradeoff in the direction of screening? As for changes in case processing, the most direct effect should be measurable: fewer plea bargains. The kinds of plea bargains that are easiest to track are charge reductions after cases are filed. A jurisdiction with hard screening practices should produce fewer and smaller charge reductions than a jurisdiction with weaker screening practices.

A second measurable impact of screening policies might be a smaller number of charges dismissed (whether mandated by judges or voluntarily entered by prosecutors) because the prosecutors should remove weaker cases from the system early. We might also expect higher levels of declination and perhaps greater use of diversion programs. Traditional assumptions about the plea bargain/trial tradeoff would predict an increase in trials from a decrease in plea bargains, but we have shown the traditional assumptions are misguided, and the actual effect on trial rates of implementing the screening/bargaining tradeoff is hard to predict.

The city of New Orleans would probably not appear at the top of most lists of progressive criminal justice systems. When the system has received national attention, it has been for alleged police corruption, including instances of officers killing people for profit. Criminal justice in Louisiana makes national news for gambling charges against notorious figures such as former Governor Edwin Edwards, not for any causes dear to reformers. Locally, the large and stressed NODA office has received criticism for its discovery practices and its aggressive use of habitual felon laws. But all of this turbulence on the surface of New Orleans criminal justice obscures a deeper reality about the local system. The New Orleans District Attorney's Office follows principled screening practices that make it one of the most interesting prosecutor's offices in the country. Those aspects of the NODA office deserve widespread attention from other prosecutors and scholars.

A. Harry Connick Sings a Reform Tune

Harry Connick was elected as the District Attorney for Orleans Parish in 1974. He has remained in that office for the past twenty-eight years. Connick first ran for office in 1969 against incumbent Jim Garrison, the flamboyant District Attorney made famous in the film JFK. His first unsuccessful campaign did not focus on plea bargaining. He promised faster prosecution and better tracking of defendants who failed to appear for trial. His 1973 campaign began with a similar emphasis on swift prosecution. As the campaign wore on, however, Connick's speeches began to feature attacks on plea bargaining.

At first he criticized reduced charges for murder cases and later expanded the critique to other crimes. He complained that the part-time prosecutors in the office used plea bargaining solely to "move" cases and avoid trial. Connick told voters that widespread plea bargaining was wrong; years later, he explained that victims were right to resent it when cases were bargained away simply because of a "lazy" prosecutor. He promised to eliminate "baseless" plea bargaining and to hire full-time prosecutors who would not use plea bargains just to move cases from the docket.

As in other American cities, the criminal courts in New Orleans deal with enormous volume. In the face of this large urban caseload, Connick needed a strategy to carry out his campaign statements about plea bargaining. During the weeks between his election victory and taking office, he started speaking publicly about a plan with two central components. First, Connick planned to devote expertise and resources to screening. He proposed a screening procedure that "would weed out those cases really not worthy of being on the criminal docket, so more courtroom emphasis can be devoted to the violent offender." Second, he instructed his prosecutors not to engage in plea bargaining—particularly charge bargaining—except under very limited circumstances. In other words, Connick recognized and tried to implement the screening/bargaining tradeoff. Connick bolstered this policy change by assigning some of his more senior trial attorneys into the screening office and by instituting a variety of procedures to monitor and reinforce screening norms. Furthermore, Connick recognized that the huge flow of cases, the large staff, high staff turnover, and the inevitable pressures for bargaining would hinder this plan. Thus, he developed data and information systems that allowed him to review and guide the work of his staff, and to defend the work of the office to the legislature and the public.

The distinctiveness of the screening process in the NODA office is apparent from a closer examination of the path each new case takes through the system. Police officers develop a case folder after they complete an investigation and file charges with the magistrate. The first stop for the case folder in the NODA office is the Magistrate Section, where the least experienced assistants work. They typically have logged six months or fewer on the job. The ADA from the Magistrate Section appears for the state at the first appearance and bail hearing before the magistrate. A public defender is also present for the first appearance, but the case is reassigned immediately after the hearing and there is typically no further defense presence or participation in the case until after the DA files an information or obtains an indictment.

After any proceedings in the Magistrate Division, the folder moves to the Screening Section of the NODA office. Connick devotes extraordinary resources to this operation. For instance, in the late 1990s, about fifteen of the eighty-five attorneys in the office worked in Screening. The Screening Section is no political backwater within the office: The last two First Assistants in the office moved up to that position after serving as head of the Screening Section. All attorneys in the Screening Section served previously (usually a couple of years) in the Trial Section. This level of experience comes at a premium in New Orleans, where the turnover among prosecuting attorneys is quite high. The average tenure of an ADA in the NODA office is around two years....

If screening prosecutors overcharge cases too often, the Chief of the Trial Section might send the screening attorney back into the courtroom on at least one of those overcharged matters to "get his teeth kicked in." Supervisors review all refusals to charge. Attorneys say they often compare notes, especially in early morning discussions, and this helps to educate and develop shared charging norms in the office. Office policy discourages refusal for select categories of crimes, notably domestic violence cases. For the most serious crimes, including rape and homicide, the office conducts "charge conferences" with senior prosecutors and police present to discuss the facts and potential charges.

Neither Connick nor any attorneys in his office claim to have abolished plea bargaining entirely from the New Orleans system. Prosecutors in the office acknowledge that sometimes new information appears and changes the value of a case. Witnesses leave town, victims decide not to testify, new witnesses appear, and investigators find new evidence. On occasion, the screening attorney makes a bad judgment and overcharges, and a plea could save the case. Connick's hope to minimize plea bargaining and the screening techniques he chose to pursue that goal would by themselves make NODA practices an important case study. But Connick added another critical tool to his administrative kit. From the earliest times, he relied on computerized information systems. Connick often invoked the slogan, "If you can't measure it, you can't manage it." During his first term in office, he combined this interest in data with his commitment to screening cases and suppressing negotiated guilty pleas.

This data system operates primarily as an internal office management tool. The office does not issue standard public reports based on the data. The system collects details about each step of the process, from intake through final disposition. It identifies both the decisionmaker (such as the screening attorney) and the reasons for each processing decision along the way. A standardized set of codes capture the reasons attorneys invoke most frequently to explain their choices. Data systems are not cheap. In addition to the costs of hardware, software, and expertise to run the system, Connick employs as many as five people to enter data. Why would a prosecutor in an environment with sharply limited resources invest in data systems? Information systems respond to limited resources and rapid turnover of lawyers since they make it easier to supervise the constant stream of new attorneys. In part because the NODA data system operates for internal administration purposes, it provides reliable information to test the claims of the office.... Although Connick refers occasionally to summary statistics, no detailed reports go to the public regarding particular cases or particular units of the office. The system exists more for management than for public relations purposes. Thus, there is little temptation to obscure important decisions in the data. The next section of this Part describes some of the initial findings from this internal data....

There is direct and indirect evidence in the New Orleans data about the success of the screening/bargaining tradeoff. The direct evidence points to the proportion of cases resolved in a manner where plea bargains are unlikely; the remainder of the cases describe the pool where plea bargains are more likely. The NODA office received around 430,000 charge recommendations in around 280,000 cases between 1988 and 1999. Plea bargains are unlikely (though not impossible) for all cases resolved through trial. Of the cases filed in state court, 74% were resolved through pleas and 13% through trials. Charge bargaining is also unlikely for cases where the defendant pleads guilty as charged. Of the 74% of cases filed that are resolved through guilty pleas, the first direct indication of the absence of charge bargaining appears in the category "pled guilty as charged."... [T]he plea was guilty as charged in 65% of all cases filed.

Combining the proportion of all filed cases resolved through trials (13%) and through pleas of guilty as charged (65%), 78% of all cases filed are resolved in a manner consistent with the goals of the screening/bargaining tradeoff, and inconsistent with charge bargaining. This is the strongest direct statistical evidence in support of the viability of the screening/bargaining hypothesis. What does the data show about charge bargaining? Since 78% of all cases filed are resolved in a manner inconsistent with charge bargaining, at most 22% of all cases fall in categories that may reflect charge bargaining. The closeness of the link between the remaining categories and charge bargaining varies greatly, and provides clues rather than direct evidence....

Based on our limited information about rates of pleas to lesser charges, New Orleans appears to be one of the few jurisdictions that combines low rates in both indicators of potential charge bargaining. Even though only part of the category of dismissed cases should be attributed to charge bargaining, these figures do suggest that much less charge bargaining occurs in New Orleans than elsewhere. Together, the two central statistics (guilty pleas to a lesser charge plus nolle pros after filing of case) provide the key empirical evidence of the screening/bargaining tradeoff at work. By this measure, New Orleans looks different from some other jurisdictions. The data suggest an unusually high level of open pleas in the New Orleans criminal justice system, a strong sign of success.

We believe that hard screening policies are more attractive than plea bargaining on a number of fronts. In particular, we believe that screening improves the honesty and accessibility of criminal justice. The vices of plea bargaining are legion; many of them, however, grow from the fact that prosecutors who decide to file charges can send false signals about the value of a case. Indeed, prosecutors can send false signals multiple times. A properly functioning policy of hard screening forces the prosecutor to send a single consistent signal about the case. It allows the defendant and the public to see more clearly how the prosecutor's office uses limited resources. When prosecutors screen effectively enough to make plea negotiations uncommon, they combine many (but not all) of the virtues not only of bargain-centered systems, but also of trials.

Notes/Questions

1. Would reducing over-charging through the changes Wright & Miller outline reduce prosecutorial hard bargaining?

2. As a defense lawyer, what are the advantages and disadvantages of improved prosecutorial screening of cases? As a prosecutor, what are the advantages and disadvantages of improved prosecutorial screening of cases?

3. Increase the Role of Judges

The federal system prohibits judges from being involved in plea negotiations with the defense and prosecution. That prohibition, however, is not the norm at the state level. One suggestion for reform is to increase the role of judges to have them act as a counterbalance against the disproportionate power of prosecutors. A recent study found that judges are already taking a more active role in plea bargaining and that this role can help to better protect defendants. The next article reports interviews with judges, prosecutors and defense attorneys and includes their views on judicial involvement in plea bargaining. As a prosecutor, what can you learn from the defense by how some defense lawyers view judicial involvement in plea bargaining? As a defense lawyer, what do these quotes tell you about how some prosecutors view plea bargaining? And what can you learn about the judges' views?

Nancy J. King & Ronald F. Wright, *The Invisible Revolution in Plea Bargaining: Managerial Judging and Judicial Participation in Negotiations*

95 Tex. L. Rev. 325, 326–327, 366–375, 380–385 (2016)

...

We learned that judicial involvement in negotiations is now institutionalized and embedded in the very structure of many court systems in ways never dreamed of in the 1970s. With no fanfare from scholars, "managerial judging," the philosophy that transformed civil litigation in the late twentieth century, has finally taken hold in criminal litigation, more than thirty years later. Along with this shift in philosophy, the judge's participation in negotiations has matured into a standard managerial tool. What once were informal, sometimes-illicit interactions between judges and parties in criminal cases have in many courts evolved into highly structured best practices for docket management....

In addition, we learned that judges and lawyers value judicial contributions to negotiations for many reasons other than efficiency. Our interviewees turned upside down some of the well-worn objections to judges' involvement. Information deficits and potential coercion of the defendant, for example, raised concerns only for a small portion of our interviewees. Instead, defense attorneys, prosecutors, and judges alike explained to us how the judge's involvement often mitigated the uncertainty and compulsion a prosecutor's early offer can present. Prosecutors accepted the judge's input, sometimes grudgingly, as an additional route to settlement; meanwhile, many defense attorneys felt confident that they could use the judge's presence to benefit their clients, while shielding them from coercion....

1. Better (Not Just Faster) Outcomes.—Judges reported that participating in discussions about potential sentences allowed them to educate prosecutors about why the sentence terms they had offered were excessive. In these conferences, said one, "I'll say that a lot, 'Why should the public have to pay to house him for three or four years when you and I know this guy is no danger?'" Explained another, "We get some [state's] assistants that aren't too smart; they don't realize they won't get anything better." The judge continued, "If I had to wait until the plea colloquy, I can't talk to them then.... I say to the state, 'You really think you are going to win this case?'" Some considered their participation to be an essential source of impartial information for an assistant prosecutor who is bound by office policy and may have less experience: "The judge has the neutral role and is not an advocate for one side.... [S]omeone not beholden to the prosecutor's office or food chain politics, who is able to look at a case and provide some balance ...."

Prosecutors with management responsibility also remarked that judicial participation in plea discussions is helpful when the attorneys involved are inexperienced or overzealous....

Judges also noted that their involvement can help to reach a more just resolution when they are concerned that inexperienced defense attorneys are going astray, against the best interests of their clients. Judges who conduct these discussions in a group setting reported that it allows the more experienced defense counsel to teach the rookie attorneys about law and strategy. A number of judges also suggested that a defense attorney might occasionally need education from the judge, as when the attorney is out to prove a point at the expense of her client, has overlooked a problem, or has an unrealistic view of the case. Stated one judge, "[I]f there is an unreasonable defense practitioner who is looking to jam up the system, wanting to have as many cases set for trial or push things as far as they can to gum up the works, the judge is able to impact things then." One judge recalled a colleague who was known to have said to defense attorneys: "Are you kidding? This deal is so good, if he doesn't take it I will!"...

Finally, several judges noted that, in talking with the parties, they would suggest dispositions or conditions of probation that neither party had thought about, but that they believed were appropriate for the particular case....

2. The Strategic Utility of Judicial Participation to Prosecutors.—In past years, some prosecutors have voiced opposition to proposals to authorize judicial participation; several of the prosecutors we interviewed were not fans of it, either. We were somewhat surprised, then, to hear from many prosecutors that judicial participation held several advantages for them. Most even said they prefer it over a system in which judicial input was not available before the plea. We have already seen that prosecutors value judicial participation for its efficiency effects and that they appreciate how judges train and moderate assistants who are inexperienced or overzealous.... One former prosecutor put it this way:

> [I]t is unusual, but in politically sensitive cases—sex crimes, domestic violence cases—there are times when the DA has to take a really hard position politically, but maybe they have a weak case.... They'll want to do what I call, "pass the poop." They want the judge to offer on the deal, so, if the guy goes out and sexually assaults somebody else, the judge would have been the one who let him out early.... [Prosecutors] are elected. If the cops think the DA is going too lenient, the cops can go AWOL.... The media won't know who the line deputy was.... It would be the *elected* district attorney who would get the flak if the police got mad.

Another California prosecutor emphasized the utility of a judge's indication of sentence when dealing with victims: ... "Victims call and voice their displeasure. You say, 'I'm sorry this wasn't our offer, it was the court's offer. We encourage you to come to sentencing and let him know your views.'" A Michigan prosecutor explained that some prosecutors might "actually [be] glad the judge does this—keeps the pleas moving—it allows the prosecutors to look like they are tough on crime."...

Assistant prosecutors had another reason to appreciate judicial input: it allowed them to avoid having to enforce a boss's rigid office policy in particular cases. "If I had an unreasonable boss that was gung ho on a case that was hopeless," explained one former assistant DA, "[and] my supervisor said I can't dump this, so I said, 'If the court does this I won't object, but I'm constrained.'"

Judges and defense attorneys mentioned this as well. As one defense attorney described it, when the line prosecutor "doesn't want to get in trouble with the boss, but wouldn't mind if the outcome were lower than office policy allows.... [He'll] just signal to me, saying something like, 'Let's ask for a conference on this one.' Wink, wink."...

3. For the Defense: Better Sentences.—In describing judicial participation and why they favor it, most interviewees told us that judicial input usually leads to sentences that are more lenient than the sentences defense attorneys would obtain for their clients if they had to deal with the prosecutor alone.... Said [a defense lawyer], "If you do have a prosecutor who won't deal, you still have an avenue to seek leniency for the client." And, we heard, when the prosecutor does offer a deal, the judge's view of the appropriate sentence is often more lenient than the prosecutor's offer. The judge's input offered a "face-saving" way for "gung ho" prosecutors to acknowledge weaknesses in their case: "[T]hey [hear] the judge say the same words that the defense lawyer was telling them about the problems with the case." Another said, "The judge backs them down, and the prosecutor will then bow to reality." In sum, defense attorneys agreed that judicial participation systematically helped their clients to receive lower sentences, not just in a few unusual cases. Judges acknowledged that they regularly try to persuade the prosecutors to take a more lenient stance....

4. Increased Certainty for All.—The most important thing, many interviewees told us, was that hearing from the judge on the sentence provided certainty—for defendants, victims, and attorneys....

b. The Certainty that Judicial Input Brings.—For the parties, the judge's advance views on sentencing provided welcome assurance that, if they proposed a sentence, the judge would probably accept their proposal. The sentence preview was especially important, said a North Carolina attorney, in "serious, victim" cases, which "all attract media attention." In those cases, "if I'm dealing with an open plea, I'm not doing my job. A charge bargain without a sentence recommendation is just way too much leeway to allow the judge, even with structured sentencing." Summed up by a Maryland attorney, it is "a big deal to be able to tell a client with confidence that a certain disposition will follow from a guilty plea." California attorneys echoed that, when a defendant was considering pleading guilty as charged ("eating the sheet") instead of taking the prosecutor's offer, knowing what sentence the judge would impose was crucial. "It would be like standing there naked," said one; "pleading guilty without a sentence indicated is crazy." "You don't *need* it, but it is sure nice to have. Like a tightrope walker, I like the net."

Judges agreed: increased certainty about the sentence is the key advantage of judicial involvement before the plea for defendants. Explained one Michigan judge, pleading guilty without knowing what the sentence will be is "a white-knuckle ride."...

6. Accommodating Early Discovery for the Defense.—Another criticism leveled against any early plea negotiations—not limited to negotiations that involve judicial input—is that defendants are compelled to consider offers before they have had time to investigate the case or receive discovery materials. A few attorneys in two states complained about this, but we found little of this concern in the other states included in our study. Instead, in these states, the practice of judicial involvement may actually prompt prosecutors to reveal more to defense counsel, and to reveal it earlier. Defendants generally receive the discovery they need in time, well before a settlement conference, or can request early discovery if a client wishes to settle before a preliminary hearing. Some interviewees reported that the settlement conference itself serves as a discovery device for the defense because prosecutors had to relate some information to the judge that they may not have disclosed in negotiations with defense counsel alone. Just as judicial involvement in bargaining may, depending on the practice, generate more information for the judge than the judge would have in a case without judicial involvement, it could also generate more information for defense counsel.

7. Informing Clients Who Won't Believe Their Lawyers.—In addition to the information benefits of judicial participation noted above, defense attorneys also perceived judicial participation as particularly helpful when clients are stubborn or do not listen to their advice. We heard this from practitioners in places where judges sometimes talked directly with defendants, as they do in some counties in Oregon, Kansas, and California. The same point came from practitioners in other states where judges met only with the attorneys, and defense counsel relayed to clients what the judge had said.

"It helps to have someone else, someone in the robe, explaining the facts of life," stated one Oregon defense attorney. As one California attorney explained, the client may treat the judge as more authoritative and therefore more believable:

> [B]ecause I'm appointed they call us "public pretenders." They don't think we're real lawyers. They don't trust what I'm saying. They want to hear it from the judge.... So I'll go back—judges are very good at this—and I'll say, "Judge, the client wants to hear from you," and the judge will give 'em a real rundown: "This is why it is serious—have you considered the victim?"... [T]here are some clients who are so used to getting away, particularly abusers. They are bullies; they are used to strong-arming their way. They need someone stronger than they are to boom down on them with a strong voice.... They used to stuff people like me in lockers. I'm saving them from themselves.

Prosecutors and judges also mentioned this. A California judge explained how, upon the request of a defense attorney, he reviews the DA's offer with the defendant and then comments along these lines:

I'm not here to choose for you—it is entirely your decision and it doesn't matter to me—but at the same time, to the extent your lawyer is saying that is a good offer and to give it some thought, I would echo that's probably right. But it's your call....

These conversations between the judge and the defendant raise the specter of coercion. Indeed, one of the perennial risks of judicial involvement in negotiations is the prospect that the judge might create too much pressure to plead guilty for defendants who believe they are innocent or would rather go to trial. We pursued this topic with our interviewees. Several defense attorneys, judges, and even prosecutors acknowledged some risk that a judge might cross the line while speaking with a defendant. But they also believed that standard limits on the judge's involvement kept that risk low, and that the benefits to the defense far outweighed that risk. In their view, judicial involvement made an already coercive situation a little less so....

Even where settlement conferences were reportedly mandatory, a defendant could opt out if he was intent on going to trial. Judges, for their part, told us that they had no time to get involved if the defendant had not already decided to plead guilty. "I don't have *time* to work on you," said one. "I've got too many cases. [I]t's like Lucy and Ethyl in there; we *have* to keep it moving, to preserve resources to be able to fully litigate the cases that need to be fully litigated." Some noted that some judges would try to get the parties to settle even when the defendant had not asked for it, but these attorneys did not perceive this as a problem.

Notes/Questions

1. What do you think about this proposal? What are the potential risks? What are the possible benefits? What are the possible unintended consequences?

2. What role might victims play as the judges increase their role in plea bargaining?

C. Systemic Change

Another approach to reform is to look at the system as a whole. This approach could incorporate all of the changes suggested above, plus others that are focused on systemic issues, such as collecting better data about the criminal legal system as a whole.

In 2019 the ABA formed a Task Force on Plea Bargaining. The task force collected written and oral testimony from experts around the United States about plea bargaining and how it works in practice. The Task Force wrote a report summarizing the concerns expressed through this testimony. The Task Force then recommended a set of fourteen Guiding Principles on Plea Bargaining. As the report points out, given that plea bargaining works differently in every jurisdiction, and sometimes in every courtroom, it is not possible to have one comprehensive set of recommendations for reform. Instead, the Task Force adopted guiding principles that should be considered in any discussions about plea bargaining reform and larger criminal legal system reform.

ABA Task Force on Plea Bargaining Guiding Principles on Plea Bargaining[12]

1. A vibrant and active docket of criminal trials and pre- and post-trial litigation is essential to promote transparency, accountability, justice, and legitimacy in the criminal justice system.
2. Guilty pleas should not result from the use of impermissibly coercive incentives or incentives that overbear the will of the defendant.
3. In general, while some difference between the sentence offered prior to trial and the sentence received after trial is permissible, a substantial difference undermines the integrity of the criminal system and reflects a penalty for exercising one's right to trial. This differential, often referred to as the trial penalty, should be eliminated.
4. Charges should not be selected or amended with the purpose of creating a sentencing differential, sentencing enhancement, punishment or collateral consequence to induce a defendant to plead guilty or to punish defendants for exercising their rights, including the right to trial.
5. The criminal justice system should recognize that plea bargaining induces defendants to plead guilty for various reasons, some of which have little or nothing to do with factual and legal guilt. In the current system, innocent people sometimes plead guilty to crimes they did not commit.
6. A defendant should have a right to qualified counsel in any criminal adjudication before the defendant enters a guilty plea. Counsel should be afforded a meaningful opportunity to satisfy their duty to investigate the case without risk of penalty to their client.
7. There should be robust and transparent procedures at the plea phase to ensure that the defendant's plea is knowing and voluntary, free from impermissible coercion, and that the defendant understands the consequences of their decision to plead guilty.
8. The use of bail or pretrial detention to induce guilty pleas should be eliminated.
9. Defendants should receive all available discovery, including exculpatory materials, prior to entry of a guilty plea, and should have sufficient time to review such discovery before being required to accept or reject a plea offer.
10. Although guilty pleas necessarily involve the waiver of certain trial rights, there are rights that defendants should never be required to waive in a plea agreement.
11. An adequate understanding of the collateral consequences that may flow from a guilty plea is necessary to ensure the guilty plea is knowing and voluntary.

12. ABA Task Force on Plea Bargaining Report, 2023.

12. Law students, lawyers, and judges should receive training on the use and practice of plea bargaining consistent with the findings and recommendations of this Report.
13. Court systems, sentencing commissions, and other criminal justice stakeholders, including prosecutor offices and public defenders, should collect data about the plea process and each individual plea, including the history of plea offers in a case. Data collection should be used to assess and monitor racial and other biases in the plea process.
14. At every stage of the criminal process, there should be robust oversight by all actors in the criminal system to monitor the plea process for accuracy and integrity, to ensure the system operates consistent with the Principles in this Report, and to promote transparency, accountability, justice, and legitimacy in the criminal system.

Questions

1. Which of these Guiding Principles are most relevant to prosecutors? To defense lawyers? To judges?

2. The ABA Task Force on Plea Bargaining Report noted that some of these guiding principles, if turned into changes in practice, could require more resources. Which of these Guiding Principles are most likely to require more spending to implement?

As you have read in this chapter, some of the proposals for reform of plea bargaining require changes in prosecutorial policies. Some require changes in policy and some require changes in the law. As the ABA Task Force on Plea Bargaining acknowledged, changing how plea bargaining works requires attention to the larger system, and not simply to individual pieces. In Chapter 14 you will read more about how a process called Dispute System Design could contribute to making meaningful systemic reforms.

Notes/Questions

1. We know that well over 90% of convictions in the United States are due to plea bargaining. But why might it help to know more about the details about how plea bargaining works? What if you found out that more cases plead guilty on the eve of trial and not at arraignment? Does that indicate that fewer defendants are being pressured to plead guilty? Or does it concern you that more defendants are going back and forth to court and not resolving their cases earlier in the process?

2. New York passed bail reform in 2019. As part of the bail reform law a new database was made publicly available starting in 2020 that reports data about how criminal cases are processed statewide and includes an ability to examine what is going on in individual counties and courtrooms (the judges names are reported for each case). One interesting finding from this data is that the majority of misdemeanor cases in the state are dismissed. If you were a prosecutor and discovered that 73% of misdemeanor cases

What We Don't Know about Plea Bargaining and the Need for Better Data

We know the number of cases resolved through plea bargaining in each state and nationally. However, we do not know much beyond that simple statistic. For example, what percentage of the entirety of criminal cases:

- have a plea offer?
- have a plea offer at arraignment?
- plead guilty at arraignment?

We do not know:

- how long the offer stays open
- what percentage of cases plead out to the charges as filed
- what percentage of cases plead to fewer charges or charges that are entirely different from the charges filed at arraignment.
- how many cases ultimately plead out to a higher offer made by the prosecution after the defense rejected the original offer
- how frequently defense lawyers make the first offer, or if they make a counter offer
- how many cases prosecutors refuse to make any offer
- if defendants reliably get better deals if they wait until their trial date, or if they would get a better deal if they plead out at arraignment.

We also do not know if the type of case might mean there are different answers to these questions. Do misdemeanor cases get essentially the same deal at arraignment as they do on the day of trial? Is it worse for sexual assault or child abuse cases on the day of trial, or on the first date in the process when a witness would testify (such as a preliminary hearing)? Do defendants get significantly worse sentences in felony possession of drug cases if they go to trial?

Andrea Kupfer Schneider & Cynthia Alkon, *Bargaining in the Dark: The Need for Transparency and Data in Plea Bargaining*, 22 New Crim. L. Rev. 434 (2019).

in your jurisdiction were dismissed (as they are in King County, New York), would you think that demands a systemic change in how cases are processed? Would you want to screen cases differently to file fewer cases instead of dismissing more cases? Cynthia Alkon, et al., *Disposing of Misdemeanors: An Empirical Study*, 99 St. John's Law Review 101 (2025).

Additional Resources

ABA Criminal Justice Section Plea Bargaining Task Force, *Plea Bargain Task Force Report* 9–11 (February 2023).

Emily Bazelon, Charged: The New Movement to Transform American Prosecution and End Mass Incarceration (2019).

Stephanos Bibas, *Prosecutorial Regulation Versus Prosecutorial Accountability*, 157 U. Pa. L. Rev. 959 (2009).

Stephanos Bibas, *Regulating the Plea-Bargaining Market: From Caveat Emptor to Consumer Protection*, 99 Cal. L. Rev. 1117 (2011).

Stephanos Bibas, *Incompetent Plea Bargaining and Extrajudicial Reforms*, 126 Harv. L. Rev. 150 (2012).

Julian A. Cook, *Compassionless Plea Bargaining*, 113 Geo L. J. Online 1 (2024).

Russell D. Covey, *Longitudinal Guilt: Repeat Offenders, Plea Bargaining, and the Variable Standard of Proof*, 63 Fla. L. Rev. 431 (2011).

Russell D. Covey, *Toward a More Comprehensive Plea Bargaining Regulatory Regime*, 101 Or. L. Rev. 257 (2023).

Lucian E. Dervan, Vanessa Edkins & Thea Johnson, Vanessa and Johnson, Thea, *Victims of Coercive Plea Bargaining* American University Law Review, Vol. 72, No. 6, (December 19, 2023).

Brandon L. Garrett et al., *Open Prosecution*, 75 Stan. L. Rev. 1365 (June 2023).

Rebecca K. Helm, *Cognitive Theory and Plea Bargaining*, 5 Policy Insights from the Behavioral and Brain Sciences 195–201 (2018).

Thea Johnson, *Trial Ambivalence*, 20 Ohio St. J. Crim. L. 269 (December 2023).

Caitlin Kennedy, *A Plea for Justice: Making the Case for Increased Regulation of Vermont's Plea Bargaining Procedures: A Proposal for the Vermont Supreme Court Advisory Committee on Rules of Criminal Procedure*, 48 Vt. L. Rev. 103 (Fall 2023).

Maximo Langer, *Rethinking Plea Bargaining: The Practice and Reform of Prosecutorial Adjudication in American Criminal Procedure*, 33 Am. J. Crim. L. 223 (2006).

Chapter 6

Plea Bargaining as Negotiation

As the Supreme Court wrote in *Premo v. Moore* in 2011, "The art of negotiation is at least as nuanced as the art of trial advocacy...."[1] We agree. This chapter will discuss the skills and behaviors needed to be more effective advocates on behalf of clients and the state. Yet the understanding that negotiation is a skill that can be taught is, perhaps, not obvious. Justice Stevens, in *Missouri v. Frye*, after citing the above statement, noted that "Bargaining is, by its nature, defined to a substantial degree by personal style. The alternative courses and tactics in negotiation are so individual that it may be neither prudent nor practicable to try to elaborate or define detailed standards for the proper discharge of defense counsel's participation in the process."[2] While we agree with Justice Stevens that these choices in negotiation are individual, we also believe that these skills can be taught.

As you have already figured out from this book, both prosecutors and defense attorneys resolve an extraordinary percentage of cases through plea bargaining. It is the second part of that term—bargaining—that we turn to in the next two chapters. The skill of negotiation is often lost in plea bargaining, and we believe that focusing on this skill is something that will help lawyers be more effective on behalf of their clients and the public.

For years, lawyers have assumed that learning on the job after graduation will teach them the practical skills of what they need to know. Yet, the MacCrate Report studying law school education in the early 1990s noted that negotiation, among other skills, is lacking in the law school curriculum.[3] More recent reports such as the Carnegie Report[4] and *Best Practices for Legal Education*[5] have made it abundantly clear that law schools can and should do a better job with practical skills. High on all lists for skills that lawyers need is negotiation. Recognizing the importance of this, the NextGen Bar (NCBE) has now added problem-solving and negotiation skills to the list of items that will be tested.

---

1. Premo v. Moore, 562 U.S. 115, 125 (2011).

2. Missouri v. Frye, 566 U.S. 134 (2012).

3. ABA, Section of Legal Education & Admissions to the Bar, Report of the Task Force on Law Schools and the Profession: Narrowing the Gap (Robert MacCrate ed., ABA 1992).

4. Stuckey, et al., Educating Lawyers: Preparation for the Profession of Law (2007) (aka the Carnegie Report).

5. Stuckey, et al., Best Practices for Legal Education (2007); Maranville, et al., Building on Best Practices: Transforming Legal Education in a Changing World (2015).

And while we might assume that your negotiation skills are developed before you arrive at law school (based on everything from family dynamics to culture to birth order to professional training, etc.), negotiation training can jump start students to begin the process of improving and continually learning how to improve their negotiation skills. These skills are more than inherent traits given to you at birth—they can be learned, practiced, and expanded throughout your career.

Most popular negotiation books (see *Getting to Yes, Bargaining for Advantage,* and *Difficult Conversations* just to name a few), start from the premise that awareness is step one. Are you aware of negotiations around you? How you yourself negotiate? What opportunities there are for negotiation? These books and most negotiation trainings will build on that awareness by adding skills to your repertoire and pointing out different strategic choices that can be made while proceeding in the negotiation. Our goals in these chapters are to raise your awareness about negotiation in the criminal context and then to start your process of improving those crucial negotiation skills.

The first part of this chapter will briefly outline how criminal lawyers use negotiation, and the remainder of this chapter will focus on how to prepare for negotiation. Lawyers often go into negotiation just to see what the other side has to say and let it unfold from there. They would never dream of going to trial that way, and our best advice is to treat negotiation like a trial in terms of preparation, particularly since we know how many cases will actually settle. Both in this chapter and the next, we will also learn about the skills—and mistakes—that lawyers can make while negotiating. And while the Supreme Court has yet to decide what effective assistance of counsel in a negotiation is, there are numerous empirical studies that can already tell us what will make *you* more effective when negotiating on behalf of a client or the state.

I. Plea Bargaining Is Negotiation—with Constraints

Before turning to the concepts of negotiation, we want to highlight (perhaps obviously) that plea bargaining negotiation is a special type of negotiation. As we have already seen in previous chapters, the power imbalance is often significant in terms of the underlying law, the amount of money that defendants can spend hiring attorneys, the ability of some defendants to help in their case, and a host of additional reasons that make this context particularly fraught. This first excerpt highlights some of these differences, and the second excerpt argues that the plea-bargaining system is its own type of administrative system.

Cynthia Alkon, *Plea Bargaining: An Example of Negotiating with Constraints*

THE NEGOTIATOR'S DESK REFERENCE, 684–685, 696–697
(Honeyman & Schneider, eds. 2017)

...

Although [plea bargaining] is the method by which well over 90% of cases are resolved, the defendant has no right to a plea bargain. Once a criminal case begins, it is the prosecutor's decision whether to make a plea offer. Some of the factors that influence what kind of offer a prosecutor will make, or if they will make an offer, are the seriousness of the charges, the possible maximum sentence, the defendant's criminal record, and the strength of the evidence. In an average criminal case, the prosecutor will make an offer at or before the first court appearance, the arraignment. With electronic discovery becoming increasingly common, prosecutors routinely give an initial plea offer with the discovery in the case. This means that the first offer is often made before there is any conversation between the defense lawyer and the prosecutor, before the defense attorney has seen the case, and often before the defense lawyer has met her client....

Once the prosecutor makes an offer, the defense lawyer may make a counter-offer and/or try to negotiate with prosecutors at a higher level within the particular office. As the negotiation literature suggests, there can be good reasons to make the first offer and defense lawyers may decide to start the plea negotiation process themselves and not wait for the prosecutor to make the first offer on the case. Defense lawyers have an ethical duty to convey any plea offer to their clients, and failure to convey an offer is also a violation of the constitutional right to competent assistance of counsel (*Missouri v. Frye* 2012). It is up to the defendants themselves to decide whether to accept or reject the deal, ideally after conferring with counsel and making an informed decision....

Nonetheless, plea bargaining is a multi-party negotiation, with each plea bargain including at least the prosecutor, the defense lawyer, the defendant, and the judge (who must agree to accept the plea deal including any sentencing terms). In addition to the multiple parties involved, plea bargaining is complicated by the constraints created by the underlying structures of our criminal justice system. These structures include the extraordinary power of prosecutors, the often limited resources of defense lawyers, and the existing criminal law including the potential maximum sentence for each charge. Each player in the criminal justice system experiences these constraints differently. The way in which each player moves beyond these constraints is also different; although each has in common the fact that strong negotiating skills help....

For outsiders, plea bargaining can appear to happen with little negotiation and can often appear, even to judges and other lawyers, as a form of negotiation where one party (the defense), has few options. Plea negotiations where the defense is left with few options and has limited abilities to negotiate better deals for their clients are still the norm. Defendants are regularly faced with a choice between a bad plea bargain and a worse sentence if they go to trial. However, despite this all too common experience, and the serious constraints built into plea bargaining, it is also a form of negotiation that has potential for great flexibility and could allow for far-reaching reform.... As discussed above, negotiators with strong negotiation skills can move beyond the constraints in negotiating plea bargains.... Negotiators who recognize that plea bargaining is a highly flexible process are able to craft plea deals beyond the often narrow constraints that the criminal code drafters envisioned. Arguably the most overlooked value of plea bargaining is this flexibility, which has allowed skilled negotiators to experiment with new and innovative ways of handling criminal cases without waiting for new laws to pass.

Gerard E. Lynch,
Our Administrative System of Criminal Justice

83 Fordham L. Rev. 1685–1688 (2015)

...

V. PLEA "BARGAINING"

Seen in the light of this administrative adjudicatory structure, it becomes apparent that the very term "plea bargaining" is something of a misnomer. The term itself is a barrier to seeing our existing system of justice as a *system* rather than as an improvisation. In effect, the very language we use to describe the phenomenon presumes the primacy of the adversarial trial, and interferes with our ability to understand existing practice.

For all but the most doctrinaire free market micro-economists, the very term "plea bargaining" is distasteful. Justice, critics of plea negotiations point out, is not a matter of bazaar haggling, but of thoughtful adjudication of claims. "To bargain" is different than "to present reasoned arguments," and to reach a "bargain" or even an "agreement" is different than to obtain a "judgment." The more colloquial meaning of "bargain" is even worse. A "bargain" is a discount, something obtained at a cut-rate. If judges and scholars squirm at the notion of "bargained justice," the public, especially in our fearful times, is even more unhappy about defendants who "get off cheap."

In either case, the language used implicitly condemns the process. Something called "plea bargaining" can hardly be other than an expedient stepchild in a judicial system. It may be, and frequently is, defended as an unpleasant necessity in overcrowded courts, but no one pictures "plea bargaining" as a rational way to determine guilt or innocence.

Of course, any look at what actually goes on in plea bargaining undermines the applicability of both senses of the word. First of all, in many courts not all that much haggling goes on. Many, perhaps most, cases are processed pursuant to fairly standard rules: the policies of a particular United States Attorney may permit a drug courier or "mule" to plead to a standard reduced charge, for example, or a district attorney may offer any mugger who does no physical injury a standard disposition (perhaps further varied depending on whether a weapon was used) somewhere short of the theoretically-applicable offense of robbery. The rules are more like those of the supermarket than those of the flea market: there is a fixed price tag on the case, and you will get no farther "bargaining" with the prosecutor than you will by making a counteroffer on the price of a can of beans at the grocery.

On the other hand, not every case comes off the rack; some need, and receive, custom tailoring. As suggested by the description above, in a typical white-collar fraud investigation, defense counsel do not look like shoppers at a "take-it-or-leave-it" department store. They will often spend hour after hour in the prosecutor's office, making presentations and arguments, eventually perhaps making and receiving proposals and counter-proposals for the disposition of the case, looking, in short, very much like negotiators.

But the burgeoning literature of negotiation tells us of a process very different from the untutored image of "haggling." After all, even the simplest bargaining is not usually just a matter of "I'll give you five dollars"; "I'll take ten"; "Seven-fifty?"; "Done." The response to the five dollar bid is likely to be more in the nature of an *argument* than a counter-offer: "But these are *magic* beans"; "I paid nine dollars for them myself"; "If I weren't hard-up for cash I could go to the next village and get twelve for sure"; "Everybody else has been happy to pay ten." And as the negotiations become more sophisticated, and the parties' goals, interests, and information become more complex, the early stages of the discussion come to focus even more on exchange of information and positions than on the ultimate terms of the bargain. Negotiators of complex mergers or international treaties do not begin by putting positions on the table, to be traded back and forth, but by describing the goals of their side, their expectations of what the other side wants, needs or deserves, and the considerations of justice or fairness that should govern the outcome.

Such broader concerns are especially central in the case of plea negotiations, because of the self-perceptions of the parties. The prosecutor in particular does not see herself as an interested party seeking personal advantage, or even as a representative of the narrow interests of another. Rather, she will typically define herself as a public official, seeking "justice" or "the public interest." My point is not that the prosecutor's self-defined purity of motive makes her a worthier or more trustworthy negotiator, or one more likely to advocate a substantively fair result—though this may on occasion be true. Rather, the point is that the self-definition of the prosecutor affects the nature of the arguments that can be used in negotiation. Because the prosecutor is, in principle, looking for a "fair" price rather than the highest price, arguments couched in terms of justice will have more currency than they might in a purely economic negotiation. The ideology of at least some marketplaces permits the merchant openly to rely on superior bargaining power and to reject arguments from fairness; prosecutors, who will often have the power to impose terms, would be sharply criticized if they declined to consider arguments that the terms imposed are unjust.

The prosecutor's proclaimed commitment to fairness, moreover, will typically permit defense counsel to appeal not only to general considerations of justice but to specific precedent. As in any adjudicatory system, constant reversion to first principles is fatiguing, unpredictable, and inefficient. "Fairness" may come to mean not abstract justice—about which debate can be endless—but satisfaction of the more limited but still important goal of horizontal equity among similarly-situated persons. In most prosecuting offices, the argument that a disposition similar to that being sought was granted to another defendant on similar facts counts as a strong argument for according the same leniency to the present defendant. In effect, a kind of common law of plea bargaining may arise, sometimes shaped by formal office "policy," and sometimes by individual negotiation. Within a single investigation, a prosecutor who accepts a particular plea from one defendant will generally feel bound not to insist on more severe treatment for another defendant unless she can give a reasonable explanation for the distinction: the first defendant was less culpable, more cooperative, or less readily proven guilty. And, at least among counsel who are aware of the dispositions in that case, the prosecutor will be hard put to take a radically different stance in the next investigation. Of course, unlike the opinions of courts, such decisions are not published, permitting discriminatory advantage to defendants represented by "insider" counsel who are well informed about local prosecutorial practice, and leaving the precise "holdings" of prior cases subject to reinterpretation, shifting memory, and policy change.

The frequent disparity of power between the prosecutor and the defendant makes the role-definition of the prosecutor particularly important to the outcome of the negotiation. At the extreme, as noted above, the prosecutor's terms may be non-negotiable; at least when secure in a strong case, the prosecutor's self-definition as a seeker of justice may lead to an insistence that only one outcome is acceptable. But even in cases in which individualized bargaining is being conducted, the prosecutor may hold the virtually unilateral power to inflict pain on the defendant. In many cases, for example, potential defendants perceive that an indictment alone, even if it ultimately results in acquittal, is an unbearable outcome; the financial and reputational costs associated with a lengthy trial might make even a not guilty verdict a Pyrrhic victory. In other situations, conviction may be a certain and harsh outcome at trial, given the elastic definitions of substantive crimes, the severe and unpredictable (or in the case of mandatory sentences, all too predictable) sentences that may be applicable, and the strength of the evidence that may be available. In such cases, the defendant is often likely to take, in the end, whatever plea the prosecutor can be persuaded to offer. Defense counsel's bargaining posture may implicitly threaten a trial, but both sides may know that the defense is very likely arguing to the ultimate decision-maker about the nature of a fair outcome, rather than proposing an exchange of values based on relative bargaining strength."

Notes/Questions

1. Which of the views above of plea bargaining make sense to you? Is the criminal legal system an administrative one or more like the "Wild West," where the prosecutor is both sheriff and executioner?

2. In the following paragraph, Ron Wright and Marc Miller argue that Lynch's view of the administrative system does not really apply.

> Such thorough give-and-take on the merits of the case, with the defense lawyer testing the prosecutor's view of the facts and the law, might indeed take place routinely in white-collar criminal cases, and in particular in the Southern District of New York.... But plea negotiations look nothing like this in most places. In state systems, and especially in the high-volume systems of urban areas, defense attorneys have far less time and money to devote to each criminal defendant. More defendants in the state systems rely on publicly funded attorneys, and the funding for those attorneys is less generous than in the federal system.

Ronald Wright & Marc Miller, *Honesty and Opacity in Charge Bargains*, 55 STAN. L. REV. 1409, 1414 (2003).

What do you think about their argument? How might each of the views about the plea-bargaining system above impact your approach to negotiation?

* * *

We now turn in the next two excerpts to the type of negotiation that is happening between lawyers. In examining the landscape of criminal negotiation, Schneider found that criminal lawyers rate each other as particularly problem-solving. We will discuss the importance of negotiation styles in the next chapter. For now, we raise the question of *why* lawyers might be more problem-solving in their approach to negotiation and what this might reflect about the system under which plea bargaining occurs.

Andrea Kupfer Schneider, *Cooperating or Caving In: Are Defense Attorneys Shrewd or Exploited in Plea Bargaining Negotiations?*

91 MARQ. L. REV. 145, 156–161 (2007)

...

III. Why Are Criminal Lawyers More Problem-Solving?

There are several different reasons why criminal lawyers might be more problem-solving than their peers in other practice areas. This section of the essay outlines these theories.

A. Repeat Play and Reputation

... In the criminal law context, ... it is clear that extremely high levels of problem-solving behavior are exhibited between the prosecutor and the defendant's attorney. In criminal law, the geographic area of practice is narrow and the population of prosecutors and criminal lawyers is also limited. Criminal lawyers deal with each other repeatedly. In the civil law context, Jason Johnston and Joel Waldfogel demonstrated how lawyers that have already dealt with one another were more likely to reach a settlement the next time they interacted. As Richard Birke has discussed, this cooperative behavior can be expected when there are relationships with no known end and that are likely to continue. Furthermore, the bargaining relationship is straightforward with little complexity or worry over miscommunication that might distort otherwise cooperative behavior. So, given the small population of criminal lawyers, the likelihood of ongoing relationships, clear communication, and problem-solving behavior could be understood to occur as a result of repeat play among the lawyers.

B. Docket Load

Problem-solving behavior could also result from the clear need to settle cases and move work along. For example, in the two primary counties examined in this study, the caseloads for both prosecutors and public defenders were impressive. The average prosecutor in Chicago had 600 total cases while prosecutors in Milwaukee had over 280 cases. In order to focus on the cases that will be proceeding to trial, in order to actually go home at night, criminal lawyers need to move the bulk of their cases quickly to the plea bargaining stage in order to get to the next one....

C. The Alternative to Negotiation Is Clear (and Punitive)

When the law is relatively clear, lawyers have an easier time "bargaining in the shadow of the law." In most criminal cases, the facts, the law, and the likely sentence are relatively clear. Prosecutors and defenders are negotiating over relatively few contentious issues and are negotiating over the sentence at the margins. With the trial outcome predictable in many cases, there is little reason (or ability) to be adversarial since the alternative (trial outcome) is clear.

D. Incentives to Plea for Both Sides

It may be that prosecutors are more problem-solving than other lawyers because of the cases they take. Prosecutors have an incentive to maximize their conviction rate and, therefore, are more likely to only go to trial with sure winners. Less clear cases on either the law or procedure will result in pleas. Doubtful or hard cases can be avoided by a prosecutor who does not press charges....

Defense attorneys also have a large incentive to plead their cases rather than go to trial. As Russell Covey explains, sentences reached in plea agreements versus at trial are significantly shorter; this trial penalty can be as high as 300% to 500% in some cases. So, for example, a plea agreement for unlawful entry might be six months while the sentence after trial on burglary charges could be a maximum of thirty years. Given the punitive effect of risking trial, only the most confident defendants will pursue trial. More likely, they will be forced to reach a plea agreement. Similarly, prosecutors, knowing the punitive effect of risking trial, can let the alternative speak for itself and have no need to engage in adversarial behavior....

E. Clients and Victims Are Not as Involved with "Their" Lawyers

... In criminal law, there is a different kind of client involvement on both sides. First, on the prosecutor side, the prosecution officially represents the "state." The victim or victim's family is not officially represented by the prosecutor and is often not part of the case at all unless the case proceeds to trial where testimony might be needed. What this means is that the person most likely to push for a harsh sentence and take a more adversarial approach in any plea bargaining negotiation is actually not involved. On the defendant side, there is also a difference between typical civil litigation clients and defendants. Criminal defendants, unless this is a high-end white collar prosecution, tend not to have the education, social status, or ability to direct their attorneys in the same way as other litigants. Furthermore, in many of these cases, the defendant is not paying the attorney and, therefore, has even less power to be directive in how the case is handled. Again, in the criminal law context compared to other contexts, the client here has little ability to push for adversarial approaches in negotiation or to hold out for better bargains.

F. Pretrial Detention

One last reason that plea bargains might be so cooperative is how they are framed to the defendant. Richard Birke, Stephanos Bibas, and others have written about the impact of loss aversion on the view of the defendant. One could hypothesize that a defendant might want to avoid the certain "loss" encompassed in a guilty plea and, therefore, would hold out for trial. In reality, however, the typical loss aversion reaction and avoidance of plea bargains does not occur. When the defendant is already in jail, a plea that gets him or her out of jail with time served looks like a gain. With close to three-fourths of federal felony defendants in jail prior to trial and close to two-thirds of state felony arrestees not out on bail, a large proportion of defendants are calculating the impact of their plea from a jail cell. With the horrors of pretrial detention well documented, the guilty plea is the most effective method to ensure the end of the legal process and getting out of jail as soon as possible.

IV. What Is the Story? Caving or Cooperating?

One could tell two different kinds of stories about what is going on in the criminal law bar. On the one hand, this study could show how well repeat play, long term reputations, and a joint interest in justice, promote problem-solving behavior. Prosecutors and defense attorneys could be working efficiently and fairly together in resolving an overwhelming number of cases appropriately. On the other hand, this study could be merely confirming just how stacked the system is. The fact that defense attorneys appear to be so overwhelmingly problem-solving could be evidence of a system that forces ill-informed, jailed, poor defendants working with underpaid, overworked defense lawyers to accept pleas despite legal rights, evidence, and even possible innocence. It could also be that prosecutors are feeling benign toward their counterparts—after all, the prosecutors generally win—and "reward" defense attorneys with a positive assessment of their negotiation behavior. Defense attorneys could be no better or worse than other attorneys but just could be getting better ratings from their prosecutorial peers. Or possibly the answers lie in the combination of all of these theories....

Notes/Questions

1. What do you think is going on in the criminal bar given all our reading on plea bargaining? Are defense attorneys caving? Does the law give too many advantages to prosecutors?

2. Note that we return to this question at the end of these two chapters, particularly after we have covered negotiation styles and psychological errors (like loss aversion discussed above) to try to understand the behavior of the criminal lawyers studied.

* * *

This next excerpt is from a national study published in 1986 surveying criminal defense lawyers on what skills they use and what skills they wish they had more of to be successful. It also starts our conversation on how to prepare.

Robert L. Doyel, *The National College-Mercer Criminal Defense Survey: Preliminary Observations about Interviewing, Counseling, and Plea Negotiations*

37 Mercer L. Rev. 1019–1021, 1023, 1025–1027 1985–1986

III. PRENEGOTIATION INVESTIGATION

[P]rofessional responsibility demands that a lawyer should not permit a client to proceed to trial when the lawyer has no idea what legal outcome will result. When a lawyer is totally uncertain about what the outcome will be, the lawyer should gather the data necessary to predict the outcome, or withdraw from the case. The ABA Standards for the Defense Function contemplate a 'full investigation' in every case, and always before entering a plea agreement." Commentators usually urge that fact investigation is a necessary precondition to plea bargaining because defense counsel "should be able to predict the likely outcome if the case were to go to trial and to predict whether the sentence imposed after a guilty verdict would be greater [than] the sentence possible under a plea agreement." The courts are somewhat less emphatic about the need for thorough prenegotiation investigation. Most courts tolerate less extensive investigations in cases in which the defendant pleads guilty. One federal court of appeals has gone so far as to hold that no preplea investigation is required. [Ed. Note *Missouri v. Turley* (8th Cir., 1971).] In actual practice, it seems that many defense lawyers conduct little or no prenegotiation fact investigation. The Phoenix study found that in 47.3% of felonies and 69.2% of misdemeanors, defense counsel did not interview any prosecution witnesses before entering plea negotiations. In 30.3% of the cases, no defense witnesses were interviewed. Attorneys participating in the National College survey reported prenegotiation investigative practices consistent with those of Phoenix criminal lawyers. One-fourth of the respondents indicated that they personally interviewed defense witnesses in no more than 40% of their cases, and more than one-third said that they interviewed prosecution witnesses in only 40% or fewer cases." Furthermore, the ability to predict the outcome of the guilt phase of a trial received a relatively low

3.100 mean importance rating. [F]ully half of the attorneys in the survey did not conduct a thorough investigation, do legal research, or develop a theory of defense before plea negotiations.

The widespread lack of pre-negotiation preparation is significant when compared with factors recognized as important in plea bargaining. In the Phoenix study, 94.7% of the lawyers believed that weaknesses in the prosecution's case were always or usually an important factor. Similarly, 90.6% thought that the strength of evidence for the defense was always or usually important to plea bargaining. The Phoenix study also disclosed that in nearly half of the felony cases reviewed, the evidence at trial was either weaker or stronger than it had appeared before trial in police reports and other discovery materials. The strength or weakness of the evidence for or against the accused is concededly a critical factor in plea negotiations, and police reports and other discovery materials are apparently poor indicators of how strong the evidence will be at trial. The only way for defense counsel to gauge the strength of a particular case is to conduct an independent investigation, including witness interviews. The absence of adequate fact investigation in a substantial proportion of cases raises a serious question about the adequacy of defense services in those cases. It would be easy to point the accusing finger of inadequacy at defense lawyers because of the frequent failure to investigate. All that can justifiably be said here, however, is that an apparent problem exists and that further research is required into the problem's existence, causes, and potential remedies.

Ronald F. Wright, Jenny Roberts & Betina Cutaia Wilkinson, *The Shadow Bargainers*

42 Cardozo L. Rev. 1295 (2021)

. . .

IV. DEFENDERS' IMPLICIT THEORIES ABOUT PLEA BARGAINING

Our survey questions asked about the "importance" of various factors to the outcome of negotiations and to preparation for bargaining. Hence, the attorney responses to these questions make it possible to identify their aspirations for the bargaining process-the actions they believe they should take and the external conditions they hope to find or create for their clients. Their ratings of the importance of different factors amount to an implicit theory of negotiation based on field experience. In this Part, we compare two of these implicit theories of negotiation; each account offers a simplified narrative to explain how one might understand a complex practice.

The first take on what matters in bargaining comes from negotiation theory, which scholars and practitioners developed in civil cases and later applied to the criminal context. Negotiation theory highlights two principles as central to bargaining. The first principle is that parties bargain in the shadow of trial, meaning that the predicted outcomes at trial, and at sentencing after trial, form the baseline for negotiations. A second theoretical principle, much studied in the civil negotiation context, is that the

Table 1. Ranking of Factors Important to Negotiation Outcomes

How important to the outcome of the negotiation are each of the following factors when you are discussing potential dispositions with a prosecutor?	Average Score
Your client's criminal history	4.63
Your knowledge of the relative facts	4.48
What your client wants and needs	4.43
Category/type of case (e.g.,drugs, property, robbery)	4.34
Your knowledge of the relevant legal issues	4.18
Whether client is currently in custody	4.15
Sentencing range under state law	3.90
Probability of conviction after trial	3.89
Your knowledge of alternatives to incarceration	3.88
Prosecutor's personality	3.88
What the judge is likely to do at sentencing	3.87
Application of prosecutor office policy	3.81
Strength or weakness of any suppression issues	3.81
Your relationship with the prosecutor	3.78
Relevant collateral consequences	3.74
Your personality	3.62
Your reputation as a trial attorney	3.61
Victim's wishes	3.41
Your reputation as a negotiator	3.35
Number of cases on the prosecutor's docket	3.08
Law enforcement witness's wishes	2.85
Prosecutor's reputation as a negotiator	2.70
Prosecutor's reputation as a trial attorney	2.63
Number of cases you are defending	2.01

Scale: 1 = not important at all, 2 = relatively unimportant, 3 = moderately important, 4 = relatively important, 5 = extremely important

negotiators' personal styles, as well as their reputations as trial attorneys and as negotiators, play a significant role in the actual bargaining process.

A second theory of negotiation is also visible in the survey data, one that we call "bargaining in the shadow of the client." This strategy emphasizes the individual qualities of the client, such as the importance of collateral consequences for some defendants. Attorneys treat a wider range of factors as important to negotiation outcomes,

Table 2. Importance of Preparation Activities

Rate the relative importance of the following preparatory activities *before* negotiating, in order to be effective during negotiations.	Average Score
Having a clear sense of the client's goals	4.76
Getting timely receipt of discovery (before bargaining)	4.71
Investigating the facts of the case	4.55
Researching the legal issues in the case	4.41
Ability to predict outcome of sentencing phase of trial	4.34
Ability to predict outcome of guilt phase of trial	4.33
Developing a theory of the case (or theory of the defense)	4.13

Scale: 1 = not important at all, 2 = relatively unimportant, 3 = moderately important, 4 = relatively important, 5 = extremely important

including equities that reveal the client's relative lack of blameworthiness, rather than a central focus on legally sufficient proof of crime elements.

Defender responses to two categories of survey questions capture the choice between these two theories of negotiation. First, in the "Negotiation Practices" section of the survey, we asked defenders to score the importance of twenty-four factors to the outcome of a negotiation on a scale of one to five ("not important at all" to "extremely important"). The attorneys who place the highest priorities on several trial-centered factors-such as "likely outcome after trial" and the "likely sentence"-signal their belief in the "shadow of the trial" theory.

Second, the "Preparation for Bargaining" section of the survey asked defenders to rate seven preparatory activities for their importance to effective bargaining. The attorneys who assigned higher importance to predictions of trial outcomes and sentences point once again to the traditional "shadow of the trial" theory. Tables 1 and 2 list the average scores for these two foundational questions.

....

In theory, we would expect defenders who adopt a shadow-of-client approach to negotiation to assign a higher score to the importance of "collateral consequences of a conviction for your client." And indeed, attorneys handling misdemeanor caseloads did score the importance of collateral consequences at 4.09, "relatively important." This result reinforces the special importance of client priorities for these attorneys, since collateral consequences are comparatively more important in misdemeanor cases, where they can easily be the most severe consequences for some defendants, such as those who need to keep their occupational licenses or driving privileges.

....

Table 6. Frequency of Activities in Preparation for Negotiation

How often do you engage in the following activities as you prepare for any bargaining session in a typical case?	Average
Ask client about possible please	4.69
Review file	4.69
Explore collateral consequences	3.99
Legal research	3.63
Interviewed defense witnesses	3.52
Discuss or moot with colleague or supervisor	3.12
Interview prosecution witnesses	3.01
Investigate scene of crime	2.80
Ask witnesses about possible pleas	2.50

Scale: 5 = Always, 4 = Usually, 3 = Sometimes, 2 = Infrequently, 1 = Never

Third, the survey asked attorneys to note the frequency with which they personally engaged in nine activities as they prepared for negotiations in their own cases, from "never" to "always." The full list of those preparation activities appears in Table 6.

Defense attorneys do link their ideas about negotiation outcomes to their views about how best to prepare for bargaining. That linkage reflects a consistent and coherent theory of negotiation on their part. Thus, attorneys who stress shadow-of-trial factors as important to the outcomes of negotiations also say that shadow-of-trial factors are important to their preparation for bargaining. The same is true for shadow-of-client factors: attorneys link their beliefs about outcomes to their preparation.

When we turn, however, to the self-reported practices of attorneys during negotiation (as opposed to preparation before negotiation begins), the relationship between attorney beliefs and their self-declared practices becomes weaker. A theory-to-practice gap opens up.

For instance, one might associate a willingness to signal a vigorous motions practice with the shadow-of-trial theory of negotiation, because this practice stresses legal factors relevant at trial rather than equitable factors related to the client's larger story. Yet this bargaining practice happened (or reportedly happened) less often for attorneys who otherwise seem committed to the shadow-of-trial theory. Strong attorney views about the importance of trial predictions and sentence prediction to the outcomes of negotiations (two indicators of a shadow-of-trial viewpoint) have a statistically significant negative impact on scores for the self-reported frequency of signaling a vigorous motions practice. The attorneys most committed to shadow-of-trial theory are the least likely to say that they make a strong investment in pretrial motions.

Notes/Questions

1. Did any of the results for these studies surprise you? Are lawyers performing these tasks more or less than you expected? Did any of the skills listed here surprise you?

2. Of the list of skills covered by the two studies, which do you think are the most critical? How should we be teaching this in law school?

3. Note that both of these studies were of public defenders. Do we think the amount of time devoted to these tasks differs between defense attorneys and prosecutors? What might be the differences in what prosecutors spend time on or how they value other factors? How do you think that the skill set might be different for each?

4. Should the percentage of time spent on each skill be different depending on the seriousness of the case? For example, should a lawyer handling a misdemeanor spend as much time counseling their client or investigating the case? What if the misdemeanor conviction would have serious immigration consequences? What if the misdemeanor conviction could act as a prior making any future convictions much more serious?

5. Both studies show that the level of preparation can vary widely among attorneys. Cynthia Alkon writes about plea bargaining:

> Defense lawyers should do appropriate follow-up investigation after discovery or when new information is provided by their clients. The Court has shown a willingness to hold that the failure to investigate constitutes ineffective assistance of counsel when lawyers fail to investigate and present mitigation evidence in death penalty cases. Although the *Strickland v. Washington* Court cautioned that "reasonable professional judgments support the limitations on investigation," the Court went on the say that:
>
> > [i]n other words, counsel has a duty to make reasonable investigations or to make a reasonable decision that makes particular investigations unnecessary. In any ineffectiveness case, a particular decision not to investigate must be directly assessed for reasonableness in all the circumstances, applying a heavy measure of deference to counsel's judgments.
>
> In examining the duty to investigate in the specific context of plea bargaining, the Court should focus on three basic questions: (1) was it reasonable to investigate; (2) did the failure to investigate result in bad advice to the defendant regarding whether to accept a plea deal or not; and (3) did the failure to investigate result in a failure to make a counter-offer when there were grounds to do so? For example, if the defendant tells the lawyer that he has an alibi witness, it is reasonable to expect the lawyer to try to find that witness. If the defendant says that he knows he had not had enough to drink to be over the legal limit, it is reasonable for the defense to re-test the blood, or order the maintenance records on the breath machine. The Court should consider such examples of basic investigation when reviewing a lawyer's preparation for plea negotiations, and should hold such preparations to be a fundamental requirement for effective assistance of counsel.

> Related to the requirement that defense lawyers investigate possible defenses to the underlying charges is the duty to investigate alleged prior convictions or enhancements. For example, if there is an enhancement due to an allegation that drugs were sold in a "school zone," it is reasonable to expect the defense lawyer to verify that the location was in fact a school zone. Defense lawyers should also investigate any priors that are alleged and that form the basis for increasing the penalty due to habitual offender statutes. For example, if only felony convictions count for the particular habitual offender statute, then the defense lawyer should order the records on the prior to verify that the charge the defendant was convicted of was actually a felony and was not reduced, for example, to a misdemeanor.

Cynthia Alkon, *Plea Bargain Negotiations: Defining Competence Beyond* Lafler *&* Frye, 53 American Criminal Law Review 377 (Spring 2016). Do you think there should be an ethical standard for the level of preparation required? Should this level differ between the plea-bargaining stage (where most cases are handled) versus the trial stage?

II. Preparation for Plea Bargaining

We now turn to the skills that lawyers can use to improve their negotiation effectiveness. Preparation is the easiest skill in negotiation, because it is the one item over which you have the most control. Preparation in advance of negotiation requires your time and your focus, but it does not ask you to modify your conversational style, learn to read body language, or even work with your negotiation counterpart. So, while it does take time, it is *your* time. And numerous commenters in criminal law have noted for years that this preparation—or lack thereof—is one of the key factors of success in plea bargaining.

Cynthia Alkon & Andrea Kupfer Schneider, *How to Be a Better Plea Bargainer*

66 Wash. U. J. 65, 69–72 (2021)

...

The fact that plea bargaining is a form of negotiation with significant constraints is exactly why negotiation skills matter.

Strong negotiation skills are what can help both prosecutors and defense lawyers move beyond the constraints. Prosecutors are constrained by office policies, which are sometimes political, since the local district attorney is usually an elected official. There may be mandatory minimums or prosecutors may have office policies preventing them from reducing certain charges or dropping enhancements, such as gun enhancements. Defense lawyers are often constrained by the existing laws that leave them with few options for their clients.

By focusing on negotiating skills, lawyers can move beyond these constraints. However, mastering the skills of assertiveness, empathy, flexibility, social intuition, and ethicality is predicated on going into each negotiation prepared. For example, a defense lawyer who has fully investigated their case and knows that the evidence is weak on a key element (for example, that the witness to the crime has recanted), can use the skill of assertiveness with the prosecutor to explain why the case, or the particular charge, should be dropped. A well-prepared defense lawyer will also know what the standard offers are for particular charges so they will know if, or when, to be assertive about negotiating a better offer. Our preparation sheet illuminates each of these skills by helping lawyers prepare to be flexible, ask good questions, and pay attention to communication choices. Each of these elements on the preparation sheet helps to build negotiation effectiveness.

Attention to preparation in advance of a negotiation would seem to be an easy place to start to improve one's negotiation skills. In other areas of leadership, we regularly hear adages on the wisdom of preparation and, in fact, the likelihood of failure when we do not. Unfortunately, in the U.S. criminal legal system, the simple calculus of taking time to prepare is often lost, or difficult due to the heavy caseloads, lack of resources, and surrounding institutional culture.

This lack of preparation is evidenced to some degree by empirical studies on defense attorneys, showing that many of them do not engage in comprehensive interviewing of defense and prosecution witnesses. This is true even though defense attorneys recognize that weaknesses in the prosecution's case are some of the main leverage points in a plea bargain.

A. Goals for the Preparations Sheet

We have several goals in the preparation sheet. First, a prep sheet organizes our thinking. Whether or not you fill out each box, it helps a negotiator conceptualize the major pieces that are needed prior to sitting down for a negotiation. As the late Public Defender of San Francisco, Jeff Adachi, observed, "checklists combat complexity" and "checklists prevent mistakes." Adachi said, "in most cases, our missteps and oversights could have been avoided by using checklists." 30 Good negotiation requires good preparation. The plea preparation sheet is a checklist to make sure that the lawyers (or students in the role of a lawyer) go into the negotiation as prepared as possible. Ineffective negotiation comes from winging it using the plea preparation sheet helps to prevent this.

Second, this prep sheet in particular brings together both typical negotiation training prep sheets, with the particular elements of plea bargaining preparation. There have been attempts at plea bargaining preparation aids before, but these often miss the nuances of negotiation theory and focus only on facts or law without really forcing negotiators to think about how these elements get used in a negotiation. As we walk through each element below and how we have already used this in classes, we hope that negotiators can see the benefit of merging these perspectives.

Third, this prep sheet is created to be used by both prosecutors and defense attorneys. The skills that you need to be a good negotiator, as a prosecutor or defense lawyer, cut across these professional identities. For example, delivering a strong closing argument is a skill that both types of lawyers need, and the skill is not fundamentally different between prosecutors and defense lawyers. It is the same with negotiation skills they are not fundamentally different for prosecutors and defense lawyers. We think that it is important for both sides to recognize more clearly that there are often shared interests and goals, perhaps shared gaps in knowledge or facts, shared mistakes that can be made, and shared concerns as one proceeds through the negotiation process. While prosecutors and defense lawyers could use the same checklist in a variety of areas, such as driving under the influence of alcohol cases, this is not the norm in practice. CLE programs, how-to manuals, and training programs are more commonly divided by role. Prosecutors train with prosecutors and defense lawyers with defense lawyers.

The plea prep sheet intentionally is not divided by professional role. We believe that what matters in plea negotiation is good preparation. The answers to the questions, the information filled in, will be different. Needing to understand the underlying interests and setting goals for the negotiation, however, are not different.

Finally, like all good prep sheets, this is designed so that each negotiator learns from this prep sheet and then makes it their own. If one creates muscle memory from practice, each negotiator will note the things that they do on autopilot versus the elements that need more work. The best prep sheets become individualized over time to the negotiator's strengths and weaknesses, to the particular cases they are handling, and to their particular jurisdictions.

* * *

The preparation sheet below is one way of organizing your thinking before going into a negotiation. We will use this sheet to organize this chapter and the next in order to give you a framework for thinking about negotiation both before and during it.

Plea Preparation				
Case Name				
Charge				
Sentence Minimum/Maximum				
Interests & Goals				
	Defendant	Defense Attorney	Prosecutor	Victim/ Public/Press
Interests				
Goals				

Investigation & Criteria	
Facts	
Good/Bad	
Defendant's Priors	
Defendant's Personal History	
Defendant's Confidential Information?	
Prosecutor Exculpatory Information?	
Law & Policy	
Min/Max/Standard offers?	
Collateral Consequences (Immigration, Family Court, Professional Licensing, etc.)	
Motions/Procedure?	
Prosecutorial Policies?	
Court History/Judge	
Element of Agreement/Plea Bargaining Options/BATNA	
Charge(s) (Minimum/ Maximum)	
Possible Other Charges?	
Enhancements?	
Leverage (Law? Facts? Procedural? Jurisdictional?)	
Alternative Processes Available? (Diversion, Problem-Solving Courts, Restorative Justice Processes, Other?)	
Dismiss?	
Approach/Communications	
Reputation & Relationship between lawyers	
Negotiation Style (Yours & Counterpart)	
Timing (What stage? How close to trial?)	
Concession Management (1st offer, 2nd offer, etc.)	
Potential Negotiation Errors?	
Communication Mode (Email, Face-to-Face, Phone, etc.)	

You will note that the preparation sheet begins with the basic information (case/client name, charge, maximum and minimum sentence) and highlights the importance of knowing your interests and your goals. These are the items you need to keep front and center during the negotiation. However, we also know that finding out your client's interests (or thinking about prosecutorial interests) and setting your goals in a negotiation occur once other fact finding and legal research has happened. We will come back to filling in the top section of this sheet once we have a more complete investigation. You can use the problem below to fill it out as we go through the chapter.

Problem

JoAnna Adams, 19 years old, got into a fight with her older sister, Susanna Adams. The fight started with yelling in Susanna's apartment. It escalated, and JoAnna ran out of the apartment, down the stairs, and to her car. Susanna followed. Multiple witnesses saw both sisters running and heard them yelling at each other, but could not distinguish what was actually said until JoAnna reached her car, opened the door and pulled out a gun. She yelled, "I'm going to kill you," and shot her sister from a distance of 20 feet. The four witnesses all said they clearly heard the threat. Susanna was shot in the leg. The police were called, and JoAnna was arrested at the scene. Susanna was taken to the hospital and is expected to make a full recovery. JoAnna has no previous criminal record. She is charged with Attempted First Degree Murder. This offense carries a life sentence in this state (this means that if convicted of this offense, the judge can only sentence to life in prison). This offense is parole eligible (which means the parole board will consider granting parole after the defendant has served 22 years). This jurisdiction also has the charges of assault, assault with a deadly weapon, and assault causing great bodily injury. The maximum for each of those offenses is 5 years, 10 years, and 20 years, respectively.

The police report includes interviews with all the witnesses, a medical report about Susanna's injury (stating it was not life threatening and that she is expected to make a full recovery), and a statement from Susanna saying that she and her sister are always fighting, and "I thought she was gonna kill me when I saw that gun." There is no indication that any of the witnesses, including Susanna, will be unwilling to testify.

A. Facts, Law and Policy Investigation— What Makes a Plea Fair?

Our first focus in investigating is figuring out what happened and what law applies. This is all under the heading of criteria—what makes an outcome fair.

Why is this investigation important even in negotiation, rather than trial? As you know from criminal law, each element of the crime must be proven. Yet, as you will

Collateral Consequences

The following are additional examples of perhaps surprising collateral consequences to a felony conviction:

- Ineligible to fundraise for a bingo game
- Revocation or denial of barber license
- Ineligible for and removed from public housing
- Ineligible to receive federal funding for education
- Denial of chiropractic license
- Ineligible for landscape architect registration
- Denial of temporary veterinarian permit
- Ineligible for certification as a driving instructor
- Ineligible for a milk dealer license
- Ineligible to hold ownership interest in a business entity owning a funeral firm

For more, see https://niccc.nationalreentryresourcecenter.org/.

See NATIONAL INVENTORY OF COLLATERAL CONSEQUENCES OF CONVICTIONS (https://csgjusticecenter.org/publications/the-national-inventory-of-collateral-consequences-of-conviction/).

note from the prep sheet, we actually think that much more is needed in order to help you prepare effectively. Most attorneys tend to divide their facts as "good" and "bad" depending on what side they are on. Remember to look for the facts that not only help your case but also harm your case. A defendant's prior history might also come into play regarding the charging of the crime or likely sentence. And each side might have particular information: the defendant's confidential information known only to the defendant and her attorney or, on the other side, the prosecutor might have exculpatory evidence (witnesses that identify someone else, non-matching blood samples, etc.) that she is required to turn over.

Your preparation on the law seems also obvious prior to a negotiation—and yet is more than just the statute or prior case law. Yes, you should research what the maximum and minimum sentence is for any particular charge and what are typical plea offers. As we have discussed in previous chapters, defense counsel specifically should be aware of any collateral consequences that could happen to the defendant with any plea (from immigration to family court to professional licensing). Not all collateral consequences will matter to each defendant, but without properly interviewing and counseling your client, you cannot know what matters to them or what else is going on in their lives that might be impacted. For example, as a defense lawyer, you will want to find out if your client is employed and what he does. If your client needs a professional license or registration, you want to be sure the conviction will not impact the license or registration. These rules are often unexpected and something you may need to research. For example, in Texas, any criminal conviction or deferred adjudication can, unsurprisingly, make a person ineligible to serve as a director of a state bank (Tex. Finance Code § 33.103) or, oddly, unable to register as an air conditioning/refrigeration technician (16 Tex. Admin. Code §75.27).

Once you know the facts and some law, you could also consider what motions might be filed (e.g., to suppress evidence) and how that might impact the case. You should also think about any prosecutorial policy that might apply in your jurisdiction (an office that, for example, has announced it will prosecute gun crimes particularly harshly or, on the other hand, is known for diverting as many veterans as possible to other programs). If you know the judge, you could also find out that judge's reputation for sentencing.

For one such dramatic shift in sentencing, see Senior Judge Jack Weinstein's opinion from June, 2018 in *U.S. v. Trotter*, 321 F. Supp. 3d 337, 339 (E.D.N.Y. 2018), in which he announced he would no longer revoke probation for smoking marijuana:

> I conclude: (1) I, like other trial judges, have in many cases imposed longer periods of supervised release than needed, and I, like other trial judges, have failed to terminate supervised release early in many cases where continuing supervision presents such a burden as to reduce the probability of rehabilitation; and (2) I, like other trial judges, have provided unnecessary conditions of supervised release and unjustifiably punished supervisees for their marijuana addiction, even though marijuana is widely used in the community and is an almost unbreakable addiction or habit for some. As a result of these errors in our sentencing practice, money and the time of our probation officers are wasted, and supervisees are unnecessarily burdened. In summary, in this and my future cases I will: (1) impose shorter terms of supervised release as needed; (2) give greater consideration to the appropriateness of conditions; (3) provide for earlier termination where indicated; and (4) avoid violations of supervised release and punishment by incarceration merely for habitual marijuana use.

Consider how this shift in sentencing would change the potential plea-bargaining stances of the prosecution and defense when drug use is part of the charge.

This next article discusses much of what happens in the initial investigation of your case from the perspective of the defense attorney. Note how he argues that much of this preparation is like planning a dance where you need to know the music and steps. We agree that strong preparation will make you a much better dancer!

Rodney J. Uphoff, *The Criminal Defense Lawyer as Effective Negotiator: A Systemic Approach*

2 CLINICAL L. REV. 73, 95, 98–100, 102–106 (1995)

...

II. THE NEGOTIATION PROCESS: PLANNING THE DANCE

A. Learning the Music and the Steps

Good criminal defense lawyers do not start out assuming their client is guilty or that a plea bargain is the best resolution of the case. Rather, as the ABA Standards for Criminal Justice recognize, the competent, committed advocate will "conduct a prompt investigation of the case and explore all avenues leading to facts relevant to the merits of the case and the penalty in the event of a conviction." Even if the defendant expresses a clear desire to plead guilty, the lawyer still has the responsibility to undertake an appropriate investigation to ensure that the client's intended guilty plea has a basis in fact and in law. Admittedly, the extent of that investigation and the lawyer's ability to push for a trial will be significantly hamstrung if the defendant lacks the will or desire to contest the charge. Nonetheless, the diligent defense lawyer understands that the defendant may not recognize potential defenses or appreciate legal challenges so she will carefully evaluate the merits of the case before even considering jettisoning the trial option....

Effective preparation for a plea bargaining session—like effective preparation for trial—begins with a thorough client interview. Rarely will defense counsel be able to effectively represent a client without learning as much as possible about the client and his or her knowledge of the facts surrounding the charges. It is also critical that defense counsel learn as much as possible about the client's personal circumstances and background....

To negotiate effectively, defense counsel must be so familiar with the defendant and her life experiences that counsel can personalize or humanize the defendant when talking with the prosecutor. Defense counsel who is unaware or unprepared when the prosecutor inquires about the defendant's present job status or work history may seriously undermine the effort to obtain a favorable sentencing concession. Finally, defense counsel who is informed about and ready to present effectively the defendant's mitigating personal circumstances also will be able to afford the defendant zealous representation at sentencing.

In addition, it is critical that defense counsel inquire about the defendant's personal situation so counsel can advise the client about the collateral consequences of a guilty plea or conviction. A criminal conviction can cost a defendant the right to drive, a professional license or even the ability to remain in this country....

As part of the investigation leading up to settlement negotiations, defense counsel also should attempt to ascertain if the prosecutor has any significant proof problems. Counsel should try to determine if the state's witnesses are still around and actually available to testify. This is easier to discover in a state like Oklahoma where the prosecution's witnesses must be identified on the initial charging document. Similarly, talking to prospective defense witnesses, particularly alibi witnesses, is an important part of the preparation process. Counsel must not only be able to assess the strength of the defense witnesses' testimony but be able to realistically predict whether those witnesses will actually show up and testify at trial. In addition, counsel must judge the strength of the defendant's own testimony and the merits of the defendant's taking the witness stand.

Another aspect of counsel's preparation is to determine the status and positions of any co-defendants, co-conspirators or other persons involved in the events underlying the charge facing the defendant. The existence of other individuals who also are implicated in the crime often complicates counsel's task. These people may play a key role in exonerating or burying defense counsel's client. Again, it may be difficult to figure out in advance of a negotiating session whether these other persons are planning to plead guilty or to testify against counsel's client. Nonetheless, the more information that defense counsel has about the role that others played in an offense and the defendant's relationship with these other persons, the better able counsel will be to assess the risks the defendant faces....

Before initiating plea bargaining, a few final preparatory steps are necessary. Defense counsel should scour the statutes to try to find lesser offenses which directly or indirectly deal with the defendant's conduct. There may be another felony offense, a misdemeanor or even a municipal ordinance violation that defense counsel can argue is a better fit or a suitable compromise in the defendant's case. In some instances, defense counsel may even be able to find an administrative regulation that covers the defendant's behavior. Counsel also should determine if there are any local conventions—e.g., a dismissal upon payment of terms—which represent a suitable resolution of the defendant's charges.

Just as it is important for defense counsel to be aware of any local conventions which may provide a simple and satisfactory resolution of the defendant's case, it is critical to learn the "standard deal" in a case such as the defendant's. Although a prosecutor's initial offer will depend on a number of variables, prosecutors generally work from a starting point or "standard deal" that is based primarily on the nature of the charge and the defendant's record. The extent to which a prosecutor ultimately will be willing to deviate from that "standard deal" generally depends on a host of factors including: time and resources; defense counsel's ability, reputation and relationship with the prosecutor; evidentiary concerns; the victim's wishes; and the aggravating and the mitigating circumstances of the case. Nevertheless, the criminal defense lawyer who is aware of the "standard deal" prior to going into a negotiating session will be better able to plan for that session as well as to respond to developments in the negotiating process.

Notes/Questions

1. Do good defense lawyers really assume all of their clients are innocent? Are you a bad defense lawyer if you don't assume your client is innocent and if you think that a plea bargain is the best resolution of the case? What if you represent a client charged with driving while under the influence of alcohol and the blood alcohol level is a .14 (well over the .08 limit)? If a client admits to drinking a "bunch of beers," is your job done? Should the client take the standard deal that is offered? Or should you order the records on the breath machine that was used to test the blood alcohol level or retest the blood before the defendant pleads guilty? Are you failing to give effective assistance of counsel if you plead a driving under the influence case out at arraignment before doing any kind of investigation?

2. What steps do you need to take for proper preparation prior to plea bargaining? The article already lists knowing the law, understanding the facts of the alleged crime, and life experiences of the defendant. How does an attorney accomplish this? Interviewing about the accused's childhood? Peers? Work history? Family structure? How many witnesses should defense counsel interview? Should this level of detail also be required of the prosecutor? Note where you would place all of this information in the prep sheet.

* * *

This next article outlines some of the legal preparation that each lawyer needs to do as well. Not only should we understand the law, the charges and enhancements, and potential sentences, but we also need to think about motions and other procedures that might occur and impact the plea bargaining.

Cynthia Alkon, *Plea Bargain Negotiations: Defining Competence beyond* Lafler *and* Frye

53 American Criminal Law Review 377, 396–399 (Spring 2016)

...

2. Possible Pretrial Motions

The second basic determination a lawyer needs to make to be minimally competent in the negotiation preparation phase is whether there are possible pretrial motions, such as a motion to suppress evidence due to an illegal search. A minimally competent defense lawyer should always ask basic questions about the circumstances of the police stop and the search. For example, if the reason for pulling over the car is a broken taillight, the defense lawyer should confirm that the taillight was in fact broken.

However, pretrial motions can be difficult for the defense to win. And, in some courts, the threat of running a pretrial motion can be a reason for the prosecutor to "pull all plea offers off the table." It is also possible that the threat of a pretrial motion can act as leverage, particularly if the prosecutor thinks it is well founded, to get a better plea offer. Therefore, a minimally competent defense lawyer should know where, when, and how to use the threat of pretrial motions to a client's advantage. This is not to suggest that it is ineffective assistance of counsel to proceed with a pretrial motion even after the prosecution has threatened to increase the plea offer, or to revoke it if the motion is lost. In determining whether the lawyer was competent, the first question is: Did the lawyer know whether there were any possible pretrial motions? Secondly, did the lawyer fully advise the client about what might happen—including the probability of winning the motion—giving the client an opportunity to decide whether to proceed or take the deal? A lawyer should do both to meet the minimal standards of competency.

3. Possible Additional Charges or Sentencing Enhancements

The third basic determination a minimally competent lawyer needs to make in the negotiation preparation phase is to find out if the defendant could be facing more time due to additional sentencing enhancements or charges. A minimally competent lawyer should know the possible sentencing enhancements and ask questions to determine if any additional enhancements might apply. Defense lawyers should also determine if there are other related charges that could be filed in the case. Prior convictions can add years to a defendant's sentence. Prosecutors regularly allege prior convictions as part of the charging document. Rap sheets and other records of prior convictions can also be part of the standard discovery prosecutors give to defense lawyers.

The question, then, is what is the defense lawyer's duty when the prosecutor may not be immediately aware of the prior conviction? It can be a challenge for defense lawyers to find this information before the prosecutor does and to secure a plea deal without enhancements. Prosecutors often do not have information about prior convictions at arraignment when they make the initial plea offer. If they know the record is incomplete, they may delay making an offer, but prosecutors are often unaware that they do not have this information for a few reasons. For example, the prior may be from another state, so it may take a little longer to discover it, and it may not show up on the initial rap sheet. Another common situation is that the prior may be under a different name, and the defendant's various "AKAs" may not have caught up with him. This is a minefield for many defendants. And, this is an important issue in the context of discussing whether to accept or reject a particular plea offer as a defendant's prior convictions could radically change the possible punishment. A competent defense lawyer will routinely explain this to their clients. A competent defense lawyer will also specifically ask a client if they have any priors that the defense lawyer does not currently know about.

However, as every defense lawyer knows, asking clients these questions does not always mean that they will receive truthful or accurate answers. Sometimes defendants have serious cognitive deficiencies, causing them to neither understand nor be able to articulate their own prior convictions. Sometimes defendants think that if they just keep quiet, their prior convictions will never be discovered. Sometimes the priors are so old that defendants think they "aren't good" anymore or have forgotten about them. Regardless of why a defendant fails to give an accurate answer, the key in terms of analyzing whether the defense lawyer is competent is not whether the defendant gave the information, but whether the lawyer asked the question and explained its significance—including why the defendant should take the plea deal if there is any chance of a prior being found that could be used to enhance the sentence. Further, if the defendant acknowledges the existence of a prior that could be used to enhance the sentence, the defense lawyer should advise the client about whether to take the deal as offered without the additional enhancement. It may not always be advisable to take the deal even in the face of possible enhancements. If, for example, there is a strong defense or a strong likelihood that the case could ultimately be dismissed, a lawyer could competently advise his or her client to not plead guilty.

A minimally competent defense lawyer should also be aware of factual circumstances that could increase the defendant's maximum penalty. For example, the use of a gun or possession of a larger amount of drugs can add time to the possible maximum sentence. If there is a gun mentioned in the police report, or lab results with the weight of the drugs, but no gun or other appropriate enhancement added to the charges, a defense lawyer should recognize that there has been a possible oversight. A minimally competent defense lawyer will advise their client about the possible enhancement and, if the plea offer is an otherwise good deal, advise their client to take it before the enhancement is added.

Notes/Questions

How much should a lawyer be able to rely on their client in providing answers? How much work/what type of work should a lawyer be required to do to investigate a case outside of the answers provided by his client to satisfy the *Strickland* Court's three questions above to avoid a finding of incompetence?

What are the prosecutor's duties to investigate? As we discussed in Chapter Two, the prosecutor has significant discretion. Recall that under the ABA Standards on the Prosecution Function, Standard 3-3.9 Discretion in the Charging Decision:

> A prosecutor should not institute, or cause to be instituted, or permit the continued pendency of criminal charges when the prosecutor knows that the charges are not supported by probable cause. A prosecutor should not institute, cause to be instituted, or permit the continued pendency of criminal charges in the absence of sufficient admissible evidence to support a conviction.

Does this standard require a prosecutor to investigate the case? Can a prosecutor simply interview the witness and not do any future investigation?

B. Elements of an Agreement, Bargaining Options, and BATNA

The previous article started to outline the next part of our preparation sheet—elements of an agreement. To understand those elements—the charge that the prosecutor will make, other possible charges as well as enhancements, whether there are any alternative processes that might satisfy both prosecution and defense, or even whether the charge can be dismissed—each attorney should think carefully about the law, policies or programs that are already in place in that jurisdiction, and all of the facts that we have already outlined.

The next three articles focus on why investigation is crucial for attorneys trying to figure out how to resolve a case in a negotiation by understanding the choices that the defendant will face. Both consider the negotiation concept BATNA, or Best Alternative to a Negotiated Agreement, made famous in the well-known negotiation book *Getting to Yes* by Roger Fisher, William Ury, and Bruce Patton. The alternative to a plea, for most defendants, is proceeding to trial. On the other hand, the prosecutor could also have the choice to not charge the alleged crime at all. As the article below outlines, making a determination about whether to offer or accept a plea depends, in part, on how you view your alternatives. And understanding the best of those alternatives, your BATNA, takes preparation.

Preparing for a negotiation by determining your BATNA ensures that there is always a point in which you can confidently walk away from the negotiation. These next three excerpts discuss BATNA in greater detail. The first excerpt covers the basics, and the following two articles place BATNA within the plea-bargaining system.

Cynthia Alkon & Andrea Kupfer Schneider, *How to Be a Better Plea Bargainer*

66 Wash. U. J. 65, 88–89 (2021)

....

BATNA is perhaps the most ubiquitous term in negotiation literature, discussed everywhere since it's coinage in *Getting to Yes* forty years ago. It literally translates as Best Alternative to a Negotiated Agreement. The concept is that a negotiator should know at what point she would walk away from this negotiation and go to her "best alternative." This prevents the negotiator from making a bad deal, a deal that would be worse than the alternative. In negotiating the rent for an apartment, for example, one might prefer an apartment with a nice view but, if the price is not lowered sufficiently, determine that the second-choice apartment with less sunlight makes more sense for her budget. The BATNA is the action one would take (rent the other apartment) without needing the agreement of the negotiation counterpart. In plea bargaining, if a negotiation is not successful, the BATNA for the defense attorney will almost always be going to trial (the prosecutor would have no choice but to proceed). The prosecutor, on the other hand, might determine that the BATNA would also be going to trial or that the BATNA might be dropping the charges completely (and yet is unlikely to signal that during the negotiation).

The second part of the BATNA analysis is knowing when to proceed to that BATNA—a concept that the negotiation literature often refers to as the reservation point or the walk-away point. Understanding the point at which to go to the BATNA also takes separate preparation. In plea bargaining, it might be easy to figure out that going to trial is the BATNA, but then one should predict what will happen in trial. Looking at recent outcomes in this court, by this judge, with this jury pool, will help. And yet, with the paucity of cases going to trial, it is often hard to predict-and therein lies one of the challenges of plea bargaining. BATNA may be, therefore, a less important concept in plea negotiations. Depending on the case, the facts, the particular prosecutor and judge, a defendant may be left with two choices: take a bad deal or go to trial and risk an even worse outcome. In these situations, the defendant may simply have a WATNA, worst alternative to a negotiated agreement. Prosecutors, by contrast, may think of trial as a BATNA. If their facts are strong, and the law supports them, they can often expect a much tougher sentence after trial, due to the trial penalty.

Rebecca Hollander-Blumoff, *Getting To "Guilty": Plea Bargaining as Negotiation*

2 Harv. Negotiation L. Rev. 115, 121–125 Spring 1997

II. Options and Alternatives

...

A. Defense

In determining whether a plea agreement is the best course of action in a particular case, defense counsel must assess the risk of going to trial. One defense counsel defines that assessment simply: "the minimum penalty [if convicted] at trial, and the strength of the government's case." This attorney would also compare a plea offer on the table with his "overall core sense of what similar cases are worth." One scholar highlights determining a case's worth as an essential element of plea negotiation:

> Once an attorney has a feel for cases, he knows whether to try or plea bargain a case; if he chooses plea bargaining, he knows how to weigh factors as diverse as the defendant's record, the facts of the case, the prosecutor's personality, the prosecutor's willingness to go to trial, the judge's reactions to specific types of crimes, the precedents in terms of prior dispositions for this type of offense, and so on. He is confident that he can predict early what disposition is obtainable.

Of course, such confidence may be misplaced; nonetheless, most defense attorneys perform this mental calculus to determine whether to advise a defendant to accept a plea agreement. As a complicating factor, defense counsel must consider the defendant's risk preferences and circumstances in order to assess the BATNA accurately.

The BATNA calculation may depend, to a large extent, on the rules and traits of particular jurisdictions; legal precedent and adherence to sentencing guidelines may necessitate further readjustment of one's risk assessment equation. When a case is slated to be heard before a particular judge, the identity and past actions of the judge further influence the determination of the litigation BATNA. As one attorney explains, "You sometimes know what a judge will do.... [You have to assess] the likelihood of the judge figuring things your way." Information about or past experience with a judge helps to make such an assessment more accurate.

Defense counsel also note, surprisingly, that there is a less obvious alternative to an offered plea agreement than going to trial. Simply dragging a case out and making it somewhat stale for prosecutors may create additional opportunities for several reasons. Prosecutors may want to get older cases out of their office quickly; they simply may not know such cases as well as their newer ones. In addition, they may no longer feel the same pressure from supervisors or law enforcement agencies to attain a particular outcome. Finally, other experiences in the interim may enable prosecutors to judge the worth of a case more accurately. As one defense counsel explains, "My feeling is that the older a case gets, the less interest [prosecutors] have in it. It moves to another assistant [U.S. attorney], or [that assistant] has gained perspective, which results in a better offer."

B. Prosecution

Prosecutors, like defense attorneys, look at the triability of the case as a key determinant of whether to plea bargain in given cases. Explains one state prosecutor, "Would I want to try this case?" is the crucial question that guides the plea bargaining process. Prosecutors weigh factors including the strength of the evidence against the defendant, the relative strength of the government and defense cases, legal precedent, and the qualities of the court, judge, and opposing counsel to decide whether and how to plea bargain in a particular case. One prosecutor notes that "the stronger [the] evidence, the more likely [there will be] a plea." Another notes, "There's room to be more brazen and arrogant, depending on how strong your evidence is." In addition, prosecutors may consider criteria such as the nature of the crime and the history of the defendant in determining what, if any, plea to offer.

Plea bargaining scholar Albert Alschuler posits that prosecutors have the greatest incentive to offer highly favorable plea deals when evidence against the defendant is very weak. This seems consistent with the notion of a BATNA—prosecutors should agree to any deal that is better than their best alternative, which, in a weak case, is a losing trial. Pleas also are advantageous because they represent a certain conviction, which precludes prosecutors' exposure to what one prosecuting attorney calls "the vagaries of the jury system."

However, empirical studies have limited Alschuler's holding somewhat; research shows that prosecutors do sometimes "bluff" when evidence against a defendant is weak or deficient, but not to an unethical or deceitful extent. Indeed, anecdotal evidence undercuts Alschuler's conclusion. For example, one prosecutor who defines "triable" somewhat counterintuitively—as a case in which there may be issues in doubt on which the defendant might prevail—explains that triable cases "are more difficult to plead out, and they should be." She notes that the less "triable" a case is, the more pressure she will bring to bear on defendants to plead—she "will try very hard to get a plea if the proof [in a given case] is overwhelming." In other words, on an open-and-shut case, she is more likely to press for a plea disposition, while in a weaker case she "will understand" the defense's reluctance to take a guilty plea, and thus "won't try so hard to get a plea." Conversely, she notes, the more triable a case is, the more likely it will be that defense counsel has less interest in accepting a plea.

Prosecutors do, of course, have the final option of dismissing charges. While it is unlikely that this is a prosecutor's BATNA in many cases, it may be an option in a case in which certain key witnesses fall through or the judge decides a crucial evidentiary issue—such as a motion to suppress important evidence—in the defense's favor. When such legal entitlements seriously influence the outcome at trial, the BATNA may well be dismissal rather than trial of a losing case.

While it may be uncommon for attorneys to perform the detailed expected value calculations so often utilized by economic theorists, each party in the criminal context roughly determines its chances of success and failure at trial using a complex array of factors based in large part upon experiential knowledge. This broad assessment then informs both prosecutors' and defense counsel's decisions about how to view plea agreements compared to trial outcome or other possible alternatives.

Jenny Roberts & Ronald F. Wright, *Training for Bargaining*

57 William & Mary L. Rev. 1445, 1479–82 (2016)

B. Training About Preparation: Understanding BATNA

...

At first impression, it seems that the BATNA for a plea agreement in a criminal case will either be a trial, a dispositive evidentiary hearing (especially in drug or weapon possession cases), or an open guilty plea to all charges. Those are certainly likely alternatives should negotiations fail, and thus defense counsel must determine the BATNA by carefully calculating: (1) the likelihood of acquittal on each count in the charging document, and (2) the likely sentence the particular judge would impose after (a) a plea to all charges or (b) a conviction after trial.

While many defense attorneys may feel confident in their ability to determine quickly and intuitively the likelihood of success at trial, training to take a step back and more methodically determine a BATNA is likely to improve bargaining outcomes. Fisher and Ury, who coined the term, recommend a three-step process for determining a BATNA: brainstorming a list of actions to be taken if there is no agreement, converting the most promising ideas into tangible alternatives, and selecting the best alternative.

To give one example, consider a drug sale case in which the police officer will testify that he observed the defendant hand a small packet to another person in exchange for money. The police found cocaine on that person; they also found cash and several small baggies of cocaine on the defendant. Obvious potential actions if there is no plea agreement are to win at trial or to get the defendant a pre- or post-plea diversionary deal (success in drug treatment in exchange for eventual dismissal of the charges). Too many defenders will do a quick calculation of the likelihood of winning the trial or getting into the program and will then enter the actual negotiation.

However, more emphasis on Fisher and Ury's second step—making promising alternatives more tangible—could significantly improve the defendant's negotiation position. For example, even if the prosecution is unlikely to offer diversion, helping the client enter drug treatment may convince a judge to keep the defendant in that program even after a trial conviction or nonnegotiated guilty plea. Even if acquittal seems unlikely, a visit to the scene and an interview of the alleged buyer might uncover facts that increase the likelihood of acquittal on the top count. These efforts might reveal poor lighting at the corner of the alleged transaction, or that the buyer had drugs in a red baggie while those on the defendant were in clear baggies. Though these steps are fairly typical for counsel to take as a case approaches trial, they are not always considered part of the preparation process for negotiation. Training about BATNAs would emphasize the importance of early investigation and planning to the negotiation process. Using the BATNA method would lead to a different calculation of the best alternative to agreement, and thus a stronger position from which to negotiate, as well as a better sense of when to walk away from the negotiation. One of the few empirical studies of defense counsel's actual preparation for plea negotiation stated that "[d]efense attorneys who interviewed prosecution witnesses and conducted extensive fact investigations would, ... in a great majority of cases, improve the bargaining position of their clients involved in plea negotiations." This conclusion was based in part on surveying criminal defense attorneys about their most recent felony cases that went to trial, and learning that in three-fourths of those recent cases, respondents perceived the prosecution's evidence at trial to be weaker than the evidence in the police reports disclosed during discovery. The conclusion about the likely effect of thorough preparation (in the form of investigation) before bargaining was also based on survey responses from about fifty-two felony cases involving violent crime victims. Lawyers reported getting better outcomes in cases in which they interviewed victims than in cases without an interview. In another study, despite rating the skill of negotiation as very important to pretrial practice, one half of respondents "did not conduct a thorough investigation, do legal research, or develop a theory of defense before plea negotiations." These studies offer strong support for the hypothesis that negotiation training can result in more effective negotiation, meaning better outcomes for defendants in criminal cases.

Although a defense attorney should not counsel accepting a deal that leaves the defendant worse off than if he went to trial, calculating the BATNA in a criminal case is more complicated than calculating the likelihood of conviction and likely sentence if convicted because failure to reach an agreement can lead to outcomes other than trial. Failing to agree can lead to an unexpectedly better bargain later in the process, or even dismissal of the charges. This is particularly true in misdemeanor cases, in which simply waiting until the trial date approaches can lead to a better outcome. Again, though these alternative outcomes to a failed negotiation may seem obvious, training can, at the very least, remind defenders about the various possible results in a criminal case and highlight that not all options surface in an initial negotiation.

Notes/Questions

1. What type of training would prepare an attorney properly to analyze BATNA in criminal cases? Law school course? Student internship? Do you feel prepared to do this yourself? Do you feel better able to do this as a prosecutor or as a defense lawyer?

2. Assume you are the prosecutor negotiating with a first-time defendant charged with theft from a local retailor. Evidence against the defendant is weak, as there were no cameras that caught the defendant stealing. A clerk called the police after allegedly witnessing the defendant stuff an item into their coat pocket and walk out the door. The police stopped the suspect as he was exiting the parking lot. However, the allegedly stolen item did not have tags or packaging of any kind. The defendant maintains he did not steal the item.

a. From each of the prosecutor and defense attorney perspective, how would you approach negotiating a plea deal? What would be your opening offer? What would be your strategy? What would be your BATNA?

b. Do your answers to the questions above change if the defendant is a repeat offender? What if the previous crime was not related to theft but rather operating a vehicle while intoxicated? Would your strategy change?

A Note on Options and Flexibility in Negotiation

Effective negotiators are also flexible in *what* they are willing to receive or what goes into a settlement. While they know that they need to remain protective of their own interests and goals, they understand that they must also remain open about which outcome might meet their interests. Recognizing that you can get what you need and want in a number of ways will actually improve your chances of success. Note that flexibility does not mean giving in or compromising your key interests. It does mean thinking about how those interests can be met—and if there is more than one way to do that.

In the preparation sheet, we outline some ways to think about flexible outcomes. Other charges and enhancements can make the charge (and the plea) more onerous. Alternative processes that may be available in the jurisdiction or even dismissal are options that should also be thought about in advance as well. Which options fit this particular case often is the heart of a plea bargain when the facts are not really in doubt. And so preparation here is crucial as well.

The problem-solving courts that we will discuss later in the book are examples of where judges have thought creatively about how to better meet the needs of the public to be safe and the defendants to be rehabilitated. Delayed and diversion sentencing, restorative justice, and other variations of outcomes in the criminal legal system all are the results of prosecutors and defense attorneys thinking creatively about how to accomplish all of the interests of the legal system. Again, this will take preparation—what are the alternatives in your jurisdiction? How will the prosecutor need to sell this to her office? And how can the defense attorney sell this to their client?

C. Outlining Interests and Setting Goals in Plea Bargaining

The investigation section of the prep sheet shows how knowing the law and the facts can help you establish what is likely to happen at trial—your alternative to a plea agreement. But effective negotiation preparation is more than knowing what your limits are—you also need this preparation in order to understand the interests of all parties and to set your goals. What is justifiable to ask for? How high (or low) should you aim?

1. Understanding Interests of All Parties

You should first start this next step by outlining your interests—*and the interests of the other parties involved in this case.* In fact, as we talk about plea bargaining, we want to remember that all of these concepts apply to the multiple negotiations going on throughout the process under the umbrella of plea bargaining. Clients and defense attorneys will negotiate; prosecutors will be talking to victims, perhaps the press or public, and might also be negotiating with their supervisor; and, if we increase judicial involvement in plea bargaining, that too becomes another negotiation. Understanding the interests of all of these potential parties is crucial preparation.

We know intuitively that the defendant and the defense attorney are not exactly aligned, so we want to take time to consider that. As the defense attorney, your goals might be to minimize jail time or to avoid a loss or to manage an overwhelming caseload or to change the law using a case that has particularly egregious facts. The defendant might have other interests—protecting his reputation, minimizing jail time, perhaps getting help for an addiction, or proving his innocence. We should note that sometimes these interests will overlap but, other times, they will not. Furthermore, defendants are often particularly suspicious of defense attorneys that have been appointed for them, and this can make the relationship much more fraught.

Consider the following excerpt advising numerous strategies to pressure defendants.

Abbe Smith, *The Lawyer's "Conscience" and the Limits of Persuasion*

36 Hofstra L. Rev. 479, 486–487, 490–491, 495–496 (2007)

...

All criminal lawyers might take a page from the American Bar Association's 2003 ABA Guidelines for the Appointment and the Performance of Defense Counsel in Death Penalty Cases, which repeatedly refer to enlisting family members, friends, clergy, and other prisoners to help persuade the client not to make a self-destructive decision. The commentary to Guideline 10.9.1, "The Duty to Seek an Agreed-Upon Disposition," states:

> In addition to persuading the prosecution to negotiate a resolution to the case, counsel must often persuade the client as well.... The entire defense team must work from the outset of the case with the client and others close to him to lay the groundwork for acceptance of a reasonable resolution.

Experienced capital defender Kevin Doyle suggests that defenders enlist the following allies: capital experts (someone who will tell the client "horror stories" and convince him that a trial will be disastrous); family members (a parent who will beg the client to take a plea to spare the family); God (telling the client who has found religion that taking a life plea is what God wants because of how much good the client can do teaching God's word in prison). Though Doyle acknowledges that this is "hardball," he expresses no concern about it being unduly coercive. He worries instead about not being forceful enough: "If you don't pull out all the stops, you will only regret it on the eve of an execution."

IV. A Note on Client-Centeredness

Much has been written about client-centered representation. But sometimes the ideal of client-centeredness—lawyer "neutrality," lawyer "humility," the "primacy of client decision-making," the customer is always right—sits uncomfortably in the rough and tumble of practice. Moreover, as one recent commentator has noted, client-centered representation means different things to different lawyers, depending on the circumstances.

I believe that, in criminal defense, client-centeredness is spending the time to counsel and ultimately convince a client to hang on to as much liberty as he or she can. As a prominent capital defender put it, client-centered criminal defenders "take off" their watches and earn the client's trust with "patience," spending "hours and days with a client to persuade him to ... make the right decision ... and to own it fully." Client-centered defenders do not take a client's ill-considered, irrational, or immature "no" for an answer. Instead, they lend perspective and guidance. They give the client the wisdom and strength to make a difficult, unpleasant decision.

So-called client-centered lawyers can do damage to their clients by "simply acquiescing" to their foolish wishes. This is an abdication of professional duty out of a "false sense of respect for [client] autonomy." It can also be a cover for laziness, for being afraid to really engage with a client, or worse.

Moreover, uncovering a client's autonomous wishes is more complicated than simply asking the client what he or she wants to do. The words "I ain't takin' no plea" can mean many different things: I'm scared about what is happening to me; I don't like any of the choices available to me; I don't trust you; I don't trust anyone....

VI. Conclusion

There is no one-size-fits-all approach to client counseling, no single method that works with every client. Some clients are more vulnerable than others. Some are more easily manipulated. Some are more stubborn.

Lawyers should be resourceful in the techniques they employ in client counseling. They should be responsive to individual clients, dogged in their efforts, and not easily discouraged. They should be able to be both gentle and tough, depending on what works best. They should not refrain from the most forceful persuasion when to do otherwise would be destructive.

The approach I propose applies to the innocent and guilty alike. Innocent clients face the same dangers at trial and sentencing as guilty clients, sometimes worse. Although no lawyer likes advising innocent people to plead guilty, sometimes this is the wisest course. If refusing a plea would be destructive, lawyers should employ the same degree of persuasion with an avowedly innocent client as with an admittedly guilty one.

Of course, ultimately the decision to plead or not is the client's. No matter how strongly the lawyer may feel, the client has the last word on whether he or she pleads guilty or goes to trial. This fact distinguishes the plea situation from "strategic decisions" where lawyers are generally allowed to override client wishes. It is clearly the client's right to make a bad decision here.

... I can coerce with a clear conscience if doing so helps a client ward off disaster or make the better of two bad choices. In a sentencing regime that routinely sends the convicted away for decades—or kills them—so long as the client makes the final choices, there is nothing wrong with a little coercion.

Notes/Questions

1. How does Smith seem to view the negotiation with the client? What style does she seem to recommend? Thinking back to preparing on interests, how might understanding both your and your client's interests assist with this conversation?

2. Do you think additional counseling guidelines should be put in place for attorneys with clients that are facing capital punishment? What about requirements to counsel about other lifelong consequences like sex offender registration or deportation? Should there be yet even more requirements when counseling juveniles? Why or why not? How would new guidelines potentially change the outcome of a plea deal?

3. Alma Magaña notes how public defenders play the unique role of interpreting their clients' interests in any plea bargain—and may value certain consequences differently than the defendant.

> "I have a fiduciary duty to my client," stated one public defender in explaining her refusal to litigate bail. This public defender believed the best interest of her client included not litigating bail. The public defender's client, Shawn Smith, was charged with a misdemeanor assault and had been arrested several times for assault on medical staff while hospitalized. Smith was not a U.S. citizen and, if convicted of the charge, would become deportable due to prior convictions he already had. With no guarantee the government would grant relief for humanitarian reasons or cancel the removal, Smith would likely be forced to return to a country where he would experience persecution. Smith's attorney provided representation conforming to the attorney model professional expectations: counseling the client about the choices they get to make; negotiating with the prosecutor for a favorable disposition on the case; and composing a pre-pleading memorandum detailing the great harm the client would suffer if convicted and deported for this crime. Arguably, she even went beyond the norms by discussing available bail litigation options with the Decarceration Project.
>
> But Smith's attorney refused to continue to litigate his bail and did not consult with him about this decision. She cited teachings from more senior attorneys, some of them supervising attorneys, stating zealous advocacy meant achieving the so-called right outcome as determined by the attorney. This attorney indicated her role was to protect—although her refusal to consult with Smith on ending bail litigation certainly puts her so-called protective nature into doubt—the person accused of a crime from themselves. For Smith's case, this meant usurping his decision to litigate bail, while still working toward mitigating the immigration consequences.
>
> For attorneys like Smith's, the purported right outcome is one minimizing the harms of the criminal legal system. The public defender, guided by their experience, will often determine what this outcome is based on the particulars of a case, including the charges, the assigned prosecutor, and the presiding judge. And, as sociologist Matthew Clair points out, "[l]awyers' efforts to control their clients are often well intentioned: passionate defense attorneys view their jobs as reducing their client's legal costs, costs sometimes resulting from the exercise of certain legal rights." In the above example, the attorney sincerely believed her decisions were in her client's best interest based on her assessment of the case. The danger, however, is that one's understanding of the supposed right decision is highly subjective and can vary greatly from public defender to public defender. Further, a public defender's view can depart substantially from the views of those they represent, which, as discussed here, can severely undermine the interests of the person charged with a crime.

Alma Magaña, *Public Defenders as Gatekeepers of Freedom*, 70 UCLA L. Rev. 978, 1005–1006 (2023).

What would you do in a similar case? How can public defenders be sure that they advocate for their client's interests, as the client defines them, even if the public defender disagrees with those?

* * *

Similarly, the prosecutor should take the time to understand her interests—maintaining a high conviction rate, protecting the public, serving justice, putting someone dangerous away—and understand how those interests may or may not align with other players in the criminal legal system. What are the interests of the elected head of the office? Is there an election coming up? And might the district attorney feel other political pressures from either the public or press that will impact how you individually conduct this case? In addition, how do the interests of the victim impact your behavior? Does this victim even want to testify, or does he want revenge or prefers to be uninvolved or is particularly prominent or eloquent to the point that the victim can also influence the press and public? All of these pressure points and interests need to be understood well for the prosecutor to set her goals in the negotiation.

Finally, you will note that the preparation sheet encourages each attorney to prepare for the interests and goals of both sides. Why is this so? Putting this in very simple terms, when you are negotiating, you are trying to change someone's mind. The negotiation skill of empathy—called perspective taking in the psychological literature—helps you figure out what the other person is thinking. That insight into his or her mind can greatly improve your chances of changing it. Think of the other person's interests, positions, and wishes as the map of the territory you are trying to navigate.[6] When you understand what the other side thinks—and why he or she thinks it—you can start factoring that into the method of reaching your own goals. If you take time to consider the other person's (or the other side's) perspective, you will be more likely to be able to frame arguments in the way that will be persuasive to him or her. And empathizing with someone makes it more likely that he or she will empathize—or at least listen—to you. Finally, empathy helps build relationships through trust and respect. With that improved relationship, you will get more information and better, lasting outcomes. (We discuss the lawyer relationship later in this chapter as well.)

Empathy is *not* sympathy or agreement. You do not have to agree that the prosecutor has a slam-dunk case. But if you understand why she thinks that, you'll have better insight into the strength of the evidence as she sees it. Or, if the defense attorney is arguing that *this* defendant does not deserve the typical sentence, you might disagree. Nonetheless, that information about the defendant could help you persuade the defense attorney down the road that part of the sentence, for example, should be that the defendant needs to stay in school.

---

6. R. Fisher, E. Kopelman & A.K. Schneider, Beyond Machiavelli: Tools for Coping with Conflict (London, Penguin Books 1994).

Even before you start the conversation, take a minute to think. What is your best prediction of what the other party, your counterpart, might say or how he or she views this situation? Assess the current situation through the other person's perspective and think about how the other person might feel about you or your interests. As you enter the conversation, ask questions that will allow the other person to tell his or her story.

Problem 1

Imagine that you are a defense attorney who has a client who is a first-time offender charged with a drug offense. You know there are problems with the search and have one civilian witness who will verify your client's story. That witness also has a criminal record for drugs. What are your options?

- Filing a search and seizure motion?
- Telling the prosecutor that you have this evidence and use it in the plea negotiation?
- Filing the motion and see what happens?
- Are there any alternative measures you could think of that would keep your client (a first-time offender) out of prison?

2. Setting Goals and Asking for Them

Effective negotiators know how to ask for what they want. They know how to frame their arguments in a way that will be persuasive, they know how to support their arguments, and they know how to remain calm and confident throughout the negotiation. This is the key negotiation skill of assertiveness.

One way of understanding assertiveness is to think about the difference between knowledge and performance. You can't be assertive—you can't effectively ask for what you want—unless you first fully understand exactly *what* you want, *how* your priorities in any case line up, and *why* your desire is fair. Begin by setting some goals, that are specific, reasonable, and aspirational. Think about exactly what you want to get out of the negotiation and detail why your request is reasonable. This is the preparation described above. Without this preparation, you cannot base your argument on legal standards, past practice or even your knowledge of this defendant and this particular incident.

For example, a typical DUI case in a jurisdiction might have a typical punishment—2 days in jail and an alcohol treatment requirement. But if you knew from your research and experience that someone serving in the military who receives a DUI actually goes through a much more thorough (and punitive) alcohol treatment program, you might be able to persuade the prosecutor to waive the jail time or the additional treatment requirement. Only if you have done the proper research into the law and into your client, would you know that this should be your goal.

If you want to get what you're asking for, once you have looked thoughtfully at your goal, you'll need to think about your performance. How can you best ask for what you want? Think about when you've been on the receiving end of a request. If someone is confident, patient, and tells a persuasive story, aren't you much more inclined to say yes?

In the context of negotiation, assertiveness is *not* being aggressive, negative, or threatening. It is *not* pounding the table or raising your voice. Bullies do sometimes get their way, but over the long run, in an arena where reputation is crucial, bullying is not a recipe for long-term success. Walking that line—firmly and pleasantly asking for what you want, holding onto your goals and trading off graciously, explaining why what you want is fair—is a skill that can lead to success and an excellent reputation. (And we will come back to the importance of a good reputation in the legal field later.)

At a minimum, a good assertive performance includes not negotiating against yourself. With or without knowing it, many of us can be our own enemy in negotiations, especially ones in which much is at stake, rushing through our own statements, anticipating (rather than listening to) the other person's response, interrupting others, or reacting too hastily to what's said or done during the meeting. Think about this in advance and remember to listen and take things slowly: at the very least, wait for the other side to respond to your request verbally or in writing. Do not let his or her flinch, frown, or hesitation cause you to back away from your request too soon.

Then, in terms of negotiating strategy, think about your opening offer. Since most people expect every negotiation to have some give-and-take, don't ask for your ultimate goal at the start—you must aim reasonably higher than that and give yourself some room to bargain. Have an optimistic and fair opening offer and think about what your successive offers will be as the other side starts to negotiate. (This is the part of the preparation sheet that asks you to think about your concession strategy—from your first, optimistic offer, to your second and third back up positions.)

Notes/Questions

How can defense attorneys use information about the law in order to be more persuasive? In *Standards of Legitimacy in Criminal Negotiations*, the authors note that

> One less obvious advantage of raising criteria to justify offers is simply that raising criteria provides a justification for defense counsel to make a demand. Research has shown that the simple step of providing a justification for a demand, even a frivolous one, has the power to induce compliance. In a fascinating study, researchers shut down all but one of the copy machines in a library, causing long lines to form at the remaining one. The experimenters compared two types of asking when students were trying to convince people to allow them to cut in front of them in the line. In one condition, the experimenter simply said, "Excuse me, I have five pages. May I use the Xerox machine?" Sixty percent of those approached this way allowed the experimenter to cut in front of them. In the other condition, the experimenter said, "Excuse me, I have five pages. May I use the Xerox machine *because I have to make some*

copies?" Even though the second approach added an entirely inane justification (as the purpose of cutting in line at a copy machine is to make copies), providing a reason induced compliance in ninety-three percent of subjects. The researchers for this study suggest that this technique is effective because humans are hardwired to accommodate the seemingly legitimate demands of others, as doing so allows us to build mutually rewarding relationships. People tend to resist demands imposed on them but will consider them if the asker thinks the demands are justified, because the asker may then be obligated to them in the future. In order to make judgments about what demands are legitimate, the authors suggest that humans use rules of thumb rather than performing a full analysis, and the very existence of the word "because" is often sufficient to gain compliance. Defense counsel, then, may find themselves at an advantage by using norms for judicial exercise of prosecutorial discretion. They will be able to better justify their offer and thus increase the likelihood that prosecutors will not reject the offer out of hand. By saying, "I think this offer is acceptable because ...," defense attorneys can bolster their bargaining position and induce the same psychological effect on their negotiation partners—prosecutors—as in any other negotiation context. Much of what happens in a plea bargain also depends on the chemistry between specific prosecutors and defense attorneys, who are often in repeat relationships with each other. Defense counsels' use of justification can persuade prosecutors to grant legitimized demands and build a mutually rewarding relationship for future plea bargains.

Wesley MacNeil Oliver & Rishi Batra, *Standards of Legitimacy in Criminal Negotiations*, 20 Harv. Negot. L. Rev. 61, 69–78 (2015).

Problem 2

You are a prosecutor. You just got a case where the defendant assaulted his younger brother. Both brothers have a history of minor violence with each other. This case is charged as a felony, but the injury is minimal (a black eye). The defendant is 21 years old. The parents of both brothers are in court urging you to dismiss the case because "Johnny didn't mean to hurt Billy, things just got out of hand, like they do when they drink." Billy is also in court and also wants the case dismissed, because "I incited him, I knew what I was doing and that he would blow up at me and I did it anyway."

What do you do? What if your boss has told you, "I don't care what you do, but I'm tired of seeing these two kids in our court"?

What if your boss said, "I don't care what you do, but I want a conviction for something because I'm tired of seeing these two kids in our court"?

Would it change your analysis if your court had an active diversion program? Would it change your analysis if the court had a domestic violence specialty court?

The excerpt below explains how negotiation training might help in terms of setting better goals, drawing on the concept of anchoring. In negotiation, when you make the first offer, you are said to be "anchoring" the negotiation to that offer. This helps us to consider optimistic goals, to anchor high, and also how a concession strategy might play out. Your counterpart must now respond given the frame you have already set. With this in mind, negotiators are advised to anchor as favorably as reasonably possible. Roberts and Wright show that public defenders, by contrast, typically do not make optimistic first offers.

Jenny Roberts & Ronald F. Wright, *Training for Bargaining*

57 William & Mary L. Rev. 1445, 1485–1486 (2016)

...

Responses to our surveys show that public defenders do not often try a first offer or a low offer. As Table 2 illustrates, when asked to characterize their own first offers in typical cases, defenders typically answered that their offers were closer to unfavorable than favorable for their own clients.

Table 2. Defense First Offer Characterized

	Number of Responses
Very Unfavorable = 1	34
Unfavorable = 2	88
Reasonable = 3	54
Favorable = 4	50
Very Favorable = 5	41
Average Rating	**2.9**

There were no meaningful differences in the responses to this question based on the gender or race of the attorney or the type of caseload they carry. Across all of these groups, the less ambitious first offers were the most common. Indeed, the average offer from a defense attorney was less than one level higher than the typical first offer from the prosecutor (defense attorneys on average scored the prosecutor's first offer at 2.0). The governance structure of the office in which the defenders work did matter in the response to this question. Attorneys working in state-operated offices rather than local offices were more likely to characterize their own offers as more favorable to their clients (at 2.7 for local offices and 3.1 for state offices).

The average rating for defenders' characterization of their own first offers is, surprisingly, just below "reasonable" for their clients. Training about anchoring would highlight how making a "very favorable" offer (made more reasonable by developing a sound BATNA) might be the better approach in many cases.

Notes/Questions

1. What would your advice to attorneys be now knowing this information? How can you set your goals in a negotiation?

2. How does an understanding of your BATNA impact your goal-setting? How should this (or should it not)?

Problem 3

Two defendants with long records of prior convictions are charged with the sale of crack cocaine to an undercover police officer. The prosecutor has added enhancements that made a drug sales case a potential life-in-prison case.

The two defense lawyers had several conversations with the prosecutor and convinced him that this case was not worth that much time and got a plea deal for eight years.

The defendants both said that eight years was "too much time" and as one said, "it was just one small rock of crack, it ain't worth that much time." The lawyers both spent a considerable amount of time with their respective clients explaining the options, explaining what would happen at trial, and explaining the minimum and maximum sentence after trial.

Despite being told they would most likely lose at trial (because the defendants had sold the rock to an undercover police officer), the defendants both rejected the plea offer. The case went to trial and the jury returned a guilty verdict. Because of the enhancements, the minimum sentence was 25-years-to-life, which is what the defendants were sentenced to.

- Is this a situation of a failure to properly advise?
- Or is this a situation where the defense lawyers just didn't understand their client's interests?
- What could the lawyers do to better understand their clients' interests?
- Overall, could they have done a better job persuading them to take the eight years and not risk significantly more time after trial?

Additional Resources

Michal Alberstein & Nourit Zimerman, *Constructive Plea Bargaining: Towards Judicial Conflict Resolution*, 32 OHIO ST. J. ON DISP. RESOL. 279 (2017).

Cynthia Alkon, *Plea Bargain Negotiations: Defining Competency Beyond* Lafler & Frye, 53 AM. CRIM. L. REV. 377 (Spring 2016).

Cynthia Alkon & Andrea Kupfer Schneider, *How to Be a Better Plea Bargainer*, 66 WASH. U. J. 65, 69–72, 88–89 (2021).

Marcus T. Boccaccini & Stanley L. Brodsky, *Characteristics of the Ideal Criminal Defense Attorney from the Client's Perspective: Empirical Findings and Implications for Legal Practice*, 25 L. & PSYCHOL. REV. 81 (Spring 2001).

Richard Delgado, *Prosecuting Violence: A Colloquy on Race, Community, and Justice*, 52 STAN. L. REV. 751 (2000).

Lucian E. Dervan, Vanessa A. Edkins & Thea Johnson, *Victims of Coercive Plea Bargaining: Defendants who give False Testimony for False Pleas*, 72 AM. U. L.REV. 1919 (August 2023).

ROGER FISHER & WILLIAM URY, GETTING TO YES: NEGOTIATING AGREEMENT WITHOUT GIVING IN (1991).

Gabriel Hallevy, *The Defense Attorney as Mediator in Plea Bargains*, 9 PEPP. DISP. RESOL. L.J. 495 (2009).

Rinat Kitai-Sangero, *Plea Bargaining as Dialogue*, 49 AKRON L. REV. 63 (2016).

Thea Johnson, *Measuring the Creative Bargain*, 92 IND. L.J. 901 (Summer 2017).

Gary T. Lowenthal, *Theoretical Notes on Lawyer Competency and an Overview of the Phoenix Criminal Lawyer Study*, 1981 ARIZ. ST. L.J. 447.

HONORABLE JAMES P. MANAK, PLEA BARGAINING: THE PROSECUTOR'S PERSPECTIVE (1973).

Jenny Roberts, *Effective Plea Bargaining Counsel*, 122 YALE L.J. 2650 (June 2013).

Jenny Roberts, *Prosecuting Misdemeanors*, WASH. COLL. L. (Research Paper No. 2020-28).

Jenny Roberts & Ronald F. Wright, *Training for Bargaining*, 57 WM. & MARY L. REV. 1445 (2016).

RICHARD SHELL, BARGAINING FOR ADVANTAGE: NEGOTIATION STRATEGIES FOR REASONABLE PEOPLE 34 (2d ed. 2006).

DOUGLAS STONE, BRUCE PATTON, AND SHEILA HEEN, DIFFICULT CONVERSATIONS: HOW TO DISCUSS WHAT MATTERS MOST (1999).

Rodney J. Uphoff, *The Criminal Defense Lawyer as Effective Negotiator: A Systematic Approach*, 2 CLINICAL L. REV. 73 (1995).

Ronald F. Wright, Jenny Roberts & Betina Cutaia Wilkinson, *The Shadow Bargainers*, 42 CARDOZO L. REV. 1295 (2021).

Chapter 7

Plea Bargaining: Sitting Down at the Table

We have thus far focused on preparation in advance of the plea bargain and, you'll note, primarily outlined how knowing the case and the law can help you figure out what to ask for in terms of a deal. We then discussed understanding interests and setting goals. In fact, this preparation is just the tip of the iceberg.

The preparation sheet from the previous chapter has an entire section labeled approach and communication. These are elements that we want you to think about in advance of the negotiation and then to be cognizant of during the negotiation as well. In part, we know that effective negotiators are flexible in terms of how they approach each situation. This seems logical—not all cases are the same even when the crime is charged the same, and not all lawyers are the same even if their respective title is. Your counterpart, your client, and the context should help determine how you approach each negotiation. To understand this further, we outline several negotiation variables below.

We first turn to reflecting about the lawyers with whom you will be negotiating, as your relationship matters in terms of your communication choices. We then turn to the discussion about negotiation styles and how each of these styles can play out in a plea-bargaining negotiation. Not surprisingly, there are advantages and disadvantages to each of these. We then outline further particular elements of communication: when, where, and how. Finally, we will review some of the literature about common errors in negotiation and show how these psychological mistakes can impact your success in plea bargaining. Again, we want to note that the negotiations under plea bargaining occur not only between the lawyers themselves but also include negotiations with clients, judges, victims, and others. So, the strategies outlined here should also be considered in these contexts.

I. Lawyer Reputation and Relationships—Preparing to Communicate

Our first section in this chapter turns to the research and preparation you can do about your counterpart before you even sit down together. We have already noted that effective negotiators try to understand the situation from the other's perspective to be more persuasive. Similarly, thinking carefully about the other lawyer's reputation and the relationship that you currently have, as well as the one you aspire to create, are important elements in a negotiation.

In negotiation, it is wise to consider this in advance. What is the reputation of that particular lawyer? That office or firm? And what is your own reputation: What behavior might your counterpart expect from you? This rubric of ethicality, another negotiation skill, operates in three ways: reputation, trustworthiness (can they trust you?) and trustfulness (can you trust them?).

Your reputation is how others perceive you. It is connected to whether others can trust you, but it is not completely the same as trust, because reputation encompasses more than trust. Furthermore, trust and distrust operate separately from each other—you might trust your counterpart to pursue justice, for example, but distrust her to put her own interests aside while doing so.[1]

The reputation of the negotiator is a crucial part of negotiation. In almost all the interactions within a legal setting, each time you negotiate, you will be operating from the foundation of your established reputation—and at the same time adding to or even remaking that reputation. Think back to your previous dealings with counterparts. What has been your typical approach to dealing with them? How does your counterpart perceive you?

Negotiations are inherently uncertain, and a reputation helps manage this uncertainty by giving others signals for predicting how you will behave and why. The phrase "your reputation precedes you" is apt; just as you researched the person you were going to negotiate with, you should expect that the other person has done research on you, at the least asking around about what to expect from you in the coming meeting. If you have a reputation for working well with others, for instance, your actions will be interpreted in that light—with that "halo" of a cooperative approach influencing your current negotiation. If word has it that you often see the merits in compromising, your counterpart will be thinking about that during your meeting. As empirical negotiation studies have clearly demonstrated, different reputations can lead to different outcomes.[2]

Your counterpart's reputation can also affect the negotiation significantly. Not surprisingly, when a counterpart is known to be adversarial and have a competitive approach to negotiations, negotiators share less information, waste more time talking around the subject, and achieve less beneficial and creative outcomes. One of us had a law student with a terrible reputation—one he had developed in the negotiation workshop no less! He bluffed and lied to enough classmates in the exercises that, by the end of the semester, many classmates avoided him. And when he became a defense attorney after graduating, one of his classmates happened to be in the prosecutor's office in the same jurisdiction. For at least several years, any time they had a case together, it went to trial. As the prosecutor told us, given the defense attorney's overly competitive behavior and reputation, it was just self-defense to plan for trial and assume that negotiations would fail.

---

1. R. Lewicki, *Trust and Distrust*, *in* 1 The Negotiator's Desk Reference 201 (A.K. Schneider & C. Honeyman eds., St. Paul, DRI Press 2017).

2. Catherine H. Tinsley et al., *Tough Guys Finish Last: The Perils of a Distributive Reputation*, 88 Organizational Behav. & Hum. Decision Processes 621, 623 (2002).

Having a reputation for being competitive, of course, can be useful in certain situations, especially when you are trying to deter someone from even beginning to negotiate with you or when you are making threats and want the other side to believe you will carry them out. In most repeat negotiations, however, these interactions will benefit from a long-term perspective that seeks to bring together multiple interests.

When parties have the reputation for being integrative or problem-solving, the result is likely to be more satisfying. Facing someone with a good reputation makes people more inclined to share information and to share it more efficiently and earlier in the negotiation, which saves time. This increased information-sharing then leads to better, more comprehensive agreements. For example, in a study examining lawyers negotiating with each other in the civil context, lawyers who had negotiated with each other before were more apt to reach agreement than those who had never done business together—even if their first meeting had not ended in agreement.[3]

You will also want to consider your reputation moving forward. Particularly if many of your negotiations will be repeat interactions, occurring with the same parties, looking ahead is essential to your long-term success.

When reflecting on your own actions and how they create your reputation, look at them from a variety of perspectives. Years from now, will you look back on your conduct and be proud or ashamed of it? Was your behavior impressive enough that it might contribute to some sort of good policy that your institution might adopt? If one of your parents had behaved as you did, what would you think? If an account of your behavior appeared tomorrow on the front page of *The New York Times* or on TikTok, would you be embarrassed? Today, there are far too many stories of zealous prosecutors who, perhaps, might have thought more carefully about their reputation before hiding evidence or continuing to prosecute. And, in the worst of these stories, a lack of ethicality will get you disbarred.[4]

The study below (from which you've already read a brief excerpt) asked attorneys to rate the *other* attorney with whom they had most recently negotiated, regardless of outcome. In other words, what reputation did the lawyer create with you over the course of the negotiation? The over 600 respondents first described their negotiation counterpart using a list of 89 adjectives (and the top 20 are shown below). They then rated the other attorney in terms of effectiveness on behalf of their client. The general results for all attorneys are discussed to demonstrate the linkage between negotiation behavior and your reputation for effectiveness. The style labels used in this study are not what we will use later in this chapter, as these were based on the statistical analysis model used. More importantly, focus on the types of behaviors (outlined in the adjective lists) that resulted in better reputations for lawyers in all practice areas.

---

3. J.S. Johnston & J. Waldfogel, *Does Repeat Play Elicit Cooperation Evidence from Federal Civil Litigation*, 31 J. Leg. Stud. 39 (2002).

4. Tom Jackman, *Disbarred Duke lacrosse prosecutor Mike Nifong is back, along with more misconduct allegations*, Wash. Post, Aug. 30, 2016.

Table 1. Top 20 Adjectives for Four Cluster

	True Problem-Solving	Cautious Problem-Solving	Ethical Adversarial	Unethical Adversarial
1	Ethical	Ethical	Confident	Irritating
2	Experienced	Experienced	Assertive	Stubborn
3	Personable	Personable	Arrogant	Headstrong
4	Trustworthy	Self-Controlled	Headstrong	Argumentative
5	Rational	Confident	Experienced	Quarrelsome
6	Fair-Minded	Rational	Demanding	Arrogant
7	Agreeable	Agreeable	Egotistical	Egotistical
8	Communicative	Dignified	Ambitious	Manipulative
9	Realistic		Stubborn	Assertive
10	Accommodating		Argumentative	Demanding
11	Perceptive		Tough	Complaining
12	Confident		Irritating	Hostile
13	Sociable		Forceful	Suspicious
14	Self-Controlled		Firm	Conniving
15	Adaptable		Quarrelsome	Greedy
16	Dignified		Masculine	Rude
17	Helpful		Dominant	Angry
18	Astute		Ethical	Confident
19	Poised		Deliberate	Ambitious
20	Flexible		Hostile	Deceptive

Andrea Kupfer Schneider, *Cooperating or Caving In: Are Defense Attorneys Shrewd or Exploited in Plea Bargaining Negotiations?*

91 Marq. L. Rev. 145, 147–150 (Fall 2007)

...

In comparing the behavior of criminal law attorneys with that of attorneys in other practice areas, we will use the results of the four-cluster analysis, so I have reprinted the table of top twenty adjectives for the four clusters from the original study in order to understand the four different styles under discussion later in the article.

The four-cluster analysis is interesting because there are striking differences even when comparing similar groups. For example, the cautious problem-solvers were engaged in completely positive behavior. All of the adjectives describing them are favorable, and they have good behavioral characteristics such as ethical, experienced,

Table 2. Four Cluster Breakdown by Effectiveness

	Ineffective	Average	Effective	Total Percentage of the Bar by Cluster
True Problem-Solving	1.3%	26.9%	71.8%	38.5%
Cautious Problem-Solving	11.8%	64.7%	23.5%	27.5%
Ethical Adversarial	39.8%	44.4%	15.8%	21.5%
Unethical Adversarial	75.3%	22.1%	2.6%	12.5%
Totals	21.7%	40.5%	37.8%	N = 618

rational, confident, agreeable, and dignified. Yet, the effectiveness rating of the cautious problem-solvers versus the true problem-solvers was dramatic—23.5% versus 71.8% (see Table 2 below). What was the difference? Those lawyers in the cautious group were cautious—cautious about truly engaging in problem-solving behavior. The true problem-solvers had far more skills in their repertoire and were effective in a triangle of skills—assertiveness, empathy, and flexibility. The lawyers with these two approaches share ethical behavior and a pleasant personality, but the true problem-solver goes further in these three skills. The true problem-solver is better at asserting the case (rated highly in preparation, astuteness about the law, and being realistic) and better at talking about the case as well (rated highly in being poised, forthright, communicative, reasonable, and sincere). The true problem-solver is better at understanding that negotiation can have mutual benefits ... and is also better at working with the other side (rated highly in accommodating, agreeable, helpful, perceptive, and tactful). Finally, the true problem-solver is highly rated in adaptability, facilitating the agreement, and flexibility. These are all skills that, apparently, the cautious problem solvers do not have.

However, these cautious problem-solvers were still rated far more highly in effectiveness on behalf of their clients than either group of adversarial lawyers. It is perhaps heartening to see the perceived effectiveness of lawyers drop rather dramatically as the level of adversarial behavior rises. While there are dramatic differences between ethical and unethical adversarial behavior, we should still note that the ethical adversarials have several strong negative adjectives attributed to them (such as arrogant, egotistical, and irritating) and are significantly less effective for their clients than cautious problem-solvers.

The differences between the ethical and unethical adversarial lawyers (as shown in Table 1 above) can be found in four areas. First, the ethical adversarial lawyers still are considered trustworthy (that is, rated highly in ethical behavior) while the unethical adversarial lawyers are highly rated in being manipulative, conniving, and deceptive—not at all trustworthy. Second, unethical adversarial lawyers are also not trusting, rated highly in being suspicious of the other side. Third, there is a difference of tone. While the ethical adversarials are tough and firm, unethical adversarials are generally considered to be rude and angry. Finally, the only group of lawyers not viewed as experienced is the unethical adversarials who are also missing the adjective of deliberate, perhaps reflecting a lack of preparation or thoughtfulness about their case. The bipolar behavior ratings ... further differentiate between the ethical and unethical adversarial attorneys, describing the unethical group as untrustworthy, unpleasant, inflexible, and not understanding of or caring to understand the other side. It should be of little surprise, as shown in Table 2 below, that only 2.6% of these unethical adversarial lawyers were perceived as effective by their peers.

So, in comparing lawyer behaviors across the clusters, it is clear that there are strong differences in style—and that these differences result in a clear disparity in effectiveness ratings as well.

Notes/Questions

1. There are real differences in perceived effectiveness between the styles. For true problem-solving, over 70% of these negotiators were perceived as effective. That drops rather dramatically for other styles. Note the middle ground of "average" negotiators populated by those attorneys who chose a cautious problem-solving approach to negotiation. The numbers for adversarial approaches are also notable. Even ethical adversarial is mostly ineffective or average. Do any of these results surprise you? How does this compare to the portrayal of lawyers in popular culture?

2. Studies have shown that trustworthy and respected reputations among your peers makes it more likely that better information exchange, efficient processes, good relationships and a more integrative outcome will occur. How do criminal lawyers build their reputations with each other?

3. How might a true problem-solving defense lawyer handle a case differently from an ethical adversarial lawyer?

4. Despite the high plea rates, most prosecutors and defense lawyers would describe their jobs as being that of "trial lawyers." Is a possible for a good trial lawyer to also be a true problem solver?

5. As a prosecutor, what do you think the attributes for a good reputation would be for defense lawyers? As a defense lawyer, what do you think the attributes for a good reputation for a prosecutor would be? Are the attributes that a defense lawyer might think makes for a good reputation for a prosecutor the same attributes that would get a prosecutor promoted?

6. How might a lawyer's reputation impact whether their counterpart will be more likely to cave (reflecting the title of the article)? For example, if a defense lawyer has a reputation as a tough trial lawyer, might that change how the prosecutor negotiates? What if a defense lawyer (or prosecutor) is known for being dishonest? Would that make their counterpart less likely to "cave"?

7. Looking at the list of adjectives, which ones are how you would like to be described as a lawyer? Which ones are adjectives that you would not like used to describe you as a lawyer?

II. Negotiation Styles

The chart below details negotiation style along three axes: level of assertiveness, level of empathy, and level of flexibility (or effort and creativity) needed to implement the style. You will note that we have already discussed preparation for these skills in the previous chapter.

Negotiation Styles

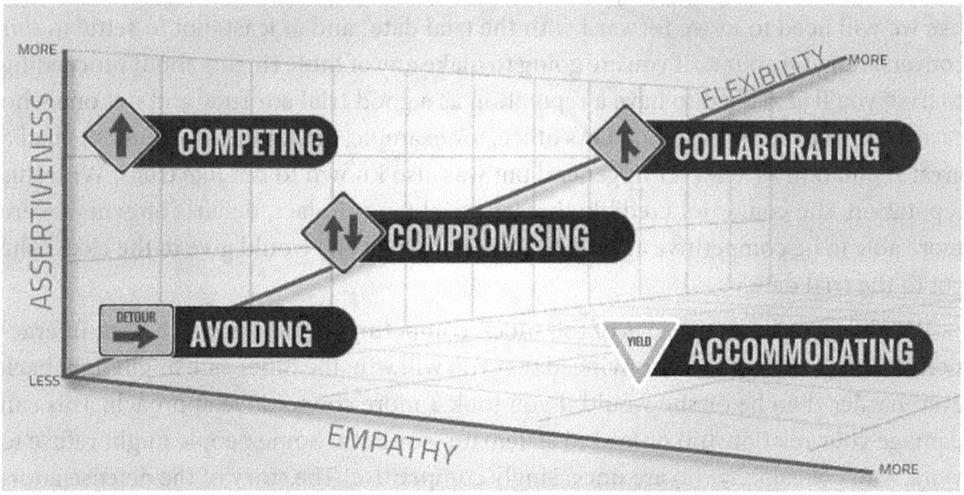

A. Competing

Competing is probably the most commonly understood style of negotiation. Most of us mastered this at age 2 (and some of us never moved past).[5] Because competing tends to be dramatic, it makes good theater and good stories. If you think of your favorite television shows about lawyering, this is often the style conveyed. Because we so often see people competing on the playing field, on the movie screen, and in the political arena, you might mistakenly think that this is how most conflicts are resolved. It's not. In real life, most legal disputes are resolved through communication and problem solving and, as you know from previous chapters, plea bargaining is no different.

A competing strategy is high in assertiveness on your own behalf and low in empathy or understanding the other side. It can have relatively less flexibility as an approach. To compete effectively, you must make a strong case for your client, you must be per-

5. A. Schneider & D. Kupfer, Smart & Savvy: Negotiating Strategies in Academia (Park City: Meadows Communications 2017).

suasive and firm, and you must often appear to be taking charge or controlling the conversation. The power of this style is the clarity of your position, and often the persuasiveness that goes along with being convinced that you are correct.

The advantages of competing are clear: If you set forth a strong position, the other side might agree with you right off the bat and you might get your way with relatively little effort. Competing can be efficient: If you get your way within minutes, you don't waste much time.

In the context of plea bargaining, a threat to proceed to trial sounds competitive—and tends to be an inelegant way of proceeding. From a defense lawyer perspective, threatening trial in the plea negotiation process can seem like a rookie move since the case will go to trial if it doesn't settle. A more common (and experienced) tactic is for the defense attorney or prosecutor to say, "ok, let's set it for trial" or "it looks like we will need to move forward with the trial date" and at least, not to settle in *this* conversation. Of course, if you are going to make any of these threats about proceeding to trial, you'll also need to have a reputation as a good trial attorney and not one who caves at the last minute. In one DA's office, for example, one of the assistant DAs had a great reputation as a lawyer in general but was also known to not like trials. With this reputation, she could not credibly threaten trial (and, in fact, defense attorneys were more able to be competitive against her, knowing that she would give in the closer she got to the trial date).

We all know the downsides of too much competing. If you approach each interaction looking for a fight and convinced that you will win, the other side might fight back even harder than he or she would if you took a more cooperative approach. This can damage your relationship or lead to stalemate—or both. Some people might refuse to work with colleagues who are unceasingly competitive. The story of the defense attorney forced to go to trial each time with a particular prosecutor comes from having a lousy, overly competitive reputation and not being trusted that he would keep his deals.

Under what circumstances is competing most effective? It makes sense when important values (such as safety) are at stake, when a quick decision is needed (for example, when a deadline is approaching or a decision is urgent), or when you know the other side is likely to give up easily. And, in some prosecutor's offices, competing is the expected cultural norm. So, even if there might be other approaches that would work, individuals feel pressure to fit in and match styles with others in their office.

B. Accommodating

At the opposite spectrum of behavior is the accommodating style of negotiation. This is low assertiveness and high empathy, usually characterized by quickly agreeing to what the other side wants. This results in "giving in," and agreeing with the other side. The power behind this style is that if your greatest concern is making the other side happy, accommodating accomplishes that quickly and completely.

Accommodating offers distinct advantages: If you give in, the other side will probably appreciate your bowing to his or her wishes, and that could improve your relationship. It also eliminates the conflict (at least in the short term) and can be efficient and easy to implement.

The big disadvantage to an accommodating style is that you don't get what you want. There are other drawbacks: Other people (like your client or the DA) might be frustrated by your lack of effort, especially when they do want to work with you, or might lose respect for you and your interests. If you accommodate everyone all the time, a reputation of always giving in can damage your reputation and can make it increasingly difficult for you to stand up for yourself. It also denies you and your counterpart the opportunity to work through conflict in a productive or creative manner.

In plea bargaining, accommodating is easiest to see on the defense side when you have a very bad case or when the offer is a very good one. For example, if the prosecutor has already knocked off one strike (under a three strikes and you're out law), the defense attorney is much more likely to accommodate and agree quickly to a sentencing recommendation without that enhancement. An article excerpted below also discusses how a power imbalance between prosecutors and defense attorneys might lead to more accommodating than is warranted. Accommodating from the prosecutor's side is also more likely to show up in weak cases or those lacking proof. For example, if a prosecutor knows that a witness may not be a good witness, she may be more willing to offer a better deal. (Note, however, that there are ethical issues if a prosecutor offers a better deal when they know they cannot prove the case or when they know that a witness is unavailable and they have not yet notified defense counsel of that fact.)

C. Avoiding

Moving to another corner of the table above, a strategy of temporarily avoiding a negotiation shows low assertiveness and low empathy as well as low creativity and flexibility. It also has the lowest level of energy devoted to dealing with the conflict. In dealing with plea bargaining, this kind of strategy can make sense as a temporary delay to negotiations.

A good example of avoiding in plea bargaining from the defense side can be when you are waiting for a different attorney or different judge to handle the case. In some jurisdictions, the prosecutor and defense attorney handling the arraignment might each change as you prepare for trial. The judge for the preliminary hearing might not be the judge for the trial. And, even when you are not going to trial, having that different person with whom to negotiate could change the dynamic. Similarly, waiting for the case to get "stale" and not draw as much attention from the prosecutor might also make sense. Avoiding a plea discussion on the prosecutor side, however, could have other implications. As we have read, some jurisdictions have (unsuccessfully) tried to eliminate plea bargaining. Avoiding offering a plea in order to force the defendant to sit in jail and pressure them to accept a deal veers toward unethical and immoral behavior.

We encourage you to use the preparation sheet on timing to think carefully about when to conduct negotiations. Perhaps you are not yet prepared to discuss a plea, you had a terrible day or a bad night's sleep, or the other side is particularly cranky and it doesn't look like you'll have a fruitful conversation. Perhaps you need more time to research the law or the facts and figure out how to approach it. Perhaps you are too busy to really focus on the negotiation. Perhaps you need to schedule the conversation for a time when you can really focus. All of these are smart reasons for delaying your own engagement until you can be most effective. Most crucially, avoiding is a necessary component of time management and sanity maintenance.

On the other hand, if you use this strategy too often or for too long, the disadvantages can be notable. People—you as well as others—might periodically explode from frustration if you are always not responding. You could be frozen out from discussions on some matters, and others could feel negatively about your avoidance.

D. Collaborating

At the last corner of the grid is collaborating, a strategy that engages the most energy by requiring assertiveness, empathy, and creativity for resolving the situation. If accommodating means "yes—we'll do it your way," collaborating is characterized by a "yes and ..." style, one in which you are both firm in your own interests while inquiring about the interests of the other side. The strategy is problem-focused, and multiple points of view are welcome in thinking about how to solve the dispute. The power of this style is in the complete involvement of everyone present and potentially integrative, imaginative solutions.

The advantages to collaborating are primarily located in your ongoing relationship with the other party and in the substance of the solution. First, because the lawyers work together in creating the solution, they build trust between them. Because the dynamic of working together is often energetic and cooperative, collaborating increases the chances that the relationship will be improved and that the solution will be carried out. Second, because the lawyers' (and client's) perspectives have been merged and they have probably shared more ideas in the collaborative process, any solution they devise is likely to be based on sound, relevant information and to be more durable than one that was decided unilaterally. Many of the more creative diversion sentencing or restorative justice work that we will discuss later in the book comes from these collaborative conversations between judges, defense attorneys, and prosecutors.

On the other hand, collaborating can be exhausting or just impossible in some contexts. Working with others takes time and motivation and can distract those involved from other pressing problems. Especially when several parties are involved, just trying to enlist everyone in a collaborative process can take longer than the issue is worth. Not every case has a creative solution; not every defendant, as we will discuss later in the problem-solving court chapters, can succeed through diversion sentencing or problem-solving courts.

E. Compromising

Finally, in the middle of these styles is compromising, a strategy characterized by finding middle ground. A compromising style will urge moderation, use techniques like splitting the difference or a trade off, and move the parties toward finding a solution that offers something for everyone.

The advantages to compromising are numerous: it can be relatively fast, it can move the agreement forward and give parties a way out of a stalemate, it is easy to understand and implement, and it appears reasonable. It is also familiar to all, because ever since childhood, when we had to take turns and share toys, most of us have long understood compromise as procedurally fair.

On the other hand, when it is not moored to standards, compromising can feel like horse-trading. If we move to agreement and to creating a solution too quickly, it can be at the expense of better answers, and we may miss a chance to hear the other's point of view before deciding. And if the trade-off is one defendant's harsher sentence for another defendant's lighter one, this could also be unethical.

Compromise is best used in two instances: when the issues are relatively unimportant to all concerned and an easy, efficient trade-off ("You pick the time to negotiate; I'll pick the location") makes sense. Compromising is also an excellent "second-choice" style to conflict. At the end of a collaborating style, when few issues remain, compromising can get the deal done. And if competing is leading to what could be a stalemate, compromising can move the agenda forward. For plea bargaining, when the prosecutor has made an offer, the defense attorney has countered, and the judge is pressuring the parties to plead before trial, this middle ground might make sense to get the deal done.

This next excerpt discusses how we need to be trained to understand each of these styles in negotiation.

Jenny Roberts & Ronald F. Wright, *Training for Bargaining*

57 William & Mary L. Rev. 1445, 1474–1479 (2016)

...

A. Training About Negotiation Strategies and Styles

One early article calling for legal scholars to study negotiation noted how, "[i]n all negotiations, regardless of the context, certain strategic decisions must be made by each party," and stated that "such decisions can and should be planned systematically, according to general principles applicable to all negotiations." Negotiation theory offers various names for different strategies and styles, but as a general matter, the current legal negotiation literature distinguishes between a cooperative/problem-solving/integrative approach and a competitive/adversarial/distributive approach. The former refers to a situation in which the parties can add value to the negotiation in a mutually beneficial manner, whereas the latter describes a zero-sum situation in which one negotiator's concession is a loss that leads to the other side's gain.

Plea bargaining might seem to be a purely distributive situation calling for a highly competitive approach because it appears that one negotiator's concession is a loss that leads to the other side's gain. In fact, the repeat-player nature of the relationships in criminal law practice—working together in one courthouse, over and over—may move some aspects of the negotiation away from competitive to a necessarily more cooperative strategy. Indeed, as Andrea Kupfer Schneider's important negotiation work demonstrates, "it is clear that extremely high levels of problem-solving behavior are exhibited between the prosecutor and the defendant's attorney."

Further, "results from [Schneider's study] suggest that criminal law may be an unexpectedly fertile environment to maximize positive problem-solving methods." Another legal negotiation scholar, applying specific factors to choose a negotiation strategy for a particular context, concluded that criminal defense attorneys should adopt a "predominantly cooperative strategy coupled with some early competitive tactics and integrative solutions whenever feasible." Consider the following example of the potential to create win-win situations in plea bargaining. A nineteen-year-old defendant is charged with misdemeanor assault in an incident resulting in some injury to the victim. An assault conviction will mean the defendant will lose his job, but the charge of disorderly conduct (a different misdemeanor in the jurisdiction, carrying a lower potential sentence than assault) will not result in that outcome. The jurisdiction also has a mechanism for deferred judgment in which, after a guilty plea, entry of judgment is stayed while the defendant serves a period of probation; successful completion results in discharge without a judgment of conviction. Defense counsel interviews the victim and takes a statement from him that describes how payment of medical bills is a primary concern and how the victim is upset the defendant has neither offered to pay nor contacted the victim (an acquaintance) to apologize. The prosecution has an office policy requiring a memo to a supervisor when there is a plea offer made on an assault case. Defense counsel offers to share the victim's statement with the prosecutor so the statement (once confirmed by the prosecutor) can form the basis for the memo to the supervisor (thus saving the prosecutor time and effort). Counsel also shares a letter from the defendant's boss about how an assault conviction will result in job loss—and thus inability to pay the medical bills—and describes how the deferred judgment will allow the young defendant to continue to develop in the workplace and pay off the bills over time.

These opportunities for cooperative strategies, which may come as a surprise to some criminal law practitioners, deserve some place in a training focused on effective negotiation. One reason for the surprisingly noncompetitive dynamic in criminal case negotiations could be that clients are not in a position—as a matter of education, physical liberty, or accessibility—to push their state-funded lawyers to be more aggressive. At the very least, defenders could learn to interview clients to get information they need to determine the most effective negotiation approach and to counsel clients in a manner that allows them to make a truly informed and uncoerced decision about whether to plead guilty.

Negotiation style and strategy often go hand in hand simply because, to take one example, someone with a competitive style will feel comfortable with competitive strategy. But separating personal style from negotiation strategies "yields new flexibility for the negotiator.... Further, a negotiator should often make competitive, cooperative, and integrative moves within a single negotiation." Consider a situation in which defense counsel has decided to adopt a competitive strategy but a cooperative style with respect to a certain aspect of the case—for example, the client is not incarcerated and will not plead guilty to anything involving jail or prison time. Counsel must then find a "nice" way to withhold information—such as an upcoming trial in another of the attorney's cases—that would not undercut the planned cooperative style....

Understanding how to implement a particular style or strategy is an undervalued skill in plea bargaining. Many defenders view themselves as simply begging or as needing to threaten to take everything to trial to get anything good out of a negotiation. Yet just as training can teach attorneys how to cross-examine or interview without antagonizing the witness—or to decide when one might want to antagonize the witness—training can be aimed at exploring different styles and strategies of negotiation. One negotiation scholar (who also conducts trainings) described how lawyers may spend hours "gathering the factual, legal, economic, and political information" for a negotiation, but spend only 10–15 minutes preparing a negotiation strategy. This strategy usually focuses only on "[w]here they plan to begin; [w]here they hope to end up; and [t]heir bottom lines. In between the starting point and the conclusion of their interactions, they wing it, thinking of their encounters as wholly unstructured." In short, a little training about particular negotiation strategies and styles, as well as the skills to implement them, could go a long way.

Notes/Questions

1. How much influence should a client or the supervising attorney have on an attorney's negotiation style? If the client is aggressive and refuses to accept anything but one specific plea deal, how should the attorney adjust their negotiation style? (Note that we raise the issue of counseling later in the chapter as well.)

2. Many prosecutors' offices have long-standing cultures that encourage (or demand) competitive styles and tough charging. What if the DA is pushing for a deal that the ADA does not think is fair? On the other hand, what happens when the DA wants to change that culture?

3. Most jurisdictions have a relatively cohesive criminal bar in which people know each other well. Does the fact that you will likely see that attorney again make a difference in how you negotiate? (Recall that this was one of the possible explanations for problem solving behavior among criminal attorneys.)

4. Now that you have thought about negotiation styles, we also want to note that effective negotiators are flexible in terms of *how* they approach a negotiation. They understand the various styles of negotiating—competing, accommodating, avoiding, collaborating, and compromising—and know how to choose a style to suit the context and the counterpart. One style may not be enough: these negotiators also are alert to signs that they need to change negotiation styles over the course of the negotiation, as the situation evolves. What might be signs in a negotiation that you should shift styles? Can you think of shifting from competing to collaborating? Either of those to compromising? Why would these potential shifts make sense?

As discussed previously, in January of 2018, Philadelphia elected a new District Attorney, Larry Krasner. On February 15, 2018, Krasner announced the following policy regarding plea offers:

1. Make plea offers below the bottom end of the mitigated range of the PA Sentencing Guidelines for most crimes.
2. Where an individual ADA believes an offer below the bottom end of the mitigated range is too low due to specific factors, that ADA must seek supervisory approval of a higher offer.
3. Where the applicable sentencing guidelines range is between 0 and 24 months, ADAs should seek more house arrest, probationary, and alternative sentences in appropriate cases.

Imagine you are a defense attorney in the Philadelphia area and read the news that in his first 3 months, Krasner has dismissed 30-plus prosecutors and instituted the above policies. With this knowledge and culture change, how would you handle plea negotiations? Would you be more aggressive? Would being aggressive be more effective for your client?

Now imagine you are a prosecutor that has survived the mass dismissals. How would you adapt to this new culture? What if you do not agree with the new policies? Is there a way to adhere to the new policies but still be "a tough prosecutor"?

III. Communication

There are three aspects of communication we will cover in this section. (If you are following along on the preparation sheet, you'll note that we've already discussed relationship and reputation, negotiation styles, and timing.) First, as with all negotiations, when we sit down with the other side, we are also still investigating. What facts do they have that we do not? What is their view of the law, the possible charges or enhancements? How does each lawyer view the defendant and the defendant's situation, mitigating circumstances or other personal details that may impact the bargain? This is the verbal part of the negotiation where questions and their answers can be crucial to setting up the actual plea deal. The second part of communication—and another skill in negotiation—is more non-verbal and can be understood as social intuition. The last part of communication is the mode of communication, or how the negotiation is being conducted. Each one of these elements is covered in this section.

A. Information Exchange

In this next excerpt, the authors discuss how you need to work with your counterpart during the information exchange part of the negotiation to be effective. The second excerpt discusses what happens with the information and communication when the prosecutor's office changes the way it deals with defense attorneys as part of a progressive DA's policies.

Jenny Roberts & Ronald F. Wright, *Training for Bargaining*

57 William & Mary L. Rev. 1445, 1487–1488 (2016)

...

2. Strategic Information Exchange

Another aspect of communication during the actual negotiation is strategic information exchange—formulating a specific plan in advance of the bargaining session for what information to seek out, what information to share, and what information to withhold. Plea bargaining discussions offer an excellent opportunity to learn something about the state's evidence, case theory, and views on sentencing in the particular case.

While bargaining has the added benefit of providing discovery to defense counsel in the event the case goes to trial, it can also allow defense counsel to understand the underlying interests of the prosecution. This understanding is critical to an integrative bargaining approach, which "requires crafting proposals to take advantage of differences in interests and preferences between the negotiators." Simply asking for such information in a straightforward manner might work in some instances, but there are more sophisticated ways to get information. Training can address how to accomplish this goal, just as training addresses different ways to get information during a witness interview or cross-examination. Indeed, G. Nicholas Herman's treatise, *Plea Bargaining*, recommends that practitioners prepare a "Plea Bargaining Preparation Outline" that includes lists of "Information 'To Find Out,' Information 'To Reveal,' and Information 'To Protect.'" Discussing the actual bargaining session, Herman offers five methods for "dodging" questions that seek to elicit information on the "To Protect" list.

To offer just one example of the myriad ways in which defense counsel might prepare for negotiation by carefully planning for potential information exchange, consider a scenario in which the only prosecution witness is a police officer. The charges are drug possession and resisting arrest, and the defendant was released after arraignment and went immediately to the hospital for medical treatment relating to nonminor injuries sustained during the arrest. Planning for and then working to strategically elicit information about the particular police officer during the negotiation will shed some light on the government's underlying interests in the case. Does the prosecutor know or appear to know of any brutality complaints against this police officer? Does the prosecution or police officer know that the defendant visited the hospital? On the flip side, defense counsel must carefully consider what information to withhold in the bargaining session. What will counsel say if the prosecutor asks if her client was injured during the arrest? Is this information that would foreclose a good offer based on the government's desire to protect against the possibility of a civil lawsuit for injuries sustained during the arrest, or would it help facilitate such a plea on the theory that evidence of those injuries at trial would make a jury trial difficult to win in the particular jurisdiction and would lead to bad publicity for the police department? These are not easy decisions, and should not be made in the heat of the negotiation without careful advance preparation.

Catherine A. Grodensky, William E. Crozier and Brandon L. Garrett, *Understanding Plea Bargaining in a New Progressive DA's Office: How Line Prosecutors Understand and Implement Progressive Goals Through Plea Decisions*

50 Criminal Justice and Behavior 434–435, 440–442 (2023)

Prosecutors articulated five main goals they felt were being promoted by the new DA regime and aligned with progressive prosecution: (a) dismissing low-level drug possession charges; (b) avoiding over-penalization, particularly for "victimless" crimes; (c) declining to prosecute weak cases; (d) communicating with the defense through mitigation and discovery; and (e) promoting racial equity in plea processes and outcomes.

Communicating with the Defense through Mitigation and Discovery

Goal and Rationale

Considering information provided by defense attorneys was seen as another important component of prosecutors' work in this office. Prosecutors uniformly expressed willingness to consider mitigating factors in developing plea offers, particularly details about the charged individual as a person and factors that may have contributed to the crime. Like other goals, the desire for information from the defense attorney stemmed both from prosecutors themselves and rom office leadership. Prosecutors reasoned that receiving information from defense attorneys was important because the defense has the only contact with the person charged with the crime and can learn about factors that motivated the crime and may affect charging, or factors that exacerbated the crime such as substance abuse or mental illness that may need to be addressed through sentencing conditions. Without this information, prosecutors have an incomplete understanding of the crime and are less able to design a just plea. One described,

> [The DA] told us to encourage [defense attorneys] to bring us their mitigation ... I know nothing about the person charged with the crime personally but you may know something. You may know that he got dropped on his head as a kid and that affected his brain ... you need to let us know that so when the issue comes up, it can be addressed with the court and we can take a position, 'Judge, if the guy's got brain damage, do what you need to do.'

Another important aspect of sharing information with defense attorneys is providing discovery, which prosecutors generally felt aided defense attorneys and the individuals they represent in plea bargaining and were therefore willing to provide. One prosecutor stated that turning over everything "... eliminates 90 percent of the what-ifs and the unknowns. If you have all the information, everyone can make a better, informed decision." Another said, "it just makes the job easier. It makes it easier to administer justice when everybody's cards, you know, are on the table.

Implementation

State law requires prosecutors to provide the defense with a full open-file discovery in felony cases, and interviewees explained that they were required to share their files through the court's case management system at the point when charges were indicated to the Superior Court as felonies. Several prosecutors stated that they were willing to share their files even in District Court because they felt it would help both sides reach the best solution in a plea deal. One prosecutor explained,

> So in District Court there's no general right to discovery until its indicated to Superior Court. I have an open file policy where if I haven't indicated it yet and a defense attorney asks for a copy, I'll offer them the plea support and the things that I have in my file because it just makes it more efficient to be able to—they know what I have and then they'll maybe give me what's called "reciprocal discovery" and tell me what they have so we can come to a good resolution, and so my file is open to anyone that wants it.

Although prosecutors were alike in intending to consider information from the defense, they differed in how and when they incorporated the information into their plea decisions. One difference among prosecutors was whether they discussed cases with the defense attorney prior to making a first plea offer. A few prosecutors typically sent offers without discussing it with the defense beforehand, expecting the defense to negotiate changes if they possessed relevant information. Other prosecutors preferred to communicate with the defense attorney before making the first plea offer, thereby necessitating less negotiation afterward. As one explained, "I'm usually talking to them before I make a plea, so, you know, we're sort of baking in the negotiation into my first offer." Another explained this choice as a matter of efficiency: "I don't want to waste writing them a plea if it's gonna be way different based on the information that I get. It could be worse or it could be better for that—more mitigation for that defendant.

Prosecutors also varied in their willingness to change their initial plea in response to requests by the defense. A few prosecutors said that they were hesitant with defense attorneys after making their initial plea offer, especially when they had already negotiated prior to the plea, when they had overwhelming caseloads, or when the criminal charges were not very serious. But by and large, prosecutors expressed willingness to consider changes requested by defense attorneys to their initial offers. One described their attitude toward counter-offers or modification requests from the defense this way:

> I'm going back to the defense attorney and I'm like, so, what's the issue? Does this person not want to be on probation? Is he just saying that he didn't do it? What's going on? So, I always want to know the rationale. Depending on what the why is or the reason will determine what my nest steps are.

Although prosecutors may prefer to receive information from the defense, they may be unable to do so. Sometimes prosecutors said they were unable to connect with the defense attorney early in a case and had to create an initial plea offer without their input. Defense attorneys may lack time to provide information on a case given their caseloads. Communication may also vary depending on their relationship with the specific defense attorney assigned to the case, or on the defense attorney's preferences for negotiation. One prosecutor described a close relationship with a defense attorney: "It could be via text message like, 'Hey, does your guy want to do whatever?' because we have this working relationship to where you are comfortable enough to contact me." Other relationships between prosecutors and defense attorneys may be less conducive to open communication. Some prosecutors described tension with defense attorneys due to the adversarial nature of their relationship and the adversarial tactics used by some prosecutors and defense attorneys. One prosecutor explained that in the past, the DA's office would bias the negotiation by crafting artificially high initial offers:

> The car salesman haggling thing was just like natural. So you always start with twice as much as you want, which I find reprehensible, like hate that idea. Like we're talking about liberty and you're talking about justice here—'Well, I'll just start twice as much and then we'll see what happens.'

Such an adversarial stance can work against open communication and lead defense attorneys to withhold necessary information. Ultimately, prosecutors acknowledged that the resulting lack of information during plea bargaining can worsen outcomes. As one lamented,

> Sometimes I'll have this terrible experience where I think I know the person charged with the crime and then they pipe up in Superior Court and they start talking. And it's clear that the psychological profile I had about them is just totally wrong, you know what I mean? Because it's based on just very dry bits of information on a page, right? So I try to encourage the defense lawyer to tell me what they think is just. But many defense lawyers are reticent to do that.

Notes/Questions

1. In the first excerpt above, the authors refer to the deflection techniques suggested by G. Nicholas Herman in his excellent book on Plea Bargaining. These are: (1) Ignore the question and change the topic; (2) Answer the question by asking another question; (3) Answer the question by answering another question; (4) Over-answer or under-answer the question; and (5) Rule the question out of bounds. Practice these with your classmates. How can each of these be used when faced with awkward questions in any negotiation?

2. In the second article above, one prosecutor described the friendly relationship they had with a defense attorney and how that shaped their communication style. What are the advantages to maintaining cordial relationships with opposing counsel? What are the disadvantages?

3. As discussed in Chapter 3, one key question in plea bargaining is what information is turned over to the defense and when. While *Brady* requires exculpatory information to be turned over before trial, not all states have requirements for full disclosure prior to plea bargaining. Some states have passed reforms to the rules governing mandated discovery:

i. Texas Code of Criminal Procedure Article 39.14, also known as the Michael Morton Act, an requires the prosecution to disclose all evidence to the defense regardless of whether the prosecutor considers it to be exculpatory or not;

ii. The New York CPL § 245.20 requires the prosecution to turn over almost all evidence within a specified period of time before a plea deal is executed;

iii. The California Penal Code 1054.1 requires prosecutors to turn over all exculpatory evidence and all relevant real evidence to the defense including written or recorded statements of witnesses.

What are the advantages and disadvantages of these new discovery rules for both the prosecution and the defense? Have these rules made it easier to come to a seemingly fair plea bargain?

B. Social Intuition

In negotiation, getting what you want from your counterpart has much to do with how she or he feels about you. We have already discussed relationships but now turn to the skill that actually helps create that. Does your counterpart trust you? Like you? How can you communicate over the course of the negotiation in ways that will increase the likelihood of building rapport and trust? Issues such as trust, rapport, and power are all translated through this intuitive communication. The degree to which one is adept at navigating this terrain is captured by the term social intuition.[6]

---

6. This section is based on Schneider & Ebner, *Social Intuition*, *in* 1 NEGOTIATOR'S DESK REFERENCE 127 (A.K. Schneider & C. Honeyman eds., St. Paul, DRI Press 2017).

To understand this phrase and consider its practical implementations in negotiation, think of it in three elements:

- **Self:** This aspect might be best understood as self-awareness regarding your own emotions, cognitive patterns, biases, attributions, and reactions. Studies have long shown that people with more self-control (those who are willing and able to delay gratification, for example) are more successful. This kind of self-control can show up as monitoring your emotional tenor during the negotiation, which then brings better control of how you come across. You can measure this part of social intuition by examining your tone, your pace of conversation, how you carry yourself physically in the negotiation (are you tense? are your shoulders elevated?), and even how your emotions show on your face.[7] Do your words (the content) match your conduct (the process)?
- **Other:** This aspect is essentially the ability to read your counterpart. Can you note and understand his signals in body language, nuance, attention span, laugh, volume, tone, and voice responses? Does her behavior seem consistent (or incongruent) with what she is saying substantively and what you understand to be her interests? In this aspect, you are working to stay attuned to the other person's emotional state and how it is reflected through conscious and unconscious signals.[8]
- **Bridging:** This third aspect involves *action* you take to form connections with the other through the interactional exchange, in turn creating connections that support you in *affecting* the other. How do you use this to focus your goals? Your actions, or the things you do to help the other person feel more at ease (or not), fall under bridging. Actions under this aspect of social intuition include physical and tonal mirroring. When your counterpart leans forward, so do you. As she picks up the pace of conversation, you respond in kind. Bridging actions can fall under body language, space, pace of communication, tone, and humor and can include all sorts of little responses you might not even be aware of.

This triad of capacities—being self-aware, reading others, and bridging—join together to form the essential negotiator attribute or skill we call social intuition. Social intuition is different from empathy, which is the cognitive understanding of what your counterpart is thinking and feeling. Social intuition is the ability to read yourself, read your counterparts, and manage *their* emotions, experiences, attributions, and responses through your own actions.

Being attuned to your counterpart's emotional state during the conversation will also help alert you to any impending hazards in the conversation. We have one criminal defense attorney colleague who has told us that she carefully watches what is going on in court between the prosecutor and the judge and will avoid speaking to them about

7. D. Goleman, Social Intelligence: The New Science of Human Relationships (New York: Bantam Books 2007).

8. J. Thompson, N. Ebner & J. Giddings, *Non-Verbal Communication in Negotiation, in* 1 Negotiator's Desk Reference 449 (A.K. Schneider & C. Honeyman eds., St. Paul, DRI Press 2017).

any deal until she thinks that they are ready to listen. And she will never approach one particular prosecutor until the first cup of coffee is finished! Studies of moods in negotiation show that happier people tend to be more creative and integrative,[9] while those who are unhappy more often end up in competitive situations.[10] When you can listen to the other person's emotions and show that you understand the emotions and the person, you are more likely to build trust and improve the relationship.[11] ("I think I see that you might be a bit hesitant to grant this request. Is that correct?") An extra advantage of these kinds of emotion questions is that they double-check your reading of the other person. Maybe you are right—or maybe you've misread her pursed lips and hesitant responses. Either way, by either reflecting the emotion accurately or correcting your misimpression, you have improved the negotiation. If you see a very busy docket, a stressed judge and a tired prosecutor, now would not be the day to negotiate at length over your client's sentence. Read the situation and try to set another time to meet. Think about how you can affect the mood of your counterpart positively.

Notes/Questions

1. Part of social intuition is being attuned to the metaphors your negotiation counterpart uses as these often reveal hidden assumptions. For example, Levine and Wright found that prosecutors use consistent metaphors to describe the players in the system.

> Four stock images that prosecutors use most often when they describe their own duties and those of their counterparts across the aisle. Prosecutors speak frequently about "wearing the white hat" in reference to themselves, "going over to the dark side" in reference to prosecutors who become defense attorneys, and "being a true believer" as well as "drinking the Kool-Aid" to refer to those attorneys on either side who are overly zealous. These images, and the narratives in which they are embedded, reveal important aspects of the prosecutors' professional self-image and their relationship with defense attorneys.

Kay L. Levine & Ronald F. Wright, *Images and Allusions in Prosecutors' Morality Tales*, 5 Virginia Journal of Criminal Law 38 (2017). How might a defense attorney use other negotiation or societal metaphors to shift a prosecutors' narrative about themselves or the defense?

2. One challenge of criminal practice is that defendants are often unhappy with and openly hostile to their lawyers. Imagine a situation where you are a criminal defense lawyer, and your client does not like the job you are doing and decides to make a motion to remove you as the lawyer. This type of motion is often made on the

9. C. Freshman, A. Hayes & G. Feldman, *The Lawyer-Negotiator as Mood Scientist: What We Know and Don't Know About How Mood Relates to Successful Negotiation,* Journal of Dispute Resolution 1 (2002).

10. *Id.*

11. R.J. Lewicki & E.C. Tomlinson, *Trust, Trust Development and Trust Repair, in* The Handbook of Conflict Resolution: Theory and Practice (M. Deutsch, P.T. Coleman & E. Marcus, eds., San Francisco: Jossey-Bass, 3d ed. 2014).

record, but without the prosecutor present in the room. During such a motion, your client would tell the judge all the reasons s/he doesn't want you as a lawyer anymore. You then have to respond to make sure the record is clear and accurate as to what you have done (or not), since this type of motion can be grounds for a bar complaint. What if the client, on hearing your response, became agitated and yelled "Liar!" and slammed into you in open court? You aren't injured, but what do you need to think about? Do you want to step aside and allow the client to get a new lawyer? Do you want to demand to be removed from the case? How does social intuition play into this scenario? Should you be thinking about the impact of this incident on the judge? What about the prosecutor (who wasn't in the room)? Would this incident help or hurt you in negotiating the case?

C. Choosing among Modes of Communication

Much negotiation advice assumes that these meetings are all conducted face to face. Yet we know that most of us are communicating using multiple devices—texting and emailing, sometimes video-chatting, etc.—and then still meeting in person or calling as needed. Effective negotiators will consider which mode makes sense: which serves the context or counterpart (as in your counterpart prefers to text offers back and forth) and which serves you (perhaps you are more persuasive in writing when you can consider your arguments than in person when your passion for a case might get in the way). The point is that we are all using multiple modes and that we should be thinking about these proactively and how we can best utilize each in negotiation. The chart below provides further details.[12]

12. A. Schneider & D. Kupfer, Smart & Savvy: Negotiating Strategies in Academia (Park City: Meadows Communications 2017).

Mode of Communication	Pros	Cons
Face-to-face conversation (in-person)	• Allows for tracking of multiple social cues (i.e., interpret body language, tone, eye contact, and facial expressions)	• Limited time to develop a response
Phone call	• Allows for tracking of certain social cues through the tone, pauses, and inflections (i.e., can learn about how the other party is feeling) • Synchronous communication (i.e., ability to explain in real time, ask questions, and clarify ambiguities)	• No chance to interpret certain important social cues (i.e., body language, eye contact, and facial expressions)
Email	• Flexibility of choosing when to read and respond • Ability to reread and reflect before responding • Good for task-oriented communications	• Does not incorporate contextual elements (i.e., can misread social cues) • Asynchronous communication (i.e., potential for slow response time and communication stack-up) • Certain mirroring skills are impossible (i.e., body language, level of eye contact, and nodding) • Developing trust is difficult (i.e., higher potential for deceptive practices) • Difficult to demonstrate empathy
Text	• Same pros as email, except less formal	• Same cons as email, except less formal • Harder to keep a record of communication • Easier to miss or lose thread
Video-conferencing	• Allows for tracking of multiple social cues (i.e., interpret body language, tone, eye contact, and facial expressions) but may miss some body language off screen; harder to mirror their social cues	• Limited time to develop a response

Notes/Questions

1. Take a moment to think about your own strengths and weaknesses in communication. And what tends to be your default mode of communication for work? Recognizing the benefits and risks of each mode can help you think carefully about how to communicate most effectively with your counterpart (and your client) in negotiation.

2. Face-to-face is usually considered the gold standard of communication. On the other hand, not all face-to-face opportunities are of equal value. What would be your advice to a defense attorney negotiating a complicated case with a prosecutor in a

courthouse that has a more structured place to have these types of negotiations, for example a "plea room," where other defense attorneys are also lined up waiting to talk with a single prosecutor?

IV. Don't Screw It Up—Understanding Negotiation Errors

While we talk about negotiation as a rational endeavor, years of psychological research show that there are often elements that can throw us off and make us less effective. They can also lead to the ethical lapses described above. Thinking about the errors that you might make (as the prosecutor or defense attorney) can help you avoid them. Thinking about the errors that your counterpart might make can help develop a negotiation strategy to minimize them.

A. Working with Defendants in the Context of Plea Bargaining

These next two excerpts focus on how these errors or psychological barriers can impact plea bargaining from the defendant's perspective.

Richard Birke,
Reconciling Loss Aversion and Guilty Pleas

1999 UTAH L. REV. 205, 210, 247–250

...

My analysis begins with the basic economic assumption that individuals choose their actions in attempts to maximize personal utility. When faced with a decision, they analyze the array of choices available to them, assign each choice a value, and opt for the choice that yields the greatest net value.

In a world of decision makers who seek risk in the face of loss, pleas can only be obtained if Vp [the value of the plea] is high, EVt [the expected value of the trial] is low, defendants are manipulated by framing effects, or there exists a combination of these events. As I have argued, it seems to me that prosecutors could not consistently offer deals that are so good that the defendants overcome loss aversion, diminishing pain, the sentencing guidelines and mandatory minima, and political accountability. Defendants plead because they are misinformed about the values of trials and pleas, and because pleas are framed as gains.

Defendants are manipulated into pleading because they possess too little information to overcome framing effects inherent in the valuation of pleas and trials, and because they lack information to accurately value that which they so readily trade away—the right to trial. Naturally, defense attorneys respond to incentives of the court that encourage pleas, and these responses manifest themselves as information that distorts defendants' views of their alternatives. Trial looks worse than it really is, and so the plea looks relatively better.

This conclusion, that the defense attorney—not the defendant—is the true player in the plea bargain, is corroborated by game theory applications. The heuristic prisoner's dilemma suggests that one-shot players in a binary choice game will rationally defect, but that repeat players will cooperate. If defendants were driving the decision, then the one-shot defection rule dominates other strategies. However, because defense attorneys are repeat players playing the game with prosecutors who are repeat players, cooperation dominates. In fact, when the players in the game are defense attorneys and prosecutors involved in a local practice, all the theoretical underpinnings for a cooperative regime are in place: an iterated game with no known end, with no ability to commit for future rounds, and with the spectre that the value of the next round may match or exceed that of the current round.

There is also some empirical evidence that defense counsel take what has been called a "lawyer-centered" approach to decision making in the context of criminal law. While the data are few, they are consistent with the suggestion that lawyers, and not clients, are "doing the deals."

The blame for the current state of affairs lies not with the hapless defense attorney, but rather with the public desire to have "the punishment fit the crime" but not to fund the effective pursuit of that punishment. The lack of funding for courts and judges has spawned a regime in which prosecutors must produce sentences that the public and the judges will respect, and without the resources to take all close cases to trial. Of course it would be a disastrous corruption of the criminal justice system if prosecutors were to dismiss all cases in which a conviction appears less than certain—and the prosecutor dare not waste scarce resources bringing too many cases to trial that ultimately produce acquittals. The prosecutor must produce sentences that fit the crimes, not sentences that fit crimes indexed for resource shortfalls. The only choice is to create pleas, and the prosecutor must enlist the help of the defense attorney. Combined with a courthouse staff that is similarly overburdened, the prosecutor has much companionship in this effort, and the defense attorney also must cooperate to survive. And none of these players could fulfill their desires to create pleas if defendants possessed information suggesting that the EVt [expected value of trial] was higher than Vp [value of the plea].

If this conclusion is correct and the fundamental problem in the criminal plea bargaining process is with the way that defendants get information—through an agent whose self-interest and self-preservation lies in cooperating with a systemic need to create pleas—then it is the information channel that needs fixing. This problem is exacerbated if the agent does not have appropriate information to give to the defendant about the actual value of trial. Alternatively, if the defendant actually possessed accurate information about the value of trial, the defendant would be in a better position to determine what, if any, was the appropriate level of expected loss at which to set a baseline, and what the value of a trial in the defendant's case would be.

The question that remains is how to provide better information to defendants. Perhaps the answer lies in more thorough colloquies between defendants and judges, or in the creation of a class of neutral individuals whose job is to advise defendants about the value of their case and to talk generally about the trial process. However, these agents of the criminal justice system may not be sufficiently divorced from their own interests in docket clearing to provide unbiased information.

A more effective remedy involves collection and direct transmission of trial data to accused defendants. If government would create a better data base that all defendants could access, the problem would be remediated significantly. Currently, only very mediocre records exist about what penalty a given crime actually carries after trial if there are certain facts and a certain record and a certain judge. If these records were better kept and made more widely available, then attorneys would be in a better position to apprise defendants of the going rate for their case.

Better information would inform defendants about the relative values of pleas and trials. With better information, defendants would plead less, as they do in cases with mandatory sentences where the relative values of trial and pleas are better known. First, defendants would make better comparisons. Second, defendants would understand the unavailability of their non-time-and-money utilities. Third, defendants would stand better equipped to draw baselines and reference points, and be less subject to psychological manipulation. Finally, given better information about trial values and plea bargains, the public would be in a better position to seek legislation preventing assistant district attorneys from selling cases for less than their trial value—a move that might prod the police to conduct better investigations, so as to keep trial values as high as possible. In some sense, determining the "going rate" of a trial is a circular problem. So many cases plead, that it is easier to know the value of a pled case than that of a tried case. If more cases went to trial, then everyone in the judicial system would have better information about the value of a trial, which could produce pleas more in conformity with the expected value of trial. That way, it would be the intangible non-punishment-related interests that would produce trial, and government (in the form of prosecutors, judges, public counsel, and private counsel who are subject to retribution by the public employees and are forced to act as their minions) would be out of the business of producing covert incentives to plead.

Of course there would be more trials in a world of better informed defendants. Unfortunately, society probably does not wish to allocate the resources necessary to have more trials. However, as long as government continually patches the system by artificially depressing trial rates and underpunishing crime, it does a disservice to the constitutional right to trial as it is currently understood, and the citizenry deludes itself into believing that both the rights of individual defendants to be free from government coercion and the rights of citizens to be free of the fear of crime are being honored.

Notes/Questions

1. Richard Birke argues that more information for defendants would make plea bargaining fairer. Would providing this information solve the issue for illiterate or poor defendants who may not have internet access or knowledge of how to access the database?

2. Should prosecutors be required to give information beyond exculpatory information, so information sharing does not depend on defense lawyers?

3. In the chapter on plea bargaining reform, some suggest that judges play a role in plea bargaining. How might this help correct bias?

4. In focusing on bias and fairness, is access to information the most serious problem, or do other factors, such as potentially high sentences, cause more of a problem both in terms of defense decision making and fairness?

5. Do the cognitive errors explained by Birke help explain negotiation strategy choices outlined by Schneider? How do you think these studies link together?

Stephanos Bibas, *Plea Bargaining Outside the Shadow of Trial*

117 Harv. L. Rev. 2463, 2498–2500, 2502–2507, 2509–2512, 2514–2519 (2004)

...

A. Overconfidence, Optimism, and Self-Serving Biases

The rational-actor model presumes that parties evaluate options and odds dispassionately, correctly weighing pros and cons. Hundreds of psychological studies, however, show that people are consistently too optimistic and therefore overconfident in their chances of achieving favorable outcomes.

A related problem is self-serving bias, which leads people to interpret information to fit their opinions or interests. People tend to recall selectively the information that is favorable to their preexisting views and to interpret that information in self-serving ways. In fact, the more information people have, the more room there is for bias. This bias skews litigants' interpretations of the facts and so their evaluations of the equities. Because people's senses of fairness influence bargaining, each side thinks it deserves a better deal than the other side thinks is warranted. For example, one set of studies asked students to play the part of attorneys trying to negotiate a settlement for either the plaintiff or the defendant in a tort suit. Though each side received identical case files, plaintiffs' estimates of the fair settlement value and the likely judicial award were substantially higher than defendants' estimates. Divergent predictions about the judge's award correlated strongly with failures to settle. Even when both parties have complete information, they tend to interpret that information asymmetrically. As a result, each party's notion of fairness gravitates toward proposals that favor its own interests. Each side is inclined to see its own offers as fair and the other side's as unfair.

Similarly, overconfidence and self-serving biases may impede plea bargaining. If one side overestimates the chances of winning at trial, it is likely to make unreasonable settlement offers and to reject reasonable offers. Overconfidence leads each side to more extreme aspirations and reservation prices in negotiations, reducing the incentive to compromise. There are two distinct strands of overconfidence at work here. First, each side is overconfident in predicting its chance of prevailing. Second, each side is overconfident or biased in viewing its own position as fair. Because each side sees a different, distorted shadow of trial, the parties may fail to settle when doing so would be in the best interests of both. Or, to overcome a client's overconfidence, counsel may resort to strong pressure or persuasion....

Finally, overconfidence varies greatly by demographic and personal characteristics. Across various age groups, men are consistently more overconfident in their own performance than are women. Younger adults are more overconfident than older ones. And there is some evidence that those who are less intelligent, as measured by test scores and grades, are more overconfident than others. Neophytes have plenty of room to be overconfident because they are unfamiliar with the justice system, whereas recidivists' knowledge and experiences may limit their overconfidence. Each of these effects produces distributive inequities that skew punishment for certain classes of defendants. These results suggest that less intelligent, young, male first offenders are most likely to reject beneficial plea bargains in favor of worse trial outcomes. This overconfidence becomes a particularly large problem in plea bargaining because young men are overrepresented among defendants in the criminal justice system.

B. Denial Mechanisms and Psychological Blocks

Whereas optimism skews predictions about the likelihood of conviction and sentence, the related phenomena of denial mechanisms and psychological blocks skew assessments of one's own guilt, which in turn affect predictions. Offenders find it hard to acknowledge guilt to their lawyers, and even to themselves, because feelings of guilt and shame are painful and depressing. Offenders use denial, excuses, and rationalizations to avoid taking responsibility and to block painful awareness of the harm they have done to others. Denial is a particularly large problem for certain especially shameful crimes, such as sex offenses. Denial takes many forms. Offenders often deny the facts, their deeds, their knowledge, or their culpability; or they minimize how harmful or wrong their actions were. These denials are not simply public-relations ploys. They reflect offenders' fears of admitting the truth to themselves. They flow from underlying attitudes and cognitive distortions that impede clear perception of the truth. For example, offenders who falsely claim innocence to others begin to deceive themselves and to distort what they remember and how they interpret those memories.

Offenders who falsely believe they are innocent probably overestimate their chances of acquittal at trial because they think juries will share their own distorted perspectives. They also likely underestimate their expected sentences after trial, particularly under indeterminate sentencing, as they expect sentencing judges to see these cases from their perspectives. This overconfidence helps to explain why many defendants in denial find it hard to take advantageous guilty pleas even when they are "obviously guilty." If a defendant cannot see the weaknesses in his own case and the merit in the other side's case, he cannot appreciate the reasonableness of the bargain offered. Prosecutors may sweeten their plea offers to try to buy off these defendants, but those in hard-core denial may reject all reasonable plea offers. The results will often be jury convictions and much heavier sentences after trial, which will surprise no one except the defendants....

C. Discounting of Future Costs

A third psychological influence on plea bargains is the discounting of future costs. Put simply, a day of freedom today is worth more than a day of freedom ten years from now. Some defendants will discount future costs only modestly, while the impatient or those with less self-control will discount greatly. Discount rates vary widely from person to person. Many people discount future losses (such as imprisonment) even more steeply than they discount future gains.

Some discounting is rational because it reflects the expected future value of the sentence rather than variations in preferences based on timing. Because an inmate may die or win early release before his tenth year of imprisonment, the tenth year of the sentence is not as certain to occur as the first year. Even if he does serve the tenth year, he will be more used to imprisonment by then, so the hardship will not be as great as in year one. These reasons partly explain why we all discount to some extent. But many people's discount rates greatly exceed the chance that things will change or that they will become accustomed to prison. This divergence bespeaks impulsiveness rather than rational calculation.

The plea-bargaining literature has recognized that defendants discount the future costs of imprisonment. What it has not addressed, however, is the import of varying discount rates. High discount rates are closely tied to impulsiveness and lack of self-control. Impulsiveness, in turn, contributes greatly to criminal behavior, aggression, and drug abuse. In particular, violent offenders are much more impulsive than nonviolent offenders. Thus, repeat offenders, particularly violent and drug offenders, are likely to be more impulsive than average and so to have higher discount rates. They will therefore demand larger discounts before taking plea bargains, which means that they will drive harder bargains or else go to trial. Conversely, occasional offenders and those innocent of any crime are likely to be less impulsive than habitual offenders. They will therefore be more eager to plea bargain to secure future sentence benefits. The counterintuitive result is that many hardened recidivists will likely get more favorable plea bargains, proportionally speaking, than first-time offenders. The most impulsive offenders, however, may bargain too hard, leading to bargaining impasse and, likely, a worse result at trial....

Finally, impulsiveness correlates with youth, being male, and low income. Older, female, and well-off defendants will discount bargaining concessions less, making them more ready to accept smaller concessions and less likely to insist on trial. The impulsive, poor, young men who bargain too hard, insist on trial, and are convicted will grow older in prison. As they age and their discount rates decline, they may regret their earlier rash decisions to go to trial. All of these effects distribute punishment inequitably across members of these various groups.

D. Risk Taking and Loss Aversion

The decision to go to trial is a gamble: the payoff can be acquittal and complete freedom, but often the more likely outcome is conviction and a longer sentence. In contrast, plea bargains barter away this chance of acquittal for a lower but more certain sentence. Defendants' attitudes toward risk and loss will powerfully shape their willingness to roll the dice at trial. Furthermore, those who have successfully taken risks are more self-confident. Self-confident people may think that they personally have succeeded in managing risks in the past and that they will continue to succeed in the future, so they underestimate future risks. Those who have successfully taken risks in the past are thus more likely to take risks again in the future. In negotiations, risk-averse people prefer sure settlements, while risk preferrers insist on better deals or walk away from the table....

Once again, the plea-bargaining literature acknowledges in passing that risk aversion may influence bargains, but it does not explore interpersonal variations in risk aversion, nor does it address loss aversion. As suggested above, one's personality powerfully shapes one's risk preferences, so that impulsive gamblers will be more likely to take risks. Those who are cautious or anxious will be more amenable to plea bargains than gambling types and so will demand smaller discounts and be less likely to go to trial. Most criminals are less risk averse (at least with regard to imprisonment) than law-abiding citizens. This understanding fits with the view of criminals as reckless thrill-seekers who fail to exercise self-control over their impulses to commit crime. Likewise, substance abusers and psychopaths are risk takers. Though defendants with little or no criminal history may be somewhat loss averse, caution will probably temper their loss aversion and make them more willing to take plea bargains. In contrast, self-confident recidivists will be more inclined to reject plea bargains and gamble on acquittal at trial. They will also be more inclined to engage in risky brinkmanship and reject plea offers in the hopes of extracting better plea offers. Because these recidivists are much less intent on avoiding risks by plea bargaining, prosecutors must offer them better deals or else go to trial. Recidivists who take these bargains may receive sweet deals, while those reckless enough to reject them may well face heavier punishment after trial. Therefore, defendants with the most self-control, who are least likely to recidivate and thus need punishment the least, may receive smaller plea discounts.

Just as with overconfidence and impulsiveness, risk preferences vary with demographics, including sex; adolescence and age generally; wealth, social class, self-employment, and education; church attendance; and marital status. Single men, infrequent churchgoers, and perhaps the educated and well-to-do are more willing to gamble and so might insist on more generous plea bargains or else go to trial. Once again, the result is inequitable distribution of punishment according to demographic characteristics instead of to trial shadows, retribution, or deterrence.

Likewise, people who are especially loss averse are more willing to gamble on a complete acquittal at trial, even at the risk of a much longer sentence. Loss aversion also varies with one's personality, cautiousness, and demographic traits. For example, females are loss averse more often and to a greater extent than are males. Loss aversion also depends on one's baseline endowment or entitlement, as the next section discusses more fully.

E. Framing

People tend to gamble to avoid sure losses, but they prefer to lock in sure gains. They assess gain and loss relative to the perceptions of both their options and their current state or baseline. Psychologists have found that gain and loss are malleable concepts and that people's choices vary greatly depending on the wording used to relate the options. Options that are packaged as gains (for example, "lives saved") induce risk aversion; when the very same choices are packaged as losses ("lives lost"), they induce risk taking because of loss aversion. This phenomenon is known as framing, and more than a hundred studies have documented the framing effect....

Framing plays a powerful role in plea bargaining. Ordinarily, defendants view plea bargaining through a loss frame: they are used to being free and are being asked to accept months or years in prison. Prosecutors stand to gain convictions by plea bargaining. So one might expect gain-framed prosecutors to be more amenable to concessions and plea bargains than are loss-framed defendants. Indeterminate sentencing lets overconfident defendants view acquittal or probation as the baseline and anything worse than that as a loss. This loss frame should impede concessions and produce unwillingness to bargain.

Not all defendants view plea bargains through loss frames, however. A defendant who is in pretrial detention is more likely to view prison as the baseline and eventual freedom as a gain, particularly if freedom is possible in weeks or months. Thus, one side effect of pretrial detention is that detained defendants may become more pliable in plea bargaining. The same thing may happen if mandatory minima, three-strikes laws, or sentencing guidelines set clear base penalties. A defendant who knows the proof of guilt is strong and the fixed base penalty is an automatic fifteen years may view anything less as a gain. This outcome is particularly likely if the bargain involves cooperating with the government, which is almost the only escape hatch from the Federal Sentencing Guidelines and mandatory minima. A proposal of cooperation looks like a significant gain: the parties discover a cooperative, win-win solution by agreeing to a massive sentence discount in exchange for assistance in convicting others. The rhetoric of "sentencing discounts" for cooperators reinforces the gain frame, even if the absolute level of punishment is quite high. This gain-framing effect of sentencing guidelines may partially explain why federal plea rates have risen dramatically since the enactment of the Guidelines. Even in indeterminate-sentencing states, prosecutors can set baselines and frames by developing going rates for certain crimes and recurring situations.

Thus, under sentencing guidelines, gain-framed defense lawyers come to view small downward adjustments as golden nuggets instead of as pathetic sops. When sentencing is more automatic and prosecutorial concessions are harder to come by, each concession seems more valuable. Sentencing guidelines will have this effect, however, only on those defendants who are familiar with them. Defendants who are used to indeterminate sentences in some state courts will keep framing outcomes as losses and continue to resist bargaining. Those who know about sentencing guidelines or statutes, perhaps because they have prior federal convictions or have heard three-strikes ads, will more readily adopt gain frames and strike deals. The former may thus reap more generous deals than the latter, except for those few who are so stubborn that they hold out, go to trial, and probably receive worse results. This result distributes punishment inequitably according to defendants' experience.

F. Anchoring and Adjustment

Selection of a reference point affects not only framing, but also anchoring. People come up with or evaluate numbers by focusing on a reference point (an anchor) and then adjusting up or down from that anchor. This anchor may come from a guess or from an analogous case.

Anchoring poses three main problems. First, the selection of an anchor is often biased. Because assessments of fairness are self-serving, each side may choose a different anchor. This was the case, for example, with the teachers' unions that compared themselves to high-salary districts while the school boards compared themselves to low-salary districts.

Second, even arbitrary, random, or irrelevant numbers can serve as anchors and distort calculations. Numbers that are obviously manipulable likewise produce strong anchoring effects. For instance, the asking price of a house strongly influences appraisals of its value, even for experts who consider the asking price completely uninformative and who have plenty of other information. Anchoring depends not so much on relevance as on recency. Experiment subjects are most influenced by information that they receive just before they make judgments, even if that information is obviously useless.

Third, people usually do not adjust away from their anchors enough. As a result, their initial choice of anchors has an inordinate effect on their final estimates. This underadjustment happens because the anchor brings to mind features of the target that resemble the anchor, thus leading people to overemphasize similarities and underestimate differences. Additional information, standing alone, is no cure for anchoring. On the contrary, more information permits more selective recall of similarities and creates stronger anchoring effects....

The same dynamics help to explain the course of plea bargaining. For example, a prosecutor might initially offer a robbery defendant twenty years' imprisonment by piling on every plausible enhancement. The defendant, of course, rejects this unreasonable offer out of hand, but the initial offer serves as a high anchor. When the prosecutor comes back with a revised offer of fifteen years, that offer sounds more reasonable. By the time the prosecutor comes down to twelve years, the defendant is ready to jump at the deal. If the prosecutor had started out at twelve years, however, the defendant might have anchored on that number as the highest likely sentence and rejected it as a bad deal.

Defendants who have been sentenced for similar crimes before in the same court system may start off with more relevant anchors. Thus, on average, anchoring will confuse neophyte defendants more than it will savvy recidivists. But, as noted earlier, a recent anchor may carry great weight even if it is not logically relevant or plausible. So, even if a defendant thinks he is innocent and deserves zero punishment, the prosecutor's opening offer may serve as an anchor and influence the defendant.

Anchoring also gives prosecutors great power to influence judges' sentences. A team of researchers asked both new and experienced German trial judges to sentence a hypothetical rape case. The researchers held all facts constant while varying the prosecutors' sentencing demands. Their findings were striking: when setting sentences, judges anchor heavily on prosecutors' demands. This anchoring occurs even if the judge is experienced, even if the judge knows the prosecutor is inexperienced, and even if the judge claims that the prosecutor's demand is irrelevant. Thus, a judge who is uncertain how to rule on certain sentencing-guidelines factors in a close case may anchor on whatever position the prosecutor takes. In about one-third of all federal districts, federal prosecutors follow a policy of not recommending specific sentences for cooperating defendants. This policy allows defense counsel to set low anchors unilaterally, without having to compete with prosecutorial anchors. Anchoring might also mean that defendants who receive and reject low plea-bargain offers may nonetheless be able to use these offers as low anchors if they mention them in passing to judges.

Finally, anchoring adds another reason why prosecutorial overcharging is effective. The conventional explanation for overcharging is that it gives prosecutors additional plea-bargaining chips. There is much truth to this explanation. But overcharging works for another reason as well: it provides high anchors for defendants. Defendants who anchor initially on maximum life sentences are more likely to think that they are getting good deals when they are offered lower sentences. This is doubly true if prosecutors can frame charge reductions as gains. If the initial charge and sentence serve as anchors and baselines, any prosecutorial concessions look like discounts or savings—wins for defendants instead of reduced losses.

Notes/Questions

1. Bibas notes in his article that lawyers can serve a key role with their clients as "de-biasers." How do you think you can do this? For example, what would you say to a young defendant who faces a significant trial penalty but wants to "take a chance" and go to trial?

2. What kind of negotiation training would you suggest to the criminal bar to better understand the impact of cognitive biases in negotiation?

3. How do you think these cognitive biases play out differently between prosecutors and defense attorneys? As a defense lawyer, how might you use your understanding of cognitive biases to get a better plea deal for your client? As a prosecutor, how might you use your understanding of cognitive biases to encourage a defense lawyer's client to take the deal you are offering?

B. Understanding Prosecutor Motivations and Perspectives

This next article examines how similar psychological errors might impact the prosecution in plea bargaining as well.

Alafair S. Burke, *Prosecutorial Passion, Cognitive Bias, and Plea Bargaining*

91 Marq. L. Rev. 183, 186–187, 192, 194–203 (2007)

I. DEFINING PROSECUTORIAL PASSION

The most common portrait of the plea bargaining prosecutor is, to put it mildly, unflattering. Much of the plea bargaining literature depicts prosecutors as motivated entirely by their own interests, crassly and singularly defined by the maintenance of high rates of conviction. From this view, the power that such prosecutors enjoy permits them to manipulate the plea negotiation process to maximize their self-serving statistics. Using leverage gained through overcharging and from determinate sentencing laws, prosecutors can extract guilty pleas in weak cases. Meanwhile, by refusing to offer meaningful concessions in stronger cases, prosecutors can reserve their easiest cases for trial to establish an impressive conviction record....

Perhaps, however, prosecutors' values are more complex. Obtaining desirable conviction rates through the manipulation of plea bargaining is not a task that drives most prosecutors into their profession. Prosecutors might accept plea bargaining as the pragmatic side of justice, but ultimately prosecutors are drawn to their jobs because of the identity that comes with it, the well known obligation to be a minister of justice—an obligation, prosecutors frequently and pridefully boast—that sets them apart from other lawyers....

II. PROSECUTORIAL PASSION AND PLEA BARGAINING

Prosecutorial passion could conceivably affect plea bargaining in two different ways. First, passion might affect a prosecutor's cost-benefit analysis as a rational decision maker, causing the prosecutor either to refuse to engage in plea negotiations altogether, or to insist upon deep concessions from the defendant to compensate the prosecutor for relinquishing her advocacy role at trial. Second, and outside of a rational decision-making model, prosecutorial passion might skew plea negotiations by inducing or exaggerating cognitive biases that cause the prosecutor to inflate both the likelihood of a conviction in the case and the length of the likely sentence after a conviction obtained at trial....

However, to the passionate prosecutor, the cost of plea bargaining is not only the possibility of obtaining a higher sentence after trial, but also the toll on the prosecutor's pride if she surrenders without a fight....

B. Skewed Plea Bargaining

Prosecutorial passion might affect plea bargaining not only by altering the prosecutor's rational cost-benefit analysis, but also by injecting irrationality into the prosecutor's decision making.... Even when a prosecutor relinquishes her advocacy role and attempts to negotiate a resolution, her passion may induce or exaggerate cognitive biases that can skew plea bargaining outcomes.

1. Selective Information Processing

Consider, for example, the ways that selective information processing can cause a passionate prosecutor to overestimate both the likelihood of a defendant's conviction and the probable post-conviction sentence and therefore inflate the appropriate negotiated outcome. Selective information processing is the tendency for people to recall stored information and interpret new information to conform to their pre-existing views. As a result of selective information processing, people readily accept evidence that is consistent with their current beliefs and find reasons to distrust or dismiss contradictory evidence. A growing body of scholarship on prosecutorial decision making explores the ways that the biased assimilation of evidence can prevent prosecutors from believing defendants' claims of innocence....

Accordingly, the more passion a prosecutor feels for her case, the more likely she will be to overestimate both the likelihood of conviction and the stiffness of the ultimate sentence, thereby making her less compliant in plea negotiations.

2. Loss Aversion and Framing

The phenomena of loss aversion and framing can also affect a passionate prosecutor's plea bargaining decisions. Cognitive research shows that people are averse to risk when given the opportunity to lock in gains, but are risk seeking if a gamble will help them avoid a loss. Moreover, gain and loss are not intrinsically fixed concepts. People are risk averse when an outcome is framed as a gain (e.g., "money retained") and risk seeking when the same result is framed as a loss (e.g., "money lost").

Scholars have previously noted that framing can cause defendants to perceive plea outcomes as either gains or losses, thereby promoting either risk aversion or risk seeking....

Prosecutors might view plea bargained outcomes as gains in their typical cases. Plea bargaining, after all, guarantees prosecutors a conviction and permits them to dispose of a case without the work of a trial. However, if prosecutors are passionate about a case, they will not view it as a typical case to be plea bargained away to make time for other (i.e., trial) cases. They will instead view the file as a case to be tried so they can request a far weightier sentence than they could receive through plea bargaining. Any disposition of the case that deprives a prosecutor of the chance to go to trial, and results in a sentence short of the sentence requested after trial, would be viewed as a loss. Accordingly, a prosecutor will be more accepting of the risks of a trial and less willing to negotiate a plea.

3. Over-Optimism and Hindsight Bias

The cognitive literature suggests that passionate prosecutors might underestimate the odds of an acquittal. As an initial matter, prosecutors have good reason to be confident about their cases; they win the vast majority of their trials. Moreover, people in general are unrealistically optimistic about themselves and their talents, routinely overestimating the likelihood that good things will happen to them and underestimating the probability of less desirable events. Accordingly, a prosecutor may persuade herself that, although her case might be a difficult one, she is more likely than others to win it, particularly because it is a case that she has decided to treat as a priority. A prosecutor's confidence is only inflated by hindsight bias, the tendency for people to overestimate ex ante the likelihood of an event once it has already occurred. Each time a prosecutor wins a difficult trial, it reinforces her perception that a conviction was inevitable. A prosecutor who overestimates the likelihood of conviction will be less malleable in plea bargaining.

4. Anchoring

Prosecutorial passion can also affect the anchors that parties use during plea negotiations. Overwhelming psychological research demonstrates that people estimate or evaluate numbers by "anchoring" on a preliminary number and then adjusting, usually inadequately, from the initial anchor....

Prosecutorial passion can exaggerate this anchoring effect by triggering an even higher initial anchor. In cases that provoke a prosecutor's passion, the prosecutor will charge the case more aggressively....

Finally, high demands made by passionate prosecutors can also influence judges, who tend to anchor on the prosecutors' positions at sentencing.

5. Sunk Costs

Finally, prosecutorial passion can decrease prosecutors' willingness to negotiate because of sunk cost effects. Although a rational decision maker should evaluate the utility of his options prospectively, ample evidence demonstrates that people are affected by sunk costs and permit prior investments of time, money, and resources to influence their current choices ...

In contrast, when a prosecutor is passionate about a case, she has selected it as special among the competing files in her caseload. She has chosen the case as one she is willing to take to trial to maximize the possible sentence against the defendant. Accordingly, she will estimate the likelihood of a trial in that case as being higher than in the cases in which she is flexible about negotiations. Because the chances of a trial are higher, she will complete more and earlier trial preparation. Once she has expended substantial time and energy preparing for the trial, those efforts become sunk costs that will reduce her willingness to negotiate a plea bargain.

Notes/Questions

1. How would involving judges or other reforms suggested in Chapter 6 on plea bargaining reform mitigate these errors?

2. What if you are a new district attorney elected to bring change in sentencing (and therefore plea bargains)? How might you need to retrain prosecutors to deal with these common errors?

3. Stephanos Bibas has written about the criminal legal system in the U.K. where barristers switch sides from day to day. In other words, barristers act as both prosecutors and defense attorneys over the course of their careers. *See* Stephanos Bibas, *Prosecutorial Regulation Versus Prosecutorial Accountability*, 157 U. Pa. L. Rev. 959, 960 (2009). How might this shift in roles affect the impact of the cognitive biases outlined above?

***

We close the chapter with a focus on prosecutor perspectives in plea bargaining. Ron Wright and Kay Levine's important study of state prosecutors and how their identity evolves over time shows one possible avenue of reform. Might the age and experience of prosecutors make them even more susceptible to the cognitive biases discussed above? They discuss the impact of the "Young Prosecutors' Syndrome" on plea bargaining and what changes might be needed to fix this.

Ronald F. Wright & Kay L. Levine, *The Cure for Young Prosecutors' Syndrome*

56 Ariz. St. L. Rev. 1065, 1068–1071 (2014)

...

The effects of Young Prosecutors' Syndrome can distort the outcomes in high-volume state criminal courts. About half of the 25,000 prosecutors who work in the state systems are the "junior" prosecutors that we discuss here. They handle less serious cases at the start of their careers, but fast turnover typically means that relatively inexperienced prosecutors also handle more serious crimes. Prosecutors who lack judgment about which cases to try, or who are inclined to goad defendants into trials to prove their professional worth, aggravate already overcrowded trial dockets. They subject defendants, victims, and witnesses to unnecessary courtroom drama and delay just to test their skills. Junior prosecutors who distrust defense attorneys may be more inclined to skirt the edges of their disclosure obligations, in violation of their constitutional and statutory duties. Lastly, inexperienced prosecutors might also press for overly broad categories in their sentencing recommendations, when more individualized judgments could produce more proportional and economical sentencing.

The cure for Young Prosecutors' Syndrome appears to be experience. Our interview data ... suggest that, like experts in other fields, many prosecutors mature over the years in their professional self-image and embrace a more pragmatic, individualized approach to the job. As a result, seasoned prosecutors see the true variety of cases on their docket and are able to calibrate their responses in individual cases. The experienced prosecutors we met said that, even though they feel the effects of cynicism at times, they reserve trials and harsh consequences only for a small subset of defendants; where the public benefits very little from a trial, they aim for a resolution through diversion programs and reasonable plea offers. Moreover, seasoned prosecutors appreciate the value that defense attorneys add, in contrast to the begrudging and abstract descriptions of the defense attorney role that junior prosecutors are likely to offer.

The dark side of prosecutorial discretion dominates most academic portrayals of prosecutors, which treat discretion as a source of race, class, or gender discrimination. We do not mean to diminish the risk that discretionary behavior poses, but this Article treats prosecutorial discretion as a mixed bag of effects, a combination that changes over the life cycle of a prosecutor's career. While some experienced prosecutors' behavior might reflect laziness or unwarranted sympathy for defendants who seem familiar to the prosecutor, veterans believe that their maturity serves the public well. They emphasize that a tempered approach produces more substantive justice, balancing the competing interests of victims, defendants, and society. According to our data, that belief is largely absent among new prosecutors, which leads us to wonder why such a disparity exists.

... [W]e develop several explanations for the transformation toward balance during a prosecutor's career. The first source of balance is confidence based on past success. Fortified by their past experiences, veteran prosecutors can resist manipulation and ignore criticism dished out by defense attorneys and judges; they can also deliver disappointing news to police officers, crime victims, and supervisors without fearing that they appear weak. The second source of balance is pragmatism based on a legacy of past mistakes. Because they have been burned by witnesses, police errors, and unexpected defense techniques in the past, experienced prosecutors approach witness evaluation and trial preparation with a skeptical eye, stemming from the intuition that a prosecutor's success depends on separating half-truths from reliable evidence. The third influence on balance is an increased ability to distinguish small crimes from large crimes. As prosecutors move up the career ladder, their caseloads become packed with very serious crimes, causing the less serious ones to drop from view; they learn to look for some proportionality between the seriousness of a case and the resources they devote to that case. Lastly, we consider the effects of life experience. Many of our interviewees emphasized the link between their personal experiences and their sense of compassion and restraint as a prosecutor. A prosecutor who lives alongside human frailty—as a parent or a community member—tends to become more grounded, more just, and more careful in her use of criminal justice resources.

Many of the prosecutors we interviewed told us that years of experience guided them towards a more pragmatic and individualized approach to the job. But does their decision-making actually change over the years? Do they in fact decide cases differently than their less experienced counterparts?... [W]e review survey data relevant to this question. It appears that prosecutors do change their plea offer practices, becoming more pragmatic and proportional as they gain more experience. Those changes in practice, however, seem to be more muted than the emphatic shifts in prosecutors' self-images might suggest.

If the cure for Young Prosecutors' Syndrome is experience, is there anything that senior prosecutors can do to make the cure take effect more quickly and completely?... [W]e discuss the ways that chief prosecutors can structure their offices to speed the transformation of their individual prosecutors. These measures include the hiring of prosecutors with a mix of experience levels and the use of training programs designed to simulate the lessons that experience will inevitably teach. We also discuss the role that office organizational schemes play in promoting balanced prosecution. Junior prosecutors who frequently interact with their senior counterparts tend to learn more quickly the lessons that experience can offer. For this reason, office arrangements that place senior and junior prosecutors alongside one another on the same teams, in the same courtrooms, and in the same trials, are likely to speed up the development of expertise. Finally, we address the role of law schools in producing the adversarial mentality that new prosecutors bring into their early years, and suggest how law schools can modify the academic curriculum to plant the seeds of balance before graduation.

Promoting balance for young prosecutors could be the most important single step our criminal justice system can take to improve its health and sustainability. Because of the absence of functional checks and balances in criminal charging and sentencing, prosecutor decisions are central to any effort to restore balance to a bloated and expensive prison system that is far out of proportion to historic and international comparison points. If we can get this right—increasing the maturity of prosecutors earlier in their careers, we can transform the individual attorneys involved, improve the lives of individual defendants, and further the goals of reasoned judgment and rough equality.

Notes/Questions

1. How might the reforms outlined above help prosecutors mature earlier and gain perspective?

2. If you are the defense attorney negotiating with a relatively inexperienced prosecutor, how does understanding their perspective help you develop a strategy for the upcoming negotiation?

3. Wright and Levine also blame law schools for young prosecutors and their overly adversarial mentality. What else should we be teaching or training in law school to avoid this?

4. If you want to become a prosecutor, what does this article suggest in terms of what you should be looking for regarding the type of prosecutor's office and their policies?

Consider the following from a Louisiana prosecutor after the exoneration of a defendant that he tried, Glenn Ford. The defendant was convicted and sentenced to death in 1983. He was released and exonerated in 2014—after serving over 30 years in prison. After reading this, what errors did the prosecutor likely commit? And, thinking back to the importance of reputation, how might prosecutors think about their reputations to help overcome any biases?

> At the time this case was tried there was evidence that would have cleared Glenn Ford. The easy and convenient argument is that the prosecutors did not know of such evidence, thus they were absolved of any responsibility for the wrongful conviction.
>
> I can take no comfort in such an argument. As a prosecutor and officer of the court, I had the duty to prosecute fairly. While I could properly strike hard blows, ethically I could not strike foul ones.
>
> Part of my duty was to disclose promptly any exculpatory evidence relating to trial and penalty issues of which I was made aware. My fault was that I was too passive. I did not consider the rumors about the involvement of parties other than Mr. Ford to be credible, especially since the three others who were indicted for the crime were ultimately released for lack of sufficient evidence to proceed to the trial.
>
> Had I been more inquisitive, perhaps the evidence would have come to light years ago. But I wasn't, and my inaction contributed to the miscarriage of justice in this matter. Based on what we had, I was confident that the right man was being prosecuted and I was not going to commit resources to investigate what I considered to be bogus claims that we had the wrong man.
>
> My mindset was wrong and blinded me to my purpose of seeking justice, rather than obtaining a conviction of a person who I believed to be guilty. I did not hide evidence, I simply did not seriously consider that sufficient information may have been out there that could have led to a different conclusion. And that omission is on me.
>
> Furthermore, my silence at trial undoubtedly contributed to the wrong-headed result.
>
> I did not question the unfairness of Mr. Ford having appointed counsel who had never tried a criminal jury case much less a capital one. It never concerned me that the defense had insufficient funds to hire experts or that defense counsel shut down their firms for substantial periods of time to prepare for trial. These attorneys tried their very best, but they were in the wrong arena. They were excellent attorneys with experience in civil matters. But this did not prepare them for trying to save the life of Mr. Ford.

The jury was all white, Mr. Ford was African-American. Potential African-American jurors were struck with little thought about potential discrimination because at that time a claim of racial discrimination in the selection of jurors could not be successful unless it could be shown that the office had engaged in a pattern of such conduct in other cases.

And I knew this was a very burdensome requirement that had never been met in the jurisprudence of which I was aware. I also participated in placing before the jury dubious testimony from a forensic pathologist that the shooter had to be left handed, even though there was no eye witness to the murder. And yes, Glenn Ford was left handed.

All too late, I learned that the testimony was pure junk science at its evil worst.

In 1984, I was 33 years old. I was arrogant, judgmental, narcissistic and very full of myself. I was not as interested in justice as I was in winning. To borrow a phrase from Al Pacino in the movie "And Justice for All," "Winning became everything."

After the death verdict in the Ford trial, I went out with others and celebrated with a few rounds of drinks. That's sick. I had been entrusted with the duty to seek the death of a fellow human being, a very solemn task that certainly did not warrant any "celebration."

In my rebuttal argument during the penalty phase of the trial, I mocked Mr. Ford, stating that this man wanted to stay alive so he could be given the opportunity to prove his innocence. I continued by saying this should be an affront to each of you jurors, for he showed no remorse, only contempt for your verdict.

How totally wrong was I....

A.M. "Marty" Stroud III, *Lead prosecutor apologizes for role in sending man to death row*, Shreveport Times, March 8, 2015 (https://www.shreveporttimes.com/story/opinion/readers/2015/03/20/lead-prosecutor-offers-apology-in-the-case-of-exonerated-death-row-inmate-glenn-ford/25049063/).

Additional Resources

Alafair S. Burke, *Improving Prosecutorial Decision Making: Some Lessons of Cognitive Science*, 47 Wm. & Mary. L. Rev. 1587 (2006).

Brite Englich, Thomas Mussweiler & Fritz Strack, *The Last Word in Court—A Hidden Disadvantage for the Defense*, 29 L. & Hum. Behav. 705 (2005).

F. Andrew Hessick III & Reshma Saujani, *Plea Bargaining and Convicting the Innocent: The Role of the Prosecutor, the Defense Counsel, and the Judge*, 16 BYU J. PUB. L. 189 (2002).

Gregory M. Gilchrist, *Counsel's Role in Bargaining for Trials*, 99 IOWA L. REV. 1979 (2014).

Catherine A. Grodensky, William E. Crozier & Brandon L. Garrett, *Understanding Plea Bargaining in a New Progressive DA's Office: How Line Prosecutors Understand and Implement Progressive Goals Through Plea Decisions*, 50 CRIM. JUST. AND BEHAV. 429, 434–435, 440–442 (2023).

Peter A. Joy & Rodney J. Uphoff, *Systemic Barriers to Effective Assistance of Counsel in Plea Bargaining*, 99 IOWA L. REV. 2103 (2014).

Nancy J. King & Ronald F. Wright, *The Invisible Revolution in Plea Bargaining: Managerial Judging and Judicial Participation in Negotiations*, 95 TEX. L. REV. 325 (2016).

Brandon J. Lester, Note, *System Failure: The Case for Supplanting Negotiation with Mediation in Plea Bargaining*, 20 OHIO ST. J. ON DISP. RESOL. 563 (2005).

Jenn Rolnick Borchetta & Alice Fontier, *When Race Tips the Scales in Plea Bargaining*, SLATE (Oct. 23, 2017), http://www.slate.com/articles/news_and_politics/jurisprudence/2017/10/new_research_finds_that_prosecutors_give_white_defendants_better_deals_than.html.

Abbe Smith, *Lawyering at the Edge: Unpopular Clients, Difficult Cases, Zealous Advocates: The Lawyer's "Conscience" and the Limits of Persuasion*, 36 HOFSTRA L. REV. 479 (Winter 2007).

Steven Zeidman, *To Plead or Not to Plead: Effective Assistance and Client-Centered Counseling*, 39 B.C. L. REV. 841 (1998).

Part II

Introduction to Part II

We have spent the first half of the book on the process of plea bargaining. This is for a number of reasons. First, this is the defining process for the vast majority of criminal defendants. It is crucial that we understand both the advantages and disadvantages of that process, concerns that we have, and the role each actor—prosecution, defense, judge, victim—has in that process. Once we understand that process, we can then compare other, newer processes to that. Second, as we turn to discussing alternative processes, we need to acknowledge that many of these occur *through* plea bargaining. In other words, you only get into a drug court as part of a plea. Or, after a restorative justice process, your stance in plea bargaining (either as defense or prosecution) might shift. Finally, although much writing in the upcoming section will compare these processes to trial, we, in fact, need to remember that we are comparing these other processes to other sentences or deals that would happen through plea bargaining.

With that, let's turn to the second half of the book. We will start with two chapters on problem-solving courts and understanding the theories of therapeutic jurisprudence on which at least some of these courts are based. Problem-solving courts—whether they are drug courts or mental health courts or another kind—pull certain kinds of cases out of the typical trial court to treat defendants differently. Perhaps it is based on who the defendant is—as in veteran's court or juvenile court—or perhaps it is by the offense—drug court or prostitution court, etc. These courts have been primarily started by judges, limited to their jurisdictions, in response to particular concerns.

We then turn to restorative justice processes, often started in the United States in the opposite way—by grassroots organizations or nonprofits. These processes—conferences, circles, and victim-offender mediation—can occur before or after sentencing, as part of the system or apart, and in very small groups or in large community gatherings. The commonality between these—in addition to the goals and underlying theory—is the process of facilitated dialogue. And the roles of the actors here are quite different from either plea-bargaining processes or even problem-solving courts.

We conclude our coverage of the criminal alternative processes with three chapters on the juvenile legal system. We do this because the juvenile system brings all of these processes together. To the extent that we have concerns about plea bargaining or mass incarceration, these are magnified in the juvenile system. The juvenile system was also the first problem-solving court, so it gives us the opportunity to examine its progress and compare it to other more recently created problem-solving courts. Moreover, at least in the United States, it is often with juveniles that we are most willing to use restorative justice practices. So these last three chapters give us the opportunity to see all of the criminal legal system in action and to pull these streams together.

The concluding chapter at the end of Part II brings the threads of alternative criminal processes together through a dispute system design lens. Looking forward with an eye on meaningful reform, how would we (and how should we) design processes to meet the myriad goals of the criminal legal system? Who should be consulted in this design? How would we measure success? And who is accountable for ongoing evaluation?

The concluding chapter at the end of Part II brings the threads of alternative criminal processes together through a dispute system design lens. Looking forward with an eye on meaningful reform, how would we (and how should we) design processes to meet the myriad goals of the criminal legal system? Who should be consulted in this design? How would we measure success? And who is accountable for ongoing evaluation?

Chapter 8

Problem-Solving Courts/ Therapeutic Justice

One fundamental criticism of the criminal legal system in the United States is that it is overly focused on punishment and does not treat the underlying problems that may lead to criminal behavior. Some professionals within the system responded to this concern and high incarceration and recidivism rates by looking for non-adversarial methods of dealing with crime that are more focused on treating offenders. Unlike restorative justice (as you will read in a future chapter), the problem-solving court movement was led by those from within, not outside, the criminal legal system. It is in many ways a uniquely American invention, although the developments in the United States have influenced other countries (such as the UK, Canada, and Ireland) to start their own versions of problem-solving courts. Problem-solving courts are courts designed to pull certain offenders out of the system, recognizing their needs or special circumstances, and treat these offenders differently. This different treatment usually includes alternative sentencing, but more importantly provides various support programs along the way. Problem-solving courts are now common throughout the United States and include drug courts, mental health courts, veterans' courts, gambling courts, and prostitution courts.

This chapter will begin with a basic explanation of the history of problem-solving courts and how they developed. We then turn to different examples of the courts to show the wide variety of applications. The focus in these courts is on treatment of the offender. Unlike in restorative justice processes, the victim often has no formal role in problem-solving courts. You will read about the changing professional roles for lawyers and judges in problem-solving courts as they change certain processes that had previously been standard in our adversarial court system. Problem-solving courts can be pre or post-conviction and generally require the defendant to agree to attend counseling and adhere to other requirements (such as remaining drug-free or not using alcohol). For example, the ten "key components" for many problem-solving courts, including veterans' and drug courts are:

1. Courts integrate alcohol and other drug treatment services with legal system case processing.
2. Using a non-adversarial approach; prosecution and defense counsel promote public safety while protecting participants' due process rights.

3. Eligible participants are identified early and promptly placed in the alternative court program.
4. Courts provide access to a continuum of alcohol, drug and other related treatment and rehabilitation services.
5. Abstinence is monitored by frequent alcohol and other drug testing.
6. A coordinated strategy governs court responses to participants' compliance.
7. Ongoing judicial interaction with each court participant is essential.
8. Monitoring and evaluation measure the achievement of program goals and gauge effectiveness.
9. Continuing interdisciplinary education promotes effective planning, implementation, and operations.
10. Forging partnerships among courts, public agencies, and community-based organizations generates local support and enhances effectiveness.[1]

The next section addresses the theories of why these courts work. We start with explaining neuroscience as it relates to both legal culpability and addiction. Increasingly, neuroscience is gaining the attention of policymakers, courts, and lawyers. Some claim that our improved understanding of how the brain works should change how we sentence offenders. Others take the view that this research demands that the criminal legal system rethink concepts of criminal liability and responsibility. (In the chapter on Juvenile Courts, you will read about how our increased understanding of how the brain develops, and the differences between the adolescent and adult brain, have led to direct changes in the law including whether it is constitutional to execute a minor or sentence a minor to life in prison without the possibility of parole.) We also examine the theory of therapeutic jurisprudence. Finally, we examine if these courts work in practice.

I. How Problem-Solving Courts Got Started

A. Introduction

In this first article, Bruce J. Winick, former Professor of Law and Professor of Psychiatry and Behavioral Sciences at the University of Miami, explains the transformation of the court system. Winick is considered one of the co-founders of the school of therapeutic jurisprudence. The new types of court systems involve a collaborative, interdisciplinary approach to problem-solving where the judge plays a leading role.

1. *See, e.g.*, Bureau of Justice Assistance, U.S. Department of Justice, *Defining Drug Courts: The Key Components*, January 1997.

Bruce J. Winick, *Therapeutic Jurisprudence and Problem Solving Courts*

30 Fordham Urb. L.J. 1055–1061 (2002)

...

I. PROBLEM SOLVING COURTS: A TRANSFORMATION IN THE JUDICIAL ROLE

In the past dozen or so years, a remarkable transformation has occurred in the role of the courts. Courts traditionally have functioned as governmental mechanisms of dispute resolution, resolving disputes between private parties concerning property, contracts, and tort damages, or between the government and an individual concerning allegations of criminal wrongdoing or regulatory violations. In these cases, courts typically have functioned as neutral arbiters, resolving issues of historical facts or supervising juries engaged in the adjudicatory process.

Recently, a range of new kinds of problems, many of which are social and psychological in nature, have appeared before the courts. These cases require the courts to not only resolve disputed issues of fact, but also to attempt to solve a variety of human problems that are responsible for bringing the case to court. Traditional courts limit their attention to the narrow dispute in controversy. These newer courts, however, attempt to understand and address the underlying problem that is responsible for the immediate dispute, and to help the individuals before the court to effectively deal with the problem in ways that will prevent recurring court involvement.

The new courts, increasingly known as problem solving courts, are specialized tribunals established to deal with specific problems, often involving individuals who need social, mental health, or substance abuse treatment services. These courts also include criminal cases involving individuals with drug or alcoholism problems, mental health problems, or problems of family and domestic violence. The juvenile court is the forerunner of these specialized courts; it was started in Chicago in 1899 as an attempt to provide a rehabilitative approach to the problem of juvenile delinquency, rather than the punitive approach of the adult criminal court. The modern antecedents of this movement are the drug treatment courts, founded in Miami in 1989.

The drug treatment court was a response to the recognition that processing nonviolent drug possession charges in the criminal courts and then sentencing the offender to prison did not succeed in changing the offender's addictive behavior. Criminal court dockets had become swollen with these drug cases, and the essentially retributivist intervention of the criminal court and prison seemed to do little to avoid repetition of the underlying problem. The result was a "revolving door effect in which [drug offenders typically] resumed their drug-abusing behavior after [being] released from prison." Instead of relying on the traditional criminal justice approach, the drug treatment court emphasized the offender's rehabilitation, and placed the judge as a member of the treatment team. Offenders accepting diversion to the drug treatment court, or pleading guilty and agreeing to participate in the drug treatment court as a condition of probation, agreed to several conditions; to remain drug-free, "to participate in a prescribed course of drug treatment, to submit to periodic drug testing in order to monitor their compliance [with the treatment plan], and to report [periodically] to court for judicial supervision of their progress."

These courts' success in helping many addicts to end their addiction and to avoid re-involvement with the criminal court led to a tremendous growth in the number of drug courts nationally and internationally, with the result that, as of December 2000, there were 697 such courts in America, and many more in the planning stage. Indeed, there now are juvenile drug treatment courts, which specialize in juveniles with drug abuse problems, and dependency drug treatment courts, that deal with families with drug problems that are charged with child abuse or neglect.

Other specialized treatment courts or problem solving courts, as they are now known, include domestic violence courts, which attempt to protect the victims of domestic violence, to motivate perpetrators of domestic violence to attend batterer's intervention programs, and to monitor compliance with court orders and treatment progress. More than two hundred domestic violence courts now exist.

Reentry courts are another form of problems solving courts. These courts were designed to assist offenders that are released from prison into a form of judicially-supervised parole, to effect a successful integration into the community. A recently proposed application of the reentry court model deals with sex offenders and attempts to manage the risk of their reoffending through close supervision and monitoring through the use of polygraph examinations.

Another example is the dependency court, a branch of family court that deals with issues of child abuse and neglect. This is a civil court that adjudicates whether child abuse or neglect has occurred, and when it has, it attempts to provide services designed to avoid its repetition. When such services appear fruitless, the dependency court works to terminate parental rights and arrange foster care for the child.

Teen court, sometimes known as youth court, is another problem solving court This court deals with cases involving juveniles charged with minor offenses. In addition, it allows other juveniles who have been through the teen court process, and who have received special training, to play the role of prosecutor, defense attorney, or member of the jury. This special process provides the juveniles charged with minor offenses with the ability to see their behavior from the victims' or society's perspective and to receive an inoculation of empathy training.

One of the most recent types of problem solving courts to emerge is the mental health court, started in 1997 in Broward County, Florida. The mental health court is a misdemeanor criminal court designed to deal with people arrested for minor offenses whose major problem is mental illness rather than criminality. This is a revolving door category of patients who are periodically committed to mental hospitals where they are treated with psychotropic medication. Due to the use of medication, they experience sufficient improvement, which allows hospitals to discharge them, but, when they are back in the community, they fail to take their medication. As a result, they frequently decompensate, sometimes committing minor offenses that result in their arrest. Mental health courts seek to divert them from the criminal justice system and to persuade them to voluntarily accept treatment while in the community. In addition, they link them with treatment resources, and provide social service support and judicial monitoring to ensure treatment compliance.

All of these courts grew out of the recognition that traditional judicial approaches have failed, at least in the areas of substance abuse, domestic violence, certain kinds of criminality, child abuse and neglect, and mental illness. These are all recycling problems, the reoccurrence of which traditional interventions did not succeed in bringing to a halt. The traditional judicial model addressed the symptoms, but not the underlying problem. The result was that the problem reemerged, constantly necessitating repeated judicial intervention. All these areas involved specialized problems that judges of courts of general jurisdiction lacked expertise in. Moreover, they involved treatment or social service needs that traditional courts lacked the tools to deal with.

In response to these failures, courts decided that they needed new judicial approaches. These new approaches involve a collaborative, interdisciplinary approach to problem solving where the judge plays a leading role. Not only is the judge a leading actor in the therapeutic drama, but also the courtroom itself becomes a stage for the acting out of many crucial scenes. On this stage, the judge also assumes the role of director, coordinating the roles of many of the actors, providing a needed motivation for how they will play their parts, and inspiring them to play them well.

The new problem solving courts are all characterized by active judicial involvement, and the explicit use of judicial authority to motivate individuals to accept needed services and to monitor their compliance and progress. They are concerned not merely with processing and resolving the court case, but in achieving a variety of tangible outcomes associated with avoiding reoccurrence of the problem. Problem solving courts generate the need for new kinds of information not typically collected by courts, and, in the process, have significantly improved the quality and quantity of information needed to understand the problem and deal more effectively with it. They play an educative role in raising community consciousness about the problem in question, its causes, and the resources that courts need to resolve it. In addition, they become advocates for the populations they deal with and for the increased allocation of community resources needed to resolve their problems. Finally, they work closely with community agencies and treatment providers, and, in the process, monitor and improve their effectiveness.

Problem solving courts represent a significant new direction for the judiciary. These judges seek to actively and holistically resolve both the judicial case and the problem that produced it. They extend help to people in need by connecting them to community resources, motivating them through creative uses of the court's authority to accept needed services and treatment, and monitoring their progress in ways that help to ensure their success. By targeting recurring problems that seem to be the product of behavioral, psychological, or psychiatric difficulties or disorders, and intervening to prevent their reoccurrence, these courts can be seen as applying a public health approach to social and behavioral problems that cause serious individual suffering and deterioration in the quality of community life. Not only have these techniques emerged in the specialized problem solving courts described above, but also judges in general courts have begun to apply the problem solving approaches derived from these courts.

Notes/Questions

In May 2024, according to the National Treatment Court Resource Center, there are approximately 4,000 drug courts in the United States, just under half of which are adult treatment courts, up from 697 in 2000. As you have read, and will read, some of the strongest advocates for these courts are judges.

Judges are often the leaders in starting drug courts, often without any law mandating that they must establish these courts. This means that problem-solving or specialty courts are often established due to informal agreements and negotiation between the judge, the prosecutor's office, and the defense bar (or public defender's office).

Below is an excerpt from the *ABA Journal* detailing the opioid epidemic currently being faced by the U.S. and ways the criminal legal system is reforming as a response.

> The need for problem-solving courts, especially drug courts, has been on the rise in recent years in part because of the opioid epidemic facing our country today. The desire to combat chronic pain has quickly turned into a society dependent on pain pills, and when that habit gets too expensive, many turn to cheaper options like heroin. According to the DEA, the black market demand for pills like OxyContin has increased so much that one 30-milligram pill can cost up to $40, while heroin has gotten cheaper by the year, with one bag costing as little as $5. Heroin itself is usually cut with a cheaper and more dangerous drug—fentanyl. Dennis Wichern of the DEA was quoted an article by the ABA stating that "taking heroin now, with fentanyl involved, it's like playing with a fully loaded gun." Many court systems across the country are working to combat the issue in a humane way while still punishing offenders. In Buffalo City, Judge Craig Hannah of the city court decided individuals needed treatment for their addictions at the beginning of their criminal case, not the end. He stated "we put their criminal case on pause while we focus on their medical case"—an approach that has never been done before. The Opiate Crisis Intervention Court "links participants with medication and behavioral treatments within hours of their arrest. The goal is intervention before adjudication—and quickly." This problem-solving court model demonstrates the changing criminal justice system as a response to a national crisis, and hopefully will lead to other cities following suit and developing similar drug treatment programs in their own courts.
>
> Liana Jackson, *Opioids, Justice & Mercy: Courts Are on the Front Lines of a Lethal Crisis.* ABA JOURNAL, June 2018.

The following is an example of how a drug court actually works. The information below is from the Milwaukee County Drug Treatment Court Participant Handbook.[2] The handbook includes guidelines for the program, definitions of the roles of individuals they will be working with, information about court sessions, and tips on how to succeed in the program.

Program Description

The Milwaukee County Drug Treatment Court is a court supervised, comprehensive treatment program for non-violent felony offenders or habitual misdemeanants. This is a voluntary program, which includes regular court appearances, alcohol and drug treatment, drug testing, and weekly appointments with your case manager. The Drug Treatment Court is a combined effort of the Milwaukee County District Attorney's Office, Public Defender's Office, Court Administration, Milwaukee County Behavioral Health Division, and Justice 2000, Inc. Program participants will be assisted with obtaining skills assessments and will be provided referrals for vocational training, education, job placement services, mental health services, "wraparound" services, and restorative justice programs. The program length will be determined by each participant's progress but will be no less than one year.

Some Definitions

Assessment: To gather information about your drug and alcohol use and lifestyle to find the best treatment for you.

Case Manager: The person who monitors your progress during the program to make sure that all Drug Court requirements are satisfied.

Confidentiality: The requirement not to discuss specific names and personal information learned during treatment and court sessions with anyone outside of the treatment group or court.

Counselor: The person who provides your treatment services, in group and individual sessions, and gathers information about your efforts.

Defense Attorney/Public Defender: The person who represents you and provides legal advice and information as to your legal options. This attorney and another attorney will be present at all court hearings and staffings.

District Attorney/Prosecutor: The person who represents the State of Wisconsin and is responsible for ensuring community safety.

Drug Treatment Court Team

The Drug Treatment Court Judge serves as a lead partner in the Drug Treatment Court Team and presides at all team staffings and all court sessions. The Judge

2. https://wilawlibrary.gov/topics/justice/drugcourts.php.

and other team members will make all decisions regarding your participation in the drug treatment court program based upon information from the various team members, providers, and other support services. In addition to the Judge, the team is made up of:

- Defense Attorney
- District Attorney
- Drug Treatment Court Coordinator
- Drug Treatment Court Case Manager
- Evaluator
- Law Enforcement
- Probation/Parole
- Treatment Provider

Drug Treatment Court Sessions

As a participant in this program, you will be required to appear in the Drug Treatment Court on a regular basis. Missing a Drug Treatment Court Hearing may result in a warrant being issued for your arrest. Prior to each court session, the team will meet, at a staffing to review your case and your progress report. This report will discuss your drug testing results, attendance, participation and cooperation with treatment, and compliance with the Drug Treatment Court Rules.

During your court appearance, the Judge may ask you questions about your progress and discuss any problems you may be experiencing. You must speak directly with the Drug Court Judge concerning your progress. You are responsible for your own behavior. Please be on time and remain seated and quiet while the court is in session.

The following documents were developed and provided by the National Drug Court Institute (NDCI) as templates and are expected to be adapted to a specific program's policy and procedures based on the Adult Drug Court Best Practice Standards. (They are free to use and available at https://allrise.org/sample-documents/.)

Phase 1 Requirements

Name: ____

Staff: ____

Date Reviewed: ________________

Review each requirement with staff and initial you understand the expectation

___ I will attend court every week at: ____.

___ I will follow my treatment plan.

___ I will comply with supervision and meet weekly with my supervision officer on time. I will notify my supervision officer of any conflicts at least one hour prior to my appointment in case of an emergency.

___ I will allow law enforcement and/or supervision officers associated to the treatment court program into my residence for home visits.

___ I will submit to random urine analysis testing as determined by the treatment court team. UA testing call number: ______________________ Color: ______________

___ I will reside in a safe environment that supports my recovery. I will keep my supervision officer informed if my residency changes.

___ I will obtain a medical assessment as directed by my treatment team.

___ I acknowledge my curfew is at 9 p.m.

I have reviewed the requirements for phase 1 and understand my responsibilities to the treatment court program.

______________________________ ______________

Client Signature Date

Phase 2 Requirements

Name: ______________________________________

Staff: ____________________________________ **Date Reviewed:** __________

Review each requirement with staff and initial you understand the expectation

___ I will attend court bi-monthly at: ______________________________.

___ I will follow my treatment plan.

___ I will comply with supervision and meet weekly with my supervision officer on time. I will notify my supervision officer of any conflicts at least one hour prior to my appointment in case of an emergency.

___ I will allow law enforcement and/or supervision officers associated to the treatment court program into my residence for home visits.

___ I will submit to random urine analysis testing as determined by the treatment court team. UA testing call number: ______________________ Color: ______________

___ I will reside in a safe environment that supports my recovery. I will keep my supervision officer informed if my residency changes.

___ I start attending peer recovery groups.

___ I will develop a financial plan and follow it.

___ I will address all medical needs identified.

___ I acknowledge my curfew is at 10 p.m.

I have reviewed the requirements for phase 2 and understand my responsibilities to the treatment court program.

______________________________ ______________

Client Signature Date

Phase 3 Requirements

Name: ____

Staff: ____

Date Reviewed: ________________

Review each requirement with staff and initial you understand the expectation

___ I will attend court monthly at: ____________________________________.

___ I will follow my treatment plan.

___ I will comply with supervision and meet bi-monthly with my supervision officer on time. I will notify my supervision officer of any conflicts at least one hour prior to my appointment in case of an emergency.

___ I will allow law enforcement and/or supervision officers associated to the treatment court program into my residence for home visits.

___ I will submit to random urine analysis testing as determined by the treatment court team. UA testing call number: ______________________ Color: _____________

___ I will reside in a safe environment that supports my recovery. I will keep my supervision officer informed if my residency changes.

___ I will maintain attending peer recovery groups and establish a recovery network.

___ I will start life skills classes identified by the treatment court team.

___ I will begin a criminal thinking program.

___ I will engage in a pro-social activity.

___ I will maintain my financial plan.

___ I will address all medical needs identified.

___ I acknowledge my curfew is at 11 p.m.

I have reviewed the requirements for phase 3 and understand my responsibilities to the treatment court program.

_________________________________ ________________

Client Signature Date

Phase 4 Requirements

Name: ____

Staff: ____

Date Reviewed: ________________

Review each requirement with staff and initial you understand the expectation

___ I will attend court monthly at: ____________________________________.

___ I will follow my treatment plan.

___ I will comply with supervision and meet bi-monthly with my supervision officer on time. I will notify my supervision officer of any conflicts at least one hour prior to my appointment in case of an emergency.

___ I will allow law enforcement and/or supervision officers associated to the treatment court program into my residence for home visits.

___ I will submit to random urine analysis testing as determined by the treatment court team. UA testing call number: ______________________ Color: ____________

___ I will reside in a safe environment that supports my recovery. I will keep my supervision officer informed if my residency changes.

___ I will maintain attending peer recovery groups and my recovery network.

___ I will find employment, vocational training, or school.

___ I will continue my criminal thinking program.

___ I will maintain participating in a pro-social activity.

___ I will address ancillary services as needed (parenting classes, family support, etc.).

___ I will maintain my financial plan.

___ I will address all medical needs identified.

___ I acknowledge my curfew is at 12 a.m.

I have reviewed the requirements for phase 4 and understand my responsibilities to the treatment court program.

______________________________ ______________

Client Signature Date

Phase 5 Requirements

Name: ____

Staff: ____

Date Reviewed: ______________

Review each requirement with staff and initial you understand the expectation

___ I will attend court monthly at: ______________________________________.

___ I will follow my treatment plan and develop a continuing care plan.

___ I will comply with supervision and meet monthly with my supervision officer on time. I will notify my supervision officer of any conflicts at least one hour prior to my appointment in case of an emergency.

___ I will allow law enforcement and/or supervision officers associated to the treatment court program into my residence for home visits.

___ I will submit to random urine analysis testing as determined by the treatment court team. UA testing call number: ______________________ Color: ____________

___ I will reside in a safe environment that supports my recovery. I will keep my supervision officer informed if my residency changes.

___ I will maintain attending peer recovery groups and my recovery network.

___ I will maintain my employment, vocational training, or school.

___ I will complete my criminal thinking program.

___ I will maintain participating in a pro-social activity.

___ I will address ancillary services as needed (parenting classes, family support, etc.).

___ I will maintain my financial plan.

___ I will address all medical needs identified.

I have reviewed the requirements for phase 5 and understand my responsibilities to the treatment court program.

________________________________ ______________

Client Signature Date

Notes/Questions

1. What are the differences between the different phases? For example, what are participants doing in Phase One that is different from Phase Five?

2. A Texas judge who has started several different specialty courts in his jurisdiction (including a drug court, veteran's court and mental health court) once commented that "the big difference with the people in these courts and people who don't end up in the criminal justice system is that they never learned basic life skills. Some had parents who were addicts, or they spent their childhood in the foster system, or had parents who couldn't teach them these basic life skills, so we spend a lot of time in these specialty courts focused on the basics." He went on to say that he often sees himself in the role of the parent the participants never had. What are the life skills included in the different phases in these forms?

3. Are these requirements different from simply being on probation? How?

The next article, *A Day at the Drug Court*, gives us a fuller picture of how a court operates. Sarah Beller provides stories from actual participants in drug court.

Sarah Beller, *A Day at the Drug Court*

The Fix, March 05, 2013 available at
http://www.thefix.com/content/drug-courts91363?page=all

A mural by participants at the computer learning center of the Brooklyn Drug Treatment Court

Derrick, a thin black man in his 20s, stands handcuffed under the fluorescent lights of the Brooklyn Drug Treatment Court. A few people occupy pew-style benches in the back, awaiting their turn in the spotlight; a girl cuddles with her nervous-looking boyfriend, who is absentmindedly playing with his braids. A policeman chews gum. Derrick has been arrested on a felony charge of heroin possession; the prosecutor has agreed to offer treatment as an option, instead of prison.

Judge Jo Ann Ferdinand tells Derrick's lawyer, a public defender, "If he's interested in treatment, he needs to plead guilty to a class A possession of controlled substance in the seventh degree [a misdemeanor]."

Derrick nods and is sworn in.

"So Mr. S—, you were in possession of drugs?" she asks, almost conversationally.

"Yes."

"What was it?"

"Heroin."

"You could be sentenced to a year, but we will delay so you can enter a methadone-to-abstinence program. If you successfully complete this plan, the plea will be vacated and dismissed. Otherwise, one year in jail. Are you ready to be drug-free and law abiding?"

He blows into his hands as if he's cold. "Yes."

Bottles of Purell line Judge Ferdinand's desk. "There's no reason you can't be successful. All your criminal history is connected to drug use. Let's make your future different than your past."

For two decades, scenes like this have been playing out nationwide in more and more drug courts—state-level programs that offer treatment instead of prison to some defendants arrested on drug or drug-related felonies. (The first known drug treatment court in the US was established in Miami in 1989, in response to the crack epidemic.) Developed locally, their operations vary significantly. Defendants are diverted to drug court programs at various stages in the judicial process. And while many people arrested for non-violent offenses are eligible, prosecutors ultimately determine who gets offered the option of treatment. Participants must usually plead guilty as a prerequisite, and they're drug tested throughout treatment. Judges can reward or punish their behaviour: Incentives include certificates, cards and applause from the courtroom. Sanctions include admonishments, assigned essays, increased drug testing and court appearances, and, sometimes, a few days or weeks in jail.

This model is now fast spreading on the federal stage, where judges increasingly reject restrictions on their sentencing discretion. This year, according to the National Association of Drug Court Professionals (NADCP), 2,734 drug courts will serve about 120,000 clients in all 50 states, thanks to a "historical 250% increase in federal funding for Drug Courts this year." New York, for example, has invested heavily in this format—which is heartily backed by the Obama administration.

"Drug courts are one of the most important pieces of evidenced-based drug policy reform we have seen in generations," US drug czar Gil Kerlikowske says in an email to *The Fix*. "By providing non-violent drug offenders with a chance to reclaim their lives through treatment rather than wasting away in prison, we save lives, save taxpayer dollars, reunite families, and reduce rates of incarceration. Decades of research and experience reveal that addiction—the underlying cause of too much crime in our communities—is a disease that can be successfully treated. Drug courts are what today's discussion about drug policy should be about."

This sounds great. But do the numbers back his claims?

Yes, says the NADCP's director of communications, Chris Deutsch, whose nonprofit organization trains drug treatment court staff and advocates for drug court funding. According to the NADCP, some 75% of drug court graduates remain arrest-free for at least two years. And for every dollar invested in drug courts, taxpayers can save as much as $3.36 in avoided criminal justice costs. So what's not to like?

Plenty, argues the Drug Policy Alliance (DPA), the major advocacy group promoting progressive alternatives to the war on drugs—and its position on drug courts is broadly shared by groups such as the Justice Policy Institute and The Sentencing Project. In 2011, the DPA issued a report entitled "Drug Courts Are Not the Answer," claiming, "Drug courts have not demonstrated cost savings, reduced incarceration or improved public safety." The report attacks some of the methodology of the research cited by the NADCP, and also challenges the basic premise behind drug courts: "Combining principles of treatment and punishment distorts the delivery of effective legal and health services. Punishment will always dominate in this arrangement."

How does the NADCP aim to balance public health and criminal justice concerns? "More and more, there is widespread acceptance that addiction is a public health concern and should be treated as such," Chris Deutsch tells me. "We're moving away from trying to deal with addiction strictly through criminal justice. But there are still instances where the two intersect—and that's where drug courts exist. Addicts who are committing crimes, breaking and entering to feed an addiction, or drunk driving—how can you both have a criminal justice response and treat the addiction in the community?"

But what about people like Derrick, who enter drug court on charges of possession, not DUI? "As long as drugs are illegal, drug courts will be there for serious addicts who get arrested for crimes like possession," Deutsch says. The advantage of drug courts, compared to voluntary treatment, Deutsch continues, is that "you can keep people out of jail, but you can also use the leverage of the court to keep them in treatment long enough to be successful. People spend a year minimum—not 30 or 60 days."

In Brooklyn, the oversight of participants is intense. One man, who looks about 20, has come to court for drug testing at the state-of-the-art on-site urinalysis lab. After he tests positive for alcohol, he is sent to Judge Ferdinand for something between a reprimand and a speed-therapy session.

"What did you drink?" she asks bluntly.

"Hennessy," he says.

"You knew you had court today?"

He takes a breath: "To be honest, I need serious help. I don't know what's going on with me. I know it was stupid, but you know . . ."

"No," says Judge Ferdinand grimly. "I don't know. I really don't."

"I just need to be a stronger individual and get support, and use consequential thinking," he says, rocking gently from side to side.

"Why do you drink?" she asks.

"I don't know. I be trying hard to change. I just want to go to school. I keep sabotaging myself."

The judge turns to the defense attorney: "OK, I want to see Mr. C— here every Friday. The next positive test for alcohol I see, I want this case remanded. Good luck, Mr. C—." . . .

Mr. C— picks up his book bag and ducks out through the back door, head down.

Judge Ferdinand later tells me that she and her colleagues are trained to understand the disease model of addiction. "We recognize that drugs take away the brain's ability to hold you accountable," she says. "Relapse is part of addiction, and we try to figure out what to do about it." Courts like hers draw a distinction between relapse and non-compliance: "Relapsing but doing treatment is a treatment issue," Deutsche says. "But If they're not complying with what the court is asking them to do, we have a waiting list of people trying to get in. We sometimes say, 'we're gonna have to let you go,' though it's not an easy decision."

The DPA's director, Ethan Nadelmann, sees a "fundamental paradox" in a drug court based on the disease model. "How do you justify imprisoning people for manifesting the symptoms of their disease?" he asks me. The DPA also disputes drug courts' overwhelming use of abstinence-only programs, rather than more harm reduction. "Whether [the disease] is hypertension, diabetes or drug use, punishing people for straying from their treatment plans, falling short of treatment goals, or relapsing is contrary to core health principles," says the DPA report. The participants with the best chance of compliance are those who do not actually have an addiction, the DPA notes, while those genuinely struggling with compulsive drug use are more likely to end up in prison.

The DPA doesn't dismiss drug courts outright, but argues that they divert scarce funds from approaches that it considers more effective, like community-based treatment. This is especially important, says Nadelmann, when arrests and incarceration statistics reflect a profound race and class bias. In 2009, for example, the NYCLU reported that black people and Latinos comprise over 90% of those imprisoned in New York for drug offenses—although most users of illegal drugs were white. The figures at the Brooklyn Drug Treatment Court are similar, confirms Joseph Mandino, director of the Brooklyn Treatment Court Program: About 75–80% of their clients are black, about 15% Latino and about 10% white. "Wealthy people who struggle with addiction often can deal with it in a private setting. Poor people can often only access treatment through the criminal justice system," Nadelmann says. Even within the drug court system, according to the DPA, the disparities are striking: Black participants are at least 30% more likely than whites to be expelled from drug court.

Changes the DPA would like to see in the drug court system include pre-plea rather than post-plea entry criteria, ensuring that people like Derrick don't have to plead guilty to certain crimes—thus waiving their right to a trial—to be accepted into treatment. There's also "huge evidence" that harm reduction is effective for many people who fail at abstinence, says the DPA. The organization wants drug courts to adopt more objective admission criteria, too. But even if these adjustments were made, the DPA would ultimately prefer to see a US drug-law model more like the one in Portugal—where low-level possession of all drugs was decriminalized in 2001. "When you see Portugal succeeding," Nadelmann says, "it raises policy and moral issues about continuing to invest in a drug court approach, as opposed to the health system."

For now though, drug courts are a growing element of national drug policy. What they uniquely offer, Judge Ferdinand says, is a sanction-and-reward system and a set-up that allows clients waiting for their own session to get the message. "If the person is not complying," she says, "I immediately sanction them—they get a penalty. The other people see, 'Here's what's gonna happen to you if you don't comply.' And they also see the success stories and think, 'maybe I could do that.' There's no reason to want to stop [using] if you believe life will still be shitty after. These people need to believe that if they stop using, life will be better."

Notes/Questions

One argument for requiring defendants to plead guilty before participating in a drug court or other problem-solving court is that it gives them an incentive to comply with the requirements, as they could be sentenced to time in custody if they do not complete the requirements. The National Association of Criminal Defense Lawyers (NACDL), in their 2009 report *America's Problem-Solving Courts: The Criminal Costs of Treatment and the Case for Reform,* recommended that no defendant should have to enter a guilty plea to participate in a problem-solving court. (We and several excerpts will refer to this report over the next two chapters.) As a criminal defense lawyer, would you agree? As a prosecutor, would you agree? As a judge, would you agree? What are the advantages and disadvantages to each approach? You may want to think about whether a guilty plea should be required for participation as you start reading the next chapter.

Assume that, one month ago, two undercover police officers from the Task Force saw Sarah Jones and Reggie Mills outside a suspected Methamphetamine (meth) lab. The officers asked how much it would cost and agreed to pay $10 per baggie and bought three baggies. They gave one bag (per agreement) to Sarah and gave Reggie $30. After the transaction was complete, both Reggie and Sarah were arrested and charged with two counts each felony sales and felony possession of a controlled substance. Sarah was also charged with a misdemeanor of being under the influence of a controlled substance as the officers decided she was under the influence of meth at the time of the transaction and arrest. Two years ago, Sarah was convicted for a misdemeanor petty theft and completed probation on that offense. Reggie has a prior spousal battery arrest, but the case was dismissed (it did not involve Sarah). Reggie has one prior conviction for carrying a concealed weapon without a permit, a misdemeanor. He completed probation four years ago and did not serve time on that offense. Reggie also has a ten-year-old conviction for possession of marijuana as a juvenile, which was a misdemeanor at the time (the law has now changed and possession of the same amount would be an infraction under the current law). He was fined in that case and did not serve time.

What are the pros and cons of sending each or either of these defendants through drug court?

Another type of problem-solving court is mental health courts. These courts focus on providing mental health services to prevent the offender from committing future crimes. This next excerpt discusses the goal of mental health courts, and how judges work to help the offenders find a place in the community, rather than a jail or prison cell.

The following article is written by Aaron Levin, senior staff writer for *Psychiatry News*, who specializes in science and medicine.

Aaron Levin, *Mental Health Courts: A Strategy That Works*

Psychiatry News, Vol. 42, No. 18, p. 6, September 21, 2007

...

Criminal defendants with mental illness stay out of jail longer when they are enrolled in programs that divert them from the prison system to the mental health system.

Mental health courts offer an alternative to sending still more people with mental illness to jail. Judges, public defenders, district attorneys, case managers, therapists, probation officers, and psychiatrists together closely supervise defendants selected for these diversion programs, helping with housing, medical care, psychotherapy, education, and job training or coaching.

The goal is to prevent these defendants from committing more crimes and to help them find a place in the community. Offenders who complete the program can have charges dropped or expunged (Psychiatric News, April 21, 2006).

About 90 mental health courts operate around the country, yet little is known about the extent to which they reduce the chances of a defendant's committing another crime.

Now a study of the mental health court in San Francisco documents reduced levels of recidivism, as measured by the time to re-offending, although questions remain about what accounts for outcomes and who gets to participate in the programs.

Dale McNeil, Ph.D., a professor of clinical psychology in the Department of Psychiatry, and Renée Binder, M.D., a professor in residence in the Psychiatry and the Law Program at the University of California, San Francisco, compared 170 criminal defendants who entered the mental health court with 8,067 other offenders who received treatment as usual, consisting of passage through the criminal justice system. All subjects had been diagnosed with some mental illness, and two-thirds were charged with felonies. Defendants selected for diversion included a higher proportion of persons with developmental disabilities or severe mental illness—like schizophrenia, delusional disorder, or bipolar disorder—than the control group....

Participation in the mental health court program predicted a longer time before offenders faced any new charge or a new violent charge, wrote McNeil and Binder in the September American Journal of Psychiatry.

After at least six months of follow-up, 81 (48 percent) of the enrollees had completed the program, 45 (26 percent) were still in it, and 44 (26 percent) had left, whether voluntarily, for noncompliance, or other reasons. The mental health court graduates remained at a lower risk of recidivism even after they left the court's supervision, according to follow-up analysis.

At 18 months, mental health court participants were 26 percent less likely to be charged with any new crime and 54 percent less likely to be charged with a violent crime, they said (see chart).

Their findings, said McNeil and Binder, "provide evidence of the potential for mental health courts to achieve their goal of reducing recidivism among people with mental disorders who are in the criminal justice system."

Furthermore, since many defendants in the San Francisco program were charged with violent crimes or felonies, results with this more-difficult population argued for expanding the use of mental health courts beyond individuals who have committed minor offenses, as is the case in some other areas, they said.

Other studies have shown that outcomes vary little between violent and nonviolent offenders or for those diagnosed with more severe illness, said mental health court

Mental Health Courts Reduce Recidivism

Defendant's participation in mental health court was found to reduce the average likelihood of any new charges being filed. Violence was uncommon in the mental health court participants and other defendants, but new violent charges were less likely with participation.

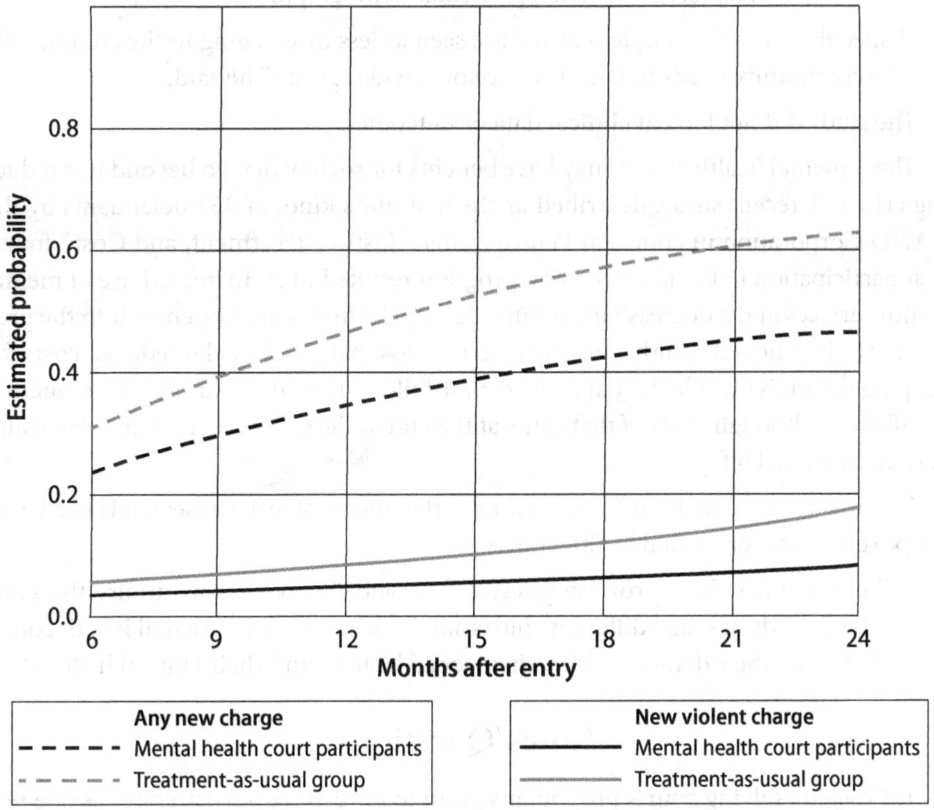

Source: Dale McNeil, Renée Binder, *American Journal of Psychiatry*, September 2007

expert Henry Steadman, Ph.D., of Policy Research Associates in Delmar, N.Y., in an interview with Psychiatric News. "No research shows that a particular type of person does more poorly."

Steadman directed a study of 21 mental health court programs sponsored by the Substance Abuse and Mental Health Services Administration. He found that 42,518 screenings, assessments, and evaluations resulted in 32,917 decisions about whether to divert them to a treatment program. Only 2,001 of those decisions recommended diversion to mental health courts, and 1,237 of those were accepted by judges.

Although many decisions were needed to divert a few individuals, ultimately, disproportionate groupings by age, race, and gender predicted those chosen to take part.

Enrollees were more likely to be older, white, and female, wrote Steadman in the study published in the August Psychiatric Services. "That could represent bias, or it could result from the mechanism of assessment."

An array of people feed information into the system, he said—prosecutors, judges, mental health experts, public health nurses in the jails—making it hard to tease out the source of any overrepresentation of a particular demographic.

"I speculate that the people selected are seen as less threatening to the community, but the community needs to take a chance on a wider group," he said.

The study did not look at clinical data or outcomes.

These mental health courts may have benefits for society that go beyond just reducing crime. A recent study, described as the first of its kind, of 352 defendants by the RAND Corporation in courts in Pennsylvania, "Justice, Treatment, and Cost," found that participation in the jail-diversion program resulted in an increased use of mental health services and a decrease in jail time during the first year after entry into the program. Higher mental health care costs were almost balanced by the reduced costs for keeping the individual locked up. A two-year follow-up found a "dramatic" reduction in jail costs, although most of that came at the end of the second year, as mental health care costs leveled off.

Steadman agreed with McNeil and Binder that more intensive research is needed to support the case for mental health courts.

"All case studies show promising results," he said. "Now we need to use the same research methods in many different courts and look at for whom mental health courts work. What are their demographics, their social history, and their clinical history?"

Notes/Questions

1. Problem-solving courts proponents point to lowered recidivism rates as one reason to support the continued use of these courts. However, the numbers are widely variable. *See* Bryanna Fox et al., *Assessing the Effect of Mental Health Court on Adult and Juvenile Recidivism: A Meta-Analysis*, 46 Am. J. Crim. Just. 644 (2021), finding that mental health courts lower recidivism by 74%. Consider why might some programs report reductions as low as 5% and other types of courts seem to have much higher rates.

2. Are there other measures that we should be using to analyze these problem-solving courts? Does a lower reduction in recidivism mean the court is not working as well? As you continue reading you may want to think about the variety of factors that can play into whether a particular problem-solving court has a better or worse recidivism rate. For example, see Hadar Dancig-Rosenberg & Tal Gal, *Success Stories in Community Courts: Listening to Participants' Voices*, 25 Cardozo Journal of Conflict Resolution 255 (2023), for a qualitative study examining how participants in problem-solving courts find success and outlining ideas for building on this achievement in the future.

Here is an example of taking these problem-solving courts and applying it in a different context, namely, gambling treatment court.

> At first glance, Justice Mark G. Farrell's docket looked like a broad array of small-time crime, filled with offenses like petty larceny, attempted burglary, and check forgery. The one thing these crimes have in common is the offenders' motivation—money to gamble.
>
> This is the norm in the country's first gambling treatment court in Amherst, NY. This gambling treatment court follows the model of many other treatment courts that have begun in the U.S. in recent years. The participants are able to avoid jail time by following a court-supervised program, including counseling sessions, credit checks, and twice-monthly meetings with Justice Farrell.
>
> This problem-solving court demonstrates the ability for this concept to be applied to many different types of crimes, allowing a more holistic approach to offender treatment and subsequent punishment. By giving criminals the tools to work through addictions that have led to crime, the goal is to avoid reoffending and encourage offenders to abide by conditions of probation or parole and continue with good behavior to avoid jail time.
>
> Ken Belson, *Stressing Help, Not Penalties, In Gambling Treatment Court*, N.Y. Times, May 01, 2007.

Another growing area of problem-solving courts is the creation of veterans' courts throughout the United States. There are many resources available for existing courts to develop their own veterans courts within their own court system. For example, the website "Justice for Vets" (https://justiceforvets.org/) has a vast array of online videos, documents, and forms that can be utilized across the country to create uniformity within these veterans' courts. Some of the Justice for Vets forms, which are essentially the forms also used by the National Association of Drug Court Professionals (which appear earlier in this chapter to give you an idea of the program requirements and the process that must be followed for successful completion of the program).

The next excerpt in this section is a portion of the policy brief from the Texas Public Policy Foundation discussing the emergence of veterans' courts and the need for specialized treatment of veterans.

Center for Effective Justice, *Texas Public Policy Foundation, Veterans Are Frequently Incarcerated*

Policy Brief, November 2009

...

The Bureau of Justice Statistics found in a 2000 survey—the most recent information available—that 12.5 percent of state prison inmates reported military service. Similarly, 11.7 percent of county jail inmates reported military service. All told, more than 200,000 veterans are behind bars. Of veterans in state prisons, 30 percent were first-time offenders, compared to 23 percent of non-veterans. Veterans were more likely to have a history of alcohol dependence than non-veterans. Of veteran inmates, 30.6 percent reported alcohol dependence compared with 23.6 percent of non-veterans.

Additionally, 70 percent of veterans in state prisons were employed prior to being arrested, compared with 54 percent of non-veterans. Veterans behind bars were more likely to be mentally ill, with 19.3 percent reporting mental illness compared with 15.8 percent of nonveterans. More than three-quarters of veterans behind bars were honorably discharged.

What Are Veterans' Courts? These courts are similar to drug and mental health courts. Not all veterans are, or should be, eligible and these courts don't let offenders off the hook simply because they are veterans. Rather, these courts hold them accountable through a strict schedule of court appearances and treatment appointments, and, if necessary, sanctions imposed by the judge that can include jail time. Some courts also utilize probation officers to ensure the offender is properly monitored.

Typically, only misdemeanants and, in some cases, non-violent felons are eligible for a veterans' court. The veterans' court in Orange County, California is limited to mentally ill offenders. In the veterans' court being created in El Paso, Texas (home to 20,000 soldiers), participants must have a service-related disability such as primary diagnosis of post-traumatic stress disorder (PTSD), traumatic brain injury, or severe depression. Eligible offenses will include marijuana possession and family altercations. The El Paso court will have the authority to require participants to attend rehabilitation, educational, vocational, medical, psychiatric, or substance-abuse programs. Like drug courts, rather than issue a sentence and move to the next case, a judge holds regular hearings to monitor the offender's progress through treatment and compliance with the terms of probation. The El Paso court is actually a docket of an existing court so there is not an expense associated with creating a new court, and the county expects to save money on jail costs.

Notes/Questions

1. Do veterans need a special court? Why not include them in a general drug court or mental health court? The shared experience of military service can provide a useful peer group for the recovery process. Veterans, who have completed their service hon-

orably, are also eligible for benefits that may help them to access mental health care that may not be available to other defendants.

2. Do veterans deserve a special court due to their service to the United States? Some veterans suffer from mental illness (such as post-traumatic stress disorder) and drug addiction due to their military service. Does this mean the criminal legal system should treat them differently from other defendants who commit crimes?

II. Why Does This Work? (Or What Is the Theory Behind These Courts?)

This next section turns to the understanding of science and psychology of addiction and mental health as it relates to these courts. Many individuals with patterns of criminal behavior often have underlying mental health conditions, addictions, or both, that have gone untreated which has led to the rise in specialty courts that aim to treat these conditions before or during the offender's criminal punishment.

David M. Eagleman, Mark A. Correro & Jyotpal Singh, *Why Neuroscience Matters for Rational Drug Policy*

11 Minn. J.L. Sci. & Tech., 7–15, 19–20, 26 (2010)

I. INTRODUCTION

Drug addiction is an ancient problem for society, leading to crime, diminished productivity, mental illness, disease transmission, and a burgeoning prison population. According to the Bureau of Justice Statistics, nearly seven out of ten jail inmates met the criteria for substance abuse or dependence in the year before their admission. One study found that 35.6% of convicted jail inmates were under the influence at the time of their criminal offense. The cost to society of drug abuse has been estimated at $180.9 billion, of which $107.8 billion is derived from drug-related crime. The linkage between drug abuse and crime has been thoroughly established elsewhere. Promising new developments relating to emerging knowledge and technologies may provide a bridge between the failed policies of the past and novel solutions in the future. Drug addiction is rooted in the biology of the brain, and society's best hope for breaking addiction lies in new ideas for rehabilitation, not in repeated incarceration.

The past two decades have witnessed remarkable progress in understanding the neural basis of drug addiction. Chronic drug use leads to enduring physical changes in the structure of the brain, and these are thought to undermine what we understand as voluntary control. Drug addiction manifests itself as an irrepressible drive to take a drug despite its undesirable consequences. For decades it was thought that drug addiction resulted from physical dependence on the drug; because withdrawal symptoms could be serious, even life-threatening, drug addiction was thought to be the same as physical dependence. By contrast, a new way of thinking suggests that drug addiction is more than dependence; it is the result of a reconfiguration of the circuitry of the reward and decision-making systems, leading to increased cravings and diminished impulse control. In other words, addiction may be reasonably viewed as a neurological problem that allows for medical remedies, just as pneumonia may be viewed as an affliction of the lungs that allows for the same. As we progress in our understanding of the underlying circuitry of addiction, how that circuitry leads to drives, and how drugs hijack and reregulate that circuitry, we have the opportunity to leverage that understanding into more effective drug policy that rests on treatment rather than punishment.

Part II briefly reviews the extent of the drug addiction problem in the United States and describes where American drug policy has fallen short in its attempts to move from punishment toward rehabilitation. Part III reviews the modern neuroscientific understanding of reward and addiction, building the argument that treating addiction requires an understanding of the neural mechanisms involved in reward systems, craving, and impulse control. Given the growing biological understanding of addiction, we argue that science must play a critical role in reforming drug policy....

II. WHAT TO DO ABOUT DRUG ADDICTS?

A. Historical Tensions Between Punishment and Rehabilitation

For centuries, societies have grappled with complex ethical questions about how to deal with drug addicts. In Robinson v. California, Justice Douglas wrote that an approach of moral condemnation "continues as respects drug addicts.... [T]hose living in a world of black and white put the addict in the category of those who could, if they would, forsake their evil ways." Rather than looking at drug addiction as a scientific and medical phenomenon, many continue to cast the issue in moral terms. It is perhaps not surprising that the criminal justice system has generally used retributive justice to deal with addicts, much like it once did for the mentally ill. The retributive stance generally extols "just deserts" and diminishes rehabilitative attempts, even those guided firmly by physiological understandings of the underlying pathologies. Nevertheless, rehabilitative efforts have made meaningful appearances throughout the twentieth century....

In 1962, the Supreme Court found unconstitutional a California statute that made addiction a crime. The statute stated that "[n]o person shall ... be addicted to the use of narcotics...." Rather than criminalizing conduct, the California statute mandated a minimum ninety day jail sentence based on a person's status as an addict. In striking down the statute, the Court reasoned that addiction is a physiological condition requiring treatment rather than punishment.

By the late 1960s, however, the failure of science to find biological solutions for addiction led to increased skepticism about rehabilitation in the Supreme Court. In 1968, the Court rejected Leroy Powell's argument that alcoholism excused him from being drunk in public. Powell argued that his public intoxication was not volitional and, therefore, punishing him for it was cruel and unusual. The psychiatrist who testified in the case acknowledged that there was no medical consensus over a definition of alcoholism or whether alcoholism was a disease; however, he asserted that the defendant, as a "chronic alcoholic" was "not able to control his behavior." But the Court found his argument a stretch because it went "much too far on the basis of too little knowledge." At that time, there existed a lack of effective treatment options and consensus regarding treatment efficacy. Moreover, treatment facilities and trained providers were scarce. Finally, without adequate treatment and facilities, a civilly committed addict could be held indefinitely without being criminally confined due to the fact that he had virtually no chance of being successfully rehabilitated. Finding no viable treatment alternatives, the Court concluded that criminal process was still necessary.

The 1970s heralded the "era of harsh prison sentences." Between 1972 and 2000, the incarcerated population grew to more than two million. According to recent studies, the "sharp rise in incarceration for drug-related offenses" directly fueled this increase. This trend was further driven by societal problems in the 1980s, the crack cocaine epidemic began, and with it came the "War on Drugs." The role of crack was implicated by researchers in the rise of violence and crime, leading to calls for longer prison sentences and cleaning up of the streets.

By the 1990s, the trend began to shift back toward rehabilitation. In 1990, President George H.W. Bush and Congress officially designated the 1990s as the "Decade of the Brain." In parallel with the acceptance and developments of neuroscience, the shift from a retributive criminal policy toward a more rehabilitative stance has continued. Recent government and American Bar Association data bear out this trend, with examples coming from jurisdictions across the United States. The American Bar Association's 2007 recommendations demonstrate this shift. Currently, programs across the nation are shifting from retribution to rehabilitation. Promising changes such as the increased use of drug courts, civil commitments, community-supervised treatment programs, and other rehabilitative strategies are beginning to supplant the old focus on incarceration. Neuroscience is critical to this new wave of treatment and rehabilitation.

Now, at the dawn of the twenty-first century, the decades-long demand for punishment is straining the criminal justice system. Recidivism rates are high. In fact, "more than two-thirds of those being released from prison [are] rearrested within three years of release, and 42% of parolees [are] returning to prison or jail within 24 months of their release...." This prison exodus means that 650,000 prisoners are temporarily returning to their communities every year. Do addicts benefit from their incarceration? If not, can we do more to enhance treatment outcomes and potentially reduce the future societal costs? Rather than cataloging addiction's cost to society, new neuroscientific developments illuminate knowledge and technologies that provide a bridge between the doctrinal literature about criminal punishment and new treatment solutions for the future.

B. Scientific Explanations of Behavior

Many people share a concern about incorporating scientific explanations for behavioral problems into the law, and this may stem in part from historical misuse. As Zedi and Goodenough state:

> Incorporating biology into legal doctrine is ... problematic. To the extent that biological approaches had been included in the great arguments of the twentieth century between fascism, communism, capitalism, socialism, dictatorship and liberal democracy, they often wore a distorted and appropriately discredited aspect that had more to do with political expediency than with any accurate application of the admittedly limited science of the times.

Considering recent history, apprehension to the use of science in making social policy is justified. "But that biology should have been thus misused in the past is not a good reason for not taking account of its findings in the future, always of course with appropriate safeguards."

A second concern, also shared by many, is that a neuroscientific understanding may exculpate criminals, allowing them to "blame their brains" for their behavior. Most people believe that there is some sense in which criminals should be held responsible for their actions, irrespective of the states of their brains, and therefore the idea of exculpation is unpalatable. We suggest that this belief does not need to be a concern. Societies will continue to remove dangerous people from the streets. Explanation does not equal exculpation; instead it can equal rational sentencing and customized rehabilitation. Rehabilitative treatments remove the threat addicts pose to innocent people and save society the associated costs that would be incurred were the addicts incarcerated. In this respect, a consequentialist or utilitarian approach may be more effective and less expensive than retribution and punishment. The ultimate issue, then, from a scientific perspective, is not how the criminal justice system can exact revenge for an evil act, but, instead, whether the underlying problem can be fixed through utilization of what is known of the neuroscience of addiction so that neither the addict nor the next victim has to suffer.

We suggest that the most fruitful path is to forego the arguments of responsibility in favor of concentrating neuroscientific efforts on rehabilitation. The onus is on neuroscience to prove that it has something to offer. If it can, then the legal system can act accordingly to leverage those assets. In this article we review the neuroscientific understanding of addiction and propose new treatments for breaking addiction and the consequent cycles of incarceration. In this paper we illustrate how neuroscience can back up its claims of addiction as a biological problem and bring actionable solutions to the table....

B. Why the Science Should Shape the Policy

The United States has a history of combating the drug problem with increased law enforcement rather than customized intervention and rehabilitation. For years, experts have weighed in on this topic and come to similar conclusions about current drug policy. One author has stated: "[D]rug treatment programs remain notoriously underfunded, turning away tens of thousands of addicts seeking help even as increasing billions of dollars are spent to arrest, prosecute, and imprison illegal drug sellers and users." Another author approached the issue in this way: "The investment of more than 70% of the federal [U.S.] drug control money into supply reduction seems misplaced ...

[c]urtailing the supply of demanded drugs has been compared to squeezing a balloon: constrict it in one place and it expands somewhere else."

In light of the current science, it would appear there is a better strategy for combating the drug trade: instead of concentrating on controlling the supply, concentrate on controlling the demand. Below we will consider biologically-based strategies for addressing demand—those strategies that are currently in use, and some that are on the horizon. The new frameworks remove the emphasis on punishment in favor of reducing craving while strengthening impulse control....

IV. CONCLUSION

Drug addiction reflects abnormal operation of normal neural circuitry. More than physical dependence, addiction represents changes in the brain that lead to increased craving and diminished capacity for the control of impulses. Given the growing biological understanding of addiction, it is critical for scientists to play an active role in drug policy. As neuroscientific understanding develops, we will, to a much greater degree, be able to target specific behavioral, pharmaceutical, and neurological treatments for specific addictions. It is important to emphasize that biological explanation will not somehow become equivalent to exculpation. Instead, the goal of explanation is to introduce rational sentencing and the opportunity for customized rehabilitation. This approach is likely to show more utility and less cost than incarceration. The neuroscientific community should continue to develop rehabilitative strategies so that the legal community can take advantage of those strategies for a rational, customized approach to drug addiction.

Notes/Questions

1. Given what we understand about the science of addiction, should drug addicts be charged with crimes or handled in some other way?

2. The 2009 NACDL report on problem-solving courts recommended against continuing to treat drug cases in the criminal legal system and instead recommended that drug addiction be treated as a public health problem. Would you agree with this approach if the crime were drug possession? What if it were drug sales? What if it were theft to support a drug habit? And would it matter to you what type of drug? What if it is abuse of prescription medication? Or heroin? Or PCP? Or cocaine? Would you advocate treating every drug the same? What about marijuana?

***

As you continue reading this chapter, consider the implications that neuroscience may have on the practice of law, including the development of problem-solving courts, in the coming decades as the science continues to evolve and develop.

The next article is an additional excerpt from Bruce Winick's article. We read at the beginning how the role of judges works in these courts. Now that you have learned about the varieties of these courts, it is useful to understand the thinking behind them. This excerpt focuses on therapeutic jurisprudence and explains the underlying theories of how problem-solving courts can work.

Bruce J. Winick, *Therapeutic Jurisprudence and Problem Solving Courts*

30 Fordham Urb. L.J. 1055, 1062–1066 (2002)

...

II. THERAPEUTIC JURISPRUDENCE AS A THEORETICAL FOUNDATION FOR PROBLEM SOLVING COURTS

The problem solving courts' revolution has been largely atheoretical. It grew out of experimental approaches used in drug treatment courts to facilitate the substance abuse treatment process, which, because of their success, were transplanted into other judicial arenas. These programs appear to be successful, although the empirical research on their efficacy remains preliminary and often methodologically flawed. Why these programs seem to work, however, has remained largely unexamined.

Therapeutic jurisprudence can be seen as a theoretical grounding for this developing judicial movement. We can understand the problem solving courts' revolution by situating it within the scholarly and law reform approach known as therapeutic jurisprudence. Therapeutic jurisprudence began in the late 1980s as an interdisciplinary scholarly approach in the area of mental health law. It criticized various aspects of mental health law for producing antitherapeutic consequences for the people that the law was designed to help.

Legal rules and the way they are applied are social forces that produce inevitable, and sometimes negative, consequences for the psychological well-being of those affected. Therapeutic jurisprudence's basic insight was that scholars should study those consequences and reshape and redesign law in order to accomplish two goals—to minimize antitherapeutic effects, and when it is consistent with other legal goals, to increase law's therapeutic potential. Thus, therapeutic jurisprudence is an interdisciplinary approach to legal scholarship that has a law reform agenda. Although it started in the area of mental health law, therapeutic jurisprudence soon spread to other areas of legal analysis, and has emerged as a mental health approach to law generally.

Therapeutic jurisprudence is not only concerned with measuring the therapeutic impact of legal rules and procedures, but also of the way they are applied by various legal actors—judges, lawyers, police officers, and expert witnesses testifying in court, among others. Whether they know it or not, these legal actors are therapeutic agents, affecting the mental health and psychological wellbeing of the people they encounter in the legal setting. For example, how lawyers deal with their clients in the law office and the courtroom can have a significant impact on a client's emotional well-being, and therapeutic jurisprudence has spawned a growing literature concerning how attorneys should act in this regard.

In a similar way, therapeutic jurisprudence has much to offer judges concerning how they treat the people appearing before them and courts concerning how they should be structured and administered to maximize their therapeutic potential. Therapeutic jurisprudence uses insights from psychology and the behavioral sciences to critique legal and judicial practices, and to suggest how they can be reshaped to increase their therapeutic potential and avoid the risk of psychological harm.

Therapeutic jurisprudence is one of the major "vectors" of a growing movement in the law towards a common goal of a more comprehensive, humane, and psychologically optimal way of handling legal matters. Problem solving courts are also one of these "vectors," and thus, share many common aims with therapeutic jurisprudence. Thus, one may see problem solving courts as related to therapeutic jurisprudence, but they are not identical with the concept. Problem solving courts often use principles of therapeutic jurisprudence to enhance their functioning. Indeed, the Conference of Chief Justices and the Conference of State Court Administrators, following a joint task force analysis, recently adopted a resolution approving the growing movement in the direction of problem solving courts, and their use of principles of therapeutic jurisprudence in performing their functions. These principles include "integration of treatment services with judicial case processing, ongoing judicial intervention, close monitoring of and immediate response to behavior, multidisciplinary involvement, and collaboration with community-based and governmental organizations."

Although problem solving courts developed separately from therapeutic jurisprudence, their development occurred at the same time, and they share similar aims. Drug treatment courts, domestic violence courts, and mental health courts, for example, can be seen as taking a therapeutic jurisprudence approach to the processing of cases, inasmuch as their goal is the rehabilitation of the offender and their use of the legal process, in particular, the role of the judge, to accomplish this goal. All of these courts seek to deal with the offender's underlying problem, and emphasize its resolution through the provision of treatment and rehabilitative services where the judge is an important member of the treatment team. Judges in these specialized courts receive special training in the nature and treatment of drug addiction, domestic violence, and mental illness, and themselves function as therapeutic agents through their supervision and monitoring of the offender's treatment progress. Unlike traditional judges functioning in traditional courts, judges in problem solving courts consciously view themselves as therapeutic agents, and, therefore, one can see them as playing a therapeutic jurisprudence function in their dealings with the individuals who appear before them.

Moreover, principles of therapeutic jurisprudence can help problem solving court judges play this function well. Therapeutic jurisprudence has already produced a large body of interdisciplinary scholarship analyzing principles of psychology and the behavioral sciences, and probing the ways in which they can be used in legal contexts to improve mental health and emotional well-being. A growing body of therapeutic jurisprudence scholarship has also addressed how judges in specialized problem solving courts can apply principles of therapeutic jurisprudence in their work. For instance, a recent symposium issue of Court Review, the official publication of the American Judges Association, was devoted entirely to therapeutic jurisprudence and its application to judging. An understanding of therapeutic jurisprudence's approach and of the psychological and social work principles it uses can thus provide considerable help in the structuring of problem solving courts and in defining the role played by judges functioning within them.

Both therapeutic jurisprudence and problem solving courts see the law as an instrument for helping people, particularly those with a variety of psychological and emotional problems. Our society has not done a particularly good job of dealing with many social problems, with the result that society often dumps them at the doorstep of the courthouse. When courts deal with such vexing problems as drug addiction, alcoholism, domestic violence, mental illness, child abuse and neglect, and juvenile delinquency, they can be seen to function as psychosocial agencies. In order for problem solving courts to succeed and function well, however, they need to be aware of some basic principles of psychology and social work. Thus, therapeutic jurisprudence can be understood as providing a theoretical foundation for much of the problem solving court movement, and a variety of principles that can help judges play this new and exciting role.

III. Does This Work in Practice?

These last articles begin to address the question of whether these courts actually achieve their goals of treating the offender's addiction and mental health conditions while still providing justice for crimes committed.

Richard C. Boldt, *The "Tomahawk" and the "Healing Balm": Drug Treatment Courts in Theory and Practice*

10 U. Md. L.J. Race, Rel., Gender and Class 45, 46–50, 56–60, 63–64, 67–69 (2010)

...

Given the association between substance misuse and offending, success in drug treatment appears to have a measurable impact on lowering crime rates. Persons who enter into a sustained period of abstinence from (or substantially lower rates of) substance misuse tend to have reduced levels of criminal offending and fewer involvements in the criminal system. These data thus suggest that interventions that effectively reduce alcohol and other drug use disorders are likely to have a beneficial impact on the incidence of crime, on rates of incarceration, and on public safety....

More than eighty percent of drug-abusing offenders resume drug use within one year of release from prison, and well over ninety percent do so within three years. Even offenders who have received drug abuse treatment while incarcerated tend to exhibit a high rate of relapse, and those who receive no transitional care upon release appear to do no better than other drug abusing ex-offenders who receive no treatment while in prison....

According to some research, three months of participation in drug treatment ordinarily is the minimum threshold for producing positive results, and twelve months in treatment may be the median point in the distribution of outcomes.... More than 2,000 drug courts now operate throughout the U.S. and in a number of other countries.... In a recent essay entitled, "The Verdict on Adult Drug Courts," longtime drug court watcher, Douglas Marlowe, reported on the results of five meta-analyses of adult drug treatment courts. Marlowe concluded that the meta-analyses, which encompassed scores of empirical evaluations of these courts, showed that "drug courts significantly reduce crime by an average of approximately 8% to 26%, with most estimates falling around 14%." Another recent report, issued by the Sentencing Project, also found support in the research data for the conclusion that drug courts produce reduced rates of either re-arrest or re-conviction relative to control groups of substance misusing offenders processed through the traditional criminal system, although the averages reported in this study were in the eight to thirteen percent range. The Sentencing Project authors warned, however, that "there is some reason to be cautious when interpreting these results." The basis for their caution is interesting, and worth quoting at length: Some studies show little or no impact from drug court participation and it can be difficult to specify which components of the program or the research design may be contributing to these results. For example, are the evaluation models appropriately specifying relevant factors that may impact outcomes, but are external to the treatment design? Gender, age, race, socioeconomic background, criminal history, and substance abuse history have all been shown to impact treatment outcomes. Many of these variables are not accounted for in analyses of drug court effectiveness. Operationalizing drug court variables can be difficult and outcome measures may be reflecting the interaction of these variables with the treatment modality....

These data, then, support the conclusion that some treatment courts can be efficacious for some participants, which is a different claim than the more ambitious conclusion that this model is effective generally. With respect to virtually all of the outcome studies, the reports are comparative and the absolute rates of reoffending are still extremely high. In addition, the positive results with respect to recidivism hold only for those participants who have completed the program; those who drop out recidivate at a rate comparable to persons in the control groups....

After collecting data at the three-year mark from a group of participants in the Baltimore Drug Treatment Courts and a randomized control group, these researchers concluded that "with the exception of welfare status, the positive effects of the drug treatment courts do not extend to the broader set of outcomes claimed by advocates," including employment status and family and social functioning....

The RAND evaluators reported that frequently encountered problems included: a lack of regular and formalized communication between court personnel and treatment providers; inadequate case management resources; a lack of resources to support needed residential treatment and nursing services; ongoing tensions between the "supervision and rehabilitation objectives" of the program; and persistent pressure to process a large number of clients, which often exceeded the treatment providers' clinical capacity....

The RAND report concludes that "many treatment programs utilized by drug treatment court programs may not be delivering the best treatment to clients," and that "more attention" should be given "to the type and quality of treatment services." The limited access of many drug courts to residential treatment facilities and to specialized services for women, persons with co-occurring mental illnesses and others with special needs is a significant shortcoming. The Sentencing Project's analysis reports a shortage of treatment slots for women, observing that women are "likely to have to wait twice as long as men for an open treatment slot." In addition, many drug courts have chosen not to work with methadone maintenance programs and other treatment providers who use opiate-replacement medications, despite the fact that overwhelming evidence suggests that a segment of the client population who do not respond to other forms of treatment benefit from these kinds of pharmacological interventions. Indeed, methadone maintenance treatment consistently has been demonstrated to reduce drug use and criminal activity among opiate addicts far more effectively than other forms of drug-free outpatient therapy....

Even in instances where clients gain access to appropriate rehabilitative services and experience treatment successes, their long-term prognosis may depend substantially on their ability to hold a job and maintain stable family relationships. Because federal and state laws restrict people with drug convictions from public housing, prevent them from qualifying for certain occupational licenses, and impose a variety of other barriers on full community participation, and because many employers ask about convictions and make job decisions based on past criminal records, the drug conviction alone may, as one expert has put it, "condemn drug court graduates to failure."...

[T]he reintegrative shaming approach suggested by Braithwaite links this initial certification event with an eventual termination ceremony intended to decertify that deviance and return the offender to his or her community. In between these certification and decertification events, the theory calls upon designated actors within the immediate community to convey to the offender their disapproval of his or her transgressive conduct, but to do so within a developing relationship of respect and social interconnectedness. Finally, the theory insists that these expressions of disapproval should be directed at the offender's conduct and not at the offender himself or herself....

Finally, Miethe, Lu, and Reese report that the goal of reconnecting drug court participants to their families and other social support networks was ill-served in many cases by the concrete interactions that took place in the drug court process. They explain that the effort to increase offenders' embeddedness in social institutions and interdependencies through repeated contact with court officials, and in particular the judge, failed to produce the expected results. It is theoretically sound that requiring offenders to meet with the judge frequently and making the judge serve multiple roles of court official, social worker, and psychologist will enhance the relationship between the offender and the judge and, consequently, improve the offender's rehabilitation. In reality, our field research shows that offenders do not generally regard court officials, including the judge, as persons they highly respect. We also found only a few instances in our field observations in which the judge encouraged greater family interdependencies by telling family members to help the defendants "keep up the treatment." Hence, the effect of reintegrative shaming is necessarily reduced....

The moral disapprobation that attends drug misuse complicates efforts to provide supportive, reintegrative treatment within the context of the criminal blaming system. This stigma has undermined the adoption of a harm minimization philosophy of the sort that informs practice in the drug treatment courts established in a number of other countries. As Zimring and Hawkins have put it, the moralism of the legalist school drives a conception of drug treatment "in which the participants are forced or frightened into treatment programs and threatened into abstinence during and after treatment." One astute observer who has written a comparative study of drug courts in the U.S. and elsewhere has explained that "[t]he goal of most U.S. drug courts is 'total abstinence' or what some have referred to as 'demand reduction.'" By contrast, in many other jurisdictions the abstinence model has given way to a harm minimization approach in which the goals of the program are defined in terms of reduced use and reduced offending....

Given the procedural informality of drug courts, this discretionary judicial decision making carries the potential for real harm. The National Association of Criminal Defense Lawyers reports that "[t]he sentences in many courts are significantly higher for those who seek drug treatment and fail than for those who simply avoid drug treatment and take a plea, at the both the misdemeanor and felony level." In some instances these harsher sentences are built into the process, while in others they reflect an effort on the part of the drug court judge to "set an example" for other participants or are merely an expression of the fact that the judge is "offended at failure in drug court."

* * *

A more recent analysis dives into the continuing challenges of problem-solving courts.

Erin Collins, *The Problem of Problem-Solving Courts*

54 UC Davis L. Rev. 1573 (2021)

Introduction

A common response to the persistent problem of the overburdened criminal court system is to create a specialized, or "problem-solving," court to focus on a particular type of offense or offender. In the thirty years since the first modern problem-solving court—the drug court—opened its doors, the problem-solving court movement has gained tremendous momentum. There are now more than 4,000 specialized courts throughout the country dedicated to an ever-expanding roster of issues, which currently includes mental health courts, veterans courts, human trafficking courts, re-entry courts, and opioid intervention courts, along with many others. And while this reform method emerged as a state-court innovation, there is growing interest in expanding its presence in the federal arena. For example, the President's Commission on Combatting Drug Addiction and the Opioid Crisis recommended in 2017 that every federal district court establish a drug court and that the Department of Justice "urge states to establish drug courts in every county." And President Biden has expressed his support for drug courts.

A survey of problem-solving court literature leaves little doubt as to why this reform has become so popular. Problem-solving courts purport to harness proven, "evidence-based" practices to address the underlying problems that lead to repeated interactions with the criminal justice system. By doing so, they promise to reduce recidivism and save money. What's more, these laudatory claims are backed with data. And they are even enshrined in legislation and reiterated in judicial opinions. Nebraska, for example, has declared that "problem-solving courts, including drug, veterans, mental health, driving under the influence, reentry, and other problem-solving courts, are effective in reducing recidivism...." In short: problem-solving courts work.

However, the empirical landscape of problem-solving court efficacy is more complicated than most proponents acknowledge. What is perhaps the most striking about problem-solving courts is how little we actually know about their impact. With the exception of drug courts, which have been the subject of great empirical scrutiny, other types of specialized courts have not been rigorously assessed. And the data regarding drug courts does not actually tell the unmitigated success story their proponents recite. For example, a recent analysis of drug court evaluations found "mixed" results. Some studies showed drug courts reduced recidivism (at "modest" levels), while others indicated they had no impact on recidivism, and one even found they increased recidivism rates. And a recent Federal Judicial Center study found that participation in the federal re-entry courts (which are essentially post-incarceration drug courts) produced no statistically significant difference in recidivism rates for court participants. It concluded that the reentry court model "cannot be said to be a cost-effective method for reducing revocation and recidivism."

Thus, much of the available data about problem-solving court performance undermines or at least tempers the unqualified claims that this is an effective and efficient reform mechanism. Nevertheless, the problem-solving court movement not only persists, but also appears to be gaining momentum. While this reform has been spreading across the country for thirty years, much of the growth has occurred over the last decade. For example, as of 2012, there were approximately 1,300 drug courts nationwide, and more than 3,400 by 2020.

What explains this disjuncture between the actual data on problem-solving court performance and the sustained—and growing—enthusiasm for this purportedly data-driven practice? Part of the answer, which has been explored in existing scholarly analyses, undoubtedly lies in how the rhetoric (if not the practice) of problem-solving justice aligns with the growing consensus that we should use data-driven practices to ration scarce carceral resources. Indeed, problem-solving courts embody the current "neo rehabilitative" impulse in criminal justice reform, which seeks to selectively revive the rehabilitative ideal for those individuals deemed sufficiently low-risk for, or deserving of, non-carceral punishment without sacrificing traditional principles of accountability or judicial authority.

This Article identifies another answer to this question by looking beyond the rhetoric and examining the courts themselves. Specifically, it focuses on the role of the problem-solving court judges in creating and sustaining this reform movement. It argues that problem-solving courts persist in part because they revive a sense of purpose and authority for judges in an era marked by diminishing judicial power. In other words, one factor that explains the growth of problem-solving courts is their positive impact on judges. Indeed, while much of the data about problem-solving court efficacy is ambiguous or inconsistent, one metric of success seems clear: judges like them. Problem-solving court judges describe presiding over these courts as the most rewarding and satisfying experiences of their careers. And they report higher job satisfaction than judges in traditional court assignments and are more likely to report that their court assignment has a "positive emotional effect" on them.

This insight helps resolve the puzzle posed above. If a primary impetus for the rise of problem-solving courts is judicial satisfaction, whether the courts actually reduce recidivism or save money is of no moment. In other words, problem-solving courts do effectively solve a problem—it is just not the problem we think.

That judges reap professional and personal benefits from presiding over a problem-solving court is not, on its own, troubling. But it becomes so in light of another dynamic this Article uncovers—problem-solving courts are largely unregulated institutions. Despite the voluminous scholarly interest in problem-solving courts, scant attention has been paid to how or whether the courts are regulated. This Article fills that gap, demonstrating that the judges themselves often wield tremendous power over these courts, deciding whether they will open in the first place and how they will operate.

Thus, those who find much satisfaction in this court process also play a central role in creating and sustaining these institutions. As a result, they have become self-reinforcing institutions that are protected from meaningful external scrutiny. Examining problem-solving courts from this new perspective raises new questions and concerns about their propriety. First, it casts doubt on what we know—or think we know—about the impact of this reform method, as the judges themselves often influence the metrics of success. Second, it reveals a new cause for concern: the judicial investment in, and control over, problem-solving courts can create resistance to new approaches to reforming or transforming the system. This resistance has taken many forms. For example, some drug court judges have lobbied against statutory reforms that would reduce penalties for low-level drug offenses or create diversion opportunities that do not involve drug court participation. And resistance also occurs more implicitly, through problem-solving court judges' unwillingness to incorporate new knowledge about both the nature of the purported "problem" to be solved and the most effective solutions.

Problem-solving courts were one of the early reforms of this data-driven era of criminal justice reform. One scholar has even suggested that the drug court model has become a "paradigm" for current sentencing reform efforts. Thus, this Article—which suggests that problem-solving courts are not driven by actual data and may in fact resist incorporating new scientific knowledge—raises questions and identifies implications for other purportedly evidence-based, data-driven reforms....

Problem-solving courts are specialized criminal or quasi-criminal courts that often offer treatment and enhanced supervision in addition to or in lieu of incarceration. The prototypical problem-solving court—the drug court—opened thirty years ago and has served as a model for courts dedicated to a range of issues. The various courts are "defined by their diversity"; they differ in topic, methodology, and organizing principle. But they generally fall into three categories. Treatment courts, such as mental health courts, drug courts, and homelessness courts, attempt to address an issue that is believed to be criminogenic. Accountability courts, such as domestic violence courts and community courts, stress the need to enhance accountability for certain kinds of offenses. And status courts, such as veterans courts and girls courts, aim to address the purportedly "unique needs" of certain populations. But despite this diversity, the universe of problem-solving courts is united by a common claim, namely, that these courts solve a problem that would otherwise lead to repeated interaction with the criminal legal system.

Much problem-solving court literature recites a common account of the origins of these specialized courts. A pioneering judge notices a problem with the way the criminal justice system treats a certain kind of offense or offender and creates a specialized court to address that problem. For example, as Judge Robert T. Russell, reflecting on the impetus behind his decision to open the nation's first veterans court, explained, "As presiding Judge over Buffalo's Drug Treatment and Mental Health Treatment courts, I noticed that many of the participants on my docket had something in common—they were veterans." From this observation, Judge Russell extrapolated that veterans are a "niche population with unique needs" that were not being met in the traditional criminal justice system, so he created a new court.

This account is recited anew seemingly every time a jurisdiction opens a new specialty court. In May 2018, the Chief Judge Daniel Guierin of the Eighteenth Judicial Circuit in DuPage County, Illinois reflected on his recent decision to open a court for first-time opioid offenders: "It became apparent to me there was a significant and growing gap in how drug offenders are treated," Guerin said....

Thus, around the same time as the problem-solving court model was emerging, judicial authority over sentencing—the core power allotted to judges in the plea-dominated system—was diminishing. Simultaneously, the war-on-drugs was ramping up, but state trial court judges, who daily witnessed the devastating impacts of these harsh policies, were relatively powerless to counteract their effect. Judges have reflected that these changes to structured sentencing systems left them feeling that they were essentially "rubber-stamp bureaucrats" or "judicial accountants." It is unsurprising, therefore, that the problem-solving court model emerged and gained popularity as this sense of judicial dissatisfaction and disempowerment was taking hold. Early reflections of drug court judges indicate that they were attracted to the emerging specialty court model precisely because of these systemic changes. Many have noted that they felt frustrated and constrained by mandatory minimum sentences, and that they found the drug court approach "liberating," in contrast, because it offered more flexibility in sentencing....

Moreover, and perhaps because these courts return to judges some of the discretion and authority that diminished as a result of sentencing reform, problem-solving court judges regularly report higher levels of job satisfaction than their conventional peers. A judge who presided over both a drug court and conventional criminal court in Roanoke, Virginia, reflected, "I get more personal satisfaction out of what I'm doing with the drug court population than with anything I do for the remainder of the week." A drug court judge from Louisville, Kentucky, similarly noted that, "When I'm in my regular [conventional] court it's more like work.... Drug court, I don't have to do it. I'm there because I want to do it." These individual reflections are not isolated experiences. Jeffrey Tauber, a former drug court judge and the founding president of the NADCP, reflected that he had talked to hundreds of problem-solving court judges and had "not found a judge yet who has done this work for a significant period of time who hasn't said it is the most satisfying work that he has done in his career as a judge."...

During the "problem-solving" phase of the court process (i.e., after the defendant has pled guilty and been admitted to the court), there are no facts to adjudicate, laws to apply, or plea-bargains to review. The sole judicial task is to oversee the administration of the conditions of sentence. For these reasons, some have suggested that problem-solving courts are not actually "courts," but rather some sort of program or agency. In the agency context, scholars have suggested that robust oversight by an independent body may guard against agencies' self-aggrandizing tendencies. However, in criminal law, generally, and in the problem-solving court context in particular, there is no such independent oversight. State legislatures may provide a remaining source of potential oversight. As this subpart demonstrates, however, they do not do so. Although legislation regarding problem-solving courts is increasingly common, it largely affirms existing practices....

Nevertheless, the evaluation does not conclude that the drug courts do not work. Rather, it then states that recidivism is an incomplete metric, as it "does not account for some offenders who had undesirable outcomes," such as those who were incarcerated based on a probation revocation. And when these "undesirable outcomes" are accounted for, drug courts become a success. The evaluation found that drug court participants had "the lowest rate of undesirable outcomes" amongst the groups that were studied. In addition to selectively choosing metrics, problem-solving court practitioners also selectively invoke empirical findings to support their success narrative. The website of the NADCP illustrates this phenomenon. NADCP is the "premier training, membership, and advocacy organization for the treatment court model," and overseen by a Board of Directors comprised primarily of state court judges. It was created in 1994 after a meeting of judges and other professionals working in the twelve drug courts that were then in existence. This organization exercises great influence over the practices and attitudes of problem-solving court judges. One researcher concluded, based on interviews, that the judges "appear to respect and trust the NADCP" more than they respect and trust statements and guidance from the federal government. She opined that this respect was because judges are the "primary members" of NADCP.

...

While drug court participation reduced or eliminated the length of incarceration for those who graduated from the program for the precipitating case, those who failed out of the program faced dramatically higher sentences. Graduates averaged 24.5 days of incarceration as compared to an average of 272.6 for those who failed the program. In a separately published summary of their findings, the researchers explained, "drug courts do not appear to operate as a reliable 'alternative to incarceration' on the precipitating case." This example is not offered to suggest that NADCP intends to mislead its audience about the MADCE study. The point, rather, is that this organization of drug court judges and other drug court professionals emphasize only the parts of the study that support their worldview—that problem-solving courts work, full stop—and disregard the rest...

Nevertheless, and despite decades of research highlighting the efficacy of MAT [medicated assisted treatment], many U.S. drug courts have resisted this treatment method. A nationwide survey of drug courts in 2013 found that nearly half (44%) of all respondents did not permit any form of MAT for court participants. Some respondents indicated they did not provide MAT because it was not available or was cost prohibitive. A sizeable percentage, however, refused to allow agonist MAT medications due to "negative attitudes" or "incorrect information," including opposition from the judge, prosecutor, or local government, because it was the court's policy to not allow it, and because it was not believed to be beneficial to the drug court participant. Some respondents specified that they believed drug court participants would abuse MAT or that MAT would simply replace addiction to one substance with another substance. The attitudinal resistance to MAT highlighted in this study has been reflected in recent journalistic interviews with drug court judges. In 2014, a drug court judge in Nassau County, New York, defended his policy against methadone and suboxone, even after a court participant died of a heroin overdose after the judge ordered him to quit his methadone treatment. The judge described methadone and suboxone as "crutches" and "substitutes for drugs and drug cravings" that constitute another addiction....

Nevertheless, drug court proponents repeated many of the same concerns when California considered Proposition 5 in 2008, the Nonviolent Offender Rehabilitation Act ("NORA"), which would have reduced penalties for certain drug offenses, and again in 2014 when the state considered and adopted Proposition 47. Proposition 47 was crafted as part of the state's ongoing effort to reduce prison overcrowding. It reclassified certain drug possession offenses from felonies to misdemeanors, which reduced the sentencing exposure of eligible offenders from a year or more in state prison to up to a year in county jail. The NADCP "strongly oppose[d]" the measure, because it "removes the legal incentive" for offenders to seek treatment. A San Diego drug court judge recently reflected that Proposition 47 "really hurt our numbers" and removed the "hammer to threaten (drug users) with incarceration." Under Proposition 47, some defendants will face a jail sentence of a few months, which the judge opined, they "can do ... standing on their heads" and therefore would choose jail over drug court.

This resistance to drug sentencing reform is not limited to California. In 2018, Ohio voters considered (and ultimately rejected) Issue One, which would have reclassified certain nonviolent drug offenses from felonies to misdemeanors, and also would have prohibited jail time for these offenses under certain circumstances...

On a more systemic level, the deep judicial investment in this institutional response helps perpetuate the notion that the criminal legal system—and particularly the courts—are the best and most appropriate mechanism for responding to complicated social and structural issues. The creation of a new court for every newly discovered (or newly acknowledged) issue that overlaps with the criminal legal system has been normalized as a natural and effective response. With each iteration of this story of court creation and success, it becomes easier to forget that the decision to respond through the criminal legal system (as opposed to, for example, the public health system) to issues such as substance abuse and mental illness, is in fact a choice.288 And it is a choice that ultimately strengthens, rather than reduces or dismantles, the tie between these social issues and the criminal legal system...

Problem-solving courts solve a problem. But the problem they solve has more to do with disaffected judges than the issues for which they are named. This insight helps explain their otherwise perplexing persistence, raises new questions, and uncovers new problems. But it also enables a conversation about what is really driving one of the most celebrated developments in modern criminal justice reform: judicial dissatisfaction and disempowerment. Instead of dealing with the symptom by creating new courts, we should focus on the cause. Perhaps it is time to find ways to allow judges to judge again.

Notes/Questions

1. Assume the County of Thompson in the State of Amelia does not yet have a drug court. It has a population of 350,000 people and an active criminal court docket. As in most places in the United States, felony drug possession, possession for sales, and sales cases take up a significant amount of the docket—at least 30%. Defendants with substance abuse problems account for an even higher percentage of the total number of defendants, as many are arrested for other offenses, such as theft or driving while under the influence.

If you were setting up a drug court, what are some parameters you should consider?

2. As you consider setting up your court, how will you determine selection? One concern with all problem-solving courts is who gets selected for (and gets to benefit from) them. As one scholar notes writing about what she calls *specialized criminal courts* instead of problem-solving courts:

> Consistent with data on discretionary bias in charging and sentencing, early evidence shows that Black and Hispanic defendants are less likely to be selected for specialized court admission than their white counterparts. For example, data from California State Drug Courts showed that, "[d]espite the disproportionate number of minorities who are charged with low-level drug offenses, minority offenders are less likely to be given the opportunity to enter drug court programs compared with white offenders because of the strict screening requirements of many drug courts." "The National Drug Court Institute has [reported] that state drug court participants are 62 percent [w]hite, 17 percent Black, and [10] percent Hispanic; by contrast, state prisoners are 32 percent [w]hite, 37 percent Black, and 22 percent Hispanic, and state probationers are 54 percent [w]hite, 30 percent Black, and 13 percent Hispanic." These statistics demonstrate that "[w]hite offenders are substantially overrepresented compared to their representation in the regular state probation and prison populations, while Black and Hispanic participants are underrepresented."

Shanda K Sibley, *The Unchosen: Procedural Fairness in Criminal Specialty Court Selection*, 43 Cardozo L. Rev. 2261 (2022).

What system and metrics would you use when setting up your problem-solving court to mitigate these biases? And is Professor Sibley's term a more accurate reflection of what these courts are?

Additional Resources

Greg Berman & John Feinblatt, Good Courts: The Case for Problem-Solving Justice 5–7 (2005).

Richard C. Boldt, *Drug Policy in Context: Rhetoric and Practice in the United States and the United Kingdom*, 62 S.C. L. Rev. 261 (2010).

Richard C. Boldt, *Rehabilitative Punishment and the Drug Treatment Court Movement*, 76 Wash. U. L.Q. 1205 (1998).

Erin Collins, *The Problem of Problem Solving Courts*, 54 U.C. Davis L. Rev. 1573, 1573 (2021).

E. Lea Johnston & Conor P. Flynn, *Mental Health Courts and Sentencing Disparities*, 62 Vill. L. Rev. 685 (2017).

Milwaukee County Drug Treatment Court Policy and Procedure Manual 2010, available at https://ndcrc.org/resource/milwaukee-county-drug-treatment-court-policy-and-procedure-manual/.

James Nolan, Legal Accents, Legal Borrowing: The International Problem-Solving Court Movement (Princeton University Press, 2009).

James Nolan, Reinventing Justice: The American Drug Court Movement (Princeton University Press, 2001).

Chapter 9

Problem-Solving Courts: Concerns

The previous chapter outlines different types of problem-solving courts and shows how these have been effective in a variety of settings. Yet, as the final readings note, not every actor involved in the courts is in favor of these continuing. Critiques of the problem-solving courts note concerns in a variety of areas. First there are concerns with what is happening to the offenders themselves. In the process of going through a problem-solving court, are they waiving constitutional rights (like trial or agreeing to searches) that they would not otherwise relinquish? And are offenders actually being punished more by going through the problem-solving courts? Second, regarding the attorneys and judges involved in these courts—how do the roles of the judge and lawyers change? Is the involvement and oversight by judges appropriate? Are prosecutors (still) given too much power? Are defense attorneys conceding too much (and are they even trained for this new role in these new courts)? Finally, there are systemic concerns—who gets chosen for these courts? Are there class and racial biases that play into these choices? And what is the role of these courts vis-a-vis the rest of the criminal legal system. Do problem-solving courts relieve the tension to fix the underlying law or process (by cherry-picking the most sympathetic offenders) and leave the vast majority of defendants to still deal with an overly harsh sentencing regime? Do police officers now pick up even minor infractions to send offenders to drug court (a net-widening effect) so that more people are in the system in drug courts, for example, than would be there otherwise? And are lawyers and criminal justice professionals the right people to be managing these problems instead of health professionals?

The readings in this chapter start to wrestle with this list of questions and also provide some responses and ideas for how to manage these concerns. We first start with a critique of the efficacy of problem-solving courts—do they really work? We then turn to critiques of the roles of judges and attorneys. Then we examine the impact on the offenders and the treatment they receive. The chapter ends with responses and suggestions.

Erin R. Collins, *Beyond Problem-Solving Courts*

25 Cardozo Journal of Conflict Resolution,
229–230, 233–241 (2023)

The problem-solving court movement is now more than thirty years old and the results of this experiment in court reform are underwhelming. Although these specialized criminal courts are widely celebrated as a successful evidence-based reform with demonstrated success in reducing recidivism, as I have argued elsewhere, "the empirical landscape of problem-solving court efficacy is more complicated than most proponents acknowledge." While drug court outcomes have been subject to robust empirical scrutiny, other problem-solving courts have been tested only sporadically, if at all. The claims of success for these other courts are based on the supposed success of drug courts—but the actual studies of drug courts hardly depict an unmitigated success story. Overall, some drug court studies show that some of the people who graduate from some drug court programs are then arrested for or convicted of crimes less frequently than people who follow traditional punishment paths. Meanwhile, the 40% to 60% of people who begin but do not complete problem-solving court programs often fare worse than they would have otherwise: many are ultimately incarcerated for at least as long as they would have been if they had been convicted in a traditional court, after having already spent time attempting the treatment court process. Many court participants, regardless of whether they graduate from the court process or not, are saddled with extra debt from the court-imposed cost of participation. Moreover, these underwhelming outcomes cost more money than traditional punishment processes. For nearly as long as these specialized courts have existed, there have been efforts to reform this reform model to increase court retention, decrease recidivism, and save more money....

A key to these underwhelming results is that many, and sometimes most, people who enter the court programs are dismissed from the court before program completion. Graduation rates for adult drug courts hover around 40% to 60%, and studies have found similar rates for mental health courts. Most specialized courts operate on a post-adjudication model, which means that most of the 40% to 60% who do not complete the process have already pleaded guilty to the underlying crime. When they are terminated from the specialized court program, they face the same original sentencing range from before they entered the program, and often end up with a total sentence that is substantially longer than they would have otherwise faced if they had pursued a traditional path. One study demonstrated that even those who graduate from mental health court serve terms of supervision that exceed the term they would have received from a traditional court by a year or more....

Even if these courts achieved the recidivism reduction they claim, there would remain many other reasons to move beyond problem-solving courts. Medical and public health experts have questioned the propriety, efficacy, and safety of combining therapy with punishment. A 2017 Physicians for Human Rights ("PHR") assessment of drug courts concluded the courts "largely failed at providing treatment to those who truly needed it" while prioritizing participation for those who did not, and documented instances in which "court officials with no medical background mandated inappropriate treatment not rooted in the evidence base." As a result of these and other observations, PHR concluded that drug courts "posed significant human rights concerns." In March of 2019, independent human rights experts for the United Nations Special Rapporteurs similarly warned that drug courts "pose dangers of punitive approaches encroaching on medical and health care matters."

Moreover, as I have argued previously, problem-solving courts—despite their supposed evidence-based commitments—often fail to embrace scientific evidence that casts doubt on their practices or their foundational premises. Once a particular conception of treatment is baked into the court process, those who are dedicated to and vested with authority in the court process may be reluctant or even antagonistic to changing it—even if new or previously overlooked insights from the relevant medical or scientific communities support making such changes....

Scientific research also reveals that some problem-solving courts are based on faulty assumptions about the connection between particular characteristics and criminal behavior. As Professor Lea Johnston has revealed, the two foundational premises of mental health courts—namely that there is a strong causal connection between mental illness and criminal behavior and, therefore, that providing mental health treatment instead of incarceration will prevent future criminal activity—is "belied by scientific evidence." Rather, a robust body of scientific research demonstrates that having a mental illness does not cause people to engage in criminal behavior and, in fact, people with mental illness who commit crimes "often simply exhibit the same risk factors—such as substance abuse, family problems, and antisocial tendencies" as other people who commit crimes." Professor Johnston concludes "[i]t is these risk factors, not symptomatic mental illness, that directly contribute to criminal activity for a majority of individuals with mental illness."...

Status courts, such as veterans courts and girls courts, depart from this framing slightly. These courts seek to address the way that past trauma resulting from external sources, such as military combat or sexual assault, contribute to current behavior and can render people vulnerable to criminal system involvement. Status courts aim to address the purportedly "unique needs" that stem from this trauma and provide a court process that acknowledges the dignity of court participants by treating them with empathy, respect, and honor. The problem these courts attempt to solve, therefore, is the inhumane and careless treatment that a select few receive in the traditional system. However, by providing special treatment for some people based on a notion of desert, these courts, too, ultimately shore up the pathologies of the traditional system in a few key ways. First, their justificatory discourse supports the notion that those who do not fall into these select status groups—in other words, the vast majority of those whom the system targets—deserve the inhumane and dysfunctional treatment they receive. Moreover, the courts overlook the similarities between those they deem deserving of better treatment and those they exclude. For example, many young people who grow up in urban areas experience post-traumatic stress disorder at rates that match or surpass those of military veterans. This trauma, like that of military veterans, often stems from witnessing or being a victim of violence. And people of all genders experience sexual assault, and presumably most if not all who do experience trauma from those experiences. And yet, there has not been a robust effort to extend the status court model to include other populations that suffer from trauma....

Despite their diversionary ideals, the authority of problem-solving courts depends on the ever-present threat of incarceration–regardless of whether that threat becomes a reality. The courts draw their power of "persuasion" from the prison itself and can and do frequently use that power. While "[t]he judge's range of options for securing compliance with drug treatment or other requirements may range from hugs to jail ... in the end, jail remains a viable sanction." As problem-solving court judges readily admit, these institutions wield their carceral authority all the time. These courts are not, judges reassure skeptics, soft on crime. This intimate and inextricable relationship between problem-solving courts and incarceration reveals the impossibility of pursuing decarceration through this method of reform. History casts further doubt on the ability of problem-solving courts to achieve decarceration. Problem-solving courts have entered their fourth decade and, as of yet, have not made an appreciable difference in recidivism rates.

I. Concerns with Judges and Attorneys

These first two articles address how the behavior of the judges and lawyers differ from their roles in the typical, adversarial criminal procedure.

Richard C. Boldt, *Rehabilitative Punishment and the Drug Treatment Court Movement*

76 WASH. U. L. REV. 1205, 1246–1250, 1252–1255 (January 1998)

A. The Adversary System, Attorney Role, and Rehabilitative Penal Practice

An adversarial system of decision making has three primary characteristics, and each directly relates to the role of counsel. First, the parties initiate and control the process, by pursuing their respective positions through affirmative presentations of evidence and argument coupled with challenges to their opponent's version of law and fact. Second, these forensic narratives and counternarratives are brought to the attention of the decision maker according to formal procedural rules. Third, the decisional figure is charged with being neutral with respect to the conflict until such time as a decision is rendered through the application of substantive decisional rules to the parties' evidence. Given these characteristics, most adversarial adjudications require the parties to seek the assistance of counsel. Laypersons usually lack the skill to present their partisan account according to formal procedural rules. Additionally, requiring that parties present these accounts with an eye toward satisfying substantive rules of decision generally militates against pro se advocacy by nonlawyer litigants. Taken together, the three defining characteristics of the adversary system have been said to yield a standard conception of the lawyer's role that largely is reflected in the A.B.A.'s Model Code of Professional Responsibility, the A.B.A.'s Model Rules of Professional Conduct, and various standards governing criminal defense practice. Because the function of a lawyer in an adversarial proceeding is to represent the client by directing his or her expertise toward the accomplishment of the client's self-interested goals, the standard conception imposes upon the lawyer a set of mutually reinforcing duties. The first is a duty of partisanship, which recognizes that the advocate is in some senses standing in the shoes of his or her client. This duty is satisfied, according to this conception, when the lawyer adopts the client's ends as his or her own. Additionally, the attorney is bound to avoid conflicts between the client's interests and his or her own interests or those of another client This duty to avoid conflicts of interest is designed to insure that the lawyer's partisan zeal, his or her unity of purpose with the client, is not diluted by some competing agenda. Finally, the lawyer is forbidden from disclosing information learned in the course of the representation, unless permitted to do so by the client This duty of client confidentiality is intended to encourage clients to speak freely with their lawyers, again in order to safeguard the unity of purpose between advocate and the client and to facilitate the lawyers' partisan efforts on their clients' behalf.

On occasion, each of the defining features of the adversary system comes into conflict with rehabilitative penal practice. As a consequence, the standard role conception sometimes is ill-suited to the tasks facing counsel for defendants in such proceedings. The first feature, that the process is driven by opposing parties who seek to accomplish their respective partisan goals through the vigorous advocacy of their representatives, does not account for cases where a defendant recognizes the need for therapeutic measures and genuinely desires to have the prosecution resolved by way of treatment. In such cases, it is difficult to describe the process as fully adversarial, although the unity of partisan purpose formed by the relationship between the defendant and his or her counsel is not jeopardized by any conflict between the client's expressed desires and judgments by the attorney regarding the client's best interests. By contrast, in cases where the defendant's expressed goal is to avoid all coercive measures, including rehabilitative treatment, defense counsel may or may not be able to adopt a familiar partisan role. If the defendant's objective of avoiding therapy is well-grounded, the adversarial model likely will hold, because the defendant's attorney will be able to pursue this outcome without doing violence to the standard role conception. If, on the other hand, the defendant's desire to avoid therapeutic measures is not well-grounded, as is often the case with defendants whose addictive disorders include a fair degree of denial, the defense attorney will be placed in a difficult situation. According to the standard conception, the attorney should adopt the defendant's goals as his or her own and should pursue them with partisan zeal, despite the fact that the lawyer may believe that it would be in the client's best interests to undergo treatment. A very different role conception for defense counsel obtains, however, in some institutional settings where the expressed purpose of the proceeding is the provision of treatment rather than the imposition of blame and punishment. Attorneys who adopt this alternative role conception often view their clients as incapable of identifying appropriate goals that further their best interests and so impose their own judgments regarding the objectives of the representation. This alternative role conception, which treats the defendant as impaired in his or her capacity to make sound decisions, is incompatible with an adjudicatory model characterized by party control. It may be possible to avoid this conclusion by locating party control in defense counsel instead of the defendant, but this conceptualization only works if some sort of strong identification between the defendant and his or her lawyer can be found. If the defense lawyer has significant links with the other ongoing participants in the process, including prosecutors, corrections officials, and judges, and shares with these actors a common set of interests, this sort of an identification between the defendant and his or her attorney may be difficult to establish or maintain. In such circumstances, a key element of the adversarial system is absent....

B. Drug Treatment Courts and Attorney Role

While treatment-based drug courts vary considerably according to each jurisdiction's statutory context, political environment available resources, and operational goals, virtually all of these institutions possess certain similar core features. Almost without exception, these courts seek to accomplish their goals by muting the traditional adversarial positions of prosecutor and defendant, and by making the process judge-driven rather than lawyer-driven. This inversion of the traditional adversary system paradigm, which ordinarily assumes that the parties' lawyers will play an active, partisan role while the judge remains passive and neutral, tends to be coupled with a high degree of procedural informality. Taken together, these features yield a setting in which familiar role expectations rarely serve as accurate predictors of actual practice. As one commentator described it:

> [W]hat makes these drug treatment calendars unique is the nonadversarial nature of their proceedings and the active and ongoing role that the drug treatment calendar judge plays—generally with the support of both the prosecutor and defense counsel—in working with the treatment provider and motivating the defendant to complete the treatment program. Essentially, these "drug courts" are not courts at all, but diversion-to-treatment programs, which are supervised through regular (usually monthly) quasi-judicial status hearings at which the drug court judge enters into a dialogue with each defendant about his or her progress in the treatment/re-habilitation program.

The underlying rationale for this situation recalls the thinking of the leading rehabilitationists of a generation ago. As noted earlier, a key feature of the rehabilitative ideal was the conviction that antisocial or criminal conduct was the product in part or whole of some pathology operating within the offender. Given this starting point, it was entirely logical that rehabilitationist thinkers urged the criminal justice system to respond to offenders with therapeutic treatment instead of retributive punishment, either to assist the offender or, in the case of social defense theorists, to protect society from future harmful conduct. Furthermore, because rehabilitationists thought that criminal conduct was linked to individual pathology, they concentrated less on the specific facts and circumstances of the completed criminal offense and more on information about the offender's personal characteristics that were necessary for accurately determining the offender's diagnosis and prognosis. Translated into the contemporary drug treatment court context, these ideas generate a powerful set of related premises: Substance abuse is a disease that contributes directly to the commission of criminal conduct. Most offenders with drug abuse problems, who are prosecuted and sentenced in the traditional punishment-oriented criminal justice system, do not receive treatment for their disease. Therefore, upon release, they resume the addictive use of drugs and associated criminal behaviors. If the disease is treated, however, this linked cycle of addiction and criminality can be disrupted. Although formal notions of guilt and responsibility as to particular instances of past criminal conduct are not made irrelevant in the drug treatment court setting, it is clear that the primary focus, and therefore the design of the system, is centered upon the offender's future conduct and the characteristics of his or her disease and progress in treatment that permit useful predictions as to future criminality. This shift in focus is responsible for the push toward a relatively nonpartisan, informal procedural approach by drug treatment courts. In light of this redirected emphasis and procedural informality, defense attorneys must make difficult choices in formulating an appropriate role conception. These choices fall into several broad categories. First, attorneys must decide what posture to adopt when their clients are faced with deciding whether to enter a treatment court program or to have the charges resolved through the traditional adjudicatory system. Second, attorneys must decide whether to play an active or a passive role in limiting the potentially severe sanctions their clients may receive in instances of relapse. An important question here is whether defense counsel should interpose himself or herself between the defendant and the treatment court judge, or acquiesce in the common practice of permitting the judge to interact directly with defendants in open court. The final choices defense attorneys are likely to face involve the degree to which potentially damaging or inculpating information will be shared with the court and the prosecutor.

Notes/Questions

1. A defense lawyer was quoted as saying, "In fact, as drug courts are part of the criminal justice system, treatment plans were negotiable issues between defense lawyers and prosecutors.... [We] suggested treatment options for expediency rather than therapeutic reasons. Did we consult a medical professional? No. It's more of a legal determination...." Physicians for Human Rights, *Neither Justice nor Treatment: Drug Courts in the United States* (June 2017).

2. In Milwaukee, District Attorney John Chisholm "decided that his office would undertake initiatives to try to send fewer people to prison while maintaining public safety." In an article published by *The New Yorker* he echoed the national sentiment that the criminal legal system has failed African Americans. He believes that prosecutors

"have to redefine their proper role in a new era" and "should also be judged by their success in reducing mass incarceration and achieving racial equality." *How to Stop Mass Incarceration*, THE NEW YORKER, 2015. If you were a prosecutor, how could you carry this out using problem-solving courts?

3. Do you believe that problem-solving courts are a way to combat mass incarceration, particularly that of the African American and Latino populations? What potential problems do you see with this theory?

In this article, Professor Tamar Meekins raises concerns about problem-solving courts and the impact they could have on the criminal defense system. Professor Meekins served as both a public defender and Deputy Attorney General over the course of her career. Note how her experience on both sides informs her critiques.

* * *

Tamar M. Meekins, *"Specialized Justice": The Over-Emergence of Specialty Courts and the Threat of a New Criminal Defense Paradigm*

40 SUFFOLK U. L. REV. 1, 2–4, 37–44, 46–49 (2006)

Introduction

Over the past ten to fifteen years, many judges, court officials, legislators, academics, and other policy-makers confronted with rising recidivism and failed attempts to rid society of "the criminal element," embarked upon a campaign to address social problems thought to lead to criminal activity. The so-called specialty courts or "problem-solving courts" are the embodiment of the therapeutic and restorative justice movements at work. Hundreds of criminal court systems around the country have implemented various forms of courts which offer the promise of "specialized justice," to address a myriad of social issues, including drug addiction, domestic violence, sexual dysfunction, nuisance crimes, and homelessness. An unintended and, as yet, largely ignored consequence of this burgeoning movement, however, may spell a threat to our adversary system. The standard premise behind these courts is the emasculation of the traditional role of the criminal defender as a zealous advocate fighting against the system. Despite the importance of defenders insuring courts adhere to principles of substantive and procedural due process, the defender in specialty courts becomes, in most instances, a collaborator. He collaborates with the judge and prosecutors, thereby taking on a role that works to diminish the effectiveness of the defender overall, decreases the confidence defendants have in the outcome, and supports a culture of ineffectiveness and under-representation. More importantly, citizens most in need of justice and traditionally overrepresented in the criminal justice system may be adversely affected the most by this turn of events. Statistics and research from specialty courts indicate that indigent criminal defendants and those from racial and ethnic minority groups are often over-represented in specialty courts, thus bearing more than their fair share of the danger of indifferent representation.

In the majority of criminal specialty courts that have been developed and implemented in recent years, the defense lawyer is relegated to the role of team player whose only purpose serves to fulfill a constitutional mandate. A client may face a significant period of incarceration due to a defender who does not zealously advocate for the dismissal of the case in appropriate circumstances, does not expose and challenge police abuse and illegality, does not voice the client's position, and does not challenge the automatic imprisonment of the defendant as a sanction for failed compliance....

With the advent of the first drug court in Miami, Florida, in 1989, court systems in many states and localities created specialty courts, which seek to address the need for services and problems in defendants' lives that bear upon their ability to follow court orders and remain free of the criminal justice system. Some of these courts seek to integrate the community's voice in determining appropriate penalties and behavior modification systems that will appease community members as well. Amidst these laudable goals, few have ventured to comment on the abandonment of the notion of adversarial justice in favor of a more treatment-oriented approach that emphasizes the team concept. Such an approach finds its roots in, and has been accepted by, other social science disciplines such as psychiatry, and is tied to several academic approaches to criminal law theory, namely rehabilitation, therapeutic jurisprudence, and restorative justice. But the approach carries potential danger for the indigent or racial minority defendant who is counting on a committed zealous defender to be their voice, their sword, and their shield in the criminal justice system. The wide acceptance and silence regarding this model of criminal defense representation signals a change in the way our criminal justice system works.

Defenders, who litigate in these courts, encounter a dilemma between their instinctual desire to be an advocate for their clients and the desire to do whatever they can to seek treatment for their clients and keep them out of prison. As difficult as this dilemma is for a good number of committed defenders, an even more interesting issue concerns whether the nature of the treatment court and defenders' role in it negatively affect clients' interests by instigating a culture of indifference and incompetent advocacy.

Part III: The Good, the Bad and the Ineffective:
Defender Roles in Theory and Practice

Defenders need to look at this as a new approach that requires a level of team work and partnership that is not often seen. It requires defenders to take a step back, to not intervene actively between the judge and the participant, and allow that relationship to develop and do its work, and basically to understand the importance of working within a team concept. It really does demand that they partner and work very closely with both the court, treatment, and their former adversary, the prosecutor.

This comment about the role of defense lawyers in drug courts by Judge Jeffrey Tauber of the National Association of Drug Court Professionals succinctly summarizes the view of specialty court advocates who are strongly in favor of the main precepts of the specialty court movement. It asserts that defense counsel in specialty courts cannot function in their traditional role. In other words, those judges and officials who have designed the specialty courts require that the traditional adversarial role of the criminal defense attorney be subordinated to the notion of teamwork. Unfortunately, this means that the zealousness that is essential to the functioning of the defense attorney, as well as the intervention that is necessary to protect important rights, may be lost in specialty courts. In essence, the very premises of drug courts, and by extension other specialty courts, are at odds with standard notions of zealous advocacy. The notion that the defense attorney in a specialty court must work as a team player engaged in the social rehabilitation of the defendant is antithetical to the traditional role of the criminal defense lawyer and invokes musings of the kinder, gentler defense practice advocated by Professor Simon. In fact, some advocates argue that these new specialty courts "empower a new type of prosecutor and defense counsel," one that will press all of his or her energies toward serving the best interests of the defendant. This is at least in so far as those best interests include treatment according to the modalities offered by the particular specialty court. According to the rhetoric, this new type of defender places a premium on the stated goals of the treatment court rather than on the defendant, and focuses all of his or her energy on that narrow goal.

Thus, the "role" of the defense attorney in specialty courts embodies no vestiges of the adversarial defender, and therefore takes on a "best interests" mantra. When a defendant is found to be in need of treatment by the court, prosecutor, social workers, or case managers, the defense attorney is expected to behave in a way that falls in line with the treatment recommendation and to act in a way that supports and furthers the treatment goals. The expected behaviors and actions of the defense attorney—what can be termed the "role markers"—are thus guided by the dictates of the court, and not the wishes of the defendant. Consequently, the defense attorney is expected to forgo any action or challenge any treatment, the process of adjudication, or interaction between the judge and defendant. This is true even when that interaction treads upon important constitutional rights, such as the right against self-incrimination. The defense attorney stands idly by, as part of the team, while the specialty court process takes effect. The only affirmative conduct expected of the defense attorney is to encourage the defendant to follow through with the treatment and any other requirements of the specialty court modality.

Advocates of specialty courts argue that the team-player defense attorney model is superior to other models because of the beneficial results which come from treatment courts. They further state that the apprehension of defense attorneys is "unfounded." They argue that defense attorneys "should view treatment courts as being in their clients' best interest" and as "the best method for 'ending the cycle of drugs and crime.'"

While the "good" that can come from specialty courts, i.e., getting needed treatment for criminal defendants, is important and necessary, questions still remain as to whether the specialty court model is sufficient to meet ethical and practice standards, and whether the loss of constitutional and other protected rights will deprive the specialty court defendant of procedural justice. Indeed, practicing lawyers and some commentators continue to raise several issues and voice their apprehension about the legal representation that is provided in specialty courts. Their comments continue to raise the specter of diluted due process and procedural justice. Unfortunately, the danger inherent in these concerns is heightened if the emergence of specialty courts has shifted the paradigm upon which our criminal justice system operates.

A. Greater Concerns than Realized at First Review

In an important article that reinvigorated the debate on representation in drug courts, and by extension other specialized courts, Public Defender Mae Quinn advocated "pulling back on the reins of the present high speed drug court movement." Quinn reviewed one of the seminal articles written on the drug treatment court movement and evaluated several role markers of defense attorneys working in the therapeutic justice model. She noted substantial concerns with each noted area of defense attorney action in specialty courts and argued that such concerns could not be dismissed. Quinn found that greater discussion was needed about the ethical and legal issues surrounding these new role markers for defense attorneys practicing in drug treatment courts. Quinn's analysis yields more implications when considering whether the concerns regarding defense attorney practice in specialty courts are magnified or enhanced given the widespread acceptance of such a mode of court administrations.

For example, Quinn showed great concern for the notion that in order to enter a specialty treatment court, a defense attorney must counsel her client to waive important constitutional rights without knowing what the final outcome might be for the defendant. Unlike a plea bargain, where the defendant knows what will happen because there has been a negotiated sentence, or where there are clear boundaries that limit a judge's options in sentencing the client, the defendant and defense attorney in a specialty court scenario do not know the results if the defendant fails treatment. Looking through the results lens, therefore, the advice to the client about whether to enter the treatment court program is meaningless, or at the very least, uninformed.

The magnitude of this issue cannot be measured solely through an analysis of results. In the fictional scenario at the beginning of this article, the defense lawyer is in the same position: counseling a client to enter a specialized court program without having any idea as to the potential results for the client. The lawyer, however, is also counseling the client on this important decision without having adequate information about the client, the case, or the extent of the defendant's so-called problem. In this post-adjudication specialty court scenario, the attorney is incapable of fully explaining the rights that are waived when a defendant enters the specialty court. From the interaction between this client and his attorney, it is clear the trepidation upon which the decision to enter a treatment court rests. Many of a defendant's basic questions do not get answered because the decision to enter the treatment court must be made very quickly, often on the day of the first appearance in court or very shortly thereafter. At other times, the questions do not get answered because the attorney has developed a mode of practice in the specialty court that does not lend itself to further attorney-client interaction.

Some commentators theorize that the answer to this quandary is to allow for additional time before the defendant makes a decision to accept or deny the specialty court program. Even allowing the additional time that some commentators believe sufficient—up to a couple of weeks—within which to make the decision, does not cure all the problems inherent in this scenario. Looking at the need for more time, one to two weeks additional is just not enough time to: allow the attorney to make informed decisions about the strength of the case through investigating the facts, obtaining discovery, and filing motions; foster a strong relationship between attorney and client that rests upon a sense of trust; or permit the attorney to find out information about the client's background to determine the appropriateness of treatment. Undoubtedly, specialty court advocates, including judges and prosecutors, would balk at expanding the time even more, since immediate treatment is one of the main foundational principles behind therapeutic justice.

Consequently, the defense attorney either has to leave the decision entirely to the client or counsel the client without any basis, as in our scenario. Both courses of action create serious implications for the attorney-client relationship. The transactional trust that underlies the traditional adversarial defense attorney-client relationship may never develop, or where there was at least some predisposition by the defendant to trust the defense attorney by virtue of her position, it may be lost. The trust is replaced by a kind of indifference when a client enters a specialty court. The attorney may not ascertain the extent of the rights the defendant forfeits or may neglect to fully explain them to the defendant either out of a belief that it is not needed given the treatment focus of the specialty court, or that other professionals who are looking out for the defendant's best interests, such as case managers, will explain this and other important aspects to the defendant. Such a course is neither competent nor effective, and may violate ethical rules and render the assistance of counsel ineffective.

Quinn also notes concern with the notion of collaboration and the team-player model in treatment courts. Specialty court advocates equate the role of the defense attorney in specialty courts with that of the judge, prosecutor, and drug treatment professional. The defense lawyers, however, have no real power in the process. The defense lawyer does not make charging decisions, has no power to dismiss an unjust charge, and has no power to dismiss a charge after successful completion of treatment. The prosecutors retain these decisions and have a large role in system-wide decisions. These are decisions retained by the prosecutor, who has a greater role in decisions in the treatment court on a macro, or system-wide, and micro, or individual case, level.

One of the biggest decisions in the design and initial implementation of a specialty court is whether the court will employ a pre- or post-adjudication model. Prosecutors have been particularly powerful in their ability to "persuade" judges and court officials that the new specialty court should only allow treatment after a defendant has entered a guilty plea. The prosecutors often argue that their ability to go forward on a case when a defendant fails in treatment after many months is compromised without a guilty plea. Their persuasion in this design process often amounts to a veto. Since the prosecutor has charging authority and is an independent branch of government, the court cannot force the prosecutor to allow a case to be dismissed, diverted, or held in abeyance until treatment or restitution is completed.

The veto power by the prosecution is just one example of the fallacy of the team-player mantra in specialty courts. The notion of a team, at least in this example, is one in which all players have an equally important role, voice, and input into the pursuit of a particular goal. This is not the case for the defender in the specialty court; the defender has no veto power during the design phase or thereafter.

Even in those instances where an institutional defender is present at the design and implementation table, the concerns, suggestions, and questions that are brought forth may be weighed down against the momentum that drives the establishment of the specialty court. In other words, the driving forces behind these courts, or their initial laudable or other goals, sometimes do not include defenders and defender organizations in the coalitions of stakeholder groups that have substantial input in the design, formulation, and initial implementation of specialty courts. Perhaps this phenomenon is a recognition by some judges, prosecutors, and other court officials of the very nature of the defense function in the criminal justice system, which is to defend and advocate on behalf of the individual and champion the accused's traditional rights. Under the traditional adversarial model, defending and advocating takes the form of resistance to government-imposed restrictions on liberty, way of life, or any part of self-determination. Some tension might appear when a defender is asked to take part in designing a system that institutionalizes automatic sanctions for defendants who violate conditions of treatment and does not allow defendants to challenge the sanctions or the parameters of the treatment. The extent to which the defenders' powerlessness leads to feelings of inadequacy of purpose and role is an interesting and compelling issue that specialty court advocates should study.

Additionally, Quinn is concerned about the possibility that prosecutors will "dump" non-meritorious cases into treatment courts. That is, cases that would not survive the normal adversarial process, like those vulnerable to a dismissal or motion to suppress, would be charged because in all likelihood the defendant would accept entry into the specialty court. Quinn argues that defense lawyers have little or no power to ensure that case dumping does not occur in jurisdictions using specialty courts.

The case dumping issue that Quinn describes has further ramifications. Even before a prosecutor charges a non-meritorious case, the police may arrest an inordinate number of defendants simply because the specialty court exists. In other words, police discretion may send many defendants into the court adjudication process who normally may be diverted to other systems or not be arrested at all. For example, defendants who exhibit mental health issues when confronted by police officers may more likely be arrested and jailed, on the theory that they will end up in mental health court, than be sent to a locality's mental health system with its overwhelming delay and red tape that officers might have to endure.

Judge Hoffman calls this phenomenon the "popcorn effect," whereby the existence of the specialty courts, specifically drug courts, cause "police to make arrests in" the types of cases that they would normally "not have bothered with." Hoffman focuses on how the increased number of cases funneled through drug courts strains court staff and the docket, and theorizes that this strain on resources leads to "demoralized and ineffective drug courts." Hoffman does not, however, address the issues raised by this problem for the delivery of defense services and the quality of defense representation.

Institutional defender services organizations have been inundated by an increase in the number of cases, particularly those with little to no merit.... Institutional defender organizations should be given additional resources to deal with the increased volume of cases, and court appointed systems should be restructured to allow for higher per-hour payments or additional lawyers to represent the increased number of defendants. Lawyers struggling to deal with the increased caseload may skimp on the quality of representation that they are able to provide.

Although specialty court advocates argue that the defender is part of the team, such rhetoric if often disputed by reality. An additional concern in specialty courts is the right to status hearings and role of defense counsel at such hearings. As noted above, attorneys often are not present at the many status hearings that can occur during the life of a case in specialty court. Sometimes their absence is attributed to the standard operating procedures of the court as hearings are often called immediately to address violations by defendants. This is a precept of specialty courts: immediate reaction to violations or problems with treatment, with the goal of addressing the treatment issue to insure that a defendant can succeed in treatment. Specialty courts focus more on outcomes and pay less attention to the formality of process and notions of procedural justice, which are central goals of the provision of counsel in criminal proceedings.

While Quinn's article was written almost five years ago, the high speed of the drug court movement that she cautioned against shows no signs of slowing down, and has even broadened its focus to include other courts as set forth above. And while some discussion has focused on the defense role in specialty courts, including the extent and quality of the representation, the widespread nature of these courts raises even more issues regarding the new forced non-adversarial role of defense attorneys practicing in these courts.

B. Treatment at Any Cost? Additional Issues that Plague the Forced Non-Adversarial Role of Defense Attorneys in Specialty Courts

Additional issues exist with respect to the new role of defense attorneys in the different court variations which embody principles of therapeutic and restorative justice. From a review of literature and my practice experience, I believe that questions still remain on the issue of whether the changed defense attorney role in specialty courts can provide zealous, effective, and competent representation to defendants.

1. Prosecutors Remain Adversarial

Conventional wisdom dictates that the prosecutor's job is to seek justice and not just win cases. The reality is, at times, different. With respect to a host of issues in the criminal justice system, prosecutors "hold the cards" and retain greater power than their counterparts in the defense bar. Some might argue their power exceeds that of judges. This very often holds true in the context of specialized courts. While the mantra of specialized courts is that prosecutors and defenders have to shed their traditional adversarial roles and work together as a team in the best interests of the defendant, the reality is that prosecutors in specialty courts still retain many vestiges of adversarial lawyering. Even though specialty court advocates might insist to the contrary, instances of adversarial prosecuting abound in the various incarnations of specialty courts....

Moreover, a good number of these courts will only allow the defendant to enter treatment if the prosecution consents. In determining whether to consent, prosecutors look at more than just the need for treatment or whether the defendant meets the program's previously set guidelines. Prosecutors often take into account prior criminal history (whether charged or uncharged), the desires of people in the community or law enforcement officers familiar with the defendant, factors surrounding the particular factual allegations, such as the crime rate in the neighborhood where the crime took place, and whether denying consent will provide leverage in some other matter, such as encouraging cooperation. With respect to the last factor, the action by the prosecution is both highly adversarial and not the least concerned with the best interests of the defendant. In such an instance, the "teamwork" between the prosecution and defense closely resembles plea bargaining, a classic example of traditional adversarial lawyering....

2. Getting the Treatment and Bearing the Burden:
Poor and Minority Populations in Specialty Courts

Statistics from drug courts indicate that the overwhelming majority of clients in this variation of specialty courts are poor and working class people who belong to minority groups. This may be explained, in part, by the historical evidence tending to show that law enforcement drug initiatives more frequently target urban areas where larger communities of color and poor people reside. Therefore, since there are more drug arrests among these populations, minorities and poor persons represent a large percentage of the individuals assigned to specialty courts. It is "almost inevitable" that individuals from these groups who have drug problems, or who fit the criteria for adjudication in other specialty courts, will also more acutely face any problems that are inherent in such courts, including the danger of inadequate defense representation.

Notes/Questions

1. Are you concerned that problem-solving courts require role changes for attorneys and judges? Are you concerned that one of the basic tenets of problem-solving courts is that defense lawyers should move away from their traditional role as advocates?

2. Can lawyers be expected to perform these new roles better (or worse) than adversarial behaviors? What additional skills might need to be taught?

3. Should judges be required to receive special training before operating these types of problem-solving courts? What might that training entail?

4. As this article notes, prosecutors often insist on a post-adjudication model for problem-solving courts. At the same time, defendants are often rushed into making decisions about whether to plead guilty and go into a problem-solving court, usually without knowing the consequences if they fail to comply with the problem-solving court rules/requirements. As we have discussed earlier in this book, prosecutors have extraordinary power in the criminal legal system and in the plea bargaining process. If you were a judge or defense lawyer who was concerned about this extraordinary power, how might you design a problem-solving court to lessen this power? What if the prosecutor will only agree to refer cases into these courts if it is post-adjudication? What else could you propose to lessen the power imbalance?

5. One concern is that drug courts often operate informally, and defendants may be unrepresented. As Tamar Meekins notes:

> For example, the Drug Court sets aside one to two days each week for new defendants to enter the program. On these days, the judge addresses all program entrants only after the court's case managers have found them to be eligible and the entrants have signed the appropriate waiver forms. Case managers ensure the entrant's eligibility to obtain waivers while interviewing the entrant outside the courtroom. However, no designated time exists for the court to call cases and because the court will often call cases without the defense attorney being present, the defense attorneys often do not attend the interview or court hearing. During the interview, the defendant is asked to sign legal documents which may have constitutional implications, and is asked about the extent of their drug use. Truthful answers to such questions may implicate Fifth Amendment protections against compelled self-incrimination. Such action may violate ethical rules because the attorney is not counseling the client as to a critical decision in the case. The decision is akin to determining whether to accept a guilty plea, to waive a trial by jury, or to testify; decisions, which under the rules, are exclusively left to the defendant. It is one of the most important decisions a defendant can make in a criminal case and should be undertaken only upon full advice and consultation with counsel.

II. Concerns with Offenders and the Law

These next two articles argue that drug courts are unfair to the offenders in terms of due process, sentencing, and actual punishment, and they continue the conversation around the NACDL 2009 report.

Norman L. Reimer, *Addicted to a Flawed Solution: Drug Courts Revisited*

35-APR Champion 7–8 (April 2011)

...

It has been two years since NACDL [National Association of Criminal Defense Lawyers] released a seminal study that focused on the burgeoning drug court phenomenon. The report, *America's Problem-Solving Courts: The Criminal Costs of Treatment and the Case for Reform*, fundamentally challenged the growing national acceptance of drug courts. For the first time, a major investigation conducted under the auspices of the criminal defense bar documented flaws in what many had perceived as a universally popular and effective alternative to lengthy incarceration.

NACDL based its report upon hearings conducted around the country. The task force received testimony from an array of stakeholders, including defense lawyers, prosecutors, drug court professionals, judges and ex-addicts. It found a widely disparate approach to drug courts. A few featured open admissions, did not require irrevocable waiver of rights, and carried minimal negative consequences for failure in treatment. But those were the exception.

All too often, drug courts denigrate fundamental rights, extracting broad waivers as the cost of admission, and expose even the most well-intended to dire consequences, often worse than if they avoided drug court and simply pleaded guilty. They tend to place a premium on early guilty pleas, thereby insulating questionable law enforcement search and seizure practices, and provide a convenient means for prosecutors to shed defective cases. And some drug courts impede the attorney-client relationship and undermine an accused person's Sixth Amendment right to a vigorous defense. Worse, many drug courts operate without transparent admission criteria, and most bar eligibility to recidivists and those most in need of treatment. These factors tend to exacerbate racial and economic disparities in the criminal justice system.

NACDL's report spawned a great deal of discussion. While some commentary has been critical, others are beginning to take a second look at drug courts and whether this approach is the best solution. On March 22, 2011, two new reports were released, both of which confirm NACDL's concerns.

The Justice Policy Institute (JPI) issued *Addicted to Courts: How a Growing Dependence on Drug Courts Impacts People and Communities*. The report makes the case that drug courts not only widen the net of criminal justice control, but they are less cost-effective, less fair, and no more successful in treating addiction. The report identifies several of the same problems NACDL detailed in its earlier report—"cherry picking" of those most likely to succeed, increased racial and economic disparity, and harsher outcomes for those who try and fail to complete drug court treatment programs.

The Drug Policy Alliance (DPA) released *Drug Courts Are Not the Answer: Toward a Heath-Centered Approach to Drug Use*. The DPA's report finds that drug courts have not demonstrated cost savings, reduced incarceration, or improved public safety. In fact, the report finds that drug courts leave many worse off for accepting that approach and have made the criminal justice system more punitive toward addiction. The DPA report asserts that there is an urgent need for a non-criminal, health-centered approach to drug use, and cites a wide range of data to support the contention that such an approach saves a fortune and reduces crime....

Let there be no mistake. Drug courts have helped many people. They have saved lives. They have probably saved hundreds of thousands of prison years. For clients facing a lengthy prison sentence, even a long shot at successful diversion must be considered. And therein lies the dilemma. As long as draconian penal policies drive America's drug policy, drug courts will thrive—irrespective of their flaws.

The JPI and DPA reports both cite a report finding that over 55,000 enter drug courts annually. This number represents only a tiny and select percentage of drug defendants. But if drug courts can only treat a sliver of those who need help, if they perpetuate inequity, reject the individuals most in need of treatment and divert precious resources toward a dead end solution, then they are not the answer. Drug courts may be a stop-gap measure that allows some to avoid harsh prison sentences and others to recover and end the cycle of self-destruction and despair. But they are no substitute for a long-term solution.

NACDL has long believed that addiction to any substance, whether legal or illegal, is really a health problem best treated by the medical community. The Association reiterated that view when it released its report on problem-solving courts. At the same time, the report listed a panoply of reforms that would make the drug court approach fairer and more widely available. With little progress toward real reform and the release of these new reports urging a public health approach, it is time to underscore NACDL's fundamental position: drug abuse and addiction are health problems. They are not criminal problems. Drug abusers are someone's sons and daughters, brothers and sisters, colleagues and neighbors. They are not inherently bad or evil. They are not criminals, and they should not be treated as such. A serious national conversation about the merits of decriminalization is long overdue.

Notes/Questions

1. Do you think the due process concerns raised above are sufficient to not start or shut down a drug court?

2. One scholar writes that those who are most likely to complete drug court are the recreational drug users who figure out how to "game" the court to avoid traditional sentences and get treatment they don't need. Meanwhile, serious addicts are far less likely to complete and more likely to "receive harsh termination sentences that often outstrip conventional plea prices." Josh Bowers, *Contraindicated Drug Courts*, 55 UCLA L. Rev. 783 (2008).

James L. Nolan, Jr., *Redefining Criminal Courts: Problem-Solving and the Meaning of Justice*

40 AMCRLR 1544–1562 (2004)

...

IV THE CONSEQUENCES OF JUST TREATMENT

If justice now means just treatment, what are the consequences of such a radical judicial reorientation? To answer this question, let us consider defenses of the "therapeutic ideal" offered by drug court judges in response to the more theoretically based criticisms previously leveled against the "rehabilitative ideal" in the 1970s. The rehabilitative ideal—commonly associated with the introduction of such practices as probation, parole, and a separate juvenile justice system—came under serious criticism when its characteristic practices of individualized treatment, indeterminate sentences, and unwieldy judicial discretion were increasingly viewed as inconsistent, disproportionate, and unfair. Do drug courts (and problem-solving courts more generally) result in similar unintended consequences—their evident differences with prior rehabilitative practices notwithstanding—and do these consequences challenge fundamental principles of justice? If so, how do judges respond to questions about these possible consequences?...

Critical assessments of drug courts likewise detect some coercive tendencies. Richard Boldt observes that though defendants in drug court "may receive needed rehabilitative services, they still face potential coercive, even punitive, dispositions." Likewise, William McColl comments that some drug court clients "experience greater criminal justice system involvement than the ordinary nonviolent offender in a like position." Drug court judges do not object to these characterizations. Indeed, the judges themselves highlight the punitive features of the court, and often warn defendants that noncompliance may result in more serious sanctions than would be experienced in a traditional criminal court. How, then, does the drug court judge respond to the argument that such practices are unjust—the basis of earlier critiques of the rehabilitative ideal?

Addressing this question, Judges Hora and Schma acknowledge that drug court "requirements may prove more onerous than the equivalent traditional court sanctions for the same offenses" and that this particular quality of the drug court "tends to disturb defense attorneys." Moreover, they recognize that drug courts "generally obligate a defendant to make more frequent court appearances and force the defendant to undertake forms of treatment which place more burdens on the defendant than normal probation." In response to the criticism that this may be unjust, they simply assert the preeminence of the therapeutic jurisprudence perspective. Accordingly, Hora and Schma maintain that the defense attorney who worries about potentially draconian judicial interventions has "unfounded apprehension" that stems from a "lack of understanding about ... the concept of therapeutic jurisprudence." From the enlightened therapeutic jurisprudence perspective, one understands that the "significant requirements of [the drug court] reflect the court's understanding that drug addiction is a disease and that intense court supervision provides the incentive for the defendant to stay in the program." In other words, the arduous demands of drug court must be considered in the context of the therapeutic benefits it offers the defendant.

So complete is this reinterpretation of judicial practices that sanctions themselves get relabeled. As one drug court judge put it, "he did not see himself as 'imposing punishment but as providing help.'" Similarly, Hora and Schma assert that "treatment regimens are not punishment, but the restructuring of the defendant's lifestyle." Notice that these judges do two things. First, they argue that the drug courts are indeed more demanding than the normal court. Second, they assert that these coercive interventions are not really punishment, but a "restructuring of the defendant's lifestyle." One response to this rather remarkable statement is that promoting lifestyle change is not the role of the judiciary. As the American Friends Service Committee argued in their influential 1971 critique of rehabilitative practices, "The whole person is not the concern of law. Whenever the law considers the whole person it is more likely that it will consider factors irrelevant to the purpose of delivering punishment."

Furthermore, simply altering the nomenclature (e.g., "lifestyle restructuring" instead of "punishment") does not make therapeutic legal practices any less punitive. Previous critics of the rehabilitative ideal denounced the practice of judicial label changing. Francis Allen, in his 1981 book The Decline of the Rehabilitative Ideal, derided the rehabilitative relabeling of solitary confinement as "constructive meditation"; of a detention facility as "Cloud Nine"; the disciplinary use of a powerful fire hose on the back of juvenile offenders as "hydrotherapy"; latrine cleaning as "work therapy"; and incarceration as "milieu therapy."

Problem-solving courts employ similar euphemisms. One domestic violence court judge uses "constructive intimidation" (i.e., substantial periods in jail) to motivate defendants. In drug courts, short-term incarceration has been called "shock therapy," "motivational jail," and "my motel." The imposition of a "sanction" is not a form of punishment, but a parent-like "response." Indeed, all aspects of drug court are interpreted in terms of their therapeutic effects. Hora and Schma have labeled drug court sanctions, "smart punishment," but even this is qualified. "Smart punishment is not really punishment at all, but a therapeutic response to the realistic behavior of drug offenders in the grip of addiction." Or again, as they put it, sanctions are really just the "restructuring of a defendant's lifestyle." Drug court judges defend compulsory "lifestyle change" on the ground that it is in the best interest of clients, whether or not the client himself realizes it. "These lifestyle changes provide the defendant with the very best chance of avoiding any further contact with the criminal justice system." Therefore, though the drug courts "may appear exhaustive and prohibitive," they "in fact work to ensure that the defendant successfully completes treatment." Because of this benevolent end, defense attorneys should get over their "unfounded apprehension" and embrace their new role of assisting in the "total improvement of the lives of their clients." This, according to Hora and Schma, is defense counsel's "best option," the realization of which simply "requires a therapeutic jurisprudence perspective." Once acquired, they argue, that perspective will enable defense attorneys "to more completely represent their clients."

A second and related issue for critics of the rehabilitative ideal was the matter of indeterminate sentences—sentences which varied according to one's performance in rehabilitative correctional settings. Ridding the criminal justice system of indeterminate sentences was one the main goals of the 1984 Sentencing Reform Act. Indeterminacy is also a reality in the drug courts. Most programs are publicly expected to last one year, though they commonly last much longer. In fact, clients are sometimes asked to sign waiver forms permitting the court to keep them in the program for an indeterminate period.

Unlike previous rehabilitative practices, indeterminacy in the case of the drug courts relates not to the length of a prison sentence, but to the amount of time a client spends under the authority of the judge-led drug court program. Therefore, the issue of indeterminacy plays itself out in the adjudicative rather than the correctional setting. This structural relocation may make less apparent and less glaring the issue of indeterminacy in the drug court. Still, recent critics have made the comparison to previous rehabilitative judicial practices.

Proponents of drug court have made several responses to criticisms regarding the injustice of indeterminacy. First, as McColl summarizes, "in relationship to the disease theory of addiction, such measures are necessary to break through the mechanism of denial and to institute a feeling of responsibility in otherwise unresponsive defendants." Thus, the therapeutic jurisprudence perspective argues that the length of one's participation in drug court should be evaluated in therapeutic rather than legal terms; under this approach, lengthy participation is justified if it serves to break down denial and contribute to recovery. Additionally, applying the treatment perspective means being patient with relapse. Relapses typically translate into extended periods of program participation. Allowing for relapse, as Hora and Schma argue, represents the "unknowing application of therapeutic jurisprudence in the [drug court] setting."

The indeterminate nature of the drug courts is also curiously defended on the ground that indeterminacy and concomitant lengthy periods of participation are evidence that the drug courts are tough on crime.

Some prosecutors worry that [drug court] sentencing of a defendant to a treatment program lets the defendant "get away" without accounting for his or her crime. This derivative of the soft on crime idea appears groundless when one compares the length and rigor of traditional incarceration and probation sentences and the length and requirements of [drug court] mandated treatment programs. Recent statistics show that a person convicted of a drug possession offense is just as likely to get probation as jail time and that median length of jail sentence for a drug possession offense is three months, while probation time is twenty-four months. Considering the fact that most [drug court] treatment programs last at least one year, not including recycle periods for relapse, the time commitment for treatment may not be much less than probation and probably will be greater than that of incarceration.

Drug court advocates thus defend indeterminacy by conceding that participation in the program rarely lasts the anticipated one year, and may well include a probation term that lasts two years or longer. This is asserted to fend off potential criticisms that drug courts coddle criminals.

William McColl likewise notes that, as with indeterminacy in previous judicial practices, indeterminacy in the drug courts typically leads to longer sentences. Like the drug court judges, he notes that indeterminacy and longer sentences actually provide a defense for drug court activists against the accusation that the drug courts are too easy on drug offenders. "The probability of receiving jail time and years of court-enforced treatment could serve to mollify those who favor punishment over other competing goals." However, while this may assuage the concerns of the "tough on crime" crowd, it also makes the drug court more vulnerable to criticism regarding the unjust nature of indeterminacy—a criticism that plagued previous advocates of the rehabilitative ideal.

In this regard, one issue that was taken up by liberal critics of the rehabilitative ideal is that indeterminacy and other features of rehabilitative justice can lead to serious violations of individual rights. Consider, for example, that the defense attorney—whose conventional role is to defend and guard the constitutional rights of his or her client—is compelled, in the context of the drug court's team approach, to put aside some of his or her traditional predilections. The forfeiting of such rights was precisely the kind of thing that bothered earlier critics of rehabilitative justice. These were among the first concerns expressed in opposition to the juvenile courts of the first part of the twentieth century. The lawyers of families involved with the early juvenile courts "questioned the court's right to deprive a child of liberty without due process, to forego trial by jury, to deny the right to appeal, to impose unequal penalties, and to disregard provisions for the equal protection of the law."

Recent critiques of the drug court have likewise raised questions about possible violations of individual constitutional rights. Boldt, for example, argues that for many drug court defendants, "the decision to participate in the treatment court process means that they effectively forego the presumption of innocence and the panoply of trial rights guaranteed by the Constitution." In fact, drug court clients typically sign forms waiving a host of constitutional rights in order to participate in drug court, including the right to trial by jury, the right to a speedy trial, the right to a preliminary hearing, and the requirement of probable cause for a search and seizure. Hora and Schma acknowledge that the waiving of "certain legal rights in order to gain entrance into the treatment program," is "[c]hief among defense attorneys' concerns" with the drug court program. However, they assert that the "preadjudicative model appears most consistent with the therapeutic orientation of the [drug court] concept." This is so because it facilitates the therapeutic goal of getting a client immediately into treatment, even if the client must waive fundamental rights to do so.

Another common defense for the drug court's provisional denial of constitutional rights is that participation in the drug courts, at least in preadjudicative programs, is entirely voluntary. In postadjudicative courts, on the other hand, where drug courts can in essence be a rather intensive condition of probation, they are clearly not voluntary. But even in preadjudicative courts, where it is more common for clients to sign waiver forms, there is some evidence to suggest that client participation is not always purely a voluntary decision. Consider one example a drug court judge provided during an interview.

Now this morning, for instance, there is this guy who is eligible. I tell him about the program. He says, "Well I'm about to get a job. I'm not interested in that." I said, "Okay, if you want to see a lawyer, that's fine." I said, "If you are going to have a job, you say you want to go through the public defender, well the public defender, unless you are very low income, won't be able to represent you. So do you want to hire a private attorney? Is that what you think you would like to do and then have about 15 pre-trials before this finally gets resolved? Or would it be more convenient for you if you are already working and then have to go to jail? Or would you like to come hear about the [drug court] program?"

The judge admitted to having pushed this client too hard. "Now I probably pushed too hard on that one. That probably I shouldn't have done, but I felt like doing that this morning. So I did." Consider similar practices in the Washington D.C. community court. As with many drug courts, the D.C. community court is pre-adjudicative. "In most cases, defendants don't plead guilty. Instead, the charges stand until the court-ordered resolution is completed; then the charges typically are dismissed." Defendants may refuse to participate, but if they are later tried and convicted Judge Noel Kramer takes "their refusal into account at sentencing."

Comments like these suggest that clients may not always have the kind of choice that is commonly asserted by court officials. But the fact that judges help clients to "volunteer" in this manner is actually consistent with the overall therapeutic jurisprudence philosophy and the conviction that treatment is what is best for the client, even if the client doesn't initially realize it. In fact, drug court advocates now have data pointing to the ostensible efficacy of coerced treatment. As reported in one drug court document, "Research indicates that a person coerced to enter treatment by the criminal justice system is likely to do as well as one who volunteers."

Coerced treatment is most apparent in post adjudicative assignments to the drug court. According to a 1997 Justice Department survey, in approximately 16 percent of the drug court programs all participating clients are post-plea clients; they enter drug courts before trial, but after a plea of guilty. In another 12 percent, drug court clients participate post-conviction but with deferred sentencing. In the second case, they are simply assigned participation in drug court, with virtually no choice in the matter. Drug court judges admit that "the post-adjudicative model does present some problems," and that a client "may also risk waiving certain defenses to charges, as well as the right to a trial." While Hora and Schma see the pre-adjudicative model as more in keeping with therapeutic jurisprudence theory, they also believe that the post-adjudicative model "may have great therapeutic impact." They believe this because having to publicly admit to drug use can force a client out of denial. As they put it, "the court proceedings may force the offender to accept her addiction and may help her overcome denial, one of the hallmarks of drug abuse and addiction." It is admitting to "drug use," not "guilt," that they view as therapeutically beneficial. In fact, inasmuch as the post-adjudicative model forces the client to admit guilt, this may be "anti-therapeutic because post-adjudication [drug courts] which require guilty pleas often meet with resistance."

As illustrated in these discussions, the just desert model isn't so much resisted as it is replaced. The judges do not really debate whether certain legal sanctions or methods of adjudication are fair or unfair, too harsh or too lenient, proportional or excessive. Rather, practices are interpreted according to the extent to which they promote or discourage therapeutic outcomes. Inasmuch as therapeutic jurisprudence becomes an increasingly dominant paradigm, debate over the traditional goals of punishment won't so much be resolved as made irrelevant. But will the therapeutic jurisprudence model ever become that dominant? This question relates to another concern expressed by the earlier critics of the rehabilitative ideal, namely the net-widening tendencies of rehabilitative programs in the judicial system.

The net-widening effect has been a defining feature of the drug court movement. Contrary to the typical claims of drug court advocates, drug courts can actually increase rather than relieve the burden of an individual court's heavy caseload. In Denver, Colorado, for example, the number of drug cases grew dramatically after the initiation of drug courts, from 1,135 filed cases in 1993 (the last full year before the implementation of drug court) to 3,223 in 1996 (the second full year of drug court). According to Judge Morris Hoffman of the Denver criminal court, "The very presence of the drug court, with its significantly increased capacity for processing cases, has caused police to make arrests in, and prosecutors to file, the kinds of ten-and twenty-dollar hand-to-hand drug cases that the system simply would not have bothered with before...." The expansion of cases in the Miami drug court led to one of the few critical media accounts of the movement. Reacting to reports on the Miami drug court's inclusion of serious offenders with long criminal histories, Seminole County Circuit Judge O.H. Eaton, Jr., worried that the program was becoming a "dumping ground"; and a Miami drug court prosecutor compared the expansion of the Miami drug court to a "rubber band that is being stretched and stretched and stretched.... [V]ery soon, it may snap."

The net-widening qualities of the drug court involve more than programmatic expansion. Therapeutic jurisprudence also allows the court to extend its authority into the lives of drug court clients in unprecedented ways. Consider a discussion among California drug court judges who sought to amend the California penal code so that drug courts might have authority to randomly search drug court clients and their homes. The proposed amendment called for a "requirement that the defendant submit to a search by a probation officer or peace officer of his or her person, personal effects, automobile or home, any time of the day or night, with or without probable cause." Most judges supported the measure. In fact, several admitted to already employing the practice. The one judge who did object to the amendment was offered the following defense of the practice by another drug court judge:

> I support a search clause for drug treatment court clients because I think a search clause is therapeutic.... Random [urine] testing keeps clients clean and so will a search clause. It also enables us to do other interventions such as getting a using partner into couples counseling, anger management, etc. and provid[ing] parenting classes if the home situation is not good. It helps keep participants from associating with the "wrong people" and with being in the "wrong place at the wrong time".... I don't see a search clause as a sanction so much as an additional therapeutic intervention that will help them succeed.

Notice that the therapeutic perspective not only justifies random searches of the drug court client's person and home without probable cause; it also allows the court to make judgments regarding persons associated with the drug court client, the result of which may be further judicially sanctioned therapeutic intervention (e.g., parenting and anger management classes).

Notes/Questions

1. Nolan notes concerns with indeterminate sentencing, judicial bullying and the lack of constitutional rights in these courts. Which of these are most concerning to you? Do you think these risks outweigh the benefits outlined by other articles?

2. Another scholar points out the issue of voice and perceived procedural justice in these courts:

> Notably, the rhetoric of the treatment program complex advances the principles of therapeutic jurisprudence, which hold that the court should "adapt its practices to assist in the therapeutic process of recovery," including by ensuring that a defendant's voice is heard. And treatment courts have been lauded for adhering to the principles of procedural justice, including (1) enabling litigants to have a voice in the proceedings; (2) treating litigants with respect; (3) unbiased decision-making; and (4) ensuring that litigants understand their rights, obligations, and the decisions that were made.
>
> However, proponents of treatment courts also view giving defendants a voice as a means to the end of ensuring compliance. As one report stated, defendants are more likely to "defer to or comply with the decisions made by the judge and others in authority" when they perceive a greater degree of procedural justice. Thus, even if treatment courts encourage defendant speech—and defendants may actually speak more frequently during the multiple status hearings each case may entail—in reality, the opportunity provided for defendants to speak is primarily meant to make defendants "feel [as if] they have input when they may not." Moreover, despite offering defendants opportunities to speak, the treatment program complex ultimately embraces a "paternal-

istic notion that the court is best able to identify and meet the client's best interests and needs."

Evelyn L. Malave, *Distorted Narratives in the Treatment Program Complex*, 93 FORDHAM L. REV. 843 (2024).

3. If you were advising a client accused of drug use who was given the opportunity to either go through the drug court or "regular" court, which option would you advise? What factors would you consider in deciding what to advise your client?

What Do Medical Professionals Have to Say?

As Erin Collins discussed in the previous chapter, in 2017, Physicians for Human Rights published a critical report on drug courts, declaring them "Neither Justice nor Treatment." The physicians were more concerned about whether drug courts are appropriately treating the medical condition of drug addiction. Both the National Association of Criminal Defense Lawyers and Physicians for Human Rights share the concern that these courts may not be the right place to treat drug addiction. The report went on to conclude that,

> In many cases, court officials with no medical background mandated inappropriate treatment not rooted in the evidence base, or mandated treatment for people who didn't need it.... The most egregious example of this was the refusal, delay, or curbing of medication-assisted treatment... to people with opioid use disorders, despite evidence that treatment for such disorders in many cases required long-term—sometimes permanent—medication.

Physicians for Human Rights expressed concern about "involuntary treatment," as doctors consider the patient voluntarily consenting to treatment to be a key principle to ethical medical care. The report also expressed concern about the impact of treatment when it is not voluntary:

> From a medical perspective, there is little evidence to support enhanced effectiveness of involuntary treatment for substance use disorders. A systematic analysis of the scientific evidence on the effectiveness of compulsory drug treatment published in 2016 concluded that the limited literature on this subject did not, on the whole, suggest improved outcomes from compulsory treatment, with some studies suggesting potential harms. From a human rights perspective, as well, the voluntary nature of the treatment is paramount, as the rights to health and physical autonomy require informed and meaningful consent to treatment.[1]

As you continue reading, you will want to think about the role of legal professionals both traditionally and in the context of problem-solving courts. In fact, in 2022 the Department of Justice successfully sued several states for discrimination against people

---

1. PHYSICIANS FOR HUMAN RIGHTS, NEITHER JUSTICE NOR TREATMENT: DRUG COURTS IN THE UNITED STATES 19 (2019).

with opioid use disorder by preventing people under court supervision from taking prescribed medications to treat their disorder (including methadone). The allegations stated that even in drug and mental health courts, judges were preventing people from following their doctors' orders. As the DOJ put it, court policies meant that defendants had an agonizing choice: "take their medication and face incarceration and termination from their treatment court program or forgo their medication and suffer painful withdrawal symptoms while risking relapse, overdose and death."[2]

Should doctors be part of drug courts or mental health courts to ensure best practices in medical care? Or does the structure of problem-solving courts prevent medical professionals from being able to insist on particular treatments?

III. Ideas for Moving Forward

The two articles below defend problem-solving courts and provide suggestions for improving them. As you read, are your concerns from the previous section sufficiently alleviated?

Greg Berman, *Redefining Criminal Courts: Problem-Solving and the Meaning of Justice*

41 AMCRLR 1313–1319 (2004)

...

The central argument of James Nolan's "Redefining Criminal Courts: Problem-Solving and the Meaning of Justice" seems to be that problem-solving courts have become so blinded by the seductive rhetoric of "therapeutic jurisprudence" that they have lost sight of fundamental legal principles like due process and proportionality. At the heart of Nolan's critique is the concern that, if the advocates of problem-solving courts have their way, treatment will somehow come to replace fairness as a central value of the American justice system.

To illustrate his point that problem-solving courts are attempting a "radical judicial reorientation," Nolan cites a number of harrowing stories from the frontlines of American drug courts—stories of judges coercing defendants into treatment, of courts that use Orwellian doublespeak when sanctioning offenders, of drug court advocates seeking to extend the authority of the court into the homes of drug court participants. The cumulative impact of these anecdotes is to paint a dire portrait of drug courts. Indeed, reading Nolan, one might easily conclude that drug courts are, to quote from another critic, a "caricature of a courtroom, in which judges are anything but impartial, defense lawyers are virtually invisible, prosecutors are making most of the decisions about who may or may not participate ... and service providers are the primary information source."

2. DOJ Press release, Justice Department Secures Agreement with Pennsylvania Courts to Resolve Lawsuit Concerning Discrimination Against People with Opioid Use Disorder, Feb. 1, 2024.

As Nolan's stories of bullying judges and the importation of twelve-step vocabulary into the courtroom make clear, it is possible to find some examples of shoddy practice happening in drug courts across the country. It would be foolish not to admit this. It would be even more foolish to try to defend such practices. The truth is that any system staffed by idiosyncratic and fallible humans will occasionally result in bad practice. Bad practice should be rooted out of problem-solving courts, just as it should be rooted out of conventional courts.

Nolan does a great service to the field by identifying some of the more egregious examples of misbehavior in drug courts. He fails to make the case, however, that bad practice is somehow intrinsic to drug courts. Put simply, there is no evidence to suggest that shoddy judging and substandard lawyering is any more widespread in drug courts than in conventional state courts. Quite the contrary. There is good reason to believe that these closely-watched experiments, with their emphasis on state-of-the-art technology, accountability and formalized systems of sanctions and rewards, actually reduce the potential for judges and other court players to run amok.

Beyond the issue of bad practice, Nolan's critique of drug courts raises a number of other questions, four of which are worth sharing here.

I. ARE PROBLEM-SOLVING COURTS EXAMPLES OF THERAPEUTIC JURISPRUDENCE?

Nolan's argument is built on the assumption that drug courts are "a direct application of therapeutic jurisprudence theory." As articulated by its two leading proponents, David Wexler and Bruce Winick, therapeutic jurisprudence has been defined as "the use of social science to study the extent to which a legal rule or practice promotes the psychological and physical well-being of the people it affects."

To support his claim that drug courts are real-life examples of therapeutic jurisprudence in action, Nolan relies on a law review article by two drug court judges (and a co-author) that argues that "without being conscious of its use" drug courts have been applying therapeutic jurisprudence to the problems of addicted criminal defendants. Thus, therapeutic jurisprudence provides "the legal and jurisprudential foundations of this new criminal justice concept."

There are good reasons why some drug court practitioners have been attracted to therapeutic jurisprudence: it's outcome-oriented, multi-disciplinary, emphasizes empirically verifiable results and asks practitioners to think outside of the confines of individual cases. That's all part and parcel of the daily work of not only drug courts, but community courts, mental health courts and other problem-solving initiatives as well.

While there is significant overlap between therapeutic jurisprudence and problem-solving courts, it would be a mistake to conflate the two. While some drug court practitioners have embraced therapeutic jurisprudence, many others blanch at the concept. Their concerns are two-fold. First, they worry that therapeutic jurisprudence is a political liability as a label, an instant turn-off for those who, like Nolan, immediately conjure images of Clockwork Orange and judges leading twelve-step programs.

More substantively, there is a concern that the therapeutic label does not adequately describe either the origins or the methods of problem-solving courts—that it places these courts too squarely in the business of rehabilitation. Problem-solving courts are, of course, concerned with rehabilitation, and they do, in fact, rely on therapeutic interventions to change the behavior of offenders. But this represents just part of their work. Much of what problem-solving courts do has no explicit therapeutic dimension. When community courts sentence low-level offenders to perform community service, it is not because they are trying to "heal" the offenders, but because they want to pay back the local neighborhood that has been harmed by crime. When domestic violence courts require batterers to return to court for judicial monitoring of their compliance with orders of protection, it isn't with any therapeutic intent, but to try to make sure they don't continue to abuse their partners.

The point here is not to deny that there is a relationship between problem-solving courts and therapeutic justice, but rather to suggest that it is a more complicated one than Nolan's reading suggests. Nolan's article simply elides the differences. It also elides the differences between and among various problem-solving models. Drug courts are different than community courts. Community courts are different than mental health courts. Mental health courts are different than domestic violence courts. It is worth keeping these distinctions in mind before drawing broad conclusions.

II. WHERE ARE THE DEFENSE ATTORNEYS?

Given Nolan's concerns about "possible violations of individual constitutional rights" in drug courts, it is worth spending a few moments looking at the role of defenders. Defense attorneys are explicitly charged with representing the interests of defendants in order to ensure the fairness of the justice system. What role do they play in these new experiments?

Reading Nolan, it would be easy to come away with the impression that there were no defense attorneys in drug courts or that the ones who practice there are effectively bound and gagged by overzealous judges and prosecutors. This is simply not true.

The reality is that both drug courts and conventional state courts are fundamentally collaborative enterprises that require the active participation of prosecutors, judges and defenders if they are going to work. Simply put, defense attorneys could effectively shut down drug courts if they wanted to by refusing to participate or let their clients plead guilty and enter treatment. By and large, of course, this hasn't happened.

Why not? One answer can be found in a letter written by Daniel Greenberg, the head of the Legal Aid Society in New York City, to the New York Law Journal. In the letter, Greenberg argues on behalf of judge-driven alternatives to incarceration programs like drug courts as compared to diversion programs that operate out of prosecutors' offices:

Common sense tells us we are all better served when accused criminal defendants with addiction problems are treated rather than incarcerated for unconscionably long periods.... The Legal Aid Society has supported effective alternatives to incarceration programs and we hope that their success will expand the willingness of others to use them.... We believe that greater promise of fairness and success lies with returning discretion to judges to fashion appropriate remedies and programs.

It would be facile to suggest that Greenberg's letter is emblematic of widespread enthusiasm for drug courts within the defender community; defenders have had a wide range of responses to drug courts—from open hostility to grudging acceptance to growing endorsement. But it is worth asking why defender agencies like the Legal Aid Society have expressed support, however conditional, for these programs.

By and large, it is because the good drug courts have included defenders in the planning process, giving them a seat at the table when determining eligibility criteria, treatment mandates and sanctioning schemes. It is because the good drug courts have delivered what defenders have wanted from courts for years—treatment instead of incarceration for their clients. And it is because the good drug courts have not, in fact, lost sight of proportionality. The moment that drug courts start trying to send first-time offenders arrested for shoplifting to eighteen months of in-patient treatment is the moment when public defenders will opt for trial instead of encouraging their clients to plead. Defenders vote with their feet; if drug courts didn't offer them (and their clients) a good deal, they wouldn't agree to play.

III. COMPARED TO WHAT?

What is the alternative to drug court? By implication, Nolan's article suggests that the alternative is a "classical" due process model in which each case receives a full-blown adversarial trial.

The reality is that, by and large, our state courts no longer operate on a classical adversarial model (if indeed they ever did).... A couple of points about standard practice in the state courts are worth underlining:

<u>Plea Bargaining</u>—More than nine out of ten cases in state courts are resolved not by trial but by plea bargain. Prosecutors and defenders have effectively been transformed into negotiators and deal-makers rather than adversarial litigators.

<u>Intermediate Sanctions</u>—The most common form of punishment in state courts is, in fact, probation—close to half of felony offenders receive probation sentences (this doesn't include misdemeanants, which would only increase the numbers). According to the U.S. Bureau of Justice Statistics, close to fifteen percent of felony offenders also receive either drug treatment or community service mandates. The bottom line is that, with or without problem-solving courts, the American criminal justice system is in the business of linking offenders to community-based services and supervision.

<u>Effectiveness</u>—Courts may already be in the business of community-based sanctions, but they don't do a particularly good job of it. Probation caseloads in some cities are as high as 1,000 cases per officer. It should come as little surprise that half of all probationers fail to complete their sanctions as ordered and two-thirds of probationers are re-arrested within three years.

As currently constructed, state courts are something less than a complete success in terms of either fairness or effectiveness. That is, business as usual in the courts can boast neither the due process protections of the classical adversarial model nor the emphasis on effective sentencing of the problem-solving model. Put simply, it is difficult to marshal a persuasive argument in favor of maintaining the status quo in the state courts.

Problem-solving courts represent an honest acknowledgment on the part of court administrators that the criminal justice system disposes of a high percentage of cases in a non-adversarial fashion and that the outcomes of these cases are often community-based treatment and supervision. Problem-solving courts didn't create these realities. What problem-solving courts have done is to improve court infrastructure, bringing new tools—technology, accountability mechanisms, research data, links to effective treatment regimens—into the courthouse. In doing so, problem-solving courts have improved the compliance of offenders with intermediate sanctions and encouraged courts to make greater use of alternatives to incarceration where appropriate. They have also changed the life-trajectories of thousands of offenders, helping them move from addiction to sobriety and from crime to law-abiding behavior.

All of which begs the question: Do problem-solving courts represent a "transformation of the adjudicative setting"? Do they alter the underlying theory of justice upon which our courts were founded? Or are they instead simply a change in methodology? Is it like doing addition with a calculator instead of by hand—the technology is different, but the underlying math is the same?

IV. IS THIS A FALSE CHOICE?

Throughout his essay, Nolan sets up a dangerous dichotomy between efficacy and justice, between problem-solving and due process. Is this fair? Do we have to choose between them? Can the two co-exist comfortably side by side? What might this look like? A trip to the Red Hook Community Justice Center, a community court in Brooklyn that handles low-level criminal cases (along with selected civil and family court matters), offers some hints.

Visitors who sit in the courtroom in Red Hook are often surprised to discover that every defendant is represented by counsel and that the prosecution stands up on every case. On a typical day, the majority of the offenders who plead guilty to crimes like drug possession, shoplifting and prostitution in Red Hook end up receiving alternative sanctions like community restitution, job training or treatment rather than incarceration. But a typical day also finds a handful of cases dismissed because the prosecution has not presented a convincing case. And a typical day also sees a few cases receiving jail sentences because the judge deems the offenders a risk to public safety. What this suggests is that the problem-solving approach has not affected the court's ability to weigh the merits of each case. On the contrary, a problem-solving court like the one in Red Hook gives judges and attorneys more options so they can provide more individualized justice to defendants.

At the end of the day, if they are done right, problem-solving courts have the potential to improve not just the effectiveness of sentencing, but the fairness of case processing as well. The good problem-solving courts are already achieving this vision. The challenge is to make sure that all problem-solving courts are good ones.

Tamar M. Meekins, *"Specialized Justice": The Over-Emergence of Specialty Courts and the Threat of a New Criminal Defense Paradigm*

40 Suffolk U. L. Rev. 1, 50–55 (2006)

...

Part VI. Proposed Solutions for the Provision of Defense Services in Specialty Courts

While it remains to be seen whether specialty courts will continue or whether they represent the paradigm shift some have noted, there is a growing sense that the problems and issues that have been noted by many scholars and practitioners, especially with regard to the defense role, must be studied, evaluated, and addressed cautiously. As such, there must be more and more consideration of not only the theoretical foundations of this new system of jurisprudence or the rhetorical statements of what these courts wish to do, but more importantly, the practical issues that are raised every day in these types of courts. Court reformers, judges, lawyers, and scholars have to be concerned with real solutions and modifications to address any inequalities, injustices, and ethical or practice issues. At this juncture in the life of specialty court jurisprudence, some modifications can be implemented to make sure that the real and perceived non-zealous representation does not blossom into a blight on the nation's specialty courts. The following proposals seek to counteract this danger.

A. Institutionalize Adversarialism into the Defender's Role

If prosecutors retain many vestiges of adversarialism, and the judge is a central figure with the power to direct the treatment provided in the specialty court, then there is no good reason for the defender to remain in this category of "forced non-adversarialism." In fact, such an imbalance of power in the specialty court is troubling and may lead to further issues of defense inadequacy. Moreover, the therapeutic and restorative goals of specialty courts can still be accomplished with the traditional model of adversarial defense representation. Since there would still be the provision of treatment and interaction with the judge regarding treatment, the central principles of the specialty court would be met....

In specialty courts, therefore, the everyday model of a defender should be one who is zealous, competent, and effective. No matter what the guidelines, eligibility requirements, or rules of the specialty court, defenders should be trained always to: ask for more time to determine if the defendant wishes to enter the treatment program; file any appropriate motions while in treatment court, including motions to dismiss or suppress evidence; challenge the level or extent of treatment if seemingly inappropriate or unworkable for the client; file and assert due process challenges against the imposition of sanctions; argue the substantive inappropriateness of sanctions; thoroughly investigate the factual allegations of the case, with no time bar; and intervene when the judge seeks to illicit incriminating or secret and confidential statements from the client. Such zealous advocacy will not frustrate the goals of the specialty court, but will potentially increase its effectiveness because these actions by defenders will have system-wide beneficial implications. For example, if law enforcement groups understand that abusive and illegal police practices are still challenged in the specialty court, then they might abandon the use of the specialty court as a dumping ground for non-meritorious cases. Additionally, prosecutors might be more careful in determining what cases to bring and which cases to divert completely from the criminal justice system, thereby reducing the number of non-meritorious cases on the specialty court docket. Moreover, specialty court stakeholders, including prosecutors, case managers, and judges, should be trained that when a defender is adversarial and advocates for the rights and wishes of her client, it does not detract from the potential benefit of providing treatment, when appropriate, to a client.

B. Additional Training for Defenders in Specialty Courts

Many scholars and practitioners have called for increased financial resources in order to upgrade the level of practice for indigent defenders. In the context of specialty courts, both institutional defender agency attorneys and private bar attorneys should be trained thoroughly on all aspects of the treatment court, including the science of addiction, therapeutic and restorative justice principles, procedural and substantive due process, "available treatment programs and sanctions, client assessment tools, treatment cycles and methodologies, and … the court's documentation and processes." Additionally, attorneys should receive training in basic ethics and practice standards, trial and courtroom skills, and legal writing. Only with adequate education and training can we expect to elevate the level of practice in specialty courts.…

C. Make Real Changes to the System for Appointment of Counsel

As noted above, judges can assert economic power by controlling the appointments that private attorneys receive in specialty courts. This can chill the zealous advocacy that a lawyer should provide to his client. To combat this possibility or perception, specialty courts should not allow individual judges to appoint lawyers, nor should the court use only a small cadre of attorneys to represent defendants in the particular specialty court. Use of a central lottery appointments process and a system of vertical representation will lessen the impact of economic disincentive to zealous representation.

D. Incorporate a Dual Track System for Specialty Court Cases

Specialty court clients should have the opportunity to contest illegal and abusive police conduct and to assert their innocence at trial without the loss of needed treatment services. In order to accomplish this, cases in which the client wishes to contest the allegations against her should remain on a traditional calendar for normal case adjudication and should, at the same time, proceed on the specialty court calendar where the defendant can receive treatment and services. The specialty court should refrain from any action that will impair the defendant's rights when contesting the case.

Court rules should be amended to forbid eliciting incriminatory statements in court and using such statements in any prosecutions....

E. Evaluate and Study the Perception of Defender Role Among Specialty Court Clients

The necessity and value of the criminal defender to our legal system is significant. Even those scholars who question and challenge our current adversarial system and the overzealousness of some advocates recognize the importance of the criminal defender, particularly one who provides indigent defense services. The ability of the attorney-client relationship to transform perceptions about the legal system, improve satisfaction with its outcomes, and boost acceptance of its dispositions is substantial and important in both traditional and specialty courts. To clarify the defender's role in specialty courts, court systems and non-profit agencies require more empirical data. Accordingly, they should study defenders', victims', and witnesses' perceptions of lawyering. Additionally, they should examine the effect defense lawyering roles, strategies, and skills have on client decision-making and satisfaction with the process.

F. Conclusion

I am not the first to call for caution in the entrenchment of the methodology and theory of specialty courts in the criminal justice system. Indeed, several authors have noted that the subject demands more discussion, study, and evaluation. If the recent emergence of variations on the drug court model signals a paradigm shift in our system's administration of cases, then the way criminal defenders practice may also shift. We must remain aware of how such a change in defender practice might imperil our legal system and the cultural and impact-setting effect of silent approval of ineffective, under-zealous, and unethical practice. Because defenders are crucial to the principle of justice in all judicial settings, courts must be vigilant about the reality of the defender role and the quality of defender services in emerging models of justice.

* * *

This final excerpt concludes that problem-solving courts can provide examples for how to change the entire criminal legal system combining the goals of the abolitionist movement with the original goals of the problem-solving courts.

Erin R. Collins, *Beyond Problem-Solving Courts*

25 Cardozo Journal of Conflict Resolution,
242–249, 252–254 (2023)

A. Beyond Criminal Courts

There are a few existing models within the criminal system that share the specialized court goal of providing treatment and services for certain people, such as people who are exhibiting signs of substance use disorder or mental health illness, or people who are suspected of or charged with certain crimes. Prosecutor-led diversion programs, which allow prosecutors to divert people arrested for certain offenses into treatment instead of instituting official charges, share many similarities with problem-solving courts.

Another model empowers law enforcement officers to refer people to drug or mental health treatment services instead of arresting them for certain low-level crimes. Some of these programs feature Crisis Intervention Teams, which are collaborative efforts by law enforcement and community-based mental health service providers to intervene with services and support instead of arrest when someone is experiencing a mental health crisis. Other programs allow law enforcement to "deflect" people suspected of drug-related crimes to treatment instead of arresting them. The law-enforcement models improve on some of the shortcomings of prosecutor-led diversion.

But there are fundamental shortcomings of both models. First, and perhaps most problematically, both approaches—like problem-solving courts—position criminal system actors as gatekeepers to treatment services, services that are in short supply and often inaccessible independent of the criminal system. This linkage between criminal system actors and services continues to imbue treatment with the specter of carceral consequences for failure to complete treatment. This threat—real or imagined—will necessarily deter participation by those who are skeptical of the criminal system and wary of promises that they will not be arrested, prosecuted, or punished.

Positioning criminal system actors as treatment gatekeepers has another significant downside. While prosecutor diversion and law enforcement deflection models change the identity of the diversion decision-maker, they do not resolve the problems that arise when we ask system actors to adopt new roles and responsibilities as treatment advocates or managers, roles that conflict with their traditional powers. Furthermore, each of these models involve discretionary decisions by prosecutors and law enforcement to divert people to treatment, decisions that will remain deeply susceptible to racial bias. And by positioning criminal system actors as service gatekeepers, these models, like problem-solving courts, require dedicating more money to criminal system actors and programs—money that will further cement the criminal system as a primary provider of much-needed social services.

B. Beyond The Criminal System

The problem-solving court movement emerged as an experiment in helping people avoid contact with the criminal system in the future by providing them with access to treatment and other supportive services. Another robust contemporary movement—carceral abolition—shares this experimentalist spirit, the goal of providing people with the services and support they need to thrive, and a vision for the future in which interactions with criminal system are minimized or non-existent. But abolitionist principles provide a different conceptualization of the problem that causes criminalization and a vision for the future that is distinct from that that embraced by the problem-solving court movement. These differences reveal strategies for achieving this shared goal in in ways that can avoid the pitfalls of criminal system-centered approaches....

While abolitionism and problem-solving courts are both dedicated to providing support as a way to reduce future harm, there are many important differences between the two approaches. For abolitionists, the problem that must be addressed is not with the people who enter and re-enter the system. Rather, abolitionists focus on the way the system and its many actors repeatedly target the same people and communities for arrest and prosecution while simultaneously creating conditions that leave people particularly vulnerable to state surveillance and intervention, such as lack of meaningful education and employment opportunities, and housing instability. And this conceptual shift leads to a very different, and much more expansive, reform agenda: a demand to change the system itself. In other words, abolition supports providing aid and treatment services in ways that do not perpetuate or enlarge the power, scope, or authority of the carceral state—through "non-reformist reforms." In contrast, abolitionists resist "reformist reforms," or "changes that tinker at the edges of the existing system and fail to target the structural origins of inequality and injustice....

With regards to access to drug treatment, mental health care, and other life-sustaining services, however, abolitionist principles do offer a unitary vision: such services should be available to all who want them, independently of the criminal system....

Abolitionist principles would also support funding efforts to address other needs that can leave people vulnerable to criminal system targeting, such as safe and secure housing. An abolitionist perspective understands that the experience of being unhoused puts stress on people that may cause or exacerbate other vulnerabilities, such as substance use, which can then lead to criminalization. The Housing First model, for example, focuses on providing permanent supportive housing to people experiencing homelessness. Importantly, this model emphasizes that safe housing—not treatment—should be provided first, with very few barriers to entry, and then people should be given the opportunity to access other supportive services on a voluntary basis. It is thus a shift from the "treatment first" model that requires people to complete treatment programs or demonstrate abstinence from all substances before they are offered stable housing....

In sum, abolitionist experiments in supportive service provision can and do look like a lot of different things. Crucially, however, any abolitionist experiment resists restricting access to such services to certain populations based on the notion that only certain people are deserving of support or that others are too risky to merit such access....

Conclusion

The problem-solving court model emerged as a genuine experiment aimed at helping some people avoid the harms of traditional punishment. Now, more than thirty years later, it is time to admit that the experiment has not succeeded in achieving its goals for many, and to acknowledge the ways in which this reform model itself can cause unintended harm. It is not time to give up on the experimentalist spirit, but rather to use it as inspiration to seek other ways of achieving these noble goals. Meanwhile, in the decades during which this particular experiment has been underway, it has become increasingly clear that the criminal system enacts deep and enduring harm on the people it targets and their communities. If we want to meaningfully address this problem, we must look for new solutions not just beyond problem-solving courts, but beyond the criminal system entirely.

Notes/Questions

1. So now that you have finished both chapters on problem-solving courts, do you agree that it is appropriate for the criminal legal system to engage in drug treatment?

2. Do you think that lawyers (including judges) have the right professional backgrounds to engage in therapeutic justice? What special training or background do you think should be required for legal professionals to work in drug courts (if any)?

3. Many states authorize judges to create problem-solving courts as they see fit and a few actually require it. For example, Texas requires drug courts for all jurisdictions with a population over 200,000.[3] And Missouri's new law in 2021 required state circuit courts to create a treatment court division.[4] Do you think it makes sense for every state to have similar requirements? Why?

4. One criticism of the Texas legislation is that it does not specify exactly how the drug courts should work (whether it should be a diversion program or post-conviction) or who should be eligible (only first time offenders or those with more serious criminal records). This means that where a defendant with a drug problem is arrested is the key determining factor of whether they will be eligible for drug court within Texas. Is that a concern? What structural changes would you make to this law (or any state law) to improve the operation of drug courts?

5. One of Berman's main arguments is that problem-solving courts are still better than plea bargaining in a typical criminal court. Is this the correct comparison to make? And do you agree with him?

6. Which of Meekins' suggestions from this last article are easiest to implement? Which are the most important? Do you have other suggestions for improving problem-solving courts or would you follow Collins' suggestion to perhaps eliminate these completely?

---

3. Texas H.B. 530 (80th legislature 2007). This requirement is contingent on state or federal funding being available. This is an expansion of the requirement, as originally, only counties with a population over 550,000 were required to have drug courts. *See also* Texas H.B. 1287 (77th legislature, 2001).

4. H.B 547, 100th Gen. Assemb., Reg. Sess (Mo. 2019). See also W.Va. Code 62-15-4 requiring all West Virginia judicial circuits to be participating in a drug court or regional drug court program.

Additional Resources

Erin Collins, *Beyond Problem Solving Courts*, 25 Cardozo J. Conflict Resol. 229, 229–230, 233–241, 242–249, 252–254 (2023).

David J. Cronwell, John Blad & Martin Wright, Civilising Criminal Justice: An International Restorative Agenda for Penal Reform (2013).

Jane Donoghue, Transforming Criminal Justice? Problem-Solving and Court Specialisation, Routledge Frontiers of Criminal Justice (2014).

Michael O'Hear, The Failed Promise of Sentencing Reform (2017).

Mae C. Quinn, *Whose Team Am I On Anyway? Musings of a Public Defender About Drug Treatment Court Practice*, 26 N.Y.U. Rev. L. & Soc. Change 37 (2000–01).

Chapter 10

Restorative Justice

"Restorative justice is defined as much through the processes it employs to redress harm as it is through its goals."

—Leigh Goodmark[1]

Restorative justice is not a new idea. As you will read in the excerpts below, the theories and practices of restorative justice have existed in many different cultures around the world for years. It is, however, a fairly new option within the criminal legal system of the United States.

The term restorative justice refers to a wide range of practices that might be in lieu of, alongside, or after a formal criminal prosecution. In 2000, the United Nations passed a resolution entitled "Basic Principles on the use of restorative justice programmes in criminal matters."[2] The UN defined "restorative process" as "any process in which the victim, the offender and/or any other individuals or community members affected by a crime actively participate together in the resolution of matters arising from the crime, often with the help of a fair and impartial third party. Examples of restorative process include mediation, conferencing, and sentencing circles."[3] The resolution went on to recommend that restorative justice "should be generally available at all stages of the criminal justice process."[4]

As you will read, one of the distinguishing features of restorative justice programs in the United States is that they have started for the most part due to interested (some might say passionate) individuals who have lobbied for changes in the criminal legal system. Often these individuals are "outsiders" who are not lawyers or professionals within the criminal legal system. However, once programs begin, a large number of professionals, including lawyers, judges, police officers, and probation officers, become advocates for continuing or increased use of restorative justice.

In many European countries, the development of restorative justice has been from within the criminal legal system, and it is often from the "top down" and not the reverse. This means that the national government funds restorative justice programs, and restorative justice program staff are often state employees. In contrast, U.S. restorative justice programs are funded through some governmental funding and

1. *Law and Justice Are Not Always the Same: Creating Community-Based Justice Forums for People Subjected to Intimate Partner Abuse*, 42 FLA. ST. U. L. REV. 707, 722 (2015).

2. U.N. Doc E/2000/INF/2/Add.2 at 35 (2000).

3. *Id.*

4. *Id.*

through non-governmental sources and, therefore, often run by private individuals and non-profit organizations.

In this chapter, we will read about the theories behind restorative justice, the practice of it in the U.S., and the roles of the various parties in restorative justice. In the next chapter, we will read about evaluations of restorative justice (Does this really work? And what does that actually mean?), as well as larger concerns with fairness and justice in the running of these programs.

I. What Is Restorative Justice?

Our first excerpt discusses a conferencing session within the Green Bay Correctional Institution in Wisconsin. Journalist Zach Brooke had the opportunity to come with Virginia VandenBranden, administrator of the prison program, and law professor Janine Geske as they worked to restructure the inmates in the institution, and they start their work with this conference circle, with a goal to create "positive ripples."

Zach Brooke, *Behind the Walls*

MILWAUKEE MAGAZINE, February 24, 2016 available at https://www.milwaukeemag.com/behind-the-walls-restorative-justice/

The coffered rotunda at the Green Bay Correctional Institution often catches the uninitiated off guard. Exiting the lobby of the maximum-security prison—the last place your movements are solely subject to your own free will—visitors filter through a succession of five gates, each opening only after the former is secured with a heavy clank.

Passing through the final gate exposes a vast two-story, 4,900-square-foot room supported by four massive, chalky rose terrazzo columns. Inmates built this room a century ago, as they did the cell blocks now confining their spiritual progeny. Inmates also painted the murals displayed atop the high walls. They depict scenic landscapes that are the antithesis of confinement.

Impressive as the structure may be, Virginia VandenBranden and Janine Geske are more concerned with restructuring the inmates themselves. For nearly two decades, they have run seminars focusing on restorative justice, challenging inmates to develop the emotional tools needed to place their crimes in context.

Broadly explained, restorative justice looks at the ripple effects of criminal actions. Less concerned with questions of guilt and innocence than asking who suffers from crime and why, restorative justice is an approach that's gained traction in the United States and abroad over the past 25 years. That's especially true in South Africa. After the abolition of apartheid there, a Truth and Reconciliation Commission was formed—based on restorative justice theory—to solicit testimony from victims and perpetrators of human rights violations, allowing, Geske says, "everybody to hear and put into light the harm that had happened."

I've come to witness the program at Green Bay as one of its sessions unfolds. Joining me are a group of law students from Marquette University and the University of Wisconsin-Madison, as well as community members and other restorative justice advocates. For the next three days, we will sit alongside some of Wisconsin's worst offenders and work to create a dialogue about the multifaceted ramifications—physical, emotional and spiritual—that happen when crimes are committed.

The program is part of a larger class called Challenges and Possibilities, taught by VandenBranden and developed to help convicted men regain their self-worth while aligning their outlook with accepted social values. Geske, a former Marquette University law professor and Wisconsin Supreme Court justice, leads the restorative justice component.

Geske was appointed to the Supreme Court in 1993 by Republican Gov. Tommy Thompson. And though she's now a staunch advocate of restorative justice, there was a time when she wanted nothing to do with it. "Somebody had talked to me about restorative justice, and my reaction was, 'Why would a victim, particularly of a violent crime, ever want to sit down with somebody who's committed that crime?' That just seemed crazy. It seemed like some wacko liberal idea," she says....

What happens during these sessions that could persuade a former doubter like Geske to adopt such reverence toward restorative justice? I'm here to find out....

Geske says the circle we are arranged in comes out of Native American traditions intended to strengthen a community. Throughout the program, we will pass a hand-painted stone around the circle, talking only when it's in our possession, listening otherwise....

"People open up in circles with a talking piece," she says. "If you ask a question that can potentially go deep, there will be some people who go deep. And when people do that, then others will open up as well." ...

Geske draws a large triangle on an easel. Each side of the triangle, she says, represents a party affected by crime: victims, perpetrators and the community. Approaching crime from a restorative justice standpoint involves looking at these sides and asking questions. Who was harmed, in what way were they injured, and what can be done to repair the damage?

"There are all sorts of people that are impacted who are never involved in the court system," Geske says. Burglaries can affect neighbors of the victim by destroying their sense of security. A community hit by multiple burglaries can grow paranoid and unravel....

Geske divides the circle into groups. She tells us about three teenagers who robbed a Sears at Bayshore mall by jumping over a counter to steal money from a cash register, knocking over an elderly employee in the process and breaking his hip. She asks the groups to find the ripples caused by the crime.

My groupmates begin by listing the injured man. He's harmed physically, financially and emotionally by the loss of personal dignity obtained by working. We also list the man's family and the families of the teens, one suffering from a victimized relative and the others from the criminal prosecution of loved ones. We then list Sears and Bayshore as affected parties, reasoning that both organizations will now have to spend more money on security. Even then, the store and mall may still lose business from people who perceive the area as a dangerous place to shop. This is on top of the direct financial loss to Sears caused by the robbery.

Digging deeper, we also identify ripples spreading to other Sears employees, determining that they may be concerned for their safety, or sad over the harm done to their colleague, or just burdened with having to work extra hours with one fewer co-worker. The group places other teens on the impact list as well, believing they will now be profiled by mall security. . . .

After returning to the prison and passing through all those gates, we encounter several new faces. Some, we would find out, belong to survivors of violent crimes. They have come to share their stories.

It takes a special brand of people to discuss the worst experiences of their lives with complete strangers, some of whom have done the same things to other people. But their participation is vital to restorative justice. . . .

The next speaker is a woman whose face exudes strength. Her hair is cropped short, and she tells us that few people understand why she talks about being sexually assaulted, but she receives a certain measure of healing and empowerment from addressing the group.

"What I get back in support in this room allows me to be a survivor," she says. A lot of people expect her to be angry, she says, but she tells the men—seven of whom have sex crimes convictions—that her words don't stem from anger. She doesn't want to be dismissed as purely emotional. She wants to prevent more rapes.

I'll call her Joan, which is not her real name, and her story begins while she's living and working in another state. She tells us that, while out for a run one morning, she saw a car passing her, moving too fast for the residential street they were on. It disappeared around a curve. Moments later, Joan rounded the same curve, and "the absolute first thing I knew was a hand over my mouth and a gun in my back." . . .

The man drove Joan to a secluded area of a state park, marched her to a field at gunpoint and ordered her to undress. "There is nothing more humiliating than having someone with a gun pointed at you asking you to take your clothes off," she says.

A profound sense of disassociation swept over her as she was raped. "I was not present at that experience. When something that traumatic happens, you retreat to a little spot in here," she says, pointing to the back of her head.

Afterward, the attacker looked at her and said, coldly, "What am I going to do with you now?" Her thoughts drifted toward her husband and 3-year-old child, both about to lose her in the middle of a field, and "how sad it was I wouldn't be able to say goodbye."

Thinking fast, Joan told her rapist it was safe to let her live, because her husband was incredibly jealous and would blame her if he found out what happened. Joan promised to not say anything or look at the man's face, but she needed to get back soon or her husband would grow suspicious.

It worked. The man returned Joan to her neighborhood. Three weeks later, he turned himself in to police after failing in an attempt to abduct a teenage girl. He was himself married, with young children....

A quick discussion follows the speakers. Many in the room are deeply moved, and a heavy atmosphere hangs over the circle, laden with the silence of weighty reflection. Many speak of the deleterious role violent crimes have played in their lives. Several prisoners have lost friends and family to murder or drunk drivers, or they know people who have been sexually assaulted....

"These guys who, as they say, put masks on in the prison—don't cry, always a tough guy—break down in this circle and really become vulnerable," Geske says. "That they are able to do that in the context of a maximum security prison is amazing."

Others begin to talk about the hurt they caused. A man convicted of robbery says he now sees the ripples of what he thought were victimless crimes.

"I hurt for each and every one of you," says another. "I hurt for my victims. I have a lot to think about."...

As the time to depart approaches, Geske has a few more words. "How do we make a difference? We make a difference in the moments. Think of the moments during the day someone was kind to you."

She closes by asking us to recall one specific action we've done over the last few weeks that has helped another person, and then ask ourselves what more we can do.

Going around the circle a final time, a room full of convicted men dwell not on the crimes they've committed, nor their punishments, nor the wrongs visited upon them, but instead speak eagerly of plans to create positive ripples for others.[5]

* * *

We started this chapter with an example of restorative justice in action. We now read from an article that gives us more background on the concept and history of restorative justice by Professor Carrie Menkel-Meadow.

5. Sadly, this program was closed down in 2019 and has not been restarted. Many of the prison-based RJ programs depend on the approval of the prison warden—who shift over time and may or may not be in favor of such programs.

Carrie Menkel-Meadow, *Restorative Justice: What Is It and Does It Work?*

3 Ann. Rev. L. Soc. Sci. 161, 162–164 (2007)

Introduction: Concepts, Definitions, and Purposes of Restorative Justice

To its conceptual and practical founders (John Braithwaite, Howard Zehr, and Mark Umbreit, among others), the field of restorative justice is an effort to transform the way we think of punishment for wrongful acts. When a crime or serious bad act (which may include more classes of activity than those legally labeled criminal) occurs, it effects the victims, offenders, interested bystanders (such as family members, employees, or citizens), and the larger community in which it is embedded. To paraphrase one of the field's founders, these bad acts or ruptures in human interaction create needs and responsibilities for the direct participants in the act, as well as for the larger society in which their act(s) occur. Restorative justice is the name given to a variety of different practices, including apologies, restitution, and acknowledgments of harm and injury, as well as to other efforts to provide healing and reintegration of offenders into their communities, with or without additional punishment. Restorative justice usually involves direct communication, often with a facilitator, of victims and offenders, often with some or full representation of the relevant affected community, to provide a setting for acknowledgment of fault by the offender, restitution of some sort to the victim, including both affective apologies and material exchanges or payments, and often new mutual understandings, forgiveness, and agreed-to new undertakings for improved behaviors. In its most idealized form, there are four Rs of restorative justice: repair, restore, reconcile, and reintegrate the offenders and victims to each other and to their shared community.

Restorative justice raises deep philosophical, sociological, and empirical issues. The philosophical literature focuses on the purposes and nature of wrongdoing and punishment and is only briefly reviewed here. At both the philosophical and sociological level, restorative justice raises important questions about who should have power, control, and possession over crime, acts of wrongdoing, punishment, restitution, reconciliation, and community interests.... This article reviews the extant findings, which do demonstrate some support for restorative justice claims, while also raising questions about the (limited) conditions under which restorative justice may be most effective.

The next major issue of evaluation in the field is whether even successful victim-offender restorative justice can be scaled up to national levels of political and civic reconciliation, either through truth and reconciliation-like processes or through reparations....

From the beginning, restorative justice practices were intended to heal at both the individual and group or social level. Attention in both practice and theory was placed on healing those directly affected by a crime or bad act and on institutional and social reform. At its most aspirational or utopian, restorative justice has been seen as a potentially transformative social practice that could, under the right conditions, obviate the need for harsh criminal punishment and incarceration. In this conception, restorative justice was linked as a social movement to community organizing, criminal justice and prison reform, the civil alternative dispute resolution (ADR) movement, and the peace movement in that it sought alternative processes for different and more humane and tailored outcomes. In its more grounded and practical institutionalized forms, restorative justice was often supplemental, not substitutive, to conventional criminal proceedings. In an early core definition of restorative justice, it is a "process that brings together all the parties affected by an incident of wrongdoing to collectively decide how to deal with the aftermath of the incident and its implications for the future". Although some think restorative justice is most appropriate in the context of small, interpersonal wrongful acts, such as petty thefts, simple assaults, drug- or alcohol related crimes, and family abuse, restorative justice has been adapted for cases involving murder, rape, genocide, and other serious transgressions against large groups or even a whole society. It has also been used effectively as a model for pre- or nonlegal disputes in schools, organizational and corporate conflict management, neighborhoods, communities, and families.

Established in the mid-1990's, South Africa's Truth and Reconciliation Commission (TRC) was a pioneering restorative justice effort. The TRC was enacted through the South African Parliament and was put in place in response to gross human rights violations that spanned decades. Divided into three committees (Amnesty, Reparation and Rehabilitation, and Human Rights Violations), the TRC set out to help heal violence and abuses inflicted by all parties during apartheid.

> A central theme of the TRC in South Africa is that "these measures cannot bring back the dead, or adequately compensate for pain and suffering, but they can improve the quality of life for victims of gross human rights violations and/or their dependents."

A Summary of Reparation and Rehabilitation Policy, Including Proposals to Be Considered by the President, available at: http://www.justice.gov.za/trc/reparations/summary.htm.

TRC's impact has spread across the planet where it has touched almost every continent. The importance of these committees or their equivalents in the international restorative justice realm cannot be understated.

What began as a domestic social reform movement (simultaneously developed in Australia, New Zealand, Canada, the United States, the Netherlands, Austria, and others), restorative justice and its basic principles became a process of international interest when Desmond Tutu (1999) led a truth and reconciliation process to transform and heal South African society's transition from apartheid to a just, multiracial society. Variations on indigenous [such as Rwandan gacaca and Ugandan mato oput] and newly minted restorative processes have now been used in more than 25 national efforts to move more peacefully through political, racial, ethnic, and civil wars and transitions to more peaceful, democratic, and just states. Restorative justice principles thus helped form a new field of international law and political structure: transitional justice.

Restorative justice has several foundational concepts that have now been elaborated and extended to many arenas of social and political interaction:

- Personalized and direct participation in a process of speaking and listening of both a wrongdoer (offender) and a victim of an act of wrongdoing;
- Narration of what an act of wrongdoing consisted of and the harm or injury it caused to those affected (including both direct victims and often others, including bystanders and the larger community);
- Explanation by the offender of what was done and why;
- Acknowledgment and acceptance of fault for the wrong committed by the offender with recognition of the harm caused (with apology, if not coerced);
- Opportunity for appreciation or understanding of why the wrong occurred (root causes) and, in some cases, forgiveness of the individual, without forgetfulness of the act;
- Consideration of appropriate outcomes or restitution to those wronged by all participants, including victim, offender, family members, and/or larger community, often with expert facilitation;
- Reintegration of the wrongdoer into the larger community, through apology, restitution, and/or support and social services provided (alone or in conjunction with formal punishment as well);
- Reconciliation of wronged and wrongdoer, within a renewed commitment to shared social norms (often reconstituted within the restorative process);
- An orientation to the wrongdoer that treats the act separate from the person so that the person may be redeemed as the victim/community is repaired;
- An orientation to the future, to the extent possible, to make right what was wrong and to rebuild new relationships and new communities.

These foundational concepts come from a belief that conventional legal processes (criminal, international tribunals, and even civil processes) are often ineffective in their bureaucratic separation of offender from the actual consequences of acts, in the timing of any remedial actions (delayed incarcerations or other punishments), and in the inattention to the personal nature of the wrong (both for rehabilitation of the offender and restitution of the particular harm suffered by the victim), not to mention in their failure to deter or reduce crime. Restorative justice hopes to harness the commission of wrongful acts to the making of new opportunities for personal, communal, and societal growth and transformation through empowerment of both victims and offenders in direct and authentic dialogue and recognition. It also hopes to reduce recidivism and reintegrate wrongdoers into more positive roles and relationships.

Notes/Questions

In Carrie Menkel-Meadow's *Restorative Justice: What Is It and Does It Work?*, she brings up several questions regarding important philosophical and criminological issues: When an act of wrongdoing is committed, who has an interest in its rectification, the victim, the community, the offender, those affected by the act, or the larger society?

- Who decides what justice is: the victim (who might want vengeance or restitution), the state (who will want to deter future crimes and acts of wrongdoing, set precedents for others, and establish social control), or the community in which the wrongdoing is embedded (where motivations may vary from revenge to the desire to reclaim every community member)?
- Who has the power to forgive and accept restitution or reconciliation: the victim, the victim's family, the community in which the wrong occurred, or the state? What if acts of wrongdoing affect both individuals and a larger community, such as hate crimes or genocides?
- If crime or other acts of wrongdoing are a collective hurt or tear in the social fabric, can individuals forgive on behalf of anyone besides themselves?
- Are crime victims adequate proxies for the rest of a society that may define justice differently (more harshly, less harshly)?

***

Before reading any further, take a moment and think how you would answer each of these questions. The readings in the rest of this chapter wrestle with these questions that underpin the foundations of restorative justice. Note how your opinions may or may not change as you learn more about this process.

Scholars have argued that restorative justice has both historical and global antecedents, yet these claims can also lead to confusion as to what restorative justice actually is. Consider this in our next reading:

Aparna Polavarapu, *Myth-Busting Restorative Justice: Uncovering the Past and Finding Lessons in Community*

13 U.C. Irvine L. Rev. 953, 956, 959,970 (2023)

I. DEBATING THE "GLOBAL" AND "HISTORIC" ROOTS OF RESTORATIVE JUSTICE

Claims connecting modern restorative justice to historic dispute resolution practices are common, sweeping, and emphatic. Such claims range in their focus, emphasizing process, underlying philosophy, or types of consequences as the proof of restorative justice. As such, they do not offer consistent evidence of the existence of restorative justice in historic practices. What they do reveal is inconsistency in how restorative justice is defined or conceptualized....

What becomes evident in reviewing these examples is that exactly what makes these historic practices or ideas "restorative" seems to vary, often depending on the person making the claim but sometimes even across examples being offered by the same person. As I have described, different philosophies and practices are viewed as restorative because they adhere to a certain process, they require compensation to be made for those who suffered harm, they emphasize forgiveness, or they present a view of humanity as interconnected. With each of these examples highlighting some different characteristic as being "restorative," the overall strength of the claim, which frames restorative justice as a widespread historic practice, is weakened. Which characteristic is most important in identifying restorative justice? Is the existence of any one on its own enough to constitute restorative justice? Is restorative justice simply an amalgam of these ideas? If so, is it truly accurate to claim any of these practices are the same as restorative justice, as opposed to simply sources of inspiration?...

II. WHAT IS RESTORATIVE JUSTICE?

Settling on a singular definition of restorative justice is challenging. Restorative justice as a label is used broadly to describe a number of practices, some of which have very little in common with one another. Some use the term to describe any alternative to the most traditionally understood implementation of the criminal system. The term has thus been used to describe new types of penalties or any non-adversarial proceedings. In addition, the term "restorative" is used to describe practices that are related to restorative justice practices but are not exclusively designed to respond to harm practices but are not exclusively designed to respond to harm....

Restorative justice (1) reframes how we consider harm by focusing on the harm that has been committed, what needs must be fulfilled, and who bears the obligations to fulfill those needs; (2) involves a process that brings together the interests of the responsible party, the harmed party, and community stakeholders; (3) allows all parties to engage in a free discussion and exploration of the harm and the circumstances surrounding it; (4) includes collaborative determination of what accountability looks like; and (5) seeks to support the responsible party in arriving at accountability and reintegrating into the community, which requires making reparation, taking responsibility for the harm and its impacts, and sometimes also taking steps to avoid committing future harm. Encapsulated in this definition is the notion that parties will be treated with dignity and respect for their humanity. As a concept, it is certainly an alternative to the criminal legal response, but it is also much more expansive than that.

* * *

The next two excerpts provide an overview of the restorative justice movement in the 21st century. Umbreit, Vos, Coates, and Lightfoot go into detail on the movement's distinguishing characteristics, as well as its history and development. Professor Gonzalez then updates their findings with her study of restorative justice programs across the U.S., published in 2020.

Mark S. Umbreit, Betty Vos, Robert B. Coates & Elizabeth Lightfoot, *Restorative Justice in the Twenty-First Century: A Social Movement Full of Opportunities and Pitfalls*

89 Marq. L. Rev. 251, 253–260 (2005)

I. Introduction

A burglary victim comes face-to-face with the young offender and his father. She is able to express the full impact of the crime, get answers to many questions, and help develop a plan to repair the harm. Her involvement in this community-based victim-offender mediation program leads to a deep sense of satisfaction, fairness, and ability to move on with her life. Meeting his victim has a huge impact on the young offender and leads to his getting his life in order and staying out of further criminal activity.

A family group conference is convened to allow the parents of the young offender who vandalized a home in the neighborhood to meet the victim's family. Several other support people are present as well. Together, along with the young offender, they talk about the impact of the crime on their lives and the community, and they develop a plan to repair the harm. All involved feel good about the process, believing it to be a very practical way of holding this young person accountable.

In response to a racial incident, a group of thirty community members, including both victims and offenders, come together in a peacemaking circle to openly discuss what led up to this crime, its impact on the community, the need for greater understanding and tolerance among diverse community members, and a detailed plan for both repairing the harm and meeting several more times to foster healing within the community.

Juvenile offenders appear before neighborhood accountability boards or community justice conferences to discuss the impact of the crime with members of the community who will determine, in coordination with the probation department, specific requirements that address the need for accountability, victim reparation, and competency development within their own lives.

Local and national justice systems and corrections departments, along with victim advocates and community members, develop policies and practices to be more responsive to the needs of crime victims and the community, while providing increasing opportunities for both juvenile and adult offenders to be actively involved in repairing the harm and increasing their victim empathy and skills for becoming productive members of the community.

In their quest for meaning and healing following the death of their loved ones, surviving family members of homicide victims from both criminal and political violence are seeking to meet the offenders through restorative dialogue opportunities in North America, Europe, Israel, Palestine, South Africa, and other parts of the world.

These stories of finding hope, meaning, and healing in the process of creating justice and promoting accountability are representative of an important social reform movement that has been developing throughout the world over the past thirty years. The movement has spawned thousands of individual programs in many countries, has led to a rising number of system-wide policies across various components of many justice systems, and increasingly has gained the attention of scholars throughout the world. In addition to a growing number of books devoted to the topic, more than 750 articles in law journals and hundreds more in other related journals have addressed restorative justice. The scholarly discussion rests on a rapidly expanding database from studies in both the United States and abroad examining the process and outcome of restorative responses. Clearly, restorative justice has become a social movement that impacts the way we understand and respond to crime and conflict in diverse communities throughout the world....

II. Overview of Restorative Justice

A. Distinguishing Characteristics

Most contemporary criminal justice systems focus on law violation, the need to hold offenders accountable and punish them, and other state interests. Actual crime victims are quite subsidiary to the process and generally have no legal standing in the proceedings. Crime is viewed as having been committed against the state, which, therefore, essentially owns the conflict and determines how to respond to it. The resulting criminal justice system is almost entirely offender driven.

Restorative justice offers a very different way of understanding and responding to crime. Instead of viewing the state as the primary victim in criminal acts and placing victims, offenders, and the community in passive roles, restorative justice recognizes crime as being directed against individual people. It is grounded in the belief that those most affected by crime should have the opportunity to become actively involved in resolving the conflict. Repairing harm and restoring losses, allowing offenders to take direct responsibility for their actions, and assisting victims to move beyond vulnerability towards some degree of closure stand in sharp contrast to the values and practices of the conventional criminal justice system with its focus on past criminal behavior through ever-increasing levels of punishment.

Within the English-speaking world, roots of the prevailing focus on harm to the state can be traced back to eleventh-century England. Following the Norman invasion of Britain, a major paradigm shift occurred in which there was a turning away from the well-established understanding of crime as a victim-offender conflict within the context of community. William the Conqueror's son, Henry I, issued a decree securing royal jurisdiction over certain offenses (robbery, arson, murder, theft, and other violent crimes) against the King's peace. In the years preceding this decree, crime had been viewed as conflict between individuals, and an emphasis upon repairing the damage by making amends to the victim was well established.

Restorative justice values, principles, and practices hearken back to such earlier paradigms, not only in British and American history, but also in numerous indigenous cultures throughout the world. Among these are many Native American tribes within the United States, the Aboriginal or First Nation people of Canada, the Maori in New Zealand, Native Hawaiians, African tribal councils, the Afghani practice of jirga, the Arab or Palestinian practice of Sulha, and many of the ancient Celtic practices found in the Brehon laws.

In addition, the values of restorative justice are deeply rooted in the ancient principles of Judeo-Christian culture that have always emphasized crime as being a violation against people and families, rather than "the state." Many biblical examples are found in both the Old and New Testaments setting forth the responsibility of offenders to directly repair the harm they caused to individuals, harm that has created a breach in the "Shalom community."

The most succinct definition of restorative justice is offered by Howard Zehr, whom many consider the leading visionary and architect of the restorative justice movement. His seminal book, *Changing Lenses*, provided the conceptual framework for the movement and has influenced policy makers and practitioners throughout the world. According to Zehr, "Restorative justice is a process to involve, to the extent possible, those who have a stake in a specific offense and to collectively identify and address harms, needs, and obligations, in order to heal and put things as right as possible."

Instead of focusing upon the weaknesses or deficits of offenders and crime victims, restorative justice attempts to draw upon the strengths of these individuals and their capacity to openly address the need to repair the harm caused. Restorative justice denounces criminal behavior yet emphasizes the need to treat offenders with respect and to reintegrate them into the larger community in ways that can lead to lawful behavior.

From a restorative perspective, the primary stakeholders are understood to be individual victims and their families, victimized communities, and offenders and their families. The state and its legal justice system also clearly have an interest as a stakeholder but are seen as more removed from direct impact. Thus the needs of those most directly affected by the crime come first. Wherever possible, opportunities for direct engagement in the process of doing justice through various forms of dialogue are central to the practice of restorative justice.

Like many reform movements, in its early years the restorative justice movement focused on contrasting its values and principles with those of the status quo. The phrase "retributive justice" emerged to describe the conventional criminal justice system approach, particularly regarding its emphasis on offenders getting what they deserved.

Following more than twenty-five years of practice, research, and continuing analysis, Zehr has come to a different understanding, stating that such a sharp polarization between retributive and restorative justice is somewhat misleading. The philosopher of law, Conrad Brunk, argues that on a theoretical level, retribution and restoration are not the polar opposites that many assume. He notes that both actually have much in common: a desire to vindicate by some type of reciprocal action and some type of proportional relationship between the criminal act and the response to it. Retributive theory and restorative theory, however, differ significantly in how to "even the score"—how to make things right. Retributive theory holds that the imposition of some form of pain will vindicate, most frequently deprivation of liberty and even loss of life in some cases. Restorative theory argues that "what truly vindicates is acknowledgement of victims' harms and needs, combined with an active effort to encourage offenders to take responsibility, make right the wrongs, and address the causes of their behavior."

Even so, Zehr notes that restorative justice can be contrasted with conventional criminal justice along at least four key variables:

Table 1. Two Different Views of Justice

Criminal Justice	Restorative Justice
Crime is a violation of the law and the state.	Crime is a violation of people and relationships.
Violations create guilt.	Violations create obligations.
Justice requires the state to determine blame (guilt) and impose pain (punishment).	Justice involves victims, offenders, and community members in an effort to put things right.
Central focus: *offenders getting what they deserve.*	**Central focus:** *victim needs and offender responsibility for repairing harm.*

The conventional criminal justice system focuses upon three questions: (1) What laws have been broken?; (2) Who did it?; and (3) What do they deserve? From a restorative justice perspective, an entirely different set of questions are asked: (1) Who has been hurt?; (2) What are their needs?; and (3) Whose obligations are these?

Restorative justice is not a list of specific programs or a clear blueprint for systemic change. It requires a radically different way of viewing, understanding, and responding to the presence of crime within our communities. Thus, an increased interest is emerging in addressing the broader, system-level implications of restorative justice principles. Among others, Braithwaite speaks of restorative justice with these larger dimensions in mind, emphasizing that restorative justice is far more than reforming the criminal justice system. It offers a way of transforming the entire legal system, while also impacting family life, workplace behavior, and even political conduct. Braithwaite's vision of restorative justice is nothing less than changing the way we do justice in the world.

Whether at the level of system-wide interventions or in individual programs, we are working toward restorative justice when our work meets the following criteria:

1. focus on the harms of wrongdoing more than the rules that have been broken;
2. show equal concern and commitment to victims and offenders, involving both in the process of justice;
3. work toward the restoration of victims, empowering them and responding to their needs as they see them;
4. support offenders while encouraging them to understand, accept, and carry out their obligations;
5. recognize that while obligations may be difficult for offenders, they should not be intended as harms, and they must be achievable;
6. provide opportunities for dialogue, direct or indirect, between victims and offenders as appropriate;
7. involve and empower the affected community through the justice process, and increase its capacity to recognize and respond to community bases of crime;
8. encourage collaboration and reintegration rather than coercion and isolation;
9. give attention to the unintended consequences of our actions and programs; and
10. show respect to all parties including victims, offenders, and justice colleagues.

B. History and Development

In the mid- to late-1970s, restorative justice principles and its precursor, victim-offender reconciliation, were advocated by a small and scattered group of community activists, justice system personnel, and a few scholars in both North America and Europe. Though these advocates began establishing connections with one another, they remained largely on the margins of the criminal justice system as a whole and were not initially connected with efforts to reform the system. Few of those involved in the early years would have ever thought their passionate yet modest efforts to promote restorative justice would trigger a widespread social reform movement with international impact.

In its more than a quarter century of development, the restorative justice movement has gone through a number of stages quite similar to other social movements. The mid-1970s marked the birthing phase of what would become known as the restorative justice movement. The "child" of this birthing process was the first Victim Offender Reconciliation Program ("VORP") in Kitchener, Ontario, in 1974. From the late 1970s to the early 1980s, a number of experimental programs based on restorative justice principles and modeled after the Kitchener program were initiated in several jurisdictions in North America and Europe, with the first VORP in the United States located in Elkhart, Indiana, in 1978.

Through the mid-1980s, in many jurisdictions, restorative justice initiatives remained small in size and number and continued to have little impact on the larger system. Few criminal justice officials viewed such programs as a credible component of the system. From the mid-1980s to the mid-1990s, the movement slowly began to be recognized in many communities as a viable option for interested crime victims and offenders, though still impacting a very small number of participants. England initiated the first state supported Victim Offender Mediation Programs ("VOM") during this period.

In 1994 the American Bar Association ("ABA") endorsed victim-offender mediation. This followed a yearlong study and considerable skepticism over the previous years. The ABA recommended the use of victim-offender mediation and dialogue in courts throughout the country and also provided guidelines for its use and development. Specific guidelines emphasized in the ABA endorsement included that participation by both offenders and victims be entirely voluntary, that offenders not incur adverse repercussions, and that statements and information shared be inadmissible in criminal or civil court proceedings.

Victim organizations were initially skeptical about victim-offender dialogue and other restorative justice initiatives in part because of the early history of focusing on offenders and their needs. However, in 1995, the National Organization for Victim Assistance ("NOVA") endorsed the principles of restorative justice by publishing a monograph entitled Restorative Community Justice: A Call to Action. As dialogue programs and other restorative initiatives continue to demonstrate a strong commitment to the needs and wishes of crime victims, victim organizations are increasingly supportive.

Thalia González, *The State of Restorative Justice in American Criminal Law*

2020 Wis L. Rev. 1147 (2020)

Restorative justice has been part of the American criminal justice system for more than three decades. As a philosophy and set of practices, it garnered the attention of legal reformists aiming to reenvision justice in the United States as early as the 1970s. These early theorists viewed restorative justice as a new paradigm that might replace the existing criminal justice system. In contract to punitive or retributive justice, which both largely perceive crime as harm to protected social values, they argued that restorative justice emphasizes relational harms caused by crime or deviance from social norms....

Since the mid-2000s, there has been rapid expansion of restorative justice laws, developing what can now be appropriately characterized as a restorative justice scheme. However, a prominent gap in the field exists: there has yet to be a comprehensive empirical examination of the codification of restorative justice into American criminal laws. This leaves policymakers, academics, and reformists often operating not only in disciplinary silos but also jurisdictional ones as they seek to advance new policies and practices aimed at diminishing the United States' overreliance on punitive justice and mass incarceration. While their efforts are well-intentioned and laudable, without a contemporary accounting of the risks and benefits of the current state of restorative justice laws, opportunities for true reform may be missed. Following the death of George Floyd and nationwide protests in response to racial violence and anti-Blackness, there is an even greater urgency to understand how states have structured restorative justice in their juvenile and adult criminal justice systems....

The aim of this study is not to be prescriptive as to whether reformists should continue to expand restorative justice in criminal law, nor does it seek to answer the theoretical debate as to whether restorative justice should exist in the legal system. The fact is that restorative justice already exists in law and also across multiple public systems, including education and child welfare. Instead, this study provides macro- and micro-analyses of restorative justice laws in the United States so that any discourse promoting, or rejecting, restorative justice as part of criminal justice reform no longer necessarily exists in a vacuum.

In isolation, each of this study's findings warrant consideration. Yet, when viewed as a whole, particularly in light of the contemporary social and political landscape, this study affirms the need for careful examination of the risks and benefits of the rapid legalization and expansion of restorative justice in law and policy. The current restorative justice scheme offers an important alternative to the status quo but, in its present form, should not be viewed as a ready-made solution to contemporary justice issues. Amid a moral and political reckoning on Black dignity and citizenship, reformists must instead look to these laws as a basic infrastructure from which to begin radically reorienting the criminal justice system, and hopefully, by extension, society....

As of July 2020, 46 jurisdictions have codified "restorative justice" into their juvenile and/or adult criminal justice systems. As Figure 1 indicates, these jurisdictions include 45 states and the District of Columbia for a total of 264 laws, including statutes, court rules, and regulations. The color gradient in Figure 1 illustrates the total number of restorative justice laws in each jurisdiction ranging from zero (white) to more than 30 (black). Data shows that 26 jurisdictions have passed between 1 and 5 laws; 15 jurisdictions between 5 and 10 laws; 1 jurisdiction between 15 and 20 laws; 1 jurisdiction between 20 and 25 laws; and 1 jurisdiction between 25 and 30 laws. Only 1 jurisdiction has passed more than 30 laws....

Analysis of the combined data reveals that there is no universal form, practice, or process of restorative justice across the country. This leaves each jurisdiction to interpret what is or what is not restorative justice in an attempt to reach aspirational goals for system reform. Disaggregated data indicates that the most commonly codified forms of restorative justice are victim-offender conferencing, mediation, and dialogue, followed by impact panels and family group conferencing. In the absence of macro-level uniformity, one might hypothesize the presence of a preferred form based on the respective system (e.g. juvenile versus adult). Yet, no such association is present in the data. Furthermore, very few jurisdictions even attempt to define restorative justice, which creates significant ambiguity in law and practice no matter what scheme a jurisdiction adopts. Moreover, most often, different forms of restorative justice appear within a list of options available to justice system actors, which can include law enforcement officers, prosecutors, judges, departments of corrections, and parole and

Figure 1. Restorative Justice Laws Distributed by Jurisdiction

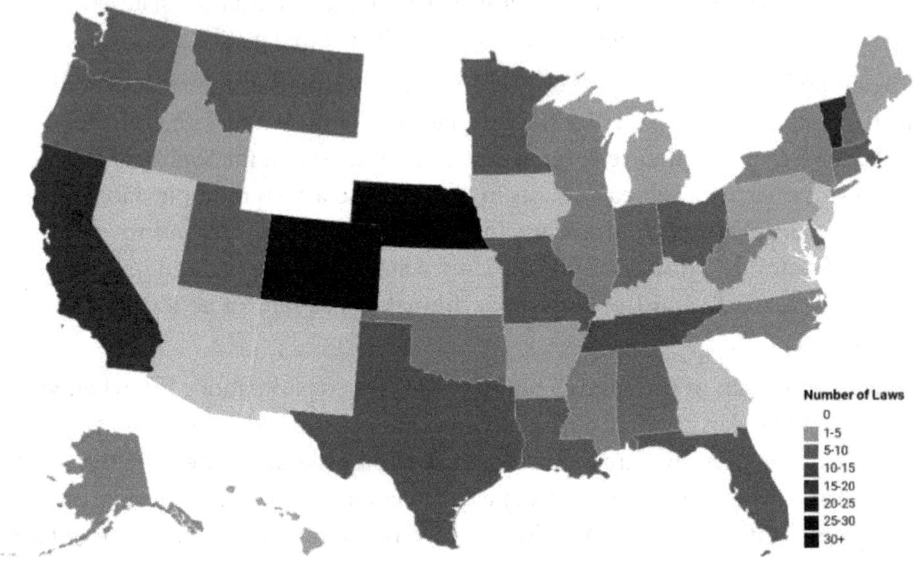

probation offices. Absent a definition of restorative justice, this long list of actor creates still more ambiguity....

Nevertheless, while there is no universal form of restorative justice or universal procedural application, 6 trends did emerge from the data. First, and related to the above discussion, a substantive body of procedural restorative justice laws is noticeably absent. While some states, like Colorado and Minnesota, have delineated the scope and use of restorative justice in their juvenile and adult justice systems, the level of delineation is highly variable across all jurisdictions. This is true whether restorative justice is codified at high, medium, or low levels.

Second, restorative justice laws that express aspirational goals of justice are highly present. Again, in contrast to procedural laws, aspirational laws seek to frame restorative justice as a remedy to existing tensions within the current criminal justice system, including victim satisfaction, offender accountability, rehabilitation, public safety, recidivism, high fiscal costs, and even reduced reliance on incarceration.

Third, participating in restorative justice often comes without a confidentiality guarantee. More than 84% of the jurisdictions examined do not protect statements made prior to or during restorative justice processes. This presents a risk for all participants (offenders, victims, and practitioners) in restorative justice, especially for cases at the pre-adjudication stage.

Fourth, participation for victims is voluntary. No jurisdiction in the United States mandates victim participation in restorative justice. This stands in sharp contrast to mandated participation by offenders in restorative justice in multiple jurisdictions.

Fifth, certain categories of crimes are exempted. Restorative justice processes do not replace or modify formal legal procedures at either the pre-adjudication or post-adjudication stages for crimes in such categories as unlawful sexual behavior, domestic violence, or an offense resulting in serious bodily injury or death. A restorative justice process, however, may be available for such crimes following conviction and/or during confinement.

Sixth, there is an offender-centered orientation, whereby restorative justice is defined relative to an offender's movement through criminal justice systems. Results also indicate 2 emerging trends: the use of fees to access restorative justice (e.g. "pay to play") and discretionary decision-making authority granted to probation or parole divisions and offices.

The primary objective of the foregoing analysis is to identify characteristics, forms, and trends in American restorative justice to provide a more comprehensive typology. But, the analysis also demonstrates opportunities for further micro-level examination to provide a framework for criminal justice reform vis-à-vis restorative justice laws. Detailed empirical analysis of this nature provides the necessary foundation for any broader reform efforts across the United States since, until now, much of the debate has centered on anecdotal claims or limited empirical studies of single jurisdictions or localities.

* * *

ConTextos—El Salvador & Chicago

An interesting example of an international program that has migrated to the U.S. is ConTextos. The program is based off the African Proverb "until the lion learns to write his own story, the tale of the hunt will glorify the hunter." ConTextos uses writing and storytelling to help not only juvenile offenders but has also expanded to reintegration centers and prisons. "We don't teach how to read and write. Instead, we use reading and writing as essential tools to develop dialogue and debate, self-reflection and self-actualization." ConTextos has recently expanded to Chicago due to both communities facing similar levels of gun violence.

Since 2011, the El Salvador program has worked with over 47,000 kids, 1,200 teachers, and 730 authors. The Chicago program, which started in 2017, has over 100 authors and 74 memoirs published. https://www.contextos.org/.

This next reading outlines the theories behind restorative justice compared to the typical theories of criminal punishment. As you read this, consider how different theories lead to different practices in the criminal legal system. What are our goals for our criminal legal system? Who should decide these? Also note the very different role of victims and the broader community within restorative justice.

Hadar Dancig-Rosenberg & Tali Gal, *Restorative Criminal Justice*

34 Cardozo L. Rev. 2313, 2319–2329, 2331–2333 (2013)

...

B. Punitive and Restorative Approaches Compared

The criminal process opens with an investigation of the reported crime. The investigative material is passed on to the prosecution for indictment. Once an indictment has been filed, the legal process begins, with adjudication as its first stage and sentencing as the second. Adjudication becomes unnecessary in many cases, when the parties agree to a plea bargain. The decision on whether a trial is to be conducted is forced on both the victim and the offender. The process culminates in the imposition of punishment, which often ravages the defendant's freedom and dignity.

The restorative justice approach offers processes that differ substantially from the criminal processes. A precondition for a restorative justice process to take place is the offender's admission of the crime. Secondly, both the offender and the victim are required to consent to a face-to-face restorative dialogue, and this voluntarism is reexamined throughout the process. The practical significance of these two conditions is that restorative justice is inapplicable in many cases.

In restorative processes the interested parties themselves—as well as affected community members—are direct parties to the process. The professionals involved act largely as suppliers of information and service providers rather than as decision-makers. Attorneys are generally not invited to be part of the process, and if they are present, their role is limited to the provision of information. Each participant's voice is heard in its authentic form, without being processed through procedural or evidentiary filters. The only restriction is a prohibition against pressure, violence, and domination.

Crime victims are called to speak of their needs and the damage which they incurred as well as to propose ways of repairing the harm and preventing additional damage. Offenders are expected to take explicit responsibility for their actions, to listen and respond to what the victims have to say, and to propose their own ways of repairing the harm and preventing any recurrence of the offenses. Consequently, the outcomes of restorative justice processes are shaped by the parties themselves according to their needs and can be unique in nature. The restorative process has therefore often been described as an empowering experience, by contrast to the criminal process, which is commonly criticized as reawakening the trauma and disempowering the victim.

Finally, the restorative process is not adversarial. Because restorative justice processes follow the offender's admission, there is no need to convince anyone present of the veracity of one party at the expense of the other, or to agree on a plea bargain. Since the objective of the process is not to penalize, the offender may take off the mantle of defense and engage in a sincere dialogue toward the formulation of a reparation plan. A reparation plan typically includes both monetary reparation and a rehabilitative program. Community work is also often agreed upon by the participants.

There are several models of face-to-face restorative justice processes, the most common being Victim-Offender Mediation (VOM), Conferencing, and the Circle. The models differ primarily by the number of participants and the level of community involvement in them. VOM involves an intimate encounter between the victim and the offender, together with a mediator. Conferences include the victim, the offender, and their respective communities of support, as well as community representatives and professionals. Circles are practiced mainly in native communities. They often involve members of an entire community and include spiritual and traditional elements representing the uniqueness of the specific community. In all three models, the processes are conducted by a neutral, professional facilitator. Before the encounter, a thorough preparation phase takes place, administered by the facilitator. During the gathering the participants discuss the offense and its implications, and collectively shape the reparation plan. When necessary, an additional meeting is held. After the gathering, the implementation of the decisions is monitored and reported to the state authorities. When a criminal process has begun, the state authorities decide whether or not to pursue it according to the results of the restorative process. In cases where the reparation plan has not been carried out, the case is transferred to (or remains in) the criminal process. Although the community plays a dominant role in all of these models, state officials participate in the processes and monitor their implementation, thus retaining the state's involvement.

Beyond the practical differences between restorative and criminal processes, proponents of each approach have emphasized the weaknesses of the respective rivals, continuing to portray the two approaches as irreconcilable with each other. Restorativists argue that the criminal process is based on a confrontational paradigm that excludes victims. The trial is perceived as a rivalry between the prosecution and the defense, and the binary structure of the verdict in the criminal process creates a "zero-sum game," whereby the victory of one party is perceived as the failure of the other.

Punitivists, on the other hand, have raised serious concerns regarding the ability of restorative justice processes to protect offenders' due process rights, and in particular the presumption of innocence. The admission requirement creates a risk of false admissions, particularly among offenders belonging to minority groups, those with mental illnesses, and juveniles. When restorative processes begin after the admission or finding of guilt, due process rights protect the offenders' interests other than maintaining their innocence. But when restorative justice is used as a diversion from the criminal process or takes place before the admission or finding of guilt, the risk of false admission raises constitutional concerns. Punitivists also question the ability of restorative justice to provide deterrent, effective, and "just" reactions to serious crimes. Restorative justice, in other words, is perceived as a "soft option" by punitivists.

In practice, restorative justice processes are currently being used in thousands of programs throughout the world. Many studies consistently indicate the effectiveness of restorative processes in reducing recidivism rates. Empirical findings also indicate the satisfaction of victims and the improvement in their emotional state as a result of their participation in restorative processes. Therefore, irrespective of one's position toward restorative justice, it is clearly "here to stay." Our purpose in this Article is to identify the position of restorative justice vis-à-vis punitive justice, focusing on their respective goals.

II. The Goals of the Criminal Process

Whereas the punitive approach generally considers retribution, deterrence (general and personal), rehabilitation, incapacitation, and denunciation of the crime as the goals of penal sanctions, many restorative justice scholars present it as promoting entirely different goals. Restorative justice, however, can in fact achieve the punitive goals in addition to its unique consequentialist objectives. Section A presents the arguments explaining how both approaches may achieve the goals of criminal law as well as those presenting the unique objectives of restorative justice. The dispute largely revolves around the question of whether requital is either attainable or desirable within the restorative philosophy. We will address this question in Section B.

A. What Do Punitive and Restorative Approaches Try to Accomplish?

Table 1. The Goals of the Retributive and Restorative Paradigms

		Punitive Justice	Restorative Justice
Utilitarian Goals: Crime Reduction	Personal Deterrence	External incentives: escalating punishments combined with strict enforcement	Internal incentives: reintegrative shaming and procedural fairness encouraging self-regulation
	General Deterrence	Consistent and predictable sanctions	Increasing reporting rates and strengthening community ties
	Rehabilitation	Rehabilitation programs as alternatives or supplements to punishment	Focusing on the crime, not the criminal; offender's involvement in decision-making; rehabilitation within the community
	Incapacitation	Imprisonment; death penalty	Spreading responsibility on many among offender's community
	Denunciation, Norm-Setting	Public judicial decisions	Authentic expressions by process participants backed up by reparation plan; offender's remorse
Additional Consequential Goals	Reparation of Harm		Addressing needs of anybody affected by crime
	Community Empowerment		Recruiting communities of support in crafting and implementing reparation plan
Deontological Goals	Requital	Just desert, proportionality	Illegitimate goal; reparation plan as a burden; reparation as restoration of justice

In what ways can restorative justice serve the utilitarian objectives of the punitive approach? Punishment, according to utilitarianism, may be justified only when it is imposed in order to attain objectives which result in benefit to society: for the sake of deterrence, the prevention of recidivism and the rehabilitation of the offender. As Table 1 demonstrates, restorative justice can potentially achieve the objectives of the classic utilitarian school in addition to its own stated goals. Accordingly, criticism is not directed principally at the utilitarian goals themselves, but rather at the inefficient, unjust, and coercive methods that the punitive approach adopts in pursuing them.

Punitive justice justifies punishment for its deterrent effect. Deterrence theory assumes rationality, but at least in certain types of offenses and certain segments of the population, it is doubtful whether the severity of the punishment affects the future behavior of offenders. In a reality of high case attrition, the certainty of enforcement is low as well. What actually deters people from committing crimes, according to restorativists, is shame. According to Braithwaite's reintegrative shaming theory, restorative justice provides a more efficient personal deterrent, because it creates a space in which the community shames offenders for their deeds, while expressing commitment and concern toward them. The combined message of denunciation of the wrongful act with the acceptance of the wrongdoer enables the offender to reintegrate into society after having taken measures to repair the harm caused by the crime.

Tom Tyler's procedural justice theory establishes that respectful and inclusive processes are more effective than threatening, aggressive discourses. Offenders who took part in restorative justice processes reported feelings of fairness, attentive listening, neutrality, and the ability to influence, which encouraged them to fulfill their undertakings. The theory of procedural justice and the theory of reintegrative shaming provide two prominent explanations for the empirical findings that restorative justice is generally more efficient than the criminal process in reducing recidivism rates.

Consistent and predictable penal sanctions are also intended to achieve general deterrence, according to punitivists. Proponents of restorative justice, however, question the validity of the punitivists' general deterrence theory. Instead, they suggest that systemic use of restorative justice processes will lead to general deterrence and to a decrease in the crime rate. The alliance between victims and community members that is created through restorative processes produces greater satisfaction and trust, consequently increasing the percentages of reported new crimes. The rise in the reporting rates increases the risk of being caught and hence the reluctance of potential offenders to commit offenses.

Indeed, punitivists question the ability of restorative justice to achieve general deterrence because restorative processes are contingent upon the victim's consent. This variability decreases the certainty of legal reactions to crime and reduces public trust in the justice system. The restorativist response is that as restorative practices become more visible and more attuned to victims' expectations, victims' consent rates increase, thus increasing the probability of enforcement through restorative processes. Yet, as long as restorative justice remains at the margins of legal systems, it is impossible to expect a "critical mass" of cases handled restoratively and an increase in reporting rates thereby; and as long as the general deterrent effect of restorative justice is not substantiated by empirical evidence it is unlikely that it would become the mainstream enforcement mechanism. A realistic view of restorative justice, then, acknowledges its limitations in achieving general deterrence. At the same time, a realistic view of punitive justice acknowledges its own weakness in achieving this goal.

Offenders' rehabilitation is another utilitarian goal of punitive justice. Imprisonment is expected to provide rehabilitative measures in addition to its incapacitative roles, while other (non)-punitive measures involve even more explicit rehabilitative goals. But according to critics the criminal process condemns offenders, not only their deeds; their imprisonment removes them from the law-abiding community, and prison is known as "the best school of crime." In restorative justice processes, by contrast, the active involvement of offenders and their supporters in selecting the rehabilitation program, along with the strengthening of their own familial and societal bonds, make restorative justice an effective means of rehabilitating offenders.

Incapacitating offenders is considered an additional utilitarian goal of punitive justice. Proponents of restorative justice, however, point out the high percentage of violence in prisons and the increase in recidivism post-release. Erroneous identifications and speculative risk assessments are additional obstacles toward effective incapacitation. In restorative justice, it is suggested, the community can incapacitate offenders in creative ways, such as placing in-house inspectors in scofflaw businesses, having a relative move into the offender's home, or taking away the offender's car keys on weekends. If activity at this level does not accomplish prevention, it will be necessary to move up in the enforcement pyramid toward more coercive measures....

Beyond the utilitarian goals of punitive justice, the restorative approach has its own unique consequential objectives. By contrast to the punitive approach, restorative justice focuses on victims, and the reparation of the harm done to them and to others constitutes its primary goal. The restorative approach criticizes punitive justice for taking a high toll from victims in the promotion of societal goals. As an alternative, it offers processes that can empower victims, strengthen social bonds, and heal, irrespective of their outcomes. In fact, findings have shown that victims who participated in restorative justice processes experienced a dramatic decrease in their post-trauma symptoms. The therapeutic effect was so dramatic that those processes were compared to cognitive-behavioral therapy, an effective psychological treatment method for reducing post-trauma symptoms. Victims' rights reforms across the globe have brought the punitive approach closer to restorative justice in terms of empowering victims. But the gap between the two approaches is still significant; promoting the wellbeing of victims is not a primary goal of punitive justice.

An additional stated goal of restorative justice is to repair and strengthen community ties. While the punitive approach focuses on offenders as individuals and considers the community a passive victim at most, the restorative approach places the community at the center of the process. Indeed, "community" is a vague, illusive concept in our modern urban society. A "community" in the restorative sense is not an entity defined by geography. Rather, it is a network of different social, familial, and professional ties. Restorative justice processes awaken inactive ties and strengthen functioning ones by recruiting acquaintances of offenders and victims to sit together and discuss the crime and the appropriate reactions to it. The community is perceived as (secondarily) responsible for the occurrence of the offense and as a (secondary) victim. Community members, representing the shared responsibility of the community, are invited to restorative processes to take part in the design of the restoration plan. As a (secondary) victim, the community needs are strengthening social bonds, regaining residents' sense of security, and reducing crime rates. Community bonds are strengthened through the intensive discussion of the consequences of the offense, as well as by the active participation in, and supervision of, the reparation plan.

Restorative justice, then, can potentially address the utilitarian goals of the punitive approach, all aimed at reducing crime. Restorative justice deters offenders from committing additional crimes through the use of fair and rehabilitative shaming ceremonies. System-wide restorative justice may potentially achieve general deterrence as well, by raising the level of certainty that offenses will be reported and handled. Restorative justice processes also constitute effective community mechanisms for censuring offenses and confirming norms. Incapacitation can be achieved through the recruitment of family, community, and governmental enforcement mechanisms that prevent offenders from reoffending. Restorative justice also provides a response to two additional distinct consequentialist objectives, namely the reparation of harm and community empowerment.

Notes/Questions

In Michael O'Hear's article *Is Restorative Justice Compatible with Sentencing Uniformity?* 89 Marq. L. Rev. 305 (2005), he discusses the five different types of paradigms of uniformity: (1) pre-offense predictability; (2) retributive proportionality; (3) in-system predictability; (4) purposeful sentencing; and (5) anti-subjugation. O'Hear concludes with plausible reasons that retributive proportionality cannot truly accomplish what it sets out to do without the use of processes that embody respect for offender dignity, give a meaningful opportunity for all interested parties to be heard, and give voice to community values on a localized basis. Restorative justice can be used by those who seek a transformative restructuring of the criminal legal system.

The static paradigms of uniformity (pre-offense predictability and retributive proportionality) should be differentiated factors that exist outside and before the criminal legal system. O'Hear provides an example.

> For instance, in a bank robbery case, the sentence might be determined by reference to such factors as whether the offender was armed, whether anyone was physically hurt by the crime, and whether the offender played a major or

minor role in planning the crime. The sentence, however, would not be determined by such considerations as whether the offender apologized, pled guilty, or successfully addressed a drug dependency problem after arrest.

Pre-offense predictability requires sentencing laws to be constructed with some specificity prior to the commission of the crime laying out what the offender may receive if convicted.

Retributive proportionality requires a sentence that is proportionate to the blameworthiness of the crime that was committed. Blameworthiness is assessed by the amount of harm caused or risked to the victim, and the offender's personal culpability.

O'Hear's dynamic paradigms of uniformity (in-system predictability, purposeful sentencing, and anti-subjugation), are discussed below:

- In-system predictability requires that the consequences of the offender's conduct be made clear while he or she is in the criminal legal system. It does not mean that the sentences need to be made clear once the crime is committed.
- Purposeful sentencing requires sentences to be linked in a clear, intentional manner to publicly accepted purposes of punishment. The goal of this approach is to advance these objectives.
- Anti-subjugation requires the offender to not be made subject to the unrestricted will of another. This approach works to make sure the offender is not being degraded, and essentially does not look like they have "merit no higher regard than, say, a domestic pet."

What paradigms of uniformity would work the best with the criminal legal system? The worst? How do these paradigms specifically work within the restorative legal system?

II. Parties and Process in Restorative Justice

This next section in the chapter focuses on the particular roles of each party in the restorative justice process. We also outline the wide variety of processes that have been created under restorative justice theories. Consider, as you read, how the roles of offender, victim, and lawyers change in each of these processes. What do you think would be the advantages and disadvantages of each of these? How does this compare to the roles of each in plea bargaining? Note, in particular, the role of the community and the victim and how that differs from their roles during a traditional criminal prosecution.

George Mousourakis, *Understanding and Implementing Restorative Justice*

11 Tilburg Foreign L. Rev. 626, 629–639, 643–644 (2003–2004)

1. THE IDEA OF RESTORATIVE JUSTICE

As has already been noted, in a restorative justice process all parties with a stake in a particular crime come together to resolve collectively, through dialogue and mutual understanding, how to deal with the aftermath of the crime and its implications for the future. Willingness to participate and truth telling are essential elements of any restorative justice program—participation cannot be the result of fear, coercion or manipulation brought to bear on either the offender or the victim. A successful outcome presupposes that the parties are allowed to relay the story of the incident and their experience of it fully and honestly. Of special importance is the offender's willingness to acknowledge what happened and assume responsibility for his wrongful acts or omissions. Besides voluntary participation and truth telling, it is crucial that the parties are brought together to hear and challenge each other's stories of the incident directly and express their feelings. Bringing the parties face to face with one another makes it possible for the offender to hear the experience of his victim in the latter's own words and for the victim to see the offender as a person rather than as a faceless criminal, dispelling the myths and stereotypes each has of the other.

The disparity in terms of power between the state and the accused in the conventional criminal justice process has justified the introduction of procedural protections intended to guard against abuse of rights by state organs. Although in a restorative justice process the offender is no longer pitted against the immense power of the state, the largely informal character of the process gives rise to rights concerns pertaining to possible power imbalances between the parties, as well as to the use of pressure tactics to make individuals participate in the process. In order to be able to address such concerns the process must embody mechanisms designed to protect the rights of the participants. The requirement of voluntariness with respect to participation has already been drawn attention to. Voluntary participation presupposes that the parties are informed about the nature and objectives of restorative justice and are given the time and support they need in deciding whether to participate or not. Once willingness to participate has been assured, the problem of possible power imbalances within the process needs to be addressed. Such imbalances might be the result of a previous relationship between the parties, or differences as to their social status.

One way of dealing with this problem is by ensuring that the parties are adequately supported by persons close to them throughout the process. As far as the conduct of the process is concerned, it is required that a balance is struck between the need for free expression of experiences on the one hand, and the need to protect the integrity and sense of security of the parties on the other. Allowing the parties to play a role in setting the ground rules governing the process is of particular importance here, as it offers the parties a feeling of empowerment and strengthens their commitment to the restorative justice process and its objectives. As has been pointed out by commentators, the process of setting ground rules is a vital "part of establishing an atmosphere and state that will be conducive to open communication and reconciliation."

Besides the victim and the offender, other parties with a stake in the process include the people in the lives of the victim and offender who care most about them, such as the families of each, and any other members of the community who may be affected or who may be able to contribute to the reconciliation process. Of particular importance is the role of the facilitator or coordinator. Besides having a symbolic role of community involvement in the process, it lies with him to bring the parties together and direct the discussion so as to ensure that the needs of the parties are considered and integrated and their rights protected. It rests with the parties and not the facilitator, however, to determine the content of the process according to what they believe is important in the situation and to decide how to arrive at an outcome that would best meet their needs. Any agreement reached must be consistent with restorative justice principles—it must be a product of a genuine commitment to restore the relationship between the parties to one of equal dignity and respect and not simply an acceptance of the offender's offer by the victim. Ultimately, justice is measured by the extent to which responsibilities are assumed, needs are met and healing is effected.

1.1 Victims

When persons are wrongfully attacked or injured, when their possessions are stolen or when their homes are broken into, they experience a loss of self-respect and dignity, accompanied by feelings of grievance, resentment and disempowerment. It is argued that victims need to express and have validated their sense of injustice and, more importantly, to be restored to a sense of control and safety in their lives based on a feeling that their rights have been vindicated. The latter presupposes that their injuries, both material and psychological, are identified and repaired as far as possible. When it comes to dealing with the injuries brought about by a crime the distinction between primary and secondary victims is important in determining priorities, especially in the case of limited resources. In general it is fair that priority is given to the primary victims, i.e. those directly harmed by the offender's actions. With respect to secondary victims, one should note that other factors beyond the offence may have contributed to or aggravated their injuries. Such victims are unlikely to have all their injuries adequately addressed unless the relevant factors are identified and explored. An important need of many victims of crime is reintegration into the community, as often the very fact of being a victim can lead to further victimization by society. Indeed victims often share the offenders' experience of being stigmatized and isolated. This can happen when a victim or his experience is disregarded or explained away as being the result of the victim's own acts or omissions.

Restoration cannot be attained unless the harm done to the relationship between the victim and the offender, as well as to that between each of the parties and the community is addressed. From this point of view, participation of the victim, the offender and the community in the restorative justice process is of vital importance. Reference

A Victim's View

Janine Geske, in *Why Do I Teach Restorative Justice to Law Students*, 89 MARQ. L. REV. 327 (2005), discusses the various things that students can learn from crime victims, like the surviving daughters of a murdered armed robbery victim who met face to face with their father's killer and then wrote this letter:

> It has been two weeks since our visit with [the offender] and we were still feeling blessed. Something has happened in our souls that will last through eternity. This has brought a new dimension to forgiveness. We've been seeing people differently. It seems quite clear that if we can forgive the man for shooting and causing the death of our father, then we can certainly forgive anyone else of anything.

should be made at this point to the central role which apology plays in the process. The goal of apology is the granting of forgiveness and, when both occur, victim and offender join in a ritual of reconciliation through which social harmony is restored. Apology is here seen as a goal to be sought, and as an expression of the victim's satisfaction and a sign of reconciliation when it is given.

1.2 Offenders

The injuries of offenders are usually a complex mix of those preceding and directly or indirectly contributing to the commission of the offence and those resulting from it. Of the latter probably the most serious is their stigmatization as deviant and dangerous individuals cut off from the rest of society. The reintegration of offenders is necessary if they are to be reconciled with the community to which they belong so that they may participate on equal footing in relationships with fellow citizens. Moreover, reintegration is crucial if reparation is to be achieved, for in order for offenders to be able to make amends for the damage they caused, access to the means to do so must not be impeded. Reintegration as a condition of restoration is facilitated by the participation of the community in the restorative justice process and the removal of barriers to active involvement of offenders in the community life. It presupposes, further, that offenders are given an active role in the restorative justice process, being encouraged to confront the shame which crime entails and to help decide what is to be done to reverse or minimize the harm they caused.

A few things need to be said in this connection about reintegrative shaming, an idea that has played an important part in the designing and implementation of restorative justice programs. According to some criminologists, the incorrect use of shaming has been one of the main reasons behind the failure of mainstream criminal justice systems to deal effectively with the problem of crime, especially with juvenile offending. The type of social shaming generated and perpetuated by traditional systems through their formal processes and punitive measures is said to create outcasts, for it entails the stigmatisation of the offender. Once a person has been singled out as a deviant and

An Offender's View

A convicted murderer sent Geske and her students this letter:

> Crime has no face or age. I was always aware of what I was doing, but I never knew just how much pain I caused my victims and to what extent my victims hurt until [my restorative justice experience]. I stopped pretending to be the victim. I was no longer being beaten [by family members as a child], so there was no need for me to hurt someone. In one blink of an eye, I made a stupid mistake that not only affected me for the rest of my life but everyone around my victims and me.... I now give every effort in my being to helping myself, others who show signs of my past, and to kids, so they will never become who I used to be. My incarceration is my way to show people a different way to live their lives.

Janine Geske, *Why Do I Teach Restorative Justice to Law Students,* 89 MARQ. L. REV. 327 (2005).

dangerous individual, the label attached may become the dominant label, or "master status", which is seen as more important than all the other aspects of the person. As his role in society is undermined by his stigmatisation, deviance for him then "becomes a way of life that is difficult to change and is rationalized as a defensive lifestyle within the deviant subculture." In the words of Gerry Johnstone, "By segregating and ostracising offenders we render them more rather than less of a threat to us. We drive them into criminal subcultures where they become more and more like alien enemies of the community. We lose whatever chance we have of influencing them to behave better and to subject themselves to various forms of supervision and control."

The challenge for a new approach to crime is to develop ways of responding to offenders which would counter the naturally occurring stigmatising processes and provide mechanisms for the reintegration of offenders into mainstream community life. As John Braithwaite has pointed out, communities characterized by high levels of cohesion and low delinquency rates make substantial use of practices in which young people who violate social norms are "shamed" and then "reintegrated" into family and community life. Reintegration presupposes that the shaming of an offender takes place within his circle of acquaintances or his own community, and that the disapproval of the offending behaviour is not accompanied by the stigmatization or "labelling" of the offender but, rather, by the re-affirmation of his value as a person and of his role as a community member. Thus the door is left open for the offender to re-enter the community after he has assumed responsibility for the harm he caused, apologized to the victim and made some kind of reparation. Clearly, a successful outcome depends on whether the procedure adopted succeeds in invoking feelings of genuine shame and remorse in the offender. In this respect, choosing the right participants to be present in supporting roles is of paramount importance. If shaming is to have a reintegrative and

Healing Circles—The Catholic Church

Community circles have been used throughout the U.S. in response to the sexual abuse scandals.

> A group—now of priests, parish leaders, abuse survivors—gathers, though just for a day....
>
> They assemble in a private room, sit on chairs in a circle and take turns sharing their pain, one with another. A hand-sized object, in this case a painted, polished stone, is a token of voice, the "talking piece." It is passed among those circled, giving the holder permission to share his or her story. There are no arguments here: Only the one holding the stone may speak. Everyone gets a turn.
>
> Geske explains, "The reason I brought this to parishes is that so many times I've heard, 'Why don't those victims just get over it? We've been through this for a long time and it's time to move on.'" She wanted people in the parishes to have firsthand experience of sexual-abuse survivors. "Once you hear the experience of a survivor, you don't ask, 'Why don't they get over it?' anymore."

Hon. Janine P. Geske, *Circles of Healing*, FRANCISCAN MEDIA, available at: https://www.franciscanmedia.org/judge-janine-p-geske-circles-of-healing/.

deterrent effect, an offender must be made powerfully aware of the disapproval of his wrongful conduct by persons for whom he maintains maximum respect. In the words of John Braithwaite, "the discussion of the consequences of the crime for victims (or consequences for the offender's family) structures shame into the [restorative justice] conference; the support of those who enjoy the strongest relationships of love or respect with the offender structures reintegration into the ritual. It is not the shame of police or judges or newspapers that is most able to get through to us; it is shame in the eyes of those we respect and trust."

1.3 Community

The notion of community is central to the restorative justice philosophy and thus formulating a workable definition of community is a prerequisite for the development of a restorative justice practice. Such a definition might be based on geography, relationship, interest, or it might refer to society as a whole. While the nature of restorative justice and the different ways in which communities may be affected by crime leave room for various types of community involvement, commentators agree that one can make the generalization that communities are harmed when the safety of their members is threatened. Of particular importance is the notion of community based on relationship or immediate interest. Immediate interest communities, such as the victim's and the offender's family groups, are expected to provide counsel and support to each of the principal parties to the process. In some cases, members of the victim's family may be required to serve in place of the victim, if the latter is not able to participate in the process.

The restorative justice approach is said to restore the deliberative control of justice by citizens by transforming those concerned from being passive participants in an impersonal process to being active players required to understand the nature and consequences of the crime and deliberate over how to deal with the problem and prevent its recurrence. It prevents the closed shop of the legal expert and, by infusing non-legal, ethical, values into the justice system, constitutes a constraint on legalism, arbitrariness and bureaucracy.

2. RESTORATIVE JUSTICE IN PRACTICE

2.1 Victim-Offender Mediation

These programs seek to mediate between victims and offenders with a view to providing an opportunity for the offender and the victim to develop a mutually acceptable plan on how to deal with the harm caused by the offence. During the relevant process victims and offenders come together in a safe, controlled setting and engage in a mediated discussion of the crime and the circumstances in which it was committed. With the assistance of the mediator the victim describes the physical, emotional and financial impact of the crime, asks questions about the crime and the offender and helps develop a plan for restoring losses. The offender is given the opportunity to learn about the impact of the crime on the victim, describe what happened from his point of view and take direct responsibility for his conduct. Paying close attention to the needs of the victim is of vital importance here, and the mediator is expected to do everything possible to ensure that the victim will not be harmed in any way during the process. Moreover, both the victim's and the offender's participation must be voluntary—the parties should never be coerced into taking part in the process—and cases should be carefully screened regarding the readiness of the parties to participate. Furthermore, it is important that the parties are given choices, whenever possible, about procedural matters, such as when and where the mediation session will take place, who will be present and who will speak first.

Cases may be referred to victim-offender mediation programs by judges, probation officers, prosecutors, victim or defense lawyers and law enforcement agents. In some programs cases are referred as a diversion from prosecution, on the understanding that any agreement reached during the mediation process is to be successfully implemented; in other programs, cases are referred after the offender has been found guilty by the court, with the mediation being a condition of probation or other disposition, if the victim has agreed to participate. Mediation can take place at any time during the criminal justice process, or outside the system altogether, but only after the offender's guilt has been established as a result of a conviction or an admission of responsibility by the offender. In many countries, such as the US, Canada, England, Belgium and the Netherlands, victim-offender meetings are held in prison, usually after sentencing (even when mediation will have no effect on the sentence imposed). In some coun-

Victim-Offender Mediation in Practice—Beyond Conviction

One documentary details the story of three crime victims and their journey through restorative justice conferences with the offenders. The first conference is between a woman and her brother who violently raped her when she was a teenager. He was convicted of the crime and now serving his sentence in prison. This was the first time they met since then and talked about the impact the crime had on both of them as well as why he took his rage out on his sister, whom he was supposed to protect. Another victim participant was just 4 years old when her mother was murdered by her boyfriend. She decided to meet the man who took her mother away in hopes of answering lingering questions about why he killed her. The third conference deals with a mother whose son was found dead in his jail cell in what was ruled as a suicide. She decided to meet with her son's cellmate in hopes of confirming her suspicions that her son's death was gang related. The conference was emotional for both individuals, as the inmate thought about his own mother when speaking to the victim, and the victim was reminded of her deceased son. In the end, both individuals embraced one another in a hug and promised to see each other again someday.

See Robert Koehler, *Beyond Conviction*, VARIETY, available at: https://variety.com/2006/film/reviews/beyond-conviction-1200514789/.

tries, moreover, meetings are organized which involve groups of unrelated victims and offenders.

2.2 Conferencing

Over the past fifteen years special attention has been given to issues concerning the nature and extent of the community's role in a restorative justice process. A restorative justice practice that has attracted much attention in recent years is conferencing. Conferencing is essentially an extension of the victim-offender mediation process involving not only offenders and victims but also their wider "communities of care", such as their respective families and other community members who may be able to contribute to the reconciliation process. It aims to involve the young offender, the victim and their families in a decision-making process with the objective of reaching a group-consensus on a "just" outcome. At the same time it seeks to increase the offender's awareness of the human impact of his behaviour and to allow both offender and victim to reconnect to key community support systems. Conferencing is being used or experimented on in many countries, and there are now several versions of conferencing found in New Zealand, Australia, Asia, Southern Africa, North America and Europe. The way in which conferencing operates in different countries varies considerably. The relevant process has been implemented in schools, police departments, probation agencies, community mediation programs, residential programs and neighbourhood groups. In

Conferencing Applied—Burning Bridges

A community conference was used after the arson of Mood's Bridge, a historic covered bridge in Bucks County, PA. The bridge was destroyed by arson in June of 2004 and the town went into mourning over the loss of this historic landmark, something that reminded the community of its history. Two months later, the identity of the arsonists came out and the community was shocked again to find that six well-known young men from the town were responsible for the fire. The community didn't know how to deal with their emotions after finding out the details of the fire and turned towards restorative justice to cope. The International Institute for Restorative Practices (IIRP) offered to run a restorative conference with the young men, their families and members of the community. The men, their parents, and other community members who participated in the conference were moved by it. The young men's parents were able to express their emotions in front of their sons in a way they never have before.

The judge in the arson case was also impacted. He watched the entire video of the conference and used it as a sentencing tool. He said the footage allowed him to see the impact that the fire had on the community, and he also got to see the young men apologize and take ownership of the incident. This is yet a different example of how restorative justice practices can be implemented in a variety of ways.

The young offenders were able to apologize for their wrongs, the parents were able to express their emotions to their children, and the community was able to sort through their own emotions and come to terms with what happened, all because of a restorative justice conference.

See Laura Mirsky, *Directing Burning Bridges, a Documentary about a Restorative Conference*, IIRP, available at: https://www.iirp.edu/eforum-archive/directing-burning-bridges-a-documentary-about-a-restorative-conference.

general, however, conferencing is most often relied upon as a diversion from the court process for juvenile offenders or used after adjudication to address unresolved matters or to determine appropriate forms of restitution. Cases dealt with through conferencing involve a variety of offences, including property and drug offences, minor assaults, vandalism and, in a number of countries, domestic violence....

2.4 Circle Sentencing

Circle sentencing has its roots in the traditional sanctioning and healing practices of aboriginal peoples in Canada and American Indians in the United States. The first sentencing circles were set up by supportive judges and community justice committees in the early 1990s in the Yukon Territory, Canada, and other northern Canadian communities. In the mid-1990s the use of sentencing circles spread to the United

States with the introduction of a pilot project in Minnesota. Circle sentencing is a community-based process conducted in partnership with the criminal justice system. Its aim is to develop an appropriate sentencing plan by taking into account the needs of all the parties involved in or affected by a crime, as well as those of the broader community. The focus of the process is again on reconciliation and the restoration of peace, rather than on retribution and deterrence, although sanctions can play a part if they are deemed necessary for achieving the goal of restoration. Circle sentencing has been used in cases involving a variety of crimes committed by both juvenile and adult offenders. Of course, not all cases can be dealt with through circle sentencing. Community concerns, the expectations of the victim and his family, the victim's and the offender's willingness to participate and the dedication of the parties' support groups are all key factors in determining whether a case is suitable for the circle process.

A sentencing circle is constructed as an open court. Within the "circle", crime victims, offenders, family and friends of both, justice and social service personnel, and interested community members talk about the crime and assess its impact freely and openly with a view to arriving at a consensus for a sentencing plan that would address the concerns of all interested parties. The objective, in other words, is to allow the best information to emerge from all the participants in the process so that a solution can be identified that would assist in healing all affected parties and prevent future crimes. In addition to offenders undertaking to make amends, the relevant plan may incorporate commitments by the justice system, the community and the families concerned. It is important to note here that circle sentencing usually involves a procedure that includes more than one step (application by the offender to participate in the circle process, a healing circle for the victim, a healing circle for the offender, a sentencing circle to reach an agreement on a sentencing plan and subsequent circles to monitor and assess the progress of the offender). The elements of the circle process vary from one community to another depending upon local needs and culture. They also evolve over time based on the community's changing needs, knowledge and experience. The successful implementation of a circle sentencing process presupposes adequate cooperation between the formal criminal justice system and the broader community—between criminal justice professionals and community members. Moreover, participants must be skillful in applying consensus-building techniques and implementation procedures must be flexible and adaptable to the requirements of the individual case.

* * *

Conferencing in New Zealand was introduced primarily as a response to problems pertaining to the treatment of juvenile offenders. It is now used in the disposition of all but the most violent and serious delinquency cases.

The conference begins with a prayer or blessing after which the participants are welcomed and introduced. The facilitator then explains to them the nature and objectives of the conference. The conference usually proceeds with the police representative outlining the offence. The offender admits or denies involvement. Unless the offence has been proved in court, the offender must admit involvement if the conference is to proceed. Once responsibility is acknowledged, the victim is given the opportunity to describe his experience and feelings, explain the effects of the offence on him, and direct questions to the offender. At this point the rest of the participants enter the discussion and views are put forward regarding the gravity of the offence, the circumstances in which it was committed and its impact on the victim, his family and the community. The facilitator then directs the participants into a discussion of what should be done to repair the damage caused by the offence, and the victim is given the opportunity to state his expectations. Following this, the offender and his family are left to deliberate privately with a view to formulating a plan on how to put things right. The meeting is then reconvened, and the offender's proposal is discussed. If the victim accepts the offender's proposal, the details of it are recorded and the [conference] comes to an end.

If agreement is not reached, the case will be referred to the appropriate court for further consideration. It is important to note here that the agreement which is aimed at is concerned not only with restitution but with a broader plan of action designed to address the underlying causes of offending conduct and thereby prevent reoffending. The relevant plan of action may include an apology, reparation, community work, an undertaking by the young offender to attend school or not to associate with delinquent elements and, occasionally, a sanction. George Mousourakis, *Understanding and Implementing Restorative Justice*. 11 Tilburg Foreign L. Rev. 626 (2003–2004).

Notes/Questions

1. Having read about examples about different restorative justice processes, what do you think some of the key differences are? In which contexts do you think each process is most appropriate?

2. Restorative justice was sometimes prohibited in domestic violence or sexual assault cases. Yet scholar Rachel Wechsler argues that not permitting victims to select into certain types of restorative processes continues the harm to them and notes that many states are reconsidering this prohibition. See Rachel J. Wechsler, *Victims as Instruments*, 97 Wash. L. Rev. 507 (2022). Who should get to choose what type of process is appropriate? And how much control should victims be given in the criminal legal system?

3. What type of criteria should a court, defense attorney, or judge consider when picking cases to proceed through restorative justice? Should courts ever require restorative justice? Should courts have a say in which parties are allowed to participate?

4. The ABA House of Delegates adopted a resolution in February 2009 (Report 101B) urging federal, state, territorial, and local governments to initiate, continue and expand the use of mediation as a means to resolve criminal matters, specifically at a time prior to actual case filing, thereby providing a means for diversion from the

criminal system. The House of Delegates was particularly concerned with the racial and ethnic minorities in the many jurisdictions throughout the United States that do not have meaningful access to legal representation. The resolution recommends that judges, prosecutors, and defenders be informed of these issues, with a goal to reduce disproportionate minority representation. The resolution asks local and state bar associations to decrease disproportionate minority representation by informing judges, prosecutors and defense attorneys about these disparities.

How would restorative justice—mediation in a criminal context—help reduce racial disparities? Would you have any concerns that restorative justice could make this worse? We will consider this question again in Chapter 14.

5. Daniel W. Van Ness and Pat Nolan, in *Legislating for Restorative Justice*, 10 REGENT U.L. REV. 53 (1998), discuss the difference restorative justice provides within the fields of juvenile and criminal justice. VanNess and Nolan go into detail on the general issues that should be confronted when one considers legislating for restorative processes or outcomes, and particular legislative approaches that have been taken in implementing restorative features in the criminal legal system. They discuss several questions:

- Is legislation needed to eliminate or reduce legal or systemic barriers to use of restorative programs?
- Is legislation needed to create a legal inducement for using restorative programs?
- Is legislation needed to provide guidance and structure for restorative programs?
- Is legislation needed to ensure protection of the rights of offenders and victims participating in restorative programs?
- Is legislation needed to set out guiding principles and mechanisms for monitoring adherence to those principles?

How would you answer these questions?

Additional Resources

ANNALISE ACORN, COMPULSORY COMPASSION: A CRITIQUE OF RESTORATIVE JUSTICE (LAW AND SOCIETY) (2015).

Alliance for Safety & Justice, *Crime Survivors Speak: The First Ever National Survey of Victims' Views on Safety and Justice* (2016), available at: https://www.allianceforsafetyandjustice.org/wp-content/uploads/documents/Crime%20Survivors%20Speak%20Report.pdf.

Douglas Evan Beloof, *The Third Model of Criminal Process: The Victim Participation Model*, 1999 UTAH L. REV. 289 (1999).

JOHN BRAITHWAITE, CRIME, SHAME AND REINTEGRATION (1989).

JOHN BRAITHWAITE, RESTORATIVE JUSTICE & RESPONSIVE REGULATION (STUDIES IN CRIME AND PUBLIC POLICY) (2002).

NILS CHRISTIE, CRIME CONTROL AS INDUSTRY (2000).

JIM CONSEDINE, RESTORATIVE JUSTICE: HEALING THE EFFECTS OF CRIME (1995).

CHRIS CUNNEEN & CAROLYN HOYLE, DEBATING RESTORATIVE JUSTICE (DEBATING LAW) (2010).

European Forum for Victim-Offender Mediation and Restorative Justice, *Victim-Offender Mediation in Europe* (1999).

John Feister, *Judge Janine P. Geske: Circles of Healing*, FRANCISCAN MEDIA, https://www.franciscanmedia.org/judge-janine-p-geske-circles-of-healing/.

Thalia González, *The State of Restorative Justice in American Criminal Law*, 2020 WIS. L. REV. 1147 (2020).

CAROLYN HOYLE & RICHARD YOUNG, NEW VISIONS OF CRIME VICTIMS (2002).

MICHAEL KING, ARIE FREIBERG, BECKY BATAGOL & ROSS HYAMS, NON-ADVERSARIAL JUSTICE (2009).

Marquette University Law School Restorative Justice Program, https://law.marquette.edu/rji/.

Aparna Polavarapu, *Myth-Busting Restorative Justice: Uncovering the Past and Finding Lessons in Community*, 13 U.C. IRVINE L. REV. 949, 953, 956, 959, 970 (2023).

HEATHER STRANG & JOHN BRAITHWAITE, RESTORATIVE JUSTICE CIVIL SOCIETY (2001).

Paul Tullis, *Can Forgiveness Play a Role in Criminal Justice?*, N.Y. TIMES, Jan. 4, 2013, www.nytimes.com/2013/01/06/magazine/can-forgiveness-play-a-role-in-criminal-justice.html?pagewanted=all.

MARK S. UMBREIT, THE HANDBOOK OF VICTIM OFFENDER MEDIATION: AN ESSENTIAL GUIDE TO PRACTICE AND RESEARCH (2000).

MARK S. UMBREIT & ROBERT B. COATES, VICTIM MEETS OFFENDER: THE IMPACT OF RESTORATIVE JUSTICE AND MEDIATION (1994).

Mark S. Umbreit & Marilyn Peterson Armour, *Restorative Justice and Dialogue: Impact, Opportunities, and Challenges in the Global Community*, 36 WASH. U. J.L. & POL'Y 65 (2011).

ANDREAS VON HIRSCH ET AL., RESTORATIVE JUSTICE AND CRIMINAL JUSTICE (2004).

LODE WALGRAVE, RESTORATIVE JUSTICE AND THE LAW (2002).

David B. Wexler, *New Wine in New Bottles: The Need to Sketch a Therapeutic Jurisprudence "Code" of Proposed Criminal Processes and Practices*, 7 ARIZ. L. REV. 463 (2014).

HOWARD ZEHR, CHANGING LENSES: RESTORATIVE JUSTICE FOR OUR TIMES (25TH ED. 2015).

HOWARD ZEHR, THE LITTLE BOOK OF RESTORATIVE JUSTICE: REVISED AND UPDATED (JUSTICE AND PEACEBUILDING) (2014).

HOWARD ZEHR & BARB TOEWS, CRITICAL ISSUES IN RESTORATIVE JUSTICE (2004).

Chapter 11

Restorative Justice Effectiveness and Concerns

Now that you have read about restorative justice theories and processes in the previous chapter, we turn to studying whether it actually works. The first part of this chapter reviews the evidence of how restorative justice processes impact particular measures including recidivism and party satisfaction. We then turn to issues of restorative justice in the legal system—how it relates to the law, concerns with fairness, and responses to these concerns.

I. Does Restorative Justice Work?

In the previous chapter, we read Carrie Menkel-Meadow's article on restorative justice. She asks the following questions in order to measure whether restorative justice actually works:

- Does it meet its own claims of reduced recidivism, restored communities, and reintegrated offenders?
- Is restorative justice more efficient (less costly, more deterrent, more restitutionary) than more conventional forms of punishment?
- Is it more fair or just (as perceived by participants or as analyzed by external, objective, and professional measures of these illusive concepts)?
- How should we integrate both the public and private aspects of crime and wrongdoing?
- Should right-making of wrongdoing be backward facing (punishment and legal justice) or future facing (reconciliation, restoration, and social justice)?

Consider how you would answer these questions and what criteria we should use to measure success. In the following article, part of which you read in the previous chapter, Umbreit and his co-authors analyze the variety of ways to measure success. In the following article, they examine participant satisfaction, perceptions of fairness, restitution, the use of diversion sentencing (and getting offenders out of the prison system) and focus on lowering the rate of recidivism and costs, as well as an increase in keeping people out of jail, amount of restitution, and perceptions of fairness.

Mark S. Umbreit, Betty Vos, Robert B. Coates & Elizabeth Lightfoot, *Restorative Justice in the Twenty-First Century: A Social Movement Full of Opportunities and Pitfalls*

89 Marq. L. Rev. 251, 269–270, 273–290 (2005)

...

The present review examines participation rates and reasons, participant satisfaction, participant perception of fairness, restitution and repair of harm, diversion, recidivism, and cost. A total of eighty-five studies were reviewed for the present report, including fifty-three mediation studies, twenty-two group conferencing studies, five circle studies, two studies of other dialogue programs, and three meta-analyses....

2. Participant Satisfaction

i. Victim-Offender Mediation

The vast majority of studies reviewed reported in some way on satisfaction of victims and offenders with victim-offender mediation and its outcomes. Expression of satisfaction with VOM is consistently high for both victims and offenders across sites, cultures, and seriousness of offenses. Typically, eight or nine out of ten participants report being satisfied with the process and with the resulting agreement. Two studies that utilized shuttle mediation yielded slightly lower satisfaction rates for those participants than for participants who met face-to-face.

Secondary analysis of satisfaction data from a United States study and a Canadian study yielded similar high rates of satisfaction. Using step-wise multiple regression procedures to determine those variables most associated with victim satisfaction, the authors discovered that three variables emerged to explain over 40% of the variance. The key variables associated with victim satisfaction were as follows: (1) the victim felt good about the mediator; (2) the victim perceived the resulting restitution agreement as fair; and (3) the victim, for whatever reason, had a strong initial desire to meet the offender.

When asked, typically nine out of ten participants would recommend a VOM program to others.

These high levels of satisfaction with victim-offender mediation also translated into relatively high levels of satisfaction with the criminal justice system. Where comparison groups were studied, those victims and offenders going through mediation indicated being more satisfied with the criminal justice system than those going through traditional court prosecution.

In a meta-analysis covering both VOM and group conferencing programs, Latimer, Dowden, and Muise found that in twelve of the thirteen VOM and group conferencing programs that reported satisfaction rates, victims were more satisfied than those in traditional approaches. Satisfaction rates were somewhat higher in VOM than in group conferencing; the authors felt one reason might be that conferences typically have more participants, making it more difficult to find as much satisfaction with an agreement.

The meta-analysis found a "moderate to weak positive impact" on offender satisfaction as compared to offenders in non-restorative programs.

ii. Group Conferencing

Group conferencing also yields fairly high satisfaction responses from participants. Apart from an early New Zealand study, in which only 53% of victims reported being satisfied, more recent group conferencing studies have yielded satisfaction rates ranging from 73% into the high 90% range. Two recent studies reported participant agreement rates from 90% to 100% across a range of items tapping dimensions of satisfaction.

Victims in a Minnesota study of group conferencing listed the most helpful component of their experience as the opportunity to talk to the offender and explain effect of crime on them and to hear the offender's explanation. The least helpful aspect of group conferencing was the "negative attitude of [some] parents."

Three studies found that over 90% of victims and offenders would recommend the group conferencing program to others. One of these further compared recommendation rates to the control sample, in which only 25% of the victims would so recommend. For the juvenile offenders in this study, 85% would recommend the program compared with 38% of the control group.

iii. Circles

Fewer studies regarding participant response to restorative justice or peacemaking circles are available to us. Circles are most often imbedded in a broader community response to conflict.

Preliminary research efforts suggest that talking circles, healing circles, and sentencing circles have positively impacted the lives of those who have participated in them. In an early evaluation of the Hollow Water First Nation Community Holistic Circle Healing approach to sex victimizers, their victims, families, and the community pointed to positive outcomes as well as lingering concerns. Having a voice and a stake in justice outcomes, mutual respect, and renewed community and cultural pride were cited as benefits of participation. On the other hand, lack of privacy, difficulty of working with family and close friends, embarrassment, unprofessionalism, and religious conflict were cited by others as negative aspects of the circle process.

Victim satisfaction is cited as "very high" in the Healing/Sentencing Circles Program in Whitehorse, Yukon Territory. Participant satisfaction with restorative justice circles for misdemeanors and low level assaults in South St. Paul, Minnesota, was also high. Each of the thirty victim and offender participants who were interviewed indicated that he or she would recommend the circle process to others who were in similar circumstances. Offenders indicated that what they liked most about circles was "connecting with people in the circle," "changed attitude and behavior," "opportunity to pay back the victim and community," and "avoid court." Victims liked "being able to tell their story," "listening to others," and "connecting with people in the circle." Community representatives liked feeling that "they were giving something back to the community" and that "they were helping people."

Three Minnesota school districts used a three-year prevention grant to train staff in the circle process and implement the use of circles in the schools as an alternative response to discipline problems. Satisfaction was mixed and was related to levels of success in implementing the program. South St. Paul had the highest satisfaction. In surveys collected at the conclusion of "circles to repair harm," a majority of participants (students, staff, parents, applicants, and victims) indicated satisfaction with the process, with higher reports of feeling "hopeful, grateful, confident, and supported after the process." School staff felt circles had a positive impact and felt the process was fair to teachers and students.

Satisfaction data was less complete for the other two districts. In one, the training received a positive evaluation, and by the end of the third year, 70% of teachers were using the circle process in community-building activities in the classroom. Return rate on staff surveys in the other district was only 27%; of these, 70% were positive, 19% neutral, and 11% negative....

3. Fairness

i. Victim-Offender Mediation

Many studies of victim-offender mediation asked participants about the fairness of the mediation process and of the resulting agreement. Not surprisingly, given the high levels of satisfaction, the vast majority of VOM participants (typically over 80%) across setting, cultures, and types of offenses reported believing that the process was fair to both sides and that the resulting agreement was fair. Again, these experiences led to feelings that the overall criminal justice system was fair. Where comparison groups were employed, those individuals exposed to mediation came away more likely feeling that they had been treated fairly than those going through the traditional court proceedings. In a study of burglary victims in Minneapolis, Umbreit found that 80% who went through VOM indicated that they experienced the criminal justice system as fair compared with only 38% of burglary victims who did not participate in VOM.

> The Australian Reintegrative Shaming Experiments ("RISE") operate by offenders facing the victims they harmed, while in the presence of friends and family. The program was designed to take into account both the victims' and offenders' perceptions of justice and their satisfaction after conferencing. Reintegrative shaming conferencing both focuses on the past harm done and preventing future recidivism. RISE conferences usually last one to two hours and bring together not only offenders and victims, but also supportive individuals for both parties to help discuss what happened (the crime), its impact, and how to best move forward.
>
> Lawrence W. Sherman, John Braithwaite, Heather Strang & Geoffrey C. Barnes, *Reintegrative Shaming Experiments (RISE) in Australia, 1995–1999* (Inter-university Consortium for Political and Social Research [distributor], Ann Arbor, Mich. 2006), available at: https://doi.org/10.3886/ICPSR02993.v1.

ii. Group Conferencing

Fairness is also an issue of concern for participants in group conferencing and is often a focus of research. In an Australian study, 80% to 95% of victims and offenders reported that they were treated fairly and had a say in the agreement. Similarly, preliminary data from the Australian Reintegrative Shaming Experiments ("RISE") found that 72% of the offenders felt the outcome of group conferencing was fair, compared with 54% of comparison offenders prosecuted in the traditional courts. Interestingly, the conference offenders were also more likely to feel that they would be caught if they re-offended.

In three United States studies, about 95% of victims indicated the process or outcome was fair. Regarding offenders, 89% of the juvenile offenders in a Minnesota-based study indicated that the resulting conference agreement was fair....

4. Restitution and Repayment of Harm

The form of restitution, or what is called reparation in some jurisdictions, is quite varied and can include direct compensation to the victim, community service, work for the victim, and sometimes unusual paybacks devised between victim and offender. Apologies are also often included in program reports as a component of repairing the harm. In some settings, restitution amounts are established before cases are referred for mediation; in others, deciding whether the victim should receive restitution and how much is seen as an important domain for the mediation session.

i. Victim-Offender Mediation

About half the studies under review addressed the issue of restitution or repair of harm. Of those cases that reached a meeting, typically 90% or more generated agreements. Restitution of some sort was part of the vast majority of these agreements. Looking across the studies reviewed here, it appears that approximately 80% to 90% of the contracts are reported as completed.

Results from comparative studies have been somewhat mixed, with some studies reporting higher amounts of restitution or greater completion rates for VOM participants than comparison groups, while another reported no difference. The meta-analysis covering both mediation and group conferencing found that offenders participating in these programs had substantially higher completion rates than offenders processed in other ways.

ii. Group Conferencing

Restitution or reparation is often a major focus of conferences, and high agreement rates are reported, usually reaching the high 90% range, and in one instance achieving 100%. Apologies play a central role in group conferencing outcomes with well over half of the victims receiving apologies across studies that report this distinction. Other frequently reported agreement components included monetary restitution and work for the victim or the community.

When victims were present for the conference, any work performed by offenders was more likely to be done for the victim than when victims were not present, although this still happened in only two-fifths of the cases. In addition, reparation occurred 42% of the time when victims were present, compared to 29% across all cases that harmed victims.

Group conferencing studies using comparison groups have found much higher rates of receiving repair for victims who participated in group conferencing than victims whose cases were processed through other channels. In one instance, the overall rate of receiving repair (including apology) was ten times that of traditionally processed cases.

Completion rates for agreements developed during conferences are quite high, ranging from the middle 80% range to the middle 90% range....

5. Diversion

Among other reasons, many restorative programs are nominally established to divert offenders from the traditional justice system processes. While such diversion was a goal lauded by many, others expressed concern about the unintended consequence of widening the net—that is, sanctioning offenders who otherwise would not have received sanctions through traditional procedures. Only a handful of the studies reviewed here address this question.

i. Victim-Offender Mediation

Two mediation studies, both in the United Kingdom, have reported a net-widening impact for the intervention. One concluded that at least 60% of the offenders participating in mediation were true diversions from court prosecution, and overall there was a 13% net-widening effect, much less than expected. In the other, fully 43% of the comparison group cases were not prosecuted and received no sanction, a fairly broad net-widening result.

In contrast, two United States-based studies found that the mediation programs successfully diverted offenders from court. One North Carolina program apparently reduced court trials by as much as two-thirds. An Indiana-Ohio study compared consequences for seventy-three youth and adults going through VOM programs with those for a matched sample of individuals who were processed in the traditional manner. VOM offenders spent less time incarcerated than did their counterparts, and when incarcerated, they did county jail time rather than state time.

ii. Group Conferencing

Results for group conferencing are likewise mixed across the few studies addressing the issue. The Bethlehem, Pennsylvania group conferencing program left police and courts largely unaffected. On the other hand, an Australian program greatly reduced the total number of police interventions involving young people and increased the proportion of cases handled through cautioning rather than in court. A school-based group conferencing program reported that all of its conferenced cases were diversion; 70% were in place of suspension, and 35% (with some overlap) were in place of criminal charges.

The New Zealand experience offers a perspective on system wide change. New Zealand's Children, Young Persons and Families Act of 1989 established new procedures for state intervention into families and the lives of children and young people, replacing many court processes with family group conferencing. Similar results were found; that is, the changes dramatically reduced the court load from up to 13,000 cases per year to as little as 2587 in 1990. On the other hand, the authors point out that only three out of five youths who appeared in court previously received any formal penalty, while fully 95% of conferenced youths either received a penalty or made an apology. Again, this demonstrates a net-widening impact.

iii. Circles

The Hollow Water First Nation Community Holistic Circle Healing Process was designed, in part, as a way of keeping victimizers in the community. Over a ten-year period, ninety-four individuals were diverted within the four communities making up Hollow Water. Forty-one of these persons had assault charges, and thirty-seven had sexual assault charges. An additional seven adult males came to the program from other reserves, resulting in a total of 101 individuals who were diverted from the provincial or federal justice system.

A school-based circle project in Minnesota succeeded in reducing behavioral referrals by 75% over the three years of its implementation. Whether this qualifies as diversion (reduction of referrals) or recidivism (prevention of further infractions) may be subject to debate, but the result is nonetheless impressive.

6. Recidivism

The goal of restorative processes is to meet the needs of all parties affected by crime—victims, offenders, and communities. Preventing recidivism is often used as a long-term measure of the "effectiveness" of such programs; such prevention benefits offenders directly, and more broadly, benefits communities. There has been some concern that the demonstrable outcome of reduction in recidivism should not be the only measure of effectiveness, but rather it should be placed in a broader context that includes the range of restorative goals.

A large number of the studies reviewed here have addressed recidivism; we will confine our discussion to those studies that provide some type of comparison group. Studies simply reporting overall re-offending rates with no comparison will not be addressed.

i. Victim-Offender Mediation

Results from studies examining the impact of mediation on recidivism have been mixed overall. Several studies found lower rates for mediation participants than for offenders processed through traditional means. In addition, five of the six programs examined by Evje and Cushman also found reduced recidivism. Two studies also found that youths who did re-offend tended to incur less serious charges than their counterparts. Others reported little or no difference, as did one of the six programs studied by Evje and Cushman. A study of a county-wide restorative program that included VOM as one component found virtually equal recidivism rates between the sample and the control group.

One United Kingdom study compared recidivism data on the VOM offenders who went through face-to-face mediation with those who were exposed only to shuttle mediation. The former group did somewhat better than the latter: 15.4% and 21.6%. As with satisfaction measures reported earlier, face-to-face mediation seems to generate better results both in the short run and in the longer run than the less personal indirect mediation. Another United Kingdom study, examining seven varying restorative justice schemes, found that "the only scheme that routinely involved victims ... was for the most part both lower cost and more effective than the other schemes." The program reduced both the frequency and the seriousness of subsequent offenses.

A few studies have examined participants' offense rates before and after mediation. All of these studies found an overall reduction in offense rates for participating offenders.

Three meta-analyses have addressed recidivism issues. Nugent, Umbreit, Wiinamaki, and Paddock conducted a rigorous reanalysis of recidivism data reported in four previous studies, involving a total sample of 1298 juvenile offenders, 619 who participated in VOM, and 679 who did not. Using ordinal logistical regression procedures, the authors determined that VOM youth recidivated at a statistically significant 32% lower rate than non-VOM youth.

In a subsequent report, Nugent, Williams, and Umbreit expanded their database to include fifteen studies. This analysis relied on a combined sample of 9037 juveniles and similarly found that the mediated adolescents committed fewer and less serious offenses than their counterparts.

The third meta-analysis included both mediation and group conferencing, and found that the two types of programs together yielded reductions in recidivism compared to other, non-restorative approaches, and that offenders in the two program types were significantly more successful during the follow-up periods.

ii. Group Conferencing

As with mediation, results have been somewhat mixed. Several studies have reported a positive difference between conferenced offenders and those who were traditionally processed.

Other studies have found different effects for different groups of participants. A series of reports on the RISE experiments showed a reduction in re-offending for the violent crimes but not for the other three categories of offense [drunk driving, juvenile property offending with personal victims, and juvenile shoplifting offenses]. McCold and Wachtel similarly found that group conferencing had a more positive impact on recidivism rates for participants whose offenses were relatively more violent. Walker found no overall difference in re-offense rates between conferenced youths and all youths in Honolulu but noted that nonviolent conferenced youths did not tend to escalate to violence in subsequent offenses, while similar youths who did not participate in group conferencing had significantly higher arrest rates for subsequent violent crimes.

A number of recent studies have begun to attempt to sort out factors that make a difference in the rate of re-offending among conferenced offenders. In 1996 Maxwell and Morris were able to contact 108 young people (67% of their original sample) and 98 parents who had participated in family group conferencing in 1990–91. Several multivariate analyses were conducted to sort out predictors of reconviction and pathways to re-offending. Critical factors that were correlated with lessened re-offending included the following: having a conference that was memorable, not being made to feel a bad person, feeling involved in the conference decision making, agreeing with the outcome, completing the tasks agreed to, feeling sorry for what they had done, meeting the victim and apologizing to him or her, and feeling that they had repaired the damage. As the authors point out, "These factors reflect key restorative values, processes and outcomes."

Hayes and Daly examined factors associated with re-offending in a juvenile group conferencing program and found that there was an interaction effect between age at first offending and whether or not the first offense was conferenced. They concluded that young, first-time offenders are less likely to re-offend if the response to that first offense is group conferencing than if it is court referral or cautioning. This finding has relevance for the net-widening concerns because early intervention has some potential to be more effective even if it temporarily widens the net.

In a related study, Hayes and Daly found that youths who expressed remorse at conferences had one-third fewer re-offenses than youths who did not, and youths who felt their conference outcome was arrived at by a genuine consensus had one-fourth fewer re-offenses than youths who did not. Both variables are recognizable restorative concepts. However, as the authors point out, the study could not rule out that these differences may have been pre-existing characteristics of the involved youths, rather than something "caused or encouraged" by the conference process.

iii. Circles

While recidivism is not a primary focus of any of the circle studies surveyed here, it was mentioned in two of the reports. Matthews and Larkin note that an internal self-study was completed for the Healing and Sentencing Circles Program at Whitehorse, Yukon Territory by an outside consultant. Over a two-year period the program served sixty-five clients. Follow-up tracking showed that there was an 80% decrease in recidivism.

Also, the Hollow Water study conducted by the Native Counseling Service of Alberta reported that only two clients (approximately 2%) over the ten years had re-offended. They suggest that typical "recidivism rates for sex offenses is approximately 13% and for any form of recidivism the figure rises to approximately 36%." It remains unclear if these latter comparative figures refer to provincial data, federal data, or both....

7. Costs

i. Victim-Offender Mediation

The relative costs of correctional programs are difficult to assess. Several studies reviewed here addressed the issue of costs.

Cost per unit case is obviously influenced by the number of cases handled and the amount of time devoted to each case. The results of a detailed cost analysis in a Scottish study were mixed. In some instances, mediation was less costly than other options and in others more costly. The author notes that given the "marginal scope" of these programs, it remains difficult to evaluate their cost if implemented on a scale large enough to impact overall program administration.

Evaluation of a large scale VOM program in California led the authors to conclude that the cost per case was reduced dramatically as the program went from being a fledgling to being a viable option. Cost per case was $250. A Missouri program reported total cost per case that ranged from $232 to $338, but did not provide comparison data.

As noted earlier, some programs have impacted either total incarceration time, place or cost of incarceration, or reduction of trials. Additionally, time spent to process a case has implications for overall cost. Stone, Helms, and Edgeworth found that the total time required to process mediated cases was only one-third of that needed for non-mediated cases.

In an evaluation of a large-scale restorative program (of which VOM was one component) for youths who would have been referred to state custody, Bradbury found that the yearly cost per case was less than for the state custody program ($48,396 versus $65,866). Since recidivism was virtually the same between the two groups, the restorative program was less costly on the surface. However, the author concluded that because the restorative youths spent more days in the community, they posed more risk to community residents. Therefore, neither program could be designated as "clearly superior."

ii. Circles

A cost-benefit analysis was the cornerstone of the Native Counseling Services of Alberta study of the Hollow Water's Community Holistic Circle Healing Process. Efforts were made to track the cost that would have occurred if the ninety-four victimizers participating in the program had not been diverted but rather had proceeded on to the provincial or federal justice systems. Estimates of pre-incarceration, incarceration, and parole costs were derived. These were compared to the costs of the CHCH. The estimates indicated that the total costs to provincial and federal governments without CHCH in place would have ranged from $6,212,732 to $15,902,885.231 The authors concluded that given the "very low recidivism rate ... it is appropriate to state that the value of services to both the government and community has been significantly understated."

* * *

Victim-Offender Mediation:
Could You Forgive the Person Who Murdered Your Daughter?

This was the question that the Grosmaire family faced after the death of their daughter, Ann Margaret Grosmaire, at the hands of her boyfriend, Conor McBride. Ann and Conor had been dating for three years. After a series of arguments between the two, Conor shot Ann in the head. Conor turned himself into the police around an hour after the shooting and subsequently confessed to the crime. The victim-offender mediation brought together many parties, including the Grosmaires, Conor McBride and his parents, lawyers, a victims' advocate, a restorative justice coordinator, and the Grosmaires' priest.

The Grosmaires spoke of Ann, her life and how her death affected them. "We went from when she was being born all the way up," Andy says. He spoke of what Ann loved to do, "like acting, and the things that were important in her life. She loved kids; she was our only daughter who wanted to give us grandchildren." She had talked of opening a wildlife refuge after college. "To me she had really grown up, and she was a woman," Andy says. "She was ready to go out and find her place in the world. That's the part that makes me most sad." ...

Conor was no less affected. "Hearing the pain in their voices and what my actions had done really opened my eyes to what I've caused," Conor told me later. "Then they were like, 'All right, Conor, it's on you.' And I had to give an account of what I did." He leaned forward, placed his elbows on his knees and looked directly at the Grosmaires, who were seated opposite him. It was difficult to get started, but once he did the story came out of him in one long flow....

When the group returned to the circle, Conor continued. He didn't try to shirk responsibility at the conference or in long conversations with me about the murder. "What I did was inexcusable," he told me. "There is no why, there are no excuses, there is no reason." He told Ann's parents that he had no plans to shoot their daughter. Still, he said, "on some subconscious level, I guess, I wanted it all to end. I don't know what happened. I just—emotions were overwhelming." He said he didn't remember deciding to pull the trigger, but he recognizes that it wasn't an accident, either....

The Grosmaires said they didn't forgive Conor for his sake but for their own. "Everything I feel, I can feel because we forgave Conor," Kate said. "Because we could forgive, people can say her name. People can think about my daughter, and they don't have to think, Oh, the murdered girl. I think that when people can't forgive, they're stuck. All they can feel is the emotion surrounding that moment. I can be sad, but I don't have to stay stuck in that moment where this awful thing happened. Because if I do, I may never come out of it. Forgiveness for me was self-preservation."

Still, their forgiveness affected Conor, too, and not only in the obvious way of reducing his sentence. "With the Grosmaires' forgiveness," he told me, "I could accept the responsibility and not be condemned." Forgiveness doesn't make him any less guilty, and it doesn't absolve him of what he did, but in refusing to become Conor's enemy, the Grosmaires deprived him of a certain kind of refuge—of feeling abandoned and hated—and placed the reckoning for the crime squarely in his hands. I spoke to Conor for six hours over three days, in a prison administrator's office at the Liberty Correctional Institution near Tallahassee. At one point he sat with his hands and fingers open in front of him, as if he were holding something. Eyes cast downward, he said, "There are moments when you realize: I am in prison. I am in prison because I killed someone. I am in prison because I killed the girl I loved."

Paul Tullis, *Can Forgiveness Play a Role in Criminal Justice?* N.Y. TIMES MAGAZINE January 6, 2013, available at http://www.nytimes.com/2013/01/06/magazine/can-forgiveness-play-a-role-in-criminal-justice.html.

Notes/Questions

1. More recent studies continue to show the benefits of restorative justice, particularly victim-offender mediation.

> To summarize, several key findings about victim offender mediation have emerged: (a) victims and offenders both generally report higher levels of satisfaction with the process, outcomes, and the fairness of the process than those who participate in court proceedings; (b) victims and offenders tend to derive psychosocial benefits from participating in the victim offender mediation process; (c) most victim offender mediations result in restitution agreements that are more likely to be fulfilled than those coming out of traditional juvenile and criminal justice processes; (d) victims who participate in victim offender mediation are likely to receive a direct apology from offenders, which they often value; (e) victim offender mediation tends to reduce the likelihood of offender recidivism; (f) victim offender mediation is typically less expensive than the traditional criminal justice system, producing immediate cost savings associated with the process itself (when compared to court proceedings), as well as long term financial benefits from decreases in recidivism and incarceration; and (g) more offenders tend to be diverted away from the traditional criminal justice system when victim offender mediation is made available. However, these benefits are not necessarily uniformly experienced across diverse programs, countries, ethnic groups, genders, races, ages, types of crimes, or other intervening variables, all of which need to be more thoroughly researched.

Toran Hansen & Mark Umbreit, *State of Knowledge: Four Decades of Victim-Offender Mediation Research and Practice: The Evidence*, 36 CONFLICT RES. Q. 106–107 (2018).

2. Do you think victim-offender mediation is a good process? Does the story above strengthen or weaken your view of victim-offender mediation?

3. Can victim-offender mediation be used in all cases? Should it be? What drawbacks could arise if implemented?

4. What if, in the story above, the parents asked for a restorative justice intervention and the prosecutor refused? Who should be deciding when this is appropriate?

5. The Grosmaires' positive experience in using restorative justice stems from excellent preparation. The prosecutor's office worked with them in advance and also worked with the perpetrator so that everyone was as ready as possible for the in-person meeting. Unfortunately, this is not always the case, and victims can be re-victimized when the process goes badly—the perpetrator refuses to talk or accept blame, or victims feel pressure to forgive. If you were advising a prosecutor's office about starting a restorative justice program, how might these negative experiences influence your recommendations? And, if you are moving forward, what processes or guardrails might you want to implement?

6. Does your answer to these questions change depending on whether victim-offender mediation happens entirely outside the criminal legal system and has no impact on the case or the time a defendant may serve (for example, participating in a restorative justice process will not be considered in parole or early release)?

II. Critiques and Responses to Restorative Justice

This final section of the chapter now examines the primary criticisms of restorative justice. The first article, by Richard Delgado, critiques restorative justice from the practical to the constitutional, and from the perspectives of victims, offenders, and society. The following article, by Erik Luna, is a direct response to Delgado's concerns. The next article, by Mary Ellen Reimund, examines the fairness and constitutional concerns of integrating restorative justice into the criminal legal system. And the final article takes on restorative justice from a prosecutor's perspective. As you read, continue to have both the goals of restorative justice in mind, as well as the different processes about which you have already read.

Richard Delgado, *Goodbye to Hammurabi: Analyzing the Atavistic Appeal of Restorative Justice*

52 Stan. L. Rev. 751, 758–771 (2000)

...

II. Can Restorative Justice Deliver on its Promises?
An Internal Critique

Critics of the Restorative Justice Movement and VOM voice two concerns: (1) they charge that restorative justice does not deliver what we expect from a system of criminal justice, and (2) they contend that the movement may render a disservice to victims, offenders, or society at large. The following two sections discuss these two sets of criticisms in turn.

A. Can Restorative Justice Deliver What We Expect from a System of Criminal Justice?

Among the elements that society may reasonably expect from a criminal justice system are consistency, equality of bargaining power, due process, punishment, state control, and widespread applicability.

1. Consistency.

Consider first the problem of inconsistent results. The traditional criminal justice system aims at uniformity, employing a system of graded offenses and sentencing guidelines designed to assure that like cases are treated alike. Although far from perfect in realizing this goal, the system at least holds consistency up as an ideal and includes measures designed to bring it about. Moreover, judges, prosecutors, and defense attorneys are repeat players who tend to see cases in categorical terms (e.g., a car accident: pedestrian versus driver) rather than in terms of ascribed qualities of the participants (e.g., black driver, white pedestrian). However, VOM lacks both an obvious "metric" (e.g., what is the appropriate number of hours of community service for a shoplifting offense?) and the repeat-player quality of formal adjudication. The mediator may have seen many cases similar to the one at hand, but the victim and the offender will most likely be in their situation for the first time. Without any prior experience, different victims and offenders may decide similar cases differently, leading to inconsistency in punishment.

2. Inequality of bargaining power.

VOM gives great power to the victim, and mediators and judges reinforce that power, placing defendants in an almost powerless position. For example, the mediator frequently advises the offender that he will be referred back to the court system for trial if he and the victim cannot reach a restitution agreement. The mediator may also tell the offender that the judge will take his lack of cooperation into account at the time of sentencing. This leaves the victim with the power to price the crime based on her subjective reaction, while at the same time confronting the offender with a harsh choice: cooperate or go to jail.

3. Waiver of constitutional rights.

Related to the above-mentioned coercive quality of mediation is the issue of waiver of constitutional rights. Enacted during a period when the "king's peace" view of crime and criminal justice prevailed, rather than during the earlier period when private restitution served as chief remedy, our Constitution and Bill of Rights guarantee the criminally accused certain rights, including the right to confront witnesses, to be represented by counsel, and to avoid self-incrimination. Fearing abuse by the powerful state, the Framers incorporated these protections against overzealous prosecution and police practices. However, because VOM pressures offenders to accept informal resolution of the charges against them and to waive representation by a lawyer, trial by jury, and the right to appeal, it would seem to stand on constitutionally questionable ground. Moreover, mediation takes place early in the criminal process, at a time when the offender may be unaware of the evidence against him, or the range of defenses available. Furthermore, social science evidence compiled by VOM's defenders is one-sided, adulatory, and lacking basic elements of scholarly rigor—such as blind studies, controls for variables, and randomization—that one would wish in connection with a widespread social experiment. In the current state of research, neither offenders nor their advisors can predict what mediation will really be like. Thus, a defendant may be unable to waive his rights "knowingly and intelligently" as required by the Constitution.

4. Punishment.

Our society has further expectations of any system of criminal adjudication. These include the traditional goals of criminal punishment—deterrence, rehabilitation, increased societal safety, and retribution. Mediation may accomplish some of these objectives in individual cases, but only incidentally and as a byproduct of its principal objectives of compensating the victim and avoiding incarceration for the offender. During mediation, if an offender is willing to apologize and make restitution, he is released immediately into society with little check on whether he is fully rehabilitated. Accordingly, society's need for retribution or vengeance remains unsatisfied. This is not surprising: Most restorative justice theorists consider retribution an illegitimate relic of a more barbaric age.

5. State control.

Another troubling aspect of VOM is that it may upset social expectations by casting a wider net of state control than we expect. One way this may happen is that minor cases that ordinarily would have been dismissed or treated summarily in the traditional system receive full-blown treatment under VOM. Indeed, one study showed that VOM increased incarceration because many offenders who would not have received jail time entered into a restitution agreement, but then failed to carry it out. These offenders were then referred back to court, where they were sentenced for failure to complete their restitution bargain.

6. VOM's limited applicability.

Finally, mediation cannot be applied, without radical modification, to victimless crimes, such as drug offenses or crimes of attempt, or to offenses against the state or a corporation. In these cases, no ordinary victim is available to meet with the perpetrator and discuss restitution, nor has the perpetrator victimized a specific individual or community who could be made whole.

B. Disservice Toward Particular Groups

Defenders of restorative justice and VOM frequently assert that this type of informal justice is beneficial to society, offenders, and victims. What they neglect to mention, however, is that informal justice may also have a number of downsides for both victims and offenders.

1. Victims.

Mediation may disserve victims by pressuring them to forgive offenders before they are psychologically ready to do so. Mediators, who typically want both parties to put aside their anger and distrust, may intimate that victims are being obstructionist or emotionally immature if they refuse to do so. Such victims may in fact harbor perfectly understandable anger and resentment over the crime. A victim who already blames herself may magnify that self-blame; this risk is most severe if the offender is an acquaintance or intimate partner of the victim. Furthermore, VOM casts the victim in the role of sentencer, holding the power of judgment over the offender. Not only does this lead to a lack of proportionality and consistency, but it may also place an unwelcome burden on the victim who will end up determining the fate of an often young and malleable offender. Not every victim will welcome this responsibility. In pressuring the victim to "forgive and move on" and handing him the power of sentencer, VOM may end up compounding the injury received from the crime itself.

2. Offenders.

At the same time, VOM may disserve offenders, who lose procedural guarantees of regularity and fair treatment. Offenders are urged to be forthcoming and admit what they did, yet often what they say is admissible against them in court if the case is returned. Finally, as mentioned earlier, mediation may not meet social expectations for a system of criminal justice: It dismisses retribution, a valid social impulse; abjures incapacitation, even for serious offenses; offers little in the way of deterrence (a forty-five minute session is not unpleasant enough); and reduces recidivism little, if at all, perhaps because offenders' basic attitudes are unchanged, and the compulsory nature of the mediation induces only superficial expressions of shame and regret.

III. External Critique: Larger, Systemic Problems with Restorative Justice and Victim-Offender Mediation

As we have seen, restorative justice, in some respects, falls short of achieving its professed goals, or, indeed, those that any system of criminal justice, even narrowly understood, should be expected to accomplish. This section examines restorative justice in light of broader political and social values, such as its ability to spark needed social change, moral reflection, or altered relationships between offender and victim communities. As will be seen, restorative justice raises troubling issues when viewed through this lens as well.

A. Restoration of the Status Quo Ante

One difficulty with restorative justice inheres in the concept itself. Restorative justice, like tort law, attempts to restore the parties to the status quo ante—the position they would have been in had the crime not occurred—through restitution and payment. But if that status quo is marked by radical inequality and abysmal living conditions for the offender, returning the parties to their original positions will do little to spark social change. The mediation agreement ordinarily requires payment from the offender to the victim, when in many cases it will be the offender who needs a better education, increased job training, and an improved living environment. Offenders rarely are assigned work that will benefit them or lead to new job opportunities; rather, they end up performing menial services for the victim, such as cutting his grass, painting his porch, or making simple repairs. When the offender performs services for the community, they typically take the form of unskilled labor, such as clearing brush, picking up trash in city parks, or painting over graffiti.

A key component of VOM consists of shaming the offender—making him feel the full force of the wrongfulness of his action, thus causing him to experience remorse. Yet, this adjustment is all one-way: No advocate of VOM, to my knowledge, suggests that the middle-class mediator, the victim, or society at large should feel shame or remorse over the conditions that led to the offender's predicament. Of course, many offenders will be antisocial individuals who deserve little solicitude, while many victims will have well-developed social consciences and empathize with the plight of the urban poor. But nothing in restorative justice or VOM encourages this kind of analysis or understanding. In most cases, a vengeful victim and a middle-class mediator will gang up on a young, minority offender, exact the expected apology, and negotiate an agreement to pay back what she has taken from the victim by deducting portions of her earnings from her minimum-wage job. Little social transformation is likely to arise from transactions of this sort.

B. Unlikelihood of Sparking Moral Reflection and Development

By the same token, it seems unlikely that VOM will produce the desired internal, moral changes in the offender. In theory, bringing the offender to the table to confront the victim face-to-face will enable him to realize the cost of his actions in human terms and to resolve to lead a better life. Some offenders may, indeed, have a crisis of conscience upon meeting the person she has victimized. But a forty-five minute meeting is unlikely to have a lasting effect if the offender is released to her neighborhood and teenage peer group immediately afterwards. If the offender-victim encounter is brief and perfunctory, and the ensuing punishment demeaning or menial, young offenders will learn to factor the cost of restitution into their practical calculus the next time they are tempted to commit a crime and to parrot what is expected of them when caught. Most offenders are at an early stage of Kohlberg's moral development, seeing right and wrong in pragmatic terms—the action is right if you can get away with it, wrong if you are caught and punished. A short encounter with a victim is unlikely to advance them to a higher stage. Reports of young offenders show that most have little self-esteem, yet both the mediation and the ensuing work an offender performs for the victim or his community come perilously close to degradation rituals. Rarely, if ever, is the offender ordered to do something that will benefit him. For all these reasons, VOM is apt to do little to make an offender a better person; indeed, in a few studies, recidivism increased, compared to a similar group subject to the ordinary criminal justice system.

C. Inequality of Treatment of Offenders and Victims

Mediation treats the victim respectfully, according him the status of an end-in-himself, while the offender is treated as a thing to be managed, shamed, and conditioned. Most surveys of VOM programs ask the victim if he felt better afterwards. By contrast, offenders are merely asked whether they completed their work order and whether they recidivated. Offenders sense this and play along with what is desired, while the victim and middle-class mediator participate in a paroxysm of righteousness. In such a setting, the offender is apt to grow even more cynical than before and learn what to say the next time to please the mediator, pacify the victim, and receive the lightest restitution agreement possible.

The offender's cynicism may not just be an intuition; it may be grounded in reality: Informal dispute resolution is even more likely to place him at a disadvantage than formal adjudication. In court, a panoply of procedural devices serve as a brake against state power and overzealous prosecution. Each defendant is assigned a lawyer, who has a prescribed time and place for speaking. The state bears a heavy burden of proof. Moreover, visible features of the American Creed, such as the flag, the robes, and the judge sitting on high, remind all present that principles, such as fairness, equal treatment, and every person receiving his day in court, are to govern, rather than the much less noble values we often act upon during moments of informality. In less formal settings, the same individuals who will behave with fairness during occasions of state will feel much freer to tell an ethnic joke or deny a person of color or a woman a job opportunity. This "fairness and formality" thesis, solidly grounded in social science understandings of the dynamics of prejudice, counsels against using VOM for offenders who are young, black, Latino, or otherwise different from the white, middle-class norm many Americans implicitly embrace.

D. Racial and Social Inequality

The prime architects of the VOM movement seem to believe that mediators can balance, or counter, inequalities among the parties. However, their own writing about race is replete with stereotypes. Rather than breaking down the barriers and preconceptions that parties bring to the table, mediation is apt to compound preexisting power and status differentials even more systematically and seriously than formal, in-court resolution. VOM sets up a relatively coercive encounter in many cases between an inarticulate, uneducated, socially alienated youth with few social skills and a hurt, vengeful victim. This encounter is mediated by a middle-class, moralistic mediator who shares little background or sympathy with the offender, but has everything in common with the victim. To label this encounter a negotiation seems a misnomer, for it is replete with overt social coercion.

E. Prompting Recognition of Common Humanity

Nothing is wrong with requiring persons who have harmed others without justification to make restitution. But forcing a needy person who has stolen a loaf of bread to do so is regressive, unless accompanied by measures aimed at easing his poverty. In VOM, all the onus is placed on the offender to change; the victim is required only to come to the bargaining table, discuss how the crime has affected him, negotiate a restitution agreement, and accept an apology. Why not require victims to take a bus tour of the offender's neighborhood and learn something about the circumstances in which he lives?

In traditional adjudication, judges, prosecutors, defense attorneys, and jurors will all be privy to this information and be able to consider it when charging and sentencing, but with mediation, the mediator and the victim often will not. Mediation aims at emotional closure, but without a reciprocal exchange of information, any closure is apt to occur only on the most superficial level. If the objective of VOM is to have both sides recognize their common humanity, measures of this sort ought to be considered. Why not even encourage the victim, in appropriate cases, to perform service to the offender or his or her community as a condition of receiving restitution (for example, by serving as a mentor or big brother/sister to a youth like the offender)? Countless studies of mediated crime adopt the feelings of the victim as the principal measure of success or failure—the better the victim feels afterwards, the more successful the mediation. Yet, sometimes in a successful mediation, the victim should feel worse, or at least realize that matters are not as simple as she might have thought.

F. Which Community Is to be Restored?

In a similar vein, VOM will frequently lead to a restitution agreement that includes service to "the community." Indeed, one of the principal advantages of VOM is said to be its ability to repair the breach that the offender's crime has opened between himself and that same community. Yet proponents of restorative justice rarely focus on the precise nature of that community. In a diverse, multicultural society, many collectivities may vie for that status. To which does the offender owe restitution? If, for example, the offender is to rake leaves, should he be required to do it in a park near where the victim lives? In a large municipal park serving the entire city? In one in his own neighborhood? Descriptions of successful mediation abound with stories of offenders made to perform services to victims' churches, for example. Apart from obvious issues of separation of church and state, such privatized, particularized service is troublingly reminiscent of peonage and prison labor gangs.

G. Erasing the Public Dimension of Criminal Prosecution

Moreover, such particularized mediation atomizes disputes, so that patterns, such as police abuse or the overcharging of black men, do not stand out readily. It forfeits what Owen Fiss and others call the public dimension of adjudication. Mediation pays scant attention to the public interests in criminal punishment, particularly retribution. It also lacks the symbolic element of a public trial, trying instead to compensate by formalized talking among private participants. The criminal justice system, of course, is a principal means by which society reiterates its deepest values; loss of that opportunity is cause for concern.

The timing of VOM's advent is also curious: It first appeared when the United States' demographic composition was beginning to shift rapidly in the direction of a majority nonwhite population. Juries were beginning to contain, for the first time, substantial numbers of nonwhite members, and at least one scholar of color would soon encourage black jurors to acquit young black men, who are, in their view more useful to the community free than behind bars. Could it be that VOM arose, consciously or not, in response to the threat of jury nullification?

H. Treating Conflict as Pathology

Perhaps the above concerns can be captured in the notion of conflict as pathology. Like many forms of mediation, VOM treats conflict as aberrational, and the absence of it as the desired state. Yet, in a society like ours, tension among groups may be normal, and not a sign of social pathology. With a history of slavery, conquest, and racist immigration laws, the United States today exhibits the largest gap between the wealthy and the poor of any Western industrialized society. Until recently, Southern states segregated school children by race and criminalized marriage between whites and blacks. Surely, in such a society, one would expect the have-nots to attempt to change their social position (by legal or illegal means), and the haves to resist these attempts. Conflict is a logical and expected result. One also would expect the majority group to use the criminal law, at least in part, as a control device—a means of keeping tabs on any behavior of subordinate groups that threatens or irritates, such as loud music, congregating on sidewalks, writing graffiti on freeway overpasses, and shoplifting. Insofar as restorative justice aims at smoothing over the rough edges of social competition and adjusting subaltern people to their roles, it is profoundly conservative. While restoration and healing are emotionally powerful objectives, it is hard to deny that they can have a repressive dimension as well.

Erik Luna, *Punishment Theory, Holism, and the Procedural Conception of Restorative Justice*

2003 Utah L. Rev. 205, 246–250

...

Now consider Professor Delgado's sweeping offensive against restorativism. To begin with, he claims that restorative justice somehow forces defendants to waive their constitutional rights, such as trial by jury. Yet concerns implicating the waiver of constitutional rights are not solely endemic to restorative justice, but rather to any form of diversion or plea bargaining. The pressure to waive trial-related guarantees does not seem comparable to placing a gun to the forehead, but instead appears as the standard persuasion of choosing a more lenient, humane, or satisfying option over taking one's chances with traditional court adjudication and sentencing. Delgado's concerns might be generalized against the basic idea of prosecutors offering something to a defendant—avoiding a more serious charge, for instance—in exchange for the waiver of his constitutional rights. It might instead be an implicit attack on the Supreme Court's standard for voluntary relinquishment of these guarantees. But either way, this criticism is more appropriately leveled against all alternatives to formal adjudication requiring a waiver of rights rather than restorative justice alone. One might suspect, however, that many members of the defense bar would disagree that placing such options before an offender is an unmitigated evil—at least in the current state of American criminal justice.

Along the same lines, Delgado argues that restorative justice lacks the "panoply of procedural devices" that protect defendants from state overreaching and abuses, as well as the formal trappings of the traditional court process that remind all actors of fundamental principles, such as legal equality and due process. But again, serious problems arise with this line of argumentation. The procedural protections Delgado heralds are, by and large, related to the adjudicative stage of the criminal trial rather than sentencing. The right to confront and cross-examine adverse witnesses and the constitutional mandate of proof beyond a reasonable doubt, for instance, concern the determination of guilt by the trier of fact. Restorative justice, however, is not a system for assessing evidence and adjudicating culpability; it is an alternate scheme for addressing a crime after the defendant's responsibility is no longer in doubt.

It is also less than clear that formal court trappings and procedures necessarily accrue to the benefit of the defendant. The ceremony and mystique of the courtroom can alienate rather than integrate defendants into the criminal process. The proceedings are dominated by lawyers—prosecutors, defense attorneys, and judges—who use a type of legalese incomprehensible to all but trained professionals. And as noted earlier, offenders rarely serve an active part in their trials but instead are relegated to the position of "dummy players" in the criminal process, with attorneys—the "repeat players" of the criminal justice system—doing most of the talking and making the most important decisions. It is thus discouraging but unsurprising that many defendants exit the courtroom dazed and confused by a process that squarely affects their interests.

Delgado also carps on restorative justice for the brevity of the process and the lack of public scrutiny. As for the former, he argues that a brief, "forty-five minute meeting" between victim, offender, and various stakeholders will have no lasting effect. Not to quibble, but restorative programs such as family group conferencing typically take hours or even a full day rather than the short duration cited by Delgado. More importantly, the purported brevity of a restorative process must be compared with the traditional criminal justice proceeding. A typical courtroom hearing can be measured in minutes (or even seconds), with little or no interaction between the defendant and various participants in the criminal process. If a multi-hour dialogue is unlikely to spark moral reflection in the offender, a ten-minute hearing in legalese would seem even less likely to produce the desired change.

As for Delgado's argument that restorativism lacks "the public dimension of adjudication," this objection would seem to have merit in the abstract: Open trials allow the public to scrutinize the conduct of police officers, the charging decisions and courtroom strategies of prosecutors, and the rulings of judges and juries. But in practice, this is an overly idealistic vision of the traditional criminal process. The vast majority of cases result in plea bargains, not public trials. Of those cases that are eventually prosecuted in court, few draw the attendance of common citizens or the media. And once the judge determines that police conduct was either constitutional or irrelevant to the current proceeding, law enforcement practices are generally free from further inquiry.

Throughout his critique, Professor Delgado challenges restorative justice with claims of inequality and inconsistency. He argues, for instance, that restorativism produces disparities in bargaining power between the offender and other actors in the criminal justice system. Yet despite Delgado's claims to the contrary, the defendant is not impotent in a restorative process, wholly subject to the victim's demands. Instead, the offender is empowered with veto authority over any resolution and has the absolute right to opt out of the process at any point. In the traditional criminal justice system, however, a convicted offender cannot negotiate an appropriate sanction nor reject the imposed sentence. Only the judge's sense of fairness and the loose constraints of the Constitution—not the views of the defendant—protect his interests. So when compared to the dominance of prosecutors and judges in the traditional system, restorative justice appears far more balanced in its distribution of power.

As for claims of inconsistent outcomes, Delgado notes that restorativism lacks "an obvious 'metric,'" that it is impossible to gauge, for example, "the appropriate number of hours of community service for a shoplifting offense." But, in truth, there is no such thing as "an obvious metric" for any crime under any theory. What is the appropriate sentence for rape? Or for robbery—or attempted robbery, for that matter? What about fines for drunk driving—how much should a blood-alcohol level of .15 cost an inebriated driver? As far as I can tell, there is no objectively knowable scale for punishing crimes. Instead, legislators guesstimate a palatable sanction for a given offense (or, more likely, a punishment that will give them electoral traction) without reference to a grand conversion chart of crime-to-penalty. As such, restorative justice cannot be singled out as the only theory that lacks "an obvious metric."

Moreover, Delgado offers a somewhat romantic vision of punishment equality under the traditional criminal justice system. He suggests, for instance, that "the repeat-player quality of formal adjudication" generates consistent outcomes for similar offenses. But this expectation is frequently more myth than reality. The punishment a criminal receives is more often than not correlated to the prosecutor he faces and the judge who hears his case. Government attorneys generally maintain wide discretion in their charging and plea bargaining decisions, while judges usually have some latitude in imposing punishment even under determinate sentencing schemes. In turn, some offenders are more likely to get caught than others because of geographic variations in policing, different levels of criminal experience, or relative intelligence. Likewise, some defendants are more likely to receive poor legal representation due to limited personal resources, fluctuations in caseloads, or regional disparities in the quality of the defense bar. And finally, some convicted offenders are more likely to receive severe penalties than others as a result of their demeanor, race, age, or gender. This is not to imply that these distinctions are justifiable or desirable—they are not. Instead, it is to suggest that the traditional approach to the criminal sanction is far from some imaginary bastion of equality and consistency.

Finally, Professor Delgado criticizes restorativism for ignoring the underlying societal disorders that produce criminal behavior, the so-called "rotten social background" of extreme inequality and squalid living conditions. As an initial matter, Delgado has set up a strawman that is easily knocked down. No criminal process—whether grounded in retributive, utilitarian, or restorative theories—can solve the severe socioeconomic disadvantages faced by many offenders. Remedying unemployment, substandard educational programs, and vulgar living environments is simply not within the capacity of a criminal justice system; these are issues for welfare legislation, not criminal sanctioning. To argue that restorative programs have no effect on bad schools is both true and irrelevant. The same, of course, can be said about the current court-based approach to criminal justice. More importantly, traditional criminal justice may well exacerbate social ills in ways that restorative justice does not. Court-based sentencing relies heavily on incarceration, often taking away breadwinners and caretakers from those families and communities that are least able to cope with such losses. It also brands the offender with a criminal record, thereby limiting any employment opportunities after serving his sentence.

If nothing else, Delgado has provided a degree of sobriety to the discussion of restorative justice. Much of the literature seems quixotic about the potential of this alternative to traditional punishment schemes. Unfortunately, Delgado adopts a mode of criticism sustainable only in a vacuum. Restorative justice may have many flaws, yet the correct test is not its validity in the abstract but how restorativism fares against a realistic standard, most notably, the current approach to criminal justice.

Notes/Questions

1. If you were designing a restorative justice statute, allowing for restorative justice processes pre-conviction, what provisions would you want to include? Would your ideas change if you were doing so as a prosecutor? As a defense lawyer? As a victims' rights advocate?

2. One critic of restorative justice questions what to do if offenders don't want to "reform" or "take responsibility" or "repair the harm." Professor Annalise Acorn, in COMPULSORY COMPASSION (UBC Press, 2004), also asks if we can't instead design a process where victims "aren't expected to spend their time and energy sitting down with people who have raped, assaulted, tortured, or stolen from them, or murdered their loved ones, trying to work toward an amicable agreement."

Do you agree with these concerns? Do you think they are serious enough to not have restorative justice processes at all, or just to limit their application? And, if a criminal legal system is going to limit their application, how? By type of crime, by age of offender? Or both?

3. Does it change your thinking if you think about what you would want if *you* were the victim? If your home were vandalized by teenagers, or your car were stolen, would you want to meet the offenders in a restorative justice setting? Why? Would your answer be different if you were assaulted and your arm broken? Would it be different if you were more seriously injured?

4. One of Professor Delgado's criticisms of restorative justice was based on the concern that the victim and mediator are middle class while the offender would be from a lower socio-economic group. But, what if the victim and offender are both from the same socio-economic group? Does that change the analysis? What if they are also from the same racial/ethnic group?

Mary Ellen Reimund, *The Law and Restorative Justice: Friend or Foe? A Systemic Look at the Legal Issues in Restorative Justice*

53 Drake L. Rev. 667, 668–669, 681–692 (2005)

I. Introduction

Restorative justice is another philosophy that resolves criminal conflict using a different set of principles. Restorative justice takes a victim-centered approach to crime. It recognizes the needs of victims and focuses on holding offenders accountable to victims and the community. Restorative justice asks the following: "Who has been hurt? What do they need? Whose obligations and responsibilities are these? Who has a stake in this situation? What is the process that can involve the stakeholders in finding a solution?"...

Along with the upsurge in restorative programs in the United States comes the question about the role of the law and lawyers. There is a continuing tension between whether restorative justice is a philosophy around which a new system of justice should be developed or whether restorative justice can be achieved within the confines of our current justice system. The legal issues and the role of lawyers in restorative justice can vary depending on the degree of restorativeness that permeates the criminal justice system. "The more restorative justice evolves into a kind of mainstream response, however, the more urgent it is to reflect on how to insert it into an adequate legal frame.... Legal formalism must not intrude on the restorative process, but the process must take place in a legalized context."...

V. Law and Restorative Justice

The foundations of law may be impeding the wider adoption of restorative justice within the criminal justice system....

Not only do legal systems adopt change slowly, other legal ramifications also hinder systemic adoption of restorative justice and raise the question of whether restorative justice can operate within the legal parameters currently existing within the criminal justice system. Critics of restorative justice have noted concerns about due process protection and procedural safeguards that exist in more formal processes. "[R]ights can ... be trampled because of the inferior articulation of procedural safeguards in restorative justice processes compared to [the] courts." When "the values are similar between restorative [justice] and conventional processes, such as offender rehabilitation and accountability," tension is low. However, when the rights of offenders are involved, "a value less compatible with restorative justice theory" emerges, and the divide becomes greater.

If restorative justice is fully embraced through a paradigm shift, then a different way of looking at legal issues should be considered. "Due process, legality, equality, right of defen[s]e, presumption of innocence and proportionality may be irrelevant or may need to be experienced in a different form. Maybe other legal principles need to be constructed in a manner more appropriate for the restorative perspective." One author has even explored what a restorative constitution might look like.

Since that shift has not taken place, restorative justice is practiced today within existing constitutional parameters and procedures in the criminal justice system. A closer examination of the pertinent legal concerns as they relate to restorative justice reveals that the issues may be of greater magnitude in theoretical discussions than in practice. Most restorative theorists and practitioners recognize that the rights of offenders cannot be ignored and responsibility for their protection falls on the professionals.

A. Constitutional Implications

Our Constitution guarantees the criminally accused certain rights, including due process and the right to avoid self-incrimination. The system relies on procedural rules to determine legal guilt or innocence, with lawyers and judges as the keepers of procedural expertise. Although constitutional rights are a vital part of the United States criminal justice system and have to be protected in restorative processes, how that process looks may be different under a restorative justice model because restoration of violated relationships is key. Expertise in substantive law becomes less necessary because crime is not viewed as breaking a state law, but rather as violating community norms. With direct participation by the victim, offender, and community, fewer specialized roles are needed. Restorative justice simplifies procedure by putting parties in control of a conflict's resolution.

1. Due Process

As guardians of due process, public defenders want to make sure that restorative justice programs protect the rights of offenders. Although there are concerns about the erosion of rights in restorative processes, it is a misnomer to believe that restorative justice requires abandonment of due process and procedural safeguards or that the two concepts are incompatible. There are times when the full array of procedural ... protections afforded by formal court processes are desired, especially if guilt is in dispute. "Conferences should never proceed in cases where the defendant sees him, or herself as innocent or blameless...." "Courts of law are designed to be 'truth machines'—forums for sorting out disputed facts" in those types of situations. But this machinery is unnecessary and can be "counterproductive in cases where significant facts are not in dispute." Concerns regarding due process are lessened in many restorative programs when the offender participates after pleading guilty. In those cases, the question becomes whether due process was infringed upon in any greater degree in a restorative process than through plea bargaining. Plea bargaining "circumvents ... 'rigorous standards of due process and proof imposed during trials.'"

If an offender is compelled to participate in restorative processes, the concerns about due process are greater. When VOM was endorsed by the American Bar Association in 1994, the number one item on its list of program requirements was that participation by both the offender and the victim be voluntary. Although coerciveness has been a criticism of restorative justice, the same could be said regarding plea bargaining, which occurs in ninety percent of felony prosecutions. Voluntariness can remedy coercive elements of restorative practices that have a tendency to impede due process.

An example of how voluntariness can be achieved within a restorative program is the Milwaukee Community Conferencing Program. Offenders are given two options: (1) what the penalty will be with restorative conferencing; and (2) what the penalty will be without conference participation. Coercion is lessened because the offender has the option of whether to participate, and thus an option to choose the corresponding penalty.

Another way to protect due process rights is to give an offender the opportunity to opt out of the restorative process at any time to pursue her case in the traditional criminal justice system with its full panoply of rights. In contrast would be restorative programs where offenders are ordered to engage in a restorative process as part of their sentence. Not only does the system take away the ability of the offender to be a voluntary participant in restorative justice, it softens the voice of victims since the options regarding the terms of an agreement reached during a VOM would be reduced.

2. Right Against Self-Incrimination and of Confidentiality

There is the potential that an offender participating in a restorative justice process could trigger her Fifth Amendment privilege against self-incrimination. The constitutional rights of a person accused of a crime and directed into a restorative process could be violated if she was not given any warning about rights against self-incrimination and then revealed information which later could be used against her in court. Most restorative justice programs "do not legally guarantee the American Bar Association's ... guideline that 'statements made by victims and offenders and documents and other material produced during the mediation/dialogue process [should be] inadmissible in criminal or civil court proceedings.'"

Legislation is not providing the solution to this concern in most states, because it is unclear whether restorative justice programs are covered by statutory confidentiality provisions in existence for other types of mediation, and there are few states with statutes specific to restorative processes. The Uniform Mediation Act, which has extensive provisions pertaining to confidentiality in mediation, has been adopted by several states and is being considered by others, but that Act does not provide the protections addressed in the American Bar Association Guidelines.

This issue is minimized if the person pleads guilty prior to participation in the restorative process. However, there have been instances where the offender has admitted committing crimes outside of the offense at issue during the restorative process. As a consequence, such information could potentially be used against the person in a subsequent prosecution.

B. Role of Attorneys in Restorative Justice

Most referrals to restorative justice programs come from the criminal justice system. However, there is a wide range of participation in and acceptance of restorative justice processes by prosecutors. On one end of the spectrum is Assistant Polk County Attorney Fred Gay:

Once the prosecutor accepts his role as gatekeeper, it is a short jump to the paradigm shift from the "trail 'em, nail 'em, jail 'em" mentality that pervades the traditional criminal justice system, to the restorative justice mindset that considers every case in light of what outcome best addresses the needs of the victim, community and offender. At the other end of the continuum are prosecutors who will not refer cases to restorative processes.

The perception that restorative justice takes power away from the prosecutor is also seen as a deterrent to prosecutors' participation in restorative justice. This was illustrated when the Minnesota prosecutor in *State v. Pearson* said the following in the Saint Paul Pioneer Press: "I believe it will give prosecutors pause as to their participation in those programs." The prosecutor in *Pearson* did not agree with the recommended stay of adjudication in a case where the sentencing circle's sentencing recommendation was followed.

As elected officials, prosecutors are often concerned about loss of political capital. "The perception that criminal mediation is 'soft on crime,' equates with 'political suicide' despite potential cost-cutting and restorative benefits." According to Assistant Polk County Attorney Fred Gay, restorative justice is not soft on crime. When discussing with offenders the process of meeting their victims, some say they would rather just spend their time in the jail cell.

As a restorative justice advocate and prosecutor for over twenty-six years in Austin, Texas, District Attorney Ronnie Earle also dispels these notions:

> I'd never been a prosecutor when I first became district attorney so I wasn't really sure what the job was. I thought all you had to do was be tough on crime because what people really wanted was justice. I thought at that time that justice was vengeance or pay back. And so we started being tough on crime, like all DA's are supposed to be. But pretty quickly I came to understand that vengeance wasn't making victims feel any better. And so I started looking for different ways to do my job.... For defense attorneys, restorative justice processes can be "counter-cultural to the more common practices of lawyers who are argumentative, persuasive and articulate debaters, who believe fervently and vigorously that seeking justice, on behalf of a client or cause, means advocating for and 'winning' a legal claim." The adversarial persona runs so deeply in attorneys that talk of restorative justice can cause attorneys to dismiss it by

> making flippant "Kumbaya" remarks when being exposed to the philosophy. According to prosecutors Gay and Lerman, when skeptical defense attorneys actually experience restorative justice in person, either through VOM or sentencing circles, they become more accepting of the processes.

Whether defense attorneys serve as roadblocks or bridges to restorative justice could turn on whether they believe that redemption, forgiveness, and conciliation are more important to their clients than the ultimate resolution of the criminal charge. Some defender offices see "these expanded services as new and improved ways to represent clients," but it more accurately "signals a paradigmatic shift in defense philosophy and ideology" and "marks a significant departure from the traditional defense role, which focused narrowly on the criminal case and left unaddressed the related convergent issues."

Defense attorney Terese Dick, who represented clients going through the Milwaukee Conferencing Program, has stated the following: "We are being challenged to explore and change our ways of thinking about the criminal justice system and the role we play in relation to the prosecutor, the judiciary, our clients, and the community in which we live." A handout is given to defense attorneys in that program which points out that defense attorneys are representing their clients' best interests, but not as advocates in the classic sense and reminds the attorneys to allow their clients to speak for themselves. Dick views conferencing as a way to serve clients differently and, ultimately, to their advantage.

Both prosecutors and defense attorneys who embrace the restorative justice philosophy understand that these processes make changes in the lives of offenders, victims, and the community at large. Restorative processes are not quick fixes to clear the dockets by closing large numbers of cases for prosecutors, nor are they a way for defense attorneys to get their client off easily. As a judge who participates in circle processes, Gary Schurrer points out that, from a legal perspective, it is very difficult to quantify those people who make lifestyle changes and lead a law-abiding life as a result of restorative justice, which in turn creates skepticism among prosecutors and defense attorneys. Developing an understanding about the deeper meaning of restorative justice defies easy explanation, as "written descriptions of practices and cases are not equally powerful, not enough to convince most people, and not enough to show that sentencing circles work better than traditional criminal justice approaches."

C. The Hazards of Law in Restorative Justice

One of "the greatest threat[s] to restorative justice may be the thoughtless enthusiasm of policy makers, police, magistrates, judges, and social workers who want to integrate a few techniques into traditional rehabilitative or punitive justice systems." This is because "[a] taste of mediation, a bit of conferencing, or a pinch of community services are added to the system without questioning fundamental principles." Practices stripped of personal commitment become "fast food" restorative practices, ornamenting a system that essentially remains unchanged.

There are also concerns about restorative justice becoming institutionalized within the legal system. Institutionalization brings pressures to be efficient and cost-effective. These objectives do not "square well with the emphasis on ritual, the taking of time to tell stories, and the inherent inefficiency of circle process." These all present "critical challenge[s to] whether the process of institutionalization can be accomplished without destroying the vitality of restorative justice."

VI. Conclusion

Law and restorative justice are not foes in the search for justice within the criminal justice system. When united, they provide a powerful force by giving victims a voice, holding offenders accountable to right their wrongs and allowing communities to participate in the process. There are rays of that power radiating from restorative programs in operation today. One only has to look at the programs in Iowa, Minnesota, and Wisconsin to see that restorative justice and the law can be successful complements to the criminal justice system.

Restorative justice does not advocate putting law in the closest available dumpster. To the contrary, law provides important qualities that are also espoused by restorative justice. This concept is confirmed by Howard Zehr, widely considered the grandfather of restorative justice in the United States, who has stated: "We also must not lose those qualities which the legal system at its best represents: the rule of law, due process, a deep regard for human rights, [and] the orderly development of law."

Constitutional concerns can be addressed by incorporating better practices in programs, such as clarifying what is and is not confidential. Attorneys can be involved as the vanguards of offender rights, with some variations in how they perform that role, as suggested in the guidelines set up in Milwaukee's program. The gains achieved by restorative justice would mean little if they came at the risk of offenders' rights. However, "there is no evidence that such risks have been realized in any form of restorative justice."

Value can be added to the criminal justice system through restorative justice. Restorative justice can fill voids of injustice in the system. As Assistant Polk County Attorney Fred Gay asserts: "Our adversarial system of justice, while necessary to protect the rights of defendants, insulates both the victim and the defendant from the very real human contact that is often necessary." An "exclusive focus on 'legal' needs and interests may not bring us justice," but restorative justice can get us closer. A realistic goal is to go "as far as we can toward a process that is restorative." "In between will be many cases and situations where both systems must be utilized, and justice is only partly restorative."

* * *

In the next excerpt, the role of the prosecutor in restorative justice is examined. Consider how the prosecutor's conception of restorative justice—and when it is appropriate—mirrors much of what we have learned about the role of prosecutors in plea bargaining, problem-solving courts, and other types of reform movements.

Bruce A. Green & Lara Bazelon, *Restorative Justice from Prosecutors' Perspective*

88 Fordham L. Rev. 2299–2300, 2303–2305, 2314–2318 (2020)

To begin with, conventional prosecutors are likely to be philosophically committed to the concept of delivering justice via trial or plea followed by punishment—the constitutionally prescribed response to criminal offenses, once proven. Whether or not punishment involves incarceration, it is assumed to achieve objectives that restorative justice processes are not intended to achieve. This is true even in cases of offenders who are not dangerous to the public, so that there is no need for incapacitation in order to ensure public safety. But it is particularly true in cases of violent crime, which has traditionally called for a carceral response. While restorative justice claims other advantages, traditional prosecutors may not see them as adequate to compensate for its limitations. First, criminal punishment serves an expressive function; the court's public imposition of punishment, which at minimum, entails a moral stigma, publicly reaffirms the societal norms underlying the criminal law that the offender is sentenced for violating. Restorative justice processes do not achieve this because they do not occur in public proceedings. While the process may result in the offender's public acknowledgement of wrongdoing, that is not invariably the resolution. Second, punishment is assumed to better serve the public interest in deterring future criminal wrongdoing precisely because it entails public shaming and the infliction of pain, typically through the loss of liberty. While restorative justice processes may culminate in undertakings and insights that better promote the particular offender's rehabilitation and therefore better protect the public from that one offender, no one plausibly claims that the fear of restorative justice effectively deters other wrongdoers. Third, punishment serves retributivist interests, which restorative justice does not. In part, the assumption is that retribution serves the victim. But that cannot be the principal reason to favor punishment over restorative justice, since, in cases where victims are offered the alternative and opt for a restorative justice process, the particular victims either do not want retribution at all, would prefer the outcome offered by restorative justice, or do not want to undergo the process of adjudication necessary to obtain retribution by way of punishment. Rather, the public at large is thought to have an interest in retribution and prosecutors are charged with representing the larger community. Regardless of what the victim wants or prefers, this interest may be thought to justify punishment but not restorative justice: the public sense of justice is served and its moral outrage at the violation of societal norms is mollified when offenders get their "just deserts," but not when offenders undeservedly escape punishment. That may be true even if the only punishment is the moral stigma, or shaming, that accompanies a criminal conviction. One of the principal advantages of restorative justice is that, when victims voluntarily choose it, it better serves victims' interests by respecting their agency, allowing them to avoid the burdens of the adjudicative process, and, most importantly, offering them a resolution that they believe will better serve their interests than criminal punishment of the offender. But prosecutors may not acknowledge these advantages and, even if they do, prosecutors may not see serving victims as an adequate reason to forgo the benefits of punishment. Prosecutors regard their overarching responsibility as being to serve the public, not any private individual, not even the victim. They may be concerned that, at least when the public's interests are not perfectly aligned with those of the victim, diverting a case to a restorative justice process gives priority to the individual victim's interests over those of the public....

It seems natural for prosecutors to assume that the traditional criminal justice process achieves more important objectives, or better achieves its objectives, than restorative justice processes. Mainstream prosecutors tend to be traditionalists rather than innovators. The essential work of prosecutors—investigating and prosecuting crimes—has not changed over time. Those who become prosecutors are generally attracted to that adjudicatory work, not to using prosecutorial power to address broader social problems or to address individual offenders' personal challenges. Prosecutors are lawyers, not social workers; they were taught to navigate the adversarial system, and they regard themselves as trial lawyers, notwithstanding the relative infrequency of criminal trials. While some mainstream prosecutors have proceeded in a more experimental spirit, reimagining themselves as "community prosecutors" or conceptualizing some criminal problems as mental health or other social problems, the typical prosecutor is a lawyer trained in the litigation process who is rewarded—reputationally and for purposes of internal promotion—for winning at trial and assembling a track record of convictions. The typical prosecutor is not trained to view social problems as criminal problems and to look for innovative legal or criminal justice solutions....

Further, prosecutors are trained to embrace the common-law style of reasoning that justifies the traditional criminal process. The assumptions about the retributive and utilitarian effects of punishment, for example, are deeply rooted in our jurisprudence and appear to be matters of common sense and ordinary experience. Restorative justice, in contrast, does not reflect prosecutors' everyday experiences and indeed may be an utterly foreign concept. The data that does exist to suggest that restorative justice is effective is too limited to be persuasive to most mainstream prosecutors. Even if the data were more robust, it is hard to let go of the old ways. In other aspects of their work, many prosecutors favor received wisdom over empirical evidence—for example, in assuming the reliability of eyewitness identifications and confessions despite decades of social science evidence establishing their inherent unreliability. Assumptions about the utility of punishment are, if anything, even more deeply ingrained....

Finally, wholly apart from their own conviction about the utility of punishment, prosecutors are likely to be deferential to the evident legislative belief that criminal offenses should ordinarily be addressed through prosecution and punishment. In general, prosecutors understand that they are executive branch officials whose responsibility is to carry out the law. In some jurisdictions, such as California, Colorado, and Vermont, the legislature has endorsed restorative justice processes, at least in certain criminal cases. Elsewhere, however, prosecutors may regard it as inconsistent with the legislative will or with legislative assumptions for prosecutors to unilaterally pursue restorative justice in place of conventional criminal justice strategies....

B. Issues of Power, Politics, and Fairness

There is another set of reasons why prosecutors are likely to be unsympathetic to restorative justice processes—namely, that these processes take away power and discretion from prosecutors and give it to various other actors, including social workers, community members, victims, and offenders. Prosecutors are likely to find this problematic in three respects: first, prosecutors are reluctant to cede power and influence in the criminal process; second, they are reluctant to enhance others' power and influence; and, finally, practical and political considerations may dampen interest in restorative justice....

Prosecutors' Interest in Retaining Power and Control, and the Perceived Neutral Exercise of Discretion

Prosecutors are widely considered to be the most powerful actors in the criminal justice system, given their authority to decide whom to investigate, when to bring charges, which charges to bring, which plea bargains to offer, and which sentences to recommend. When prosecutors bring charges that come with mandatory minimum sentences, the defense attorney's input is virtually irrelevant, and the judge's ultimate power to determine the offender's sentence is greatly, if not entirely, constrained. Power is difficult to give up and embracing restorative justice practices requires ceding significant ground. Because restorative justice processes are by their nature individualized, community-oriented, and victim-centered, and require participation by outside facilitators, prosecutors will perceive that they have limited involvement in the process and diminished influence over the outcome....

To some extent, the ability of restorative justice to serve traditional criminal law objectives depends on how the process is implemented. The individual process itself is private, but a detailed, publicly available description of how the program operates and its empirical outcomes can and should be public. Further, restorative justice need not always be in lieu of jail or prison. As London describes, the process can be employed in conjunction with the criminal process as a way to achieve an agreed, lesser sentence. But even where the process is used as a diversion from the criminal process, the offender can agree to undertake a public act of contrition. Where the outcome of any individual restorative justice process is public and entails the acceptance of burdens by the offender, the process can serve traditional functions of criminal punishment—deterrence, affirmation of societal norms, and retribution. Unless one concludes that only the deprivation of liberty can serve these functions—an assumption that is inconsistent with our nation's historical use of shaming punishments—the public resolution of the restorative justice process can promote traditional objectives in much the same way as carceral punishment does. To be sure, the victim will be promoting her own objectives, preferences, and interests, not the public interest in a resolution that best achieves the objectives of the criminal process. But there is no reason to assume that the victim's objectives will be vastly misaligned with those of the public. On the contrary, prosecutors often assume, when they are making discretionary decisions, that the public interests and the victim's interests are largely aligned. The same can be presumed true when victims make discretionary decisions in a restorative justice process. That leaves the interest in promoting public safety through rehabilitation of the offender. Needless to say, this is where restorative justice, which aims to restore the offender no less than the victim, makes the strongest claim.136 The empirical evidence that exists—albeit limited and lacking in longitudinal data—tends to show that the recidivism rate is lower for offenders who satisfactorily complete a restorative justice program, as compared with those who are sentenced in the criminal process. These results track programs where restorative justice processes typically result in an agreement to engage in education, receive counseling, maintain full-time employment, and/or engage in other activities that are assumed to be prosocial and rehabilitative. Restorative justice programs encourage offenders to agree on rehabilitative measures and rigorously supervise offenders to ensure they comply with their agreements. In contrast, no one would expect a prison sentence or other outcome of the criminal justice process to be particularly rehabilitative, and, on the contrary, one might expect incarceration generally to be criminogenic....

The argument that will best appeal to conventional prosecutors is that restorative justice is not unlike other diversion programs in that it will sometimes be the best way to serve the mixture of public interests that prosecutors are expected to pursue through the criminal process. Where the victim seeks restorative justice and the offender is a willing participant, this alternative may serve those individual interests better than criminal prosecution would. Provided—and this is a key caveat—that it will not result in a risk to public safety, on balance, restorative justice may be preferable. Using restorative justice in these cases is not dissimilar to the use of problem solving courts, in that these noncarceral alternatives seek to serve the public interest without radically departing from the norm. Viewed this way, restorative justice is not an abdication of control to social workers, victims, and prison abolitionists. Instead, the use of restorative justice respects prosecutorial power and discretion because offenders are diverted to restorative justice processes only when the prosecutor makes a threshold determination that the process is preferable after factoring in fairness of outcomes and public safety. This means that prosecutors must develop an understanding of available restorative justice processes and an appreciation for whom they work best. Prosecutors cannot simply shuttle cases off to social service agencies. Further, prosecutors have a responsibility to monitor the outcomes of restorative justice processes, both to confirm that the results are generally consistent with the public interest and so that prosecutors can hold themselves accountable to the public for when and how these processes are employed. Monitoring cannot simply be informal; rather, the collection and analysis of data are essential. It is reasonable to conclude that by deferring to victims' preferences for restorative justice processes, a prosecutor will serve other criminal justice interests as well. Crime victims often feel mistrustful of, or neglected by, prosecutors' offices. This attitude undermines prosecutors' effectiveness, both because it makes victims more reluctant to report crimes and because it makes them less willing to cooperate with a prosecution. Employing restorative justice as a diversionary alternative gives victims a greater say in how criminal cases are addressed—both a choice between a restorative justice process or the criminal adjudication process and, if the former is elected, a greater role in the process and outcome. One might expect prosecutors who use restorative justice to win greater trust from victims. In communities that perceive the prosecutors and police to be overly punitive, the use of restorative justice may promote public trust as well....

CONCLUSION

Proponents of restorative justice have sold progressive prosecutors on it. Newly elected progressive prosecutors will soon attempt to carry out their campaign pledges to use, or expand the use of, restorative justice. This will mean that in some felony cases, including some involving serious, violent crimes where the prosecutor would ordinarily pursue a criminal conviction and carceral punishment, the prosecutor will offer restorative justice as an alternative. If both the offender and the victim agree, the prosecutor will divert the case to a social service agency to administer a restorative justice process; and if a successful resolution is reported, the prosecutor will decline to bring, or will dismiss, criminal charges. Eventually, progressive prosecutors will gather both anecdotal evidence and data about the use of restorative justice in different types of felony cases. Assuming that proponents' claims are substantiated—i.e., if the evidence shows a lower recidivism rate and greater victim satisfaction—proponents will urge mainstream prosecutors to follow suit by implementing or expanding restorative justice programs. As this Article has shown, when it comes to mainstream prosecutors, proponents of restorative justice will have a host of concerns to allay and objections to overcome. How advocates argue their cause will matter. It is unlikely that conventional prosecutors can be persuaded to radically reimagine the criminal justice process. But they need not be. One need not conceptualize restorative justice as a rejection of the traditional adjudicatory process; instead, restorative justice is an alternative that runs parallel to traditional adjudication. Restorative justice processes can also be rhetorically deradicalized by analogizing their use to the establishment of drug courts and other diversion programs that have a proven track record of success. This analogy is not far-fetched: a restorative justice process is comparable to a drug treatment program in that the offender must undergo rigorous rehabilitative processes, and intensive supervision, and meet any number of benchmarks as a condition of a nonprosecution agreement. From prosecutors' perspective, the key question is whether the public interest is best served in a given case when, rather than being convicted and punished, an offender successfully completes a restorative justice process. The answer will turn in large part on assumptions or available data on such questions as whether restorative justice lowers recidivism rates or better serves crime victims, or whether implementing restorative justice on a selective basis meaningfully reduces the deterrent effect or the expressive value of the criminal law. No matter how much data becomes available, prosecutors' receptivity to restorative justice will ultimately turn on their interpretation of what it means to carry out their mandate to "do justice," an interpretation that, to some degree, is based on value judgments, received wisdom, and belief in the efficacy of the status quo. Even if data were to show convincingly that a restorative justice process elected by the victim and offender is more likely than a criminal prosecution to be healing for the victim and rehabilitative for the offender, there will be countervailing considerations, including public safety and the need to achieve systemic fairness by treating like cases alike. The question is which way the balance tips in any given case and whether a broad application, including in cases of serious, violent crime, can exist outside the jurisdictions of a small number of progressive prosecutors who are willing to give restorative justice a try. Ideally, as their experience with restorative justice grows, both mainstream prosecutors and the public will be in a better position to answer that question.

Notes/Questions

1. Reimund concludes that we need both the conventional law system and restorative legal system together. Are you persuaded that these can work together? What concerns do you still have?

Which would bring the most challenges of integrating restorative justice into the criminal legal system? Delgado discusses in his article above several challenges that he believes restorative justice brings. Delgado believes there are issues with restorative justice in regard to

- Consistency
- Inequality of bargaining power
- Waiver of constitutional rights
- Punishment
- State control
- Limited applicability
- Victim offender mediation

Did the other articles in this chapter address those issues? Which of these challenges still remain for you?

2. Professor Luna urged us to compare restorative justice to the criminal legal system that exists, a system where plea bargaining is the dominant form of case resolution and one where there is little consistency, in terms of outcomes, from case to case and county to county. Are you concerned that restorative justice fails to protect a defendant's rights in the way that traditional adjudication does? What specific rights are you concerned about? If you were designing a restorative justice program, how would you address those concerns in the design of the program to protect defendants? You may want to think about this as you address the question below.

3. Assume a restorative justice program is being initiated in your county. You may support this program, or you might find it to be difficult to provide support for this program, and this depends on what your position is in the county.

From the perspective of a prosecutor, judge, defense lawyer, and citizen, why might you support introducing a restorative justice program in your county? What might make it difficult for you to support introducing a restorative justice program?

In answering these questions, you may want to consider the article at the beginning of this chapter that reported high victim satisfaction, and lowered recidivism rates for those who participate in restorative justice processes.

4. Laura Merkey discusses how a new strategy in our traditional system needs to quickly be put in place in *Building Trust and Breaking Down the Wall: The Use of Restorative Justice to Repair Police-Community Relationships*, 80 Mo. L. Rev. 1133 (2015). Merkey recalls the events that occurred in Baltimore, Ferguson, New York, and Cleveland, and acknowledges that the violence and mistrust must be addressed. She states that the changes need to be both enduring and have to restructure how members of society interact with one another. This change needs to be proactive and responsive.

Merkey believes that if change occurs, society will be more likely to stabilize, and this will create the potential to move forward together to tackle more positive issues. How would you see restorative justice working in this arena? How would you go about rebuilding the relationships in the areas the events occurred in? Will restorative justice change our system for the better, or will it be detrimental to certain groups? List the concerns that both community members and police officers might have.

Additional Resources

Stephanos Bibas & Richard A. Bierschbach, *Integrating Remorse and Apology into Criminal Procedure*, 114 Yale L.J. 85 (2004).

Fania E. Davis, The Little Book of Race and Restorative Justice (2019).

Danielle Fields, *Returning Justice to the Community: Restorative Justice to Reform Oklahoma Juvenile Justice System, 85 OBJ* 333 (Feb. 15, 2014).

Janine P. Geske & India McCanse, *Neighborhoods Healed Through Restorative Justice*, Dispute Resolution Magazine 16 (2008).

Bruce A. Green & Lara Bazelon, *Restorative Justice from Prosecutors' Perspective*, 88 Fordham L. Rev. 2287, 2299–2300, 2303–2305, 2314–2318 (2020).

M. Eve Hanan, *Decriminalizing Violence: A Critique of Restorative Justice and a Proposal for Diversionary Mediation*, 46 N.M. L. Rev. 123 (2016).

Rachel King, *Restorative Justice: How Law Schools Can Help Heal Their Communities*, 34 Fordham Urb. L.J. 1285 (2007).

Gregory Dennis Paul & William J. Schenck-Hamlin, *Openness to participating in a victim-offender conference: A theory of planned behavior perspective*, 29 Int'l J. Conflict Mgmt. 659–682 (2018), available at: https://doi.org/10.1108/IJCMA-03-2018-0042.

Zari Tarazona, *Can 'restorative justice' transform school discipline in Philadelphia?*, GENEROCITY.ORG (May. 25, 2018), available at: https://generocity.org/philly/2018/05/25/restorative-justice-school-discipline-philadelphia-student-union-youth/, https://generocity.org/philly/tag/criminal-justice-month-2018/.

Eric Westervelt, *To Save Opioid Addicts, This Experimental Court Is Ditching the Delays*, NPR CRIMINAL JUSTICE COLLABORATIVE (Oct. 5, 2018), available at: https://www.npr.org/sections/health-shots/2017/10/05/553830794/to-save-opioid-addicts-this-experimental-court-is-ditching-the-delays.

Elise White, Sarah Picard-Fritsche, Yolaine Menyard, Kate Barrow, Elise Jensen & Julian Adler, *Up & Out: Toward an Evidence-Based Response to Misdemeanors*, Ctr. for Ct. Innovation (May 2018).

Chapter 12

Juvenile Legal System: An Introduction

The next three chapters of this book are about how juveniles are treated in the criminal legal system in the United States. As you will read, the juvenile legal system uses all of the different processes discussed in this book from plea bargaining to restorative justice. Juveniles are different, yet the criminal legal system has often failed to recognize that difference in meaningful ways. Juveniles have been on the front lines of changing attitudes towards crime, both when the concept of "super-predators" was born, and more recently, as there has been a steady and significant drop in juvenile incarceration rates. The scholarship and writing on juvenile justice is deep and varied. We will, in these next few chapters, only touch the surface of the field. Our goal with these chapters is to use the juvenile legal system as an example to explore in more detail the promise and pitfalls of the various processes that you have read about so far in this book.

The original problem-solving court was the first juvenile court in Illinois in 1899. Before that, juveniles were treated like adults, tried in adult courts and subjected to adult punishments. Juvenile courts were intended to focus on treating and rehabilitating children to prevent future criminal behavior. At the time, and for many decades, this was an innovative approach and one that influenced the development of juvenile courts and juvenile legal systems around the world. However, as you will read, modern juvenile courts have fallen short of these ideals and, similar to adult courts, often focus more on punishment than treatment.

There are notable similarities to the adult legal system that we have been studying thus far. As with adult offenders, the numbers of juveniles pulled into the system is significant, although the raw numbers have decreased overall since 2000. As with adults, most juvenile cases are not serious or violent. Juveniles can be prosecuted for the same crimes as adults and are also prosecuted for status offenses. Status offenses are those that are only crimes because of the age, or status, of the offender. Examples of status offenses include under-age drinking and breaking a municipal curfew. As with adults, the incarceration rates for juveniles are substantially higher for African Americans and Latinos. Poor children are far more likely to be pulled into the criminal legal system than those from wealthy backgrounds. And children who are suspended from school (who are disproportionately poor and minorities) are also more likely to end up in the adult criminal legal system in what is often called the "school to prison pipeline."

Just as the juvenile system has many of the same concerns as the adult criminal legal system, it also mirrors the adult system in the use of alternative processes. There is widespread use of plea bargaining in the juvenile system and by juveniles who are tried as adults. There are also problem-solving courts that are specific to juveniles such as drug courts and mental health courts. Restorative justice, although far from institutionalized in the juvenile system in any state, is used more widely with juveniles than adults in the United States. In addition, there are questions about how juveniles who are tried as adults should be treated once they are transferred to the adult system. Should they get the same punishments as adults, such as life in prison without parole or the death penalty?

In this chapter, you will read about the history of juvenile courts in the United States and how the practices have evolved. You will also read about the concerns about how the juvenile legal system works, including the specific concerns about juveniles pleading guilty. We will end the chapter discussing the overall decrease in juvenile incarceration rates since 2000. In the next chapter, you will read the U.S. Supreme Court caselaw that limits the use of certain punishments with juveniles due to concerns about their level of cognitive development. The final juvenile chapter will focus on alternative processes for juveniles, including problem-solving courts and restorative justice.

I. History of Juvenile Courts

This article gives the standard account (and it calls it that) of the evolution of the juvenile legal system. Note how the theories behind the system have changed over time, much like the theories of punishment that we read about at the beginning of this book. You will then read an article describing the four waves of reform in the juvenile legal system, ending with the current wave in which we have seen dramatic declines in juvenile crime rates and incarceration rates.

Daniel M. Filler & Austin E. Smith, *The New Rehabilitation*

91 Iowa L. Rev. 951, 955–58, 959–64 (2006)

...

I. The Standard History of Juvenile Justice

A. The Rise of Juvenile Courts and the Parenting Model

According to most historians, the move to create special juvenile courts was the product of a broader movement within Western culture. In the late nineteenth century, criminologists touted a new science of crime. Challenging the notion of crime as grounded in "free-will choice," they argued that criminal conduct was the result of "antecedent forces—biological, psychological, social, or environmental." In 1892, for example, Elbridge T. Gerry, president of the New York Society for the Prevention of Cruelty to Children, cited poverty, inadequate housing, and neglect as causes of juvenile delinquency. If the consensus view was that crime could no longer be explained by free will, retributive punishment—imposition of a sentence based on an offender's moral responsibility—made no sense. At the same time, scholars and Progressive activists, motivated by a growing belief in science and rationality, became convinced that experts were capable of addressing the damage caused by these "antecedent forces," thus solving the crime problem. As Barry Feld explains it, "[a] growing class of social science professionals fostered the 'rehabilitative ideal,' which requires a belief in human malleability and a consensus about the appropriate directions of personal change." Since each individual would require a particular regime of treatment, a cornerstone of the new Progressive program was the individualization of punishment. If courts were to effectively rehabilitate offenders, they would need to tailor their punishment to the precise needs of that individual.

The juvenile court, in this view, was the culmination of efforts of the positivist criminologists and Progressive activists. It would be a special tribunal designed to address the individual needs of delinquent children, provide care and rehabilitation, and ensure that they could go on to live lawful, productive lives. The Illinois legislature moved first to turn this new view of crime into substantive policy. The Juvenile Justice Act of 1899 served as a model for juvenile justice policy across the nation. This legislation, designed to "regulate the treatment and control of dependent, neglected and delinquent children," was the first attempt to create a specialized set of courts to deal with offenders under the age of sixteen. The Act "defined a rehabilitative rather than punitive function of a court of special jurisdiction for neglected, dependent and delinquent children under the age of sixteen." Within twelve years, twenty-two states followed Illinois' lead and created juvenile courts. By 1925, every state except Maine and Wyoming had created a criminal justice system specifically for juvenile offenders.

These courts operated on a paternalistic or *parens patriae* model of justice. Most state statutes provided that juvenile courts would function as civil, rather than criminal, tribunals. The judge was to serve as a loving parent—in most cases, a father—providing the helpful discipline that would lead the child to a new, crime-free life. Legislators gave juvenile courts a broad range of powers. Judges could intervene in a child's life with minimal instigation. If a child was charged with a crime, or a variety of precriminal acts such as vagrancy, truancy, and living an immoral life, the court's jurisdiction attached. Courts offered children few standard procedural protections. The judge alone would hear the facts, witnesses were not required to appear in person, defendants were not entitled to juries, and in many jurisdictions, a judge could adjudicate a child delinquent—that is, find him guilty—on a mere preponderance of the evidence. If a judge found that a child had committed a legal transgression, he could impose a wide range of sanctions—some light, and others harsh—irrespective of the severity of the underlying offense. According to the accepted history of these courts, judges focused on the individual needs and capacities of the offender, not on the characteristics of the crime. They ordered offenders into any program that the judge thought would "'cure' the youth" and left the disposition process open for as long as necessary to ensure that the child had indeed been rehabilitated.

Proponents of this approach took the parenting model very seriously. Judge Julian Mack, a leading advocate for the emerging juvenile justice system, described the process in painstaking detail in a 1909 Harvard Law Review article. Among other things, he argued that the layout of the room was essential to effective adjudication. He believed that the judge was to be "[s]eated at a desk, with the child at his side, where he can on occasion put his arm around his shoulder and draw the lad to him." Judge Mack wanted to take the juvenile into his charge "not so much to punish as to reform, not to degrade but to uplift, not to crush but to develop, not to make him a criminal but a worthy citizen." ...

A. The Fall of Rehabilitation

By the 1960s, however, the Warren Court was increasingly interested in giving clearer shape to criminal procedural protections. In the 1967 landmark case, *In re Gault*, [387 U.S. 1 (1967),] the Court held that juveniles prosecuted in juvenile courts were entitled to many procedural protections previously denied children. That case signaled the end of the unbridled discretion of juvenile court judges to conduct their hearings and trials in the manner described by Judge Mack at the beginning of the century. In *Gault*, a fifteen-year-old Arizona defendant charged with making a lewd phone call was taken into custody overnight without any notice to his parents. The probation officer filed a pro forma petition that never actually identified what offense Gault had committed. The judge never heard testimony from the victim; instead, he relied on the secondhand report of a juvenile probation officer. The offender received neither proper notice of the hearing, nor the assistance of counsel. His hearing was never transcribed, and Arizona law made no provision for an appeal. Gault was adjudicated delinquent and committed to an industrial school—the equivalent of a prison for children—until age 21 "unless sooner discharged by due process of law." For the same offense, an adult could have received a fifty-dollar fine or two months' imprisonment.

The Supreme Court rebelled. The majority held that juveniles facing delinquency proceedings in juvenile court were entitled to many of the same protections as adults. The protections include notice of the specific charges to be addressed at the delinquency hearing, the assistance of counsel, protection against self-incrimination, and the ability to appeal the order of the trial judge....

The standard description of this backlash identifies several ways in which states abandoned rehabilitation. First, legislatures narrowed the jurisdiction of the juvenile justice system by diverting some crimes to the adult system, making it easier to transfer individual defendants to adult court, and shifting the age at which juvenile court jurisdiction attaches. Most juvenile courts have long allowed prosecutors to transfer—or "waive"—particular child defendants to adult court upon consent of the judge. In recent years, many legislatures have relaxed the waiver process to make it easier to move children to adult court.

In many jurisdictions, one change has shifted the burden of proof in these waiver hearings from the state to the defendant. Other states have adopted mandatory waiver provisions, which require judges to grant transfer requests if certain preconditions are

> Thirty-four states have "once an adult, always an adult" laws—which means that once a juvenile has been convicted in adult court, all future cases will go to adult courts.
>
> CARA H. DRINAN, THE WAR ON KIDS: HOW AMERICAN JUVENILE JUSTICE LOST ITS WAY 21 (2018).

met. In South Carolina, for example, a judge must transfer a case of any child over the age of thirteen, if he has been twice adjudicated delinquent and now faces charges on an offense carrying a maximum adult sentence of more than ten years' imprisonment. Many states automatically transfer capital cases when the offender is over a certain age, such as fourteen. In other jurisdictions, the entire transfer decision has been left to the prosecutor's discretion. Finally, some states have lowered the age at which children automatically fall within the jurisdiction of adult criminal courts. For example, in New Mexico, offenders age fifteen and older charged with first-degree murder are excluded from entering the juvenile courts. The law simply prevents the offender from being defined as a "child."

Caitlin Cavanagh, Jennifer Paruk & Thomas Grisso, *The Development Reform in Juvenile Justice: Its Progress and Vulnerability*

28 PSYCHOL. PUBL. POL'Y & L. 151, 152–153 (2022)

Juvenile justice reforms follow a cyclical pattern, influenced by juvenile crime rates in the context of existing juvenile justice policies. By 2000; juvenile justice in the United States had already experienced three waves of reform in its 100-year history. The first reform beginning in the late 19th century was characterized by a civil child welfare approach: youth were to be rehabilitated instead of treated as adult criminals. In practice, however, the newly established juvenile courts had wide discretion in their responses to delinquency and often did not act in the best interests of the youth. In addition, early juvenile justice reforms were influenced by White attitudes on race and social class, For example, reformers often denied Black youth rehabilitative court services, such that Black youth experienced more severe, violent, or adult punishments, as well as disproportionate rates of institutionalization. As juvenile justice and other progressive reforms made their way through the country, juvenile treatment was naturally affected by regional laws and policies, such as Jim Crow laws and forced assimilation.

Criticism of discretionary and discriminatory juvenile court practices led to a second "due process" wave of reforms in the 1960s. These reforms provided youth procedural safeguards and recognized the rights of youth in juvenile court as similar to defendants' rights in criminal court (e.g., In Re Gault, 387 U.S. 1.,1967; see Feld, 2005). Then, in the 1980s, in the context of skepticism of the treatment and rehabilitation model, a significant increase in juvenile violent crime, and sensational media reports that construed "the crime problem as a black problem", nationwide reform in laws and practices created a third, "get-tough" era. This third wave of reforms emphasized zero tolerance and harsh penal ties for juvenile offenders, and often targeted youth of color.

The current fourth wave of juvenile justice reform emerged in the late 1990s as a response to the damage done by the "get-tough" reforms. Some philanthropic foundations began specific juvenile justice interventions, such as reduction in the overuse of incarceration for youths with minor or first-time offenses (e.g., the Annie E. Casey Foundation's Juvenile Detention Alternatives Initiative) and identifying youths with mental health needs entering the system (e.g., William T. Grant Foundation's funding of mental health screening). In 1996; the John D. and Catherine T. MacArthur Foundation embarked on eight years of funding to support a national network of developmental, child clinical, and criminology researchers, working together with juvenile legal scholars and practitioners. The collaborative studies of the MacArthur Foundation Research Network on Adolescent Development and Juvenile Justice focused on adolescents' decisional capacities, legal competencies, and delinquency trajectories, testing hypotheses about adolescents' legally relevant immaturity compared to adults.

At the same time, neuroscience researchers were performing early studies of adolescent brain development using new MRI technology. By the time the MacArthur Research Network's studies were completed, evidence of youths' behavioral and brain immaturity supported a call for broad reform in juvenile justice based on youths' relative immaturity. In both behavior and in brain development, adolescents were found to be immature in ways that accounted for their tendencies toward risk-taking and impulsiveness, and their illegal behaviors often were not signs of future criminal lifestyles in adulthood. Rather than face punishment as though they were adults, a better social response would be to avoid incarceration when possible, provide second chances and restorative justice methods, and engage youth in rehabilitative efforts. The essence of the message was later articulated succinctly by Zimring and Tannenhaus: (a) kids are different than adults; (b) kids change; (c) growing up is effective crime control; and (d) juvenile courts are well-suited to the special needs of young offenders.

During the time that this research was ongoing, issues of disproportionate minority contact in juvenile justice received increased attention when the federal government began (in 1987) requiring that states' juvenile justice programs collect data to determine the proportion of minority youth in contact with juvenile justice. By 2000; substantial research had identified racial disparity in juvenile justice, as well as specific points in the process when decisions differentially affected youth of color negatively. Yet remarkably little research or effort had been made to reduce it, thus making racial disparity in juvenile justice "the elephant in the room."

Beginning early in the 21st century, scholars and juvenile justice advocates began framing the developmental research results to suggest reforms in juvenile justice laws, policies, and practices. The MacArthur Foundation's project, Models for Change: Systems Reform in Juvenile Justice, played a major role in translating the new research into nationwide policy and practice reform. Across 10 years (2004 to 2014), this initiative provided $121 million to a coordinated network of social science and legal advocacy centers nationwide to assist 35 states willing to introduce developmentally and empirically-based reforms in their juvenile justice systems. Areas for change included, for example, reduced detention and incarceration through diversion; improved community based options; improved risk assessment and mental health screening; better indigent defense; racial and ethnic fairness and reduction in disproportionate minority contact and an emphasis on empirically supported practices in all aforementioned.

One of the first signs of the impact of this development reform research on national policy was in Roper v. Simmons, 543 U.S. 551 (2005), the first of several United States Supreme Court cases (Graham v. Florida, 2010; Miller v. Alabama, 132 S. Ct. 2455 (2012); Montgomery v. Louisiana, 136 S. Ct.718, 2016) to acknowledge developmental research in their decisions, which restricted the harshest sentences for juveniles tried in criminal court for the most serious offenses. In addition, national professional organizations for juvenile courts, detention and corrections, as well as federal agencies, adopted many of the developmentally driven practices as recommended policy. The impact was further magnified by the Models for Change collaboration with federal agencies such as the Substance Abuse and Mental Health Services Administration and the Office of Juvenile Justice and Delinquency Prevention. In 2013; the National Research Council published an extensive set of recommended policies for reforming juvenile justice stating, "The central premise of this report is that the goals, design, and operation of the juvenile justice system should be informed by the growing body of knowledge about adolescent development."

Moreover, there was much evidence that the developmental reform had taken hold. Between 2000 and 2016: (a) transfer of juveniles to criminal court for trial as adults had reduced by one third; (b) the number of youths in juvenile detention centers and juvenile corrections facilities had been reduced by about one half; (c) whereas use of risk assessment and mental health screening tools in juvenile justice decision making had been rare in the 1990s, by 2015 over one half of states had laws or uniform policies requiring their use; and (d) solitary confinement for juveniles is banned in federal prisons, and several states have reduced or banned their use of solitary confinement. Competency to stand trial in juvenile court had rarely been addressed until the late 1990s, but during the developmental reform it was recognized in all states and defined by new legislation in nearly two thirds of states. In 2020 alone, several state legislatures made it easier for youth to seal or expunge their juvenile records, and three states (NJ, MD, LA) reduced fines and fees associated with juvenile justice processing. As the result of Raise the Age reform efforts, since 1997; ten states out of thirteen that had juvenile court jurisdictions ending at the 16th or 17th birthday have raised their jurisdictions to the 18th birthday [Note from authors: as you will read later, one of those states, Louisiana, has overturned its law and returned to considering 17 year olds as adults in criminal cases].

Notes/Questions

1. If juvenile courts are different, should the same processes that are available in adult courts be available to juveniles? Should juveniles have the right to a jury trial? Should they be allowed to plead guilty? You will want to think about these questions as you continue reading this chapter.

2. Juvenile courts were first taken out of the criminal legal system and, as you have read, in most states treated as civil courts. The U.S. Supreme Court in *Gault* recognized that these were not simply civil proceedings and held that juveniles were entitled to many of the same protections as adults in criminal courts, including the right to counsel and notice of charges. After *Gault*, there were other protections, and, at the same time, legislatures passed laws making it possible, and in some states fairly simple, to transfer juveniles to adult court. You may want to consider this evolution, and how it differs from what you have read about adult courts, as you continue reading.

3. A related question to think about, as you continue reading, is when should juveniles be treated as adults? Based on age? On the crime? On the jurisdiction? Never?

II. Juvenile Courts

At first glance, a juvenile court looks similar to an adult court. There are judges, lawyers, court reporters, and bailiffs. Most juvenile courts are in courtrooms that physically also look very similar to adult courts (although, they may not have a jury box). One immediate difference is that juvenile courts are not open to the public, because there is no constitutional right to a public juvenile adjudication, unlike the right to a public trial. In most jurisdictions, District Attorneys prosecute the cases, and if there is a public defender's office, public defenders handle the representation for juveniles who cannot afford to hire a lawyer. What often looks different is that the attorneys, both prosecutors and defense lawyers, may be younger and less experienced. Juvenile court has historically been considered a training ground for new defense lawyers and prosecutors. However, the consequences for the juvenile can be serious and life altering.

> "[Juvenile Court is] where they learn to be an attorney," said Tim Curry with the National Juvenile Defender Center (NJDC), which developed training standards for juvenile defenders. "But that is not OK in other professions. We don't tell brand-new doctors they should start as pediatricians. So why do we accept that with the justice system?"[1]

Another problem can be the use of private appointed counsel who may also not be as experienced. One study in Los Angeles County found that juveniles represented by privately appointed lawyers had a much higher rate of transfer to adult courts than

1. Rebecca Beitsch, *States Push Tougher Standards for Juvenile Public Defenders*, Stateline, May 5, 2016, available at: https://www.pewtrusts.org/en/research-and-analysis/blogs/stateline/2016/05/05/states-push-tougher-standards-for-juvenile-public-defenders.

Basic Juvenile Court Process

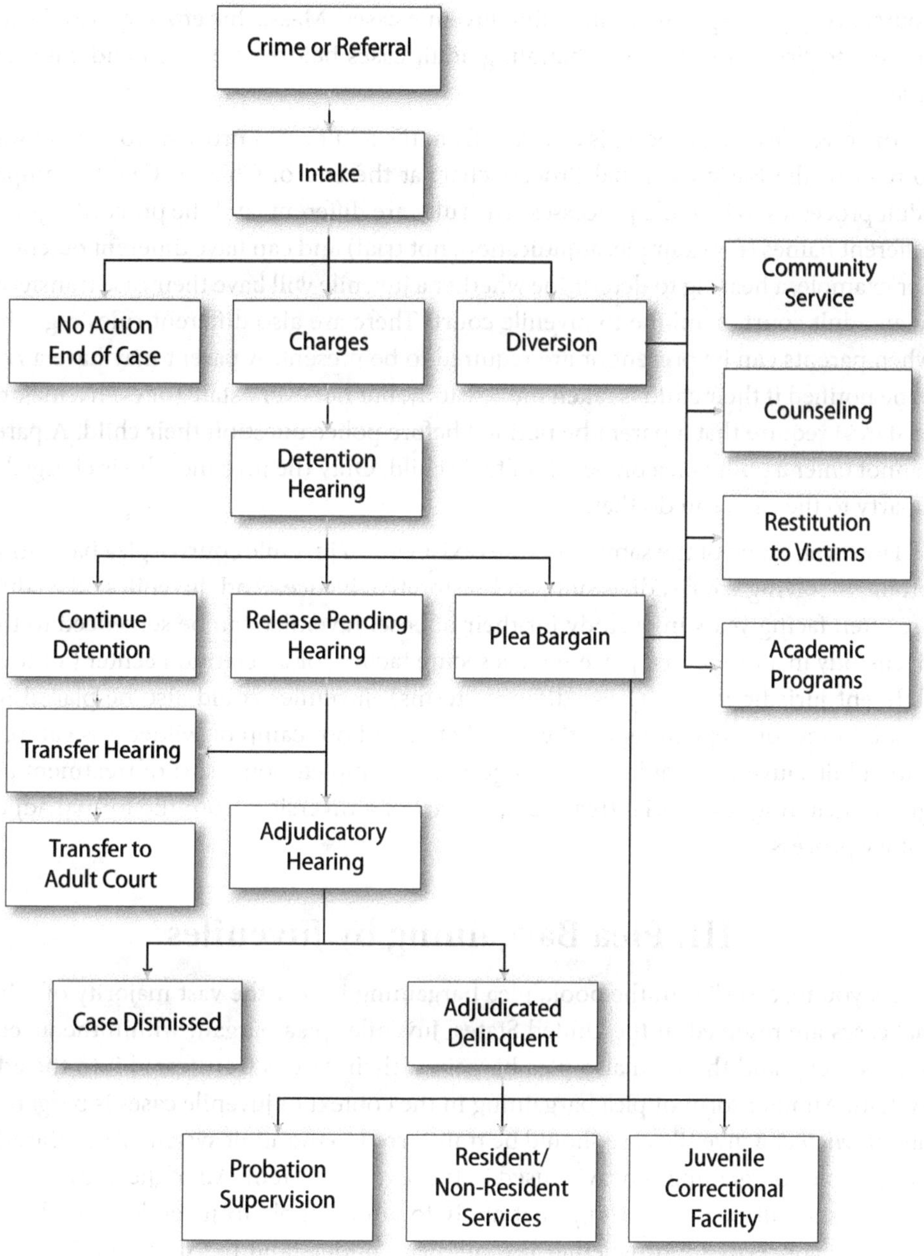

those represented by public defenders in the same county (25% were transferred as compared to 15% for public defenders).[2]

2. *Id.*

States are starting to require training and certain levels of experience for lawyers before they can handle juvenile cases. California requires continuing legal education hours, every year, specific to handling juvenile cases. Massachusetts requires defense lawyers to *first* get experience handling adult cases before they can handle juvenile cases.[3]

The juvenile court process is different from the adult court process. You might want to refer to the Basic Criminal Process chart at the end of Chapter One to compare adult processes to juvenile processes. The rules are different, and the proceedings have different names (for example, adjudication, not trial) and can have different outcomes. For example, a hearing to determine whether a juvenile will have their case transferred to an adult court is unique to juvenile court. There are also different rules regarding when parents can be present or are required to be present. A parent may have a right to be notified if their child is taken into custody, but not every state (or even a majority of states) require that a parent be notified before police question their child. A parent cannot enter a guilty plea on behalf of their child. Only the juvenile who is charged, as a party to the case, can do that.

However, many of the same processes exist within juvenile court—plea bargaining, problem-solving courts, diversion, and restorative justice. And, juveniles, like adults, are often facing years in custody for their offense. Juveniles can be sentenced to time in custody in a residential placement, a secure facility, or a detention center (although different jurisdictions may use different terms). Juveniles could also be placed in a group home, or, depending on the jurisdiction, a boot camp or wilderness camp. As with adults, juveniles could also be required to complete some sort of treatment program, including residential treatment, as part of a diversion from the formal adjudicatory process.

III. Plea Bargaining by Juveniles

As you read earlier in the book, plea bargaining is how the vast majority of criminal cases are resolved in the United States. Juveniles plea bargain within the juvenile legal system, and they can also plea bargain if their case is transferred into the adult system. Another form of plea bargaining in the context of juvenile cases is bargaining about *whether* a juvenile case should be transferred to the adult system. As in the adult system, plea bargaining is heavily used in the juvenile system. All of the questions and concerns about plea bargaining that apply to adults apply to juveniles. In addition, there are concerns about whether juveniles can understand the short and long term consequences of their pleas due to their age and stage of cognitive development.

---

3. *Id.*

Lacey Cole Singleton, *Say "Pleas"*: *Juveniles' Competence to Enter Plea Agreements*

9 J.L. & Fam. Stud. 439–40, 440–44, 447, 450–51, 455 (2007)

If a juvenile is too young to enter into a legally binding contract to purchase a set of tires, how can that same juvenile validly waive constitutional rights and enter into a legally binding plea agreement?

I. Introduction

K.M., a fifteen-year-old girl, "thought that she was merely having severe menstrual cramps" on the evening of September 4, 2002. Some time later, she "felt an 'urge to push'" and gave birth to a little boy in her bathroom. Instead of enlisting the help of her aunt, an experienced newborn intensive-care nurse who was present in the house at the time, K.M. "secreted the baby in the bathroom's window well." K.M.'s mother discovered K.M. and took her to the hospital after she lost consciousness multiple times as a result of blood loss. The baby died in the window well, and the "State brought a delinquency charge of murder, a first degree felony if committed by an adult, against K.M. for the death of the infant."

After the first day of her trial, K.M. entered into an agreement with the State in which she admitted to "an amended charge of child abuse homicide." Shortly thereafter, however, K.M. sought to withdraw her plea, but the juvenile court found that her admission was given knowingly and voluntarily at the time it was made and denied K.M.'s motion to withdraw.

Like K.M., adolescent defendants in the juvenile justice system frequently make unilateral decisions that can have profound consequences in the future, such as agreeing to enter into a binding plea agreement. By contrast, many laws stem from a paternalistic yet well-founded presumption that minors lack the necessary judgment and maturity to participate in certain activities, as evidenced by the fact that teenagers are not allowed to drive, vote, or consume alcoholic beverages until reaching a statutorily prescribed age. Why, then, is society so skeptical of adolescents' judgment in certain contexts, yet perfectly willing to believe that they are capable of making mature, rational decisions in the course of a juvenile criminal proceeding?

II. The Distinction Between Minors and Adults in the Law

The law treats adolescents substantially differently than adults in many ways, reflecting the societal belief that minors are neither mature nor responsible enough to engage in certain activities and understand the consequences of their actions. This presumption is particularly apparent in the rationale underlying minors' contractual rights, statutory rape offenses, abortion statutes, and the categorical exclusion of minors from the death penalty. The legal rights and protection of minors in each of these contexts will be discussed in turn.

The infancy doctrine in contract law allows a minor to disaffirm a contract "during minority or within a reasonable time upon achieving majority." The purpose of the doctrine is "to protect inexperienced and improvident minors from the consequences of dealing with others," largely based upon the "presumption that unequal bargaining power always exists" between adolescents and adults. Because a legally enforceable contract requires that "the 'parties to them have the psychological and intellectual capacity to understand and evaluate the consequences of their agreements,'" the law limiting minors' contractual rights and obligations recognizes that adolescent judgment and decision-making is not comparable to that of adults.

Similarly, statutory rape laws and statutes regulating minors' abortion rights exist to protect adolescents from making personal decisions that may dramatically affect the rest of their lives. Although the statutory age of consent varies in each state, minors are generally considered "too immature to rationally or legally consent" to sexual relations with another person. The asserted purpose of these laws is to safeguard the "health and welfare" of innocent children, and even "[t]he history of the offense of statutory rape indicates that from ancient times the law has afforded special protection to those deemed too young to understand the consequences of their actions."

For the same reasons, the Supreme Court has held that states may require parental consent or notification before a teenager is allowed to have an abortion.... Thus, the public policy rationale underlying all of these laws is substantially the same: society does not regard minors as mature enough to make personal decisions that may have serious consequences in the future, and as a result "adolescents are not considered autonomous agents in most contexts under the law."

Notably, the Supreme Court has also recognized a difference in criminal culpability between minors and adults. In *Thompson v. Oklahoma*, the Court declared that the "immature judgment of youth" prohibited the execution of adolescents who committed criminal offenses before reaching age sixteen. Most recently, in 2003 the Court held in *Roper v. Simmons* [543 U.S. 551 (2005)] that the Eighth Amendment prohibited the execution of a juvenile who committed a capital crime before turning eighteen, largely basing its decision on the fact that "adolescents are less culpable than typical adults because of diminished decision-making capacity." The Court's rationale in *Roper* is also supported by the vast amount of psychological research demonstrating that adolescents have underdeveloped judgment and decision-making skills, thereby reducing a juvenile's adjudicative competence.

III. Juvenile Adjudicative Competence

Adjudicative competence, otherwise known as competence to stand trial, relies heavily on cognitive maturity and generally falls into two categories: "competence to assist counsel" and "decisional competence." Each of these categories will be discussed in turn, with particular emphasis on the ways in which the unique psychological characteristics of adolescence can dramatically affect a juvenile's adjudicative competence.

A. Competence to Assist Counsel

A criminal defendant's competence to assist counsel is defined as the ability "to consult with [counsel] with a reasonable degree of rational understanding." Specifically, this involves the ability "to understand and appreciate the significance of the proceedings against oneself (e.g. the roles and motivations of participants, one's rights, and the significance of the matter at hand to one's own situation)."

Examining these requirements in light of an adolescent's developing cognitive skills, it becomes clear that a teenager's competence to assist counsel is significantly different than that of an adult. For example, juvenile defendants frequently have "an incomplete comprehension of the concept and meaning of a right," and even those "who understand the meanings of events, participants, and rights in the trial process sometimes fail to appreciate that these actually apply to their own circumstances." Other studies show that minors are not fully capable of understanding their constitutional rights, and although the "comprehension of Miranda warnings" is correlated with age, teenagers have particular "difficulty applying the right to remain silent." Furthermore, the ability to understand one's rights does not appear to increase with exposure to the criminal justice system, suggesting that this lack of comprehension stems from fundamental differences in the adolescent brain.

B. Decisional Competence

Decisional competence, the second prong of adjudicative competence, requires "decision-making abilities, including capacities for reasoning and judgment (e.g., the abilities to foresee the consequences of multiple options, compare them, and weigh both their probability of occurrence and subjective desirability in making a decision)." Due to the different cognitive skills necessary for decisional competence, it is important to recognize that "a defendant who is competent to assist counsel may not be competent to make the specific decisions regarding the defense of his or her case that are encountered as the process of criminal adjudication unfolds."

Notably, "the parts of the brain 'that govern impulsivity, judgment, planning for the future, (and) foresight of consequences' do not completely mature until the early twenties." The MacArthur Foundation Research Network on Adolescent Development and Juvenile Justice demonstrated the significance of this immaturity of the adolescent brain in the context of juvenile adjudicative competence, finding that teenagers "aged 15 and younger ... differed from young adults in their legal decision-making." Specifically, these teenagers "were less likely to recognize the risks inherent in different choices and less likely to think about long-term consequences of their choices." The study also found that adolescents fail to "put facts together and draw conclusions the way adults do," and they are much more likely to comply with authority figures. Thomas Grisso, the director of the study, explains that these findings are important because juvenile defendants "are often asked to accept or reject plea bargains that have very long-term consequences.... At that age, they are frequently not as equipped as the average adult to grasp the consequences of legal decisions that will seal their fate for the rest of their lives."

Thus, it is clear that adolescents "possess certain developmental characteristics that impair their effective participation" in a criminal trial. Moreover, a juvenile's competence "to participate in a trial may be less than the competency needed to make a judgment to plead guilty and accept the consequences of that decision." Given the substantial research supporting the immature cognitive abilities of adolescents, why are courts willing to use standards designed for adults to assess the validity of a juvenile's plea agreement?...

V. Applying an Adult Standard to K.M.

After entering into a plea agreement with the State, K.M. sought to withdraw her admission to child abuse homicide, claiming 1) that she did not know she was "admitting to causing the death" of her baby; 2) "that she was pressured or coerced into admitting the amended allegation"; and 3) "that she understood little or none of the colloquy with the Court or her counsel at the time of her admission." The juvenile court then conducted a hearing and informed K.M. of her trial rights, which she waived after assuring the court "that she understood what she was doing and that she was not acting under any coercion." Despite K.M.'s claim that the infant was stillborn because it "never made a noise and was not breathing," the juvenile court accepted K.M.'s plea of guilty to child abuse homicide.

Despite her comparatively lenient sentence of a month of detention and two-hundred-and-fifty hours of community service, K.M. then appealed the juvenile court's denial of her motion to withdraw on the ground that her admission was not knowing and voluntary due to "infirmities in her understanding at the time of her admission." Thus, the main issue before the Court of Appeals was whether or not the juvenile court wrongly denied K.M.'s motion to withdraw her plea based on an erroneous finding that she understood her rights and the consequences of her admission....

VI. Recommendations for Conducting Plea Colloquies in Juvenile Court

A. Recognizing the Effect of a Learning Disability

K.M. was sixteen years old at the time of the admission colloquy, a fact the majority found significant when applying the totality test in this case and concluding that her plea agreement was knowing and voluntary. In fact, the aforementioned MacArthur study did not find a significant difference "between juveniles aged 16 and 17 and young adults in abilities relevant to their competence to stand trial." However, it is highly likely that K.M. did not possess the same mental capacity as a typical sixteen-year-old because she "has learning disabilities, necessitating special attention and resource classes at school," a fact that the majority fails to properly consider or even mention. Interestingly, "there is a link between juvenile delinquency and learning disabilities," and the MacArthur study in particular found that "young people with below-average intelligence—an IQ under 85—were at the highest risk of lacking abilities for competence to stand trial."

Significantly, K.M. "had an I.Q. between 79 and 84," thus placing her in the category of adolescents most likely to be found incompetent to stand trial according to the MacArthur study. Furthermore, the court knew that she had a learning disability and should have weighed this factor more heavily in the totality test. Although K.M.

A study published in 2025 found that juveniles were largely unrepresented at the municipal court level in Lakewood County, Colorado. Judges routinely denied appointing counsel on the grounds that the municipal court offenses did not include jail time. The study found that only 1.5% of juveniles in this county were represented.

Attorney Hannah Seigel Proff, who practices in Denver-area municipal courts, describes the challenges that youth face in municipal court and how these challenges are magnified when youth do not have counsel: "What has become clear to me is that the majority of juvenile municipal dockets are kangaroo courts. The vast majority of the children are unrepresented, and prosecutors push youth to accept diversion sentences before they carefully review the facts of the case. Without legal representation, these families do not understand their rights. Prosecutors downplay the severity of the municipal court system, but often these cases are the first stop on the school-to prison pipeline." Gwendolyn Walker & Carly Wasserman, *Unrepresented and Unseen: A Closer Look at the Harmful Impacts of Municipal Courts on Youth, Families*, National Center for Youth Law, January 2025.

testified at the admission colloquy that she understood her legal rights, she could not correctly define terms such as "the right to remain silent" at the withdrawal hearing. The majority even admits that this is suggestive of "K.M.'s intelligence or education level," but ultimately found the fact that this right was explained to her in three different ways at the admission hearing to be determinative. However, the very nature of a learning disability is "a disorder in one or more of the basic psychological processes involved in understanding or in using language." Therefore, it is quite likely that K.M. could not comprehend the explanations of her rights in the same way that an average teenager would, as evidenced by the fact that she later offered "nonsensical" or even "absurd" definitions of those rights. Furthermore, "during moments of increased stress, the likelihood of comprehension by a juvenile with a learning disability decreases significantly," and K.M. was certainly emotional and under a great amount of stress at the time she entered into the plea agreement.

Given that learning disabilities affect many adolescents and the correlation between these disorders and juvenile delinquency, courts should address this possibility when applying the totality of the circumstances test to determine whether a plea was knowing and voluntary. A learning disorder can be a "hidden handicap" because it is not always immediately apparent, but "[s]uspicion or preliminary identification of a learning disability must be confirmed or ruled out as promptly as is feasible." Therefore, counsel should look for clues in the adolescent's "reading, writing, listening, and speaking behaviors" in order to determine whether a juvenile client suffers from such a learning disability. Further, in order to properly assess whether an adolescent knowingly and voluntarily entered a plea agreement, juvenile judges should be educated about the effects that a learning disability may have on a juvenile's comprehension of legal rights. K.M.'s case may have ended differently had the majority weighed her learning disability more heavily when inquiring as to the knowing and voluntary nature of her plea agreement....

V. Conclusion

Juvenile courts should not rely solely upon the standards used for adults in the criminal justice system to determine whether a plea agreement was knowingly and voluntarily made by a juvenile. Instead, courts should specifically tailor such inquiries to account for the juveniles' unique cognitive capabilities and maturity level, using open-ended questions and recognizing that the use of indirect forms of speech may

Is 8 Years Old Too Young to Plead Guilty?

In 2008, an 8 year old Arizona boy plead guilty in a case where he was charged with murder after shooting his father and another man (NY Times, Nov. 30, 2008, A 37). Is an 8 year old competent to plead guilty? Do you think it matters if the juvenile is represented by a lawyer? Would representation by a lawyer make a guilty plea acceptable at any age?

In this case, the juvenile pled to a lesser charge (negligent homicide instead of murder) and was sentenced to residential treatment. Pleading guilty prevented the case from having a transfer proceeding (to transfer to adult court) and guaranteed that the juvenile would get intensive psychiatric treatment. At the time the case was reported, experts questioned whether the juvenile could be competent to stand trial due to his young age. Yet, it seems, he was found competent to plead guilty.

If you were his lawyer, what would you do? Is a guilty plea appropriate, particularly if you were concerned about the more serious charge and transfer to adult court? And, as a prosecutor, should you make an offer? Why not reduce the charges and have an adjudication hearing, and allow the judge to sentence to psychiatric treatment and probation (the sentence the defendant received)? Should you threaten to do a transfer proceeding, as the prosecutor in this case apparently did? Would you want to transfer the case to adult court?

Postscript: The boy (whose name was never released), successfully finished probation when he turned 18 (in 2017). He was sentenced at the age of nine and spent nine years under intense supervision and treatment which included many years in a residential facility.

Felicia Fonseca, *St. John's Boy Killed His Father When He Was 8. Now His Probation Is Ending as He Turns 18*, Associated Press, Dec. 26, 2017.

be a sign of confusion or uncertainty. Furthermore, the totality of the circumstances test should include a consideration of any potential learning disabilities that may affect the juvenile's ability to comprehend his or her legal rights and the consequences of entering into a plea agreement. Finally, juvenile courts should view a motion to withdraw a plea prior to sentencing as analogous to a minor's right to avoid contractual obligations, in order to treat adolescents consistently within the context of both criminal and civil law.

Notes/Questions

1. Many states require any defendant convicted (either by plea or trial) of a sex offense to register as a sex offender for the rest of their lives (or risk a new offense for Failure to Register as a Sex Offender). The registration requirement exists for both juveniles and adults. What is different for a juvenile, as compared to an adult, who is required to register as a sex offender for the rest of their life? As a policy question, should a juvenile sex offender convicted as a juvenile have to register as a sex offender? Sex offender registries are open and available to the public (and on-line). Should registration requirements be the same regardless of whether the crime is sexting or a violent sexual assault? Whether the offense is a status offense (sex with an underage romantic partner) versus unwelcome? Since many juvenile proceedings are confidential, does sex offender registration violate this premise? Which value—confidentiality vs. safety—should be more protected? For more information on this issue, see Maggie Jones, *The Case of the Juvenile Sex Offender: Is he a criminal forever marked or a kid whose behavior can be changed?*, N.Y. Times Magazine, July 22, 2007, p. 32.

2. Should there be different standards if a juvenile pleads guilty in the juvenile court or in an adult court? If yes, what should the differences be? Should there be more protections in the juvenile courts or in the adult courts?

3. As you read earlier in the book, courts have standard plea colloquies when defendants plead guilty in a case. For the most part, defendants are asked questions that they can answer with a "yes" or a "no." Should a judge use the same plea colloquy with a juvenile? In discussing this questions, Lacey Cole Singleton said,

> ... [A]dolescents tend to "make choices that reflect a propensity to comply with authority figures" and are substantially more susceptible to coercion than adults, especially those teenagers who suffer from learning disabilities.
>
> Adolescent defendants in the juvenile justice system also face an "asymmetry of power" when dealing with adults throughout the adjudicative process, especially in an interrogatory environment. Interrogations, by definition, involve "a power disparity between the person asking the question and the person being questioned. The questioner has the right to control the subject matter, tempo, and progress of the questioning, to interrupt responses to questions, and to judge whether the responses are satisfactory." This dynamic tends to give the subject of interrogation a feeling of powerlessness, which in turn

> affects the manner of responding to questions. Specifically, these individuals "frequently adopt an indirect speech register" characterized by "beginning statements with 'I think,' 'I guess,' or 'I suppose,' or using 'maybe' or 'perhaps.'" These hedges tend to suggest "that the speaker is uncertain about the statement" and should cause alarm in the context of a plea colloquy designed to assess whether an admission is truly knowing and voluntary.[4]

Juveniles may want to not "sound stupid" and they may therefore answer in a way that indicates they understand. This may be even more of an issue with juveniles who have learning disabilities.

Singleton suggests that the solution would be to use open-ended questions in the plea colloquy. This would ensure that the juvenile understands and isn't simply answering "yes" to please the court or to not show confusion or misunderstanding.[5]

4. In one study of nearly 100 juveniles in the juvenile court system, ranging in age from nine to seventeen years old, the juveniles were asked about their "understanding of the thirty-six words used in the Massachusetts" plea forms and court colloquies. On average, the group that had no instruction understood only two of the thirty-six words, and the group that *was* instructed understood only five of the thirty-six words. "Examples of incorrect answers, such as "presumption of innocence" being defined as "[i]f your attorney feels you didn't do it" (age fifteen) and "disposition" repeatedly defined as "bad position" (age sixteen)." This study suggests that even juveniles represented by lawyers, who have the terms explained to them, may still not understand the rights they are waiving when they enter a guilty plea. Allison D. Redlich, *Righting the Wronged: Causes, Effects, and Remedies of Juvenile Wrongful Conviction*, 62 Rutgers L. Rev. 943, 948–949 (Summer 2010).

5. Should any of the plea bargaining reform proposals that you read about earlier in the book be considered for plea bargaining in juvenile courts? In the juvenile context?

The following reading will outline some of the additional concerns about how the juvenile legal system currently works. As you are reading, think about what types of reforms might help to address the specific concerns and whether the concerns are unique to juvenile offenders or whether we have seen these concerns for adult offenders as well.

---

4. Lacey Cole Singleton, Study Note, *Say "Pleas": Juveniles' Competence to Enter Plea Agreements*, 9 J.L. & Fam. Stud. 439, 452 (2007).

5. *Id.* at 449.

IV. Concerns about the Juvenile Legal System

There are numerous concerns and critiques of how the juvenile legal system works, how juveniles are treated within the juvenile legal system, and how or whether they should be transferred out of the juvenile system into adult courts. This section will give you a brief introduction to those concerns. You will want to pay attention to which concerns are similar to the adult system and which ones are unique to the juvenile system.

A. Discrimination

Samantha Michaels, *Black Kids Are 5 Times Likelier Than White Kids to Be Locked Up: And the Racial Disparity Is Only Growing*

MOTHER JONES, Sept. 13, 2017

Since 2001, the number of kids in detention has dropped by more than half across the country—a seemingly decisive victory for juvenile-justice reformers. But digging into the numbers reveals a much bleaker picture. Recently released data from the Justice Department shows that black juveniles are five times likelier than white juveniles to be locked up. It's not exactly a new phenomenon, but it's a worsening one.

The gap between black and white juvenile detention grew more than 20 percent from 2001 to 2015, according to the Sentencing Project, a criminal justice advocacy group that crunched the new data in a report out this week.[6] As of 2015, about 44 percent of all kids in custody were black, even though African Americans make up just 16 percent of the total youth population in the United States.

Black youths are more likely to be locked up in 49 states—all but Hawaii—though the racial gap is worse in some states than it is in others: In New Jersey, Wisconsin, Montana, Delaware, Connecticut, and Massachusetts, black kids are at least 10 times as likely to be held in custody as white kids.

The Sentencing Project

"The disparity exists because of differences in how young people of color are treated at every point of contact with the justice system, but the *growth* of the incarceration disparity is likely due to growing disparities in arrests, which feeds the rest of the system," Joshua Rovner, who studies juvenile justice at the Sentencing Project, tells *Mother Jones*.

Black kids are more than twice as likely as white kids to be arrested. But that's not because black kids are committing so many more crimes; the data proves they're not. "Black and white youth are roughly as likely to get into fights, carry weapons, steal

6. Report available at http://www.sentencingproject.org/publications/black-disparities-youth-incarceration/.

property, use and sell illicit substances, and commit status offenses, like skipping school," the Sentencing Project found in a report last year.

Inequality in Residential Placements for Juveniles?

In 2021, the white placement rate in juvenile facilities was 49 per 100,000 youth under age 18. By comparison, the Black youth placement rate was 228 per 100,000, 4.7 times higher. Tribal youth were 3.7 times as likely (181 per 100,000) and Latino youth were 16% more likely (57 per 100,000). Asian American youth were the least likely to be held in juvenile facilities (13 per 100,000).

Joshua Rovner, *Youth Justice by the Numbers*, The Sentencing Project, Aug. 14, 2024.

Still, slight behavioral differences do exist—white high school students are more likely to carry weapons or drink underage, while black students are more likely to smoke weed or get into fights, according to the Centers for Disease Control and Prevention. But they don't explain the *vast* differences in arrest rates: In the CDC study, a third of black students had gotten into a fight, compared with a fifth of white students. Yet the Justice Department data shows that black youths are about 300 percent more likely than white youths to be arrested for simple assault.

"The disparity is driven by the way that adults respond to those behaviors," says Rovner. Kids of color are more likely than white kids to go to schools with school resource officers, who provide security and also have the ability to make arrests. And cops are more likely to patrol neighborhoods where black kids live, Rovner adds. "In an era of racial segregation, especially residential segregation, black youths' lives are surrounded by police officers, and their teenaged mistakes are more likely to land in the juvenile justice system," says Rovner. "White youth's mistakes are not."

Heather Cobb, *Separate and Unequal: The Disparate Impact of School-Based Referrals to Juvenile Court*

44 Harv. Civ. Rts. Civ. Lib. L. Rev. 581, 582–85, 587–88 (2009)

II. Presentation of the School to Prison Pipeline

School administrators and security personnel enjoy wide discretion to decide which students are referred to juvenile court for behavioral infractions. Combined with preconceived notions about the ability of African American children to succeed, this discretion works to push African American students out of school at significantly higher rates than their white peers for lesser or more subjective offenses. This phenomenon, known as the school to prison pipeline, exposes a disproportionate number of African American children to the criminal justice system. The educational experience of African American and white students in terms of punishment is therefore radically different and unequal.

A. The Presence of Security Personnel in Schools

The analogy between schoolyards and detention centers has grown increasingly apt in urban, low-income communities of color. The emergence of security policies focused on zero tolerance and other harsh measures began in the 1990s. Several prominent politicians, spurred by the media's exploitation of a few high-profile juvenile crimes, convinced fellow legislators and the public that children had become incorrigible and that a generation of super-predators had begun to fill classrooms.

Yet it was white students in predominately rural and suburban areas who in fact committed the high profile violent crimes that received the most press coverage at this time. While crimes certainly increased in urban areas as well, especially due to a rise in drug and gang activity, African American youths were only one-third more likely than white youths to commit a violent offense by the time they were seventeen. Nonetheless, statistical analyses show that excessive policing takes place primarily in schools with populations consisting of a majority of African American students, and "[f]our out of five new juveniles detained between 1983 and 1997 were youths of color."

Heightened police presence in schools increases police involvement in non-criminal incidents, resulting in a spike of school referrals to the juvenile court system for largely childish misbehavior. For example, introduction of police officers to schools in Clayton County, Georgia led to a 600% increase in referrals to juvenile court over a three year period. Yet during that time there was no increase in the number of serious safety violations. At their peak in 2003, school referrals accounted for about a quarter of total referrals to juvenile court. Such an increase is not unique. In Philadelphia, between the 1999–2000 school year and the 2002–2003 school year, the number of arrests in schools increased from 1632 to 2194; in Denver, referrals rose 71% from 818 in 2000–2001 to 1401 in 2003–2004.

In 1975, 1% of schools in the United States had a sworn law enforcement officer on site. Chelsea Connery, *The Prevalence and the Price of Police in Schools*, UConn Center for Education Policy Analysis, October 27, 2020. By 2020 that number had increased to 51.4%. Kayla Susalla, *School Resource Officers: Is Police Presence in Schools Doing More Harm than Good?* CATO Institute, July 24, 2023.

One reason for the rise in referrals for minor misconduct is that a large number of these security and police officers are not subject to the supervisory authority of school administrators, and they have not been adequately trained to work in educational settings. Lacking this familiarity with the school community, they often operate with authority that extends far beyond the limited mission of ensuring the safety of students and teachers. This exacerbates the gap in communication between police personnel and school administrators, who are predominately white, and the youth of color with whom they have limited interaction outside of school. This disconnect in cultural understanding allows security officers to interpret student behavior in ways that lead to negative judgments about African Americans. Such an environment produces two results: it reinforces common stereotypes about the criminality of African Americans and fosters the African American students' insecurity about a pre-determined future that looks very different from that of their white peers.

The criminalization of schoolyards contributes more to the problems of a school than it does to alleviate them. Pedro A. Noguera, a professor at New York University's Steinhardt School of Education, explains: "Schools that rely on security guards and metal detectors to create safety may end up creating an environment that is so repressive that it is no longer conducive to learning." Evidence that schools are already generally safe indicates that these security measures are not only counterproductive, but also unnecessary. Indeed, "[l]ess than 1 percent of all violent incidents involving adolescents occur on school grounds."

B. The (In)Effectiveness of Zero Tolerance Policies

In connection with an increase in the number of police patrolling school halls, legislators have reacted to the law and order movement of the 1990s by enacting punitive laws that contain exclusionary zero tolerance clauses. These laws and their resulting school-level policies further alienate the children who are most in need of stability and guidance because they mandate that schools severely punish disruptive students regardless of the circumstances surrounding the infraction. The increase in suspensions and expulsions stemming from zero tolerance policies have proven to disproportionately affect African American students.

....

C. The Disparate Racial Impact of Well-Intended Discipline Policies and Statutes

As Beale points out, the Warren Court, for all its groundbreaking decisions, neglected to discuss race when deciding the criminal procedure cases during the Civil Rights era. As a result, legislatures and school boards lack the impetus to address the disparate racial impact of school disciplinary policies, even as race continues to be a determinative factor in the discipline of students. A meta-analysis of studies on race and the juvenile justice system found that "about two-thirds of the studies of disproportionate minority confinement showed negative 'race effects' at one stage or another of the juvenile justice process," including the initial transfer from school. Therefore, it is not surprising that the policies Beale recounts in her article, and the student discipline codes described here, have a disproportionate impact on the same group: African American youth. Studies have shown that African American students are "far more likely" than whites "to be suspended, expelled, or arrested for the same kind of conduct...." In fact, one study found that African American students are disciplined more severely even for lesser offenses, such as "disrespect, excessive noise, threat and loitering" than their white peers. For example, in 1995, African American youth with no prior criminal records were six times more likely to be incarcerated than whites for the same offense. And, as recently as November of 2008, African American students in West Hartford, Connecticut who got into fights on campus "were about twice as likely to be arrested" as whites. In East Hartford, African American students accused of offenses "involving drugs, alcohol or tobacco were ten times more likely to be arrested than were similarly situated white students." Experts on race and discipline issues, including Russell Skiba, a professor of educational psychology at Indiana University, describes this data as "structural inequity or ... institutional racism."

> "Since 1972, the suspension rate for white students increased only 2 percentage points—from 3 percent to 5 percent—while the suspension rate for black students nearly tripled from 6 percent to 16 percent."
>
> Cara H. Drinan, The War on Kids: How American Juvenile Justice Lost Its Way 51 (2018).

Whatever the name, this disproportionate minority contact with the juvenile court system reinforces stereotypes and race-based expectations that African American students are likely to require discipline. Such disproportionate punishments have resulted in an educational experience characterized by many as "learning while black." Skiba, however, notes that "there simply isn't any support for the notion that, given the same set of circumstances, African American kids act out to a greater degree than other kids."

Notes/Questions

1. A study published in July of 2021 confirmed that the school to prison pipeline continues to impact students. The study found that students who were assigned to a "stricter" middle school, a school with higher suspension rates, were "substantially more likely to be arrested and jailed as adults"[7] The same study also found that of color were impacted at much higher rates and that "Black and Hispanic students assigned to stricter schools are more likely to be arrested and incarcerated than their non-minority classmates."[8] This is just one of many studies that have continued to collect data confirming that students who are suspended from school are more likely to end up in the juvenile legal system and ultimately the adult criminal legal system. Should states limit, by law, when students can be suspended? Would taking the authority to suspend away from the local school district help to prevent bias? As you continue reading you might

---

7. Andrew Bacher-Hicks et al., Proving the School to Prison Pipeline, 21 Education Next (Fall 2021).

8. *Id.*

Arrested for Being a Teenager?

"Boisterous" behavior, "annoying conduct," "disturbing in any way or any place students or teachers of any school," or acting in an "obnoxious manner." These may all sound like typical teenage behavior, but they are also definitions of crimes in some states. These offenses are often referred to as "disturbing school," and over twenty-two states criminalize such behavior. According to *The Atlantic*, approximately 10,000 juveniles are charged with these offenses every year.

> When teenagers talk back, scream obscenities, or otherwise behave badly, adults must call them out and hold them accountable.... But the laws have ... been used to punish behavior that few reasonable people would consider criminal. Defiance is a typical part of adolescence, so putting teenagers in jail for swearing or refusing to follow an order is akin to arresting a 2-year-old for having a meltdown in a grocery store. It essentially outlaws the human condition. And the vagueness of the laws means that they are inevitably applied unevenly, depending on the moods and biases of the adults enforcing them. In South Carolina, black students ... are nearly four times as likely as their white peers to be charged with disturbing school.

Amanda Ripley, *How America Outlawed Adolescence*, The Atlantic, November 2016.

One concern with these laws is the school to prison pipeline, as once a child is arrested, they are more likely to drop out of school, and once they drop out of school, they are much more likely to be arrested again. Controlling for factors such as GPA, race, and prior offenses, being arrested makes a juvenile twice as likely to drop out, and this is for those whose case is dismissed without conviction. Those who are arrested and go to court are four times as likely to drop out of school.

want to consider if there are other approaches to decrease the number of students pulled into the school to prison pipeline.

2. Related to racial and ethnic bias is bias against students with learning disabilities or conditions such as Attention Deficit Disorder, particularly students of color who have a learning disability or disability that makes it harder for them to control their behavior. There have been numerous news reports of 4-, 5-, and 6-year-old children who were handcuffed at school either by the school resource officer or by a police officer called into the school. As a prosecutor, what would you do with a case of a 5-year-old "causing a disturbance" in their kindergarten class? Is the criminal legal system the place to manage these cases? What if the child was mentally disabled and 13 years old? Is that different? Should that become a criminal case?

3. As a prosecutor, should you make different decisions about how to handle individual cases that come before you now that you know the statistics about biased treatment of African American juveniles and how this can increase their likelihood of ending up in the criminal legal system?

4. As a criminal defense lawyer handling juvenile cases, how might you use these statistics to help your individual clients?

5. Some schools that are concerned about bias in suspensions and school discipline have moved to other practices, including introducing restorative justice and "empathetic discipline." You will read more about restorative justice for juveniles in Chapter 15. *See* Susan Dominus, *An Effective But Exhausting Alternative to High School Suspensions*, N.Y. TIMES MAGAZINE, Sept. 7, 2016 (describing the introduction of restorative justice for discipline problems at a New York high school). *See also* David L. Kirp, *Don't Suspend Students. Empathize.* N.Y. TIMES, Sept. 2, 2017 (describing empathetic discipline to reduce disproportionately high suspension and discipline rates against minority students).

B. Innocent Juvenile Defendants

Earlier in the book, you read about the concern that innocent defendants have pled guilty. The following article outlines the many concerns in juvenile court that lead to wrongful convictions. This is, of course, a danger with adult offenders as well. Note what challenges are the same and what are different from adult offenders.

Steven A. Drizin & Greg Luloff, *Are Juvenile Courts a Breeding Ground for Wrongful Convictions?*

34 N. KY. L. REV. 257, 259–60, 266, 268–69, 270, 273, 283, 284, 289, 289–90, 292–93, 302, 303–04 (2007)

Introduction

....

Although the 1990s brought increased attention to the problem of wrongful convictions in the criminal justice system, little or no attention, however, has been paid to the risks of wrongful convictions in juvenile court. There are several good reasons why it is time to start paying attention.

First, studies of wrongful convictions demonstrate that juvenile defendants may be at special risk of being wrongfully convicted in criminal court. Juveniles are prominently featured in these studies, especially when it comes to false confessions. *People v. Salaam*, the "Central Park Jogger" case, in which five teenagers falsely confessed to attempting to murder and raping a woman who was out for a run in Central Park, is just one of many examples of juveniles who have confessed, been convicted, and later exonerated.

Second, developmental differences between juveniles and adults (especially in the areas of judgment, maturity, assessing and weighing risks, vulnerability to peer pressure, and an inability to see the long-term consequences of their actions) make juveniles less competent trial defendants. Juveniles also tend to be more compliant and suggestible during police interrogations, two traits which are risk factors for false confessions.

Third, many of the same problems that cause wrongful convictions in criminal court also exist in juvenile court. For example, psychologically coercive interrogations lead to false confessions and suggestive interviewing techniques lead to mistaken eyewitness identifications.

The risk of wrongful convictions in juvenile court proceedings may also be increased by a lack of many of the due process protections afforded adult criminal defendants and the lesser capabilities of juveniles to take advantage of those due process rights. The so-called "due process revolution" of the 1960s did transform the juvenile court from a "kangaroo court" to a court system which afforded juveniles some of the same due process protections given to adults in criminal proceedings. Even in those instances where juveniles were given the same due process rights as adults, the rights were of little use because many juvenile defendants were not competent to exercise them. For example, Miranda warnings offer little protection to juvenile suspects from police coercion (because they do not understand their meaning and function), the right to counsel is of no use to many juveniles who are allowed to waive this right, and the lack of meaningful probable cause hearings and the absence of jury trials may affect the reliability of the judge-made determinations of innocence and guilt. Finally, discovering and remedying wrongful convictions is further limited by the fact that few juvenile cases are appealed and even fewer post-conviction and habeas cases are filed involving juveniles....

Part II: Procedural Deficiencies in Juvenile Court

It is beyond the scope of this article to cover all of the procedural deficiencies that continue to exist in the juvenile court. Instead, this section sheds light on just a few of the most glaring deficiencies of the juvenile court and how those deficiencies make children dangerously susceptible to wrongful convictions....

A. Miranda Rights: Words Without Meaning to Juveniles?

Miranda rights are an example of a procedural protection extended to juveniles. Miranda, however, is little more than a speed-bump for police officers when questioning adults and even less of an obstacle when interrogating juveniles. Approximately, 80–85 percent of adult criminal suspects waive their Miranda rights and well over 90 percent of juveniles waive their protection against self-incrimination....

The Miranda rights were designed as a protection for adults against the inherent compulsion present in the modern psychological police interrogation. By simply invoking the right to silence or asking for an attorney, suspects could bring the interrogation to a crashing halt. The rights were not only meant to give suspects a safeguard against self-incrimination, but also as a safeguard against false confessions. In order to make use of this protection, however, a suspect must understand the meaning of the words of Miranda rights and the consequences of giving them up. Study after study has shown that juvenile suspects fail on both counts.

Much of the underutilization of Miranda rights stems from children's lack of comprehension with regard to the privilege against self-incrimination. Children under the age of 14 and older adolescents are especially at risk for not understanding the nature of Miranda. In psychological testing, these children have scored significantly lower than adults, including adults with low intelligence. At age 15, children have basic intellectual skills similar to adults, but exposure to hearing Miranda recited does not necessarily transfer to the ability to knowingly and intelligently waive one's Miranda rights. Miranda presents a juvenile with a set of options, and while a child might know what these options are, she might not know their significance or function. Because children, and even adolescents over the age of 15, often neither understand the function of Miranda nor the consequences of waiving Miranda rights, it is impossible for them to provide a knowing and intelligent waiver.

In addition, juveniles often do not understand the concept of a right itself. Unlike adults, who conceive a right as an entitlement and something that cannot be taken away, juveniles perceive their rights as something they are allowed to do, not an entitlement.

This misunderstanding of Miranda is further exacerbated in the interrogation context because of children's susceptibility to coercive pressure to waive their Miranda rights. Children learn at an early age to answer questions directed to them by adults. Moreover, police occupy an elevated position of power in relation to juveniles, thus creating a "status differential" in the interrogation. Juveniles' "low status" compared to their adult interrogators, compounded with societal mores that children should obey adults, their dependence on adults, and their reduced ability to withstand intimidation, all serve to coerce juveniles to waive their Miranda rights. Research has demonstrated that lower status individuals yield to the authority of a higher-status figure, resulting with children making such comments as "They the police, you do what they say." ...

B. False Confessions and Children's Waivers of Miranda Rights.

Most people find it preposterous that anyone would waive her right to silence and confess to a crime she did not commit. Yet, false confessions are one of the leading causes of wrongful convictions. Data collected by the Innocence Project indicates that approximately 23 percent of exonerations involved false confessions or admissions....

... When [interrogation] tactics are used on juvenile suspects, the risk of obtaining false confessions is markedly increased. Juveniles' inferior comprehension of rights, limited language ability, and inadequate decision-making skills increase their susceptibility to interrogation tactics and thus increase the likelihood of a false confession. Studies of proven false confessions have demonstrated that juveniles (defined as those under 18), are over-represented in false confession cases. In Drizin and Leo's study, for example, juveniles comprised 33 percent of a sample of 125 known false confessions. Because juvenile courts are not covered by most news and print media and court proceedings remain confidential in many instances, it is likely that these reported juvenile false confessions are the tip of the iceberg of the juvenile false confessions problem.

Getting a child to forfeit his or her Miranda protections is an easy feat for a police officer in an interrogation room. Psychological research has shown that a child's understanding of Miranda warnings negatively correlates with false confessions—the better the Miranda comprehension, the less likely a child will falsely confess....

D. Access and Quality of Counsel in the Juvenile Court

Every study done on wrongful convictions has documented the role that poor and ineffective counsel has played in these tragedies. Ineffective assistance of counsel has been found to be "a significant contributing factor" in about 5% to 28% of wrongful convictions....

The problem of ineffective assistance of counsel may be even more serious in juvenile courts. While the punishment is nowhere near that in capital cases, children suffer the double problem of inadequate access to counsel and poor representation in juvenile court. For all the same reasons that children waive their Miranda rights, children frequently waive their right to counsel in juvenile court. Poor representation occurs for the same reasons as in adult court with the added problems of a juvenile court culture that frowns upon zealous advocacy. In many ways, access and quality of counsel in juvenile courts make children more susceptible to wrongful convictions than their adult counterparts.

....

2. Quality of Advocacy in Juvenile Court

If a child is able to survive arraignment without waiving her right to counsel, the battle is only half over as many juvenile defendants are victims of ineffective assistance of counsel....

First, investigation is essential in being able to represent competently a client. Scheck and Neufeld, as well as other innocence projects, repeatedly demonstrate the importance of investigations in uncovering wrongful convictions. Moreover, the example of the three boys cited above by Berkheiser [this case is explained in the Notes on p. 433] shows how even the most cursory investigation can make the difference between guilt and innocence. The most basic investigation begins with the client; however, the ABA studies document how infrequently juvenile attorneys meet with their clients before entering a guilty plea. As one defense attorney stated, "I don't call my clients when I receive the paperwork from the court because I don't have an obligation to chase them down. If they want to talk to me they know where to find me." The ABA study in Kentucky uncovered that only about 20 percent of youth not in custody stated that they met with their attorney prior to the day of adjudication. In North Carolina, 44 percent of juvenile attorneys stated that they rarely, or never, look at the police report or other investigative materials prior to seeing their client. Even if attorneys do meet with their clients, they often rely on the parents and children to contact witnesses and bring those witnesses into court. Juvenile attorneys rarely rely on investigators to help build a case.... The failure to investigate cannot be blamed entirely on attorneys; lack of investigation is tied to the lack of funding juvenile defenders receive. However, regardless of the reason, the fact is that a majority of juvenile cases proceed to trial with minimal or no investigation, a situation that enhances the risk of wrongful convictions.

Attorneys in juvenile court rarely, if ever, file pretrial motions. While good motion practice is considered one of the bedrock principles in zealous advocacy, only some juvenile attorneys (approximately 30 percent) surveyed by the ABA Juvenile Justice Center said they filed pretrial motions.... While a successful motion might blur the distinction between legal and factual guilt, the complete failure to file relevant motions diminishes a juvenile's ability to receive a fair and accurate trial.

Throughout the country, juvenile attorneys handle an excessively burdensome caseload. In fact, problems such as lack of investigations and motions and reliance on pleas are directly correlated with the heavy caseloads juvenile attorneys carry....

3. False Guilty Pleas

The juvenile court culture in turn creates a system in which there is an extremely high rate of guilty pleas. Guilty pleas do not, by their nature, enhance the possibility for wrongful conviction. In many ways, pleas allow for cases to be adjudicated quickly and for the child to move on, if in fact he or she is delinquent. A plea negotiation can be an opportunity for defense counsel to receive a positive outcome for her client, and it is not necessarily a failure. However, the problem is that pleas are used so often in juvenile court without investigation or advocacy that there is a high probability that innocent children are being asked by the courts and their lawyers to take guilty pleas. The literature on adult wrongful conviction is filled with stories of innocent suspects accepting false guilty pleas.

There are several reasons why false guilty pleas can occur. First, it will often be the case that innocent clients are more risk averse than guilty clients, and thus are more likely to want to avoid the risk of trial. Next, guilty pleas are often encouraged out of a desire to avoid the adversarial nature of litigation. As defense attorneys work more with prosecutors and judges in the same courtroom, defense counsel feels pressure to accept deals offered by the prosecution. Litigation requires filing discovery and pretrial motions, which defense attorneys quickly learn are frowned upon by both prosecutors and judges. Finally, defense attorneys often approach their cases with an assumption that their clients are guilty, especially in cases where their clients have confessed.

The combination of heavy caseloads, juvenile court culture that frowns upon advocacy and lawyers who only meet their clients on the day of adjudication creates a system of representation ripe for wrongful convictions. In Montana, one judge reported that he only had 2–3 trials a year and defenders stated that cases rarely go to trial. One attorney explained, "I tell the clients the rights that they have, but the risks are so low, they don't want to go through with it. The worst that they can look at is [a county facility] until 18."

The problem with this approach, besides shirking professional responsibility, is that children do not necessarily understand the plea system and could be pleading guilty when they would like to fight the charges. Youth remain uninformed about their decisions because attorneys fail to communicate with children at an appropriate language level.... The language that judges and lawyers use during plea negotiations is often in-comprehensible to children, even those children with previous involvement with the court system. Thus, unless both the judge and lawyer use language and vocabulary that does not exceed an eighth grade level and concepts are explained more than once, there is a good chance that children will simply not understand that they are waiving their right to a trial and admitting guilt. Such was the case with one youth interviewed in Montana, who stated he "didn't know that [he] could have fought the charges."

False guilty pleas, like false confessions, are higher among juveniles for a variety of developmental reasons. Juveniles tend to focus on the short-term rather than the long term, they are more likely to comply with adult authority figures, and they are not as mature in their decision-making or judgment.

Innocent children find themselves at a disadvantage in a court system where the court does not speak to them in an age-appropriate manner, their attorneys are too busy to investigate the case, and judges and prosecutors frown upon assertions of innocence and exercising a right to trial. One of the enduring lessons of *Gault* is that due process is not just about fairness, it is about accuracy, and this type of environment is not one in which accuracy is sought or encouraged. When an innocent child pleads guilty to a crime he or she did not commit, it is not only an injustice to the individual child, but it undermines our entire juvenile justice system....

B. Judicial Versus Jury Factfinding

The public discourse on wrongful convictions has examined the actions of prosecutors, defense lawyers, witnesses, and police but rarely has it assessed the role of judges in these miscarriages of justice. However, a closer examination reveals that judges are often some of the central actors in the wrongful conviction of an innocent defendant. In most false confession cases, for example, judges allowed the State to introduce confessions which were not only false, but also, in all likelihood, coerced. They are the gatekeepers of unreliable evidence and they routinely admit into evidence confessions that turn out to be false, eyewitness testimony that is erroneous, junk science, and jailhouse snitch testimony.

One of the main differences between jury and judicial factfinding is the application of proof of guilt "beyond a reasonable doubt." In *In re Winship*, the Supreme Court held that the burden to find a youth delinquent is "proof beyond a reasonable doubt."... Numerous studies have shown "that juries are more likely to acquit than are judges." This sentiment was echoed in the ABA state studies with defense lawyers readily acknowledging that judges do not apply a proof beyond a reasonable doubt standard. Judges and juries evaluate evidence, sentiments about the law, and defendant sympathy differently, with juries more likely to demand heightened proof of facts and be more sympathetic to the defendant's youthfulness. While in the majority of jurisdictions that allow juvenile court trials, juveniles rarely invoke the right, a jury can enforce the standard of proof of guilt beyond a reasonable doubt in marginal fact cases. In addition, a jury can reduce prosecutorial over-charging, a result which can reduce the incentive for juveniles to enter a false guilty plea....

Notes/Questions

1. Should juveniles not be allowed to waive their right to a lawyer? States allow juveniles to waive their right to a lawyer, and they may not be fully advised by judges when doing so. As Drizin and Luloff wrote,

> It appears that many juvenile court judges do not pay close attention to youth as they waive their right to counsel. In a recent study by Mary Berkheiser of 99 appeals challenging a juvenile's waiver of counsel, 80 of the 99 waivers were overturned on appeal. The study documented one instance of a child as young as nine who had been allowed to waive his right to counsel, and another judge accepted a boy's waiver even though the boy suffered mental health and emotional problems for which he was on medication and attended a specialized school.
>
> Permissive judges who allow children to waive their right to counsel ensure that juvenile cases are not tried on their merits. For example, Berkheiser cites an example from her study where three boys were charged for damaging a complainant's trailer by pushing it into a ravine. Two of the boys went without counsel and the judge found them delinquent and placed them on probation. The third boy asked for a lawyer, and was then referred to a law school clinic. After minimal investigation, a law student discovered that the complainant did not even own the trailer (the boy's father did) and the charges were dismissed. Thus, two boys had a delinquency record and one did not just because of the presence of a lawyer.

2. Would having jury trials for all juveniles help prevent the conviction of innocent juveniles? Consider the case of judicial misconduct in Pennsylvania, where a juvenile court judge was accused of accepting kickback payments after he sentenced children to a local detention facility. One accusation is that many of the juveniles went unrepresented after assurances that if they waived their right to a lawyer, the judge would go easier on them (and then sentenced them to time in custody). For a full account of this story, see Wendy N. Davis, *Town Without Pity*, ABA Journal, Sept. 2009. See also the documentary, *Kids for Cash* (SenArt, 2014).

3. One concern with making jury trials a right in every state in the USA is that it will put more pressure on juveniles to plead guilty, as jury trials take more time and court resources. If you were a policy-maker proposing a change in the law to give juveniles a right to a jury trial in your state, what protections might you put into the law regarding

the use of plea bargaining to prevent this from happening? Are there other limitations or restrictions that you might want to place on juveniles pleading guilty?

4. Should juveniles have more protections in juvenile courts than we provide for adult offenders in adult courts?

5. Note how these latter articles start to raise the arguments of juvenile brain development and how that can hinder decision making. In the next chapter we will turn to how the Supreme Court has addressed our increased scientific understanding of how the human brain develops.

C. Transfer to Adult Court

As you read earlier in this chapter, juveniles can be tried and sentenced as adults if their cases are transferred to adult courts. Most states set minimum ages for transfer (fourteen years old or older). There are three basic types of transfer laws: automatic transfer, judicial transfer, or prosecutorial direct file. Automatic transfer laws require transfer to an adult court if the criteria in the law are met, such as a particular crime is committed, or a juvenile has previously been tried as an adult. In judicial transfer, a prosecutor makes a motion to transfer the case to adult court, and the judge decides whether to grant the motion. Judges may look at factors such as the crime committed; specific characteristics of the juvenile including dangerousness, sophistication and maturity; and how amenable the juvenile may be to treatment. All of these factors are highly subjective and subject to bias. The final type of transfer law is prosecutorial direct file, under which the decision rests with the prosecutor alone. This type of transfer law is also highly subjective and subject to bias.

One concern about transferring juveniles to adult courts is that it is contrary to the original goals of juvenile courts, as the focus is no longer on treating the defendant but has, instead, shifted to trial and punishment as adults. A related concern is that the process and punishment may cause the juvenile more harm, both because the underlying causes aren't being treated and because the adult system is harsher in terms of both punishment and conditions, particularly imprisonment conditions. Another concern is that trying juveniles as adults does not deter future criminal behavior, as juveniles are either unaware of transfer laws or do not think they will be applied to them. The final concern that we will discuss, in the next brief excerpt, is the dramatic increase in the number of juveniles transferred out of the juvenile system.

Christopher Slobogin, *Treating Juveniles Like Juveniles: Getting Rid of Transfer and Expanded Adult Court Jurisdiction*

46 Tex. Tech L. Rev. 103–04 (2013)

...

Numerous states increased the types of crimes that trigger transfer and most also lowered the age at which it could occur; thus, for instance, a majority of states passed laws permitting waiver of juvenile court jurisdiction for ten-year-olds charged with murder, and many other states created a presumption of transfer for juveniles older than twelve or thirteen who committed a serious or second felony. A third of the states also enacted statutes authorizing prosecutorial waiver or "direct file," while the number of jurisdictions that adopted "automatic" transfer regimes for designated crimes (rather than leaving that decision to the discretion of the juvenile court or the prosecutor) more than doubled to thirty-one. Perhaps even more significant than these changes to transfer jurisdiction, thirteen states lowered the age at which juvenile court jurisdiction ends from eighteen to either fifteen or sixteen. In New York State alone, this move led to the adult prosecution of over 45,000 youths aged sixteen and seventeen in 2010.

As a result of this legislative flurry, transfers of juveniles to adult court shot up at least 70%, and the number of juveniles under eighteen prosecuted as adults skyrocketed from somewhere between 10,000 and 15,000 a year to 250,000 a year. While in the past several years some states have reduced the scope of transfer or have raised the age for criminal court jurisdiction, the latter number has stayed fairly constant since 2000. Furthermore, even those juveniles who remain in juvenile court can be subjected to "blended" sentencing, a dispositional type of transfer system that permits imposition of adult sentences on individuals convicted in juvenile court, either immediately after their conviction or when they reach eighteen.

Notes/Questions

1. Does transfer to the adult system deter future offending either by the juvenile who is sentenced, or by others who fear an adult sentence? Recidivism rates are high among juveniles sentenced as adults, which would tend to suggest that the deterrence effect is low. Juveniles tried in adult courts have higher recidivism rates and more serious new offenses than those who remain in juvenile court.7

2. One study interviewed juveniles from Georgia who were tried as adults and found that the majority did not know about the transfer law, or if they knew about it, they did not believe that they would be transferred to adult court. Richard E. Redding & Elizabeth J. Fuller, *What do Juvenile Offenders Know About Being Tried as Adults? Implications for Adults*, 55 Juv. & Fam. Ct. J. 35 (2004).

3. Another study of juvenile offenders tried as adults had similar findings: the overwhelming majority of juveniles did not understand the law and the possibility that they

might be tried as adults. Karen Miner-Romanoff, *Juvenile Offenders Tried as Adults: What they Know and Implications for Practitioners*, 41 N. Ky. L. Rev. 205 (2014).

4. As a prosecutor, what impact would these studies have on your decision about whether to try a juvenile as an adult? As a defense lawyer, what impact would these studies have on how you might talk to a prosecutor who is threatening to transfer your juvenile client to adult court?

Additional Resources

Dia N. Brannen, et al., *Transfer to Adult Court: A National Study of How Juvenile Court Judges Weigh Pertinent Kent Criteria*, 12 Psychol. Publ. Pol'y & L. 332 (2006).

Caitlin Cavanagh, Jennifer Paruk & Thomas Grisso, *The Development Reform in Juvenile Justice: Its Progress and Vulnerability*, 28 Psychol. Publ. Pol'y & L. 151, 152–153 (2022).

Michael Corriero, Judging Children as Children: A Proposal for a Juvenile Justice System (Temple University Press 2007).

Cara H. Drinan, The War on Kids: How American Juvenile Justice Lost Its Way (Oxford, 2018).

Aaron Kupchik, Judging Juveniles: Prosecuting Adolescents in Adult and Juvenile Court (NYU Press 2007).

Justice For Kids: Keeping Kids Out of the Juvenile Justice System (Nancy E. Dowd, ed., NYU Press 2012).

Rolf Loeber & David P. Farrington, From Juvenile Delinquency to Adult Crime (Oxford 2012).

Richard E. Redding, *Juvenile Transfer Laws: An Effective Deterrent to Delinquency*? (Office of Justice Programs, June 2010).

Albert R. Roberts, Juvenile Justice Sourcebook: Past, Present, and Future (Oxford 2004).

Randall T. Salekin, et al., *Juvenile Transfer to Adult Courts: A Look at the Prototypes for Dangerousness, Sophistication-Maturity, and Amenability to Treatment through a Legal Lens*, 8 Psychol. Publ. Pol'y & L. 373 (2002).

David S. Tanenhaus, *First Things First: Juvenile Justice Reform in Historical Context*, 46 Texas Tech. L. Rev. 281 (2013).

John T. Whitehead & Steven Lab, Juvenile Justice: An Introduction (8th ed. Routledge 2015).

Franklin E. Zimring, American Juvenile Justice (Oxford 2005).

Franklin E. Zimring & David S. Tanenhaus, Choosing the Future for American Juvenile Justice (NYU Press 2014).

Chapter 13

Are Juveniles Different?

The teenage brain . . . is like a car with a good accelerator but a weak brake. With powerful impulses under poor control, the likely result is a crash. And, perhaps, a crime.[1]

Are juveniles different? Should they be treated differently by the criminal legal system? Should they get the same sentences that an adult would get for committing the same crime? The basic answer is that juveniles do not think like adults, as their brains are not yet fully developed. But what impact should this have on how juveniles are treated in the criminal legal system? When should they be treated differently from adults? As you read in the last chapter, the reason juvenile courts developed was due to the concern that juveniles are different and the hope that they can be rehabilitated. But our understanding of why and how juveniles are different has evolved since the first juvenile court was established in the late 1890s. While we know this intuitively, neuroscience has allowed scientists to see that the juvenile brain is not the same as an adult brain. We have learned that the frontal cortex, the part of the brain that exercises control, is the last part of the brain to fully develop, and it may not be fully developed until a person is twenty-five years old.

The U.S. Supreme Court, in a series of cases beginning in 2005, examined what is different in terms of the juvenile brain and what this should mean in terms of how juveniles are sentenced in the United States. In 2005 the U.S. Supreme Court, in *Roper v. Simmons*, prohibited the execution of defendants who were juveniles at the time they committed their crime. In 2010, the U.S. Supreme Court, in *Graham v. Florida*, held that juveniles could not be sentenced to life in prison without the possibility of parole for non-homicide offenses. In 2012, the U.S. Supreme Court, in *Miller v. Alabama*, held that it was unconstitutional to sentence a defendant to a mandatory term of life in prison without parole if the offense was committed when the defendant was under the age of eighteen years old. As you will read, these opinions all discuss the cognitive development of juveniles and the impact this should have on their punishment. You should also consider what this might mean for the juvenile legal system beyond sentencing questions. If juveniles process information differently, and understand language differently, should the process itself be different than adults?

After reviewing the Supreme Court caselaw, this chapter will next examine what impact our increased understanding of juvenile cognitive development might have

1. Malcolm Ritter, *Experts link teen brains' immaturity, juvenile crime*, https://www.commonlit.org/en/texts/experts-link-teen-brains-immaturity-juvenile-crime.

on how we handle juveniles in the criminal legal system. This chapter will consider whether the Supreme Court's analysis can have, or should have, wider application. For example, do these cases demand changes in juvenile plea bargaining? But before reading the cases, it is useful to have a small introduction to the brain science and what we understand about the adolescent brain.

I. Introduction to Neuroscience and the Juvenile Brain

Lorelei Laird, *States Raising Age for Adult Prosecution Back to 18*

ABA Journal (Feb. 2017)

As Dr. Judith Edersheim, co-director of the Center for Law, Brain and Behavior at the Massachusetts General Hospital, explains it, there are three widely agreed-upon differences between adult brains and adolescent brains. One is that during adolescence, kids actually lose "gray matter," the brain cells that do all of the brain's computation. This "pruning" of gray matter is especially concentrated in the frontal lobes, which are responsible for self-control, planning, decision-making and other executive functions.

At the same time, Edersheim says, teenagers get more "white matter," the cells that pass messages between parts of the brain, which increases processing speed. Scientists think these two changes make the brain more efficient, even though it also loses some computational ability. This process of brain maturation continues after the body matures; some scientists think it ends as late as age 25.

But perhaps the most conspicuous difference, Edersheim says, is that adolescent brains have more circulating dopamine—a neutrotransmitter that scientists believe governs rewards and learning—and more receptors in their brains to pick it up. Dopamine is released when a person receives many kinds of rewards, including new experiences, as well as things such as food and sex. This predisposes teenagers to seek out rewards and novelty.

The thinking, Edersheim says, is that this helps push adolescents out of the nest and into the world. And what kids learn during this process, she says, helps determine what parts of the gray matter get pruned. That means a kid's environment matters a lot, and adult prison isn't the best environment.

"If you don't provide an adolescent with an opportunity to develop a social competency or self-esteem, if you don't put them in contact with pro-social peers, then you're setting trajectories which actually might persist through adulthood," Edersheim says. "Adolescents are really these neurologic sponges for their environment."

That's the science that's helping fuel the "kids are different" conversation Levick mentions. But at the same time, Levick says, that conversation is being driven by another discussion the country is having about justice reform generally. And that's very much a bipartisan conversation.

"Conservatives were the ones who stepped forward most recently and said, 'This is becoming fiscally irresponsible, to take what are now increasingly limited public resources and ... lock up a population that doesn't really pose a safety risk,'" says Levick, who co-founded the Juvenile Law Center in 1975. "And I think once conservatives began putting that message out there, liberals and progressives were more than happy to join in."

Dianna Muldrow, a policy analyst at the conservative policy organization Right on Crime, says it's about more than money—it's about creating better outcomes, for society as well as for teenagers. Three decades of research have consistently shown higher recidivism rates for teenagers sent to adult prison. For example, a 2007 review of studies by the Centers for Disease Control and Prevention found that the kids who served time in adult prison were 34 percent more likely to commit new crimes than similar kids who went to juvenile detention.

Outcomes for the kids themselves are also bad. According to the Campaign for Youth Justice, which used Department of Justice and CDC numbers, teens under 18 being held in adult jails are 19 times more likely to commit suicide than teens generally, and 36 times more likely than those held in juvenile facilities. The Bureau of Justice Statistics says youths under 18 were 21 percent of those sexually assaulted in adult jails in 2005, despite being only 1 percent of jail inmates that year.

Muldrow also notes that when teens are treated as adults, there's no requirement for the police to notify the parents. Treating kids as kids helps keep their parents involved.

***

II. The Supreme Court Cases

Unlike some of the other processes you have read about in this book, juvenile cases that are adjudicated in the juvenile system are closer to adult trial processes and are not done through an informal process with few rules or laws. Overall, how the juvenile legal system works has been shaped by Supreme Court cases. In the last chapter, you read about *In re Gault* and its importance in changing juvenile practice by requiring due process protections for juveniles within juvenile adjudication. More recently, the Supreme Court decided a series of cases, often referred to as the *Miller* Trilogy, which mandate a different approach to juvenile sentencing. The following excerpts of Supreme Court cases are included so you can get a sense of how the Supreme Court has changed its thinking and embraced the evolving science around brain development in these legal decisions. Each of the following cases has been edited to focus on the questions of whether juveniles are different and what impact this can or should have on how they are treated within the criminal legal system. You should consider whether these cases could have implications beyond sentencing, including implications for how juvenile cases are processed within the criminal legal system.

Roper v. Simmons

543 U.S. 551, 555, 556–57, 557–59, 560, 568,
569–70, 571–72, 574, 578–79(2005)

KENNEDY, J., delivered the opinion of the Court, in which STEVENS, SOUTER, GINSBURG, and BREYER, JJ., joined. STEVENS, J., filed a concurring opinion, in which GINSBURG, J., joined. O'CONNOR, J., filed a dissenting opinion, *post,* p. 1206. SCALIA, J., filed a dissenting opinion, in which REHNQUIST, C.J., and THOMAS, J., joined.

Justice KENNEDY delivered the opinion of the Court.

....

I.

At the age of 17, when he was still a junior in high school, Christopher Simmons, the respondent here, committed murder. About nine months later, after he had turned 18, he was tried and sentenced to death. There is little doubt that Simmons was the instigator of the crime. Before its commission Simmons said he wanted to murder someone. In chilling, callous terms he talked about his plan, discussing it for the most part with two friends, Charles Benjamin and John Tessmer, then aged 15 and 16 respectively. Simmons proposed to commit burglary and murder by breaking and entering, tying up a victim, and throwing the victim off a bridge. Simmons assured his friends they could "get away with it" because they were minors.

The three met at about 2 a.m. on the night of the murder, but Tessmer left before the other two set out. (The State later charged Tessmer with conspiracy, but dropped the charge in exchange for his testimony against Simmons.) Simmons and Benjamin entered the home of the victim, Shirley Crook, after reaching through an open window and unlocking the back door. Simmons turned on a hallway light. Awakened, Mrs. Crook called out, "Who's there?" In response Simmons entered Mrs. Crook's bedroom, where he recognized her from a previous car accident involving them both. Simmons later admitted this confirmed his resolve to murder her.

Using duct tape to cover her eyes and mouth and bind her hands, the two perpetrators put Mrs. Crook in her minivan and drove to a state park. They reinforced the bindings, covered her head with a towel, and walked her to a railroad trestle spanning the Meramec River. There they tied her hands and feet together with electrical wire, wrapped her whole face in duct tape and threw her from the bridge, drowning her in the waters below....

The next day, after receiving information of Simmons' involvement, police arrested him at his high school and took him to the police station in Fenton, Missouri. They read him his *Miranda* rights. Simmons waived his right to an attorney and agreed to answer questions. After less than two hours of interrogation, Simmons confessed to the murder and agreed to perform a videotaped reenactment at the crime scene.

The State charged Simmons with burglary, kidnaping, stealing, and murder in the first degree. As Simmons was 17 at the time of the crime, he was outside the criminal jurisdiction of Missouri's juvenile court system. See Mo.Rev.Stat. §§ 211.021 (2000) and 211.031 (Supp.2003). He was tried as an adult. At trial the State introduced Simmons' confession and the videotaped reenactment of the crime, along with testimony that Simmons discussed the crime in advance and bragged about it later. The defense called no witnesses in the guilt phase. The jury having returned a verdict of murder, the trial proceeded to the penalty phase.

The State sought the death penalty. As aggravating factors, the State submitted that the murder was committed for the purpose of receiving money; was committed for the purpose of avoiding, interfering with, or preventing lawful arrest of the defendant; and involved depravity of mind and was outrageously and wantonly vile, horrible, and inhuman. The State called Shirley Crook's husband, daughter, and two sisters, who presented moving evidence of the devastation her death had brought to their lives.

In mitigation Simmons' attorneys first called an officer of the Missouri juvenile justice system, who testified that Simmons had no prior convictions and that no previous charges had been filed against him. Simmons' mother, father, two younger half brothers, a neighbor, and a friend took the stand to tell the jurors of the close relationships they had formed with Simmons and to plead for mercy on his behalf. Simmons' mother, in particular, testified to the responsibility Simmons demonstrated in taking care of his two younger half brothers and of his grandmother and to his capacity to show love for them.

During closing arguments, both the prosecutor and defense counsel addressed Simmons' age, which the trial judge had instructed the jurors they could consider as a mitigating factor. Defense counsel reminded the jurors that juveniles of Simmons' age cannot drink, serve on juries, or even see certain movies, because "the legislatures have wisely decided that individuals of a certain age aren't responsible enough." Defense counsel argued that Simmons' age should make "a huge difference to [the jurors] in deciding just exactly what sort of punishment to make." In rebuttal, the prosecutor gave the following response: "Age, he says. Think about age. Seventeen years old. Isn't that scary? Doesn't that scare you? Mitigating? Quite the contrary I submit. Quite the contrary."

The jury recommended the death penalty after finding the State had proved each of the three aggravating factors submitted to it. Accepting the jury's recommendation, the trial judge imposed the death penalty.

Simmons obtained new counsel, who moved in the trial court to set aside the conviction and sentence. One argument was that Simmons had received ineffective assistance at trial. To support this contention, the new counsel called as witnesses Simmons' trial attorney, Simmons' friends and neighbors, and clinical psychologists who had evaluated him.

Part of the submission was that Simmons was "very immature," "very impulsive," and "very susceptible to being manipulated or influenced." The experts testified about Simmons' background including a difficult home environment and dramatic changes in behavior, accompanied by poor school performance in adolescence. Simmons was absent from home for long periods, spending time using alcohol and drugs with other teenagers or young adults. The contention by Simmons' postconviction counsel was that these matters should have been established in the sentencing proceeding....

We granted certiorari, 540 U.S. 1160, 124 S.Ct. 1171, 157 L.Ed.2d 1204 (2004), and now affirm.

III. B.

... A majority of States have rejected the imposition of the death penalty on juvenile offenders under 18, and we now hold this is required by the Eighth Amendment....

Three general differences between juveniles under 18 and adults demonstrate that juvenile offenders cannot with reliability be classified among the worst offenders. First, as any parent knows and as the scientific and sociological studies respondent and his *amici* cite tend to confirm, "[a] lack of maturity and an underdeveloped sense of responsibility are found in youth more often than in adults and are more understandable among the young. These qualities often result in impetuous and ill-considered actions and decisions." *Johnson* [*v. Texas*, 509 U.S.] at 367, 113 S.Ct. 2658 [(1993)]; see also *Eddings* [*v. Oklahoma*, 455 U.S.] at 115–116, 102 S.Ct. 869 [(1982)] ("Even the normal 16-year-old customarily lacks the maturity of an adult"). It has been noted that "adolescents are overrepresented statistically in virtually every category of reckless behavior." Arnett, *Reckless Behavior in Adolescence: A Developmental Perspective*, 12 Developmental Rev. 339 (1992). In recognition of the comparative immaturity and irresponsibility of juveniles, almost every State prohibits those under 18 years of age from voting, serving on juries, or marrying without parental consent. See Appendixes B–D, *infra*.

The second area of difference is that juveniles are more vulnerable or susceptible to negative influences and outside pressures, including peer pressure. *Eddings*, *supra*, at 115, 102 S.Ct. 869 ("[Y]outh is more than a chronological fact. It is a time and condition of life when a person may be most susceptible to influence and to psychological damage"). This is explained in part by the prevailing circumstance that juveniles have less control, or less experience with control, over their own environment. See Steinberg & Scott, *Less Guilty by Reason of Adolescence: Developmental Immaturity, Diminished Responsibility, and the Juvenile Death Penalty*, 58 Am. Psychologist 1009, 1014 (2003) (hereinafter Steinberg & Scott) ("[A]s legal minors, [juveniles] lack the freedom that adults have to extricate themselves from a criminogenic setting").

The third broad difference is that the character of a juvenile is not as well formed as that of an adult. The personality traits of juveniles are more transitory, less fixed. See generally E. Erikson, Identity: Youth and Crisis (1968).

These differences render suspect any conclusion that a juvenile falls among the worst offenders. The susceptibility of juveniles to immature and irresponsible behavior means "their irresponsible conduct is not as morally reprehensible as that of an adult." *Thompson* [*v. Oklahoma*, 487 U.S.] at 835, 108 S.Ct. 2687 [(1988)] (plurality opinion). Their own vulnerability and comparative lack of control over their immediate surroundings mean juveniles have a greater claim than adults to be forgiven for failing to escape negative influences in their whole environment. See *Stanford* [*v. Kentucky*], 492 U.S., at 395, 109 S.Ct. 2969 [(1989)] (Brennan, J., dissenting). The reality that juveniles still struggle to define their identity means it is less supportable to conclude that even a heinous crime committed by a juvenile is evidence of irretrievably depraved character. From a moral standpoint it would be misguided to equate the failings of a minor with those of an adult, for a greater possibility exists that a minor's character deficiencies will be reformed. Indeed, "[t]he relevance of youth as a mitigating factor derives from the fact that the signature qualities of youth are transient; as individuals mature, the impetuousness and recklessness that may dominate in younger years can subside." *Johnson, supra,* at 368, 113 S.Ct. 2658; see also Steinberg & Scott 1014 ("For most teens, [risky or antisocial] behaviors are fleeting; they cease with maturity as individual identity becomes settled. Only a relatively small proportion of adolescents who experiment in risky or illegal activities develop entrenched patterns of problem behavior that persist into adulthood")....

Once the diminished culpability of juveniles is recognized, it is evident that the penological justifications for the death penalty apply to them with lesser force than to adults. We have held there are two distinct social purposes served by the death penalty: "'retribution and deterrence of capital crimes by prospective offenders.'" *Atkins* [*v. Virginia*], 536 U.S., at 319, 122 S.Ct. 2242 [(2002)].... As for retribution, we remarked in *Atkins* that "[i]f the culpability of the average murderer is insufficient to justify the most extreme sanction available to the State, the lesser culpability of the mentally retarded offender surely does not merit that form of retribution." 536 U.S., at 319, 122 S.Ct. 2242. The same conclusions follow from the lesser culpability of the juvenile offender. Whether viewed as an attempt to express the community's moral outrage or as an attempt to right the balance for the wrong to the victim, the case for retribution is not as strong with a minor as with an adult. Retribution is not proportional if the law's most severe penalty is imposed on one whose culpability or blameworthiness is diminished, to a substantial degree, by reason of youth and immaturity.

As for deterrence, it is unclear whether the death penalty has a significant or even measurable deterrent effect on juveniles, as counsel for petitioner acknowledged at oral argument. Tr. of Oral Arg. 48. In general we leave to legislatures the assessment of the efficacy of various criminal penalty schemes, see *Harmelin v. Michigan,* 501 U.S. 957, 998–999, 111 S.Ct. 2680, 115 L.Ed.2d 836 (1991).... Here, however, the absence of evidence of deterrent effect is of special concern because the same characteristics that render juveniles less culpable than adults suggest as well that juveniles will be less susceptible to deterrence. In particular, as the plurality observed in *Thompson,* "[t]he likelihood that the teenage offender has made the kind of cost-benefit analysis that attaches any weight to the possibility of execution is so remote as to be virtually nonexistent." 487 U.S., at 837, 108 S.Ct. 2687. To the extent the juvenile death penalty might have residual deterrent effect, it is worth noting that the punishment of life imprisonment without the possibility of parole is itself a severe sanction, in particular for a young person....

Drawing the line at 18 years of age is subject, of course, to the objections always raised against categorical rules. The qualities that distinguish juveniles from adults do not disappear when an individual turns 18. By the same token, some under 18 have already attained a level of maturity some adults will never reach. For the reasons we have discussed, however, a line must be drawn.... The age of 18 is the point where society draws the line for many purposes between childhood and adulthood. It is, we conclude, the age at which the line for death eligibility ought to rest....

The Eighth and Fourteenth Amendments forbid imposition of the death penalty on offenders who were under the age of 18 when their crimes were committed. The judgment of the Missouri Supreme Court setting aside the sentence of death imposed upon Christopher Simmons is affirmed.

It is so ordered.

Notes/Questions

1. In *Roper*, the Court stated that it has held "there are two distinct social purposes served by the death penalty: 'retribution and deterrence of capital crimes by prospective offenders.'" As a prosecutor, does life in prison without possibility of parole meet these purposes?

2. Before the Court decided *Roper*, 72 defendants were on death row in the United States for crimes they committed before they were 18 years old. All of those defendants were entitled to resentencing. An additional twenty-two people who committed their crimes when they were juveniles were executed after the death penalty was reimposed in 1976, and before *Roper* was decided—approximately 2% of all executions in that period. As with other punishments, minorities were disproportionately impacted: eleven of the twenty-two executions were of African Americans, one was Latino and ten were white. One was sixteen at the time he committed the crime; the rest were seventeen.

3. The Court in *Roper* questioned whether there was an "objective indicia of consensus" in terms of how many states allowed juveniles to be executed. The Court found that a majority did not allow juveniles to be subject to the death penalty and that those who did allow it, rarely used it. Thus "evolving standards of decency" supported the Court's holding that the Eighth Amendment prohibits capital punishment for juveniles. *Roper v. Simmons*, 543 U.S. 551, 564–68 (2005).

Graham v. Florida

560 U.S. 48, 52–58, 68–69, 69–70, 70–71,
72, 72, 73, 74–75, 82 (2010)

KENNEDY, J., delivered the opinion of the Court, in which Justices STEVENS, GINSBURG, SOTOMAYOR and CHIEF JUSTICE ROBERTS joined. Justice STEVENS filed a concurring opinion in which Justices GINSBERG and SOTOMAYOR joined. CHIEF JUSTICE ROBERTS filed a concurring opinion. Justice THOMAS filed a dissenting opinion in which Justice Scalia joined, and which Justice Alito joined in part. Justice Alito filed a dissenting opinion.

Justice Kennedy delivered the opinion of the Court.

The issue before the Court is whether the Constitution permits a juvenile offender to be sentenced to life in prison without parole for a nonhomicide crime. The sentence was imposed by the State of Florida. Petitioner challenges the sentence under the Eighth Amendment's Cruel and Unusual Punishments Clause, made applicable to the States by the Due Process Clause of the Fourteenth Amendment. *Robinson v. California*, 370 U.S. 660, 82 S.Ct. 1417, 8 L.Ed.2d 758 (1962).

I

Petitioner is Terrance Jamar Graham. He was born on January 6, 1987. Graham's parents were addicted to crack cocaine, and their drug use persisted in his early years. Graham was diagnosed with attention deficit hyperactivity disorder in elementary school. He began drinking alcohol and using tobacco at age 9 and smoked marijuana at age 13.

In July 2003, when Graham was age 16, he and three other school-age youths attempted to rob a barbeque restaurant in Jacksonville, Florida. One youth, who worked at the restaurant, left the back door unlocked just before closing time. Graham and another youth, wearing masks, entered through the unlocked door. Graham's masked accomplice twice struck the restaurant manager in the back of the head with a metal bar. When the manager started yelling at the assailant and Graham, the two youths ran out and escaped in a car driven by the third accomplice. The restaurant manager required stitches for his head injury. No money was taken.

Graham was arrested for the robbery attempt. Under Florida law, it is within a prosecutor's discretion whether to charge 16- and 17-year-olds as adults or juveniles for most felony crimes. Fla. Stat. § 985.227(1)(b) (2003) (subsequently renumbered at § 985.557(1)(b) (2007)). Graham's prosecutor elected to charge Graham as an adult. The charges against Graham were armed burglary with assault or battery, a first-degree felony carrying a maximum penalty of life imprisonment without the possibility of parole, §§ 810.02(1)(b), (2)(a) (2003); and attempted armed-robbery, a second-degree felony carrying a maximum penalty of 15 years' imprisonment, §§ 812.13(2)(b), 777.04(1), (4)(a), 775.082(3)(c).

On December 18, 2003, Graham pleaded guilty to both charges under a plea agreement. Graham wrote a letter to the trial court. After reciting "this is my first and last time getting in trouble," he continued "I've decided to turn my life around." App. 379–380. Graham said "I made a promise to God and myself that if I get a second chance, I'm going to do whatever it takes to get to the [National Football League]." *Id.*, at 380.

The trial court accepted the plea agreement. The court withheld adjudication of guilt as to both charges and sentenced Graham to concurrent 3-year terms of probation. Graham was required to spend the first 12 months of his probation in the county jail, but he received credit for the time he had served awaiting trial, and was released on June 25, 2004.

Less than 6 months later, on the night of December 2, 2004, Graham again was arrested. The State's case was as follows: Earlier that evening, Graham participated in a home invasion robbery. His two accomplices were Meigo Bailey and Kirkland Lawrence, both 20-year-old men. According to the State, at 7 p.m. that night, Graham, Bailey, and Lawrence knocked on the door of the home where Carlos Rodriguez lived. Graham, followed by Bailey and Lawrence, forcibly entered the home and held a pistol to Rodriguez's chest. For the next 30 minutes, the three held Rodriguez and another man, a friend of Rodriguez, at gunpoint while they ransacked the home searching for money. Before leaving, Graham and his accomplices barricaded Rodriguez and his friend inside a closet.

The State further alleged that Graham, Bailey, and Lawrence, later the same evening, attempted a second robbery, during which Bailey was shot. Graham, who had borrowed his father's car, drove Bailey and Lawrence to the hospital and left them there. As Graham drove away, a police sergeant signaled him to stop. Graham continued at a high speed but crashed into a telephone pole. He tried to flee on foot but was apprehended. Three handguns were found in his car.

When detectives interviewed Graham, he denied involvement in the crimes. He said he encountered Bailey and Lawrence only after Bailey had been shot. One of the detectives told Graham that the victims of the home invasion had identified him. He asked Graham, "Aside from the two robberies tonight how many more were you involved in?" Graham responded, "Two to three before tonight." *Id.*, at 160. The night that Graham allegedly committed the robbery, he was 34 days short of his 18th birthday.

On December 13, 2004, Graham's probation officer filed with the trial court an affidavit asserting that Graham had violated the conditions of his probation by possessing a firearm, committing crimes, and associating with persons engaged in criminal activity. The trial court held hearings on Graham's violations about a year later, in December 2005 and January 2006. The judge who presided was not the same judge who had accepted Graham's guilty plea to the earlier offenses.

Graham maintained that he had no involvement in the home invasion robbery; but, even after the court underscored that the admission could expose him to a life sentence on the earlier charges, he admitted violating probation conditions by fleeing. The State presented evidence related to the home invasion, including testimony from the victims. The trial court noted that Graham, in admitting his attempt to avoid arrest, had acknowledged violating his probation. The court further found that Graham had violated his probation by committing a home invasion robbery, by possessing a firearm, and by associating with persons engaged in criminal activity.

The trial court held a sentencing hearing. Under Florida law the minimum sentence Graham could receive absent a downward departure by the judge was 5 years' imprisonment. The maximum was life imprisonment. Graham's attorney requested

Does Environment Matter?

Terrence Graham's grandmother gave birth to his mother when she was twelve years old. His mother grew up in a poor and abusive household. All of her brothers (Terrence's uncles) served time in prison. His grandmother was addicted to drugs and died at the age of 44. Terrence's mother was also addicted to drugs, and although she disputes using crack while she was pregnant with Terrence, she did use it during Terrence's childhood, in addition to her heavy drinking. His mother raised her children in the same environment she knew: poverty and violence. "Hunger was a constant struggle" and utilities were cut off when bills weren't paid. Terrence's mother "repeatedly told him that she was sorry she'd ever given birth to him, that he was a motherf***er and a son of a bitch, and that he would amount to nothing." He was also regularly and harshly beaten, and despite child welfare being aware of these conditions, no action was taken. Terrence was diagnosed with Attention Deficit Hyperactivity Disorder in the second grade, but his mother did not allow him to take medication. Terrence began drinking alcohol in the 4th grade, and starting smoking marijuana at 13 years old. Do these conditions support that Terrence Graham had a "great opportunity" that he had "thrown away"? Should this background have been considered by the sentencing judge?

Cara H. Drinan, The War on Kids: How American Juvenile Justice Lost Its Way 26–29 (Oxford, 2018).

the minimum nondeparture sentence of 5 years. A presentence report prepared by the Florida Department of Corrections recommended that Graham receive an even lower sentence—at most 4 years' imprisonment. The State recommended that Graham receive 30 years on the armed burglary count and 15 years on the attempted armed robbery count.

After hearing Graham's testimony, the trial court explained the sentence it was about to pronounce:

> "Mr. Graham, as I look back on your case, yours is really candidly a sad situation. You had, as far as I can tell, you have quite a family structure. You had a lot of people who wanted to try and help you get your life turned around including the court system, and you had a judge who took the step to try and give you direction through his probation order to give you a chance to get back onto track. And at the time you seemed through your letters that that is exactly what you wanted to do. And I don't know why it is that you threw your life away. I don't know why.
>
> "But you did, and that is what is so sad about this today is that you have actually been given a chance to get through this, the original charge, which

were very serious charges to begin with.... The attempted robbery with a weapon was a very serious charge....

"[I]n a very short period of time you were back before the Court on a violation of this probation, and then here you are two years later standing before me, literally the—facing a life sentence as to—up to life as to count 1 and up to 15 years as to count 2.

"And I don't understand why you would be given such a great opportunity to do something with your life and why you would throw it away. The only thing that I can rationalize is that you decided that this is how you were going to lead your life and that there is nothing that we can do for you. And as the state pointed out, that this is an escalating pattern of criminal conduct on your part and that we can't help you any further. We can't do anything to deter you. This is the way you are going to lead your life, and I don't know why you are going to. You've made that decision. I have no idea. But, evidently, that is what you decided to do.

"So then it becomes a focus, if I can't do anything to help you, if I can't do anything to get you back on the right path, then I have to start focusing on the community and trying to protect the community from your actions. And, unfortunately, that is where we are today is I don't see where I can do anything to help you any further. You've evidently decided this is the direction you're going to take in life, and it's unfortunate that you made that choice.

"I have reviewed the statute. I don't see where any further juvenile sanctions would be appropriate. I don't see where any youthful offender sanctions would be appropriate. Given your escalating pattern of criminal conduct, it is apparent to the Court that you have decided that this is the way you are going to live your life and that the only thing I can do now is to try and protect the community from your actions." *Id.*, at 392–394.

The trial court found Graham guilty of the earlier armed burglary and attempted armed robbery charges. It sentenced him to the maximum sentence authorized by law on each charge: life imprisonment for the armed burglary and 15 years for the attempted armed robbery. Because Florida has abolished its parole system, see Fla. Stat. § 921.002(1)(e) (2003), a life sentence gives a defendant no possibility of release unless he is granted executive clemency.

Graham filed a motion in the trial court challenging his sentence under the Eighth Amendment. The motion was deemed denied after the trial court failed to rule on it within 60 days. The First District Court of Appeal of Florida affirmed, concluding that Graham's sentence was not grossly disproportionate to his crimes. 982 So.2d 43 (2008). The court took note of the seriousness of Graham's offenses and their violent nature, as well as the fact that they "were not committed by a pre-teen, but a seventeen-year-old who was ultimately sentenced at the age of nineteen." *Id.*, at 52. The court concluded further that Graham was incapable of rehabilitation. Although Graham "was given an unheard of probationary sentence for a life felony, ... wrote a letter expressing his remorse and promising to refrain from the commission of further crime, and ... had a strong family structure to support him," the court noted, he "rejected his second chance and chose to continue committing crimes at an escalating pace." *Ibid.* The Florida Supreme Court denied review. 990 So.2d 1058, 2008 WL 3896182 (2008) (table).

We granted certiorari....

III.B.

....

Roper established that because juveniles have lessened culpability they are less deserving of the most severe punishments. 543 U.S., at 569, 125 S.Ct. 1183. As compared to adults, juveniles have a "'lack of maturity and an underdeveloped sense of responsibility'"; they "are more vulnerable or susceptible to negative influences and outside pressures, including peer pressure"; and their characters are "not as well formed." *Id.*, at 569–570, 125 S.Ct. 1183. These salient characteristics mean that "[i]t is difficult even for expert psychologists to differentiate between the juvenile offender whose crime reflects unfortunate yet transient immaturity, and the rare juvenile offender whose crime reflects irreparable corruption." *Id.*, at 573, 125 S.Ct. 1183. Accordingly, "juvenile offenders cannot with reliability be classified among the worst offenders." *Id.*, at 569, 125 S.Ct. 1183. A juvenile is not absolved of responsibility for his actions, but his transgression "is not as morally reprehensible as that of an adult." *Thompson*, supra, at 835, 108 S.Ct. 2687 (plurality opinion).

No recent data provide reason to reconsider the Court's observations in *Roper* about the nature of juveniles. As petitioner's amici point out, developments in psychology and brain science continue to show fundamental differences between juvenile and adult minds. For example, parts of the brain involved in behavior control continue to mature through late adolescence. See Brief for American Medical Association et al. as Amici Curiae 16–24; Brief for American Psychological Association et al. as Amici Curiae 22–27. Juveniles are more capable of change than are adults, and their actions are less likely to be evidence of "irretrievably depraved character" than are the actions of adults. *Roper*, 543 U.S., at 570, 125 S.Ct. 1183. It remains true that "[f]rom a moral standpoint it would be misguided to equate the failings of a minor with those of an adult, for a greater possibility exists that a minor's character deficiencies will be reformed." *Ibid.* These matters relate to the status of the offenders in question; and it is relevant to consider next the nature of the offenses to which this harsh penalty might apply.

The Court has recognized that defendants who do not kill, intend to kill, or foresee that life will be taken are categorically less deserving of the most serious forms of punishment than are murderers....

It follows that, when compared to an adult murderer, a juvenile offender who did not kill or intend to kill has a twice diminished moral culpability. The age of the offender and the nature of the crime each bear on the analysis.

As for the punishment, life without parole is "the second most severe penalty permitted by law." *Harmelin* [*v. Michigan*], 501 U.S., at 1001, 111 S.Ct. 2680 [(1991)] (opinion of Kennedy, J.). It is true that a death sentence is "unique in its severity and irrevocability," *Gregg v. Georgia*, 428 U.S. 153, 187, 96 S.Ct. 2909, 49 L.Ed.2d 859 (1976) (joint opinion of Stewart, Powell, and Stevens, JJ.); yet life without parole sentences share some characteristics with death sentences that are shared by no other sentences. The State does not execute the offender sentenced to life without parole, but the sentence alters the offender's life by a forfeiture that is irrevocable. It deprives the convict of the most basic liberties without giving hope of restoration, except perhaps by executive clemency—the remote possibility of which does not mitigate the harshness of the sentence. *Solem* [*v. Helm*], 463 U.S., at 300–301, 103 S.Ct. 3001 [(1983)]. As one court observed in overturning a life without parole sentence for a juvenile defendant, this sentence "means denial of hope; it means that good behavior and character improvement are immaterial; it means that whatever the future might hold in store for the mind and spirit of [the convict], he will remain in prison for the rest of his days." *Naovarath v. State*, 105 Nev. 525, 526, 779 P.2d 944 (1989)....

Life without parole is an especially harsh punishment for a juvenile. Under this sentence a juvenile offender will on average serve more years and a greater percentage of his life in prison than an adult offender. A 16-year-old and a 75-year-old each sentenced to life without parole receive the same punishment in name only. See *Roper*, supra, at 572, 125 S.Ct. 1183; cf. *Harmelin*, supra, at 996, 111 S.Ct. 2680 ("In some cases ... there will be negligible difference between life without parole and other sentences of imprisonment—for example, ... a lengthy term sentence without eligibility for parole, given to a 65-year-old man"). This reality cannot be ignored.

The penological justifications for the sentencing practice are also relevant to the analysis.... A sentence lacking any legitimate penological justification is by its nature disproportionate to the offense. With respect to life without parole for juvenile nonhomicide offenders, none of the goals of penal sanctions that have been recognized as legitimate—retribution, deterrence, incapacitation, and rehabilitation, see *Ewing* [*v. California*], 538 U.S., at 25, 123 S.Ct. 1179 [(2003)] (plurality opinion)—provides an adequate justification.

Retribution is a legitimate reason to punish, but it cannot support the sentence at issue here....

Deterrence does not suffice to justify the sentence either....

Incapacitation, a third legitimate reason for imprisonment, does not justify the life without parole sentence in question here....

Here one cannot dispute that this defendant posed an immediate risk, for he had committed, we can assume, serious crimes early in his term of supervised release and despite his own assurances of reform. Graham deserved to be separated from society for some time in order to prevent what the trial court described as an "escalating pattern of criminal conduct," App. 394, but it does not follow that he would be a risk to society for the rest of his life. Even if the State's judgment that Graham was incorrigible were later corroborated by prison misbehavior or failure to mature, the sentence was still disproportionate because that judgment was made at the outset. A life without parole sentence improperly denies the juvenile offender a chance to demonstrate growth and maturity. Incapacitation cannot override all other considerations, lest the Eighth Amendment's rule against disproportionate sentences be a nullity.

Finally there is rehabilitation, a penological goal that forms the basis of parole systems.…

A sentence of life imprisonment without parole, however, cannot be justified by the goal of rehabilitation. The penalty forswears altogether the rehabilitative ideal. By denying the defendant the right to reenter the community, the State makes an irrevocable judgment about that person's value and place in society. This judgment is not appropriate in light of a juvenile nonhomicide offender's capacity for change and limited moral culpability. A State's rejection of rehabilitation, moreover, goes beyond a mere expressive judgment. As one amicus notes, defendants serving life without parole sentences are often denied access to vocational training and other rehabilitative services that are available to other inmates. See Brief for Sentencing Project as Amicus Curiae 11–13. For juvenile offenders, who are most in need of and receptive to rehabilitation, see Brief for J. Lawrence Aber et al. as Amici Curiae 28–31 (hereinafter Aber Brief), the absence of rehabilitative opportunities or treatment makes the disproportionality of the sentence all the more evident.

In sum, penological theory is not adequate to justify life without parole for juvenile nonhomicide offenders. This determination; the limited culpability of juvenile non-homicide offenders; and the severity of life without parole sentences all lead to the conclusion that the sentencing practice under consideration is cruel and unusual. This Court now holds that for a juvenile offender who did not commit homicide the Eighth Amendment forbids the sentence of life without parole. This clear line is necessary to prevent the possibility that life without parole sentences will be imposed on juvenile nonhomicide offenders who are not sufficiently culpable to merit that punishment. Because "[t]he age of 18 is the point where society draws the line for many purposes between childhood and adulthood," those who were below that age when the offense was committed may not be sentenced to life without parole for a nonhomicide crime. *Roper*, 543 U.S., at 574, 125 S.Ct. 1183.

A State is not required to guarantee eventual freedom to a juvenile offender convicted of a nonhomicide crime. What the State must do, however, is give defendants like Graham some meaningful opportunity to obtain release based on demonstrated maturity and rehabilitation. It is for the State, in the first instance, to explore the means and mechanisms for compliance. It bears emphasis, however, that while the Eighth Amendment forbids a State from imposing a life without parole sentence on a juvenile nonhomicide offender, it does not require the State to release that offender during his natural life. Those who commit truly horrifying crimes as juveniles may turn out to be irredeemable, and thus deserving of incarceration for the duration of their lives. The Eighth Amendment does not foreclose the possibility that persons convicted of nonhomicide crimes committed before adulthood will remain behind bars for life. It does forbid States from making the judgment at the outset that those offenders never will be fit to reenter society....

The Constitution prohibits the imposition of a life without parole sentence on a juvenile offender who did not commit homicide. A State need not guarantee the offender eventual release, but if it imposes a sentence of life it must provide him or her with some realistic opportunity to obtain release before the end of that term. The judgment of the First District Court of Appeal of Florida is reversed, and the case is remanded for further proceedings not inconsistent with this opinion.

It is so ordered.

Notes/Questions

1. On remand, in 2012, Terrance Graham was sentenced to 25 years in prison by the original sentencing judge. Does remand to the same judge make sense? (Remember the language the judge used in determining that Graham seemed to be without the potential for rehabilitation and note that the Department of Corrections had only recommended 4 years!). Graham was released from prison in March 2024. "Over his 20-year incarceration, Graham earned his GED, took college classes, and found solace in his faith. He's passionate about family, sports, and prison reform. He also co-founded *Plead the 8th*, a nonprofit working to end the incarceration of children in Florida's adult system."[2] Graham described his first months after his release from prison, when he was required to live in a transition house:

> It's me and three other guys. So my family are allowed to come visit me, but I'm not allowed to go and visit them. I have elderly people in my family, such as my grandma who's 91 years old, staying in a nursing home. I just pray daily that I get to see her here in the free world before she passes. I can't leave the house but to go to work and church. I get to go to the store and the barber shop once a week. I have to fill out a weekly report of where I'm going to be and when. Basically, I left one form of confinement for another.
>
> I got my GED in 2008 for my family. I remember at first I was rebellious towards the staff for making me go to school when I wanted to review my case in the law library. They kept writing me disciplinary reports and putting me in the box [solitary confinement]. I turned 21 and then it was my choice to attend school. I was in the box when my first appeal got denied [in 2008] and it felt like I was being sentenced to life all over again. I wrote my mom and brother and they were like, "Please don't give up. Pray and focus on God if you want your freedom!" So that's what made me want to get my GED and enroll into college. I was the first of my mom's kids to graduate and the only child of hers to even enroll into college despite me being in prison. It felt good to be doing

---

2. Charlotte West, *The Supreme Court struck down his sentence 14 years ago. He only just got out now*, SLATE, March 19, 2024.

> something good instead of just being her child that's in prison. I met a lot of good guys in there that will never get a chance to get out here in the free world. So I'm living for them as well.[3]

In Chapter 14 you will read about what might be appropriate punishment for juveniles and you may want to consider Graham's story again in that section.

2. In 2017, both North Carolina and New York increased the age of adulthood in criminal cases to 18 years old. Previously, 16- and 17-year-olds were considered adults in those states. Juveniles can be transferred to adult courts under these new laws, but the default is not to treat all 16- and 17-year-old defendants as adults. Four states in the United States (Georgia, Louisiana, Texas, and Wisconsin), consider 17-year-olds to be adults when they are charged with a crime. In 2017, Louisiana passed a law increasing the age of adulthood from 17 to 18 years old. In 2024 Louisiana reversed course and passed a law returning the age of adulthood to 17 years old. Under a meme on the social media site "X" that declared, "Correct the Age," Louisiana Governor Jeff Landry wrote:

> Today marks the start to a new justice system here in Louisiana. No more will 17-year-olds who commit home invasions, carjack, and rob the great people of our state be treated as children in court. These are criminals and today, they will finally be treated as such.

You may want to consider this statement as you continue reading Supreme Court decisions about how the legal system should treat juveniles in light of the evolving brain science.

3. In 2009, before *Graham* was decided, there were approximately 2300 people serving life without the possibility of parole for offenses committed when they were juveniles.

4. The Supreme Court in *Graham* rejected that "death is different" and applied the reasoning in *Roper* (a death case). In other death cases, the Supreme Court has narrowed their conclusions to application only with death cases. In *Graham*, the Court applied *Roper*'s reasoning in a non-death case, opening the door for even wider application. Terry A. Maroney, *Adolescent Brian Science After Graham v. Florida*, 86 Notre Dame. L. Rev. 765 (2011).

Miller v. Alabama
Jackson v. Hobbs

567 U.S. 460, 465–66, 467–69, 470–71, 471, 477–80, 489 (2012)

Kagan, J., delivered the opinion of the Court, in which Kennedy, Ginsburg, Breyer, and Sotomayor, JJ., joined. Breyer, J., filed a concurring opinion, in which Sotomayor, J., joined. Roberts, C.J., filed a dissenting opinion, in which Scalia, Thomas, and Alito, JJ., joined. Thomas, J., filed a dissenting opinion, in which Scalia, J., joined. Alito, J., filed a dissenting opinion, in which Scalia, J., joined.

---

3. *Id.*

Justice KAGAN delivered the opinion of the Court.

The two 14-year-old offenders in these cases were convicted of murder and sentenced to life imprisonment without the possibility of parole. In neither case did the sentencing authority have any discretion to impose a different punishment. State law mandated that each juvenile die in prison even if a judge or jury would have thought that his youth and its attendant characteristics, along with the nature of his crime, made a lesser sentence (for example, life *with* the possibility of parole) more appropriate. Such a scheme prevents those meting out punishment from considering a juvenile's "lessened culpability" and greater "capacity for change," *Graham v. Florida,* 560 U.S. ___, ___, ___, 130 S.Ct. 2011, 2026–2027, 2029–2030, 176 L.Ed.2d 825 (2010), and runs afoul of our cases' requirement of individualized sentencing for defendants facing the most serious penalties. We therefore hold that mandatory life without parole for those under the age of 18 at the time of their crimes violates the Eighth Amendment's prohibition on "cruel and unusual punishments."

I.A.

In November 1999, petitioner Kuntrell Jackson, then 14 years old, and two other boys decided to rob a video store. En route to the store, Jackson learned that one of the boys, Derrick Shields, was carrying a sawed-off shotgun in his coat sleeve. Jackson decided to stay outside when the two other boys entered the store. Inside, Shields pointed the gun at the store clerk, Laurie Troup, and demanded that she "give up the money." *Jackson v. State,* 359 Ark. 87, 89, 194 S.W.3d 757, 759 (2004) (internal quotation marks omitted). Troup refused. A few moments later, Jackson went into the store to find Shields continuing to demand money. At trial, the parties disputed whether Jackson warned Troup that "[w]e ain't playin'," or instead told his friends, "I thought you all was playin'." *Id.,* at 91, 194 S.W.3d, at 760.... When Troup threatened to call the police, Shields shot and killed her. The three boys fled empty-handed....

Arkansas law gives prosecutors discretion to charge 14-year-olds as adults when they are alleged to have committed certain serious offenses. See Ark.Code Ann. § 9-27-318(c)(2) (1998). The prosecutor here exercised that authority by charging Jackson with capital felony murder and aggravated robbery. Jackson moved to transfer the case to juvenile court, but after considering the alleged facts of the crime, a psychiatrist's examination, and Jackson's juvenile arrest history (shoplifting and several incidents of car theft), the trial court denied the motion, and an appellate court affirmed. See *Jackson v. State,* No. 02-535, 2003 WL 193412, (Ark.App., Jan. 29, 2003); §§ 9-27-318(d), (e). A jury later convicted Jackson of both crimes. Noting that "in view of [the] verdict, there's only one possible punishment," the judge sentenced Jackson to life without parole. App. in No. 10-9647, p. 55 (hereinafter Jackson App.); see Ark.Code Ann. § 5-4-104(b) (1997) ("A defendant convicted of capital murder or treason shall be sentenced to death or life imprisonment without parole"). Jackson did not challenge the sentence on appeal, and the Arkansas Supreme Court affirmed the convictions. See 359 Ark. 87, 194 S.W.3d 757.

....

B.

Like Jackson, petitioner Evan Miller was 14 years old at the time of his crime. Miller had by then been in and out of foster care because his mother suffered from alcoholism and drug addiction and his stepfather abused him. Miller, too, regularly used drugs and alcohol; and he had attempted suicide four times, the first when he was six years old. See *E.J.M. v. State,* 928 So.2d 1077, 1081 (Ala.Crim.App.2004) (Cobb, J., concurring in result); App. in No. 10-9646, pp. 26–28 (hereinafter Miller App.).

One night in 2003, Miller was at home with a friend, Colby Smith, when a neighbor, Cole Cannon, came to make a drug deal with Miller's mother. See 6 Record in No. 10-9646, p. 1004. The two boys followed Cannon back to his trailer, where all three smoked marijuana and played drinking games. When Cannon passed out, Miller stole his wallet, splitting about $300 with Smith. Miller then tried to put the wallet back in Cannon's pocket, but Cannon awoke and grabbed Miller by the throat. Smith hit Cannon with a nearby baseball bat, and once released, Miller grabbed the bat and repeatedly struck Cannon with it. Miller placed a sheet over Cannon's head, told him "'I am God, I've come to take your life,'" and delivered one more blow. *Miller v. State,* 63 So.3d 676, 689 (Ala.Crim.App.2010). The boys then retreated to Miller's trailer, but soon decided to return to Cannon's to cover up evidence of their crime. Once there, they lit two fires. Cannon eventually died from his injuries and smoke inhalation. See *id.,* at 683–685, 689.

Alabama law required that Miller initially be charged as a juvenile, but allowed the District Attorney to seek removal of the case to adult court. See Ala.Code § 12-15-34 (1977). The DA did so, and the juvenile court agreed to the transfer after a hearing. Citing the nature of the crime, Miller's "mental maturity," and his prior juvenile offenses (truancy and "criminal mischief"), the Alabama Court of Criminal Appeals affirmed. *E.J.M. v. State,* No. CR-03-0915, pp. 5–7 (Aug. 27, 2004) (unpublished memorandum). The State accordingly charged Miller as an adult with murder in the course of arson. That crime (like capital murder in Arkansas) carries a mandatory minimum punishment of life without parole. See Ala.Code §§ 13A-5-40(9), 13A-6-2(c) (1982).

Relying in significant part on testimony from Smith, who had pleaded to a lesser offense, a jury found Miller guilty. He was therefore sentenced to life without the possibility of parole. The Alabama Court of Criminal Appeals affirmed, ruling that life without parole was "not overly harsh when compared to the crime" and that the mandatory nature of the sentencing scheme was permissible under the Eighth Amendment. 63 So.3d, at 690; see *id.,* at 686–691. The Alabama Supreme Court denied review....

II

... The cases before us implicate two strands of precedent reflecting our concern with proportionate punishment. The first has adopted categorical bans on sentencing practices based on mismatches between the culpability of a class of offenders and the severity of a penalty. See *Graham,* 560 U.S., at ___, 130 S.Ct., at 2022–2023 (listing cases). So, for example, we have held that imposing the death penalty for nonhomicide crimes against individuals, or imposing it on mentally retarded defendants, violates the Eighth Amendment. See *Kennedy v. Louisiana,* 554 U.S. 407, 128 S.Ct. 2641, 171 L.Ed.2d 525 (2008); *Atkins v. Virginia,* 536 U.S. 304, 122 S.Ct. 2242, 153 L.Ed.2d 335 (2002). Several of the cases in this group have specially focused on juvenile offenders, because of their lesser culpability. Thus, *Roper* held that the Eighth Amendment bars capital punishment for children, and *Graham* concluded that the Amendment also prohibits a sentence of life without the possibility of parole for a child who committed a nonhomicide offense. *Graham* further likened life without parole for juveniles to the death penalty itself, thereby evoking a second line of our precedents. In those cases, we have prohibited mandatory imposition of capital punishment, requiring that sentencing authorities consider the characteristics of a defendant and the details of his offense before sentencing him to death. See *Woodson v. North Carolina,* 428 U.S. 280, 96 S.Ct. 2978, 49 L.Ed.2d 944 (1976) (plurality opinion); *Lockett v. Ohio,* 438 U.S. 586, 98 S.Ct. 2954, 57 L.Ed.2d 973 (1978). Here, the confluence of these two lines of precedent leads to the conclusion that mandatory life-without-parole sentences for juveniles violate the Eighth Amendment.

To start with the first set of cases: *Roper* and *Graham* establish that children are constitutionally different from adults for purposes of sentencing....

Our decisions rested not only on common sense—on what "any parent knows"—but on science and social science as well....

So *Graham* and *Roper* and our individualized sentencing cases alike teach that in imposing a State's harshest penalties, a sentencer misses too much if he treats every child as an adult. To recap: Mandatory life without parole for a juvenile precludes consideration of his chronological age and its hallmark features—among them, immaturity, impetuosity, and failure to appreciate risks and consequences. It prevents taking into account the family and home environment that surrounds him—and from which he cannot usually extricate himself—no matter how brutal or dysfunctional. It neglects the circumstances of the homicide offense, including the extent of his participation in the conduct and the way familial and peer pressures may have affected him. Indeed, it ignores that he might have been charged and convicted of a lesser offense if not for incompetencies associated with youth—for example, his inability to deal with police officers or prosecutors (including on a plea agreement) or his incapacity to assist his own attorneys....

Both cases before us illustrate the problem. Take Jackson's first. As noted earlier, Jackson did not fire the bullet that killed Laurie Troup; nor did the State argue that he intended her death. Jackson's conviction was instead based on an aiding-and-abetting theory; and the appellate court affirmed the verdict only because the jury could have believed that when Jackson entered the store, he warned Troup that "[w]e ain't playin'," rather than told his friends that "I thought you all was playin'." See 359 Ark., at 90–92, 194 S.W.3d, at 759–760; *supra,* at 2461. To be sure, Jackson learned on the way to the video store that his friend Shields was carrying a gun, but his age could well have affected his calculation of the risk that posed, as well as his willingness to walk away at that point. All these circumstances go to Jackson's culpability for the offense. See *Graham,* 560 U.S., at ___, 130 S.Ct., at 2027 ("[W]hen compared to an adult murderer, a juvenile offender who did not kill or intend to kill has a twice diminished moral culpability"). And so too does Jackson's family background and immersion in violence: Both his mother and his grandmother had previously shot other individuals. See Record in No. 10-9647, pp. 80–82. At the least, a sentencer should look at such facts before depriving a 14-year-old of any prospect of release from prison.

That is true also in Miller's case. No one can doubt that he and Smith committed a vicious murder. But they did it when high on drugs and alcohol consumed with the adult victim. And if ever a pathological background might have contributed to a 14-year-old's commission of a crime, it is here. Miller's stepfather physically abused him; his alcoholic and drug-addicted mother neglected him; he had been in and out of foster care as a result; and he had tried to kill himself four times, the first when he should have been in kindergarten. See 928 So.2d, at 1081 (Cobb, J., concurring in result); Miller App. 26–28; *supra,* at 2461–2462. Nonetheless, Miller's past criminal history was limited—two instances of truancy and one of "second-degree criminal mischief." No. CR-03-0915, at 6 (unpublished memorandum). That Miller deserved severe punishment for killing Cole Cannon is beyond question. But once again, a sentencer needed to examine all these circumstances before concluding that life without any possibility of parole was the appropriate penalty.

> The U.S. Supreme Court has yet to rule on cases where juveniles are sentenced to de facto life sentences—sentences that are for such long terms that it is unlikely, or impossible, that the defendant will live long enough to be released. The Sentencing Project estimates that there are 11,745 people serving life or de facto life sentences for offenses committed when they were juveniles. This is 5.7% of the total life population in US Prisons. Of these, 98% are male and 80.4% are people of color.
>
> Ashley Nellis, *Still Life: America's Increasing Use of Life and Long-Term Sentences,* The Sentencing Project, May 3, 2017, available at: https://-americas-increasing-use-life-long-term-sentences/.

We therefore hold that the Eighth Amendment forbids a sentencing scheme that mandates life in prison without possibility of parole for juvenile offenders. Cf. *Graham,* 560 U.S., at ___, 130 S.Ct., at 2030 ("A State is not required to guarantee eventual freedom," but must provide "some meaningful opportunity to obtain release based on demonstrated maturity and rehabilitation"). By making youth (and all that accompanies it) irrelevant to imposition of that harshest prison sentence, such a scheme poses too great a risk of disproportionate punishment. Because that holding is sufficient to decide these cases, we do not consider Jackson's and Miller's alternative argument that the Eighth Amendment requires a categorical bar on life without parole for juveniles, or at least for those 14 and younger. But given all we have said in *Roper, Graham,* and this decision about children's diminished culpability and heightened capacity for change, we think appropriate occasions for sentencing juveniles to this harshest possible penalty will be uncommon. That is especially so because of the great difficulty we noted in *Roper* and *Graham* of distinguishing at this early age between "the juvenile offender whose crime reflects unfortunate yet transient immaturity, and the rare juvenile offender whose crime reflects irreparable corruption." *Roper,* 543 U.S., at 573, 125 S.Ct. 1183; *Graham,* 560 U.S., at ___, 130 S.Ct., at 2026–2027. Although we do not foreclose a sentencer's ability to make that judgment in homicide cases, we require it to take into account how children are different, and how those differences counsel against irrevocably sentencing them to a lifetime in prison....[4]

IV

Graham, Roper, and our individualized sentencing decisions make clear that a judge or jury must have the opportunity to consider mitigating circumstances before imposing the harshest possible penalty for juveniles. By requiring that all children convicted of homicide receive lifetime incarceration without possibility of parole, regardless of their age and age-related characteristics and the nature of their crimes, the mandatory sentencing schemes before us violate this principle of proportionality, and so the Eighth Amendment's ban on cruel and unusual punishment. We accordingly reverse the judgments of the Arkansas Supreme Court and Alabama Court of Criminal Appeals and remand the cases for further proceedings not inconsistent with this opinion.

It is so ordered.

Notes/Questions

1. *Roper*, *Graham*, and *Miller* are now often referred to as the "*Miller* Trilogy" and, "together stand for the proposition that children are different in the eyes of the law."[5]

2. Does the Supreme Court's reliance on the science of brain and cognitive development mean that the juvenile legal system needs to change how it handles juveniles in cases beyond those involving life in prison without parole and the death penalty?

---

4. Where mandatory sentencing does not itself account for the number of juveniles serving life-without-parole terms, the evidence we have of practice supports our holding. Fifteen jurisdictions make life without parole discretionary for juveniles.... According to available data, only about 15% of all juvenile life-without-parole sentences come from those 15 jurisdictions, while 85% come from the 29 mandatory ones.... That figure indicates that when given the choice, sentencers impose life without parole on children relatively rarely. And contrary to The Chief Justice's argument, see *post,* at 2462, n. 2, we have held that when judges and juries do not often choose to impose a sentence, it at least should not be mandatory....

5. Cara H. Drinan, The War on Kids: How American Juvenile Justice Lost Its Way 88 (Oxford 2018).

3. Professor Jenny Carrol suggests that courts should go beyond the narrow application of the evolving brain science to issues of punishment and sentencing and instead re-think mens rea as applied to juveniles:

> As an element, mens rea distinguishes behavior and assigns culpability. To accomplish this goal, mens rea must contemplate the actor's state of mind at the time of her act—not in the abstract but in actuality. It must consider what the defendant thought or understood her actions to mean. Admittedly, this is a complex analysis requiring fact finders to infer and discern mental states from a defendant's actions. In this process, fact finders construct their notions of the defendant's mens rea as much from their own thought processes as from what they know of the defendant's behavior. They anchor their judgment of the defendant's culpability in their own adult decision making processes.
>
> From the perspective of juvenile offenders, this grounding of mens rea in an adult-referenced standard distorts the thought processes that adolescents actually engage in. Therefore, while an adolescent offender may not be deemed as culpable as an adult for purposes of punishment, he may nonetheless be judged culpable, or guilty, in the first place based on his ability (or more accurately his inability) to conform to adult expectations and understandings of the social norms that undergird criminal law generally and mens rea particularly.
>
> To rely on an adult mens rea standard for youthful offenders in the face of scientific evidence demonstrating that such offenders do not possess the same cognitive abilities or engage in the same thought processes as an adult is to undermine mens rea's value. It effectively reduces mens rea to a wholly objective analysis that fails even to use a properly objective standard of comparison. Whatever shortcomings remain in the current state of scientific knowledge, one principle remains clear: children are different from adults, and so the calculation of their mens rea must be different.

Jenny E. Carroll, *Brain Science and the Theory of Juvenile Mens Rea*, 94 N.C.L. Rev. 539, 590–591 (2016). What impact would a different approach to mens rea for juveniles potentially have on how prosecutors evaluate cases before making charging decisions? Should prosecutors consider another approach to mens rea for juveniles before making a plea offer? Should this be extended to defendants who are legal adults but who are 25 years old or younger?

4. Do you think the reasoning in *Roper v. Simmons* and *Graham v. Florida* requires a re-evaluation of the plea bargaining system in the juvenile system? If yes, why?

5. States that sentenced juveniles to mandatory terms of life in prison without the possibility of parole in violation of these Supreme Court rulings have had to consider how to change their laws if they were not in compliance. These cases did not result in widespread releases or drastic sentence reductions. For more information, see *A State-by-State look at Juvenile Life Without Parole*, July 31, 2017, available at https://www.usnews.com/news/best-states/utah/articles/2017-07-31/a-state-by-state-look-at-juvenile-life-without-parole.

6. The dissenting opinions are not reprinted in this chapter. However, it is important to note that two of these cases were decided by a slim majority. Four Justices dissented from the majority opinion in *Roper v. Simmons* and *Miller v. Alabama*. Three Justices dissented in *Graham v. Florida*.

7. In 2016, in *Montgomery v. Louisiana*, 136 S. Ct. 718, the Supreme Court held that *Miller v. Alabama* should apply retroactively. This means that juveniles sentenced to mandatory life without parole should have their sentences reconsidered. However, in a significant number of such cases, prosecutors are continuing to seek life without parole. Should prosecutors rethink the sentences they are seeking after a case like *Miller v. Alabama*, or are they acting within their ethical duty to continue to seek the higher sentences? See Rashad Robinson, *No Child Deserves a Life Sentence. But Try Telling Prosecutors That*, N.Y. Times, Aug. 10, 2017.

8. One example of a district attorney's office that has been notably unyielding in resentencing cases, and in seeking life for juveniles in new cases, is Wayne County, Michigan, where prosecutor Kym Worthy interpreted the law to mean that she must seek the 60 year maximum on resentencing cases. Jessica Pishko, *The Troubled Resentencing of America's Juvenile Lifers*, The Nation, June 21, 2017. *See also* The Fair Punishment Project, *Juvenile Life Without Parole in Wayne County: Time to Join the Growing National Consensus*? July, 2016, available at: http://fairpunishment.org/ wp-content/uploads/2016/07/FPP-WayneCountyReport-Final.pdf.

9. The Fair Punishment Project at Harvard Law School found that nearly one third of all juvenile life without parole inmates had turned down a plea deal that averaged 20 years—significantly less time than they got after trial. Prosecutors are not tied to those original offers in cases that require re-sentencing. Jessica Pishko, *The Troubled Resentencing of America's Juvenile Lifers*, The Nation, June 21, 2017. Do you think that resentencing should include the option of taking the original plea?

10. In the *Miller* Trilogy, the defendants were each tried and sentenced as adults. Do these cases demand a change in the transfer laws? You may want to think about this question again in Chapter 15.

III. Juvenile Justice Reform

A. Are We Adults at 18?

This chapter is an example of how scientific advances can lead to changes in both law and policy. Our increased understanding of how the human brain develops, from birth to adulthood, has led to calls for changes in juvenile practices. The Supreme Court has decided cases that now limit certain kinds of punishment due to this better understanding of how the juvenile brain works. But what other reforms should be considered due to our increased understanding of the neuroscience? If you were arguing that juveniles are different, would you look to what other nations are doing to bolster your argument? Would it matter if you were arguing at the trial level, appellate level, or to the Supreme Court? What about if you were advocating for a change in legislation, such as proposing that juveniles should not be tried as adults before a certain age? Would that be a persuasive argument for your state legislature? In both *Roper v. Simmons* and *Graham v. Florida*, Justice Kennedy's majority opinions compared the punishments juveniles were receiving in the United States to what was happening in other countries. In *Roper v. Simmons*, Justice Kennedy wrote:

> Our determination that the death penalty is disproportionate punishment for offenders under 18 finds confirmation in the stark reality that the United States is the only country in the world that continues to give official sanction to the juvenile death penalty. This reality does not become controlling, for the task of interpreting the Eighth Amendment remains our responsibility. Yet at least from the time of the Court's decision in *Trop* [*v. Dulles*], the Court has referred to the laws of other countries and to international authorities as instructive for its interpretation of the Eighth Amendment's prohibition of "cruel and unusual punishments." 356 U.S., at 102–103, 78 S.Ct. 590 [(1958)] (plurality opinion)....
>
> Respondent and his *amici* have submitted, and petitioner does not contest, that only seven countries other than the United States have executed juvenile offenders since 1990: Iran, Pakistan, Saudi Arabia, Yemen, Nigeria, the Democratic Republic of Congo, and China. Since then each of these countries has either abolished capital punishment for juveniles or made public disavowal of the practice. Brief for Respondent 49–50. In sum, it is fair to say that the United States now stands alone in a world that has turned its face against the juvenile death penalty....
>
> It is proper that we acknowledge the overwhelming weight of international opinion against the juvenile death penalty, resting in large part on the understanding that the instability and emotional imbalance of young people may often be a factor in the crime. See Brief for Human Rights Committee of the Bar of England and Wales et al. as *Amici Curiae* 10–11. The opinion of the world community, while not controlling our outcome, does provide respected and significant confirmation for our own conclusions....

As in *Roper*, Justice Kennedy discussed norms around the world in his majority decision in *Graham*:

> There is support for our conclusion in the fact that, in continuing to impose life without parole sentences on juveniles who did not commit homicide, the United States adheres to a sentencing practice rejected the world over. This observation does not control our decision. The judgments of other nations and the international community are not dispositive as to the meaning of the Eighth Amendment. But "'[t]he climate of international opinion concerning the acceptability of a particular punishment'" is also "'not irrelevant.'"... The Court has looked beyond our Nation's borders for support for its independent conclusion that a particular punishment is cruel and unusual....

> Thus, as petitioner contends and respondent does not contest, the United States is the only Nation that imposes life without parole sentences on juvenile nonhomicide offenders....

Justice Kennedy's references to other countries, and international law, in *Roper v. Simmons*, was controversial at the time. *See* Comment, *The Debate Over Foreign Law in Roper v. Simmons*, 119 HARV. L. REV. 103 (2005); Robert J. Delahunty & John Yoo, *Against Foreign Law*, 29 HARV. J.L. & PUB. POL'Y 291 (2005).

In the following article, you will read about the variety of approaches to juvenile legal systems in other countries. As you read, consider whether any of these other approaches might make sense in your state. For example, does it still make sense to have separate juvenile courts or to try juveniles as adults?

Anthony N. Doob & Michael Tonry, *Varieties of Youth Justice*

31 CRIME & JUST. 1–2, 2–3, 4–5 (2004)

Like parents trying to figure how best to raise their children, countries have, in recent years, wrestled with the question of how to respond to youths who break laws. There are many different models. Few appear to work in a completely satisfactory manner from the perspective of those in each jurisdiction. There is not even consensus on what "youth justice systems" (where they exist) are trying to accomplish. Few decisions—other than that youths are different from adults—have been settled in the same way across jurisdictions. The manner in which each country has resolved the "youth justice" problem is almost certainly best understood within the broad context of that country's history and justice institutions. Hence it would be premature to carry out a true multicultural cross-jurisdictional study of youth justice systems without first attempting to understand each system within its own context....

Many jurisdictions are searching for new and better approaches for dealing with youth crime. It is as if, in the latter part of the twentieth century, many countries suddenly discovered that there was more than one way of responding to youths who offend. Principles, purposes, and procedures all changed, but the ambivalence within each community remained.

Approaches to youth justice are sometimes caricatured as falling at different points along a dimension of which one pole is a "pure" welfare model and the other is a "pure" criminal law or punishment model. Although this is an oversimplification, the tension that exists between responding to youths who have offended in terms of their social or psychological needs, and punishing them for what they have done, is part of the story of youth justice in many jurisdictions. Various essays in this volume illustrate that a criminal law approach need not be particularly punitive, nor a child welfare approach particularly effective.

Policy makers and practitioners often are not comfortable making clear distinctions between these two approaches.... [M]ost states in the United States have not been able to decide between them. Hence, they characterize thirty-two states as having both a "prevention/diversion/treatment" orientation and a "punishment" orientation in their legislated goals. The other eighteen jurisdictions are evenly split in their legislative goals between "punishment" and "child welfare" orientations. These stated goals are not unimportant, but seldom do they determine what actually happens....

I. Separate Systems?

Youth justice systems vary much more between countries than do adult systems. Adult systems vary in many detailed ways but are broadly similar in most important respects. There is a good deal of consensus about what constitutes an offense. The exact nature of the prosecution process and court structures differs (especially between common-law and European countries), but there is widespread agreement that, at the end of the process, the sentence should, to a large extent, reflect the seriousness of the offense. Whatever else a sentence was said to accomplish, it would be seen unambiguously as punishment by the community and by the person subject to it. Sentencing systems in many countries have changed in the last thirty years—sometimes dramatically—but the focus of the sentence is more likely to be on the severity of punishment, rather than its purposes.

Youth justice systems do not have these same basic similarities. To give one illustration, what are commonly known as "status offenses"—behavior that is prohibited only because of a person's status as a youth (e.g., curfews, truancy) exist in some jurisdictions (e.g., in many U.S. states) but not in others (e.g., Canada, Denmark, or Germany).

Nor do all youth justice systems feature the same core features. In England and many U.S. states, youth justice systems closely resemble adult courts in their organization and their focus on punishment as a primary aim. In Scandinavian countries, people below age fifteen are legally incapable of committing crimes, and their serious misconduct is dealt with by social welfare agencies. At and after age fifteen, young offenders are processed by the same courts as process adults. In Scotland, a strong social welfare ethos dominates handling of young offenders. In New Zealand, nearly all cases are handled by conferences that many see as premised in part on ideas akin to those embodied in restorative justice.

The most notable aspect of the treatment of youths who offend in Western countries is that every country appears to have laws or policies reflecting the belief that youths should be treated differently from adult offenders. Exactly how they should be treated differently varies from country to country. What constitutes a "youth" also varies from country to country. And the rigidity of the demarcations between a child who is not criminally responsible and a youth who might be, and the demarcations between youthfulness and adulthood, also vary....

In Denmark, there is no formally separate system for young offenders. There are no special courts, and there are no special offenses (i.e., there are no status offenses). Denmark does not appear to have had a formally separate system (with distinct youth justice laws and a completely distinct set of youth justice institutions) for youths who offend. A naive American, therefore, might think that Denmark had not progressed even as far as reforms introduced in the early twentieth century in Chicago, ... however, that does not mean that Danish youths are treated as if they are adults. Clearly they are not.

The Swedish system of youth justice has similar characteristics. Early twentieth-century American reformers would be dismayed to find that those over the age of criminal responsibility (fifteen) in Sweden are dealt with in the criminal courts. The system that existed at the end of the twentieth century—with shared responsibility between the welfare system and the justice system—for those between ages fifteen and twenty—does not sound like a "separate justice system." Nevertheless, various rules ... differentiate the treatment of a sixteen-year-old from that of a twenty-one-year-old and add up to, in effect, a separate system. Youths between ages fifteen and seventeen, for example, cannot normally be sent to prison.

These two examples highlight the importance of looking at how youth justice systems work rather than exclusively at formal laws and institutions. Furthermore, it is well established that in the United States and Canada there were many aspects of a separate youth justice system, including separate custodial institutions and probation officers for juveniles, in place long before the establishment of the youth courts in Chicago and Toronto.

The tendency of most countries ... was to establish some form of separate set of formal rules for youthful offenders. Beyond that, however, the similarity—at least at the level of the underlying operating theory—more or less disappears. It is difficult to find many similarities among England's preponderantly punitive system, the Scottish system of children's hearings, New Zealand's conferences, and the juvenile courts in the Netherlands.

Similarly, the influence of international conventions (the European Convention for the Protection of Human Rights and Fundamental Liberties and the United Nations Convention on the Rights of the Child) on European youth justice ... is not likely to have been anticipated by an American whose country is not even a signatory to the U.N. Convention.

But all of these "systems" have one important common element: all reflect the view that youths should be dealt with differently from adults. And, generally speaking, the assumption is that the youthfulness of an offender mitigates the punishment that youths should receive and that youths should be kept separate from adult offenders.

* * *

Notes/Questions

1. Assume you have been hired as legislative director for your state representative. She has told you that she doesn't like how juvenile cases are handled in your state. Your state has "automatic transfer statutes" requiring certain kinds of cases be tried in adult courts. Your state has high juvenile detention rates. What would you advise her? Would you look to any of the examples from other countries to suggest changes in your state? If so, which ones?

2. Would you suggest ending "status offenses" such as breaking curfew or underage drinking? Why or why not?

3. How would you talk to your boss about whether juveniles are different and whether they should be treated differently in the criminal legal system? You should keep this question in mind as you continue reading.

Tim Requarth, *Neuroscience Is Changing the Debate Over What Role Age Should Play in the Courts*

Newsweek, Apr. 18, 2016

"People are not magically different on their 18th birthday," says Elizabeth Scott, a professor of law at Columbia University whose work was cited in the seminal *Roper* case. "Their brains are still maturing, and the criminal justice system should find a way to take that into account."

... The 18-to-24 demographic makes up only 10 percent of the population but accounts for 27 percent of all criminal arrests. Leniency in this high-crime population, opponents argue, could compromise public safety. Yet it's also clear that the current system does not work. Recidivism rates for offenders aged 18 to 24 are breathtakingly high: 78 percent of 18- to 24-year-olds released from prison are rearrested, and half return to prison again.

Few would argue that a 13-year-old is developmentally the same as a 25-year-old, but there's a gray zone in between, says B.J. Casey, director of the Sackler Institute for Developmental Psychobiology at Cornell's Weill Medical College. For the criminal justice system, she says, "it's basically a question of, When is an adolescent an adult?"

Casey is leading an unlikely consortium of scientists and legal scholars, including Scott, to home in on the young adult mind. In a set of experiments published last month in the journal *Psychological Science*, Casey and her collaborators asked: At what age do people gain the ability to control themselves in emotionally charged situations? To try to answer this question, they placed 13- to 25-year-olds into a brain scanner while asking them to do a task that required restraint. The instructions were simple: Press a button if you see a bored or scared face, but don't press it if you see a happy face. The twist was that the subjects performed the task under three conditions: positive arousal, negative arousal and no arousal. In the first condition, they were told ahead of time that at any moment they could be awarded up to $100, while in the second condition they were told there could be a loud noise. In the third condition, the subjects were told nothing.

The idea was that the first two conditions would create a sustained period of heightened emotion. It was inspired by the circumstances of criminal behavior: Many crimes by the young are in emotionally or socially charged situations. The question, says Casey, is, Why, in the heat of the moment, under threat, do they pull the trigger, even when they know better?

The results of her experiment involving negative stimulus were striking: 18- to 21-year-olds were less able than 22- to 25-year-olds to restrain themselves from pushing the button when there was the threat of a loud sound. (This diminished cognitive control was not observed under positive or neutral conditions.) In fact, under the threatening condition, says Casey, the 18- to 21-year olds "weren't much better than teenagers." The brain scanners revealed a telltale pattern: Areas in the prefrontal cortex that regulate emotion showed reduced activity, while areas linked to emotional centers were in high gear.

These results support previous brain-imaging studies and postmortem examinations. Brain areas involved in reasoning and self-control, such as the prefrontal cortex, are not fully developed until the mid-20s—a far later age than previously thought. Brain areas involved in emotions such as desire and fear, however, seem to be fully developed by 17. This pattern of brain development creates a perfect storm for crime: Around the ages of 18 to 21, people have the capacity for adult emotions yet a teenager's ability to control them.

Fueled in part by studies such as Casey's, legal experts and policymakers are beginning to reconsider how the criminal justice system treats this age range. Vincent Schiraldi, a former commissioner of probation for New York City and now a senior research fellow at the Harvard Kennedy School's Program in Criminal Justice Policy and Management, argues that offenders should not enter the adult system until 21, with gradually diminishing protections until 25. "Anyone who has a 22-year-old living in his childhood bedroom," Schiraldi says, "knows they aren't the same as older adults."

In many countries, 18 as the threshold for adulthood is already a thing of the past. In Germany, it has been age 21 since 1953, and in Switzerland it's 25. Here in the U.S., a bill was filed last month to raise the age in Illinois to 21. Governor Dannel Malloy of Connecticut—inspired by a recent trip to Germany—has been outspoken about making similar changes in his state. Last fall, he proposed raising the juvenile age to 20 and instituting alternative ways to deal with people up to age 25, such as keeping convictions for less serious crimes confidential and establishing a special young-offender prison whose sole focus is reform and reintegration.

There are already a few places in the U.S. experimenting with some of those alternatives. This April, the Brooklyn District Attorney's Office, in partnership with the Center for Court Innovation, is piloting a separate court system for ages 16 to 24 (offenders 16 and older are currently treated as adults in New York). The court—which is beginning with low-level offenses—has a dedicated judge, defense staff, prosecutors and social workers. The San Francisco DA launched a similar program last summer but focused on felonies, including violent crimes. Both programs are working on an approach that takes developmental factors into account, and all parties receive training from an in-house expert in the field. "Neuroscience," says Katy Weinstein Miller, chief of alternative programs and initiatives at the San Francisco DA's office, "has really informed everything we do in court."

Notes/Questions

1. In 2013, new guidelines for child psychologists in the UK defined adolescence as continuing until the age of 25. Adolescence, according to these guidelines, is now broken into three phases: "early adolescence that ranges from 12 to 14 years, middle adolescence from 15 to 17 years and 18 and over is classed as late adolescence." Victoria Woollaston, *An adult at 18? Not any more: Adolescence now ends at 25 to prevent young people getting an inferiority complex*, Daily Mail, Sept. 24, 2013.

2. If adolescence ends at 25, should 18- or 20-year-olds be tried as adults? Or should this definition just change the potential punishments? If you were a prosecutor, would this knowledge change how you prosecuted younger adults?

3. As you think about these questions consider this additional reading on brain development:

> The adolescent brain may reach its adult volume by age 10; however, that does not mean that the brain is mature. Rather, that brain will take over a decade to reach what can be considered adult maturity. This means that, even when an individual turns the age of 18 and is considered to be a legal adult, his brain still has years of development and maturity ahead of it. As more is understood about this process, it will undoubtedly influence policymakers and legislators when considering certain rights granted to those deemed to be able to make reasoned, "adult" decisions. To confuse the issue even further, research has shown that different parts of the brain mature and make connections for a longer period of time than others—the occipital lobe may show a slow down of these connections by age 20, but the frontal lobe may continue development into the 30s. The most recent research suggests that brain development continues until at least the age of 26. This development can affect both emotion and cognition, playing a key role in how decisions are made that, in some cases, can put a juvenile into the criminal justice system. For example, emotional regulation and impulse control may not be adequately developed in the juvenile brain.

Michael L. Perlin & Alison J. Lynch, *"Some Mother's Child Has Gone Astray": Neuroscientific Approaches to a Therapeutic Jurisprudence Model of Juvenile Sentencing*, 59 Fam. Ct. Rev. 478, 479–480 (2021). You will have an opportunity to consider these questions more in the next chapter as we discuss the variety of alternative processes and how they work in the context of the juvenile legal system and in connection what is understood about brain development and what might be better approaches in juvenile criminal cases, particularly to decrease recidivism.

Additional Resources

Elizabeth Cauffmann, et al., *How Developmental Science Influences Juvenile Justice Reform*, 8 UC Irvine L. Rev. 21 (2018).

Cara Drinan, Graham *on the Ground*, 87 Wash. L. Rev. 51 (2012).

Cara Drinan, *Misconstruing Graham & Miller*, 91 Wash U. L. Rev. 785 (2014).

Mark R. Fondacaro, et al., *Reconceptualizing Due Process in Juvenile Justice: Contributions from Law and Social Science*, 57 Hastings L.J. 955 (2006).

Martin R. Gardner, *The Categorical Distinction Between Adolescents and Adults: The Supreme Court's Juvenile Punishment Cases—Constitutional Implications for Regulating Teenage Sexual Activity*, 28 BYU J. Pub. L. 1 (2013).

Josh Gupta-Kagan, *The Intersection Between Young Adult Sentencing and Mass Incarceration*, 2018 Wis. L. Rev. 669.

Clayton A. Hartjen, Youth, Crime, and Justice: A Global Inquiry (Rutgers University Press 2008).

Juvenile Justice in Global Perspective (Franklin E. Zimring, et al., eds., NYU Press 2015).

Carly Loomis-Gustafson, Note, *Adjusting the Bright-Line Age of Accountability within the Criminal Justice System: Raising the Age of Majority to Age 21 Based on the Conclusions of Scientific Studies Regarding Neurological Development and Culpability of Young Adult Offenders*, 55 Duq. L. Rev. 221 (2017).

Cheryl B. Preston & Brandon T. Crowther, *Legal Osmosis: The Role of Brain Science in Protecting Adolescents*, 43 Hofstra L. Rev. 447 (2014).

Christopher Slobogin, *Neuroscience Nuance: Dissecting the Relevance of Neuroscience in Adjudication Criminal Culpability*, 4 J. L. & Biosci. 577 (2017).

Victor L. Streib, *Prosecutorial Discretion in Juvenile Homicide Cases*, 109 Penn. St. L. Rev. 1071 (2005).

Chapter 14

Alternative Processes for Juveniles

This book has discussed, and asked you to look critically at, each process that we use to resolve criminal cases in the United States. As you have read in the last two chapters, although the juvenile court system started out as an alternative process, it has entered the mainstream and, in the last many decades, has focused, along with the adult system, more on punishment and less on rehabilitation. The juvenile legal system is in many ways a microcosm of the larger criminal legal system in the United States. Juveniles offenders suffer from the same bias that is embedded into the system for adults. From school suspension rates through to incarceration rates, juveniles of color are disproportionately represented. Juveniles pulled into the criminal legal system are also, as with adults, more likely to be poor and suffer from mental illness and cognitive disabilities.

In the public eye, juveniles are often viewed as more deserving of a break, particularly if their crime is non-violent. At the same time, laws and practices have evolved to address the public fear of teenage "super-predators" who are perceived to be too dangerous to remain in society. As you have read, the juvenile legal system now regularly punishes juveniles with incarceration without a focus on rehabilitation, and a significant number are tried as adults (and subjected to adult-length prison terms, including life without parole).

This chapter will ask you to look at alternative processes for juveniles. You should consider whether the questions are different when examining what processes might be appropriate for a juvenile offender as compared to an adult offender. Should the criminal legal system have different processes, depending on the age of the offender? And what processes are appropriate for juveniles? This book started by asking you to look at the underlying reasons we have criminal laws: incapacitation/public protection; deterrence; retribution; and treatment/rehabilitation. Are different goals more important with juvenile offenders than with adult offenders? And, depending on your answer, should the juvenile legal system use more alternative processes and, if so, which ones? Or should it return to its roots as a system focused on rehabilitation and not punishment? A related question is whether juveniles should be processed in separate courts and not transferred to adult courts regardless of the crime. Note that as we address these questions in the juvenile system, we may, in fact, come up with even more questions.

I. Juvenile Court: The Original Alternative Process

As you read in Chapter 13, juvenile courts were the original problem-solving courts. Many argue that the best reform for juvenile justice is to return to that process, with due process protections in place, and stop transferring juveniles into adult courts. As you will read, Christopher Slobogin argues against transfer to adult courts, especially if the goal of the process is to prevent future offending.

Christopher Slobogin, *Treating Juveniles Like Juveniles: Getting Rid of Transfer and Expanded Adult Court Jurisdiction*

46 Tex. Tech L. Rev. 103, 105, 106–107, 113 (2013)

...

Between 1979 and 2000, every state enacted provisions that eased transfer of juveniles to adult court.... [T]his Article argues that transfer should be abolished and that juvenile court jurisdiction should be expanded, not reduced. Treating juvenile offenders like adult offenders wastes resources, damages juveniles, and decreases public safety. Offenders under the age of eighteen should never be tried in adult court or subjected to adult sentences. Nor should people who are convicted as juveniles be detained for their crimes past the age of twenty-five, except in extremely limited circumstances....

[T]he best rationale for treating juveniles differently than adults is not their lesser culpability, but their lesser deterrability or, more precisely, the fact that criminal sanctions do not have the same deterrent effect on juveniles as they do on adults. The lesser deterrability rationale has long sanctioned separate justice systems for people with mental disabilities on the theory that the prospect of criminal punishment is less likely to inhibit crimes by these types of individuals and that an alternative, prevention-oriented commitment regime is, therefore, necessary. The same rationale can easily justify a juvenile justice system, because juveniles as a group are demonstrably less risk-averse and more impulsive than adults. In contrast to the lesser culpability rationale, which is focused on punishing juveniles (albeit less harshly than adults), the lesser deterrability rationale is focused on preventing juveniles from reoffending. In terms of the purposes of punishment, a prevention-oriented juvenile justice system aims not at retribution or general deterrence, but at specific deterrence and rehabilitation. Incapacitation as incarceration also plays a role, but only as a last resort.

Because these purposes of a prevention-oriented approach to juvenile justice are so different from the primary purpose of the adult criminal justice system, they provide a much more solid conceptual and pragmatic justification for a separate juvenile justice system. More to the point of this Article, a prevention-oriented approach provides a strong basis for abolishing transfer and transfer-like policies. While desert-based punishment—even discounted punishment—requires adult-style sentences for the more serious crimes, prevention can be accomplished within the juvenile system, even for the most dangerous juvenile offenders. No link between adult criminal justice and juvenile justice is necessary....

Notes/Questions

1. Should transfer to adult court be eliminated to encourage development of better treatment programs for juveniles? Consider this additional excerpt from Christopher Slobogin's article (pages 124–25):

> Numerous decisions make clear that courts have transferred a juvenile to adult court solely because of a lack of accessible programs. For instance, one court waived juvenile court jurisdiction for a fourteen-year-old because the State's experts testified that the state lacked adequate facilities to deal with a fourteen-year-old homicide offender. Another court transferred a youth who became violent when he consumed alcohol because the jurisdiction offered no substance abuse program. In perhaps the most egregious case (thankfully, now mooted by the Supreme Court's decision in *Roper*), the court rejected the argument that "the state has an obligation not to execute a juvenile who is deemed to be amenable to treatment but for whom the state offers no appropriate treatment program." Courts also routinely refuse to consider a juvenile offender treatable when the only pertinent programs are in another jurisdiction.
>
> These types of decisions led us to conclude in Juveniles at Risk that "[i]f transfer were eliminated, courts would have to confront the problems caused by the current paucity of treatment programs and might become more willing to force legislatures to [treat] them." This impetus is necessary. According to one estimate, only 15,000 juvenile offenders per year participate in MST and similar regimes; despite the success of these programs, states have been unwilling to scale them up. From a crime-prevention perspective, that failure is shortsighted.

2. Should the focus be on preventing transfer, or expanding assistance in the juvenile system, or both? You may want to consider this question about what process might be appropriate again, after you read later in this chapter about reducing recidivism through not incarcerating juvenile offenders.

3. One argument against adult sentences and terms of incarceration, as noted in the previous chapter, is that most juveniles will "age out" of crime and will stop offending at some point in their twenties, with or without incarceration. As Christopher Slobogin observed (pages 126–27),

> Young adults find jobs, get married, and, in general, acquire "stakes in life" that militate against a life of crime. Neurobiological and developmental research confirms that a person's impulsivity and susceptibility to peer influence significantly diminishes in the early to mid-twenties. Thus, if the goal is public

safety, prolonged incarceration of people who commit crimes as adolescents is excessive.

Prolonged incarceration is also counterproductive. As the research on deterrence implies, prison is criminogenic. Transfer may keep a troublesome youth off the streets, but it increases the probability that youth will turn to crime once back on the streets. Also important is the fact that adolescents in adult prisons are highly likely to be the victims of crime themselves, a fact which must be weighed on the cost side of the ledger. In short, the safety of both the public and of juvenile offenders would be enhanced by moving from detention-heavy policies to those that focus on community-based corrections.

II. Plea Bargaining

As you read in Chapter 12, plea bargaining is heavily used in the juvenile legal system and suffers from the same concerns as in the adult criminal system including that it might be overly coercive and that it can encourage innocent people to plead guilty. In addition to these concerns, you have read about the concerns that are specific to juveniles including that, due to their age and brain development, juveniles may be even more susceptible to false confessions and that they may not understand the rights they are waiving when they plead guilty. Another difference with juvenile plea bargaining is that the decision to plead guilty is not just between the juvenile and their lawyer. The juvenile's parents may also be involved in the process in a few ways. First, they may need to agree to the outcome if it includes that the juvenile will be in the parent's home and under their care. Second, they can be heavily influential in the juvenile's assessment of the case and decision about whether to accept the plea offer or not. You have already read about how plea bargaining is, by definition, a multi-party negotiation. In the context of juveniles, as you will read, parents are often another, albeit unofficial, party.

Ericka N. Fountain & Jennifer Woolard, *Negotiating with Parents: Attorney Practices in the Juvenile Plea Bargain Process*

45 Law & Hum. Behav. 112 (April 2021)

A unique feature of juvenile plea bargain decision making is the role of parents. Although parents do not have the legal authority to decide how to plead on their children's behalf, evidence suggests that some parents are actively involved in advising their children how to and, in some jurisdictions, signing their children's tender-of-plea forms. National juvenile defense standards emphasize the importance of working with the client's parents throughout court proceedings, albeit within some limits. The current study explores the strategies and decisions made by juvenile defense attorneys from a large city on the East Coast about including parents in the plea bargaining process and investigates how parental involvement may impact the ways they represent their juvenile clients.

The Attorney-Parent Relationship: Suggestions and Standards

In the absence of Supreme Court caselaw or state statutory frameworks that explicitly address the role of parents in the attorney-client relationship, national attorney associations and legal scholars alike stress the importance of clear communication and active engagement with parents but emphasize that the ultimate authority for plea decision making rests with the youth. The recommendations put forth by these scholars and organizations are based on the legal consensus that attorneys have an ethical obligation to their client and not the parent. Acknowledging that it is unrealistic to assume their juvenile clients are making decisions on their own, the NJDC standards make clear that attorneys should work "collegially with parents" for several reasons. First, they suggest parents can help the attorney evaluate potential benefits or concerns regarding disposition options and will likely be instrumental in ensuring the success of the child's disposition. Parents can also inform attorneys of important information such as if their child has any special needs that might help the attorney determine how best to confer with their client. Further, the juvenile defense attorney trial manual references the likely influence parents have over their child's plea decision in justifying why attorneys should almost always also consult with parents. They are also clear when indicating this conversation with parents should happen in the presence of the client and only after the attorney has thoroughly discussed the plea with the client alone. Additionally, because parents will likely be given a chance to address the court, attorneys will benefit from learning the parent's initial attitudes and perceptions of the client and their case. In the best-case scenario, attorneys might ensure parents support their child's decisions and preferred disposition before the court given that, unlike in adult court, what is more often being negotiated in juvenile court are potential dispositions as opposed to reductions in charges (Hertz et al., 2012). In the end, the standards warn that

> "if counsel cannot convince the parent to be an active ally in support of the client's objectives, counsel should attempt to limit the parent's negative effect on the client's outcome by limiting the parent's role in the proceedings as much as possible" (NJDC, 2012, p. 109).

Legal scholars have also discussed the importance of considering the potential for conflicting interests between parents and their child clients. Unlike other contexts such as education, parents have no legal decision-making authority in juvenile proceedings. Nevertheless, attorneys will likely be met by parents who wish to use the plea bargaining process to their advantage, perhaps even to teach their child a moral lesson. Alternatively, parents may see the plea process as an opportunity for their child to gain access to mental health resources and other services through the juvenile justice system. Furthermore, there are many ways the child's decision to plead guilty or go to trial can impact parents. For example, parents may want their child to plead guilty to reduce the amount of time the parent must be out of work and in court. Parents may encourage their children to reject a favorable plea offer to avoid having to be held civilly or financially responsible for their child's offenses. Parents may also encourage their children to reject a favorable plea if it includes a community-based disposition plan when they rather have the child placed outside of the home. Unlike in adult court, juvenile plea negotiations are more likely to focus on the specific terms of disposition. Therefore, parent conflicts of interests with the child's preferred disposition may have important implications for juvenile plea negotiations.

The greatest dilemma emerges when attorneys must convince parents to prioritize their child's stated goals and interests over their own. While attorneys should be understanding of parents' concerns or fears, they must be sure not to prioritize the parent's interests over the client's. To avoid this, attorneys must carefully explain early on that their responsibility is to the client and not their parents and that the child has the legal right to decide how to plead. As a result, lawyers may have good reason or even an ethical obligation to exclude parents from the plea bargain decision making process in order to avoid these conflicts of interest and to ensure the client's decisions are not substituted by that of their parents.

Notes/Questions

1. As a criminal defense lawyer representing juvenile clients, the parents could be both another challenge in terms of concluding a plea agreement, or an ally in arriving at a better outcome for you client. As the reading highlights, there are serious potential conflicts of interest. As a prosecutor, are you as worried about these potential conflicts of interest and/or would you want to involve the parent in you decision-making before making a plea offer in the case? As a defense lawyer, would you want to caution the parent against speaking to the prosecutor? Or encourage them to speak to the prosecutor?

2. Consider this comment from a defense lawyer from the article above:

> I had a real problem where the state wanted to offer a [type of suspended sentence]. Basically, for my kid to do well, and my kid's mom was like, "I want him locked up in detention and sent away." I can't go into court and accept [a suspended sentence] and the court's going to be like, "Mom how do you feel?" and she's like, "I want him sent away to a youth camp." Right? The court's not going to take that plea. It's a problem. So, I ended up working out a plea that did include a short term of probation ... so in that case I had to bring that mom in, I had to get her buy in because she's going to sit in court and blow my deal and that was a great deal and I wish that kid could have taken it.—Attorney No. 6.[1]

As a prosecutor, if you found out that the mother was opposed to the deal that you had offered, what should you do? What if you think that your deal is doing justice, but the mother's ideas of what is right is likely to make it so their child is at higher

1. Erika N. Fountain & Jennifer Woolard, *Negotiating with Parents: Attorney Practices in the Juvenile Plea Bargaining Process*, 45 LAW & HUM. BEHAV 112, 117 (April 2021).

risk for recidivism? You may want to consider this question as you continue reading this chapter.

III. Problem-Solving Courts in the Juvenile System

The introduction of problem-solving courts within the juvenile legal system is one indication of how far juvenile courts have strayed from their roots, as the original problem-solving court. We will start with a reading about these courts and how they operate within the juvenile system and then discuss the concerns about these problem-solving courts operating within what was originally a problem-solving court.

A. What Are Juvenile Problem-Solving Courts?

Daniel M. Filler & Austin E. Smith, *The New Rehabilitation*

91 Iowa L. Rev. 951, 968–69, 971, 973–75, 984 (2006)

...

II. Juvenile Specialty Courts

A. The Creation of Juvenile Specialty Courts

...

Juvenile specialty courts were designed to provide the same focused, rehabilitative approach, [as adult specialty courts] targeted exclusively at children. While it is hard to tell who actually created the first juvenile specialty court, Circuit Judge John Parnham in Escambia County (Pensacola), Florida has been credited with creating the first juvenile drug court in 1995. In this early, rudimentary juvenile drug court, the judge presided over both the regular family court docket as well as the separate family drug court cases. To enter the court, Judge Parnham required participants to plead guilty to contempt of court, accept a six-month suspended sentence, and comply with any additional conditions from the drug court sentence.

The most pervasive form of juvenile specialty courts is the drug court. Like adult drug courts, after the news of the perceived success of the first programs in 1995 began to spread, programs started to pop up across the country. There are also juvenile courts that address drug and alcohol abuse by children, drug use by parents whose children are processed by dependency courts, gun possession, truancy, violent acts committed by juveniles, and even teen courts that are intended to impose peer pressure on young offenders for minor violations....

The Jefferson County, Alabama, Juvenile Gun Court provides a good example of how a specialty court comes into being. In the mid-1990s, Birmingham, Alabama, was suffering from high rates of juvenile gun violence. Judge Sandra Storm, a juvenile court judge in Jefferson County, home to Birmingham, read an article in the Birmingham News discussing an adult gun court in Providence, Rhode Island. She convened a town-hall meeting to discuss the possibility of establishing such a court in Jefferson County, inviting law enforcement officials, prosecutors, criminal defense attorneys, the Alabama Department of Youth Services (the operator of the state's detention facilities), and various social service agencies such as IMPACT, a local family counseling provider. After building connections between these groups and gaining their support, the family court reallocated funds and other resources to support the program. The new court began to hear cases on a specialty gun court docket. Unlike any move requiring legislative action, this process was relatively simple and quick. The new court obtained funding beyond the standard family court line through grants. Without a single vote in the Alabama legislature, a new court—with a new agenda—was created....

B. Profiles of Juvenile Specialty Courts

Juvenile specialty courts appear, at first, anachronistic. Juvenile courts were designed, originally, to provide individualized rehabilitative justice for children. Specialty courts are supposed to provide the same thing. Why, then, are they necessary? Because legislatures have worked diligently to undermine rehabilitative juvenile courts, existing court structures have difficulty delivering rehabilitative services. Specialty courts create new forums where delinquency cases can be funneled to receive the individualized attention once dedicated to all children charged with delinquency. One purpose of specialty courts is to "abandon[] conventional adversarial roles in the interest of providing a more therapeutic and less contentious environment for the resolution of issues."

Specialty courts pull cases out of the general delinquency docket and subject them to special, intensive handling on a smaller docket. Frequently, a defendant must enter a guilty plea—or its juvenile court equivalent—to become eligible for the special jurisdiction. Depending on the jurisdiction, it may be more or less difficult to divert the most serious cases from a punitive to a rehabilitative docket. In many states, the decision of whether to prosecute a child in adult court belongs to either a judge or district attorney. In these cases, judges and prosecutors committed to specialty courts retain the power to divert suitable children to a rehabilitative regime. Even in states with juvenile sentencing guidelines, it may be possible for children to enter conditional pleas that may be withdrawn later if they successfully complete a treatment program. In these ways, specialty courts may remain open even to offenders explicitly targeted by legislators for tough sentences.

Once in these tribunals, offenders are subject to a unique sanction and reward regime that often bears little resemblance to the main line of delinquency cases. Instead of a hands-off probation, or a bid at the state "industrial school," children are brought back to court regularly so that judges can check on their progress. The offenders receive stepped sanctions to punish small transgressions and rewards to affirm small successes. They often undergo intensive, self-conscious treatment and therapeutic counseling programs. The roles of actors within the juvenile justice process have been fluid over the past quarter century. Until the civil-rights revolution in the Supreme Court, juvenile courts were driven primarily by judges, their professional staff (such as probation officers and social workers), and prosecutors. Lawyers, if they were present at all, had a peripheral role. With *Gault* and its progeny, juvenile courts began to more closely resemble adult criminal courts. They became adversarial, with a more clearly defined role for the defense attorney, and the judge became more of a fact-finder and sentencer than a parent. The advent of specialty courts has, to a significant extent, turned back the clocks, and it has done so while remaining consistent with the procedural safeguards of *Gault*....

A. Why Specialty Courts?

... This Article posits six reasons why local juvenile courts have created these tribunals ... local officials may be (1) acting on their personal beliefs and values, (2) managing scarce resources, and (3) working to preserve their jobs and autonomy.... Local courts may have created specialty courts (4) as a quick response to a new, and under-appreciated problem, (5) acting on the will of the local community, even if it conflicts with the desires of the state as a whole, or (6) for the most basic reason of all: they are effective.

Notes/Questions

1. Are the reasons that juvenile courts have created specialty or problem-solving courts different from the reasons in adult courts? Should the reasons be different?

2. How does the availability of funding contribute to the establishment of juvenile problem-solving courts?

3. In reviewing the reasons that these courts are established, think about what else you have learned in law school. Are these reasons for establishing these courts consistent with due process concerns? Are there ethical considerations that are different for lawyers handling cases in juvenile court and in juvenile problem-solving courts?

4. Should juvenile courts adopt a new model of problem-solving courts focused on particular types of juvenile offenders? Erin Collins argues against doing so in the article below.

B. Teen Courts

Teen courts are a variation of problem-solving courts and are another alternative process for juveniles. These courts, also called peer courts, youth courts, and student courts, are intended for non-serious offenses and can be a form of diversion from the formal criminal legal system. Teen courts or peer courts can also be separate from the criminal legal system and tied into a school disciplinary system. There are over 1000 youth courts in the United States. As with other forms of problem-solving courts, there is no one singular model, and non-profit organizations, schools, juvenile courts, juvenile probation departments, and law enforcement agencies operate youth court programs.

Teen courts may adopt ideas from restorative justice and focus on "determining a fair and restorative sentence."[2] However, these courts do not follow a full restorative justice process as described earlier in this book. As you will read, the focus in a teen court process may not be on repairing the harm, and the victim may or may not participate. Another difference is that many teen courts are structured as adjudication, and the offender is sentenced.

Teen courts, as with other problem-solving courts, focus on sentencing or what the offender will be required to do. However, a small percentage of these courts allow a defendant to plead "not guilty" and have a proceeding to decide guilt or innocence. Depending on how the particular teen court is structured, teens may take on the role of lawyers, judges, bailiffs, and juries. Often those roles are played by juveniles who have previously been offenders, and their continued involvement in the teen court is part of their sentence. Over 50% of teen courts use an "adult judge" model, with the rest dividing between the use of a teen judge, peer jury, or youth tribunal model.[3]

Typical teen court sentences include community service, written apologies, essays, payment of restitution, curfews, tutoring, counseling, drug testing, a jail tour, peer mediation, and participation in the teen court.

Julieta Kendall, *Can It Please the Court? An Analysis of the Teen Court System as an Alternative to the Traditional Juvenile Justice System*

24 J. Juv. L. 154, 156–60, 162–63 (2003–2004)

...

III. The History of Teen Courts in the United States

One rehabilitative juvenile system that has grown in popularity is the Teen Court. Also known as "Youth Court" or "Peer Court," a teen court is a diversion program where a juvenile offender is prosecuted, defended and sentenced by his or her peers all of whom are eighteen years of age, or younger. Some accounts trace the first teen court to 1976 in Grand Prairie, Texas. Others maintain the Naperville, Illinois teen court, which is still in operation, started as early as 1972. Despite the early beginnings, teen courts did not become a popular diversion program until the 1990s. Federal and state government support followed when popularity and anecdotal evidence of successful outcomes increased. Today, there are almost 900 teen courts operating in at least forty-six states across the United States.

Although the title suggests otherwise, a teen court is an informal diversion program. In fact, most teen court orders are legally unenforceable. A teen court is a mainly youth run diversion program that attempts to discourage juvenile delinquency among impressionable first time offenders. The local community usually takes responsibility

2. https://www.youthcourt.net/about/facts-and-stats.

3. *Id.*

for developing a teen court program. Local community involvement and development may result in a program tailored for the neighborhood, but it also leads to inconsistency and lack of uniformity among programs nation wide. Currently, teen courts operate without guidance from national laws or guidelines, although some states have legislation that addresses teen court structure and procedure.

A. Teen Court Procedure

Depending on the jurisdiction, a teen court accepts a delinquent juvenile at any point during the delinquency process, up to formal adjudication. The typical juvenile referred to teen court is a first time offender under the age of sixteen who is willing to admit guilt when the structure of the teen court is dispositional. A prior admission of guilt is not necessary when the teen court is adjudicatory in nature. A national survey of teen courts reported theft as the offense most often handled, followed by minor assault, disorderly conduct, and alcohol possession or use. After the teen court identifies the juvenile as a willing candidate for the teen court system, a program coordinator will meet with the juvenile and his or her parent or guardian to discuss the teen court process and schedule a hearing date.

B. Teen Court Structural Models

The format of the hearing depends on which of the four structural models the teen court follows. All models rely heavily on youth volunteers, many of whom once faced a teen court body, themselves. In the Youth Judge model, volunteers under the age of nineteen staff all of the standard court positions (judge, jury, attorneys and support staff), whereas in the Adult Judge model, an adult serves as the judge. Both models mimic the traditional adjudicatory hearings of the juvenile justice system. In the Youth Tribunal model, several youth judges sitting en banc will dispose of the case after youth attorneys for each side present oral arguments. In contrast, the jury plays the most active role in the Peer Jury model, where the judge and attorneys are absent. In this model, a panel of jurors disposes of the case after questioning the juvenile, the parents or guardian, and any other witnesses.

After the hearing, the deliberating body determines the appropriate sanction for the juvenile, which is often dictated by "sentencing guidelines" that take into consideration, among other things, the defendant's age, level of offense, and remorse. The most common sanctions are community service and letters of apology, followed by jury duty in a subsequent teen court trial, lifestyle classes, and restitution. The juvenile must comply with the terms of the sanction within a certain period to avoid redirection to the original referring agency. Most records related to the case are destroyed once the juvenile successfully completes the teen court process, excluding records of referral or participation that are necessarily maintained to limit teen courts to first time offenders.

IV. Teen Court Effectiveness

Although the teen court system is not a concept with universal appeal, advocates list many reasons to support trial by peers. The most cited reason is the positive use of peer pressure. Proponents argue that a teen court setting channels a negative, unavoidable life experience like peer pressure into positive energy. The same peer pressure that compels teenagers to commit minor offenses can make abiding the law "cool" and give heretofore-apathetic juvenile offenders a greater respect for law and order. Teen courts also report high levels of customer satisfaction when compared with the traditional juvenile justice system, where the customer is the juvenile and his or her parent or guardian. High levels of customer satisfaction are a logical by-product of a system that dispenses relatively mild sentences and operates without leaving a permanent record. Customer satisfaction is a good measuring device for upscale department stores and long distance service providers, but it has no place in a delinquency setting. The most powerful measure of a program's success may be the rate of recidivism. Finally, it is often argued that a combination of the above factors contribute to reduced recidivism rates in teen court participants. Until recently, the evidence to support this claim was anecdotal.

The first major study to track the effect of teen courts on recidivism was published in April 2002 by Jeffrey A. Butts, et al., entitled, "The Impact of Teen Courts on Young Offenders." Although a program's effectiveness is arguably multifaceted, this study measured effectiveness by decreased recidivism. The study compared over five hundred teen court cases from programs located in Alaska, Arizona, Maryland, and Missouri with similar cases tried within that jurisdiction's traditional juvenile justice system. The study then compared the recidivism rates of the juvenile offenders from both groups after six months.

Both the Alaska and Missouri teen court programs' lower recidivism rates were statistically significant ($p < .01$) when compared to similar cases tried in the states' traditional juvenile justice systems. The recidivism rates in the Arizona and Maryland teen court programs were not statistically significant. The attribute that contributed most to the recidivism rate in teen courts was social attitude. Juvenile offenders that reported high levels of "pro-social attitudes" before participating in the teen court were less likely to reoffend within six months. Although the study results suggested teen courts decrease recidivism rates through the positive use of peer pressure, the researchers readily acknowledged the need for more research before one could conclude teen courts effectively combat juvenile crime....

C. Widening the Net

Another concern with the teen court system is the "wider net of social control" given to the traditional juvenile system. Juveniles who may have never appeared before the court, let alone entered the system, are now fulfilling teen court sentences to avoid referral to the juvenile court for harsher sentencing. Proponents of teen court programs argue that the wider net only brings juveniles into the system sooner rather than later, and consider the teen court experience to be a much needed intervention.

D. Scope of Punishment

The greatest variation among teen courts is in the sentencing. This raises the inevitable concern that juvenile offenders that commit similar crimes do not receive similar punishment. In some teen courts, judicial intervention is necessary to reduce a punishment that is ridiculously disproportionate with the offense. In Los Angeles, California, Superior Court Judge Jaime R. Corral "reversed" a teen court sanction that imposed 750 hours of community service for a minor infraction. In Texas, a justice of the peace refused a sentence that suggested a one-month stay in a juvenile detention facility for a traffic violation. Conversely, critics argue that teen courts are too lenient. As the traditional juvenile system begins to favor punishment over re habilitation, some sentences seem inappropriate. Recently, one teen court imposed the sanction of one hug to the defendant's worried grandmother. Disparate treatment is not wrong as a rule. Factual circumstances vary with each case, and the juvenile's remorse should rightfully play a role in determining the sentence. Nevertheless, it is imperative that the teenagers impose sentences that are at least consistent, and not a reflection of personal convictions inappropriate for a court of law.

Notes/Questions

1. Should concerns about disparate treatment prevent the development and increased use of teen courts as a diversion option?

2. As a prosecutor, what policies could you introduce to prevent "widening the net" at the time that an option to divert a case to teen court was introduced?

3. Would you support a "law student" court at your law school for disputes between students? If so, for what kinds of disputes? Roommate? Study group? Physical altercations? Honor code violations? Conduct code violations? And what process would you suggest? Who should serve as the jury?

C. Concerns about Problem-Solving Courts

You have read about the variety of concerns regarding how problem-solving courts work in the adult criminal system. These concerns include: changes in how professionals such as judges and lawyers do their jobs in these courts; concerns about whether defendants' rights are protected, including due process rights; and concerns about whether the legal system is the right place to offer treatment that is usually done by medical professionals. All of these concerns apply within the juvenile system. In addition, there are concerns, as you will read, that these courts take away from providing better treatment to all juvenile offenders, as the original juvenile courts were intended to provide.

Erin R. Collins, *Status Courts*

105 Geo. L.J. 1481, 1492–96, 1497, 1498–99,
1500, 1502–05, 1511 (2017)

...

C. THIRD GENERATION: STATUS COURTS

Recently, a new generation of problem-solving courts has begun to emerge: what I call here "status courts." The organizational principle of status courts is that offenders who belong to certain status groups have unique needs that the conventional justice system does not, but should, meet. Status courts seek to solve this systemic oversight by offering services and treatment options specifically tailored to the needs of the populations they target.

To date, status courts have emerged to address two status groups: veterans and girls. Veterans courts are criminal courts that offer intensive supervision, coordinated services, and treatment as an alternative to incarceration for criminal defendants who have served in the United States military. Judge Robert Russell opened the nation's first veterans court in 2008 based on his observation that "veterans are a niche population with unique needs" who require "tailored care." The uniqueness of veterans' needs are said to derive from the impact of military service, in particular the traumatic and potentially criminogenic impact of combat. This model has proliferated quickly. By July 2014, just six years after the first court's opening, approximately 200 veterans courts had opened. [Editors' note: we have also discussed veterans' courts in Chapter 9.]

Girls courts are gender-specific juvenile courts that adjudicate delinquency charges against female offenders. Like veterans courts, girls courts reflect a judgment that those who come before them have special, unmet needs that distinguish them from the general offender population and require specialized attention. The first modern girls court opened in Oahu, Hawaii in 2004 because "[g]irls in the juvenile justice system have special needs that were not being met by a system traditionally designed for boys." The Hawaii State Judiciary specifies, "female juvenile offenders tend to be victims of physical, sexual, and emotional abuse and experience depression and low self-esteem that are linked to at-risk behaviors and delinquency." It also identifies "[s]ubstance abuse and school failure" as "prominent characteristics of at-risk girls."

Thus, the Oahu court focuses on programs that address "issues such as healing from physical, sexual and emotional abuse, family conflict, substance abuse, depression, suicidal ideation and attempts, and self-injurious behaviors." The court also emphasizes "activities that focus on empowerment, self-respect, and self-efficacy." Although girls courts predated the first veterans court by four years, they have spread less rapidly; to date only a handful of girls courts have opened nationwide, most recently in Duval County, Florida, in September 2014.

Status courts resemble treatment courts in both ideology and structure. Like treatment courts, status courts primarily adopt a therapeutic jurisprudence approach to problem-solving justice, promoting treatment and rehabilitation as a way to reduce recidivism. Veterans courts explicitly model themselves on drug courts, and aim to "successfully rehabilitate veterans." Girls courts similarly adopt a "[t]herapeutic modalit[y] and approach[]," and embrace the characteristics of many treatment courts, such as intensive supervision and therapeutic services provided by a coordinated, multidisciplinary team. And as in treatment courts, status courts regularly monitor participants and mete out positive reinforcement or graduated sanctions, depending on the participant's progress.

Because status courts are similar to treatment courts, those who have analyzed courts that fall within the category have mistakenly characterized them as simply a new type of treatment court. However, status courts differ from treatment courts in an important and definitive way: the characteristic used to filter offenders into the court is not a "problem" to be "solved." So in contrast to drug courts, for example, which aim to treat the underlying drug addiction that contributed to the criminal behavior, status courts do not seek to break the offender's connection with the characteristic around which the court is organized; when the status court offender is finished with the court process, he or she will not stop being a veteran or a girl. Instead, as the following discussion demonstrates, status courts take affirmative steps to strengthen the offender's association with his or her status group.

The animating justification for status courts is that neither the conventional court system nor existing problem-solving courts adequately address the purportedly unique needs of these particular populations. When Judge Russell opened the first veterans court in Buffalo, New York, he presided over the city's drug and mental health courts but believed that these courts were "limited" in their ability to serve veterans. Veterans, he concluded, "derive from a unique culture, with unique experiences and needs" and, therefore, require a "unique program" that specifically targets their needs.

Girls courts similarly reflect a judgment that they target a distinctive population whose needs were being overlooked by the conventional system. The first girls court opened in 2004 as part of the effort to "stem" what was perceived to be a "quickly rising tide of female delinquency"; whereas the rates of juvenile delinquency were dropping overall, the rate of girls entering the juvenile system was increasing. Although the increase eventually was determined to be the result of changes in policing strategies, not behavioral patterns, the statistics inspired the creation of "gender-responsive" juvenile justice programs, including girls courts. Girls courts embrace the twin presumptions that motivate all gender-responsive programming: that boys and girls are fundamentally different and the conventional juvenile justice system, including the "[s]taffing patterns, staff training, classification systems, physical design, and the correctional routine," were designed "for a male juvenile population."

Thus, although they serve very different populations, both veterans courts and girls courts stem from a similar concern. Both justify the specialized justice they offer with claims that the populations they serve have "unique needs" that are not—and cannot be—satisfied in the conventional system, requiring the creation of a new institution dedicated only to members of that status group. In this way, status courts—though they grew out of the modern problem-solving court movement—echo the claims offered in support of the creation of juvenile courts. In some ways juvenile courts were the first problem-solving court. For example, they were the first to make the system respond more effectively to particular types of offenders by carving out separate court processes and procedures. But there is an even stronger parallel between juvenile courts and status courts. Juvenile courts were created, in large part, because reformers believed the adult criminal court system was "unfit to address the underlying issues that brought a young person to court" and "[un]able to distinguish the special developmental needs of children in order to treat them differently than adults."

Yet, status courts strive to meet a unique goal that distinguishes them from their problem-solving court predecessors, both modern and historic: they aim to honor the experience of the offenders.... The first "Program Value" upon which the Hawaii Girls Court bases its "decision making and actions" is "[h]onoring the [f]emale [e]xperience." Thus, status courts' process is not just about what the offender should change, but also what they should respect in themselves. If the process succeeds, the offender leaves court proud of the characteristic that brought ... her into the court.

To accomplish this goal, status courts strive to create a courtroom environment in which members of the status group play a prominent role....

Like veterans courts, many girls courts strive to create a courtroom environment of mutual trust, respect, and understanding by staffing the court with people with whom the offender can identify, in this case women. The Oahu and Alameda County courts, for example, are staffed predominantly by women, featuring female judges, court officers, and attorneys who are expected to act as role models for the girls. Furthermore, in addition to traditional therapeutic programming aimed at addressing addiction and mental health issues, girls courts offer programs that aim to target what their creators have identified as needs unique to girls, such as building self-esteem and inspiring trust and respect in relationships with family members, other girls, and court personnel. The mission of Dallas County's new E.S.T.E.E.M. (Experiencing Success Through Empowerment, Encouragement and Mentoring) Court is to "provide positive experiences" for the female participants to "foster success and empowerment and thereby prevent further involvement in the legal system." And Hawaii's court offers activities and services that provide girls with a "powerful context ... to build relationship skills and maintain healthy relationships," which have included group community service projects, mother-daughter retreats for participants and mother figures, and group activities such as surfing lessons and art projects.

II. REVEALING THE TROUBLING RELEASE OF PROBLEM-SOLVING JUSTICE

... [P]roblem-solving courts are selective reforms that parcel out opportunities and resources to particular offenders or, in the case of accountability courts, particular victims. This increased funding for resources and opportunities—for some—raises the specter of unequal access to a different, and purportedly better, kind of justice for certain offenders or victims in a system that claims to treat all equally.

Surprisingly, this selective distribution of access to resources, opportunities, and perhaps alternatives to incarceration has not been met with abundant outcry. To the contrary, many have hailed problem-solving courts as the most important criminal justice system innovation of our time, with a fervor that has been compared to evangelism. Although the problem-solving court enterprise has been subjected to increasing scholarly critique, no one has yet questioned the distributive equity of the problem-solving court model itself....

A. STATUS COURTS AND MORAL SORTING

In justifying status courts selection mechanisms, proponents invoke a discourse of difference, insisting that status courts are necessary to serve the "unique needs" of particular status groups. Although these courts serve dramatically different populations, the needs of both groups are said to result from the residual influence of traumatic experiences that often accompanies group membership. However, as the following discussion demonstrates, the latent and possibly criminogenic impact of past traumatic experiences is a condition that connects girls and veterans to, rather than separates them from, other offenders. What really distinguishes these offenders from others is not the impact of trauma per se, but rather a judgment that the criminal justice system should account for the impact of trauma upon certain populations because they are more deserving of such treatment. In other words, as this section contends, the sorting in which status courts engage is moral, not empirical....

The foundational claims about the uniqueness of girls' needs similarly obscures a point of connection between them and those who are "sorted out" of these courts—boys. An organizing principle of girls courts is that girls follow "fundamentally different" pathways to delinquency than boys. The distinguishing factor many proponents invoke is that many girls have experienced past trauma—particularly sexual and physical abuse—and that this trauma contributes to their criminality. Toward that end, girls courts, like all gender-responsive juvenile justice reform efforts, seek to provide "[t]rauma-informed services" that respond to the traumatic impact of physical and sexual abuse against girls and young women. For example, the Alameda County Girls' Court dedicates itself to the creation of a "trauma-informed courtroom" that focuses on "addressing the trauma, healing, and empowerment of young women." Trauma-informed service providers aim to "be aware of consumers' history of past abuse, to understand the role that abuse plays in victims' lives, and to use this understanding to create services that facilitate their participation in treatment."

As with the link between PTSD and criminal behavior, it is undeniable that sexual and physical abuse can be criminogenic. In response to concerns over the increase in arrest rates for female juveniles, the Department of Justice's Office of Juvenile Justice and Delinquency Prevention convened the Girls Study Group in 2008 to gain insight into, *inter alia*, the causes of delinquency in girls. While the group found that some delinquency risk factors are "gender sensitive," importantly, it found that "*girls and boys experience many of the same delinquency risk factors.*" Crucially, the group found that all types of maltreatment—sexual, physical, and neglect—increase the risk of delinquency in *all* juveniles. In other words, the experience of sexual victimization may contribute to delinquency for *both* boys and girls. Although sexual victimization is more common among girls, that sexual victimization contributes to delinquency is not "unique" to them. Moreover, although many girls who come into contact with the juvenile justice system have been subjected to sexual abuse, undoubtedly not all have. The use of gender as a proxy for sexual victimization, therefore, is both under- and overinclusive.

Thus, the experience of trauma—and its potentially criminogenic influence—is hardly unique to veterans or girls. By invoking a discourse of difference, however, status court proponents avoid having to grapple with the difficult and unavoidable conclusion that a history of trauma is one that unites veterans and girls with, rather than separates them from, other offenders. For example, veterans court proponents insist that the trauma experienced by veterans is qualitatively different than that experienced by civilians.

Once the veil of uniqueness is lifted, the only remaining justification for the separation of these populations into different courts is that these offenders deserve different—and better—treatment than others. Veterans court proponents routinely insist that instead of being "churned through the courts like any common criminal," veterans "need and *deserve* something *much better*." Girls court proponents make similar claims, albeit less directly, by insisting that girls are different from boys and require a more empathetic, relational court experience than boys do. But it is undeniable that the process girls courts promise, one that values trust, respect, and empowerment, is qualitatively better than the conventional juvenile justice system.

That status courts embody a judgment about moral desert of these offenders is underscored by the intragroup sorting that occurs within status courts. Despite the broad rhetoric about the universal needs of veterans and girls, some of these courts restrict access to only a segment of these status group populations. Most veterans courts, for example, preclude those who were dishonorably discharged from participating. This restriction "reflects the sense that participants deserve the help provided in the treatment court because of their honorable service."

In sum, status courts are concerned with funneling resources not only, or even primarily, to where they can be most effective but rather to where they are most deserved. *This*—the sorting of offenders for rehabilitative opportunities based on a judgment about morality—represents a true paradigm shift. The criminal law supposedly responds to the offense and is not concerned with making moral judgments about the worth of the offender.

....

The reasoning for girls courts is less direct but equally troubling. A foundational principle of girls courts is that male and female juveniles have distinct needs and the traditional juvenile justice system was designed "for boys." Among the "Gender-Specific Programming for Girls" the Oahu court offers are programs that provide emotional and physical safety, address abuse, are culturally competent, provide positive role models, and are strength- and relationship-based. And the "gender-responsive" values it seeks to advance include "Healing," "Instilling Hope," and "Nurturing Strengths." It is difficult to imagine how male juvenile offenders would not benefit from programs that emphasize these values. Yet, by justifying the implementation of these programs through a discourse of gender difference, the courts imply that *only* girls need these specialized programs; because the traditional system was designed "for boys," it already addresses their needs and need not be changed to accommodate them. Male offenders, it follows, do not require the empathetic, relational treatment promoted in the girls court setting.

Thus, by conveying that offenders who do not belong to these status groups do not require or deserve specialized treatment, status courts risk reifying old ways of doing justice for non-status offenders, who comprise the majority of the criminal offender population. Indeed, if non-status offenders deserve the dysfunctional system, it follows that there is no need to change it.

Notes/Questions

1. Is the ultimate lesson of the problem-solving court movement, including with juvenile courts, that as a society we should move away from individual retributive approaches to crime and more to a rehabilitative focus that recognizes the societal forces that influence individual criminal behavior?

2. What are the barriers to doing as Collins recommends and shutting down status courts and problem-solving courts and instead incorporating these ideas into the juvenile legal system as a whole? How would juvenile court judges likely respond? How would prosecutors likely respond? How would defense lawyers likely respond? And how would the general public respond to this kind of restructuring?

3. If you were a prosecutor in a small county, could you think of changing how your county handles juvenile cases to bring them in line with the approach that Collins recommends? Would it be easier or tougher if you worked in a larger or smaller county?

IV. Restorative Justice for Juveniles

Restorative justice is perhaps most widely used in the United States with juveniles. A variety of restorative justice programs exist, which prevent cases from entering the criminal legal system or divert cases out of the criminal legal system. You have already read about many of these programs and the philosophy underlying the use of restorative justice. The reading for this section focuses on how restorative justice might be used to both solve disputes between juveniles and to prevent criminal acts from occurring that could be brought into the juvenile criminal legal system. The first reading gives an overview of the use of restorative justice for juveniles in the context of school discipline cases and highlights both examples and concerns about using this process in schools.

Cara Suvall, *Restorative Justice in Schools: Learning from Jena High School*

44 HARV. C.R.-C.L. L. REV. 547–48, 548–50, 550–51, 557, 559–66 (2009)

I. Introduction

Public policy debates about discipline and punishment often include a tension between punitive and rehabilitative ideals. Although policymakers and practitioners often advocate rehabilitative ideals, there is a trend in criminal and juvenile justice away from rehabilitation and toward increasingly punitive forms of discipline. This same movement is occurring in education. Punitive discipline is the dominant model in schools today. Schools rely on exclusion through suspension and expulsion, harsh mandatory punishments, surveillance, and partnership with law enforcement to address behavior problems.

Instead of being a solution, punitive school discipline is often part of the problem. Disciplinary exclusion through suspension and expulsion deprives misbehaving students of educational opportunities while still generally failing to make schools safer places for other students. Punitive discipline unilaterally imposes punishment on offenders, thereby failing to turn disciplinary violations into learning experiences. This missed opportunity is particularly problematic because of the socializing function played by schools. School communities, comprised of students, teachers, and administrators, have long been viewed as fulfilling important roles in affirming democratic norms and other positive social values. If schools do not address disciplinary violations in ways that promote positive norms within the school community, then their disciplinary policies are not meeting the needs of the school environment.

An alternative to punitive school discipline is an approach rooted in the values of restorative justice. The dominant goals of restorative justice include repairing the harm caused by an offense and community participation in disciplinary procedures. There are many models of conflict resolution that fall under the rubric of restorative justice. All of these include mechanisms for expressing a community's disapproval of an offender's actions while simultaneously reaffirming the norms of the community and reintegrating the offender back into the community. Restorative justice practices build support for victims and offenders, providing both with an opportunity to share their perspectives and to work together to reach a reparative solution. Whereas traditional school discipline cuts off discussion in favor of a swift and punitive response, restorative programs focus on improving the community's capacity to respond positively to adversity and conflict.

This Essay advances the argument that a disciplinary response rooted in restorative justice values is more appropriate for schools than the conventional punitive disciplinary approach.

A. The Problem of School Misconduct

School discipline is an extremely important issue facing schools today and it requires a strong and concerted response by schools and administrators. Disciplinary problems, ranging from minor misbehavior to outright violence, inhibit classroom learning and place students at risk. In a 1998 national survey, 40% of public school students reported that the misbehavior of other students interfered with their school performance. Students at schools with moderate to high levels of school violence see their performance particularly inhibited. They are less likely to graduate from high school or attend a four-year college, even after controlling for a range of student and school characteristics. The National Center for Education Statistics found that in 2005 approximately 4% of students ages 12–18 reported being victimized at school during the past six months, with 3% reporting being the victim of a theft and 1% reporting violent victimization. The harmful effects of victimization extend beyond the specific victim, as disciplinary violations create a threatening environment and cause heightened levels of stress for all of a school's students.

B. Punitive School Discipline Responses

As concern about school discipline has grown over the last several decades, schools have responded through punitive and authoritarian measures. Schools have adopted heightened security procedures such as controlling access to and from school buildings, using metal detectors to check for weapons, employing random dog sniffs to look for drugs, performing random sweeps for contraband, and using security cameras. Schools have also extended their disciplinary reach over incidents that occur off-campus. Congress and state legislatures have supported the growth of punitive discipline policies by increasing criminal penalties associated with offenses committed near schools. Courts similarly have generally supported schools' disciplinary efforts, for example by upholding random drug testing as a prerequisite to participation in school athletic programs....

Beginning in the late 1980s, heightened public concern about school safety and the spread of zero tolerance policies caused a swing back toward exclusion as a major school discipline strategy. As a result, there has been a significant increase in average national student suspension rates, which nearly doubled between 1974 and 1997: from 3.7% to 6.8% per year. According to the Department of Education's National Center for Education Statistics, a 2003 survey showed that 10.8% of students from kindergarten to 12th grade have been suspended at some point in their educational careers, and 2.0% have been expelled.

One of the characteristics of punitive school discipline is zero tolerance policies. Zero tolerance policies in schools are a relatively recent development. While some schools have used zero tolerance policies since the late 1980s, school boards around the country began widely adopting them beginning in 1993. Zero tolerance in schools is an outgrowth of similar policies in the military and in the criminal justice system. As in the criminal context, the mandatory punishments are designed to be highly punitive in order to send a strong deterrent message to other would-be offenders.

Under zero tolerance policies, students are suspended or expelled for a single occurrence of certain specified conduct. Zero tolerance in schools began solely for serious offenses like possession of firearms. Over the past few years, however, zero tolerance policies have expanded to include a wider range of student behavior including other violence, bullying, threatening, use of profanity, alcohol or tobacco consumption, and other offenses.

The "school-to-prison pipeline" is another characteristic of contemporary school discipline policy that highlights both its increasingly punitive nature and the infiltration of criminal justice policy into education policy. This "pipeline" includes all school and criminal justice policies that speed the removal of students from schools and their entry into the juvenile and criminal justice systems. Many referrals to the juvenile justice system stem from offenses that occur at school. This has a disproportionate effect on youth of color, who are more likely to be referred for school disciplinary offenses. The overrepresentation of students of color in the disciplinary referral process parallels and is one of the reasons for the overrepresentation of black youth in the juvenile justice system....

IV. Restorative Justice as a More Effective School Discipline Model

School discipline problems are school-wide problems.... Schools need to respond to discipline problems seriously and effectively. Focusing on punishing only the offender is insufficient. Schools must instead tailor their disciplinary responses with an eye towards addressing the community-wide impact of disciplinary violations and supporting the offender in positive behavior change. Rather than focusing solely on punishing the offender, the restorative justice movement provides a framework for a school discipline model that can focus on repairing harm by identifying community dynamics and victim and offender needs....

B. Benefits of Restorative Justice

i. Broader Understanding of Harm

A restorative justice philosophy in schools views misconduct as a harm to community members and relationships, not as an offense against the institution itself. This understanding of harm brings with it collateral benefits. As members of the school community, students are more likely to understand this idea of harm. Emphasizing the harm caused by violation of a school rule or policy will help students see the rules as more legitimate and will also help students view the disciplinary consequences as more fair. This idea of harm also creates an opportunity for the disciplinary process to address the perspectives and needs of the victims, whether discrete community members who have been individually wronged or a broader segment of the school community.

Traditional approaches to school violence fail to assess the full extent of harm that violence can cause to students within a school. This includes the psychological and emotional harms that arise from being in a community where misconduct or even violence occurs, as well as more concrete harms such as decreased instructional time due to a teacher's need to address disciplinary issues. Traditional discipline similarly does not take into account the harm to an offender and victim resulting from the school's own disciplinary policies or practices. We can view the disciplinary actions of the school as another form of "systemic violence." This concept draws on education theorist Paulo Freire's concept of liberation pedagogy and feminist and critical race theory. "Systemic violence" understands the disciplinary actions of the school as another form of violence: violating the student victims whose concerns are not met and violating the offenders who are prevented from learning due to alienation from school or physical exclusion. One broad definition of "systemic violence" is:

> any institutional practice or procedure that adversely impacts ... disadvantaged individuals or groups.... It includes practices and procedures that prevent students from learning.... This may take the form of conventional policies and practices that foster a climate of violence, or policies and practices that ... result in discriminatory effects.

This expanded notion of systemic violence and victimization includes a wide range of school practices. It identifies conventional school discipline as a form of violence and an additional source of victimization. Under this model, excluding a student from school is a form of violence against that student that school officials must take into account when they devise a disciplinary approach.

ii. Appreciation of the Context for Disciplinary Violations

Restorative justice also allows the response to address the context in which an offense occurs. Whereas conventional punitive school discipline is narrow in that it typically punishes an offender for specific misconduct, restorative justice recognizes that context is often important and that the roles of the students involved are rarely clearly defined. Because misbehavior is best understood as deriving from an interaction between people's personalities and their environment, schools using solely traditional offender-focused punishment fail to understand how school environment inhibits or exacerbates the likelihood of violence.

Understanding the context of an offense requires a nuanced understanding of victimization. A student identified as an offender in one sense is also likely a victim in another.... Often, schools' failures to create a safe environment are a root cause of violence in schools, as fear of victimization can produce more violence. For example, many fights at school are reactions to perceived needs by students to preserve social status. Even for more serious offenses, like weapons possession, studies show that the majority of youth who carry a gun into school do so for protection, not intimidation. Because the perpetrators of violence are also often in many ways victims, schools must look beyond the isolated incident leading to the disciplinary referral and must instead take a broader view of the context and school environment.

Particularly in school settings with racial tensions, failures of school administrators to address the broader context of racial conflict negatively affect the broader student community. High school students who believe that their peers are prejudiced report higher levels of emotional distress, and high levels of racial tension create hostile school environments....

iii. Repairing Community Relations and Creating Learning Opportunities

Building school community can be justified as an important goal in its own right, and strengthening school community is particularly important for addressing disciplinary issues. This is because institutionally strong communities are best able to prevent misconduct and respond to it when it happens. Restorative justice helps promote these strong community relationships through its ability to engage in a process of "relational rehabilitation." Restorative justice views the problems of violence and anti-social behavior as stemming from a breakdown in social relationships, and it uses the process of identifying harm and imposing a consequence as an opportunity to reaffirm and strengthen those relationships. The focus is not on punishment. Rather, it is on what both the offender and the community must do to reintegrate the offender and repair the bonds between youth, their school, and their broader communities.

By creating a role for the offender and the victim, restorative justice is able to serve as a learning experience and can help develop positive social norms. This is contrasted with conventional punitive school discipline, in which the student offender passively experiences punishment. Because students accused of disciplinary violations are rarely given the opportunity to explain their version of events and are instead forced into a passive role, students often resent and feel alienated from both the school's authority figures and the institution they represent. Such a student may experience the process as so unjust that she views herself as the victim.... With conventional punitive school discipline, the community witnesses only the initial punishment. In contrast, with a restorative justice approach, the community is able to participate in the process of learning about the offense and the harm, witness the offender's acknowledgement of responsibility, and support her reintegration.

V. Implementation of Restorative Justice Models in Schools

Having identified many benefits that a restorative justice framework can offer school communities, we now move on to examining how restorative justice can be implemented in schools.

A. Case Studies of Restorative Justice in Schools

The largest study of restorative practices in schools took place in Queensland, Australia. Queensland was the site of the first documented school restorative justice conference, which took place in 1994 in response to a serious assault at a high school. The Queensland schools continued to conference future disciplinary violations. The majority of these conferences dealt with assaults and serious victimization. Eighty-nine conferences were conducted during the course of two studies, and conferencing continues today. The Queensland model is an adaptation of the family conference model. The conferences are conducted by a trained facilitator who brings together the offender and her victims along with their families, supporters, and appropriate school personnel. The facilitator poses a number of scripted questions to the offender, who explains in her words what she has done. The facilitator then directs questions to the victim, then to the victim's supporters, and finally to the offender's supporters. All parties are given a chance to tell their version of events and their account of the harm done to them. The entire group then goes on to decide what should be done to repair the harm and how to minimize the likelihood that it will happen again. The group reaches an agreement that reflects the victim's wishes but which is negotiated until all parties are satisfied that it is fair and reflects the value of reparation instead of retribution. Agreements can also provide for future support for the offender or victim.

Findings from the conferences were very positive. There was a high compliance rate by the offenders with the terms of the agreement. After conferencing, a majority of offenders said they felt more accepted by other conference participants, and a majority of victims felt safer and more able to manage similar situations. All school administrators questioned in relation to the conferences felt that conferencing reinforced school values. Nearly all schools reported that they had changed their thinking from a punitive to a more restorative approach. Despite these positive findings, however, there were also a significant number of incidents that these same schools chose not to conference, but instead dealt with in a traditional punitive manner that included suspensions and expulsions.

This tension between a desire to use restorative methods and a desire to return to the more traditional punitive methods is seen in all attempts to introduce restorative justice into schools. In the United States, both Minnesota and Denver, Colorado schools have attempted to implement restorative justice practices throughout their districts. The strategy used in Minnesota was similar to the conference model in Queensland in that it included the same parties and provided an opportunity for participants to discuss strategies for repairing the harm, reintegrating the offender, and building community. The mediators in Minnesota were members of the school and general community, including teachers, administrators, corrections officers, and others who were trained in restorative conferencing techniques. Minnesota, the restorative justice approach was treated as one possible approach among many legitimate disciplinary approaches, and conventional punitive discipline continued to play an important role as well. The Minnesota Department of Children, Families and Learning, described it as "another tool to use with children and youth to repair harm and teach problem solving skills."

The implementation of restorative practices in Denver included a wider scope of practices, ranging from "informal classroom meetings where the teacher calls an impromptu circle to address a student's misbehavior to the more formal victim impact panels, where student offenders learn about the effects of their type of offense from victims of similar offenses." The schools tended to use victim impact panels and formal conferencing when the case involved a higher degree of severity, and informal methods when the offense was less severe. The results for the offenses that were conferenced in both locations were overwhelmingly positive, with sharp drops in exclusionary discipline practices. This corresponded to decreases in violent acts and other disruptive behavior and also reflected the way in which restorative justice provides an alternative means of disciplining students.

However, in both programs the schools found that the restorative model was in tension with the broader institutional policies grounded in retributive justice both within the schools and in the criminal justice system. Denver, like Minnesota, used "a loose combination of restorative justice and traditional punitive responses when dealing with the more severe criminal offenses." For example, if a student was caught selling drugs, the student would still typically be suspended, but the school would engage in restorative practices upon the student's return to school, at which point the focus would be less on making amends and more on building relationships. Because of the background norm of retributive justice in schools and the retributive practices of the criminal justice system, schools had to either develop standards for determining which offenses should get the benefit of restorative treatment, or require students to go through both a restorative and retributive process either concurrently or consecutively.

B. Limitations of Restorative Justice against the Backdrop of Punitive Discipline

Drawing on the experiences of Denver and Minnesota, we can identify the backdrop of the punitive criminal justice system as a serious impediment to implementing restorative justice in schools. Because the benefits of restorative justice can only be accessed through a process in which the offender acknowledges the harm that she has caused, restorative justice is unlikely to work when the stakes for the offender are too high. For example, if acknowledging culpability in a restorative conference can have serious implications for a pending criminal charge against a student, it would be against the student's interest to participate in a restorative process. While Denver addressed this problem by instituting a restorative process subsequent to a criminal referral, this approach is unlikely to work if the student feels that the criminal consequences were already harsh. For this reason, it is nearly impossible to imagine incorporating restorative justice in parallel or subsequent processes to the serious criminal charges faced by the Jena Six. This suggests that schools can only truly perform their socializing role if the school is able to address disciplinary issues without the involvement of the criminal justice system.

Some proponents of restorative discipline view restorative justice as one possible response in a pyramid of responses of escalating severity. Under this pyramid model, restorative justice would be used as an initial response, with more harsh responses such as exclusion or referral to the criminal justice system as options to be used further up the pyramid if a restorative approach should fail. Yet today's school discipline culture interferes with the development of a restorative model because most schools' first response is to exclude a student from school or to refer an offense to the criminal justice system. While some schools attempt to include a restorative element at a later point, it is difficult for restorative justice to play a role after the severity of the response has already been escalated.

Notes/Questions

1. New Zealand handles virtually all of its juvenile cases through restorative justice proceedings. Do you think that the United States should move towards using restorative justice in most juvenile cases? What would be the advantages and disadvantages? What would be impediments to such a change?

2. Jena High School is an example of a school that did not use restorative based practices as a part of their school disciplinary process. Jena is a predominately white town in Louisiana. Approximately 10% of the population is African American. In 2006, there were a number of incidents that exacerbated tensions between the African American and white students at Jena High School. These incidents included the hanging of nooses from a tree on the high school grounds, which is described in the excerpt below. In addition to the nooses incident, there were two violent confrontations between white and black students in which only the black students were arrested and criminally charged. One of these incidents led to the arrest of six African American students (the Jena Six) many of whom were initially charged as adults and with serious felonies, including attempted second-degree murder, and were facing long terms of imprisonment. All charges were eventually reduced to lesser offenses. Professor Suvall, below, questions whether school administrators could have prevented the incidents from inflaming had they used a restorative based approach:

> An analysis of how school administrators at Jena High School handled the series of racially-charged incidents leading up to the assault on Justin Barker provides a particularly vivid example of the failures of conventional punitive school discipline. Much attention has been paid to the problems in the criminal justice system highlighted by the prosecution of the Jena Six. However, relatively little attention has been paid to how administrators at Jena High School addressed the incidents leading up to the assault or to how a different response could have prevented the assault and the involvement of the criminal justice system. The shortcomings in the school's handling of the disciplinary issues stemmed from its failure to include the voices of those who felt victimized or to properly acknowledge the community-wide context of the conflicts and the harm to the broader student body.
>
> The series of racial conflicts in Jena, Louisiana leading up to the assault that spawned the charges against the Jena Six began on August 31, 2006, the first day of school. At an assembly, a black student asked a school administrator whether he could sit under a tree that was known as a hang-out for white students. The student was told that he could sit wherever he wanted. The next morning students arrived at school to find two nooses hanging from the tree.
>
> Jena High School Principal Scott Windham recommended to the expulsion hearing committee that the students who hung the nooses be expelled, which was the harshest punishment available in Jena High School's Code of Conduct. While the severity of this punishment indicates that the principal took the

offense seriously, the school did not publicly address the racial nature of the incident. Officials did not acknowledge the significance of the noose-hanging at the school nor its relation to the history of violent lynching and threats against blacks in the South. School officials later said that, "in reality, the nooses had nothing to do with racial bigotry, but rather were an ignorant prank taken from the mini-series, Lonesome Dove." The parish expulsion hearing committee voted to override the principal's recommendation. The committee chose instead to suspend the three students on the basis that the noose hanging was not racially motivated. After the suspension hearing, La Salle Parish School Superintendent Roy Breithaupt said that there were no plans to address the matter again before the school board, since he felt that the issue had been dealt with sufficiently.

Neither the school nor the school district provided any opportunity for input from those who perceived themselves as victims of the noose-hanging or from the broader community. The parents and students who felt harmed by the noose-hanging were never given an opportunity to have their concerns formally acknowledged or legitimized. Parents of Jena High School students began to meet as early as September 5 to discuss how they should respond to the noose-hanging incident. Many community members felt that the school board had failed to understand the seriousness of the offense, because of the board's reduction in the punishment for the white perpetrators and its refusal to address the racial implications of the noose-hanging. Many parents and community members were as concerned with the response to the noose-hanging as they were with the incident itself. The parents organized to express their concern that the punishment for the students was insufficient. However, the real problem was not the punishment itself, but rather the board's refusal to acknowledge the seriousness of the incident and the harm to the students and community.

In the days following the noose-hanging incident, there was a series of fights between black and white students, causing parents and students to feel that Jena High School was not a safe place. The school dealt with each of the fights as separate violations of the school disciplinary policy, thereby failing to address the escalating situation as a problem facing the school community as a whole. The racial tension led to such a strong sense of a lack of discipline that Superintendent Roy Breithaupt addressed parents by radio broadcast, assuring them that Jena High School was safe and that it was unnecessary to keep their children home from school.

School officials did make one attempt to address the racial conflict: they invited law enforcement to Jena High School. During the week following the noose-hanging, local law enforcement and the Jena High School principal invited District Attorney Reed Walters to speak at a school-wide assembly. District Attorney Walters warned students to behave or they would suffer the consequences. He allegedly told the students, "I can be your best friend or your worst enemy. I could take your lives away with the stroke of my pen." When this warning did not de-escalate the tension at Jena High School, police were sent to the school the following two days "as a precaution," according to the LaSalle Parish Sheriff. The school was placed on a "lockdown" after reports that a student might have brought a gun to school. Unsurprisingly, the increased police intervention at the school did not comfort the students. On this day, 150 students stayed home from Jena High School and 160 more students were pulled out of school by their parents or left on their own later in the day.

Later in the semester there was another series of racially motivated conflicts, this time off-campus. These conflicts included at least some involvement by both white and black Jena High School students. These conflicts began when a group of black students was denied admission to a mostly-white student party and was assaulted by a white party guest and taunted by a group of white guests. The next day there was another confrontation, this time at a convenience store, between black students and a white Jena resident.

On the following Monday afternoon, December 4, a white Jena High School student named Justin Barker was assaulted and knocked unconscious by multiple students in the school gymnasium. Accounts vary as to what sparked the assault and who the attackers were, with some saying it was motivated by racially charged comments Barker made about the weekend's fights, and others saying it was unprovoked. Barker was taken to the hospital and was released after three hours. He drove himself to a high school ring ceremony that evening. The school referred the assault to the police, and six black Jena High students were charged with the assault. These charges were soon increased to attempted murder and conspiracy to commit second degree murder. Local law enforcement denied connections between the Barker assault and the racial tension that had been building up since the noose-hanging, although local detectives said that they suspected that the fight at the party on Friday led to the attack. After the assault, the police and district attorney stepped in to fill the disciplinary role that the school had failed to fill. Had the school better addressed these ongoing conflicts, beginning with the noose-hanging incident, it is possible that the conflicts would not have escalated as they did and that law enforcement would not have become involved.

Cara Suvall, *Restorative Justice in Schools: Learning from Jena High School*, 44 HARV. C.R.-C.L. L. REV. 547, 554–57 (2009).

3. Would a restorative based approach have prevented the escalation at Jena High School? What exactly would constitute a restorative based approach? Professor Suvall suggests the following:

What might a restorative response to the noose-hanging at Jena High have looked like? After identifying the offenders, the next step would have been to identify the victims of the offense. The school might have provided restorative

> options at different levels of the community as a way of acknowledging how this act caused harm to the victims and the broader community. For example, at the most intimate level, three family group conferences could have been held. Each would have included one of the three offenders, a few members of the student body who felt they were harmed by the noose-hanging, family and supporters of the offender and victims, as well as appropriate school administrators or teachers. The school could have arranged a victim impact panel to include more community members who were not able to participate in the conference, opening up the conversation to those outside the student body who also felt harmed by the incident. It might have been appropriate to include victims of other racist acts in order to connect the noose-hanging to the deeper history of racism in this country and particularly in Jena. A school-wide conference would also have been appropriate, one which included both black and white students, to validate that the harm caused was to the entire community, not only to the black students and their families.

Suvall, *supra*, 44 HARV. C.R.-C.L. L. REV. at 567. Do you agree with these suggestions? Should high schools regularly act to intervene earlier to prevent student misconduct from escalating to crimes?

4. If you were a local DA, and read about the noose-hanging incident in a local high school, what would you do? Do you think you might have an obligation to step in and suggest some of the approaches listed above? Would your answer change if one of your children was a student at the same local high school? If you were a local defense lawyer who handles juvenile cases, would you have a different answer? Would it matter if you lived in a small town like Jena, or a large city like Dallas? How proactive should professionals in the criminal legal system be to prevent crime? And at what stage should they intervene?

5. One important part of decreasing juvenile criminal behavior is to increase graduation rates and decrease suspension rates. Proponents suggest that one way to move from "zero-tolerance policies" in school discipline is to adopt restorative practices, and that doing so can reduce school discipline problems and decrease suspension and dropout rates.[4] A related question, in light of continued school shootings, is whether schools with a restorative justice approach may handle problems more holistically, which could reduce bullying, suicide, and school violence.[5] One approach is to use restorative justice to handle disciplinary problems. For example, some school districts in Texas have adopted Restorative Discipline Programs. At one San Antonio middle school that adopted Restorative Discipline, the off-campus suspension rate fell by 87%,

---

4. Trevor Fronius et al., *Restorative Justice in U.S. Schools: A Research Review* 10–11 (West Ed. Justice & Prevention Research Center, Feb. 2016), https://jprc.wested.org/wp-content/uploads/2016/02/RJ_Literature-Review_20160217.pdf.

5. Anya Kamenetz, *Is there Any Way for Schools to Prevent Shootings?*, NPR, Feb. 15, 2018, available at https://www.npr.org/sections/ed/2018/02/15/586022815/is-there-any-way-for-schools-to-prevent-shootings.

and the total suspension rate fell by 44% in the first year.[6] National Public Radio has reported on a number of these programs over the years. *See* Jennifer Guerra, *School Hopes Talking It Out Keeps Kids From Dropping Out*, NPR, June 22, 2013, available at http://www.npr.org/2013/06/22/194467944/ schools-try-restorative-justice-to-keep-kids-from-dropping-out; Eric Westervelt, *What if Every High School Had a Justice Program Instead of a Cop?*, NPR, Oct. 30, 2015, available at https://www.npr.org/sections/ed/2015/10/30/452910812/what-if-every-high-school-had-a-justice-program-instead-of-a-cop.

6. In July 2017, the Office of Justice Programs for the U.S. Department of Justice reported on a research project looking at the effectiveness of restorative justice programs for juveniles. The research found that "some restorative justice programs—when compared to traditional approaches—can reduce future delinquent behavior and produce greater satisfaction for victims." https://www.ncjrs.gov/pdffiles1/ojjdp/grants/250995.pdf.

7. A follow-up study published in 2023 added additional programs and continued to find decreased recidivism rates for juveniles who participated in RJ programs compared to traditional criminal court processes. Catherine S. Kimbrell et al., *Restorative Justice Programs and Practices in Juvenile Justice: an Updated Systemic Review and Meta-analysis for Effectiveness*, 22 Criminology & Public Policy 161 (Feb. 2023).

8. If you were a prosecutor, would you want to have more options to send juvenile cases out to restorative justice proceedings? Would you want those proceedings to be as a diversion of the case, or post-conviction? Why?

9. As a defense lawyer, if restorative justice were not already an option in your county for juvenile cases, and you had a case that you thought was appropriate to send out to a restorative justice proceeding, what might you do to make that happen?

V. Is No Process the Best Process for Juveniles?

Juvenile crime rates have decreased dramatically over the last several decades, as have juvenile incarceration rates. In addition, as we understand from the science of brain development, criminal behavior in general decreases after the age of twenty-five. Should we reconsider our entire system of juvenile prosecutions and prosecuting young adults? As you will read, professionals in the juvenile legal system, scholars, and policymakers are questioning whether the lessons from the declining juvenile crime and incarceration rates are that it is better for the criminal legal system to do minimal, or no, interventions for juveniles and instead allow others, such as schools, family, and the community to be the main intervenors.

---

6. https://tea.texas.gov/Home/Commissioner_Blog/Texas_Focusing_on_Restorative_Discipline/.

A. Juvenile Incarceration Rates

From 2000–2020, juvenile incarceration rates have fallen dramatically. Even after increases of about 10% in 2021 and 2022, the rates are still lower than in the 1970s.[7]

One-Day Count of Youth Held in Juvenile Justice Facilities, 1975–2022[8]

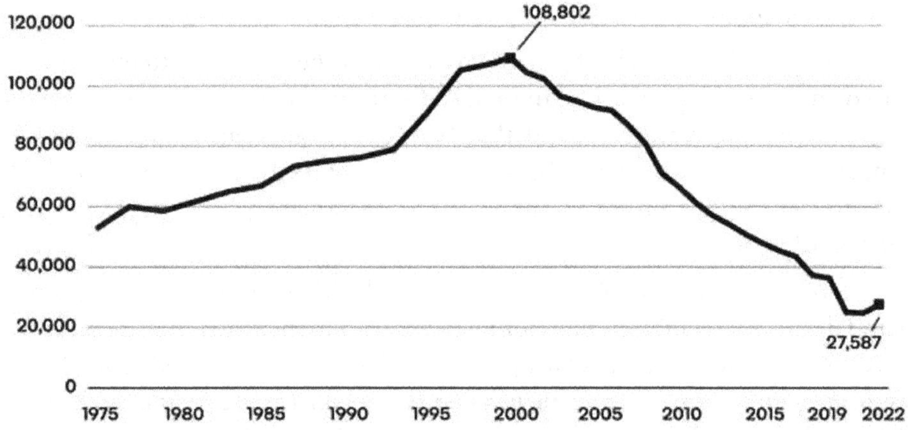

As James Foreman Jr. wrote, "between 2000 and 2020, the number of young people incarcerated in the United States declined by an astonishing 77%.... You don't have to look at the graph for long to grasp the story. First the part that won't surprise you, given the well-chronicled rise in incarceration rates since the 1970s: The number of young people behind bars increased steadily in the 1970s and the 1980s and then rose more sharply in the 1990s. What comes next *is* surprising: Beginning in 2000, each year for the next two decades there was a decline.... If you think of juvenile incarceration as a mountain, we reached the summit in 2000, and until 2020 we sprinted straight downhill.[9]

One of the arguments against decreasing incarceration rates is that doing so will increase criminal behavior. The data on juveniles contradicts this and shows not only a steady decline in incarceration rates, but also a steady decline in arrest rates.

7. James Forman Jr., *What Happened When American Emptied Its Youth Prisons*, NY TIMES MAGAZINE, Jan. 28, 2025.

8. *Id.*

9. *Id.*

Youth Arrest Rates, 1980–2020[10]

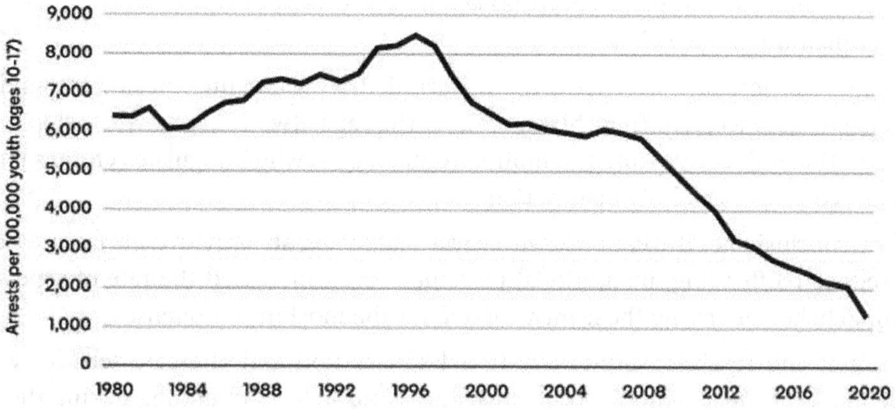

The story behind this data is a substantial shift in mindset by judges and prosecutors away from using incarceration and towards using a variety of community-based resources to help juveniles who were pulled into the criminal legal system.

B. Aging Out of Criminal Behavior

Adjusting Juvenile Justice

UC NET, May 28, 2014

"We found that about 90 percent of these kids stopped offending by the time they turned 25," [Elizabeth Caufmann] says. "A very small percentage continues committing crimes."

[Caufmann] is part of a team conducting a long-term, groundbreaking study on juvenile crime and prevention. The Pathways to Desistance project has tracked 1,300 serious felony offenders between the ages of 14 and 17 in Philadelphia, Phoenix and Orange County. Its goal is to learn what stops some juveniles from committing crimes and, conversely, why others maintain a life of crime. The results so far have surprised Cauffman and fellow researchers. The cease in criminal behavior was not due to any intervention or outreach programs, Cauffman says: "The best predictor of stopping youth crime is just growing up. It's really just due to an increase in maturity and self-control. Older adults are also more resistant to peer pressure."

She says it costs about $100,000 a year to incarcerate a child in a California juvenile detention center. For that amount, she notes, four kids could be educated in the University of California system.

---

10. *Id.*

"If I'm a businessman, that's a terrible return on investment," Cauffman says. "There's a reason rental car companies don't lease out cars to people under 25. They want to protect their investments."

Risky behaviors such as binge drinking, drunk driving and unprotected sex tend to peak in adolescence. Cauffman blames this on the gap between cognitive development and emotional development. The brain's frontal lobe—which regulates emotion and impulse control—isn't fully mature until about 25.

One conclusion of the Pathways study was that longer stays in juvenile facilities did not reduce reoffending; institutional placement even increased the rate of repeated criminal behavior among those incarcerated for the most minor offenses.

"Youth who received community-based supervision and aftercare services were more likely to attend school, go to work and avoid further offending during the six months after release, and longer supervision periods increase these benefits," Cauffman says.

Notes/Questions

1. If people "age out" of criminal offending, should that change sentencing practices both for juveniles, for young adults, and for older adults? Should life without the possibility of parole ever be used with a younger person?

2. Should it change who we prosecute? Should juveniles be prosecuted at all?

3. When we draw lines for age, should it matter how "smart" you are? Your educational level? Or your social class? Should we, for example, punish a 24-year-old law student more harshly then a 24-year-old high school graduate? Or a 24-year-old high school drop out?

4. Does our expanded understanding of the brain due to neuroscience call for entirely different approaches, such as restorative justice, for juvenile and young adult crime? Or should we simply keep juveniles in juvenile court and not transfer them to adult court? You will want to keep in mind these questions as you read the final chapter.

5. Consider this from James Forman Jr., discussing the juvenile legal system:

> Can doing nothing really be enough? For some teenagers, the University of Miami criminologist Alex Piquero says, the answer is yes. Piquero ran the Federal Bureau of Justice Statistics in 2022 and 2023; before that, he was an author of the landmark Pathways to Desistance study, which tracked over 1,300 teenagers who went through juvenile systems in Philadelphia and Phoenix into young adulthood. "One of the things that people don't understand is how many young people who commit delinquent acts will simply grow out of that phase on their own," Piquero says. "They mature, their brains develop, and they learn to make better decisions."
>
> But others need help, and in the past three decades there has been a remarkable, if largely unacknowledged, explosion of initiatives designed to pro-

> vide it. Some [programs have] the goal of helping them address the factors that have led them to break the law. Others, … pair young people with histories of violence or delinquency with mentors and advocates who offer therapy and connect them to education and employment services.
>
> What these programs have in common is evidence to support their effectiveness. As the Sentencing Project's Richard Mendel explains: "The research is clear that kids who are placed in one of these programs tend to do better than those who are sent to a juvenile facility. And the group that does best of all is those who are diverted from the system entirely."

James Foman Jr., *What Happened when America Emptied it Youth Prisons: Lessons from a radical 20-year experiment and a quiet triumph of public policy*, NY TIMES, Jan 28, 2025.

This chapter has considered how various alternative processes are being used with juveniles and has asked the question of whether any or all of these processes are a better approach. You may want to keep these questions in mind, and the specifics of the juvenile legal system, as you read the final chapter which addresses these questions for all offenders, not only juvenile offenders.

Additional Resources

Samantha Buckingham, *Trauma Informed Juvenile Justice*, 53 AM. CRIM. L. REV. 641 (2016).

Ericka N. Fountain & Jennifer Woolard, *Negotiating with Parents: Attorney Practices in the Juvenile Plea Bargain Process*, 45 L. & HUM. BEHAV. 112, (2021).

Mark R. Fondacaro et al., *Reconceptualizing Due Process in Juvenile Justice: Contributions from Law and Social Science*, 57 HASTINGS L.J. 955 (2006).

Kristin Henning, *Criminalizing Normal Adolescent Behavior in Communities of Color: The Role of Prosecutors in Juvenile Justice Reform*, 98 CORNELL L. REV. 383 (2013).

Janet C. Hoeffel, *The Jurisprudence of Death and Youth: Now the Twain Should Meet*, 46 TEX. TECH. L. REV. 29 (2013).

Tamar Lerer, *Hawai'i Girls Court: Juvenile, Gender, and Justice*, 18 BERKELEY J. CRIM. L. 84 (2013).

David Pimentel, *The Widening Maturity Gap: Trying and Punishing Juveniles as Adults in an Era of Extended Adolescence*, 46 TEX. TECH. L. REV. 71 (2013).

Joy Radice, *The Juvenile Record Myth*, 106 GEO. L.J. 365 (2018).

Kelly Richards, et al., *Children's Magistrates' View of Restorative Justice and Therapeutic Jurisprudence: Measure for Young Offenders*, 17 YOUTH JUSTICE 22 (2016).

Christopher Slobogin & Mark R. Fondacaro, *Juvenile Justice: The Fourth Option*, 95 IOWA L. REV. 1 (2009).

Chapter 15

The Promise of Dispute Resolution to Reform the Criminal Legal System[1]

In this book you have read about various processes, beyond trials, that are used to resolved criminal cases in the United States. You have read why each of these processes has advantages and you have read about the concerns related to each of these processes. You have read about various efforts to reform our criminal legal system, and yet, as you have read, it continues to be plagued by serious and systemic problems. It is easy to be swept up in pessimism when discussing the criminal legal system. Change is hard, at best incremental, and as of this writing it is hard to know if we are in the beginning of an era of backlash against recent reforms. Yet we also think dispute resolution theories hold promise for reform.

This chapter will explore the potential for dispute resolution to drive meaningful reform in the criminal legal system without overlooking hard realities that continue to stand in the way. To give us a framework for addressing those challenges, we want to use dispute resolution yet again. In this chapter, we will use dispute resolution theory to understand the problem and dispute system design as a possible framework for reforming the current system. This chapter will start with a discussion of intractable, or wicked, problems because the failure to recognize that reforming the criminal legal system is an intractable problem is one reason larger reform efforts have failed. The criminal legal system is a highly complex system (or multiple systems) with a variety of unpredictable and interconnected problems. Reformers all too often continue to propose piecemeal or isolated changes that fail to recognize this complexity and plan accordingly. This chapter demonstrates why we need to frame criminal legal reform as an intractable problem for reform efforts to have more of an impact.

As this chapter aims to encourage broader systemic thinking about how dispute resolution practices can contribute to meaningful reform, we will then introduce you to dispute system design. This framework can contribute to comprehensive reforms by providing an interest-based lens through which processes can be introduced and/or improved to meet the challenge of the intractable problem of the criminal legal system. This kind of systemic thinking could focus on improvements to the system to

---

1. This chapter has been expanded from an article: Cynthia Alkon, *Looking Forward, Reflecting Back: The Promise of Dispute Resolution to Reform the Criminal Legal System*, MISSOURI JOURNAL OF DISPUTE RESOLUTION, forthcoming, 2025.

make it a justice system (not simply a legal system) that improves safety and rehabilitates offenders.

Next, this chapter will examine the central role of plea bargaining, the challenges of reforming this entrenched practice and how it remains both a serious problem and, ironically, the process that has the greatest potential to move towards innovative improvements in the criminal legal system. Yet, the potential of plea bargaining to be a source of reform will likely remain limited and largely unrealized as long as reformers consider plea bargaining separately from the overall criminal legal system. Prosecutors have used the flexibility of plea bargaining as an integral part of exercising their largely unregulated discretion in how and what they do. But the complexity and flexibility of plea bargaining could also be harnessed for reform.

The discussion will then turn to problem-solving courts, highlighting their innovative approaches and the barriers they face. The transformative potential of restorative justice will be analyzed, along with its limitations and opportunities for broader integration. Mediation in criminal cases will also be considered as a final flexible tool for resolving cases. As we will discuss, reform efforts within and between these various dispute resolution processes should recognize that the criminal legal system is an intractable problem and move away from proposals for reform that fail to recognize complexity.

I. Intractable Problems

Planning and dispute resolution professionals recognize that intractable problems require a different approach. Intractable problems, or wicked problems, are often described as "unfixable problems." Single solutions or reforms do not fix intractable problems. For example, simply increasing criminal penalties, as was done in the 1980s–1990s in the United States, did not eliminate crime. These simple solutions can instead spark new and unintended consequences, such as mass incarceration. For the purposes of this discussion, it is first important to understand the basic definition of an intractable problem in the context of the criminal legal system. This section will then discuss the importance of being able to distinguish between a complicated and a complex problem and why that distinction matters in considering criminal legal system reform. Finally, this section will discuss the importance of approaching intractable problems differently and how this could contribute to meaningful criminal legal reform.

Intractable problems are social problems that are "inherently different from the problems that scientists" deal with.[2] Problems in the natural sciences are "definable and separable and may have solutions that are findable" and it is clear whether the

2. Horst W.J. Ritell & Melvin B. Webber, *Dilemmas in a General Theory of Planning*, 4 Pol'y Sci., 160, (June 1973).

problem has been solved.[3] In contrast, social problems "are ill-defined."[4] It is not easy to understand the various contributors to an intractable problem much less the paths forward towards resolution. For example, there are potentially numerous causes of criminal behavior including poverty, trauma, mental illness, substance abuse, violence, access to illegal drugs, access to guns and other weapons.

Taking just the first item on this list, policymakers and social scientists have struggled to understand the causes of poverty, much less to fully understand the impact of poverty on criminal behavior, and then to determine what changes might both reduce poverty and crime. As this example illustrates, an intractable problem has "an interconnected web of sub-problems."[5] Wicked problems are "unpredictable, and it may be nearly impossible to unequivocally link causes—such as plans and decisions—to their effects."[6] Consider the following excerpt and how it might apply in the context of our criminal legal system.

Calvin Chrustie, James Richard Coben & Christer Honeyman, *Negotiating Wicked Problems: Five Stories, Venturing Beyond the Classroom*

VOL. 2 RETHINKING NEGOTIATION TEACHING SERIES, 449, 453 (Christopher Honeyman, et al., eds) (2010)

The concept of tame versus wicked problems is imported from public planning; we find the distinction also useful for thinking about why negotiation works well in some situations but not in others. However, the terms cause difficulty, because while "wicked" problems have a flavor all their own, the term "tame" seems insulting as well as inaccurate for problems that can include the negotiation of multi-million-dollar deals or the settlement of complex litigation. It is important to acknowledge that "tame" is not a synonym for easy, and "wicked" is not a synonym for complex. A more useful way to think about negotiating tame versus negotiating wicked problems is to consider the types of changes negotiators need to make when dealing with a problem. Tame problems can be very complex, but they are still amenable to "technical" solutions.... [They] can be analyzed largely in terms of "technical" change—with the negotiator or intervener applying an external set of tools to solve a problem. Wicked problems, on the other hand, require "adaptive" responses that require negotiators or intervenors to modify their own views and behaviors, rather than merely applying tools to a problem outside themselves.

---

3. *Id.*

4. *Id.*

5. Calvin Chrustie, James Richard Coben & Christer Honeyman, *Negotiating Wicked Problems: Five Stories, Venturing Beyond the Classroom*; VOL. 2 RETHINKING NEGOTIATION TEACHING SERIES, 449, 451 (Christopher Honeyman, et al., eds) (2010).

6. Cynthia Alkon & Sanda Kaufman, *A Theory of Interests in the Context of Hybrid Warfare: It's Complex*, 24 CARDOZO J. CONF. RES. 581, 594 (2023).

Yet we all deal with problems that appear to be wicked; each of the cases exhibits some combination of the following features

- The problem is ill-defined and resists clear definition as a technical issue, because wicked problems are also social, political, and moral in nature. Each proposed definition of the problem implies a particular kind of solution which is loaded with contested values. Consequently, merely defining the problem can incite passionate conflict.
- Solutions to a wicked problem cannot be labeled good or bad; they can only be considered better or worse, good enough or not good enough. Whether a solution is good enough depends on the values and judgment of each of the parties, who will inevitably assess the problem and its potential solutions from their respective positions within the social context of the problem.
- Every wicked problem is unique and novel, because even if the technical elements appear similar from one situation to another, the social, political, and moral features are context specific.
- A wicked problem contains an interconnected web of sub problems; every proposed solution to part or the whole of the wicked problem will affect other problems in the web.
- The only way to address a wicked problem is to try solutions; every solution we try is expensive and has lasting unintended consequences. So, although we have only one shot to solve this wicked problem, we will have plenty of opportunities to develop our skills as we deal with the wicked problems that we create with our attempted solutions.

A tame problem, by contrast, can be—more or less—separated from the surrounding context and dealt with as a discrete issue.... A tame problem:

- Has a relatively well-defined and stable problem statement.
- Has a definite stopping point, i.e., we know when a solution is reached.
- Has a solution which can be objectively evaluated as being right or wrong.
- Belongs to a class of similar problems which can be solved in a similar manner.
- Has solutions that can be tried and abandoned.[7]

* * *

As the reading in this book has made clear, the criminal legal system is not a tame problem. Consider even the first definition of a wicked problem—something that has social, political, and moral characteristics. Are the problems with our criminal legal system any one of these? Without a well-defined or stable problem statement, it is clearly more challenging to address the problem. Some consider the problem to be

---

7. Calvin Chrustie, et al., *Negotiating Wicked Problems: Five Stories, Venturing Beyond the Classroom*; Vol. 2 Rethinking Negotiation Teaching Series, 449, 453 (Christopher Honeyman, et al., eds) (2010).

mass incarceration, some consider it to be over-policing, some consider the problem to be a lack of personal responsibility leading to criminal behavior, others look to poverty, mental illness, or substance abuse as the cause or causes of criminal behavior. This means there is no single problem statement to consider when looking at what to reform in the criminal legal system.

And, logically, without a clear problem to fix, there is also no clear stopping point. Do decreased crime rates indicate a solution? Do decreased incarceration rates indicate a solution? Do increased rehabilitative programs indicate a solution? There is also no single reform that could be objectively right or wrong. It depends on the values of the people evaluating the problem. Is it objectively right to incarcerate many more people? Is it objectively right to incarcerate many fewer people? As a society we do not have one single answer to these questions.

Intractable problems do not have tame attributes. Instead, they are complex. A complex problem is one where the "elements ... interact dynamically so their cumulative outcomes cannot be predicted with any degree of certainty...."[8] Something can be complicated but not complex. For example, "an airline engine is complicated, while air traffic control is complex."[9] Putting this in the criminal context, a criminal jury trial is complicated, while the criminal legal system is complex. The criminal legal system has numerous parts to it that interact in ways that are difficult, if not impossible to predict. For example, the policy decisions to increase penalties for criminal acts not only led to higher incarceration rates, but also impacted entire communities as more children were raised with one or both parents incarcerated during some or all of their childhood, which, in turn, impacted the child's risk for incarceration later in life. As we have read, the creation of problem-solving courts might have "fixed" a problem of excessive punishment for some but, perhaps, widened the net of violations, relieved pressure on the rest of the criminal legal system to reform, and actually not been effective for many of the participants.

Peter Coleman and Robert Ricigliano use philosopher Karl Popper's explanation of the differences between a clock problem and a cloud problem to further define intractable problems.[10] A clock problem is something that is "more mechanical, knowable, controllable, and predictable."[11] These problems can be "broken down to their component parts and systematically studied to reveal the source of the problem ... [and then] can be repaired and reassembled."[12] Cloud problems are "much more complex, murky, uncontrollable, and unpredictable."[13] These problems are "highly irregular and

8. Cynthia Alkon & Sanda Kaufman, *A Theory of Interests in the Context of Hybrid Warfare: It's Complex*, 24 CARDOZO J. CONF. RES. 581, 594 (2023).

9. Id. at 594–595.

10. Peter R. Coleman & Robert Ricigliano, Getting in Sync: *What to do when problem-solving fails to fix the problem*? 83, 84, VOL. 2 THE NEGOTIATOR'S DESK REFERENCE (CHRISTOPHER HONEYMAN & ANDREA KUPFER SCHNEIDER, EDS) (2017).

11. *Id.*

12. *Id.*

13. *Id.*

disorderly in nature ... [with] many aspects ... interact[ing] over time in unpredictable ways, and therefore evidence erratic behavior and outcomes."[14]

One marker of a complex system or problem is that it is difficult to isolate one factor and determine if that is what caused the change or if the same change happened again, if it would have the same effect.[15] For example, often individuals who are incarcerated will reflect on how time in jail helped them. But, these individual stories are not necessarily transferrable in later periods or to other individuals nor do they have a system-wide impact. For example, more recent studies of the impact of incarceration on juveniles have found that the common narrative (often cited by judges and sometimes parents) that incarceration will "scare them straight" or "give them a chance to reconsider their life choices" is not what happens to most juveniles sentenced to even short terms of incarceration.[16] The narrative is outdated (and perhaps from parent's experiences from an earlier time) and is now dangerous. We know understand that incarceration increases the chances that juveniles will end up in adult prisons with adult offenses.[17] These individual stories also do not consider whether having more readily available social services, mental health treatment, substance abuse treatment, housing assistance, or simply not imprisoning, might have been better interventions to help before people get to the point of incarceration. Beyond the question of whether some people might think they benefitted from serving time, it is still an open research question whether incarceration itself contributes to recidivism in adults, although studies have shown that pretrial incarceration does increase recidivism rates.[18]

Why does it matter that the criminal legal system is a highly complex intractable problem? It matters because intractable problems require not only different analysis to understand the problems themselves, but they also demand a different approach to have any hope of making meaningful change. Intractable problems require "adaptive" approaches in which multiple responses are implemented together.[19] This means that more time should be spent to better understand and analyze the situation. This should include looking at possible negative impacts and making sure there is an understanding of any already existing changes.

---

14. *Id.* at 471.

15. *Id.* at 595.

16. *See e.g.*, James Forman Jr., *What Happened When America Emptied Its Youth Prisons: Lesson from a radical 20-year experiment and quiet triumph of public policy*, NY TIMES MAG. Jan 28, 2025.

17. *Id.*

18. Charles E. Loeffler & Daniel S. Nagin, *The Impact of Incarceration on Recidivism*, 5 ANN. REV. OF CRIM, 133, 147–149 (January 2022).

19. Calvin Chrustie, et al., *Negotiating Wicked Problems: Five Stories, Venturing Beyond the Classroom*; VOL. 2 RETHINKING NEGOTIATION TEACHING SERIES, 449, 451 (Christopher Honeyman, et al., eds) (2010).

Notes/Questions

1. How might you apply an adaptive approach to the problem of pre-trial incarceration? You might want to first consider, from a variety of perspectives, why pre-trial incarceration is a problem. Answers could include that poor jail conditions increase the coercive atmosphere of plea bargaining, and that defendants in custody may get worse plea deals on their cases than those who are out of custody. On the other hand, concerns could be that if people are released they will not show up to court or that they may commit other crimes while awaiting disposition of their pending case.

Taking a more adaptive approach could include making sure that all of the players in the system (police, probation, pretrial services, jail personnel, prosecutors, defense lawyers and judges) are involved in examining how the system currently works and determining what may need to be done to either better implement existing bail laws or to determine what is lacking so proposals could come from the players in the system for specific changes in the law to decrease the number of people held in custody while not increasing failures to appear and addressing safety concerns.

2. Does thinking of the criminal legal system as a intractable problem help to explain why reform is so difficult? What reforms have you read about in the book that you might reconsider?

3. What about examples of where others have tried to "fix the clock" for particular pieces of the criminal legal system? Consider San Francisco or Seattle's approach to not prosecuting drug crimes—only to face serious safety issues in their respective downtown areas because they didn't take a more comprehensive approach and address the underlying problems of poverty and mental health. Another example of a cloud versus a clock fix was trying to fix mass incarceration by releasing nonviolent offenders or drug offenders—this too only gets at a small percentage of those incarcerated *See e.g.* Michael O'Hear, The Failed Promise of Sentencing Reform.

4. What reforms have we read about in the book that you might reconsider or want to expand to make these reforms more adaptive to intractable problems?

II. Dispute System Design

Dispute resolution processes are deeply embedded in the U.S. criminal legal system. Virtually every case goes through one or more of these processes. Yet, despite the heavy use of these alternative processes many are not the result of a deliberate and collaborative effort involving stakeholders to define the objectives and determine the most effective strategies to achieve them. Dispute System Design (DSD) is a dispute resolution process that could help to change that. DSD demands a more intentional, deliberate, and adaptive approach that is appropriate for intractable problems.

DSD is "the applied art and science of designing the means to prevent, manage, and resolve streams of disputes or conflict." DSD started in labor relations and has expanded far beyond that for civil conflicts. As will be discussed, DSD is an interest based process for planning and designing processes and as such can be useful when starting new programs, new processes, or considering how to reform existing programs or processes. This section will start by explaining what DSD is and how it has been used in the criminal legal system. Then this section will discuss DSD as an appropriate process for wicked problems and how it could be useful in the specific context of reforming the criminal legal system.

A. Background

As stated above, DSD is an interest-based approach to designing or changing processes for dispute resolution. There are a series of guiding principles and a framework for analyzing DSD:

1. Create a DSD that is fair and just.
2. Consider efficiency for the institutions and participants.
3. Engage stakeholders—including users—in design and implementation.
4. Consider and seek prevention.
5. Provide multiple and appropriate interest-based and rights-based processes.
6. Ensure users flexibility in choice and sequence of process options.
7. Match the design to the available resources, including training and support.
8. Train and educate system providers, users, and other stakeholders.
9. Make the DSD accountable through transparency and evaluation, with appropriate concern for privacy, to improve it continuously.

Some judges and planners have used DSD to design restorative justice processes and problem-solving courts. However, this tends to be the exception. This became clear when the COVID-19 pandemic hit and within a ten-day period, in March 2020, all criminal courts around the country shut down. There were few plans or clear processes in place for how to manage the crisis. Courts around the country tended towards top-down decision-making that did not include all of the key players, much less a larger stakeholder community, and they did not tend to look at larger systemic issues.

According to a nationwide survey conducted during the first five months of the pandemic, over 74% of defense lawyers reported that they were not consulted about key pandemic changes to court processes.[20] Some lawyers reported that this was consistent with long-standing practices in their jurisdictions where "the defense bar is never consulted regarding court procedures."[21] Defense lawyers were concerned that these changes had a direct impact on their clients and since the defense bar was left out of the decision-making process, these concerns were not considered. What was perhaps most striking about the survey results were the dramatically different perceptions of who had given input during to the changes in process. Over 82% of judges thought that

20. Cynthia Alkon, *Criminal Court System Failures During COVID-19: An Empirical Study*, 37 Ohio St. J. on Disp. Resol. 453, 456 (2022).

21. *Id.* at 225.

the defense bar had been appropriately consulted. There are two key takeaways from the survey results for the purposes of this discussion. First, the vast majority of defense lawyers, a key player in the criminal legal system, reported that they were not part of the decision-making process. This indicates that whatever processes were in place they were largely not seen as inclusive and collaborative by at least one key group. At the same time this was not true for a quarter of the courts where defense lawyers reported that they were consulted. Second, even without any formal DSD process in place, 25% or so of the courts used a process where defense lawyers did not report that they had been left out. This indicates that those courts likely used a more inclusive process.

Why does this matter? As we discussed earlier, intractable or wicked problems are best managed through processes that are inclusive so that information is gathered from a wide group of people to better analyze and understand the problems and dynamics. No single player in the criminal legal system intrinsically knows the perspective of all the players and stakeholders. For example, prosecutors and judges, unless they have been defense lawyers, are not necessarily focused on the challenge of confidential communications with clients who are in custody. Attorney client communication was a serious problem during the pandemic when jails were closed. Lawyers could not meet with their clients in person, and they had significant concerns about confidentiality of telephone and video communications with their clients in jail.[22] The use of DSD might have prevented or mitigated these issues. DSD processes, by including key stakeholders, are more likely to collect better information about the concerns or problems, which is a key step towards finding better approaches for the future.

As Stephanie Smith and Janet Martinez observed, "attorneys are rarely faced with the need to design a system from scratch. More often, they must improve existing, flawed systems, or adapt an existing system to a new context."[23]

The diagnostic elements for DSD are to determine the goals, the process and structure, the stakeholders, resources, and to access success and accountability. The element of goals includes both the types of conflicts the system will manage and what the system intends to accomplish. In the criminal legal system context this could include the basic goals of justice, fairness, rehabilitation, reducing recidivism, and efficiency. Process and structure refer to what types of processes are used (or could be), how do these processes interconnect with each other and it could also include examining how the processes have changed (or not). In the criminal legal system this could include looking at how plea bargaining impacts other processes, such as problem-solving courts. The third element requires identifying the stakeholders. In the criminal legal system this could include the judges, prosecutors, public defenders, private defense lawyers, court personnel, probation department personnel, law enforcement, healthcare and mental health professionals, community organizations, and the general public. The fourth element is to determine the resources available for the process. Criminal courts

22. Cynthia Alkon, *We Need to Talk: Modernizing Attorney-Client Jail Communications*, 59 University of Richmond Law Review 199 (Winter 2025).

23. Stephanie Smith & Janet Martinez, *An Analytic Framework for Dispute Systems Design*, 14 Harv. Negot. L. Rev. 123, 125 (Winter 2009).

and the criminal legal system in general are often constrained by a lack of funding. The final element is to access success. In the context of the criminal legal system this would require better data collection. This element is also connected to establishing the goals. If the only goal is efficiency, then the only measure of success would be how quickly cases are processed. However, if the goals include rehabilitation, then tracking recidivism rates is important.

B. The Promise of Change

DSD could change how criminal courts approach planning which could, in turn, lead to fundamental changes in criminal processes. Dispute resolution processes currently used in the criminal legal system are largely not a product of a DSD approach that first analyzed the five elements in the framework and then applied the guiding principles. There are few examples of a wider stakeholder consultative process to understand how current processes work or to set goals. Criminal courts often focus on efficiency. DSD's approach would introduce a more comprehensive process of both analysis and planning. Importantly, DSD demands the inclusion of all stakeholders and is a more comprehensive process of both analysis and planning. If courts around the country changed and adopted this process it could lead to far-reaching substantive changes in how criminal courts process cases.

For example, one area that is ripe for DSD to consider is how technology could be used in the criminal legal system to help improve access to justice. Criminal courts are not generally early adopters of technology, largely due to resource limitations. Yet, technology could improve access to justice in a variety of ways. These include using virtual appearances to limit when defendants need to come to court, increasing access to information, and gathering better information. As Malcome Feeley observed decades ago, in low-level misdemeanor cases, the "process is the punishment."[24] Defendants who chose to fight their cases must come back to court repeatedly. Using technology, defendants could call in and not be required to take a day of vacation (likely unpaid) to wait for hours for their case to be called in court.

DSD could be used to start pilot projects and to develop long-term strategies to transform the operations of criminal courts and integrate advanced technologies beyond traditional case management systems. Although efficiency does matter and is one of the guiding principles for DSD, it is not efficiency at the expense of justice. Increasing use of technology in the criminal courts demands adopting DSD so that considerations of justice and fairness are part of any expanded use of technology and not simply done for the convenience of the court without considering other stakeholders, including defendants and victims. As the pandemic illustrated, in the absence of a clear process to include key stakeholders in decisions, many concerns and viewpoints are left out. Increasing technology in the criminal legal system could be both complicated and complex—depend-

---

24. Malcom M. Feeley, The Process is the Punishment: Handling Cases in a Lower Criminal Court, 199 (1979).

ing on the technology. Either way, DSD ensures a more collaborative approach which is likely to do a better job both analyzing the problems that new types of technology may address, and avoiding problems new technology might create.

DSD could also help to address some of the underlying concerns about how plea bargaining operates. As we have discussed, plea bargaining is a complex process and an intractable problem that is highly resistant to change and reform. However, DSD could help to address some concerns in the plea bargaining process to make meaningful improvements. Using DSD demands that all the stakeholders are involved in both diagnosing the problem and proposing solutions. As was discussed in Chapter 5, plea bargaining reform that has been done through fiat — like banning plea bargaining — has hit serious resistance. In contrast, using DSD to focus on specific problems within plea bargaining, in particular jurisdictions, such as reducing the last-minute scramble for plea deals in serious criminal cases, has tremendous promise to improve how the process works. For example, one concern is the use of hard bargaining such as telling defendants that they have "today only" to make a decision, or worse, that they have to decide in minutes. DSD may be one way to approach these process concerns allowing for local changes to make plea bargaining work better and be more justice focused especially in the absence of laws regulating plea bargaining and because so few plea bargained cases are appealed. One example of a change in the process, as we will discuss, is a Missouri judicial district using mediation in the plea bargaining process. One goal of that program is to plea bargain cases earlier in the process. That can have the impact of removing pressure to settle quickly which would give defendants more time to consider the plea offer.

DSD could also be used to help improve existing programs. A DSD process will include stakeholders to evaluate what is working and might need to change while focusing on justice. Veterans courts are one example where DSD could be a useful process to reimagine how these courts work and their availability. As was discussed in Chapter 9, one of the criticisms of problem-solving courts is that they admit too few people and miss a large number who would benefit from the problem-solving approach. Critics of veterans courts point to greater need for these courts due to the large number of veterans pulled into the criminal legal system who are suffering from traumatic brain injuries, post-traumatic stress, and other trauma related to our wars in Iraq and Afghanistan. Reportedly one in three veterans have been arrested and approximately 181,000 are currently serving time. Only a fraction of those veterans have been directly involved with a veterans court. Advocates suggest revising eligibility criteria so these courts do not limit themselves to veterans with honorable discharges. Advocates also suggest increasing the capacity of veterans courts to make these courts more widely available. DSD could help at a local level, each court can evaluate whether to change the eligibility criteria and/or put more court resources into expanding the overall capacity of the veterans court in that jurisdiction. A DSD approach could also be adopted state-wide, or nationally, to analyze how these courts could better address veterans' needs. Improving specific veterans courts is a complicated problem while addressing the larger needs of veterans is highly complex.

Although it holds tremendous promise to improve how existing processes work, DSD is not a complete fix for the criminal legal system. The criminal legal system is itself a wicked problem as are many of the problems within it. As the example above of veterans courts illustrates, the problems that veterans have when they enter the criminal legal system are complex. Veterans are often injured by their military service and there are continuing criticisms about the failure of the military to address these problems. Veterans may also be more likely to be pulled into the criminal legal system due to factors beyond their military service such as childhood trauma, including poverty, and limited access to mental health services (even with the Veterans Administration). A good DSD process can help to improve veterans courts in a jurisdiction and perhaps statewide. However, DSD is limited and would not be able to address these larger wicked problems that contribute to criminal behavior by veterans, such as a need for better economic support, mental health treatment or other resources to ease the adjustment back into civilian life.

DSD also hold promise as it takes a more holistic approach and could be used to look at the criminal legal system in a more systemic and adaptive way. It could be that starting to use DSD on more defined problems, such as with veterans courts, could acclimate the players in the system to a more collaborative approach than is often taken. This, in turn, could lead to more players recognizing the potential value in the DSD approach to larger, systemic problems.

III. Plea Bargaining

As you have read, plea bargaining is the dominant process for resolving criminal cases in the United States. As you have also read, it is the entry point for other alternative processes, including problem-solving courts. Plea bargaining allows for flexibility and innovation within the criminal legal system. But there are serious concerns with how plea bargaining works in practice.

Plea bargaining has several distinct advantages. First, it allows for cases to be resolved more quickly than going to trial. Second, like with other forms of dispute resolution, it can give the parties more control over the case outcome than they might have if their case went to trial.[25] Finally, and most importantly for this discussion, plea bargaining allows for creativity in the process and case outcomes. As will be discussed below, it is due to plea bargaining that the criminal legal system can innovate and that new processes, such as problem-solving courts, can start. The informal nature of plea bargaining allows for any case outcome, or process, as long as is not a violation of the law and the defendant, lawyers, and judge agree to it.

Importantly, players in the system (judges and lawyers) both expect and rely on this form of negotiation to resolve cases and look at trial as the exception. This has created

25. Carrie Menkel-Meadow, *When Dispute Resolution Begets Disputes of Its Own: Conflicts Among Dispute Professionals*, 44 UCLA L. Rev. 1871, 1872 (August 1997).

a culture where the players in the criminal legal system are both comfortable with and expect informal negotiation to be the dominant form of case resolution.

Plea bargaining has long been the subject of intense criticism. There are five basic concerns about the process itself. First, plea bargaining is overly coercive. The second concern is the trail penalty for defendants who do not take the plea deal. Third is the concern about disparate treatment of defendants, including that innocent defendants plead guilty. Fourth is the extraordinary power that prosecutors have and can misuse in the plea bargaining process. Finally, the heavy use of plea bargaining prevents the development of better lawyering skills by both prosecutors and defense lawyers.

Due to the criticism of plea bargaining there have been numerous efforts to reform the process. As you read in Chapter 5, there have been three main types of reform efforts over the years (that one might argue in hindsight are really "clock" recommendations versus "cloud" recommendations particularly when each is considered in isolation). First, there have been recommendations to change the criminal law. Second, calls for changes in the process of plea bargaining itself. Third, calls to change how the players operate within plea bargaining. Despite repeated and sustained calls for reform, plea bargaining, and the criminal legal system itself, has been highly resistant to change.

One issue is that reform efforts often look at plea bargaining as a stand-alone process and fail to consider that it is deeply embedded into the criminal legal system requiring a more adaptive approach. Moreover, reformers fail to recognize that plea bargaining in and of itself is a wicked problem that demands a more comprehensive and adaptive approach for any meaningful change to take hold. This failure is part of the reason that plea bargaining has not had the wider impact towards reform that it could have. Imagine if plea bargaining reform included conversations with all of the stakeholders—prosecutors, defense attorneys, victim advocacy groups, judges, and even law professors. This is the kind of thinking that dispute system design would encourage moving forward.

A. Regulating Plea Bargaining

Consider the next excerpt that suggests pulling plea bargaining into the court room and formalizing the processes surrounding it. You may want to consider whether these suggestions seem to be taking a more adaptive approach to overall reform.

Russell D. Covey, *Toward a More Comprehensive Plea Bargaining Regulatory Regime*

101 Or. L. Rev. 257, 282–300 (2023)

The process of plea bargain regulation that I envision would encompass several critical components. First, bargaining would be removed from back hallways and courthouse lobbies and returned to where the resolution of significant legal accusations belongs—in the courtroom itself. What this means, in practical terms, is that plea offers must take on the characteristics of legal instruments that serve similar functions in the trial process. Plea offers, for instance, should always be in writing, and they should always be filed in court. In addition, the consequences of accepting, or declining, a plea offer should be transparent. Defendants, in all cases, need to understand what the maximum sentence will be if they accept or decline the offer. Better yet, defendants should understand the actual sentences that would be imposed if they agreed to enter a guilty plea or if they went to trial and were convicted.

Regulation of plea bargaining also necessarily means regulating the conditions under which decisions to plead guilty are made. There is no justification for forcing defendants to make high-pressure decisions to accept or reject exploding offers, or to prevent them from obtaining thoughtful, well-considered counsel from their lawyers and their loved ones before deciding which years or decades of their freedom may hinge. The amount of time that defendants have to consider whether or not to accept plea offers must be standardized. Individuals should not be forced to make critical decisions about the disposition of charges without having an opportunity to consider the implications and consequences of the decision, consult with counsel, or speak with friends or family about the decision. This means that short deadlines and high-pressure bargaining tactics must end. Defendants must be provided a reasonable time to consider and act on any offers extended.

Importantly, the range of penalties must be limited by law. As Darryl Brown has noted, plea bargaining exploded after prosecutors "recognized that the power to dictate enhanced post-trial sentences through charging decisions gave them enormous leverage in convincing defendants to plead guilty." Prosecutors simply cannot be allowed to continue to exercise unfettered discretion over the size of the trial penalty and thereby ensure that they can compel just about any defendant to plead guilty in just about every case. Other types of highly dubious pleas that deserve renewed regulatory scrutiny include "linked" pleas, in which one defendant agrees to plead guilty in exchange for an agreement not to prosecute another person—often a family member or loved one—and group pleas, in which the offer made to one defendant is contingent on other defendants also agreeing to plead guilty. A comprehensive attempt to regulate plea bargaining should entail a careful, systematic review of such tactics and mindful consideration of whether to allow their use.

Finally, the contents and terms of plea bargains should be standardized—particularly with respect to the rights that defendants are asked to waive. The range of rights currently thought to be "fair game" for bargaining runs the gamut. Defendants are regularly asked to waive their right to appeal, to challenge their sentence, to seek collateral review, to challenge the ineffective assistance of their lawyers, and to forgo discovery or to raise issues regarding the state's unconstitutional conduct, including its failure to produce exculpatory *Brady* material. The list goes on. The rights sought to be waived vary markedly between jurisdictions. Waivers held valid in some places have been held to violate constitutional rights or ethical rules in others. Effective plea bargaining regulation requires a standard plea agreement. Perhaps some waivers are appropriate and may be the proper subject of bargaining. But there is simply no justification for the anarchic scrum that constitutes contemporary waiver practice.

Notes/Questions

Russell Covey observes that "prosecutors simply cannot be allowed to continue to exercise unfettered discretion over the size of the trial penalty and thereby ensure that they can compel just about any defendant to plead guilty in just about every case." You have read about the trial penalty. Is this unfettered (and unregulated) discretion that prosecutors demand a rethinking or regulation of the flexibility of plea bargaining to make it more fair? Is this a clock or a cloud problem?

As Russell Covey notes, it is difficult to get comprehensive information about how plea bargaining works. Defendants do not know what the trial penalty might be in their individual cases, plea bargains are not required to be filed in writing in court, in advance of the defendant deciding whether to accept or deny them. The lack of information can impact the plea negotiation process in individual cases and limit efforts to do more widespread reform. And, from a dispute system design perspective, it is almost impossible to provide accountability without transparency. Consider the following readings: First, Jenia Turner offers five proposals for better transparency in plea bargaining. Next, Andrea Schneider and Cynthia Alkon explain the importance of these particular items for improving negotiation effectiveness.

Jenia I. Turner, *Transparency in Plea Bargaining*

96 Notre Dame L. Rev. 973, 1000–1022 (2021)

V. Transparency Proposals

While certain aspects of plea bargaining may need to remain confidential in order to protect candor in the negotiations, to shield cooperators, and to conserve resources, broader transparency in plea bargaining promises to make the process fairer, more truthful, and more legitimate. Enhancing transparency in plea bargaining would also be consistent with our constitutional commitment to open criminal proceedings.

B. Requiring That Plea Agreements Be in Writing and on the Record

Perhaps the easiest and most straightforward transparency measure that legislators across the United States can introduce is to require that plea agreements be in writing and filed with the court. This rule is already in place in a number of states, and if adopted more broadly, it would enhance the predictability, fairness, and public understanding of plea-bargaining outcomes.

C. Placing Plea Offers on the Record

Another way in which plea-bargaining transparency can be enhanced is to require that, before proceeding to trial, prosecutors set on the record any plea offer that they extended and the defendant rejected. The defendant would hear the offer in open court and have the opportunity to raise questions and concerns before deciding whether to proceed with trial. This requirement would help ensure that the defendant has been informed of the plea offer, a basic element of receiving effective assistance.

Placing the offer on the record would also trigger rights of public access, allowing the public to scrutinize the plea-bargaining process more effectively. This would be consistent with our constitutional commitment to public criminal proceedings and facilitate more informed criminal justice policy. In particular, it would permit the public to understand the true size of the trial penalty because the case record would reflect both the plea offer made and the disposition after trial. The public could then discuss and determine whether and how much defendants should be penalized for rejecting a plea offer and choosing to exercise their right to trial.

D. Creating Searchable Plea Databases

States and the federal system can further increase fairness in plea bargaining by requiring the recording of plea offers in digital databases that are searchable and accessible to prosecutors, defense attorneys, and judges.

The digital plea records should include, at a minimum, the date of the offer, the terms of the offer, and the date on which it expires. This information would be entered into a digital file that also contains charging information, other relevant information about the case (such as the defendant's prior record and detention status), and the final disposition of the case. The data would be shared between prosecutors and defense attorneys and would later be accessible by judges.

E. Strengthening Judicial Review of Plea Bargains on the Record

Another way to enhance transparency in plea bargaining is to strengthen judicial review of the plea process and ensure that such review occurs on the record. Judicial review exposes plea bargains to analysis by a more neutral figure with the knowledge and authority to influence the outcome of the case. And when judicial oversight occurs on the record, it can expose critical elements of the plea to broader scrutiny.

The first way in which states and the federal system can strengthen judicial oversight and transparency of plea bargaining is by encouraging or requiring judges to review the terms of the plea agreement at the plea hearing. Rules should further mandate that judges conduct a careful dialogue with the defendant to ensure that the guilty plea is voluntary, knowing, and factually based. In some states, rules or practice already encourage judges to inquire into the terms of any agreement associated with a guilty plea. Going over the terms of the plea agreement with the defendant can help the court determine whether any of the concessions exchanged might have coerced the defendant to waive his right to trial. When reviewing the agreement's terms, the court is also better positioned to examine whether the defendant understands the consequences of pleading guilty, whether the guilty plea is factually based, and whether defense counsel has adequately advised the defendant about the plea agreement.

Andrea Kupfer Schneider and Cynthia Alkon, *Bargaining in the Dark: The Need for Transparency and Data in Plea Bargaining*

22 New Criminal Law Review 434, 435–438, 447–448, 454–457, 475–485

Bargaining in the shadow of the law has become perhaps the most ubiquitous understanding of how civil negotiation occurs.... This concept—that negotiations will be impacted by the parties' legal endowments—has now been applied across fields.... The theory is simple: the existing case and statutory law casts a shadow over the negotiation, informing the parties of their rights and influencing the parameters of the settlement. This assumes, of course, that the parties and their lawyers are informed about the likely outcome of the case at trial and can then make calculations on that basis. Bargaining in the shadow of the law also assumes that parties can make informed decisions, that some minimal protections exist to keep this bargaining just, and that lawyers can help their clients navigate more complicated negotiations to bargain effectively. What happens when lawyers lack information? Their ability to bargain wisely and effectively is constrained. This happens far too often in plea bargaining. Instead of bargaining in the shadow of the law, both prosecutors and defense attorneys are often bargaining in the dark, ill-informed of similar cases except for the narrow window of their practice or jurisdiction, with little ability even to research and find out what else is happening during the plea bargaining process. This lack of information, in fact, impacts all parties in the plea bargaining process, from the prosecutors and defense attorneys to judges and even juries when the few cases do proceed to trial. Defense attorneys may or may not know what the standard deal is for that prosecutor in that courthouse. Prosecutors do not know how other offices in the same state, or perhaps even different courthouses in the same county, handle cases. Judges do not necessarily know how other judges in the same courthouse, country, or state sentence similarly situated defendants. And juries, particularly those who sentence after conviction, do not know standard sentences....

We know the number of cases resolved through plea bargaining. However, we do not know much beyond that simple statistic. For example, what percentage of the entirety of cases:

- have a plea offer?
- have a plea offer at arraignment?
- plead guilty at arraignment?

We do not know:

- how long the offer stays open
- what percentage of cases plead out to the charges, as filed

- what percentage of cases plead to fewer charges, or charges that are entirely different from the charges filed at arraignment
- how many cases ultimately plead out to a higher offer made by the prosecution after the defense rejected the original offer
- how frequently defense lawyers make the first offer, or if they make a counter offer
- how many cases prosecutors refuse to make any offer on
- if defendants reliably get better deals if they wait until their trial date, or if they would get a better deal if they plead out at arraignment.

We also do not know if the type of case might mean there are different answers to these questions. Do misdemeanor cases get essentially the same deal at arraignment as they do on the day of trial? Is it worse for sexual assault or child abuse cases on the day of trial, or on the first date in the process when a witness would testify (such as a preliminary hearing)? Do defendants get significantly worse sentences in felony possession of drug cases if they go to trial? Does the type of drug make a difference? For example, are opioid users treated differently than crack cocaine users? Does the race of the defendant make the trial penalty more or less likely?…

C. What We Could Easily Collect

All of the information that could be easily collected falls into the general category that [Andrew] Crespo identifies as information that is "already within the criminal courts' custody and control." First, courts can easily report what the charge was at filing and what the charge was for the guilty plea (if it was the same, or if it was different—did the defendant plead to fewer or different charges?).… Collecting this information would answer the question of how much charge bargaining is happening, and over what types of cases (for example, is charge bargaining more or less common with felony drug cases or misdemeanor theft cases?).

Second, courts can easily report who the defense lawyer was—was it a privately retained lawyer, a public defender, or publicly appointed private counsel?… Collecting this data is a valuable improvement, particularly if it is reported in a way that makes it possible to see what the deals were for particular cases; then we could start to see whether the type of lawyer makes a difference in terms of plea outcomes, understanding that there are many other important variables (such as the defendant's prior record).…

Third, courts could easily report dates of entry to the bar for both prosecutors and defense lawyers on particular cases.… [L]ess experienced prosecutors are more prone to the Young Prosecutor's Syndrome and may, therefore, overcharge and give worse plea deals. It might help if less experienced prosecutors had data to look at to see how cases were handled by more experienced prosecutors. These data fields would help readers later to reconstruct the 'what' and 'when' of a plea agreement.".

Fourth, courts can report on whether a case involved a first-time offender or repeat offender. Whether a person has a prior criminal record is a key fact in every plea negotiation that can, and it does impact the outcome. Therefore, knowing whether there is a prior conviction matters in evaluating whether a defendant is being treated similarly or differently....

Fifth, courts could also easily collect how the plea offer was made (as part of the written discovery, conveyed in writing through email or other means, or conveyed orally).... This would be helpful to know, particularly when combined with information regarding when cases plead out in the process. In counties with electronic discovery, it is standard practice for the prosecutor to make a first offer as part of the electronic discovery. Under negotiation theory, the first offer can have more power and create an anchor. It would be useful to know if this is happening, in practice, in counties where first offers are made electronically. Negotiation theory also posits that negotiators can be more successful when they negotiate face-to-face. Collecting data about how the offers are conveyed could help to build a better base of understanding about whether the way a defendant received an offer, and whether the defense lawyer or prosecutor was the first to convey the offer, results in different plea outcomes. We could examine outcomes, both in terms of the quality of the deal reached and the timing of the deal, depending on where, when, and how the offer is made. Are defendants disadvantaged by early plea offers given with electronic discovery? Or does it not make a difference in the ultimate plea outcome?

Sixth, and related to this, there could be a simple place to report time limits on plea offers. For example, during the plea colloquy, the judge could ask, "How was the plea offer conveyed?" And, "Was there any limit on the plea offer?" If so, "What was the limit?" The defense lawyer could be primarily responsible for answering, and the prosecutor would be able to correct the record if they disagreed. Judges are generally checking off a plea colloquy form, or their clerks are, so this information could be quickly recorded for reporting. Asking these questions would take less than a minute of precious court time.

Seventh, it would be useful to add one more question: What was the first offer in the case? The defense lawyer could respond "the same as the plea deal" or give the first offer.... Collecting first offers, and agreed offers, can help lawyers to understand both what is the "going rate" for particular types of cases in a particular county, and whether there is an advantage to pleading out earlier. Do offers basically stay the same? Or do they get worse or better? It will also help prosecutors to understand whether there is any advantage to making time-pressured or take-it-or leave-it offers....

...

V. NEGOTIATION EFFECTIVENESS RELIES ON TRANSPARENCY

Particularly in negotiations where there are large power imbalances, such as in plea bargaining, negotiation theory can be helpful in ensuring the most effective negotiation possible. Negotiation theorists have advised weaker parties in several key elements of negotiation: using criteria to set alternatives in order to avoid a bad deal; using criteria to set justifiable goals; using other examples or cases to offer options; and using criteria to avoid common negotiation errors and psychological mistakes. This section will explain each of these.

A. Setting Alternatives

One of the most important responsibilities for defense attorneys is to understand (and convey) the realistic alternatives to negotiation to defendants.... If, instead, defense lawyers knew the "standard deal" that the prosecutor's office typically ended up with, that standard deal could be the predicted BATNA and would also act as persuasive objective criteria. Defense attorneys would be bargaining in the shadow of that deal rather than the trial. And given the difference between these two, defense attorneys would have more bargaining leeway. Furthermore, for the judges who approve these deals, their perspective on what is appropriate would be shifted. Instead of the likely trial outcome (which, understandably is the number most available and obvious to judges), judges would have access to the data showing typical, standard deals for all types of case and would be able to assess the BATNA of the defendant.

B. Setting Goals

Similarly, knowledge about the deals that have been offered in the past would better allow defense attorneys to set optimistic and justifiable goals.... In plea bargaining, defense counsel either can make the opening offer or will be responding to the prosecutor. In order to know what would be a good and legitimate outcome, in this particular case, one needs information about other similarly situated defendants.... Using objective criteria is a critical part of negotiation strategy in terms of setting one's goals, and it also helps to frame persuasive arguments to the negotiation counterpart....

C. Using Other Cases to Offer Options

Yet another stream of negotiation theory focuses on the importance of offering options to achieve optimal outcomes. Instead of simple trades or splitting the difference, perhaps there is a preferable way to reach an agreement.... [I]n civil court settlements, there might be more than money that can be traded. Perhaps a dismissed employee will (happily) accept less money in exchange for good references and job retraining. Or perhaps two companies can figure out a licensing agreement rather than litigate over allegedly stolen intellectual property. In all of these instances, lawyers are helped by analogic thinking—by knowing how other similarly situated cases were handled and what other options there might be to help your client. In plea bargaining, and particularly in the face of trying to reduce mass incarceration and deal with systemic problems, both prosecutors and defense counsel would benefit by knowing how other defendants have been treated in the system. Are there options for diversion sentencing? For delayed prosecution? For a mix of community service and reparations? Even for dropping the case completely? Only if this information is widely shared can attorneys properly and consistently offer options.

D. Using Information to Avoid Negotiation Mistakes

A final area to address under negotiation theory is how a lack of information can exacerbate negotiation mistakes.... Without objective criteria that is known to both parties, negotiators often need to substitute other information. This information, being more subjective, can lead to the use of more heuristics and biases—short-cuts—in negotiation that potentially lead to problematic outcomes. Mistakes from lack of information include anchoring, the availability bias, and loss aversion [more extensively covered in Chapter 7.] ...

E. Summary: Negotiating Effectiveness

When it comes to understanding the role information plays in negotiation strategy, we can now understand why transparency is so crucial. Lawyers need knowledge to help them counsel their clients better and avoid these errors. It is one kind of the knowledge that this article focuses on: information that helps an individual lawyer in an individual case to assess the deal, and information that helps lawyers to improve their negotiation skills.

Notes/Questions

1. A team of professors, Kay Levine, Ron Wright, Nancy King, and Marc Miller, have examined different types of more open plea bargaining to note how more information has changed the negotiation landscape in these jurisdictions. For example, in Yavapai County, Arizona, for several years, there was the equivalent of group plea bargaining every Friday afternoon—dubbed "sharkfest" by local defense attorneys. They also examine other jurisdictions where judges were more openly involved in plea bargaining and far more information was shared among the defense attorneys, prosecutors, and judges than is typical in other jurisdictions. What they found supports the call for more data and more transparency. As they note: "If the criminal defense organization of a given jurisdiction encouraged defense attorneys to share among themselves the plea offers they received—much the way prospective law students share with each other admissions offers and financial aid offers received from various law schools—the pricing for pleas would become more transparent, particularly for newcomers to the profession. If defense attorneys were to report all offers received, the time to trial at the moment of each offer, various background characteristics about the defendant, and the estimated strength of the evidence, the true market price for certain crimes would be accessible to other defense attorneys before the start of negotiations.... Crowdsourced plea-bargaining data can help attorneys to connect the dots between cases and escape the illusion that they negotiate alone." Kay L. Levine, Ronald F. Wright, Nancy J. King, & Marc Miller, *Sharkfests and Databases: Crowdsourcing Pleas Bargains*, 3 Tex. A&M L. Rev. 653 (2019) Does the analogy to law school admissions help make this more clear? What can you do upon graduation as a young lawyer to gather more information before negotiating?

2. Another suggestion for transparency in the criminal legal system comes from Jocelyn Simonson who argued that, among other suggested reformers, court watchers could be a way to hold the system accountable. *See* Jocelyn Simonson, Radical Acts of Justice (2023). One could imagine that community members who consistently were in criminal court could provide another source of information to defendants on

the "going rate" as well as suggest other options, like diversion, that they had witnessed in the court room.

3. How are Professor Turner's suggestions for gathering more information fixing the cloud problem? Note the more comprehensive approach that she is advocating. How we will know that is enough? What would be required to institutionalize these suggestions and make them more sustainable? A law, or a regulation, tying funding to reporting?

4. The reading above all discusses the need for better data which is a call for more transparency in plea bargaining. Could better transparency act as a form of regulation of prosecutors?

5. In 2019 New York State passed bail reform. The law required public reporting and collecting of a wide range of criminal legal system data. The data set that now exists includes three specific types of data that Andrea Schneider and Cynthia Alkon suggested would be "easy to collect": reporting what the charge was at filing and what the charge was that the defendant plead guilty to; reporting who the defense lawyer is; reporting whether the offender was a first time offender (although this data are more challenging and not always clear). The data set goes further than recommended in *Bargaining in the Dark* and includes reporting the charge the police recommend filing, dismissals, and the reasons for dismissal. For more information see, Cynthia Alkon, et al., *Disposing of Misdemeanors: An Empirical Perspective*, 99 St. John's L. Rev. 101 (2025).

6. Erin Collins cautions against relying too heavily on what she terms the evidence-based paradigm. She cautions that "decisions about what we measure, why we measure, and how we measure" favors the status quo and will, therefore, not be a positive agent for change. Instead the "three core commitments" of the evidence based paradigm will strengthen the "influence of neoliberalism, punitive impulses, and white supremacy over criminal system policy and procedure." The three core commitments are: "the collection and analysis of data about how the system operates and how reforms impact its operation; this collection should occur through quantitative methods, and the collected evidence should be used to increase the efficiency of the criminal legal system." Professor Erin Collins is concerned that insisting on an evidence based approach can prevent actions until it can be shown that these actions will redress the problems. This can prevent any action. Erin Collins, *Abolishing the Evidence-Based Paradigm*, 48 BYU L. Rev. 403 (2022).

7. Encouraging better collection of data, as the last two articles did, is not necessarily recommending an evidence-based approach. These articles are suggesting better data collection so the players in the system are better informed and to improve the practice of plea bargaining. But, these articles also discuss the collection of data to inform reforms to plea bargaining. Erin Collins recommends caution if reforms do not challenge "existing structures of power or privilege" as reforms of this kind "will tinker at the edges of a deeply rotten system." What kind of data about plea bargaining could help to get to core problems and not simply be tinkering at the edges of a deeply rotten system?

B. Plea Bargaining Contributing to Change?

Despite all these challenges and the criticisms of plea bargaining, it remains the single most important process within the criminal legal system that has contributed to innovation and which could contribute to more serious and far-reaching changes. The criminal legal process is highly adversarial during certain processes like trials and pre-trail motions. But, the dominant use of plea bargaining, a highly informal process, means that every player in the system is accustomed to regularly using an informal process that may be less adversarial and more cooperative.[26] Due to plea bargaining, the players in the system understand through experience that if everyone agrees, (the judges, prosecutors, defense lawyers, and defendants) and if the proposed plea deal or process does not violate the law, it is possible to innovate and try new things. No one is constrained by what is already enshrined in law.

As has been discussed earlier in the book and as will be discussed in the next section, this culture of flexibility and informality is how problem-solving courts, including drug courts, were able to start without any laws or legal framework. All it took was an agreement to try something new. Although the players in the system rarely look at it this way, plea bargaining is, in fact, a conduit for innovation and flexibility that can contribute to meaningful change to focus the criminal legal system on justice and rehabilitation and away from the more simplistic retributive approaches. It is limited when plea bargaining has been used towards these ends, and even rarer when the players in the system view plea bargaining in this light. But because of its flexibility, there is tremendous potential for greater reforms through the plea bargaining process. However, as we said earlier, this potential will likely remain limited and largely unrealized as long as plea bargaining is considered a stand-alone process disconnected from the overall criminal legal system. Far reaching reform is more possible if reformers considered plea bargaining as part of larger systemic reforms, recognizing its complexity while using an adaptive process that would include the various players both to understand the impact of change and to ensure agreement so the changes would be implemented.

IV. Problem-Solving Courts

As you learned earlier in this book, problem-solving courts started with the first drug court in Dade County, Florida, in 1989. These courts tended to start because a judge decided they wanted to do things differently—that they didn't like the limited role and constrained approaches in traditional criminal courts. These courts represent a significant innovation within the criminal legal system by offering an alternative to

26. *See generally*, Andrea Kupfer Schneider, *Shattering Negotiation Myths: Empirical Evidence on the Effectiveness of Negotiation Style*, 7 HARV. NEGOT. L. REV. 143 (2002) (finding that criminal lawyers had the highest number of true problem solvers); Andrea Kupfer Schneider, *Cooperating or Caving In: Are Defense Attorneys Shrewd or Exploited in Plea Bargaining Negotiations*? 91 MARQ. L. REV. 145 (2007) (reporting the results from criminal lawyers in a survey about negotiation styles and the attitudes of criminal lawyers towards negotiation).

traditional adjudication for certain types of offenses and certain defendants. These courts focus on rehabilitation and not punishment and strive to address the underlying issues of criminal behavior including substance abuse and mental illness. As we have discussed, problem-solving courts are an example of innovation that is possible due to the plea bargaining culture, where players in the system understand that all that is needed to try something new is agreement by the players (judges, prosecutors, defense lawyers, and defendants) and to make sure that the law is not violated through the innovation. Like plea bargaining, there are no laws that outline how drug courts should work. This process, again like plea bargaining, happens largely without regulation and outside the formal legal process.

A. Criticism

Despite their promise, as you learned in Chapter 9, problem-solving courts face serious criticism. One concern is that the courts are not grounded in best practices to treat serious medical conditions such as substance abuse and mental illness. Critics call for treatment to be directed exclusively by doctors and health care professionals. From a dispute system design perspective, one might argue that additional stakeholders—the medical profession—should have been included (or added now) to give input to the creation of these courts.

Another concern is that relatively few defendants are able to participate in these courts. This can be for two reasons. First, the admission criteria may be overly restrictive, preventing defendants with prior offenses, or current offenses in certain categories, such as violent crimes from being admitted, even if they would benefit from rehabilitative programs.[27] For example, many veterans courts require that defendants be honorably discharged to qualify—despite the fact that many of those who have been less than honorably discharged could benefit from the veterans court approach and that their military service might be a cause of criminal behavior (due to PTSD and other mental illnesses contracted during military service). Second, these courts restrict the absolute number of participants regardless of whether they would otherwise qualify. The size restrictions are because these courts require more resources both in terms of personnel and court time limiting the number of people each court can realistically accommodate. A related criticism is that the restrictive criteria and limited focus of these courts can disproportionately impact people of color who are disproportionately represented in the criminal legal system.

Another concern is that how these courts work in practice can vary widely. There may be different resources in terms of treatment or other types of assistance available in different communities. Some courts prioritize punitive compliance measures, such as incarceration for minor infractions over supportive interventions that address

27. *Addicted to Courts: How a Growing Dependence on Drug Courts Impacts People and Communities*, Justice Policy Institute, 21, March 2011, https://justicepolicy.org/wp-content/uploads/justicepolicy/documents/addicted_to_courts_final.pdf.

underlying issues. Completion requirements may also vary widely with some having more steps and taking longer to complete.

There are also differences in terms of the criminal process itself within these courts. Many courts require defendants to plead guilty before they can be admitted. Some of these courts will then allow the plea to be withdrawn and the case dismissed. Others allow the conviction to stand even after successful completion.

Perhaps the biggest criticism is that problem-solving courts should not be the exception in terms of how criminal defendants are treated. Instead, critics suggest the entire criminal legal system itself should be structured to focus on providing rehabilitation services to any defendant who could benefit from this kind of help.[28] Critics urge that the problem-solving court approach should be the norm, not reserved as the exception for the lucky few.

B. Contributing to Change?

Despite these challenges, problem-solving courts have demonstrated their potential to contribute to systemic change by changing how defendants are treated and how courts operate. What if these approaches were more widely adopted and not limited to a relatively small number of courts and did not require a guilty plea for entry? Consider this next reading discussing the five problem-solving court practices that could bring wider change. Could this provide the more adaptive reform needed for intractable problems?

Cynthia Alkon, *Have Problem Solving Courts Changed the Practice of Law?*

21 Cardozo J. Conflict Resolution, 598, 617–624 (2020)

IV. WHAT WOULD IT LOOK LIKE IF PROBLEM-SOLVING COURT PRACTICES WERE MORE WIDESPREAD?

What would our criminal legal system look like if standard problem-solving court practices were applied to how all criminal cases were handled? Can our traditional legal system learn something from the best-practices of the problem-solving court approach that could improve how we handle criminal cases throughout the system? Could a more widespread use of some of these approaches reduce both recidivism rates and incarceration rates? There are five approaches that would change how our criminal courts currently work. First, if a more problem-solving approach were applied system-wide, defendants would be viewed as whole person, not simply by the offense

28. *See generally*, *Drug Courts Are Not the Answer: Toward a Health-Centered Approach to Drug Use*, Drug Policy Alliance, March 2011, available at: https://drugpolicy.org/wp-content/uploads/2023/09/Drug-Courts-Are-Not-the-Answer_Final2.pdf (recommending moving away from Drug Courts and towards better options to treat those with a drug use disorder); Avinash Singh Bhati, *To Treat or Not to Treat: Evidence on the Prospects of Expanding Treatment to Drug-Involved Offenders*, US DOJ, May 2008, available at https://www.ojp.gov/pdffiles1/nij/grants/222908.pdf, (recommending treating all "at risk" for drug dependence arrestees not just the smaller subset currently in drug courts).

they committed. Second, defendants would be congratulated for success, not simply punished for shortcomings. Third, prosecutors would focus more on rehabilitation and how to prevent future crime in deciding appropriate sentences. Fourth, we would require our traditional criminal courts to show "success" by reduced recidivism rates. Finally, the overall atmosphere in courtrooms might include more kindness and less openly unpleasant and hostile behavior.

A. Viewing the Defendant as a Whole Person

As Bryan Stevenson has said, "each of us is more than the worst thing we have ever done." Traditional criminal courts rarely see the defendant beyond the worst thing they have done that brought them to court. There may be probation reports and/ or "risk assessments" examining the defendant's prior record, his employment history, or current charge. However, these reports rarely dive deeply into the problems and challenges of a particular defendant. Problem-solving courts, when done right, do a fantastic job of seeing the defendant as a whole person and encouraging success from that viewpoint. There are social workers or other court staff whose job it is to help defendants overcome obstacles, such as finding educational programs, drug treatment programs, and employment. The judge speaks to the defendant and gets to know them, often asking questions about their family, their jobs, and their work or school.

B. Congratulate Defendants for Success

A judge in one of the problem-solving courts in Texas once said to me, "the participants in this court were never told they did anything right, so now we applaud them for any reason at all so they can feel what it is like to succeed. They know what it is like to fail." Our criminal legal system is more often premised on the ideas of deterrence and retribution.... But, what might it be like if defendants were congratulated and made to feel like successes when they did something right? What might the impact be of an approach that emphasized positive reinforcement? Clearly, some applause and words of congratulations alone cannot reverse serious drug addictions, mental illnesses, or the long-term impact of trauma. And, equally importantly, resources need to be available for defendants, such as programs and counselors, for any meaningful hope of change. Could a more positive approach encourage defendants to seek help and address their serious challenges? On its own this change in approach may not lead to long-standing change. But it might be a start.

C. Prosecutors Focus More on Rehabilitation and Less on Punishment

What if prosecutors looked at each defendant and asked the question: What would it take to rehabilitate this person? If prosecutors were expected to ask this question with each defendant, they would need more information about each defendant.... But, what if the first question prosecutors asked themselves was not, "how much time should we offer?" But instead, "how do we prevent future criminal behavior by this defendant?"

If every criminal court focused on evaluating defendants for rehabilitation, and sentenced with rehabilitation as a goal, it might start to change the existing culture in prosecutors' offices. It would no longer be an unusual or select defendant who is referred for therapeutic or rehabilitative help. It would become normal. And, if it were normal, prosecutors might more often look for therapeutic or rehabilitative outcomes for cases. This is not to suggest that over time prosecutors will stop thinking that time in prison is an appropriate sentence, but that it could help prosecutors to expand their view of who will benefit from, and be deserving of, rehabilitation.

D. Demonstrate Success Through Reduced Recidivism Rates

Related to the above is the suggestion that traditional criminal courts be required to demonstrate success through reduced recidivism rates. Problem-solving courts routinely gather data on how many defendants successfully complete the program and whether they are re-arrested for new offenses. Reduced recidivism rates are one of the important pieces of data that helps to justify continuing particular problem-solving courts. For traditional criminal courts, there is no similar requirement. A traditional criminal court could sentence people to prison, have high recidivism rates for those defendants and never be asked to report those numbers or to even collect data on recidivism rates....

E. Improved Overall Atmosphere

Criminal courts can be extraordinarily unpleasant.... Every year in one of my classes I give my students an assignment to go and observe a problem-solving court. They come back with reports about the specific requirements of the courts and the stories of the defendants they saw in court on the day they observed. Invariably, the most striking thing they see is the very different atmosphere in the court room. They report that there was applause, laughter, joking, and that the judges seemed to care about the defendants and their families. The class where I give this assignment is an upper level class, so my students have all been in traditional courtrooms and they are struck by the different atmosphere in problem-solving courts. Kindness can have healing powers. In the healthcare context, kindness promotes healing and reduces anxiety. One study found that caregivers were "found to be more resilient" when practicing kindness. What might this mean for the criminal legal system? As discussed above, judges who preside over problem-solving courts have higher satisfaction rates, in large part because judges feel good about helping people. Why limit this approach to just a smaller subset of defendants? It may be more time consuming to talk to each defendant. And, it would require a change in approach for some judges to be mindful about the atmosphere in their courtrooms and to not act as bullies or accept or reinforce a highly adversarial atmosphere where defendants and their lawyers are treated poorly. Prosecutors, defense lawyers, defendants, witnesses, and victims, would all benefit from courtrooms where people were treated differently than is so often the norm. If we take no other lesson from problem-solving courts, the lesson of treating people in our criminal courts with kindness and decency would, by itself, be a game changer.

* * *

Notes/Questions

1. To date, problem-solving courts have not been an example of a systemic approach to reform or using a more adaptive model for change while recognizing the complexity of the criminal legal system. Do you think these courts have the potential to be used differently?

2. One question is whether these courts have contributed to cultural change of the players within the system due to their exposure to the practices in these courts. We don't have any studies to answer this question, but does serving in a problem-solving court change a prosecutor's attitude towards rehabilitation? Does it change an individual judge's sentencing practices in traditional cases? What if all new prosecutors were required to have their first assignment include serving in a problem-solving court?

3. As you read at the end of Chapter 10, Erin Collins has suggested that problem-solving courts be eliminated: "The problem-solving court model emerged as a genuine experiment aimed at helping some people avoid the harms of traditional punishment. Now, more than thirty years later, it is time to admit that the experiment has not succeeded in achieving its goals for many, and to acknowledge the ways in which this reform model itself can cause unintended harm. It is not time to give up on the experimentalist spirit, but rather to use it as inspiration to seek other ways of achieving these noble goals. Meanwhile, in the decades during which this particular experiment has been underway, it has become increasingly clear that the criminal system enacts deep and enduring harm on the people it targets and their communities. If we want to meaningfully address this problem, we must look for new solutions not just beyond problem-solving courts, but beyond the criminal system entirely." Consider this suggestion from the cloud versus clock perspective—can we take the best of the problem-solving model and apply it across the board? (Is that a more adaptive solution?)

V. Restorative Justice

As you have read earlier in this book, Restorative Justice (RJ) is not new, but when used in the modern criminal legal system it represents a fundamental rethinking of how crime and harm are addressed. There are a variety of practices that fall under restorative justice and we have limited our discussion to restorative justice processes that are used as a diversion from the criminal legal system or in lieu of the standard criminal process, not post-conviction restorative justice or RJ practices that are entirely outside of the criminal legal system and used, for example in school discipline. As you read, a condition precedent to a restorative justice process is that the defendant (or offender) must accept responsibility for the act, as restorative justice is not an adjudicative process to determine guilt. Instead, restorative justice processes focus on identifying and repairing the harm, restoring relationships, and addressing the needs of all stakeholders—victims, offenders, and the community—and then reintegrating the offender back into the community. Consider how RJ incorporated many more stakeholders in its creation and the different kinds of processes that come from this approach.

And, as you have read, studies suggest RJ can reduce recidivism, improve victim satisfaction, and foster a greater sense of accountability among offenders. Victims often report feeling empowered by the opportunity to articulate the impact of the crime and participate in shaping resolutions, while offenders report gaining a deeper understanding of their actions and are offered a chance to make amends. In contrast to problem-solving courts, restorative justice proponents tend to be outsiders to the criminal legal system and not players within it. This has meant that many RJ programs are often operated by non-profits and, in the United States, the RJ process itself is more likely to happen outside the courthouse then within it.

A. Criticism

But, as you read in Chapter 11, critics of restorative justice in lieu of standard criminal processes are concerned about the use of such a fundamentally different process and the impact it can have on both defendants and victims. These concerns include whether defendants and victims are participating voluntarily; the power imbalance in restorative justice processes; due process violations; the misuse of restorative justice by people who are not adequately trained and/or don't understand how RJ should work; and finally, the inability to use it more frequently due to the additional resources it requires.

Despite these concerns, RJ represents another example of a process that can be adopted due to plea bargaining. If the parties and the judge agree to divert a case to a restorative justice process, there is nothing in the law that prevents that diversion. Unlike with problem-solving courts, in the United States the main advocates for RJ have been those outside the system advocating for the use of RJ to reform the criminal legal system.

B. Contributing to Change?

Does RJ contribute to change in the criminal legal system? It represents a fundamentally different approach to crime and punishment from the traditional legal system. RJ gives both victims and defendants a voice that is most often absent in the traditional legal process. There are higher satisfaction rates with RJ due to this part of the process. Traditional criminal courts often give no time for either victims or defendants to speak. There is no time spent trying to understand, in open court, why a defendant did what they did (unless it is a sentencing hearing or a few other processes such as a competency hearing). There is no opportunity for the victim to ask questions or be heard, outside of formal victim impact statements. There is no opportunity for family, friends, and the wider community to be involved in any meaningful way unless they are called as witnesses. RJ offers a process that changes all of this.

Illustrating the possible flexibility of the criminal legal system, Michael O'Hear, in the following excerpt, suggests that it would be better to change to a restorative justice approach in drug courts instead of the standard treatment based approach, thus merging ideas from both reforms.

Michael M. O'Hear, *Rethinking Drug Courts: Restorative Justice as a Response to Racial Injustice*

20 Stan. L. & Pol'y Rev. 463 (2009)

I will propose an alternative model for specialized drug courts, one that is built around principles of restorative justice (RJ). An RJ-based model will likely do no worse—and may do better—than the prevailing treatment-based model in reducing quantitative disparities, and seems much better suited to address concerns about stigma, trust, and collective problem-solving.

Although RJ has been used principally to address juvenile offenses and low-level property crimes, it can also be adapted for use in drug cases. Indeed—ironically enough—a pioneer in this regard has been Milwaukee's own Community Conferencing Program (CCP). Advocates for racial justice in Milwaukee would do better to expand the CCP than to develop a new drug treatment court. And advocates for racial justice in other cities would do well to consider the Milwaukee program as a model.

Drug courts should be reconceived, not as places for the administration of coerced treatment, but as meeting places for members of the community (including offenders and their families) to engage in constructive dialogue about the effects of drug-related crime on the community and the proper response of the criminal justice system. The drug court then becomes a locus for relationship-building and community empowerment. Indeed, the basic principles and processes I suggest here are nothing new: they are derived from the increasingly well-accepted theory and practice of restorative justice. What is more original is the effort to consider how RJ may be adapted to deal with drug crimes.

Despite the rapid proliferation of RJ programs nationally and internationally, drug cases have generally been omitted from their coverage. A pioneer in this regard, the CCP began taking drug cases in 2004, four years after the initial implementation of the program. The CCP Director decided to add drug cases to the program because of the absence of a Drug Treatment Court (DTC) or other diversion program in Milwaukee for low-level marijuana distribution cases, which were routinely resulting in felony convictions for young offenders. In all, about forty drug cases have been handled through mid-2008, with most involving felony marijuana distribution charges.

The CCP illustrates how RJ principles can be successfully adapted for drug offenses. The basic processes for drug cases are the same as for other cases in the CCP, although there is no distinct "victim" at the conference. Instead, community members take the lead in discussing the harms caused by drug trafficking. The agreements emerging from drug offense conferences typically include the same sorts of conditions that are found in other CCP cases, such as community service and a reflection paper. The agreements also usually require the offender to undergo drug treatment, although sometimes it is recognized that the offender (despite dealing drugs) is not a user. When treatment is required, the CCP refers the offender to a providing agency with which it has a regular relationship. If the offender fails to comply with treatment, then another conference is called to determine what to do, with second chances usually afforded. Successive failures in treatment may result in termination and conventional felony prosecution. When the agreement is satisfied, the prosecutor will typically reduce the felony charge to a ticket or a misdemeanor.

It is not clear why so few RJ programs have followed the CCP's lead in taking on drug cases, although part of the explanation must be that DTCs have already occupied the field in many jurisdictions, and RJ advocates have not seen it as helpful or politically prudent to wrestle with the DTC bureaucracy over the management of drug offenders. More fundamentally, though, it seems that RJ advocates do not conceptualize drug cases as lying within the core set of cases that RJ is best-suited to address. Thus, even in Milwaukee, which did not have a DTC, the CCP did not take drug cases in the first four years of its existence, and only began doing so to compensate for the lack of a DTC in the city, not because it seemed a necessary extension of RJ principles.

Aside from an unwillingness to come into conflict with preexisting DTCs, three additional considerations may explain the tendency of RJ programs to disregard drug cases: (1) drug crimes lack clear victims, thus potentially diminishing the meaningfulness of the direct victim-offender encounter that lies at the heart of RJ processes; (2) drug offenders are often seen as too dangerous to participate in RJ processes without compromising the safety of other participants and of the community more broadly; and (3) drug offenders are often seen as suffering from cognitive and volitional defects that may prevent them from participating effectively in conferences or complying with the agreed-to conditions.

Although these considerations may help to explain why drug cases have not been at the top of the RJ agenda, they do not justify their continued neglect. For instance, the CCP illustrates how the "victimless" nature of drug crimes can be addressed by recognizing that whole communities can be victimized by the drug trade. Once the community is recognized as a victim in its own right, then the encounter between the offender and representatives of the community can be seen as a meaningful one: meaningful to the representatives/victims as an opportunity to tell their story and secure accountability, and meaningful to the offender as an opportunity to learn about the effects of his or her offense and take responsibility for it.

Notes/Questions

1. Is it an either/or approach? Should drug cases either be handled through the treatment based model adopted in drug courts or should they be handled through a restorative justice model as Micheal O'Hear suggests?

2. Is the suggestion to change to a restorative justice model a clock or cloud suggestion?

3. Would a DSD process be useful to re-think whether to change a particular drug court to more of a restorative justice model? If yes, how would you organize the DSD process? Who are the stakeholders?

As you are considering the suggestion to shift to a more restorative approach for drug cases, consider the following article by Olwyn Conway and whether restorative justice should continue to be limited to less serious cases and juvenile cases.

Olwyn Conway, *Grasping the Third Rail: Restorative Justice and Violent Crime*

81 Wash. & Lee L. Rev. 1379 (2024) 1379–1380, 1453, 1456–1460, 1464–1465, 1468–1471, 1475

As the United States continues to reckon with the deep injustices that pervade the criminal system, restorative justice has become an increasingly popular talking point in conversations around reducing mass incarceration. Yet as state legislatures, courts, and prosecutors expand restorative justice offerings as a response to crime, they largely or exclusively focus on low-level, nonviolent offenses and juvenile matters. Crimes of violence, especially domestic and intimate partner violence and sexual offenses, are often excluded. With half of the country's incarcerated population serving time for violent offenses, expansion of restorative justice in such limited areas is unlikely to meaningfully decrease rates of incarceration. These restrictions appear to stem largely from several pervasive misunderstandings about the practices and principles of restorative justice. This Article dispels these myths and makes the case that restorative justice is most needed—and has the greatest potential impact—in addressing acts of interpersonal violence.

. . .

B. Restorative Justice Should Be Available for Sexual Offenses

Cases involving sexual offending are regularly excluded from restorative justice programs. Yet sexual offenses are often cases where both parties can most benefit from what restorative justice offers. The current criminal system approach to sexual harm is woefully inadequate, creating both a need and opportunity for restorative justice.

1. Current Approaches to Sexual Offenses Are Ineffective

... [T]he criminal system offers no meaningful challenge to denial or victim-blaming and no opportunity to learn how and why to change thinking and behavior. Through the adversarial criminal process, defendants are encouraged to deny responsibility and to adopt the defense attorney's version of the facts as their own. Common dispositions in sexual offense cases include dismissals, guilty pleas to non-sexual offenses, and no contest pleas during which the defendant takes no responsibility for the conduct. In all of these scenarios, the defendant may persist in a state of denial. Even a guilty verdict may fail to overcome denial as it allows a defendant to view themselves as the victim of an unfair process or system. There is often no point in the process when a person must meaningfully accept responsibility or acknowledge the harm they have done. In fact, they are often dissuaded from doing so to protect their rights on appeal. By failing to confront denial and promote meaningful accountability, the criminal system is unlikely to encourage changes in behavior—increasing the likelihood of reoffending.

2. Restorative Justice Can Address Unmet Needs

Because so many laws restrict the use of restorative justice for sexual offenses and so many restorative justice programs exclude sexual offenses from their programming, research in this area in the United States is more limited. However, a pilot program in Arizona produced significant and positive findings for the use of restorative justice to address sexual harm....

The findings from the study were significant. First, the study found no cases of a conference being cancelled due to safety concerns. Given that this is a primary impediment to using restorative justice in sex offenses, this finding is critical in showing that careful design and execution can adequately address safety. The study also found that for most harmed parties their primary purpose in entering the program was having control over the process. In particular, people wanted input into the consequences the responsible party would face. The study revealed near unanimous reporting from harmed parties that the procedure was fair and the outcomes were just, and cited levels of satisfaction higher than those typical of conventional criminal court proceedings. Again, given the dismal satisfaction rates in the criminal system and the critogenic harm posed by prosecuting sexual offenses in court, these findings should promote wider availability of restorative justice processes for harmed parties who seek them.

3. Restorative Justice Can Reduce Reoffending

The State of Vermont has the most robust restorative justice framework in the United States.... It is one of the few states in the nation that permits using restorative justice for violent offenders and high-risk sex offenders.... In particular, studies of CoSA programming [Vermont's restorative justice program] show increased efficacy in decreasing recidivism rates in violent offenses and even more significant reductions in sexual reoffending....

B. Restorative Justice Should Be Available in Domestic and Intimate Partner Violence Cases

Like sexual offenses, domestic and intimate partner violence cases are often precluded from restorative justice programs either by law or by practice. Yet current criminal system approaches to addressing domestic and intimate partner violence have been largely ineffective, and restorative responses—when done safely and well—have been shown to improve outcomes for all parties. When asked, people in relationships involving domestic and intimate partner violence often voice a desire for more choices, more control, and a less punitive response. The continued exclusion of domestic and intimate partner violence from restorative justice programs does not serve these interests....

The current approach to domestic violence cases appears to make people experiencing harm less satisfied and less safe and fails to meaningfully hold accountable those committing harm. It is time to reconsider whether the fears and concerns that have prevented using restorative justice in these cases are sound in the face of such a crisis....

2. Specific Concerns About Using Restorative Justice to Address Domestic and Intimate Partner Violence Can Be Resolved

... Safety concerns include fears that a restorative justice conference may give a partner committing abuse an opportunity to harm, assault, or abuse their partner or that a face-to-face conference could lead to them to be able to identify someone's whereabouts. These are serious concerns. However, they necessarily rely on the belief that all restorative interventions require a face-to-face interaction. They do not....

The study [in Canada] found no incidents of violence during any of the conferences, even though the program process had families conference their case without program facilitators or staff present. The study also found significant difference in the outcomes for the study and control groups: families who had participated in the restorative justice conferences saw significant reductions in post-conference incidents of partner and child abuse. By the end of the study period, incidents of violence among the conferencing families had been reduced by half, while control families saw increased incidents of violence during the study period. This was not due to differences in pre-conference violence among the groups: the conferencing families entered the program with higher rates of violence compared to the control families. Other randomized controlled trials comparing restorative justice with conventional court responses like batterers' intervention or imprisonment have produced similar results....

Conclusion

Recent efforts to increase the use of restorative justice in the criminal system focus primarily on low-level, nonviolent, and first-time offenses. Crimes of violence, and especially sexual offenses and domestic and intimate partner violence, are often excluded from restorative justice offerings. This approach misses the opportunity to leverage the strengths of restorative justice to address violent crime and obtain better outcomes for all involved. It is in serious crimes of violence that individuals have the highest need for both healing and accountability and where restorative justice has proven most successful in reducing rates of reoffending and delivering satisfaction. Many of the objections to using restorative justice more widely stem from misunderstandings about what restorative justice is and how flexible it can be. While valid concerns certainly exist, many can be effectively addressed through careful and deliberate program design and execution. They are not legitimate reasons to forego the use of a tool that has repeatedly been proven effective in addressing serious harm. The United States needs more tools in its toolkit to address violence, not fewer. Restorative justice can and should be one of them.

Notes/Questions

1. If you were going to advocate for increased use of restorative justice for serious criminal cases, what might you do to overcome some of the concerns that Olwyn Conway discusses that have prevented looking more widely at how restorative justice is used in the United States?

2. Is adopting wider use of restorative justice a clock or a cloud approach to reforming the criminal legal system?

3. As we discussed earlier, one challenge is that RJ is still happening largely outside of the traditional court system. This means that the insiders—the judges, prosecutors, and defense lawyers—often don't see the process so, unlike problem-solving courts, they do not get an opportunity to experience first-hand doing things differently. This can limit the impact that RJ may have on traditional criminal processes. What might be done to give greater exposure to what RJ is and how it works?

4. Rachel Wechsler has suggested that restorative justice processes could be a way of dealing with victims of sex-trafficking who then themselves commit crimes (like killing their trafficker). As she notes:

> The tailoring that restorative justice offers is especially significant in the context of crime committed by human trafficking victims. This feature makes it particularly capable of appreciating complex power dynamics present within human trafficking situations and victims' diminished culpability for their harmful actions. In the words of renowned restorative justice practitioner Danielle Sered, "restorative justice is capable of acknowledging and holding people's multiple roles as at once harmed and responsible, at once owed and in debt." Her insight based on many years of restorative justice facilitation underscores the ability of restorative justice to go beyond the myopic binary approach of the criminal legal system, to one that appreciates the nuance and complexity often involved in criminal offending and victimization....
>
> Restorative justice holds much promise for greatly expanding access to the non-punishment principle in the U.S. and for promoting healing, repair, and reintegration for trafficking victim-defendants and those who have been harmed by their criminal acts. It also holds promise as a politically feasible way to advance decarceration efforts because trafficking victims are a sympathetic population that legislators and governors have a track record of singling out for mercy. Importantly, it provides a substantive response to those who commit violent crime, who elected officials are unlikely to be willing to fully excuse (at least prior to any criminal punishment). Even if they find the circumstances of trafficking victims who commit violent offenses compelling, elected officials tend to be perpetually afraid of appearing "soft on crime." Restorative justice's emphasis on meaningful accountability is likely to ease their concerns. Thus, lobbying efforts to implement restorative justice with trafficking victim-

> defendants in place of criminal prosecution and punishment, including for those who have committed violent and serious crimes, is a worthwhile endeavor. Rachel Wechsler, THE NON-PUNISHMENT PRINCIPLE AND RESTORATIVE JUSTICE, 174 U. Pa. L. Rev. (forthcoming 2025).

As we think about adaptive, systemic reform, how might her suggestion apply across the board to defendants? The 2022 National Survey of Victims reported that 90% of people with a criminal conviction have been victims of crime in the past ten years, and 60% were victims of violent crimes.[29] This raised the question of why would we separate only sex-trafficking victims for alternative processes?

5. Recidivism rates for problem-solving courts are highly variable, while the rate for RJ seems to be more steady with lower recidivism rates overall for those who participate in RJ. Is recidivism how we should measure success? Are there other things that we should look at? Do different measures of success demand a more systemic approach?

As with the other processes discussed above in this chapter, restorative justice processes tend to stand alone and not be considered, except by RJ proponents outside the system, as a model for larger change within the criminal courts themselves. RJ proponents and programs may suggest RJ for certain classes of cases. But, so far, RJ is used for a small number of cases in the United States and not in ways that contribute to larger systemic changes. The programs discussed below about using mediation in criminal cases are examples of how exposure to practices in the civil system can transplant or influence the criminal legal system. You might want to consider whether this is a model that could increase exposure to how restorative justice works also.

VI. Mediation in Criminal Cases

Another process that could be part of broader reform efforts is mediation. Although we haven't discussed it to this point in the book, mediation, beyond restorative justice, is used in limited ways in the criminal legal system. In simple terms, mediation is a facilitated negotiation. Mediation is commonly used to resolve civil cases. In the civil context there are serious concerns about court-connected mediation. One recurring concern is that mediation should not be mandated as the process itself should be fully voluntary to protect the parties' right to self-determination. Another concern is that court-connected mediation focuses on settlements through "streamlined bargaining without addressing the deeper underlying interests and seeking creative solutions." Putting aside the serious concerns about the shortcomings of court-connected and compulsory mediation, could mediation be used more often to facilitate plea bargaining?

29. *Crime Survivors Speak 2022: National Survey of Victims' Views on Safety and Justice*, Alliance for Safety and Justice, https://allianceforsafetyandjustice.org/wp-content/uploads/2022/09/Alliance-for-Safety-and-Justice-Crime-Survivors-Speak-September-2022.pdf?utm_source=chatgpt.com.

A. Background

There are a few examples of jurisdictions that use mediation to resolve criminal cases, including in Idaho, Kansas, and Kentucky. An additional notable example of a recent adoption of mediation is in the 16th Circuit Court of Jackson County, Missouri. Judge Joel P. Fahnestock was a civil practitioner before taking the bench in 2009. In this practice area, Judge Fahnestock worked with mediation regularly and saw its benefits as a settlement tool. Judge Fahnestock therefore, saw great potential value to this process and started a voluntary program to import it into the criminal system where judges act as neutrals to facilitate plea bargaining. The prosecutor and defense lawyers who decide to use this program can decide which judge they would like to act as the neutral. One goal was to have meaningful settlement negotiations before the eve of trial, avoiding the last-minute scramble to conclude a plea deal that had been the norm before this mediation program started.

According to data collected by the District Attorney's office, as of October 8, 2024, over eighty criminal cases have gone through mediation. As is typical with innovation in the criminal legal system—there are no rules surrounding this process. The lawyers are able to pick anyone to act as a mediator. Reportedly, prosecutors heavily favor judicial officers. Judge Fahnestock has offered mediation training for judges, but they are not required to complete the training before accepting cases for mediation.

In contrast to restorative justice, and problem-solving courts, the program has focused on more serious cases. At first glance this may seem surprising. But, in terms of plea bargaining, it is often the more serious cases that have lower plea bargaining rates. Therefore, mediation could help to settle cases that are harder to settle otherwise. One marker, and perhaps the primary marker, of success in these programs has been the high settlement rates, also referred to as "success rates." For example, in Kentucky, Chief Justice John Minton Jr. testified in 2023 that the felony mediation program had been "successful in moving cases more rapidly" and had an "88% settlement rate." Although these mediation programs are supporting and facilitating the long-standing process of plea bargaining, they are doing so in new ways raising the question about their impact or potential impact.

B. Contributing to Change?

Could increased use of mediation in criminal cases contribute to meaningful reform? One concern could easily be that mediation in criminal cases could replicate mediation in civil cases where there are serious concerns that the process has been simplified to the point where the greater ideals of mediation, such as party self-control, and improving relationships, are not achieved. But, is it also possible that introducing a new process could have unintended positive consequences? In the 16th Judicial District in Missouri, one unexpected consequence was that the process gives defendants who are in custody a chance to speak with their family in a more private setting. As is typical, in the local jail there are no private phone calls or visits. The mediation process is conducted in the courthouse and there is a room for the defendant where their families can join—giving them a chance to visit and talk in a way that is otherwise unavailable. In addition, the mediations take longer than many (if not most) pre-trial court proceedings and stand-alone plea negotiations. In Jackson County, MO, 41% of the mediations are completed in less than three hours and 44% are completed in three-six hours. This may seem a short amount of time but given that plea negotiation conversations can be extraordinarily short and measured in minutes, not hours, the time is noteworthy. Defendants are often rushed to make quick decisions and may only have a few minutes to make the life-changing decision of whether to accept the plea deal or not. In contrast, mediation as practiced in Jackson County, MO, gives defendants potentially many hours to discuss their case and decide whether to take the deal. This is a significant difference and could decrease concerns about coercion as defendants are not rushed as they can be in a traditional plea bargain.

As with the other processes discussed above, one key contribution that each of these processes can have towards meaningful change is that they can show what is possible and help the players in the system to see, firsthand, the advantages of change. So far, the 16th Judicial District's mediation program hasn't led to more far-reaching changes in how in-custody defendants can communicate with their families. But, humanizing the system in a way that allows for better communication between some defendants and their families is a meaningful change.

Notes/Questions

1. Jacob Leamon recommends that Missouri should adopt a rule specific to criminal mediation—so it no longer operates on an informal basis. He suggests that this rule should "define: (1) what mediation is; (2) what matters are subject to mediation; (3) the role of the mediator; (4) who is allowed to attend; and (5) what communications are allowed between the mediator, the court, and the attorneys."[30] Do you agree that this makes sense? Are there other rules to consider? Would having such a rule constrain the use of criminal mediation?

2. In January of 2025, the Kansas Supreme Court created a 12 member ad hoc group to advise the court on creating criminal mediation rules for Kansas. The group includes sitting and retired judges, district attorneys, a representative of the Kansas Attorney General, and defense lawyers. What rules would you suggest this group recommend? Are any stakeholders missing from this group?

3. If you were a prosecutor, would you want your cases to go to a mediation? Unlike restorative justice, the prosecutor is directly involved in the mediation. This means that you would need to spend the time to attend the mediation session. Would you want to do this? What value might it hold? Would you want a judge to be the mediator, or someone else?

---

30. Jacob Leamon, *Justice Unlocked: Resolving Plea Negotiations in Missouri with Criminal Mediation*, 93 UMKC Law Review (2025).

4. If you were a defense lawyer, would you want to take your more serious cases to a mediation? Would you want a judge to be the mediator, or someone else?

5. How might the Kansas ad hoc group creating rules for criminal mediation proceed if they decided to use a DSD approach? Are all the stakeholders involved who should be? Do you have other suggestions?

6. Should DSD be required before adopting a new process, like criminal mediation? Who would be the stakeholders to bring in?

The criminal mediation examples discussed above are similar to problem-solving courts in that they were started by judges. They might reflect some larger thinking about how the criminal legal system is working, but the examples above are not products of an intentional dispute system design process. You might want to consider how using DSD could change how some of these judge-led processes, such as mediation and problem-solving courts, operate.

VII. Conclusion

As you have read throughout this book, the criminal legal system is a complex problem that has no easy fix. Yet, it uses a variety of dispute resolution processes that have changed how criminal cases are processed and have contributed changes to the culture of the criminal legal system to varying degrees. Even though the criminal legal system is highly resistant to change, change has happened and is continuing to happen. One reason for this is that dispute resolution processes like plea bargaining have opened up opportunities for innovation and change without needing to get buy-in from legislators or those outside the system.

What is largely missing is the recognition that one of the reasons that the criminal legal system is resistant to change is because it is an intractable problem. As an intractable problem, reformers need to use more adaptive processes that include information gathering and analysis from more stakeholders. In an ideal world, those working on criminal legal reform would coordinate their efforts with those working to address larger societal issues such as poverty, trauma, mental illness, education, and healthcare. At the very least, a more widespread recognition that the criminal legal system is a wicked problem would be a step forward. It would, hopefully, encourage more use of processes like dispute system design, that are more appropriate than top down or single issues approaches to reform. Recognition that reform in this area is working within an intractable or wicked problem would also be a step away from the calls for simplistic solutions such as higher jail sentences. We hope that this book has inspired you to look beyond the simpler or clock fixes—such as what you read in Chapter 5 about changing the people, the players, or the law—to thinking about the criminal legal system as a whole. All of the dispute resolution processes we discuss in this book hold promise for justice focused change and we hope that you will be part of helping to make that happen.

Additional Resources

Calvin Chrustie, James Richard Coben & Christer Honeyman, *Negotiating Wicked Problems: Five Stories, Venturing Beyond the Classroom*, Vol. 2 Rethinking Negot. Teaching Series, 449, 453 (Christopher Honeyman, et.al., eds) (2010).

Cynthia Alkon, *Have Problem Solving Courts Changed the Practice of Law?*, 21 CARDOZO J. CONFLICT RESOL. 598, 617-624 (2020).

Cynthia Alkon & Andrea Kupfer Schneider, *Bargaining in the Dark: The Need for Transparency and Data in Plea Bargaining*, 22 NEW CRIM. L. REV. 434, 435–438, 447–448, 454–457, 475–485 (2019).

Olwyn Conway, *Grasping the Third Rail: Restorative Justice and Violent Crime*, 81 WASH. & LEE L. REV. 1379, 1379–1380, 1453, 1456–1460, 1464–1465, 1468–1471, 1475 (2024).

Russell D. Covey, *Toward a More Comprehensive Plea Bargaining Regulatory Regime*, 101 OR. L. REV. 257, 282–300 (2023).

Michael M. O'Hear, *Rethinking Drug Courts: Restorative Justice as a Response to Racial Injustice*, 20 STAN. L. & POL'Y REV. 463, (2009).

Jenia I. Turner, *Transparency in Plea Bargaining*, 96 NOTRE DAME L. REV. 973, 1000–1022 (2021).

Index